Epidemiology and Prevention of Vaccine-Preventable Diseases

11th EDITION
Revised May 2009

This book was produced by the Education, Information and Partnership Branch, National Center for Immunization and Respiratory Diseases, Centers for Disease Control and Prevention, who is solely responsible for its content. It was printed and distributed by the Public Health Foundation. For additional copies, contact the Public Health Foundation at 877–252–1200 or website http://bookstore.phf.org/.

Slide sets to accompany this book are available on the CDC Vaccines and Immunization website at http://www.cdc.gov/vaccines/pubs/pinkbook/default.htm.

E-mail address for comments, questions or suggestions about the contents of this book: nipinfo@cdc.gov.

EDITED BY:
William Atkinson, MD, MPH
Charles (Skip) Wolfe
Jennifer Hamborsky, MPH, CHES
Lynne McIntyre, MALS

CONTRIBUTIONS FROM:
PerStephanie Thompson, MS Ed
Donna Weaver, RN, MN
Steven Stewart
LAYOUT AND DESIGN:
Susie P. Childrey

DEPARTMENT OF HEALTH AND HUMAN SERVICES
CENTERS FOR DISEASE CONTROL AND PREVENTION

On the cover

"Die Spanische Krankheit" ("The Spanish Flu") ink drawing by Alfred Kubin, circa 1920. Kubin (1877-1959) studied in Munich and was associated with German expressionism. He was a contemporary of Edvard Munch, who also recorded his experience with the 1918 influenza pandemic. This work illustrates the figure of Death and the victims of the influenza pandemic in a way similar to that used in European woodcuts to depict the bubonic plague centuries earlier. The drawing is in a private collection.

Suggested Citation:

Centers for Disease Control and Prevention. Epidemiology and Prevention of Vaccine-Preventable Diseases. Atkinson W, Wolfe S, Hamborsky J, McIntyre L, eds. 11th ed. Washington DC: Public Health Foundation, 2009.

Milestones in the History of Vaccination

400BCE	1100s	1721	1796
Hippocrates describes diphtheria, epidemic jaundice, and other conditions	Variolation for smallpox first reported in China	Variolation introduced into Great Britain	Edward Jenner inoculates James Phipps with cowpox, and calls the procedure vaccination ("vacca" is Latin for cow)

Table of Contents

Milestones in the History of Vaccination →

1870	1884	1885	1887	1900
Louis Pasteur creates the first live attenuated bacterial vaccine (chicken cholera)	Pasteur creates the first live attenuated viral vaccine (rabies)	Pasteur first uses rabies vaccine in a human	Institut Pasteur established	Paul Ehrlich formulates receptor theory of immunity

Table of Contents

Milestones in the History of Vaccination

1901	1909	1919	1923	1926
First Nobel Prize in Medicine to von Behring for diphtheria antitoxin	Theobald Smith discovers a method for inactivating diphtheria toxin	Calmette and Guerin create BCG, the first live attenuated bacterial vaccine for humans	First whole-cell pertussis vaccine tested Gaston Ramon develops diphtheria toxoid	Ramon and Christian Zoeller develop tetanus toxoid

Table of Contents

Milestones in the History of Vaccination

1927	1931	1936	1948	1954
Yellow fever virus isolated	Goodpasture describes a technique for viral culture in hens' eggs	Thomas Francis and Thomas Magill develop the first inactivated influenza vaccine	John Enders and colleagues isolate Lansing Type II poliovirus in human cell line	Enders and Peebles isolate measles virus Francis Field Trial of inactivated polio vaccine

Table of Contents

Milestones in the History of Vaccination

1955	1961	1963	1965	1966
Inactivated polio vaccine licensed	Human diploid cell line developed	Measles vaccine licensed Trivalent oral polio vaccine licensed	Bifurcated needle for smallpox vaccine licensed	World Health Assembly calls for global smallpox eradication

Table of Contents

Milestones in the History of Vaccination →

1967	1969	1971	1977	1979
Maurice Hilleman develops Jeryl Lynn strain of mumps virus	Stanley Plotkin develops RA27/3 strain of rubella vaccine virus	MMR vaccine licensed	Last indigenous case of smallpox (Somalia)	Last wild poliovirus transmission in the U.S.

Table of Contents

Milestones in the History of Vaccination

1981	1983	1986	1989	1990
First hepatitis B vaccine licensed	Smallpox vaccine withdrawn from civilian market	First recombinant vaccine licensed (hepatitis B)	Two-dose measles vaccine recommendation	First polysaccharide conjugate vaccine licensed
		National Childhood Vaccine Injury Act		(*Haemophilus influenzae* type b)

Milestones in the History of Vaccination →

1994	1995	1996	1997	1998
Polio elimination certified in the Americas	Varicella vaccine licensed	Acellular pertussis vaccine licensed for infants	Sequential polio vaccination recommended	First rotavirus vaccine licensed
Vaccines for Children program begins	Hepatitis A vaccine licensed			
	First harmonized childhood immunization schedule published			

Table of Contents

APPENDICES

1999	2000	2003	2004	2004
Exclusive use of inactivated polio vaccine recommended	Pneumococcal conjugate vaccine licensed for infants	Live attenuated influenza vaccine licensed	Inactivated influenza vaccine recommended for all children 6–23 months of age	Indigenous transmission of rubella virus interrupted
Rotavirus vaccine withdrawn				

E Vaccine Information Statements

F Vaccine Safety

G Data and Statistics

H Immunization Resources

Milestones in the History of Vaccination →

2005	2005	2006	2006	2006
Acellular pertussis vaccines licensed for adolescents and adults	MMR-varicella (MMRV) licensed	Second generation rotavirus vaccine licensed	First human papillomavirus vaccine licensed	First herpes zoster vaccine licensed

Vaccines and Related Products Distributed in the United States

Vaccine/Biologic	Brand Name	Manufacturer	Type	How Supplied
Diphtheria, Tetanus, acellular Pertussis	Infanrix®	GlaxoSmithKline	Inactivated	single-dose vial or syringe
Diphtheria, Tetanus, acellular Pertussis	Tripedia®	sanofi-pasteur	Inactivated	single-dose vial
Diphtheria, Tetanus, acellular Pertussis	Daptacel®	sanofi-pasteur	Inactivated	single-dose vial
Diphtheria, Tetanus, acellular Pertussis + Hib	TriHIBit®	sanofi-pasteur	Inactivated	single-dose vial
Diphtheria, Tetanus, acellular Pertussis +Hep B + IPV	Pediarix®	GlaxoSmithKline	Inactivated	single-dose vial or syringe
Diphtheria, Tetanus, acellular Pertussis + Hib + IPV	Pentacel®	sanofi-pasteur	Inactivated	single-dose vial
Diphtheria, Tetanus, acellular Pertussis + IPV	Kinrix®	GlaxoSmithKline	Inactivated	single-dose vial or syringe
Diphtheria, Tetanus (DT; ped <7yrs, P-free)	generic	sanofi-pasteur	Inactivated	single-dose vial
Tetanus, diphtheria, adsorbed (Td; >7yrs, P-free)	Decavac®	sanofi-pasteur	Inactivated	single-dose syringe
Tetanus, diphtheria, adsorbed (Td; >7yrs)	generic	Mass Biologic Labs	Inactivated	15-dose vial
Tetanus, diphtheria, acellular Pertussis (Tdap; 10-64 yrs)	Boostrix®	GlaxoSmithKline	Inactivated	single-dose vial or syringe
Tetanus, diphtheria, acellular Pertussis (Tdap; 11-64 yrs)	Adacel™	sanofi-pasteur	Inactivated	single-dose vial
Tetanus toxoid (TT; >7 yrs) adsorbed	generic	sanofi-pasteur	Inactivated	10-dose vial
Tetanus toxoid (TT; adult booster use only)	generic	sanofi-pasteur	Inactivated	15-dose vial
Tetanus immune globulin (TIG)	HyperTET™	Talecris	Human immunoglobulin	single-dose syringe
Haemophilus influenzae type b (PRP-T)	ActHIB®	sanofi-pasteur	Inactivated	single-dose vial
Haemophilus influenzae type b (HbOC)	HibTITER®	Wyeth	Inactivated	single-dose vial
Haemophilus influenzae type b (PRP-OMP)	PedvaxHIB®	Merck	Inactivated	single-dose vial
Haemophilus influenzae type b (PRP-OMP) + Hep B	Comvax®	Merck	Inactivated	single-dose vial
Hepatitis A: ped/adol & adult formulations	Havrix®	GlaxoSmithKline	Inactivated	single-dose vial or syringe
Hepatitis A: ped/adol & adult formulations	Vaqta®	Merck	Inactivated	single-dose vial or syringe
Hepatitis A immune globulin	GamaSTAN™	Talecris	Human immunoglobulin	2 mL and 10 mL vials
Hepatitis B: ped/adol & adult formulations	Engerix-B®	GlaxoSmithKline	Inactivated	single-dose vial or syringe
Hepatitis B: ped/adol & adult formulations	Recombivax HB®	Merck	Inactivated	single-dose vial or syringe
Hepatitis B dialysis formulation	Recombivax HB®	Merck	Inactivated	single-dose vial
Hepatitis B immune globulin (HBIG)	HyperHEP B™	Talecris	Human immunoglobulin	1 mL syringe, 1 mL or 5 mL vial
Hepatitis B immune globulin (HBIG): ped formulation	HyperHEP B™	Talecris	Human immunoglobulin	single-dose 0.5 mL neonatal syringe
Hepatitis B immune globulin (HBIG)	Nabi-HB®	Nabi	Human immunoglobulin	single-dose vial
Hepatitis A & B: adult formulation	Twinrix®	GlaxoSmithKline	Inactivated	single-dose vial or syringe
Human papillomavirus (HPV)	Gardasil®	Merck	Inactivated	single-dose vial or syringe
Influenza (trivalent inactivated influenza vaccine [TIV])	Fluarix®	GlaxoSmithKline	Inactivated	10 single-dose syringes
Influenza (live attenuated influenza vaccine [LAIV])	FluMist®	Medimmune	Live, intranasal	10 single-use sprayers
Influenza (TIV)	Afluria®	CSL Biotherapies	Inactivated	single-dose syringe & 10-dose vial
Influenza (TIV)	Fluvirin®	Novartis	Inactivated	single-dose syringe & 10-dose vial
Influenza (TIV)	Fluzone®	sanofi-pasteur	Inactivated	10-dose vial
Influenza (TIV; >36 mos; no preservative)	Fluzone®	sanofi-pasteur	Inactivated	single-dose syringe (0.5 mL)
Influenza (TIV; ped 6-35 mos; no preservative)	Fluzone®	sanofi-pasteur	Inactivated	single-dose syringe (0.25 mL)
Influenza (TIV; >18 yrs)	FluLaval™	GlaxoSmithKline	Inactivated	10-dose vial
Measles, Mumps, Rubella (MMR)	M-M-R II®	Merck	Live, attenuated	single-dose vial
Measles, Mumps, Rubella + Varicella (MMRV)	ProQuad®	Merck	Live, attenuated	single-dose vial
Meningococcal conjugate (A/C/Y/W-135)	Menactra®	sanofi pasteur	Inactivated	single-dose vial
Meningococcal polysaccharide (A/C/Y/W-135)	Menomune®	sanofi pasteur	Inactivated	single-dose vial
Pneumococcal conjugate, 7-valent	Prevnar®	Wyeth	Inactivated	single-dose vial
Pneumococcal polysaccharide, 23-valent	Pneumovax 23®	Merck	Inactivated	single-dose vial or 5-dose vial
Polio (IPV)	IPOL®	sanofi pasteur	Inactivated	single-dose syringe or 10-dose vial
Rotavirus	RotaTeq®	Merck	Live, oral	single-dose tube
Rotavirus	Rotarix®	GlaxoSmithKline	Live, oral	single-dose tube
Varicella	Varivax®	Merck	Live, attenuated	single-dose vial
Varicella Zoster Immune Globulin (VZIG) (IND)	VariZIG™	Cangene	Human Immunoglobulin	125-U vial
Zoster	Zostavax®	Merck	Live, attenuated	single-dose vial
Anthrax, adsorbed	BioThrax™	BioPort	Inactivated	multi-dose vial
Japanese encephalitis	JE-VAX®	sanofi pasteur	Inactivated	single-dose vial
Rabies	Imovax®	sanofi pasteur	Inactivated	single-dose vial
Rabies	RabAvert®	Novartis	Inactivated	single-dose vial
Rabies Immune Globulin (RIG)	Imogam Rabies-HT®	sanofi-pasteur	Human immunoglobulin	2 mL and 10 mL vials
Rabies Immune Globulin (RIG)	HyperRAB™	Talecris	Human immunoglobulin	2 mL and 10 mL vials
Typhoid VI polysaccharide	Typhim Vi®	sanofi-pasteur	Inactivated	single-dose syringe and 20-dose vial
Typhoid, live oral Ty21a	Vivotif®	Berna	Live, attenuated	4-capsule package
Yellow Fever	YF-Vax®	sanofi-pasteur	Live, attenuated	single- and 5-dose vial

Principles of Vaccination

Immunology and Vaccine-Preventable Diseases

Immunology is a complicated subject, and a detailed discussion of it is beyond the scope of this text. However, an understanding of the basic function of the immune system is useful in order to understand both how vaccines work and the basis of recommendations for their use. The description that follows is simplified. Many excellent immunology textbooks are available to provide additional detail.

Immunity is the ability of the human body to tolerate the presence of material indigenous to the body ("self"), and to eliminate foreign ("nonself") material. This discriminatory ability provides protection from infectious disease, since most microbes are identified as foreign by the immune system. Immunity to a microbe is usually indicated by the presence of antibody to that organism. Immunity is generally specific to a single organism or group of closely related organisms. There are two basic mechanisms for acquiring immunity, active and passive.

Active immunity is protection that is produced by the person's own immune system. This type of immunity is usually permanent.

Passive immunity is protection by products produced by an animal or human and transferred to another human, usually by injection. Passive immunity often provides effective protection, but this protection wanes (disappears) with time, usually within a few weeks or months.

The immune system is a complex system of interacting cells whose primary purpose is to identify foreign ("nonself") substances referred to as antigens. Antigens can be either live (such as viruses and bacteria) or inactivated. The immune system develops a defense against the antigen. This defense is known as the immune response and usually involves the production of protein molecules by B lymphocytes, called antibodies (or immunoglobulins), and of specific cells (also known as cell-mediated immunity) whose purpose is to facilitate the elimination of foreign substances.

The most effective immune responses are generally produced in response to a live antigen. However, an antigen does not necessarily have to be alive, as occurs with infection with a virus or bacterium, to produce an immune response. Some proteins, such as hepatitis B surface antigen, are easily recognized by the immune system. Other material, such as polysaccharide (long chains of sugar molecules that make up the cell wall of certain bacteria) are less effective antigens, and the immune response may not provide as good protection.

Principles of Vaccination

Immunity
- Self vs. nonself
- Protection from infectious disease
- Usually indicated by the presence of antibody
- Very specific to a single organism

Principles of Vaccination

Active Immunity
- Protection produced by the person's own immune system
- Usually permanent

Passive Immunity
- Protection transferred from another human or animal
- Temporary protection that wanes with time

Principles of Vaccination

Antigen
- A live or inactivated substance (e.g., protein, polysaccharide) capable of producing an immune response

Antibody
- Protein molecules (immunoglobulin) produced by B lymphocytes to help eliminate an antigen

Passive Immunity

- Transfer of antibody produced by one human or other animal to another
- Temporary protection
- Transplacental most common source in infancy

Sources of Passive Immunity

- Almost all blood or blood products
- Homologous pooled human antibody (immune globulin)
- Homologous human hyperimmune globulin
- Heterologous hyperimmune serum (antitoxin)

Passive Immunity

Passive immunity is the transfer of antibody produced by one human or other animal to another. Passive immunity provides protection against some infections, but this protection is temporary. The antibodies will degrade during a period of weeks to months, and the recipient will no longer be protected.

The most common form of passive immunity is that which an infant receives from its mother. Antibodies are transported across the placenta during the last 1–2 months of pregnancy. As a result, a full-term infant will have the same antibodies as its mother. These antibodies will protect the infant from certain diseases for up to a year. Protection is better against some diseases (e.g., measles, rubella, tetanus) than others (e.g., polio, pertussis).

Many types of blood products contain antibody. Some products (e.g., washed or reconstituted red blood cells) contain a relatively small amount of antibody, and some (e.g., intravenous immune globulin and plasma products) contain a large amount.

In addition to blood products used for transfusion (e.g., whole blood, red cells, and platelets) there are three major sources of antibody used in human medicine. These are homologous pooled human antibody, homologous human hyperimmune globulin, and heterologous hyperimmune serum.

Homologous pooled human antibody is also known as immune globulin. It is produced by combining (pooling) the IgG antibody fraction from thousands of adult donors in the United States. Because it comes from many different donors, it contains antibody to many different antigens. It is used primarily for postexposure prophylaxis for hepatitis A and measles and treatment of certain congenital immunoglobulin deficiencies.

Homologous human hyperimmune globulins are antibody products that contain high titers of specific antibody. These products are made from the donated plasma of humans with high levels of the antibody of interest. However, since hyperimmune globulins are from humans, they also contain other antibodies in lesser quantities. Hyperimmune globulins are used for postexposure prophylaxis for several diseases, including hepatitis B, rabies, tetanus, and varicella.

Heterologous hyperimmune serum is also known as antitoxin. This product is produced in animals, usually horses (equine), and contains antibodies against only one antigen. In the United States, antitoxin is available for treatment of botulism and diphtheria. A problem with this product is serum sickness, an immune reaction to the horse protein.

Immune globulin from human sources is polyclonal; it contains many different kinds of antibodies. In the 1970s, techniques were developed to isolate and "immortalize" (cause to grow indefinitely) single B cells, which led to the development of monoclonal antibody products. Monoclonal antibody is produced from a single clone of B cells, so these products contain antibody to only one antigen or closely related group of antigens. Monoclonal antibody products have many applications, including the diagnosis of certain types of cancer (colorectal, prostate, ovarian, breast), treatment of cancer (B-cell chronic lymphocytic leukemia, non-Hodgkin lymphoma), prevention of transplant rejection, and treatment of autoimmune diseases (Crohn disease, rheumatoid arthritis) and infectious diseases.

A monoclonal antibody product is available for the prevention of respiratory syncytial virus (RSV) infection. It is called palivizumab (Synagis). Palivizumab is a humanized monoclonal antibody specific for RSV. It does not contain any other antibody except RSV antibody, and so will not interfere with the response to a live virus vaccine.

Active Immunity

Active immunity is stimulation of the immune system to produce antigen-specific humoral (antibody) and cellular immunity. Unlike passive immunity, which is temporary, active immunity usually lasts for many years, often for a lifetime.

One way to acquire active immunity is to survive infection with the disease-causing form of the organism. In general, once persons recover from infectious diseases, they will have lifelong immunity to that disease. The persistence of protection for many years after the infection is known as immunologic memory. Following exposure of the immune system to an antigen, certain cells (memory B cells) continue to circulate in the blood (and also reside in the bone marrow) for many years. Upon reexposure to the antigen, these memory cells begin to replicate and produce antibody very rapidly to reestablish protection.

Another way to produce active immunity is by vaccination. Vaccines interact with the immune system and often produce an immune response similar to that produced by the natural infection, but they do not subject the recipient to the disease and its potential complications. Many vaccines also produce immunologic memory similar to that acquired by having the natural disease.

Many factors may influence the immune response to vaccination. These include the presence of maternal antibody, nature and dose of antigen, route of administration, and the presence of an adjuvant (e.g., aluminum-containing material

Monoclonal Antibody

- Derived from a single type, or clone, of antibody-producing cells (B cells)
- Antibody is specific to a single antigen or closely related group of antigens
- Used for diagnosis and therapy of certain cancers and autoimmune and infectious diseases

Antibody for Prevention of RSV

- Palivizumab (Synagis)
  - monoclonal
  - contains only RSV antibody
  - will not interfere with the response to a live virus vaccine

Vaccination

- Active immunity produced by vaccine
- Immunity and immunologic memory similar to natural infection but without risk of disease

added to improve the immunogenicity of the vaccine). Host factors such as age, nutritional factors, genetics, and coexisting disease, may also affect the response.

Classification of Vaccines

There are two basic types of vaccines: live attenuated and inactivated. The characteristics of live and inactivated vaccines are different, and these characteristics determine how the vaccine is used.

Live attenuated vaccines are produced by modifying a disease-producing ("wild") virus or bacterium in a laboratory. The resulting vaccine organism retains the ability to replicate (grow) and produce immunity, but usually does not cause illness. The majority of live attenuated vaccines available in the United States contain live viruses. However, one live attenuated bacterial vaccine is available.

Inactivated vaccines can be composed of either whole viruses or bacteria, or fractions of either. Fractional vaccines are either protein-based or polysaccharide-based. Protein-based vaccines include toxoids (inactivated bacterial toxin) and subunit or subvirion products. Most polysaccharide-based vaccines are composed of pure cell wall polysaccharide from bacteria. Conjugate polysaccharide vaccines contain polysaccharide that is chemically linked to a protein. This linkage makes the polysaccharide a more potent vaccine.

Classification of Vaccines

- Live attenuated
  - viral
  - bacterial

- Inactivated

Inactivated Vaccines

Whole
- viruses
- bacteria

Fractional
- protein-based
  - toxoid
  - subunit

- polysaccharide-based
  - pure
  - conjugate

GENERAL RULE

The more similar a vaccine is to the disease-causing form of the organism, the better the immune response to the vaccine.

Live Attenuated Vaccines

- Attenuated (weakened) form of the "wild" virus or bacterium
- Must replicate to be effective
- Immune response similar to natural infection
- Usually produce immunity with one dose*

*except those administered orally

Live Attenuated Vaccines

Live vaccines are derived from "wild," or disease-causing, viruses or bacteria. These wild viruses or bacteria are attenuated, or weakened, in a laboratory, usually by repeated culturing. For example, the measles virus used as a vaccine today was isolated from a child with measles disease in 1954. Almost 10 years of serial passage using tissue culture media was required to transform the wild virus into attenuated vaccine virus.

To produce an immune response, live attenuated vaccines must replicate (grow) in the vaccinated person. A relatively small dose of virus or bacteria is administered, which replicates in the body and creates enough of the organism to stimulate an immune response. Anything that either damages the live organism in the vial (e.g., heat, light) or interferes with replication of the organism in the body (circulating antibody) can cause the vaccine to be ineffective.

Although live attenuated vaccines replicate, they usually do not cause disease such as may occur with the "wild" form of the organism. When a live attenuated vaccine does cause "disease," it is usually much milder than the natural disease and is referred to as an adverse reaction.

The immune response to a live attenuated vaccine is virtually identical to that produced by a natural infection. The immune system does not differentiate between an infection with a weakened vaccine virus and an infection with a wild virus. Live attenuated vaccines produce immunity in most recipients with one dose, except those administered orally. However, a small percentage of recipients do not respond to the first dose of an injected live vaccine (such as MMR or varicella) and a second dose is recommended to provide a very high level of immunity in the population.

Live attenuated vaccines may cause severe or fatal reactions as a result of uncontrolled replication (growth) of the vaccine virus. This only occurs in persons with immunodeficiency (e.g., from leukemia, treatment with certain drugs, or human immunodeficiency virus (HIV) infection).

A live attenuated vaccine virus could theoretically revert to its original pathogenic (disease-causing) form. This is known to happen only with live (oral) polio vaccine.

Active immunity from a live attenuated vaccine may not develop because of interference from circulating antibody to the vaccine virus. Antibody from any source (e.g., transplacental, transfusion) can interfere with replication of the vaccine organism and lead to poor response or no response to the vaccine (also known as vaccine failure). Measles vaccine virus seems to be most sensitive to circulating antibody. Polio and rotavirus vaccine viruses are least affected.

Live attenuated vaccines are fragile and can be damaged or destroyed by heat and light. They must be handled and stored carefully.

Currently available live attenuated viral vaccines are measles, mumps, rubella, vaccinia, varicella, zoster (which contains the same virus as varicella vaccine but in much higher amount), yellow fever, rotavirus, and influenza (intranasal). Oral polio vaccine is a live viral vaccine but is no longer available in the United States. Live attenuated bacterial vaccines are bacille Calmette-Guérin (BCG—not currently available in the U.S.) and oral typhoid vaccine.

Live Attenuated Vaccines

• Severe reactions possible

• Interference from circulating antibody

• Fragile – must be stored and handled carefully

Live Attenuated Vaccines

• Viral	measles, mumps, rubella, vaccinia, varicella, zoster, yellow fever, rotavirus, intranasal influenza, oral polio*
• Bacterial	BCG, oral typhoid

*not available in the United States

Inactivated Vaccines

Inactivated vaccines are produced by growing the bacterium or virus in culture media, then inactivating it with heat and/or chemicals (usually formalin). In the case of fractional vaccines, the organism is further treated to purify only those components to be included in the vaccine (e.g., the polysaccharide capsule of pneumococcus).

Inactivated vaccines are not alive and cannot replicate. The entire dose of antigen is administered in the injection. These vaccines cannot cause disease from infection, even in an immunodeficient person. Inactivated antigens are less affected by circulating antibody than are live agents, so they may be given when antibody is present in the blood (e.g., in infancy or following receipt of antibody-containing blood products).

Inactivated vaccines always require multiple doses. In general, the first dose does not produce protective immunity, but "primes" the immune system. A protective immune response develops after the second or third dose. In contrast to live vaccines, in which the immune response closely resembles natural infection, the immune response to an inactivated vaccine is mostly humoral. Little or no cellular immunity results. Antibody titers against inactivated antigens diminish with time. As a result, some inactivated vaccines may require periodic supplemental doses to increase, or "boost," antibody titers.

Currently available whole-cell inactivated vaccines are limited to inactivated whole viral vaccines (polio, hepatitis A, and rabies). Inactivated whole virus influenza vaccine and whole inactivated bacterial vaccines (pertussis, typhoid, cholera, and plague) are no longer available in the United States. Fractional vaccines include subunits (hepatitis B, influenza, acellular pertussis, human papillomavirus, anthrax) and toxoids (diphtheria, tetanus). A subunit vaccine for Lyme disease is no longer available in the United States.

Polysaccharide Vaccines

Polysaccharide vaccines are a unique type of inactivated subunit vaccine composed of long chains of sugar molecules that make up the surface capsule of certain bacteria. Pure polysaccharide vaccines are available for three diseases: pneumococcal disease, meningococcal disease, and *Salmonella* Typhi. A pure polysaccharide vaccine for *Haemophilus influenzae* type b (Hib) is no longer available in the United States.

The immune response to a pure polysaccharide vaccine is typically T-cell independent, which means that these vaccines are able to stimulate B cells without the assistance of T-helper cells. T-cell–independent antigens, including

---

Inactivated Vaccines

- Cannot replicate
- Less interference from circulating antibody than live vaccines
- Generally require 3-5 doses
- Immune response mostly humoral
- Antibody titer diminishes with time

Inactivated Vaccines

Whole-cell vaccines
- Viral — polio, hepatitis A, rabies, influenza*

- Bacterial — pertussis*, typhoid* cholera*, plague*

*not available in the United States

Inactivated Vaccines

Fractional vaccines
- Subunit — hepatitis B, influenza, acellular pertussis, human papillomavirus, anthrax

- Toxoid — diphtheria, tetanus

Polysaccharide Vaccines

Pure polysaccharide
- pneumococcal
- meningococcal
- *Salmonella* Typhi (Vi)

Conjugate polysaccharide
- *Haemophilus influenzae* type b
- pneumococcal
- meningococcal

polysaccharide vaccines, are not consistently immunogenic in children younger than 2 years of age. Young children do not respond consistently to polysaccharide antigens, probably because of immaturity of the immune system.

Repeated doses of most inactivated protein vaccines cause the antibody titer to go progressively higher, or "boost." This does not occur with polysaccharide antigens; repeat doses of polysaccharide vaccines usually do not cause a booster response. Antibody induced with polysaccharide vaccines has less functional activity than that induced by protein antigens. This is because the predominant antibody produced in response to most polysaccharide vaccines is IgM, and little IgG is produced.

In the late 1980s, it was discovered that the problems noted above could be overcome through a process called conjugation, in which the polysaccharide is chemically combined with a protein molecule. Conjugation changes the immune response from T-cell independent to T-cell dependent, leading to increased immunogenicity in infants and antibody booster response to multiple doses of vaccine.

The first conjugated polysaccharide vaccine was for Hib. A conjugate vaccine for pneumococcal disease was licensed in 2000. A meningococcal conjugate vaccine was licensed in 2005.

Recombinant Vaccines

Vaccine antigens may also be produced by genetic engineering technology. These products are sometimes referred to as recombinant vaccines. Four genetically engineered vaccines are currently available in the United States. Hepatitis B and human papillomavirus (HPV) vaccines are produced by insertion of a segment of the respective viral gene into the gene of a yeast cell. The modified yeast cell produces pure hepatitis B surface antigen or HPV capsid protein when it grows. Live typhoid vaccine (Ty21a) is *Salmonella* Typhi bacteria that have been genetically modified to not cause illness. Live attenuated influenza vaccine has been engineered to replicate effectively in the mucosa of the nasopharynx but not in the lungs.

Selected References

Siegrist C-A. Vaccine immunology. In Plotkin SA, Orenstein WA, Offit PA. *Vaccines*, 5th ed. Philadelphia, PA: Saunders, 2008:17–36.

Plotkin S. Vaccines, vaccination, and vaccinology. *J. Infect Dis* 2003; 187:1347–59.

Plotkin S. Correlates of vaccine-induced immunity. *Clin Infect Dis* 2008; 47:401–9

Pure Polysaccharide Vaccines

- Not consistently immunogenic in children younger than 2 years of age
- No booster response
- Antibody with less functional activity
- Immunogenicity improved by conjugation

General Recommendations on Immunization

This chapter discusses issues that are commonly encountered in vaccination practice. A more thorough discussion of issues common to more than one vaccine can be found in the *General Recommendations on Immunization: Recommendations of the Advisory Committee on Immunization Practices*. These recommendations are revised every 3 to 5 years as needed; the most current edition was published in December 2006 (*MMWR* 2006;55[RR-15]:1–48). A revised version is expected to be published in late 2009 or early 2010. All providers who administer vaccine should have a copy of this report and be familiar with its content. It can be downloaded from the *MMWR* website or ordered in print version from the Centers for Disease Control and Prevention.

Timing and Spacing of Vaccines

The timing and spacing of vaccine doses are two of the most important issues in the appropriate use of vaccines. Specific circumstances that are commonly encountered in immunization practice are the timing of antibody-containing blood products and live vaccines (particularly measles and varicella-containing vaccines), simultaneous and nonsimultaneous administration of different vaccines, and the interval between subsequent doses of the same vaccine.

GENERAL RULE

Inactivated vaccines generally are not affected by circulating antibody to the antigen.

Live attenuated vaccines may be affected by circulating antibody to the antigen.

Antibody–Vaccine Interactions

The presence of circulating antibody to a vaccine antigen may reduce or completely eliminate the immune response to the vaccine. The amount of interference produced by circulating antibody generally depends on the type of vaccine administered and the amount of antibody.

Inactivated antigens are generally not affected by circulating antibody, so they can be administered before, after, or at the same time as the antibody. Simultaneous administration of antibody (in the form of immune globulin) and vaccine is recommended for postexposure prophylaxis of certain diseases, such as hepatitis B, rabies, and tetanus.

Antibody and Measles- and Varicella-Containing* Vaccines

Product Given First	Action
Vaccine	Wait 2 weeks before giving antibody
Antibody	Wait 3 months or longer before giving vaccine

*except zoster vaccine

Live Injected Vaccines

Live vaccines must replicate in order to cause an immune response. Antibody against injected live vaccine antigen may interfere with replication. If a live injectable vaccine (measles-mumps-rubella [MMR], varicella, or combination measles-mumps-rubella-varicella [MMRV]) must be given around the time that antibody is given, the two must be separated by enough time so that the antibody does not interfere with viral replication. If the live vaccine is given first, it is necessary to wait at least 2 weeks (i.e., an incubation period) before giving the antibody. If the interval between the vaccine and antibody is less than 2 weeks, the recipient should be tested for immunity or the vaccine dose should be repeated.

If the antibody is given before a dose of MMR or varicella vaccine, it is necessary to wait until the antibody has waned (degraded) before giving the vaccine to reduce the chance of interference by the antibody. The necessary interval between an antibody-containing product and MMR or varicella-containing vaccine (except zoster vaccine) depends on the concentration of antibody in the product, but is always 3 months or longer. A table listing the recommended intervals between administration of antibody products and live vaccines (MMR and varicella-containing) is included in Appendix A and in the *General Recommendations on Immunization* (2006). The interval between administration of an antibody product and MMR or varicella vaccination can be as long as 11 months. Zoster vaccine is not known to be affected by circulating antibody so it can be administered at any time before or after receipt of an antibody-containing blood product.

Although passively acquired antibodies can interfere with the response to rubella vaccine, the low dose of anti-Rho(D) globulin administered to postpartum women has not been demonstrated to reduce the response to the rubella vaccine. Because of the importance of rubella and varicella immunity among childbearing age women, women without evidence of immunity to rubella or varicella should receive MMR or varicella vaccine (but not MMRV) in the postpartum period. Vaccination should not be delayed because of receipt of anti-Rho(D) globulin or any other blood product during the last trimester of pregnancy or at delivery. These women should be vaccinated immediately after delivery and, if possible, tested 3 months later to ensure immunity to rubella and, if necessary, to measles.

Live Oral and Intranasal Vaccines

Oral typhoid and yellow fever vaccines are not known to be affected by the administration of immune globulin or blood products. This is because few North Americans are immune to yellow fever or typhoid. Consequently, donated blood products in the United States do not contain a significant amount of antibody to these organisms. Typhoid and yellow fever vaccines may be given simultaneously with blood products, or separated by any interval. The replication of live attenuated influenza (LAIV) and rotavirus vaccines are not believed to be affected by antibody-containing blood products. These can be given any time before or after administration of antibody-containing blood products.

Products Containing Type-Specific or Negligible Antibody

Some blood products do not contain antibodies that interfere with vaccine replication. Palivizumab (Synagis), used for the prevention of respiratory syncytial virus (RSV) infection in infants and young children, contains antibody directed only at RSV. Washed red blood cells contain a negligible amount of antibody. These products can be given anytime before or after administration of MMR or varicella-containing vaccines.

Simultaneous and Nonsimultaneous Administration

Products Containing Type-Specific or Negligible Antibody

- Palivizumab (Synagis)
  - monoclonal
  - contains only RSV antibody

- Red blood cells (RBCs), washed
  - negligible antibody content

GENERAL RULE

All vaccines can be administered at the same visit as all other vaccines.

Simultaneous administration (that is, administration on the same day) of the most widely used live and inactivated vaccines does not result in decreased antibody responses or increased rates of adverse reaction. Simultaneous administration of all vaccines for which a child is eligible is very important in childhood vaccination programs because it increases the probability that a child will be fully immunized at the appropriate age. A study during a measles outbreak in the early 1990s showed that about one-third of measles cases in unvaccinated but vaccine-eligible preschool children could have been prevented if MMR had been administered at the same visit when another vaccine was given.

Although all indicated vaccines should be administered at the same visit, individual vaccines should not be mixed in the same syringe unless they are licensed for mixing by the Food and Drug Administration. Only the sanofi-pasteur DTaP/Hib (TriHIBit) and DTaP-IPV/Hib (Pentacel) vaccines are licensed for mixing in the same syringe. See Appendix D for additional guidelines for vaccine administration.

Spacing of Vaccine Combinations Not Given Simultaneously

Combination	Minimum Interval
Two live parenteral, or live intranasal influenza vaccine	4 weeks
All other	None

Spacing of Live Vaccines not Given Simultaneously

- If two live parenteral vaccines, or live intranasal influenza vaccine, are given less than 4 weeks apart the vaccine given second should be repeated
- Exception is yellow fever vaccine given less than 4 weeks after measles vaccine

---

Nonsimultaneous Administration of Different Vaccines

In some situations, vaccines that could be given at the same visit are not. If live parenteral (injected) vaccines (MMR, MMRV, varicella, zoster, and yellow fever) and live intranasal influenza vaccine (LAIV) are not administered at the same visit, they should be separated by at least 4 weeks. This interval is intended to reduce or eliminate interference from the vaccine given first on the vaccine given later. If two live parenteral vaccines or LAIV are not administered on the same day but are separated by less than 4 weeks, the vaccine given second should be repeated in 4 weeks or confirmed to have been effective by serologic testing of the recipient (serologic testing is not recommended following LAIV, varicella, or zoster vaccines). An exception to this recommendation is yellow fever vaccine administered less than 4 weeks after single-antigen measles vaccine. A 1999 study demonstrated that yellow fever vaccine is not affected by measles vaccine given 1–27 days earlier. The effect of nonsimultaneously administered rubella, mumps, varicella, zoster, LAIV and yellow fever vaccines is not known.

Live vaccines administered by the oral route (oral polio vaccine [OPV] oral typhoid, and rotavirus) are not believed to interfere with each other if not given simultaneously. These vaccines may be given at any time before or after each other. Rotavirus vaccine is not approved for children older than 32 weeks, oral typhoid is not approved for children younger than 6 years of age, and OPV is no longer available in the United States, so these vaccines are not likely to be given to the same child.

Parenteral live vaccines (MMR, MMRV, varicella, zoster, and yellow fever) and LAIV are not believed to have an effect on live vaccines given by the oral route (OPV, oral typhoid, and rotavirus). Live oral vaccines may be given at any time before or after live parenteral vaccines or LAIV.

All other combinations of two inactivated vaccines, or live and inactivated vaccines, may be given at any time before or after each other.

Interval Between Doses of the Same Vaccine

GENERAL RULE

Increasing the interval between doses of a multidose vaccine does not diminish the effectiveness of the vaccine.

Decreasing the interval between doses of a multidose vaccine may interfere with antibody response and protection.

Immunizations are recommended for members of the youngest age group at risk for a disease for whom efficacy and safety of a vaccine have been demonstrated. Most vaccines in the childhood immunization schedule require two or more doses for development of an adequate and persisting antibody response. Studies have demonstrated that recommended ages and intervals between doses of the same antigen(s) provide optimal protection or have the best evidence of efficacy. Table 1 of the *General Recommendations on Immunization* (included in Appendix A) shows the recommended and minimal ages and intervals between doses of vaccines most frequently used in the United States.

Administering doses of a multidose vaccine at shorter than the recommended intervals might be necessary when an infant or child is behind schedule and needs to be brought up-to-date quickly or when international travel is pending. In these cases, an accelerated schedule using the minimum age or minimum interval criteria can be used. Accelerated schedules should not be used routinely.

Vaccine doses should not be administered at intervals less than the recommended minimal intervals or earlier than the minimal ages. Two exceptions to this may occur. The first is for measles vaccine during a measles outbreak, when the vaccine may be administered at an age younger than 12 months (this dose would not be counted, and should be repeated at 12 months of age or older). The second exception involves administering a dose a few days earlier than the minimum interval or age, which is unlikely to have a substantially negative effect on the immune response to that dose. Although vaccinations should not be scheduled at an interval or age less than the recommended minimums, a child may have erroneously been brought to the office early, or may have come for an appointment not specifically for vaccination. In these situations, the clinician can consider administering the vaccine earlier than the minimum interval or age. If the parent/child is known to the clinician and is reliable, it is preferable to reschedule the child for vaccination closer to the recommended interval. If the parent/child is not known to the clinician or is not reliable (e.g., habitually misses appointments), it may be preferable to administer the vaccine at that visit than to reschedule a later appointment that may not be kept.

Vaccine doses administered up to 4 days before the minimum interval or age can be counted as valid. This 4-day recommendation does not apply to rabies vaccine because of the unique schedule for this vaccine. Doses administered 5 days or earlier than the minimum interval or age should not be counted as valid doses and should be repeated as age appropriate. The repeat dose should generally be spaced after the invalid dose by an interval at least equal to the

Minimum Intervals and Ages

Vaccine doses should not be administered at intervals less than the minimum intervals or earlier than the minimum age

Violation of Minimum Intervals or Minimum Age

- ACIP recommends that vaccine doses given up to 4 days before the minimum interval or age be counted as valid
- Immunization programs and/or school entry requirements may not accept all doses given earlier than the minimum age or interval

Extended Interval Between Doses

- Not all permutations of all schedules for all vaccines have been studied
- Available studies of extended intervals have shown no significant difference in final titer
- It is not necessary to restart the series or add doses because of an extended interval between doses

recommended minimum interval shown in Table 1 of the General Recommendations. In certain situations, local or state requirements might mandate that doses of selected vaccines be administered on or after specific ages, superseding this 4-day "grace period."

In some cases, a scheduled dose of vaccine may not be given on time. If this occurs, the dose should be given at the next visit. Not all permutations of all schedules for all vaccines have been studied. However, available data indicate that intervals between doses longer than those routinely recommended do not affect seroconversion rate or titer when the schedule is completed. Consequently, it is not necessary to restart the series or add doses of any vaccine because of an extended interval between doses. The only exception to this rule is oral typhoid vaccine in some circumstances. Some experts recommend repeating the series of oral typhoid vaccine if the four-dose series is extended to more than 3 weeks.

Number of Doses

For live injected vaccines, the first dose administered at the recommended age usually provides protection. An additional dose is given to provide another opportunity for vaccine response in the small proportion of recipients who do not respond to the first dose. For instance, 95%–98% of recipients will respond to a single dose of measles vaccine. The second dose is given to ensure that nearly 100% of persons are immune (i.e., the second dose is "insurance"). Immunity following live vaccines is long-lasting, and booster doses are not necessary.

For inactivated vaccines, the first dose administered at the recommended age usually does not provide protection (hepatitis A vaccine is an exception). A protective immune response may not develop until the second or third dose. For inactivated vaccines, antibody titers may decrease (wane) below protective levels after a few years. This phenomenon is most notable for tetanus and diphtheria. For these vaccines, periodic "boosting" is required. An additional dose is given to raise antibody back to protective levels.

Not all inactivated vaccines require boosting throughout life. For example, *Haemophilus influenzae* type b (Hib) vaccine does not require boosting because Hib disease is very rare in children older than 5 years of age. Hepatitis B vaccine does not require boosting because of immunologic memory to the vaccine and the long incubation period of hepatitis B (which can produce an "autoboost").

Adverse Reactions Following Vaccination

Vaccines are intended to produce active immunity to specific antigens. An adverse reaction is an untoward effect caused by a vaccine that is extraneous to the vaccine's primary purpose of producing immunity. Adverse reactions are also called vaccine side effects. A vaccine adverse event refers to any medical event that occurs following vaccination. An adverse event could be a true adverse reaction or just a coincidental event, with further research needed to distinguish between them.

Vaccine adverse reactions fall into three general categories: local, systemic, and allergic. Local reactions are generally the least severe and most frequent. Allergic reactions are the most severe and least frequent.

The most common type of adverse reactions are local reactions, such as pain, swelling, and redness at the site of injection. Local reactions may occur with up to 80% of vaccine doses, depending on the type of vaccine. Local reactions are most common with inactivated vaccines, particularly those, such as DTaP, that contain an adjuvant. Local adverse reactions generally occur within a few hours of the injection and are usually mild and self-limited. On rare occasions, local reactions may be very exaggerated or severe. These are often referred to as hypersensitivity reactions, although they are not allergic, as the term implies. These reactions are also known as Arthus reactions, and are most commonly seen with tetanus and diphtheria toxoids. Arthus reactions are believed to be due to very high titers of antibody, usually caused by too many doses of toxoid.

Systemic adverse reactions are more generalized events and include fever, malaise, myalgias (muscle pain), headache, loss of appetite, and others. These symptoms are common and nonspecific; they may occur in vaccinated persons because of the vaccine or may be caused by something unrelated to the vaccine, like a concurrent viral infection, stress, or excessive alcohol consumption.

Systemic adverse reactions were relatively frequent with DTP vaccine, which contained a whole-cell pertussis component. However, comparison of the frequency of systemic adverse events among vaccine and placebo recipients shows they are less common with inactivated vaccines currently in use, including acellular pertussis vaccine.

Systemic adverse reactions may occur following receipt of live attenuated vaccines. Live attenuated vaccines must replicate in order to produce immunity. The adverse reactions that follow live attenuated vaccines, such as fever or rash, represent symptoms produced from viral replication and are similar to a mild form of the natural

Vaccine Adverse Reactions

- Adverse reaction
  - extraneous effect *caused by vaccine*
  - side effect

- Adverse event
  - *any* event following vaccination
  - may be true adverse reaction
  - may be only coincidental

Vaccine Adverse Reactions

- Local
  - pain, swelling, redness at site of injection
  - common with inactivated vaccines
  - usually mild and self-limited

Vaccine Adverse Reactions

- Systemic
  - fever, malaise, headache
  - nonspecific
  - may be unrelated to vaccine

2

Live Attenuated Vaccines

- Must replicate to produce immunity
- Symptoms usually mild
- Occur after an incubation period (usually 7-21 days)

Vaccine Adverse Reactions

- Allergic
  - due to vaccine or vaccine component
  - rare
  - risk minimized by screening

Contraindication

- A condition in a recipient that greatly increases the chance of a serious adverse reaction

---

disease. Systemic adverse reactions following live vaccines are usually mild, and occur 7–21 days after the vaccine was given (i.e., after an incubation period of the vaccine virus). LAIV replicates in the mucous membranes of the nose and throat, not in the lung. As a result, LAIV may cause upper respiratory symptoms (like a cold) but not influenza-like symptoms.

A third type of vaccine adverse reaction is a severe (anaphylactic) allergic reaction. The allergic reaction may be caused by the vaccine antigen itself or some other component of the vaccine, such as cell culture material, stabilizer, preservative, or antibiotic used to inhibit bacterial growth. Severe allergic reactions may be life-threatening. Fortunately, they are rare, occurring at a rate of less than one in half a million doses. The risk of an allergic reaction can be minimized by good screening prior to vaccination. All providers who administer vaccines must have an emergency protocol and supplies to treat anaphylaxis.

Reporting Vaccine Adverse Events

From 1978 to 1990, CDC conducted the Monitoring System for Adverse Events Following Immunization (MSAEFI) in the public sector. In 1990, MSAEFI was replaced by the Vaccine Adverse Event Reporting System (VAERS), which includes reporting from both public and private sectors. Providers should report any clinically significant adverse event that occurs after the administration of any vaccine licensed in the United States.

Providers should report a clinically significant adverse event even if they are unsure whether a vaccine caused the event. The telephone number to call for answers to questions and to obtain VAERS forms is (800) 822-7967, or visit the VAERS website at http://vaers.hhs.gov. VAERS now accepts reports of adverse reactions through their online system. (See Chapter 4, Vaccine Safety.)

Contraindications and Precautions to Vaccination

Contraindications and precautions to vaccination generally dictate circumstances when vaccines will not be given. Most contraindications and precautions are temporary, and the vaccine can be given at a later time.

A contraindication is a condition in a recipient that greatly increases the chance of a serious adverse reaction. It is a condition in the recipient of the vaccine, not with the vaccine per se. If the vaccine were given in the presence of that condition, the resulting adverse reaction could seriously harm the recipient. For instance, administering influenza vaccine to a person with a true anaphylactic allergy to egg could cause serious illness or death in the recipient. In general, vaccines should not be administered when a contraindication condition is present.

A precaution is similar to a contraindication. A precaution is a condition in a recipient that *might increase* the chance or severity of a serious adverse reaction, or that might compromise the ability of the vaccine to produce immunity (such as administering measles vaccine to a person with passive immunity to measles from a blood transfusion). Injury could result, but the chance of this happening is less than with a contraindication. In general, vaccines are deferred when a precaution condition is present. However, situations may arise when the benefit of protection from the vaccine outweighs the risk of an adverse reaction, and a provider may decide to give the vaccine. For example, prolonged crying or a high fever after a dose of whole-cell or acellular pertussis vaccine is considered to be a precaution to subsequent doses of pediatric pertussis vaccine. But if the child were at high risk of pertussis exposure (e.g., during a pertussis outbreak in the community), a provider may choose to vaccinate the child and treat the adverse reaction if it occurs. In this example, the benefit of protection from the vaccine outweighs the harm potentially caused by the vaccine.

There are very few true contraindication and precaution conditions. Only two of these conditions are generally considered to be permanent: severe (anaphylactic) allergic reaction to a vaccine component or following a prior dose of a vaccine, and encephalopathy not due to another identifiable cause occurring within 7 days of pertussis vaccination.

Conditions considered permanent precautions to further doses of pediatric pertussis-containing vaccine are temperature of 105°F or higher within 48 hours of a dose, collapse or shock-like state (hypotonic hyporesponsive episode) within 48 hours of a dose, persistent inconsolable crying lasting 3 or more hours occurring within 48 hours of a dose, or a seizure, with or without fever, occurring within 3 days of a dose. The occurrence of one of these events in a child following DTaP vaccine is not a precaution to later vaccination with the adolescent/adult formulation of pertussis vaccine (Tdap).

Two conditions are temporary contraindications to vaccination with live vaccines: pregnancy and immunosuppression. Two conditions are temporary precautions to vaccination: moderate or severe acute illness (all vaccines), and recent receipt of an antibody-containing blood product. The latter precaution applies only to MMR and varicella-containing (except zoster) vaccines.

Precaution

- A condition in a recipient that might increase the chance or severity of an adverse reaction, or

- Might compromise the ability of the vaccine to produce immunity

Contraindications and Precautions

Permanent contraindications to vaccination:

- severe allergic reaction to a vaccine component or following a prior dose

- encephalopathy not due to another identifiable cause occurring within 7 days of pertussis vaccination

Contraindications and Precautions

Condition	Live	Inactivated
Allergy to component	C	C
Encephalopathy	---	C
Pregnancy	C	V*
Immunosuppression	C	V
Severe illness	P	P
Recent blood product	P**	V

C=contraindication P=precaution V=vaccinate if indicated
*except HPV and Tdap. **MMR and varicella-containing (except zoster vaccine), and rotavirus vaccines only

Allergy

A severe (anaphylactic) allergic reaction following a dose of vaccine will almost always contraindicate a subsequent dose of that vaccine. Severe allergies are those that are mediated by IgE, occur within minutes or hours of receiving the vaccine, and require medical attention. Examples of symptoms and signs typical of severe allergic reactions are generalized urticaria (hives), swelling of the mouth and throat, difficulty breathing, wheezing, hypotension, or shock. With appropriate screening these reactions are very rare following vaccination.

A table listing vaccine contents is included in Appendix B. Persons may be allergic to the vaccine antigen or to a vaccine component such as animal protein, antibiotic, preservative, or stabilizer. The most common animal protein allergen is egg protein found in vaccines prepared using embryonated chicken eggs (e.g., yellow fever and influenza vaccines). Ordinarily, a person who can eat eggs or egg products can receive vaccines that contain egg; persons with histories of anaphylactic or anaphylactic-like allergy to eggs or egg proteins should not. Asking persons whether they can eat eggs without adverse effects is a reasonable way to screen for those who might be at risk from receiving yellow fever and influenza vaccines.

Several recent studies have shown that children who have a history of severe allergy to eggs rarely have reactions to MMR vaccine. This is probably because measles and mumps vaccine viruses are both grown in chick embryo fibroblasts, not actually in eggs. It appears that gelatin, not egg, might be the cause of allergic reactions to MMR. As a result, in 1998, the ACIP removed severe egg allergy as a contraindication to measles and mumps vaccines. Egg-allergic children may be vaccinated with MMR without prior skin testing.

Certain vaccines contain trace amounts of neomycin. Persons who have experienced an anaphylactic reaction to neomycin should not receive these vaccines. Most often, neomycin allergy presents as contact dermatitis, a manifestation of a delayed-type (cell-mediated) immune response, rather than anaphylaxis. A history of delayed-type reactions to neomycin is not a contraindication for administration of vaccines that contain neomycin.

Latex is sap from the commercial rubber tree. Latex contains naturally occurring impurities (e.g., plant proteins and peptides), which are believed to be responsible for allergic reactions. Latex is processed to form natural rubber latex and dry natural rubber. Dry natural rubber and natural rubber latex might contain the same plant impurities as latex but in lesser amounts. Natural rubber latex is used to produce medical gloves, catheters, and other products. Dry natural rubber is used in syringe plungers, vial stoppers, and injection ports on intravascular tubing. Synthetic rubber and synthetic latex also are used in medical gloves, syringe plungers, and vial stoppers. Synthetic rubber and synthetic latex do not contain natural rubber or natural latex, and therefore, do not contain the impurities linked to allergic reactions.

The most common type of latex sensitivity is contact-type (type 4) allergy, usually as a result of prolonged contact with latex-containing gloves. However, injection-procedure-associated latex allergies among diabetic patients have been described. Allergic reactions (including anaphylaxis) after vaccination procedures are rare. Only one report of an allergic reaction after administration of hepatitis B vaccine in a patient with known severe allergy (anaphylaxis) to latex has been published.

If a person reports a severe (anaphylactic) allergy to latex, vaccines supplied in vials or syringes that contain natural rubber should not be administered unless the benefit of vaccination clearly outweighs the risk of an allergic reaction to the vaccine. For latex allergies other than anaphylactic allergies (e.g., a history of contact allergy to latex gloves), vaccines supplied in vials or syringes that contain dry natural rubber or natural rubber latex can be administered.

Pregnancy

The concern with vaccination of a pregnant woman is infection of the fetus and is theoretical. Only smallpox (vaccinia) vaccine has been shown to cause fetal injury. However, since the theoretical possibility exists, live vaccines should not be administered to women known to be pregnant.

Since inactivated vaccines cannot replicate, they cannot cause fetal infection. In general, inactivated vaccines may be administered to pregnant women for whom they are indicated. An exception is human papillomavirus (HPV) vaccine, which should be deferred during pregnancy because of a lack of safety and efficacy data for this vaccine in pregnant women.

Pregnant women are at increased risk of complications of influenza. Any woman who will be pregnant during influenza season (generally December through March) should receive inactivated influenza vaccine. Pregnant women should not receive live attenuated influenza vaccine.

Any woman who might become pregnant is encouraged to receive a single dose of Tdap if she has not already received a dose. Women who have not received Tdap should receive a dose in the immediate postpartum period, before discharge from the hospital or birthing center.

Vaccination of Pregnant Women

- Live vaccines should not be administered to women known to be pregnant
- In general inactivated vaccines may be administered to pregnant women for whom they are indicated
- HPV vaccine should be deferred during pregnancy

2

Use of Tdap Among Pregnant Women

- Any woman who might become pregnant is encouraged to receive a single dose of Tdap
- Women who have not received Tdap should receive a dose in the immediate postpartum period
- ACIP recommends Td when tetanus and diphtheria protection is required during pregnancy
- Pregnancy is not a contraindication for Tdap
- Clinician may choose to administer Tdap to a pregnant woman in certain circumstances (such as during a community pertussis outbreak)

MMWR 2008;57(RR-4)

ACIP recommends Td when tetanus and diphtheria protection is required during pregnancy. However, pregnancy is not a contraindication for use of Tdap. A clinician may choose to administer Tdap to a pregnant woman in certain circumstances, such as during a community pertussis outbreak. When Td or Tdap is administered during pregnancy, the second or third trimester is preferred to avoid coincidental association of vaccination and spontaneous termination of a pregnancy, which is more common in the first trimester. Clinicians can choose to administer Tdap instead of Td to protect against pertussis in pregnant adolescents for routine or "catch-up" vaccination because the incidence of pertussis is high among adolescents. They also may consider Tdap for pregnant healthcare personnel and child care providers to prevent transmission to infants younger than 12 months of age and other vulnerable persons, and for pregnant women employed in an institution or living in a community with increased pertussis activity.

Susceptible household contacts of pregnant women should receive MMR and varicella vaccines, and may receive LAIV, zoster and rotavirus vaccines if they are otherwise eligible.

Immunosuppression

Live vaccines can cause severe or fatal reactions in immunosuppressed persons due to uncontrolled replication of the vaccine virus. Live vaccines should not be administered to severely immunosuppressed persons for this reason. Persons with isolated B-cell deficiency may receive varicella vaccine. Inactivated vaccines cannot replicate, so they are safe to use in immunosuppressed persons. However, response to the vaccine may be decreased.

Vaccination of Immunosuppressed Persons

- Live vaccines should not be administered to severely immunosuppressed persons
- Persons with isolated B-cell deficiency may receive varicella vaccine
- Inactivated vaccines are safe to use in immunosuppressed persons but the response to the vaccine may be decreased

Both diseases and drugs can cause significant immunosuppression. Persons with congenital immunodeficiency, leukemia, lymphoma, or generalized malignancy should not receive live vaccines. However, MMR, varicella, rotavirus, and LAIV vaccines may be given when an immunosuppressed person lives in the same house. Household contacts of immunosuppressed persons may receive zoster vaccine if indicated. Transmission has not been documented from a person who received zoster vaccine.

Immunosuppression

- Disease
  - congenital immunodeficiency
  - leukemia or lymphoma
  - generalized malignancy

- Chemotherapy
  - alkylating agents
  - antimetabolites
  - radiation

Certain drugs may cause immunosuppression. For instance, persons receiving cancer treatment with alkylating agents or antimetabolites, or radiation therapy should not be given live vaccines. Live vaccines can be given after chemotherapy has been discontinued for at least 3 months. Persons receiving large doses of corticosteroids should not receive live vaccines. For example, this would include persons receiving 20 milligrams or more of prednisone daily or 2 or more milligrams of prednisone per kilogram of body weight per day for 14 days or longer. See Chapter 20 for more information about administration of zoster vaccine to immunosuppressed persons.

Aerosolized steroids, such as inhalers for asthma, are not contraindications to vaccination, nor are alternate-day, rapidly tapering, and short (less than 14 days) high-dose schedules, topical formulations, and physiologic replacement schedules.

The safety and efficacy of live attenuated vaccines administered concurrently with recombinant human immune mediators and immune modulators are not known. There is evidence that use of therapeutic monoclonal antibodies, especially the anti-tumor necrosis factor agents adalimumab, infliximab, and etanercept, may lead to reactivation of latent tuberculosis infection and tuberculosis disease and predispose to other opportunistic infections. Because the safety of live attenuated vaccines for persons receiving these drugs is not known, it is prudent to avoid administration of live attenuated vaccines for at least a month following treatment with these drugs.

Inactivated vaccines may be administered to immunosuppressed persons. Certain vaccines are recommended or encouraged specifically because immunosuppression is a risk factor for complications from vaccine-preventable diseases (i.e., influenza, invasive pneumococcal disease, invasive meningococcal disease, invasive *Haemophilus influenzae* type b disease, and hepatitis B). However, response to the vaccine may be poor depending on the degree of immunosuppression present. Because a relatively functional immune system is required to develop an immune response to a vaccine, an immunosuppressed person may not be protected even if the vaccine has been given. Additional recommendations for vaccination of immunosuppressed persons are detailed in the *General Recommendations on Immunization*.

HIV Infection

Persons infected with human immunodeficiency virus (HIV) may have no symptoms, or they may be severely immunosuppressed. In general, the same vaccination recommendations apply as with other types of immunosuppression. Live-virus vaccines are usually contraindicated, but inactivated vaccines may be administered if indicated.

Varicella and measles can be very severe illnesses in persons with HIV infection and are often associated with complications. Varicella vaccine is recommended for children (but not adults) with HIV infection who are not severely immunosuppressed. Zoster vaccine should not be given to persons with AIDS or clinical manifestations of HIV infection. Measles vaccine (as combination MMR vaccine) is Recommended

---

Immunosuppression

- Corticosteroids
  - —20 mg or more per day of prednisone*
  - —2 mg/kg or more per day of prednisone*
  - —NOT aerosols, alternate-day, short courses, topical

*for 14 days or longer

2

**Live Attenuated Vaccines
for Persons with HIV/AIDS***

Vaccine	Asymptomatic	Symptomatic
Varicella	Yes	No
Zoster	No	No
MMR	Yes	No
MMRV	No	No
LAIV	No	No
Rotavirus	No	No
Yellow fever	Consider	No

Yes=vaccinate   No=do not vaccinate

*see specific ACIP recommendations for details.

**Vaccination of Hematopoietic Stem
Cell Transplant Recipients**

• Antibody titers to VPDs decline during
the 1-4 years after allogeneic or
autologous HSCT if the recipient is not
revaccinated

• HSCT recipients are at increased risk of
some VPDs, particularly pneumococcal
disease

• Revaccination recommended beginning
6-12 months posttransplant

MMWR 2000;49(RR-10)

for persons with HIV infection who are asymptomatic or
mildly immunosuppressed. However, persons with severe
immunosuppression due to HIV infection should not receive
measles vaccine or MMR. MMRV should not be administered
to persons with HIV infection. Persons with HIV infection
should not receive LAIV; they should receive inactivated
influenza vaccine (TIV). Yellow fever vaccine should be
considered for persons who do not have AIDS or other
symptomatic manifestations of HIV infection, who have
established laboratory verification of adequate immune
system function, and who cannot avoid potential exposure
to yellow fever virus.

Susceptible household contacts of persons with HIV infection
should receive MMR and varicella vaccines, and may receive
rotavirus, zoster and LAIV vaccines if otherwise eligible.

Vaccination of Hematopoietic Stem Cell Transplant Recipients

Hematopoietic stem cell transplant (HSCT) is the infusion
of hematopoietic stem cells from a donor into a patient
who has received chemotherapy and often radiation, both
of which are usually bone marrow ablative. HSCT is used
to treat a variety of neoplastic diseases, hematologic disorders, immunodeficiency syndromes, congenital enzyme
deficiencies, and autoimmune disorders. HSCT recipients
can receive either their own cells (i.e., autologous HSCT) or
cells from a donor other than the transplant recipient (i.e.,
allogeneic HSCT).

Antibody titers to vaccine-preventable diseases (e.g., tetanus,
poliovirus, measles, mumps, rubella, and encapsulated
bacteria [i.e., *Streptococcus pneumoniae* and *Haemophilus
influenzae* type b]) decline during the 1–4 years after allogeneic or autologous HSCT if the recipient is not revaccinated.
HSCT recipients are at increased risk for certain vaccine-
preventable diseases. As a result, HSCT recipients should be
routinely revaccinated after HSCT, regardless of the source of
the transplanted stem cells. Revaccination with inactivated
vaccines should begin 12 months after HSCT. An exception
to this recommendation is influenza vaccine, which
should be administered 6 months after HSCT and annually
thereafter for the life of the recipient. Revaccination with
pneumococcal conjugate vaccine (PCV) can be considered,
especially if the HSCT recipient is younger than 60 months.
Two doses of PCV followed by a dose of pneumococcal polysaccharide vaccine (at least 8 weeks after the second dose of
PCV) are recommended.

MMR and varicella vaccines should be administered 24
months after transplantation if the HSCT recipient is
presumed to be immunocompetent. ACIP has not made a
recommendation regarding the use of meningococcal and

Tdap vaccines among HSCT recipients. Use of these vaccines should be a case-by-case decision by the clinician.

Household and other close contacts of HSCT recipients and healthcare providers who care for HSCT recipients should be appropriately vaccinated, particularly against influenza, measles, and varicella. Additional details of vaccination of HSCT recipients and their contacts can be found in a CDC report on this topic available at http://www.cdc.gov/vaccines/pubs/textbks-manuals-guides.htm

Moderate or Severe Acute Illness

There is no evidence that a concurrent acute illness reduces vaccine efficacy or increases vaccine adverse events. The concern is that an adverse event (particularly fever) following vaccination could complicate the management of a severely ill person. If a person has a moderate or severe acute illness, vaccination with both live and inactivated vaccines should be delayed until the illness has improved.

Invalid Contraindications to Vaccination

Some healthcare providers inappropriately consider certain conditions or circumstances to be true contraindications or precautions to vaccinations. Such conditions or circumstances are known as invalid contraindications; they result in missed opportunities to administer needed vaccines. Some of the most common invalid contraindications are mild illnesses, conditions related to pregnancy and breastfeeding, allergies that are not anaphylactic in nature, and certain aspects of the patient's family history.

Mild Illness

Children with mild acute illnesses, such as low-grade fever, upper respiratory infection (URI), colds, otitis media, and mild diarrhea, should be vaccinated on schedule. Several large studies have shown that young children with URI, otitis media, diarrhea, and/or fever respond to measles vaccine as well as those without these conditions. There is no evidence that mild diarrhea reduces the success of immunization of infants in the United States.

Low-grade fever is not a contraindication to immunization. Temperature measurement is not necessary before immunization if the infant or child does not appear ill and the parent does not say the child is currently ill. ACIP has not defined a body temperature above which vaccines should not be administered. The decision to vaccinate should be based on the overall evaluation of the person rather than an arbitrary body temperature.

Invalid Contraindications to Vaccination

- Mild illness
- Antimicrobial therapy
- Disease exposure or convalescence
- Pregnant or immunosuppressed person in the household
- Breastfeeding
- Preterm birth
- Allergy to products not present in vaccine or allergy that is not anaphylactic
- Family history of adverse events
- Tuberculin skin test
- Multiple vaccines

Antimicrobial Therapy

Antibiotics do not have an effect on the immune response to most vaccines. The manufacturer advises that Ty21a oral typhoid vaccine should not be administered to persons receiving sulfonamides or other antibiotics; Ty21a should be administered at least 24 hours after a dose of an antibacterial drug.

No commonly used antimicrobial drug will inactivate a live-virus vaccine. However, antiviral drugs may affect vaccine replication in some circumstances. Live attenuated influenza vaccine should not be administered until 48 hours after cessation of therapy using antiviral drugs active against influenza (amantadine, rimantadine, zanamivir, oseltamivir). Antiviral drugs active against herpesviruses (acyclovir, famciclovir) should be discontinued 24 hours before administration of a varicella-containing vaccine, if possible.

Disease Exposure or Convalescence

If a person is not moderately or severely ill, he or she should be vaccinated. There is no evidence that either disease exposure or convalescence will affect the response to a vaccine or increase the likelihood of an adverse event.

Pregnant or Immunosuppressed Person in the Household

It is critical that healthy household contacts of pregnant women and immunosuppressed persons be vaccinated. Vaccination of healthy contacts reduces the chance of exposure of pregnant women and immunosuppressed persons.

Most vaccines, including live vaccines (MMR, varicella, zoster, rotavirus, LAIV, and yellow fever) can be administered to infants or children who are household contacts of pregnant or immunosuppressed persons, as well as to breastfeeding infants (where applicable). Vaccinia (smallpox) vaccine should not be administered to household contacts of a pregnant or immunosuppressed person in a nonemergency situation. Live attenuated influenza vaccine should not be administered to persons who have contact with severely immunosuppressed persons who are hospitalized and require care in a protected environment (i.e., who are in isolation because of immunosuppression). LAIV may be administered to contacts of persons with lesser degrees of immunosuppression.

Measles and mumps vaccine viruses produce a noncommunicable infection and are not transmitted to household contacts. Rubella vaccine virus has been shown to be shed in human milk, but transmission to an infant has rarely been documented. Transmission of varicella vaccine virus is not common, and most women and older immunosuppressed persons are immune from having had chickenpox as a child. Transmission of zoster vaccine virus to household or other close contacts has not been reported.

Breastfeeding

Breastfeeding does not decrease the response to routine childhood vaccines and is not a contraindication for any vaccine except smallpox. Breastfeeding also does not extend or improve the passive immunity to vaccine-preventable disease that is provided by maternal antibody except possibly for *Haemophilus influenzae* type b. Breastfed infants should be vaccinated according to recommended schedules. Although rubella vaccine virus might be shed in human milk, infection of an infant is rare. LAIV may be administered to a woman who is breastfeeding if she is otherwise eligible; the risk of transmission of vaccine virus is unknown but is probably low.

Preterm Birth

Vaccines should be started on schedule on the basis of the child's chronological age. Preterm infants have been shown to respond adequately to vaccines used in infancy.

Studies demonstrate that decreased seroconversion rates might occur among preterm infants with very low birth weight (less than 2,000 grams) after administration of hepatitis B vaccine at birth. However, by 1 month chronological age, all preterm infants, regardless of initial birth weight or gestational age are as likely to respond as adequately as older and larger infants. All preterm infants born to hepatitis B surface antigen (HBsAg)-positive mothers and mothers with unknown HBsAg status must receive immunoprophylaxis with hepatitis B vaccine and hepatitis B immunoglobulin (HBIG) within 12 hours after birth. If these infants weigh less than 2,000 grams at birth, the initial vaccine dose should not be counted toward completion of the hepatitis B vaccine series, and three additional doses of hepatitis B vaccine should be administered beginning when the infant is 1 month of age.

Preterm infants with a birth weight of less than 2,000 grams who are born to women documented to be HBsAg-negative at the time of birth should receive the first dose of the hepatitis B vaccine series at 1 month of chronological age or at the time of hospital discharge.

Allergy to Products Not Present in Vaccine

Infants and children with nonspecific allergies, duck or feather allergy, or allergy to penicillin, children who have relatives with allergies, and children taking allergy shots can and should be immunized. No vaccine available in the United States contains duck antigen or penicillin.

Allergy That is Not Anaphylactic

Anaphylactic allergy to a vaccine component (such as egg or neomycin) is a true contraindication to vaccination. If an allergy to a vaccine component is not anaphylactic, it is not a contraindication to that vaccine.

Family History of Adverse Events

The only family history that is relevant in the decision to vaccinate a child is immunosuppression. A family history of adverse reactions unrelated to immunosuppression or family history of seizures or sudden infant death syndrome (SIDS) is not a contraindication to vaccination. Varicella-containing vaccine (except zoster) should not be administered to persons who have a family history of congenital or hereditary immunodeficiency in first-degree relatives (e.g., parents and siblings) unless the immunocompetence of the potential vaccine recipient has been clinically substantiated or verified by a laboratory.

Tuberculin Skin Test

Infants and children who need a tuberculin skin test (TST) can and should be immunized. All vaccines, including MMR, can be given on the same day as a TST, or any time after a TST is applied. For most vaccines, there are no TST timing restrictions.

MMR vaccine may decrease the response to a TST, potentially causing a false-negative response in someone who actually has an infection with tuberculosis. MMR can be given the same day as a TST, but if MMR has been given and 1 or more days have elapsed, in most situations a wait of at least 4 weeks is recommended before giving a routine TST. No information on the effect of varicella-containing vaccine or LAIV on a TST is available. Until such information is available, it is prudent to apply rules for spacing measles vaccine and TST to varicella vaccine and LAIV.

Multiple Vaccines

As noted earlier in this chapter, administration at the same visit of all vaccines for which a person is eligible is critical to reaching and maintaining high vaccination coverage. All vaccines (except vaccinia) can be administered at the same visit as all other vaccines.

Screening for Contraindications and Precautions to Vaccination

2

The key to preventing serious adverse reactions is screening. Every person who administers vaccines should screen every patient for contraindications and precautions before giving the vaccine dose. Effective screening is not difficult or complicated and can be accomplished with just a few questions.

Is the child (or are you) sick today?

There is no evidence that acute illness reduces vaccine efficacy or increases vaccine adverse events. However, as a precaution, with moderate or severe acute illness, all vaccines should be delayed until the illness has improved. Mild illnesses (such as otitis media, upper respiratory infections, and diarrhea) are NOT contraindications to vaccination. Do not withhold vaccination if a person is taking antibiotics.

Does the child have allergies to medications, food, or any vaccine?

A history of anaphylactic reaction such as hives (urticaria), wheezing or difficulty breathing, or circulatory collapse or shock (not fainting) from a previous dose of vaccine or vaccine component is a contraindication for further doses. For example, if a person experiences anaphylaxis after eating eggs, do not administer influenza vaccine. It may be more efficient to inquire about allergies in a generic way (i.e., any food or medication) rather than to inquire about specific vaccine components. Most parents will not be familiar with minor components of vaccine, but they should know if the child has had an allergic reaction to a food or medication that was severe enough to require medical attention.

Has the child had a serious reaction to a vaccine in the past?

A history of anaphylactic reaction to a previous dose of vaccine or vaccine component is a contraindication for subsequent doses. A history of encephalopathy within 7 days following DTP/DTaP is a contraindication for further doses of pertussis-containing vaccine. Precautions to DTaP (not Tdap) include (a) seizure within 3 days of a dose, (b) pale or limp episode or collapse within 48 hours of a dose, (c) continuous crying for 3 hours within 48 hours of a dose, and (d) fever of 105°F (40°C) within 48 hours of a previous dose. There are other adverse events that might have occurred following vaccination that constitute contraindications or precautions to future doses. Usually vaccines are deferred when a precaution is present. However, situations may arise when the benefit outweighs the risk (e.g., during a community pertussis outbreak). A local reaction (redness or swelling at the site of injection) is not a contraindication to subsequent doses.

Screening Questions

- Is the child (or are you) sick today?
- Does the child have allergies to medications, food, or any vaccine?
- Has the child had a serious reaction to a vaccine in the past?
- Has the child had a seizure, or brain or nerve problem?
- Has the child had a health problem with asthma, lung disease, heart disease, kidney disease, metabolic disease such as diabetes, or a blood disorder?
- Does the child have cancer, leukemia, AIDS, or any other immune system problem?

Screening Questions

- Has the child taken cortisone, prednisone, other steroids, or anticancer drugs, or had x-ray treatments in the past 3 months?
- Has the child received a transfusion of blood or blood products, or been given a medicine called immune (gamma) globulin in the past year?
- Is the child/teen pregnant or is there a chance she could become pregnant during the next month?
- Has the child received vaccinations in the past 4 weeks?

2

Has the child had a seizure, or brain or nerve problem?

DTaP and Tdap are contraindicated for children who have a history of encephalopathy within 7 days following DTP/DTaP. An unstable progressive neurologic problem is a precaution to the use of DTaP and Tdap. For children with stable neurologic disorders (including seizures) unrelated to vaccination, or for children with a family history of seizure, vaccinate as usual but consider the use of acetaminophen or ibuprofen to minimize fever.

A history of Guillain-Barré syndrome is a precaution for tetanus-containing, influenza and meningococcal conjugate vaccines.

Has the child had a health problem with asthma, lung disease, heart disease, kidney disease, metabolic disease such as diabetes, or a blood disorder?

Children with any of these conditions should not receive LAIV. Children with these conditions should receive inactivated influenza vaccine only.

Does the child have cancer, leukemia, AIDS, or any other immune system problem?

Live-virus vaccines (e.g., MMR, varicella, rotavirus, and the intranasal live attenuated influenza vaccine [LAIV]) are usually contraindicated in immunocompromised children. However, there are exceptions. For example, MMR and varicella vaccines are recommended for asymptomatic HIV-infected children who do not have evidence of severe immunosuppression. Persons with severe immunosuppression should not receive MMR, varicella, rotavirus, or LAIV vaccines. For details, consult the ACIP recommendations for each vaccine.

Has the child taken cortisone, prednisone, other steroids, or anticancer drugs, or had x-ray treatments in the past 3 months?

Live-virus vaccines (e.g., MMR, varicella, zoster, LAIV) should be postponed until after chemotherapy or long-term, high-dose steroid therapy has ended. Details and the length of time to postpone vaccination are described elsewhere in this chapter and in the *General Recommendations on Immunization*.

Has the child received a transfusion of blood or blood products, or been given a medicine called immune (gamma) globulin in the past year?

Certain live virus vaccines (e.g., MMR and varicella) may need to be deferred, depending on the type of blood product and the interval since the blood product was administered. Information on recommended intervals between immune globulin or blood product administration and MMR or varicella vaccination is in Appendix A and in the *General Recommendations on Immunization*.

Is the child/teen pregnant or is there a chance she could become pregnant during the next month?

Live-virus vaccines (e.g., MMR, varicella, zoster, LAIV) are contraindicated during pregnancy because of the theoretical risk of virus transmission to the fetus. Sexually active young women who receive MMR or varicella vaccination should be instructed to practice careful contraception for 1 month following receipt of either vaccine. On theoretical grounds, inactivated poliovirus vaccine should not be given during pregnancy; however, it may be given if the risk of exposure is imminent (e.g., travel to endemic-disease areas) and immediate protection is needed. Use of Td or Tdap is not contraindicated in pregnancy. At the provider's discretion, either vaccine may be administered during the second or third trimester.

Has the child received vaccinations in the past 4 weeks?

If the child was given either live attenuated influenza vaccine or an injectable live-virus vaccine (e.g., MMR. varicella, yellow fever) in the past 4 weeks, he or she should wait 28 days before receiving another live vaccine. Inactivated vaccines may be given at the same time or at any time before or after a live vaccine.

Every person should be screened for contraindications and precautions before vaccination. Standardized screening forms for both children and adults have been developed by the Immunization Action Coalition and are available on their web site at http://www.immunize.org.

ACKNOWLEDGMENT
The editors thank Dr. Andrew Kroger, National Center for Immunization and Respiratory Diseases, CDC, for his assistance in updating this chapter.

Selected References

American Academy of Pediatrics. Active and passive immunization. In: Pickering L, Baker C, Long S, McMillan J, eds. *Red Book: 2006 Report of the Committee on Infectious Diseases.* 27th edition. Elk Grove Village, IL: American Academy of Pediatrics; 2006:1–103.

Atkinson W, Pickering LK, Watson JC, Peter G. General immunization practices. In: Plotkin SA, OrentseinWA, eds. *Vaccines.* 4th ed., Philadelphia, PA: Saunders; 2003:91–122.

CDC. General recommendations on immunization: recommendations of the Advisory Committee on Immunization Practices. *MMWR* 2006;55(No. RR-15):1–48.

CDC. Guidelines for preventing opportunistic infections among hematopoietic stem cell transplant recipients: recommendations of CDC, the Infectious Disease Society of America, and the American Society of Blood and Marrow Transplantation. *MMWR* 2000;49(No. RR-10):1–128.

Dietz VJ, Stevenson J, Zell ER, et al. Potential impact on vaccination coverage levels by administering vaccines simultaneously and reducing dropout rates. *Arch Pediatr Adolesc Med* 1994;148:943–9.

James JM, Burks AW, Roberson RK, Sampson HA. Safe administration of the measles vaccine to children allergic to eggs. *N Engl J Med* 1995;332:1262–9.

King GE, Hadler SC. Simultaneous administration of childhood vaccines: an important public health policy that is safe and efficacious. *Pediatr Infect Dis J* 1994;13:394–407.

Ljungman P, Engelhard D, de la Camara R, et al. Special report: vaccination of stem cell transplant recipients: recommendations of the Infectious Diseases Working Party of the EBMT. *Bone Marrow Transplant* 2005;35:737–46.

Plotkin SA. Vaccines, vaccination and vaccinology. *J. Infect Dis* 2003;187:1349–59.

Immunization Strategies for Healthcare Practices and Providers

The Need for Strategies to Increase Immunization Levels

An important component of an immunization provider practice is ensuring that the vaccines reach all children who need them. While attention to appropriate administration of vaccinations is essential, it cannot be assumed that these vaccinations are being given to every eligible child at the recommended age. Immunization levels in the Unites States are high, but gaps still exist, and providers can do much to maintain or increase immunization rates among patients in their practice. This chapter describes the need for increasing immunization levels and outlines strategies that providers can adopt to increase coverage in their own practice.

Vaccine-preventable disease rates in the United States are at very low levels. In 2007, only 43 cases of measles, 12 cases of rubella, no cases of diphtheria, 28 cases of tetanus, and no wild-type polio were reported to CDC. Given these immunization successes, one might question the continued interest in strategies to increase immunization levels.

However, although levels of vaccine-preventable diseases are low, this should not breed complacency regarding vaccination. For several reasons—including possible resurgence of disease, introduction of new vaccines, suboptimal immunization levels, cost-effectiveness, and gaps in sustainable immunization efforts—the need to focus on immunization rates remains crucial. The viruses and bacteria that cause vaccine-preventable disease and death still exist and can be passed on to unprotected persons or imported from other countries as demonstrated by measles outbreaks that occurred in 2008. Diseases such as measles, mumps, or pertussis can be more severe than often assumed and can result in social and economic as well as physical costs: sick children miss school, parents lose time from work, and illness among healthcare providers can severely disrupt a healthcare system. For many of these diseases, without vaccination, the incidence will rise to prevaccine levels.

Although levels of disease are the ultimate outcome of interest, these are a late indicator of the soundness of the immunization system. Immunization levels are a better indicator for determining if there is a problem with immunization delivery, and this chapter will focus on increasing immunization levels and the strategies healthcare providers can use to do this.

3

3

Specific concerns about U.S. immunization levels and areas for further study include the following:

Childhood immunization rates are still suboptimal. In 2007, for example, only 84.5% of children 19 to 35 months of age had received four doses of DTaP vaccine.

For other age groups, immunization rates are considerably lower than those for early childhood. According to Behavior Risk Factor Surveillance System data from 2005, a median of only 65.5% of persons 65 years of age and older received the influenza vaccine in the past 12 months, and 65.7% had ever received pneumococcal vaccine.

Economic and racial disparities exist. Low-income and minority children and adults are at greater risk for underimmunization. "Pockets of need" exist in our nation's inner cities.

Rates of influenza immunization are also unacceptably low among healthcare providers, an important target population for vaccination. Typically, fewer than 40% of healthcare providers receive influenza vaccine.

Improvements in adult immunization rates have tapered off. According to data from the National Health Interview Survey, after a consistent increase in rates during the 1980s and early 1990s, improvements in influenza vaccination rates for adults 65 years of age and older have leveled off since 1997.

Cost-effectiveness needs more research. More research is needed regarding which strategies increase immunization levels with the least expenditure so these strategies can be prioritized.

Sustainable systems for vaccinating children, adolescents, and adults must be developed. High immunization rates cannot rest upon one-time or short-term efforts. Greater understanding of strategies to increase immunization levels is necessary in order to create lasting, effective immunization delivery systems.

Many strategies have been used to increase immunizations. Some, such as school entry laws, have effectively increased demand for vaccines, but the effectiveness of other strategies (e.g., advertising) is less well documented. Some proven strategies (e.g., reducing costs, linking immunization to Women Infants and Children (WIC) services, home visiting) are well suited to increasing rates among specific populations, such as persons with low access to immunization services.

One key to a successful strategy to increase immunization is matching the proposed solution to the current problem. At present in the United States, most persons have sufficient

---

Why Focus on Strategies to Increase Immunization?

- Immunization levels not optimal
- Cost-effectiveness of some strategies uncertain
- Sustainable systems needed

---

interest in and access to health care and are seen, at least periodically, in healthcare systems. Those who remain unvaccinated are so largely because healthcare practices and providers do not always optimally perform the activities associated with delivering vaccines and keeping patients up-to-date with their immunization schedules. Although a combination of strategies—directed at both providers and the public—is necessary for increasing and maintaining high immunization rates, this chapter focuses on immunization strategies for healthcare practices and providers.

The AFIX Approach

The CDC, through state and other grantees, administers a program designed to move healthcare personnel from a state of unawareness about the problem of low immunization rates in their practice to one in which they are knowledgeable, concerned, motivated to change their immunization practices and capable of sustaining new behaviors. The acronym used for this approach is AFIX: Assessment of the immunization coverage of public and private providers, Feedback of diagnostic information to improve service delivery, Incentives to motivate providers to change immunization practices or recognition of improved or high performance, and eXchange of information among providers. First conceived by the Georgia Division of Public Health, AFIX is now being used nationwide with both public and private immunization providers and is recommended by governmental and nongovernmental vaccine programs and medical professional societies.

Overview

The AFIX process consists of an assessment of an immunization provider's coverage rates by a trained representative from the state or other immunization grantee program, feedback of the results of the assessment to provider staff, incentives to improve deficiencies and raise immunization rates, and exchange of information and ideas among healthcare providers. Some specific characteristics of this approach have made it one of the most effective for achieving high, sustainable vaccine coverage.

First, AFIX focuses on outcomes. It starts with an assessment, producing an estimate of immunization coverage levels in a provider's office, and these data help to identify specific actions to take in order to remedy deficiencies. Outcomes are easily measurable. Second, AFIX focuses on providers, those who are key to increasing immunization rates. AFIX requires no governmental policy changes, nor does it attempt to persuade clients to be vaccinated, but instead focuses on changing healthcare provider behavior. Third, AFIX, when used successfully, is a unique blend of advanced technology and personal interaction. Much of the AFIX

AFIX

Assessment

Feedback

Incentives

eXchange

Special Characteristics of AFIX

- Focuses on outcomes
- Focuses on providers
- Blend of advanced technology and personal interaction

3

process can be done electronically, increasing speed and accuracy of assessment and feedback and streamlining reporting. However, the personal skills of the assessor and that person's ability to establish rapport with and motivate a provider are critical to achieving lasting results.

Assessment

Assessment refers to the evaluation of medical records to ascertain the immunization rate for a defined group of patients as well as to provide targeted diagnosis for improvement. This step is essential because several studies have documented that most healthcare providers, while supportive of immunizations, do not have an accurate perception of their own practice's immunization rates. Pediatricians in these studies greatly overestimated the proportion of fully immunized children in their practices. Assessment increases awareness of a provider's actual situation and provides a basis for subsequent actions by provider staff.

CDC has developed a software program, CoCASA, that enables assessment to be done electronically, is flexible enough to accommodate whatever assessment parameters are desired, and provides results that can be printed immediately. This program will be described further in the section, "AFIX Tools and Training."

Feedback

Feedback is the process of informing immunization providers about their performance in delivering one or more vaccines to a defined client population. The work of assessment is of no use unless the results are fed back to persons who can make a change. Assessment together with feedback creates the awareness necessary for behavior change.

Feedback generally consists of the immunization program representative meeting with appropriate provider staff and discussing the results of the assessment in order to determine the next steps to be taken. This may be done at a second visit following the assessment of the provider's records, or it may take place the same day. There are advantages and disadvantages to each approach. If CoCASA has been used, the summary report that is generated can identify specific subsets of patients (e.g., those who have not completed the series because of a missed opportunity for immunization) that, if found in substantial numbers, can provide clues to which changes in the provider's practice would be most effective. This can save time and make the feedback session more focused.

The personal element of feedback, as mentioned, is also critical to its success. A reviewer who is involved and

---

Assessment

- Evaluation of medical records to ascertain the immunization rate for a defined group
- Diagnosis of potential service delivery problems
- Assessment increases awareness

Feedback

- Informing immunization providers about their performance
- Assessment with feedback creates the awareness necessary for behavior change

---

How to Provide Feedback

- With feeling and precision
- Without judgment
- With confidentiality as appropriate

---

committed to the AFIX process, who addresses deficiencies without judgment, and who respects the confidentiality of the data and the efforts of the provider will be likely to gain the trust of providers and motivate them to increase immunization rates in the practice.

Incentives

An incentive is defined as something that incites one to action or effort. Incentives are built into the AFIX process, recognizing that immunization providers, like everyone else, will accomplish a desired task more successfully if motivated to do so. The assessment and feedback components are not intended to be done in isolation; providers may have sufficient data about their practice's immunization rates, but they must recognize high immunization coverage as a desirable goal and be motivated to achieve it.

Incentives are extremely variable. No one thing will be effective for every provider, and a single provider may need different types of motivation at different stages of progress. Things like small tokens of appreciation and providing resource materials at meetings have helped providers approach their task positively and create an atmosphere of teamwork, but longer-term goals must be considered as well. Since the effort to raise immunization rates may involve an increase in duties for staff, offering assistance in reviewing records or sending reminder notices might more directly address a provider's needs. Incentives pose a challenge to the creativity of the program representative but also offer the opportunity to try new ideas.

Finally, incentives are opportunities for partnerships and collaboration. Professional organizations or businesses have been solicited to publicize the immunization efforts in a newsletter or provide funding for other rewards for provider staff. Many other types of collaboration are possible; these also have the benefit of increasing awareness of immunization among diverse groups.

eXchange of Information

The final AFIX component, eXchange of information, goes hand in hand with incentives. The more information providers have about their own practice's immunization coverage status, how it compares with state norms and with other providers in their community, and what strategies have been successful with other providers, the more knowledgeable and motivated they will be to increase their immunization rates. It is up to the AFIX representative to provide appropriate statistical and educational information and create forums for exchange of information among providers.

Incentives
- Something that incites to action
- Vary by provider and stage of progress
- Opportunities for partnership and collaboration

eXchange of Information
- Allows access to more experience than an individual can accumulate
- Motivates improvement
- Coordinates resources and efforts

3

Staff members at all levels can benefit from the exchange of ideas about immunization practices and increasing rates of coverage—what has worked or not worked with another provider, streamlining office procedures, or where to obtain educational or other resources. The forums for such exchanges vary widely from informal meetings on the local level to more structured meetings sponsored by government or professional organizations. Immunization training sessions can be combined with sharing of ideas regarding actual situations in which recommendations, such as those from ACIP, are applied.

With the increased use of electronic communication, this method should not be neglected in the information exchange component of AFIX. Although different from face-to-face communication, e-mail exchanges or newsletters sent electronically can be cost-saving and fast means of disseminating information.

VFC–AFIX Initiative

In the last several years, responsibility for immunization has largely shifted from public health departments to private providers, who now vaccinate nearly 80% of children in the United States. Many of these providers participate in the Vaccines for Children (VFC) program, a federal program whereby funding is provided for state and other immunization programs to purchase vaccines and make them available at no cost to children who meet income eligibility requirements. Because immunization program staff make periodic quality assurance site visits to VFC providers, CDC launched an initiative in 2000 to link some AFIX and VFC activities and incorporate AFIX activities during VFC provider site visits. VFC program staff are encouraged to promote the AFIX approach and, if possible, to combine VFC and AFIX site visits. This reduces the number of visits to a single provider and helps avoid duplication of staff time and effort. In addition, it increases the emphasis on overall quality improvement for a provider rather than meeting the requirements of a single program.

VFC serves more than 30,000 private provider sites, and every state participates in the program. VFC provider site visits are conducted to review compliance with VFC eligibility screening requirements and to evaluate vaccine storage and handling procedures. Linking VFC with AFIX enables AFIX to reach a large number of providers in the private sector and to reinforce the goals of both programs. Information about VFC can be found at http://www.cdc.gov/vaccines/programs/vfc/default.htm.

VFC/AFIX

- Incorporate AFIX activities during VFC site visits
- Combine VFC/AFIX site visits
- Reduces number of visits
- Extends reach of AFIX

3

AFIX Tools And Training

The CDC has developed a software program titled Comprehensive Clinic Assessment Software Application (CoCASA) to enable electronic entry of AFIX and VFC site visit data. CoCASA, first released in December 2005, is an update of previous versions of CASA and supersedes previous versions. Using CoCASA, a reviewer enters appropriate basic information about an individual provider and conducts an assessment of patient records. The user also has the option to record AFIX visit outcomes and VFC site visit information.

CoCASA can provide immediate results of the assessment, supplying the reviewer with the information needed for use in the feedback session and noting areas that need further follow-up. CoCASA saves the reviewer time and provides various analysis options. CoCASA reports provide estimates of immunization coverage levels and potential reasons for the coverage level, such as missed opportunities for immunization and patients who did not return to finish the immunization series. The program can generate reports on specific sets of patients, such as those mentioned. Data from an immunization registry or patient management system can be imported into CoCASA, and data collected during the visit can be exported for further analysis.

CoCASA is available on the CDC Vaccines and Immunization website at http://www.cdc.gov/vaccines/programs/cocasa/default.htm. Comprehensive training modules on AFIX and on how to use CoCASA are built into the CoCASA program. Additional information about AFIX is available on the CDC Vaccines and Immunization website at http://www.cdc.gov/vaccines/programs/afix/default.htm.

AFIX Endorsements

AFIX is widely supported as an effective strategy to improve vaccination rates. Many states have shown gradual and consistent improvement in their coverage levels in the public sector, and studies of private pediatricians have also documented substantial improvements in median up-to-date coverage at 24 months. Assessment and feedback of public and private provider sites are recommended by the National Vaccine Advisory Committee (NVAC) in the Standards of Pediatric Immunization Practices as well as by the Advisory Committee on Immunization Practices (ACIP) in a statement endorsing the AFIX process and recommending its use by all public and private providers. *Healthy People 2010* also supports the AFIX concept with a recommendation for increasing the proportion of immunization providers who have measured vaccination levels among children in their practice within the past 2 years.

Comprehensive Clinic Assessment Software Application (CoCASA)

- VFC and AFIX results
- Immediate assessment results
- Estimate of coverage levels
- Reasons for deficiencies
- Reports on patient subsets

3

One of the Standards for Adult Immunization Practices issued by NVAC calls upon providers of adult immunization to do annual assessments of coverage levels. Although the use of AFIX among providers who serve adults is not as widespread as among childhood immunization providers, this strategy can be a powerful tool to improve rates in the adult population.

Other Essential Strategies

Although a substantial portion of this chapter is devoted to AFIX, certain other strategies for improvement of immunization levels deserve emphasis. These are complementary to AFIX; their adoption will support the goals of AFIX, i.e., raising immunization coverage levels, and will facilitate the AFIX process and ensure a favorable outcome of an assessment.

Recordkeeping

Patient records are of vital importance in a medical practice, and maintaining these records, whether paper or electronic, is critical to providing optimal healthcare. Immunization records, specifically, should meet all applicable legal requirements as well as requirements of any specific program, such as VFC, in which the provider participates. These records should be available for inspection by an AFIX or VFC representative and should be easy to interpret by anyone examining the record.

Immunization records must be accurate. The active medical records must reflect which patients are actually in the practice; charts of persons who have moved or are obtaining services elsewhere should be clearly marked accordingly or removed. Records should be kept up-to-date as new immunizations are administered, and all information regarding the vaccine and its administration should be complete.

Because patients often receive vaccines at more than one provider office, communication between sites is necessary for maintaining complete and accurate immunization records. School-based, public health, and community-based immunization sites should communicate with primary care personnel through quick and reliable methods such as, telephone, fax, or e-mail. This will become increasingly important as new vaccines for adolescents are added to the immunization schedule and more alternative sites are available for receiving immunizations.

Strategies for High Immunization Levels

- Recordkeeping
- Recommendations and reinforcement
- Reminder and recall to patients
- Reminder and recall to providers
- Reduction of missed opportunities
- Reduction of barriers to immunization

Records

- Must be available at the time of the visit
- Must be easy to read
- Must be accurate
  - reflect current patient population
  - reflect all vaccines given

Immunization Information Systems (IIS)

Many recordkeeping tasks, as well as patient reminder/recall activities, can be greatly simplified by participation in a population-based immunization information system (IIS), also known as an immunization registry. An IIS is a computerized information system that contains information about the immunization status of each child in a given geographic area (e.g., a state). In some areas, an IIS is linked to a child's complete medical record. An IIS provides a single data source for all community immunization providers, enabling access to records of children receiving vaccinations at multiple providers. It provides a reliable immunization history for every enrolled child and can also produce accurate immunization records, if needed for school or summer camp entry.

An IIS can also generate reminder/recall notices (discussed below), relieving provider staff of an additional burden, and can automatically produce reports of immunization coverage in an individual provider's practice, or by the child's age or geographic area. A goal of *Healthy People 2010* is to increase to 95% the proportion of children younger than 6 years of age who participate in fully operational, population-based immunization registries. In 2007, approximately 71% of children in this age-group met this participation goal. Federal, state and local public health agencies are continuing their efforts to improve the registries themselves and to increase participation by immunization providers. Registries are a key to increasing and maintaining immunization levels and provide benefits for providers, patients, and state and federal immunization program personnel. More information about immunization registries is available on the CDC Vaccines and Immunization website at http://www.cdc.gov/vaccines/programs/iis/default.htm.

Recommendations to Parents and Reinforcement of the Need to Return

The recommendation of a healthcare provider is a powerful motivator for patients to comply with vaccination recommendations. Parents of pediatric patients are likely to follow vaccine recommendation of the child's doctor, and even adults who were initially reluctant were likely to receive an influenza vaccination when the healthcare provider's opinion of the vaccine was positive.

Regardless of their child's true immunization status, many parents believe the child is fully vaccinated. Parents may not have been told or may not have understood that return visits are necessary. It is useful for patients to have the next appointment date in hand at the time they leave the provider's office. An additional reminder strategy is to link the timing of the return visit to some calendar event, e.g., the child's birthday or an upcoming holiday. Even with

3

Immunization Information Systems

- Single data source for all providers
- Reliable immunization history
- Produce records for patient use
- Key to increasing immunization levels

Recommendations and Reinforcement

- Recommend the vaccine
  - powerful motivator
  - patients likely to follow recommendation of the provider
- Reinforce the need to return
  - verbal
  - written
  - link to calendar event

3

written schedules or reminders, a verbal encouragement and reminder can be an incentive for a patient's completing the immunization series and can ultimately result in higher coverage levels.

Reminder and Recall to Patients

- Reminder—notification that immunizations are due soon
- Recall—notification that immunizations are past due
- Content of message and technique of delivery vary
- Reminders and recall have been found to be effective

Reminder and Recall Messages to Patients

Patient reminders and recall messages are messages to patients or their parents stating that recommended immunizations are due soon (reminders) or past due (recall messages). The messages vary in their level of personalization and specificity, the mode of communication, (e.g., postcard, letter, telephone), and the degree of automation. Both reminders and recall messages have been found to be effective in increasing attendance at clinics and improving vaccination rates in various settings.

Cost is sometimes thought to be a barrier to the implementation of a reminder/recall system. However, a range of options is available, from computer-generated telephone calls and letters to a card file box with weekly dividers, and these can be adapted to the needs of the provider. The specific type of system is not directly related to its effectiveness, and the benefits of having any system can extend beyond immunizations to other preventive services and increase the use of other recommended screenings.

Both the Standards for Child and Adolescent Immunization Practices and the Standards for Adult Immunization Practices call upon providers to develop and implement aggressive tracking systems that will both remind parents of upcoming immunizations and recall children who are overdue. ACIP supports the use of reminder/recall systems by all providers. The National Center for Immunization and Respiratory Diseases provides state and local health departments with ongoing technical support to assist them in implementing reminder and recall systems in public and private provider sites.

Reminder and Recall to Providers

- Communication to healthcare providers that an individual client's immunizations are due soon or past due
- Examples
  - computer-generated list
  - stamped note in the chart
  - "Immunization Due" clip on chart

Reminder and Recall Messages to Providers

Providers can create reminder and recall systems for themselves as aids for remembering for which patients routine immunizations are due soon or past due. Provider reminder/recall is different from "feedback," in which the provider receives a message about overall immunization levels for a group of clients. Examples of reminder/recall messages are

- A computer-generated list that notifies a provider of the children to be seen that clinic session whose vaccinations are past due.

3

- A stamp with a message such as "No Pneumococcal Vaccine on Record," that a receptionist or nurse can put on a the chart of a person age 65 years or older.

- An "Immunization Due" clip that a nurse attaches to the chart of an adolescent who has not had hepatitis B vaccine.

Reminder systems will vary according to the needs of the provider; in addition to raising immunization rates in the practice, they will serve to heighten the awareness of staff members of the continual need to check the immunization status of their patients.

Reduction of Missed Opportunities to Vaccinate

A missed opportunity is a healthcare encounter in which a person is eligible to receive a vaccination but is not vaccinated completely. Missed opportunities occur in all settings in which immunizations are offered, whether routinely or not.

Missed opportunities occur for several reasons. At the provider level, many nurses and physicians avoid simultaneous administration of four or even three injectable vaccines. Frequently stated reasons have included concern about reduced immune response or adverse events, and parental objection. These concerns are not supported by scientific data. Providers also may be unaware that a child is in need of vaccination (especially if the immunization record is not available at the visit) or may follow invalid contraindications (see Chapter 2 for more information).

Some of the reasons for missed opportunities relate to larger systems; e.g., a clinic that has a policy of not vaccinating at any visits except well-child care, or not vaccinating siblings. Other reasons relate to large institutional or bureaucratic regulations, such as state insurance laws that deny reimbursement if a vaccine is given during an acute-care visit. The degree of difficulty in eliminating the missed opportunity may vary directly with the size of the system that has to be changed.

Several studies have shown that eliminating missed opportunities could increase vaccination coverage by up to 20 percent. Strategies designed to prevent missed opportunities have taken many different forms, used alone or in combination. Examples include the following:

- Standing orders. These are protocols whereby nonphysician immunization personnel may vaccinate clients without direct physician involvement at the time of the immunization. Standing orders are implemented in settings such as clinics, hospitals, and nursing homes.

Missed Opportunity

A healthcare encounter in which a person is eligible to receive vaccination but is not vaccinated completely

---

Reasons for Missed Opportunities

- Lack of simultaneous administration
- Unaware child needs additional vaccines
- Invalid contraindications
- Inappropriate clinic policies
- Reimbursement deficiencies

Strategies for Reducing Missed Opportunities

- Standing orders
- Provider education with feedback
- Provider reminder and recall systems

3

When used alone or in combination with other interventions, standing orders have had positive effects on immunization rates among adults.

- Provider education. Anyone responsible for administering immunizations should be knowledgeable about principles of vaccination and vaccination scheduling, to the extent required for their position. Providers are largely responsible for educating their patients, so an investment in provider education will result in a higher level of understanding about immunizations among the public in general. Numerous educational materials, in a variety of formats, are available from CDC, the Immunization Action Coalition, and some state health departments, hospitals, or professional organizations. Incorporating some AFIX principles (i.e., assessment, feedback) into a provider education program might have a greater effect on provider behavior than an education effort aimed only at increasing knowledge.

- Provider reminder and recall systems. Provider reminder and recall systems are discussed above. These reminder systems, while effective in increasing immunization levels, can also help avoid missed opportunities if they are a component of other practices directed toward this goal. For example, if a reminder system is used consistently and staff members are knowledgeable about vaccination opportunities and valid contraindications, the system can be an additional aid in promoting appropriate immunization practices.

Reduction of Barriers to Immunization Within the Practice

Despite efforts by providers to adhere to appropriate immunization practices, obstacles to patients' being vaccinated may exist within the practice setting, sometimes unknown to the provider. Barriers to immunization maybe physical or psychological. Physical barriers might be such things as inconvenient clinic hours for working patients or parents, long waits at the clinic, or the distance patients must travel. Providers should be encouraged to determine the needs of their specific patient population and take steps, such as extending clinic hours or providing some immunization clinics, to address obstacles to immunization.

Cost is also a barrier to immunization for many patients. In addition to evaluating their fee schedule for possible adjustments, providers should be knowledgeable about such programs as Vaccines for Children and the State Children's Health Insurance Program and the provisions specific to their state. Enrollment as a VFC provider is recommended for those with eligible children in their practice.

Reduction to Barriers to Immunization

- Physical barriers
  - waiting time
  - distance
- Psychological barriers
  - unpleasant experience
  - safety concerns

Psychological barriers to health care are often more subtle but may be just as important. Unpleasant experiences (e.g., fear of immunizations, being criticized for previously missed appointments, or difficulty leaving work for a clinic appointment) may lead clients to postpone receiving needed vaccinations. Concerns about vaccine safety are also preventing some parents from having their children immunized. Overcoming such barriers calls for both knowledge and interpersonal skills on the part of the provider—knowledge of vaccines and updated recommendations and of reliable sources to direct patients to find accurate information, and skills to deal with fears and misconceptions and to provide a supportive and encouraging environment for patients.

Selected References

American Academy of Pediatrics, Committee on Community Health Services and Committee on Practice and Ambulatory Medicine. Increasing Immunization Coverage. *Pediatrics* 2003;112:993–996.

CDC. Programmatic strategies to increase vaccination rates —assessment and feedback of provider-based vaccination coverage information. *MMWR* 1996;45:219–220.

CDC. Recommendations of the Advisory Committee on Immunization Practices (ACIP), the American Academy of Pediatrics, and the American Academy of Family Physicians: Use of reminder and recall by vaccination providers to increase vaccination rates. *MMWR* 1998;47:715–717.

Dietz VJ, Baughman AL, Dini EF, Stevenson JM, Pierce BK, Hersey JC. Vaccination practices, policies, and management factors associated with high vaccination coverage levels in Georgia public clinics. *Arch Pediatr Adolesc Med* 2000;154:184–189.

Dini EF, Linkins RW, Sigafoos, J. The impact of computer-generated messages on childhood immunization coverage. *Am J Prev Med* 2000;18(2):132–139.

LeBaron CW, Chaney M, Baughman AL, Dini EF, Maes E, Dietz V, et al. Impact of measurement and feedback on vaccination coverage in public clinics, 1988–1994. *JAMA* 1997;277:631–635.

LeBaron CW, Mercer JT, Massoudi MS, Dini EF, Stevenson JM, Fischer WM, et al. Changes in clinic vaccination coverage after institution of measurement and feedback in 4 states and 2 cities. *Arch Pediatr Adolesc Med* 1999;153:879–886.

Lieu T, Black S, Ray P. Computer-generated recall letters for underimmunized children: how cost-effective? *Pediatr Infect Dis J* 1997;16:28–33.

3

Lieu T, Capra A, Makol J, Black S, Shinefield H. Effectiveness and cost-effectiveness of letters, automated telephone messages, or both for underimmunized children in a health maintenance organization [Abstract]. *Pediatrics* 1998;101:690–691.

Massoudi MS, Walsh J, Stokley S, Rosenthal J, Stevenson J, Miljanovic B, et al. Assessing immunization performance of private practitioners in Maine: impact of the Assessment, Feedback, Incentives, and eXchange (AFIX) strategy. *Pediatrics* 1999;103:1218–1223.

National Vaccine Advisory Committee. Standards for child and adolescent immunization practices. *Pediatrics* 2003;112:958-63.

Poland GA, Shefer AM, McCauley M, et al. Standards for adult immunization practices. *Am J Prev Med* 2003;25:144–150.

Szilagyi PG, Rodewald LE; Humiston SG, et al. Immunization practices of pediatricians and family physicians in the United States. *Pediatrics* 1994;94:517–23. Available at http://www.aap.org/research/periodicsurvey/peds10_94b.htm.

Task Force on Community Preventive Services. *Guide to community preventive services*. Atlanta: Centers for Disease Control and Prevention. Available at http://www.thecommunityguide.org.

Yawn BP, Edmonson L, Huber L, Poland GA, Jacobson RM, Jacobsen SJ. The impact of a simulated immunization registry on perceived childhood immunization status. *Am J Managed Care* 1998;4:186–192.

Vaccine Safety

Vaccine safety is a prime concern for manufacturers, immunization providers, and recipients of vaccines. This chapter describes how vaccines licensed for use in the United States are monitored for safety, and presents general information about the provider's role in immunization safety. Further information about contraindications and precautions for individual vaccines, such as pregnancy and immunosuppression, and about potential adverse events associated with the vaccine is contained in Chapter 2, *General Recommendations on Immunization*, and in the chapters on specific vaccines.

The Importance of Vaccine Safety Programs

Vaccination is among the most significant public health success stories of all time. However, like any pharmaceutical product, no vaccine is completely safe or completely effective. While almost all known vaccine adverse events are minor and self-limited, some vaccines have been associated with very rare but serious health effects. The following key considerations underscore the need for an active and ongoing vaccine safety program.

Decreases in Disease Risks

Today, vaccine-preventable diseases are at or near record lows. By virtue of their absence, these diseases are no longer reminders of the benefits of vaccination. At the same time, approximately 15,000 cases of adverse events following vaccination are reported in the United States each year (these include both true adverse reactions and events that occur coincidentally after vaccination). This number exceeds the current reported incidence of vaccine-preventable childhood diseases. As a result, parents and providers in the United States are more likely to know someone who has experienced an adverse event following immunization than they are to know someone who has experienced a reportable vaccine-preventable disease. The success of vaccination has led to increased public attention on health risks associated with vaccines.

Public Confidence

Maintaining public confidence in immunizations is critical for preventing a decline in vaccination rates that can result in outbreaks of disease. While the majority of parents believe in the benefits of immunization and have their children vaccinated, some have concerns about the safety of vaccines. Public concerns about the safety of whole-cell pertussis vaccine in the 1980s resulted in decreased vaccine coverage levels and the return of epidemic disease in Japan,

---

Importance of Vaccine Safety
- Decreases in disease risks and increased attention on vaccine risks
- Public confidence in vaccine safety is critical
  - higher standard of safety is expected of vaccines
  - vaccinees generally healthy (vs. ill for drugs)
  - lower risk tolerance = need to search for rare reactions
  - vaccination universally recommended and mandated

4

Sweden, United Kingdom, and several other countries. In the United States, similar concerns led to increases both in the number of lawsuits against manufacturers and the price of vaccines, and to a decrease in the number of manufacturers willing to produce vaccines. Close monitoring and timely assessment of suspected vaccine adverse events can distinguish true vaccine reactions from coincidental unrelated events and help to maintain public confidence in immunizations.

A higher standard of safety is generally expected of vaccines than of other medical interventions because in contrast to most pharmaceutical products, which are administered to ill persons for curative purposes, vaccines are generally given to healthy persons to prevent disease. Public tolerance of adverse reactions related to products given to healthy persons, especially healthy infants and children, is substantially lower than for reactions to products administered to persons who are already sick. This lower risk tolerance of risk for vaccines translates into a need to investigate the possible causes of very rare adverse events following vaccinations.

Adding to public concern about vaccines is the fact that immunization is mandated by many state and local school entry requirements. Because of this widespread use, safety problems with vaccines can have a potential impact on large numbers of persons. The importance of ensuring the safety of a relatively universal human-directed "exposure" like immunizations is the basis for strict regulatory control of vaccines in the United States by the Food and Drug Administration (FDA).

Sound Immunization Recommendations and Policy

Public health recommendations for vaccine programs and practices represent a dynamic balancing of risks and benefits. Vaccine safety monitoring is necessary to accurately weigh this balance and adjust vaccination policy. This was done in the United States with smallpox and oral polio vaccines as these diseases neared global eradication. Complications associated with each vaccine exceeded the risks of the diseases, leading to discontinuation of routine smallpox vaccinations in the United States (prior to actual global eradication) and a shift to a safer inactivated polio vaccine. Sound immunization policies and recommendations affecting the health of the nation depend upon the ongoing monitoring of vaccines and continuous assessment of immunization benefits and risks.

Importance of Vaccine Safety

- Ongoing safety monitoring needed for the development of sound policies and recommendations

Methods of Monitoring Vaccine Safety

Prelicensure

Vaccines, like other pharmaceutical products, undergo extensive safety and efficacy evaluations in the laboratory, in animals, and in sequentially phased human clinical trials prior to licensure. Phase I human clinical trials usually involve anywhere from 20 to 100 volunteers and focus on detecting serious side effects. Phase II trials generally enroll hundreds of volunteers. These trials might take a few months, or last up to 3 years. Phase II trials determine the best dose for effectiveness and safety and the right number of doses. Next, the vaccine moves into phase III trials, which may last several years. A few hundred to several thousand volunteers may be involved. Some volunteers receive another already-licensed vaccine, allowing researchers to compare one vaccine with another for adverse health effects—anything from a sore arm to a serious reaction. If the vaccine is shown to be safe and effective in Phase III, the manufacturer applies for a license from the FDA. The FDA licenses the vaccine itself (the "product license") and licenses the manufacturing plant where the vaccine will be made (the "establishment license"). During the application, the FDA reviews everything: the clinical trial results, product labeling, the plant itself, and the manufacturing protocols.

FDA licensure occurs only after the vaccine has met rigorous standards of efficacy and safety, and when its potential benefits in preventing disease clearly outweigh any risks. However, while rates of common vaccine reactions, such as injection-site reactions and fever, can be estimated before licensure, the comparatively small number of patients enrolled in these trials generally limits detection of rare side effects or side effects that may occur many months after the vaccine is given. Even the largest prelicensure trials (more than 10,000 persons) are inadequate to assess the vaccine's potential to induce possible rare side effects. Therefore, it is essential to monitor reports of vaccine-associated adverse events once the vaccine has been licensed and released for public use.

Fundamental to preventing safety problems is the assurance that any vaccines for public use are made using Good Manufacturing Practices and undergo lot testing for purity and potency. Manufacturers must submit samples of each vaccine lot and results of their own tests for potency and purity to the FDA before releasing them for public use.

Prelicensure Vaccine Safety Studies

• Laboratory
• Animals
• Humans

Prelicensure Human Studies

• Phases I, II, III trials
• Common reactions are identified
• Vaccines are tested in thousands of persons before being licensed and allowed on the market

4

4

Postlicensure

Because rare reactions, delayed reactions, or reactions within subpopulations may not be detected before vaccines are licensed, postlicensure evaluation of vaccine safety is critical. The objectives of postlicensure surveillance are to

- identify rare reactions not detected during prelicensure studies,

- monitor increases in known reactions,

- identify risk factors or preexisting conditions that may promote reactions,

- identify whether there are particular vaccine lots with unusually high rates or certain types of events,

- identify signals of possible adverse reactions that may warrant further study or affect current immunization recommendations.

Historically, postlicensure monitoring of vaccine safety has relied on healthcare providers and the public to report side effects, and on "ad hoc" research studies to investigate possible rare associations between vaccines and identified health conditions of interest to scientists. Today, Phase IV trials and large-linked databases (LLDBs) have been added to improve the capability to study rare risks of specific immunizations. Phase IV studies can be an FDA requirement for licensure. These trials include tens of thousands of volunteers and may address questions of long-term effectiveness and safety or examine unanswered questions identified in Phase III clinical trials. In 2001, a clinical immunization safety assessment network was established which will increase understanding of vaccine reactions at the individual patient level.

The Vaccine Adverse Event Reporting System

The National Childhood Vaccine Injury Act of 1986 mandated that healthcare providers who administer vaccines, and licensed vaccine manufactures, report certain adverse health events following specific vaccinations. The Vaccine Adverse Event Reporting System (VAERS) is a national reporting system, jointly administered by CDC and FDA. VAERS was created in 1990 to unify the collection of all reports of clinically significant adverse events. VAERS is a passive reporting system and accepts reports from health professionals, vaccine manufacturers, and the general public. Reports are submitted via mail and fax as well as the Internet. All reports, whether submitted directly to VAERS or via state or local public health authorities or manufacturers, are coded and entered into the VAERS database. VAERS receives about 15,000 reports per year (more than 200,000 total to date). Though this seems like a very large number, it is relatively small compared with the approximately 100 million doses of childhood vaccines distributed during the past decade, as well as the millions of additional doses given to adults.

VAERS seeks to capture all clinically significant medical events occurring postvaccination, even if the reporter is not certain that the incident is vaccine related. A review of VAERS from 1991 through 2001 indicated that reports were received from manufacturers (36.2%), healthcare providers (20%), state and local health departments (27.6%), patients or parents (4.2%), others (7.3%), and unknown sources (4.7%).

Data collected on the VAERS reporting form include information about the patient, the vaccination(s) given, the reported health effect (called an adverse event—which may or may not be caused by vaccine), and the person reporting the event. Serious adverse event reports are defined as those involving hospitalization or prolongation of hospitalization, death, or reported life-threatening illness or permanent disability. All reports classified as serious are followed up to obtain additional medical information in order to provide as full a picture of the case as possible. For serious reports, letters to obtain information about recovery status are mailed to the reporters at 60 days and 1 year after vaccination. All records submitted to VAERS directly or as part of follow-up activities are protected by strict confidentiality requirements.

Despite some limitations, VAERS has been able to fulfill its primary purpose of detecting new or rare vaccine adverse events, increases in rates of known side effects, and patient risk factors for particular types of adverse events. Examples include tracking and raising the concern about intussusception after rotavirus vaccine and anaphylactic reaction to measles-mumps-rubella (MMR) vaccine caused by gelatin allergy. Additional studies are always required to confirm signals detected by VAERS because not all reported adverse events are causally related to vaccine. (See "Reporting Suspected Side Effects to VAERS" for detailed information on submitting reports.)

VAERS data with personal identifiers removed are available on the website at http://vaers.hhs.gov, at no cost or through the National Technical Information Service at http://www.ntis.gov or by phone at 800-553-6847 for a fee.

Adverse Event Classifications and Assessment of Causality

Adverse events following vaccination can be classified by frequency (common, rare), extent (local, systemic), severity (hospitalization, disability, death), causality, and preventability (intrinsic to vaccine, faulty production, faulty administration).

Adverse Event Classification

- **Vaccine-induced**
- **Vaccine-potentiated**
- **Programmatic error**
- **Coincidental**

Vaccine adverse events can be classified as follows:

- Vaccine-induced: Due to the intrinsic characteristic of the vaccine preparation and the individual response of the vaccinee. These events would not have occurred without vaccination (e.g., vaccine-associated paralytic poliomyelitis).

- Vaccine-potentiated: The event would have occurred anyway, but was precipitated by the vaccination (e.g., first febrile seizure in a predisposed child).

- Programmatic error: Due to technical errors in vaccine storage, preparation, handling, or administration.

- Coincidental: The reported event was not caused by vaccination but happened by chance occurrence or due to underlying illness.

It is natural to suspect a vaccine when a health problem occurs following vaccination, but in reality a causal association may or may not exist. More information would be needed to establish a causal relationship. An adverse health event can be causally attributed to vaccine more readily if 1) the health problem occurs during a plausible time period following vaccination, 2) the adverse event corresponds to those previously associated with a particular vaccine, 3) the event conforms to a specific clinical syndrome whose association with vaccination has strong biologic plausibility (e.g., anaphylaxis) or occurs following the natural disease, 4) a laboratory result confirms the association (e.g., isolation of vaccine strain varicella vaccine from skin lesions of a patient with rash), 5) the event recurs on re-administration of the vaccine ("positive rechallenge"), 6) a controlled clinical trial or epidemiologic study shows greater risk of a specific adverse event among vaccinated versus unvaccinated (control) groups, or 7) a finding linking an adverse event to vaccine has been confirmed by other studies.

Vaccine Safety Datalink (VSD)

In 1990, CDC established the Vaccine Safety Datalink (VSD) project to address gaps in the scientific knowledge of rare vaccine side effects. This project involves partnerships with eight large managed care organizations (MCOs) to monitor vaccine safety. MCOs' site locations as of April 2009 are Group Health Cooperative of Puget Sound, Seattle, Washington; Kaiser Permanente Northwest, Portland, Oregon; Kaiser Permanente Medical Care Program of Northern California, Oakland, California; Southern California Kaiser Permanente Health Care Program, Los Angeles, California; HealthPartners Research Foundation, Minneapolis, Minnesota; Marshfield Clinic Research Foundation, Marshfield, Wisconsin; Kaiser Permanente Colorado, Denver, Colorado; and Harvard Pilgrim Health Care, Boston, Massachusetts.

Each participating organization gathers data on vaccination (vaccine type, date of vaccination, concurrent vaccinations), medical outcomes (outpatient visits, inpatient visits, urgent care visits), birth data, and census data.

The VSD project allows for planned immunization safety studies as well as timely investigations of hypotheses that arise from review of medical literature, reports to the Vaccine Adverse Event Reporting System (VAERS), changes in immunization schedules, or the introduction of new vaccines.

In 2005, the Vaccine Safety Datalink (VSD) project team launched an active surveillance system called Rapid Cycle Analysis (RCA). Its goal is to monitor adverse events following vaccination in near real time, so the public can be informed quickly of possible risks. RCA data come from participating managed care organizations that include more than 8.8 million people annually, representing nearly 3% of the United States population. The RCA data contain no personal identifiers. The VSD project team is monitoring the safety of newly licensed vaccines, which includes conjugated meningococcal vaccine, rotavirus vaccines, MMRV vaccine, Tdap vaccine, Pentacel vaccine, Kinrix vaccine and HPV vaccine. In addition, the VSD RCA monitors the safety of seasonal influenza (flu) vaccinations. Further information about VSD is available at http://www.cdc.gov/vaccinesafety/vsd.

Clinical Immunization Safety Assessment Network

The most recent addition to the postlicensure vaccine safety monitoring system is the Clinical Immunization Safety Assessment (CISA) Network, which is designed to improve scientific understanding of vaccine safety issues at the individual patient level. The CISA network's goal is to evaluate persons who have experienced certain adverse health events following vaccination. The results of these evaluations will be used to gain a better understanding of how such events might occur and to develop protocols or guidelines for healthcare providers to help them manage similar situations. In addition, the CISA centers will serve as regional information sources to which clinical vaccine safety questions can be referred. Prior to the creation of the CISA network, no coordinated facilities in the United States investigated and managed vaccine side effects on an individual level for the purposes of providing patient care and systematically collecting and evaluating the experiences.

Established in 2001, the CISA network consists of six centers of excellence with vaccine safety expertise working in partnership with CDC. These centers are Johns Hopkins University in Baltimore, Maryland; Boston University Medical Center in Boston, Massachusetts; Columbia Presbyterian Hospital in New York City; Vanderbilt University

---

Vaccine Safety Datalink (VSD)

- Large-linked database
- Links vaccination and health records
- "Active surveillance"
  - 8 Managed Care Organizations
  - ~3% of the U.S. population
- Powerful tool for monitoring vaccine safety

Clinical Immunization Safety Assessment (CISA) Network

- Improve understanding of vaccine safety issues at individual level
- Evaluate persons who experience adverse health events
- Gain better understanding of events
- Develop protocols for healthcare providers

4

Vaccine Injury Compensation Program (VICP)

- **Established by National Childhood Vaccine Injury Act (1986)**
- **"No fault" program**
- **Covers all routinely recommended childhood vaccines**
- **Vaccine Injury Table**

---

in Nashville, Tennessee; Northern California Kaiser in Oakland, and Stanford University in Palo Alto, California. For more information about CISA, visit http://www.vaccinesafety.net.

Vaccine Injury Compensation

The topic of vaccine safety was prominent during the mid-1970s, with increases in lawsuits filed on behalf of those presumably injured by the whole-cell pertussis component of diphtheria-tetanus-pertussis (DPT) vaccine. Legal decisions were made and damages awarded despite the lack of scientific evidence to support vaccine injury claims. As a result of the liability, prices soared and several manufacturers halted vaccine production. A vaccine shortage resulted, and public health officials became concerned about the return of epidemic disease. To reduce liability and respond to public health concerns, Congress passed the National Childhood Vaccine Injury Act (NCVIA) in 1986.

As a result of the NCVIA, the National Vaccine Injury Compensation Program (VICP) was established. This program is intended to compensate individuals who experience certain health events following vaccination on a "no fault" basis. "No fault" means that persons filing claims are not required to prove negligence on the part of either the healthcare provider or manufacturer to receive compensation. The program covers all routinely recommended childhood vaccinations. Settlements are based on a Vaccine Injury Table (Appendix F), which summarizes the adverse events associated with vaccines. This table was developed by a panel of experts who reviewed the medical literature and identified the serious adverse events that are reasonably certain to be caused by vaccines. The Vaccine Injury Table was created to justly compensate those possibly injured by vaccines while separating out unrelated claims. As more information becomes available from research on vaccine side effects, the Vaccine Injury Table is amended.

VICP has achieved its policy goals of providing compensation to those injured by rare adverse events and liability protection for vaccine manufacturers and administrators. Further information about the VICP is available at http://www.hrsa.gov/vaccinecompensation/

The Immunization Provider's Role

Even though federal regulations require vaccines to undergo years of testing before they can be licensed, and vaccines are monitored continually for safety and efficacy, immunization providers still play a key role in helping to ensure the safety and efficacy of vaccines. They do this through proper vaccine storage and administration, timing and spacing of vaccine doses, observation of precautions

---

The Provider's Role

- **Immunization providers can help to ensure the safety and efficacy of vaccines through proper:**
  - vaccine storage and administration
  - timing and spacing of vaccine doses
  - observation of contraindications and precautions

---

and contraindications, management of vaccine side effects, reporting of suspected side effects to VAERS, and educating patients and parents about vaccine benefits and risks. Each of these steps is described only briefly here. Further information is available elsewhere in this book or in resource materials from CDC or other organizations.

Vaccine Storage and Administration

To achieve the best possible results from vaccines, immunization providers should carefully follow the recommendations found in each vaccine's package insert for storage, handling, and administration. Other steps to help ensure vaccine safety include 1) inspecting vaccines upon delivery and monitoring refrigerator and freezer temperatures to ensure maintenance of the cold chain, 2) rotating vaccine stock so the oldest vaccines are used first, 3) never administering a vaccine later than the expiration date, 4) administering vaccines within the prescribed time periods following reconstitution, 5) waiting to draw vaccines into syringes until immediately prior to administration, 6) never mixing vaccines in the same syringe unless they are specifically approved for mixing by the FDA, and 7) recording vaccine and administration information, including lot numbers and injection sites, in the patient's record. If errors in vaccine storage and administration occur, corrective action should be taken immediately to prevent them from happening again and public health authorities should be notified. More information on vaccine storage and handling is available in Appendix C and in CDC's Vaccine Storage and Handling Toolkit, available at http://www2a.cdc.gov/nip/isd/shtoolkit/splash.html

Timing and Spacing

Timing and spacing of vaccine doses are two of the most important issues in the appropriate use of vaccines. To ensure optimal results from each immunization, providers should follow the currently recommended immunization schedules for children, adolescents, and adults. Decreasing the timing intervals between doses of the same vaccine may interfere with the vaccine's antibody response. For more specific information on timing and spacing of vaccines see Chapter 2, *General Recommendations on Immunization*. A table showing recommended minimum ages and intervals between vaccine doses is contained in Appendix A.

Providers should also remember the following:

• Administering all needed vaccines during the same visit is important because it increases the likelihood that children will be fully immunized as recommended. Studies have shown that vaccines are as effective when administered simultaneously as they are individually and carry no greater risk for adverse reactions.

4

• There is no medical basis for giving combination vaccines, such as MMR, separately. Administration of separated combination vaccines results in more discomfort and higher risk of disease from delayed protection.

• Some vaccines, such as pediatric diphtheria and tetanus, produce increased rates of side effects when given too frequently. Good recordkeeping, maintaining careful patient histories, and adherence to recommended schedules can decrease the chances that patients receive extra doses of vaccines.

Contraindications and Precautions

Contraindications and precautions to vaccination are conditions that indicate when vaccines should not be given. A contraindication is a condition in a recipient that increases the chance of a serious adverse reaction. In general, a vaccine should not be administered when a contraindication is present. A precaution is a condition in a recipient that might increase the chance or severity of an adverse reaction or compromise the ability of the vaccine to produce immunity. Normally, vaccination is deferred when a precaution is present. Situations may arise when the benefits of vaccination outweigh the risk of a side effect, and the provider may decide to vaccinate the patient. Most contraindications and precautions are temporary and the vaccine may be given at a later time. More information about contraindications can be found in the Advisory Committee on Immunization Practices (ACIP) statements for individual vaccines. Recommendations for immunizing persons who are immunocompromised can be found in Appendix A. Information on allergic reactions to vaccines can be found in the American Academy of Pediatrics *Red Book*.

Screening for contraindications and precautions is key to preventing serious adverse reactions to vaccines. Every provider who administers vaccines should screen every patient before giving a vaccine dose. Sample screening questionnaires can be found in Chapter 2, *General Recommendations on Immunization*. Many conditions are often inappropriately regarded as contraindications to vaccination. In most cases, the following are not considered contraindications:

• Minor acute illness (e.g., diarrhea and minor upper respiratory tract illnesses, including otitis media) with or without low-grade fever

• Mild to moderate local reactions and/or low-grade or moderate fever following a prior dose of the vaccine

• Current antimicrobial therapy

• Recent exposure to infectious disease

• Convalescent phase of illness

• Pregnant or immunosuppressed person in the household

Contraindication

A condition in a recipient that increases the chance of a serious adverse reaction

---

Precaution

A condition in a recipient that might
- **Increase the chance or severity of an adverse reaction, or**
- **Compromise the ability of the vaccine to produce immunity**

Invalid Contraindications to Vaccination

- Minor illness
- Mild/moderate local reaction or fever following a prior dose
- Antimicrobial therapy
- Disease exposure or convalescence
- Pregnant or immunosuppressed in the household
- Premature birth
- Breastfeeding
- Allergies to products not in vaccine
- Family history (unrelated to immunosuppression)

4

- Premature birth
- Breastfeeding
- Allergies to products not in vaccine
- Family history (unrelated to immunosuppression)

Managing Vaccine Side Effects

Providers should use their best clinical judgment regarding specific management of suspected vaccine side effects. Allergic reactions to vaccines are estimated to occur after vaccination of children and adolescents at a rate of one for every 1.5 million doses of vaccine. All providers who administer vaccines should have procedures in place and be prepared for emergency care of a person who experiences an anaphylactic reaction. Epinephrine and equipment for maintaining an airway should be available for immediate use. All vaccine providers should be familiar with the office emergency plan and should be certified in cardiopulmonary resuscitation.

Reporting Suspected Side Effects to VAERS

Healthcare providers are required by the National Childhood Vaccine Injury Act of 1986 to report certain events to VAERS and are encouraged to report any adverse event even if they are not sure a vaccine was the cause. A table listing reportable events is available at http://vaers.hhs.gov/reportable.htm. and is contained in Appendix F. Reporting can be done in one of three ways:

- Online through a secure website: https://secure.vaers.org/VaersDataEntryIntro.htm

- Fax a completed VAERS form* to 877-721-0366

- Mail a completed VAERS form* to

      VAERS
      P.O. Box 1100
      Rockville, MD 20849-1100

*A one-page VAERS form can be downloaded from http://vaers.hhs.gov/pdf/vaers_form.pdf or can be requested by telephone at 800-822-7967 or by fax at 877-721-0366. The form is also printed in Appendix F.

When providers report suspected vaccine reactions to VAERS, they provide valuable information that is needed for the ongoing evaluation of vaccine safety. CDC and FDA use VAERS information to ensure the safest strategies of vaccine use and to further reduce the rare risks associated with vaccines.

Benefit and Risk Communication

Parents, guardians, legal representatives, and adolescent and adult patients should be informed of the benefits and

---

The Provider's Role

- Immunization providers can help to ensure the safety and efficacy of vaccines through proper:
  - management of vaccine side effects
  - reporting of suspected side effects to VAERS
  - vaccine benefit and risk communication

4

Benefit and Risk Communication

- Opportunities for questions should be provided before each vaccination
- Vaccine Information Statements (VISs)
  - must be provided before each dose of vaccine
  - public and private providers
  - available in multiple languages

risks of vaccines in understandable language. Opportunity for questions should be provided before each vaccination. Discussion of the benefits and risks of vaccination is sound medical practice and is required by law.

The National Childhood Vaccine Injury Act requires that vaccine information materials be developed for each vaccine covered by the Act. These materials, known as "Vaccine Information Statements (VISs)," must be provided by all public and private vaccination providers before each dose of vaccine. Copies of VISs are available from state health authorities responsible for immunization, or they can be obtained from CDC's website at http://www.cdc.gov/vaccines/pubs/vis/default.htm or from the Immunization Action Coalition at http://www.immunize.org. Translations of VISs into languages other than English are available from certain state immunization programs and from the Immunization Action Coalition website. Further information about VISs and their use is contained in Appendix E.

Healthcare providers should anticipate questions that parents or patients may have regarding the need for or safety of vaccination. A few may refuse certain vaccines, or even reject all vaccinations. Some persons might have religious or personal objections to vaccinations. Having a basic understanding of how patients view vaccine risk and developing effective approaches to dealing with vaccine safety concerns when they arise are imperative for vaccination providers. Healthcare providers can accomplish this by assessing patients' specific concerns and information needs, providing them with accurate information, and referring them to credible sources for more information. The CDC's website contains extensive and up-to-date information on vaccine safety issues http://www.cdc.gov/vaccines/.

When a parent or patient initiates discussion regarding a vaccine concern, the healthcare provider should discuss the specific concern and provide factual information, using language that is appropriate. Effective, empathetic vaccine risk communication is essential in responding to misinformation and concerns. The Vaccine Information Statements provide an outline for discussing vaccine benefits and risk. Other vaccine resources are available at http://www.cdc.gov/vaccinesafety/.

Rather than excluding from their practice those patients who question or refuse vaccination, the more effective public health strategy for providers is to identify common ground and discuss measures to be followed if the patient's decision is to defer vaccination. Healthcare providers can reinforce key points regarding each vaccine, including safety, and emphasize risks encountered by unimmunized children. Parents should be informed about state laws pertaining to school or child care entry, which might require that unimmunized children stay home from school during outbreaks. Documentation of these discussions in the patient's record, including the refusal to receive certain vaccines (i.e., informed refusal), might reduce any potential liability if a vaccine-preventable disease occurs in the unimmunized patient.

Acknowlegements

The editors thank PerStephanie Thompson of the Immunization Safety Office, CDC for her updating and critical review of this chapter.

Selected References

American Academy of Pediatrics. Vaccine Safety and Contraindications. In: Pickering L, Baker C, Long S, McMillan J. *Red Book: 2006 Report of the Committee on Infectious Diseases.* 27th ed. Elk Grove Village, IL: American Academy of Pediatrics;2006:39–50.

Bohlke K, Davis RL, Marcy SM, et al. Risk of anaphylaxis after vaccination of children and adolescents. *Pediatrics.* 2003;112:815–20.

CDC. General recommendations on immunization: recommendations of the Advisory Committee on Immunization Practices. *MMWR* 2006;55(No. RR-15):1–48.

CDC. National Childhood Vaccine Injury Act: Requirements for permanent vaccination records and for reporting of selected events after vaccination. *MMWR* 1988;37:197–200.

CDC. Surveillance for safety after immunization. *MMWR* 2003;52(No.SS-1):1–24.

CDC. Update: Vaccine side effects, adverse reactions, contraindications and precautions: recommendations of the Advisory Committee on Immunization Practices (ACIP). *MMWR* 1996;45(No. RR-12):1–35.

Chen RT, Hibbs B. Vaccine safety: current and future challenges. *Pediatr Ann* 1998;27:445–64.

Chen RT, Glasser J, Rhodes P, et al. The Vaccine Safety Datalink (VSD) Project: a new tool for improving vaccine safety monitoring in the United States. *Pediatrics* 1997;99:765–73.

Chen RT, Rastogi SC, Mullen JR, et al. The Vaccine Adverse Event Reporting System (VAERS). *Vaccine* 1994;12:542–50.

Diphtheria

Diphtheria is an acute, toxin-mediated disease caused by the bacterium *Corynebacterium diphtheriae*. The name of the disease is derived from the Greek *diphthera*, meaning leather hide. The disease was described in the 5th century BCE by Hippocrates, and epidemics were described in the 6th century AD by Aetius. The bacterium was first observed in diphtheritic membranes by Klebs in 1883 and cultivated by Löffler in 1884. Antitoxin was invented in the late 19th century, and toxoid was developed in the 1920s.

Corynebacterium diphtheriae

C. diphtheriae is an aerobic gram-positive bacillus. Toxin production (toxigenicity) occurs only when the bacillus is itself infected (lysogenized) by a specific virus (bacteriophage) carrying the genetic information for the toxin (tox gene). Only toxigenic strains can cause severe disease.

Culture of the organism requires selective media containing tellurite. If isolated, the organism must be distinguished in the laboratory from other *Corynebacterium* species that normally inhabit the nasopharynx and skin (e.g., diphtheroids).

C. diphtheriae has three biotypes—gravis, intermedius, and mitis. The most severe disease is associated with the gravis biotype, but any strain may produce toxin. All isolates of *C. diphtheriae* should be tested by the laboratory for toxigenicity.

Pathogenesis

Susceptible persons may acquire toxigenic diphtheria bacilli in the nasopharynx. The organism produces a toxin that inhibits cellular protein synthesis and is responsible for local tissue destruction and membrane formation. The toxin produced at the site of the membrane is absorbed into the bloodstream and then distributed to the tissues of the body. The toxin is responsible for the major complications of myocarditis and neuritis and can also cause low platelet counts (thrombocytopenia) and protein in the urine (proteinuria).

Clinical disease associated with non-toxin-producing strains is generally milder. While rare severe cases have been reported, these may actually have been caused by toxigenic strains that were not detected because of inadequate culture sampling.

Clinical Features

The incubation period of diphtheria is 2–5 days (range, 1–10 days).

Disease can involve almost any mucous membrane. For clinical purposes, it is convenient to classify diphtheria into a number of manifestations, depending on the site of disease.

Diphtheria

- Greek *diphthera* (leather hide)
- Recognized by Hippocrates in 5th century BCE
- Epidemics described in 6th century
- *C. diphtheriae* described by Klebs in 1883
- Toxoid developed in 1920s

5

Corynebacterium diphtheriae

- Aerobic gram-positive bacillus
- Toxin production occurs only when *C. diphtheriae* infected by virus (phage) carrying tox gene
- If isolated, must be distinguished from normal diphtheroid

Diphtheria Clinical Features

- Incubation period 2-5 days (range, 1-10 days)
- May involve any mucous membrane
- Classified based on site of infection
  - anterior nasal
  - pharyngeal and tonsillar
  - laryngeal
  - cutaneous
  - ocular
  - genital

5

Pharyngeal and Tonsillar Diphtheria

- Insidious onset of exudative pharyngitis
- Exudate spreads within 2-3 days and may form adherent membrane
- Membrane may cause respiratory obstruction
- Fever usually not high but patient appears toxic

Anterior Nasal Diphtheria

The onset of anterior nasal diphtheria is indistinguishable from that of the common cold and is usually characterized by a mucopurulent nasal discharge (containing both mucus and pus) which may become blood-tinged. A white membrane usually forms on the nasal septum. The disease is usually fairly mild because of apparent poor systemic absorption of toxin in this location, and it can be terminated rapidly by antitoxin and antibiotic therapy.

Pharyngeal and Tonsillar Diphtheria

The most common sites of diphtheria infection are the pharynx and the tonsils. Infection at these sites is usually associated with substantial systemic absorption of toxin. The onset of pharyngitis is insidious. Early symptoms include malaise, sore throat, anorexia, and low-grade fever. Within 2–3 days, a bluish-white membrane forms and extends, varying in size from covering a small patch on the tonsils to covering most of the soft palate. Often by the time a physician is contacted, the membrane is greyish-green, or black if bleeding has occurred. There is a minimal amount of mucosal erythema surrounding the membrane. The membrane is adherent to the tissue, and forcible attempts to remove it cause bleeding. Extensive membrane formation may result in respiratory obstruction.

The patient may recover at this point; or if enough toxin is absorbed, develop severe prostration, striking pallor, rapid pulse, stupor, and coma, and may even die within 6 to 10 days. Fever is usually not high, even though the patient may appear quite toxic. Patients with severe disease may develop marked edema of the submandibular areas and the anterior neck along with lymphadenopathy, giving a characteristic "bullneck" appearance.

Laryngeal Diphtheria

Laryngeal diphtheria can be either an extension of the pharyngeal form or can only involve this site. Symptoms include fever, hoarseness, and a barking cough. The membrane can lead to airway obstruction, coma, and death.

Cutaneous (Skin) Diphtheria

In the United States, cutaneous diphtheria has been most often associated with homeless persons. Skin infections are quite common in the tropics and are probably responsible for the high levels of natural immunity found in these populations. Skin infections may be manifested by a scaling rash or by ulcers with clearly demarcated edges and membrane, but any chronic skin lesion may harbor C. diphtheriae along with other organisms. Generally, the organisms isolated from recent cases in the United States were nontoxigenic. The severity of the skin disease with toxigenic strains appears to be less than in other forms of infection with toxigenic strains. Skin diseases associated with nontoxigenic strains are no longer reported to the National Notifiable Diseases Surveillance System in the United States.

Other sites of involvement include the mucous membranes of the conjunctiva and vulvovaginal area, as well as the external auditory canal.

Complications

Most complications of diphtheria, including death, are attributable to effects of the toxin. The severity of the disease and complications are generally related to the extent of local disease. The toxin, when absorbed, affects organs and tissues distant from the site of invasion. The most frequent complications of diphtheria are myocarditis and neuritis.

Myocarditis may present as abnormal cardiac rhythms and can occur early in the course of the illness or weeks later, and can lead to heart failure. If myocarditis occurs early, it is often fatal.

Neuritis most often affects motor nerves and usually resolves completely. Paralysis of the soft palate is most frequent during the third week of illness. Paralysis of eye muscles, limbs, and diaphragm can occur after the fifth week. Secondary pneumonia and respiratory failure may result from diaphragmatic paralysis.

Other complications include otitis media and respiratory insufficiency due to airway obstruction, especially in infants.

Death

The overall case-fatality rate for diphtheria is 5%–10%, with higher death rates (up to 20%) among persons younger than 5 and older than 40 years of age. The case-fatality rate for diphtheria has changed very little during the last 50 years.

Laboratory Diagnosis

Diagnosis of diphtheria is usually made on the basis of clinical presentation since it is imperative to begin presumptive therapy quickly.

Culture of the lesion is done to confirm the diagnosis. It is critical to take a swab of the pharyngeal area, especially any discolored areas, ulcerations, and tonsillar crypts. Culture medium containing tellurite is preferred because it provides a selective advantage for the growth of this organism.

Diphtheria Complications

- Most attributable to toxin
- Severity generally related to extent of local disease
- Most common complications are myocarditis and neuritis
- Death occurs in 5%-10%

A blood agar plate is also inoculated for detection of hemolytic streptococcus. If diphtheria bacilli are isolated, they must be tested for toxin production.

Gram stain and Kenyon stain of material from the membrane itself can be helpful when trying to confirm the clinical diagnosis. The Gram stain may show multiple club-shaped forms that look like Chinese characters. Other *Corynebacterium* species (diphtheroids) that can normally inhabit the throat may confuse the interpretation of direct stain. However, treatment should be started if clinical diphtheria is suggested, even in the absence of a diagnostic Gram stain.

In the event that prior antibiotic therapy may have impeded a positive culture in a suspect diphtheria case, two sources of evidence can aid in presumptive diagnosis: 1) isolation of *C. diphtheriae* from cultures of specimens from close contacts, or 2) a low nonprotective diphtheria antibody titer (less than 0.1 IU) in serum obtained prior to antitoxin administration. This is done by commercial laboratories and requires several days. To isolate *C. diphtheriae* from carriers, it is best to inoculate a Löffler or Pai slant with the throat swab. After an incubation period of 18–24 hours, growth from the slant is used to inoculate a medium containing tellurite.

Medical Management

Diphtheria Antitoxin
Diphtheria antitoxin, produced in horses, was first used in the United States in 1891. It is no longer indicated for prophylaxis of contacts of diphtheria patients, only for the treatment of diphtheria. Since 1997, diphtheria antitoxin has been available only from CDC, and only through an Investigational New Drug (IND) protocol.

Antitoxin will not neutralize toxin that is already fixed to tissues, but it will neutralize circulating (unbound) toxin and will prevent progression of disease. The patient must be tested for sensitivity before antitoxin is given. Consultation on the use of diphtheria antitoxin is available through the duty officer at the CDC during office hours (8:00 a.m.–4:30 p.m. ET) at 404-639-3158, or at all other times through CDC's Emergency Operations Center at 770-488-7100.

Persons with suspected diphtheria should be given antibiotics and antitoxin in adequate dosage and placed in isolation after the provisional clinical diagnosis is made and appropriate cultures are obtained. Respiratory support and airway maintenance should also be administered as needed.

Diphtheria Antitoxin
- Produced in horses
- First used in the U.S. in 1891
- Used only for treatment of diphtheria
- Neutralizes only unbound toxin

5

Antibiotics

Treatment with erythromycin orally or by injection (40 mg/kg/day; maximum, 2 gm/day) for 14 days, or procaine penicillin G daily, intramuscularly (300,000 U/day for those weighing 10 kg or less, and 600,000 U/day for those weighing more than 10 kg) for 14 days. The disease is usually not contagious 48 hours after antibiotics are instituted. Elimination of the organism should be documented by two consecutive negative cultures after therapy is completed.

Preventive Measures

For close contacts, especially household contacts, a diphtheria booster, appropriate for age, should be given. Contacts should also receive antibiotics—benzathine penicillin G (600,000 units for persons younger than 6 years old and 1,200,000 units for those 6 years old and older) or a 7- to 10-day course of oral erythromycin, (40 mg/kg/day for children and 1 g/day for adults). For compliance reasons, if surveillance of contacts cannot be maintained, they should receive benzathine penicillin G. Identified carriers in the community should also receive antibiotics. Maintain close surveillance and begin antitoxin at the first signs of illness.

Contacts of cutaneous diphtheria should be treated as described above; however, if the strain is shown to be nontoxigenic, investigation of contacts can be discontinued.

Epidemiology

Occurrence

Diphtheria occurs worldwide, but clinical cases are more prevalent in temperate zones. In the United States during the pretoxoid era, the highest incidence was in the Southeast during the winter. More recently, highest incidence rates have been in states with significant populations of Native Americans. No geographic concentration of cases is currently observed in the United States.

Reservoir

Human carriers are the reservoir for *C. diphtheriae* and are usually asymptomatic. In outbreaks, high percentages of children are found to be transient carriers.

Transmission

Transmission is most often person-to-person spread from the respiratory tract. Rarely, transmission may occur from skin lesions or articles soiled with discharges from lesions of infected persons (fomites).

Diphtheria Epidemiology

• Reservoir	Human carriers Usually asymptomatic
• Transmission	Respiratory Skin and fomites rarely
• Temporal pattern	Winter and spring
• Communicability	Up to several weeks without antibiotics

Diphtheria

5

Temporal Pattern

In temperate areas, diphtheria most frequently occurs during winter and spring.

Communicability

Transmission may occur as long as virulent bacilli are present in discharges and lesions. The time is variable, but organisms usually persist 2 weeks or less, and seldom more than 4 weeks, without antibiotics. Chronic carriers may shed organisms for 6 months or more. Effective antibiotic therapy promptly terminates shedding.

Secular Trends in the United States

Diphtheria was once a major cause of morbidity and mortality among children. In England and Wales during the 1930s, diphtheria was among the top three causes of death for children younger than 15 years of age.

In the 1920s in the United States, 100,000–200,000 cases of diphtheria (140–150 cases per 100,000 population) and 13,000–15,000 deaths were reported each year. In 1921, a total of 206,000 cases and 15,520 deaths were reported. The number of cases gradually declined to about 19,000 cases in 1945 (15 per 100,000 population). A more rapid decrease began with the widespread use of toxoid in the late 1940s.

From 1970 to 1979, an average of 196 cases per year were reported. This included a high proportion of cutaneous cases from an outbreak in Washington State. Beginning in 1980, all cases with nontoxigenic cutaneous isolates were excluded from reporting. Diphtheria was seen most frequently in Native Americans and persons in lower socio-economic strata.

From 1980 through 2004, 57 cases of diphtheria were reported in the United States, an average of 2 or 3 per year (range, 0–5 cases per year). Only 5 cases have been reported since 2000.

Of 53 reported cases with known patient age since 1980, 31 (58%) were in persons 20 years of age or older; 44% of cases were among persons 40 years of age or older. Most cases have occurred in unimmunized or inadequately immunized persons. The current age distribution of cases corroborates the finding of inadequate levels of circulating antitoxin in many adults (up to 60% with less than protective levels).

Although diphtheria disease is rare in the United States, it appears that *Corynebacterium diphtheriae* continues to circulate in areas of the country with previously endemic diphtheria. In 1996, 10 isolates of *C. diphtheriae* were obtained from persons in an Native American community in South Dakota. Eight of these isolates were toxigenic.

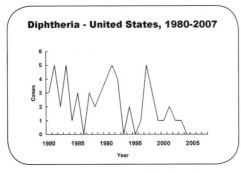

Diphtheria - United States, 1980-2007

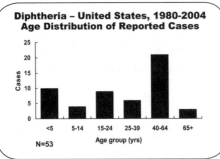

Diphtheria – United States, 1980-2004
Age Distribution of Reported Cases

N=53

None of the infected persons had classic diphtheria disease, although five had either pharyngitis or tonsillitis. The presence of toxigenic *C. diphtheriae* in this community is a good reminder for providers not to let down their guard against this organism.

Diphtheria continues to occur in other parts of the world. A major epidemic of diphtheria occurred in countries of the former Soviet Union beginning in 1990. By 1994, the epidemic had affected all 15 Newly Independent States (NIS). More than 157,000 cases and more than 5,000 deaths were reported. In the 6 years from 1990 through 1995, the NIS accounted for more than 90% of all diphtheria cases reported to the World Health Organization from the entire world. In some NIS countries, up to 80% of the epidemic diphtheria cases have been among adults. The outbreak and the age distribution of cases are believed to be due to several factors, including a lack of routine immunization of adults in these countries.

Diphtheria Toxoid

Characteristics

Beginning in the early 1900s, prophylaxis was attempted with toxin–antitoxin mixtures. Toxoid was developed around 1921 but was not widely used until the early 1930s. It was incorporated with tetanus toxoid and pertussis vaccine and became routinely used in the 1940s.

Diphtheria toxoid is produced by growing toxigenic *C. diphtheriae* in liquid medium. The filtrate is incubated with formaldehyde to convert toxin to toxoid and is then adsorbed onto an aluminum salt.

Single-antigen diphtheria toxoid is not available. Diphtheria toxoid is available combined with tetanus toxoid as pediatric diphtheria-tetanus toxoid (DT) or adult tetanus-diphtheria (Td), and with both tetanus toxoid and acellular pertussis vaccine as DTaP and Tdap. Diphtheria toxoid is also available as combined DTaP-HepB-IPV (Pediarix) and DTaP-IPV/Hib (Pentacel—see Chapter 14 for more information. Pediatric formulations (DT and DTaP) contain a similar amount of tetanus toxoid as adult Td, but contain 3 to 4 times as much diphtheria toxoid. Children younger than 7 years of age should receive either DTaP or pediatric DT. Persons 7 years of age or older should receive the adult formulation (adult Td), even if they have not completed a series of DTaP or pediatric DT. Two brands of Tdap are available—Boostrix (approved for persons 10 through 64 years of age) and Adacel (approved for persons 11 through 64 years of age). DTaP and Tdap vaccines do not contain thimerosal as a preservative.

DTaP, DT, Td and Tdap

	Diphtheria	Tetanus
DTaP, DT	7-8 Lf units	5-12.5 Lf units
Td, Tdap (adult)	2-2.5 Lf units	5 Lf units

DTaP and pediatric DT used through age 6 years. Adult Td for persons 7 years and older. Tdap for persons 10–64 years

---

Diphtheria Toxoid

- Formalin-inactivated diphtheria toxin
- Schedule   Three or four doses + booster
              Booster every 10 years
- Efficacy   Approximately 95%
- Duration   Approximately 10 years
- Should be administered with tetanus toxoid as DTaP, DT, Td, or Tdap

Immunogenicity and Vaccine Efficacy

After a primary series of three properly spaced diphtheria toxoid doses in adults or four doses in infants, a protective level of antitoxin (defined as greater than 0.1 IU of anti-toxin/mL) is reached in more than 95%. Diphtheria toxoid has been estimated to have a clinical efficacy of 97%.

Vaccination Schedule and Use

DTaP (diphtheria and tetanus toxoids and acellular pertussis vaccine) is the vaccine of choice for children 6 weeks through 6 years of age. The usual schedule is a primary series of 4 doses at 2,4,6, and 15–18 months of age. The first, second, and third doses of DTaP should be separated by a minimum of 4 weeks. The fourth dose should follow the third dose by no less than 6 months, and should not be administered before 12 months of age.

If a child has a valid contraindication to pertussis vaccine, pediatric DT should be used to complete the vaccination series. If the child was younger than 12 months old when the first dose of DT was administered (as DTP, DTaP, or DT), the child should receive a total of four primary DT doses. If the child was 12 months of age or older at the time the first dose of DT was administered, three doses (third dose 6–12 months after the second) completes the primary DT series.

If the fourth dose of DT, DTP or DTaP is administered before the fourth birthday, a booster (fifth) dose is recommended at 4 through 6 years of age. The fifth dose is not required if the fourth dose was given on or after the fourth birthday.

Because of waning antitoxin titers, most persons have antitoxin levels below the optimal level 10 years after the last dose. Tetanus toxoid should be given with diphtheria toxoid as Td every 10 years. The first booster dose may be given at 11 or 12 years of age if at least 5 years have elapsed since the last dose of DTP, DTaP, or DT. ACIP recommends this dose be administered as Tdap. If a dose is given sooner as part of wound management, the next booster is not needed for 10 years thereafter. More frequent boosters are not indicated and have been reported to result in an increased incidence and severity of local adverse reactions.

Td is the vaccine of choice for children 7 years and older and for adults. A primary series is three or four doses, depending on whether the person has received prior doses of diphtheria-containing vaccine and the age these doses were administered. The number of doses recommended for children who received one or more doses of DTP, DTaP, or DT before age 7 years is discussed above. For unvaccinated persons 7 years and older (including persons who cannot

Routine DTaP Primary Vaccination Schedule

Dose	Age	Interval
Primary 1	2 months	---
Primary 2	4 months	4 weeks
Primary 3	6 months	4 weeks
Primary 4	15-18 months	6 months

Children Who Receive DT

- The number of doses of DT needed to complete the series depends on the child's age at the first dose:
  - if first dose given at younger than 12 months of age, 4 doses are recommended
  - if first dose given at 12 months or older, 3 doses complete the primary series

Routine DTaP Schedule for Children Younger Than 7 Years of Age

Booster Doses
- 4 through 6 years of age, before entering school
- 11 or 12 years of age if 5 years since last dose (Tdap)
- Every 10 years thereafter (Td)

Routine Td Schedule for Unvaccinated Persons 7 Years of Age and Older

Dose*	Interval
Primary 1	---
Primary 2	4 weeks
Primary 3	6 to 12 months

Booster dose every 10 years

*ACIP recommends that <u>one</u> of these doses (preferably the first) be administered as Tdap

5

document prior vaccination), the primary series is three doses. The first two doses should be separated by at least 4 weeks, and the third dose given 6 to 12 months after the second. For persons 10 years and older ACIP recommends that one of these doses (preferably the first) be administered as Tdap. A booster dose of Td should be given every 10 years. Tdap is approved for a single dose at this time (i.e., it should not be used for all the doses of Td in a previously unvaccinated person 7 years or older). Refer to the pertussis chapter for more information about Tdap.

Interruption of the recommended schedule or delay of subsequent doses does not reduce the response to the vaccine when the series is finally completed. There is no need to restart a series regardless of the time elapsed between doses.

Diphtheria disease might not confer immunity. Persons recovering from diphtheria should begin or complete active immunization with diphtheria toxoid during convalescence.

Contraindications and Precautions to Vaccination

Persons with a history of a severe allergic reaction (anaphylaxis) to a vaccine component or following a prior dose should not receive additional doses of diphtheria toxoid. Diphtheria toxoid should be deferred for those persons who have moderate or severe acute illness, but persons with minor illness may be vaccinated. Immunosuppression and pregnancy are not contraindications to receiving diphtheria toxoid. See pertussis chapter for additional information on contraindications and precautions to Tdap.

Adverse Reactions Following Vaccination

Local reactions, generally erythema and induration with or without tenderness, are common after the administration of vaccines containing diphtheria toxoid. Local reactions are usually self-limited and require no therapy. A nodule may be palpable at the injection site for several weeks. Abscess at the site of injection has been reported. Fever and other systemic symptoms are not common.

Exaggerated local (Arthus-type) reactions are occasionally reported following receipt of a diphtheria- or tetanus-containing vaccine. These reactions present as extensive painful swelling, often from shoulder to elbow. They generally begin 2–8 hours after injections and are reported most often in adults, particularly those who have received frequent doses of diphtheria or tetanus toxoid. Persons experiencing these severe reactions usually have very high serum antitoxin levels; they should not be given

---

Diphtheria and Tetanus Toxoids Contraindications and Precautions

- Severe allergic reaction to vaccine component or following a prior dose
- Moderate or severe acute illness

Diphtheria and Tetanus Toxoids Adverse Reactions

- Local reactions (erythema, induration)
- Fever and systemic symptoms not common
- Exaggerated local reactions (Arthus-type)
- Severe systemic reactions rare

further routine or emergency booster doses of Td more frequently than every 10 years. Less severe local reactions may occur in persons who have multiple prior boosters.

Rarely, severe systemic reactions such as generalized urticaria, anaphylaxis, or neurologic complications have been reported following administration of diphtheria toxoid.

Vaccine Storage and Handling

All diphtheria-toxoid-containing vaccines should be stored continuously at 35°–46°F (2°–8°C). Freezing reduces the potency of the tetanus component. Vaccine exposed to freezing temperature should never be administered.

Suspect Case Investigation and Control

Immediate action on all highly suspect cases (including cutaneous) is warranted until they are shown not to be caused by toxigenic *C. diphtheriae*. The following action should also be taken for any toxigenic *C. diphtheriae* carriers who are detected.

1. Contact state health department or CDC.

2. Obtain appropriate cultures and preliminary clinical and epidemiologic information (including vaccine history).

3. Begin early presumptive treatment with antibiotics and antitoxin. Impose strict isolation until at least two cultures are negative 24 hours after antibiotics were discontinued.

4. Identify close contacts, especially household members and other persons directly exposed to oral secretions of the patient. Culture all close contacts, regardless of their immunization status. Ideally, culture should be from both throat and nasal swabs. After culture, all contacts should receive antibiotic prophylaxis. Inadequately immunized contacts should receive DTaP/DT/Td/Tdap boosters. If fewer than three doses of diphtheria toxoid have been given, or vaccination history is unknown, an immediate dose of diphtheria toxoid should be given and the primary series completed according to the current schedule. If more than 5 years have elapsed since administration of diphtheria toxoid-containing vaccine, a booster dose should be given. If the most recent dose was within 5 years, no booster is required (see the ACIP's 1991 Diphtheria, Tetanus, and Pertussis: *Recommendations for Vaccine Use and Other Preventive Measures* for schedule for children younger than 7 years of age). Unimmunized contacts should start a course of DTaP/DT/Td vaccine and be monitored closely for symptoms of diphtheria for 7 days.

5. Treat any confirmed carrier with an adequate course of antibiotic, and repeat cultures at a minimum of 2 weeks

5

to ensure eradication of the organism. Persons who continue to harbor the organism after treatment with either penicillin or erythromycin should receive an additional 10-day course of erythromycin and should submit samples for follow-up cultures.

6. Treat any contact with antitoxin at the first sign of illness.

Selected References

CDC. Diphtheria, tetanus, and pertussis: Recommendations for vaccine use and other preventive measures. *MMWR* 1991;40 (No. RR-10):1–28.

CDC. Pertussis vaccination: use of acellular pertussis vaccines among infants and young children. Recommendations of the Advisory Committee on Immunization Practices (ACIP). *MMWR* 1997;46 (No. RR-7):1–25.

CDC. Preventing tetanus, diphtheria, and pertussis among adolescents: use of tetanus toxoid, reduced diphtheria toxoid and acellular pertussis vaccines. Recommendations of the Advisory Committee on Immunization Practices (ACIP). *MMWR* 2006;55(No. RR-3):1–34.

CDC. Preventing tetanus, diphtheria, and pertussis among adults: use of tetanus toxoid, reduced diphtheria toxoid and acellular pertussis vaccines. Recommendations of the Advisory Committee on Immunization Practices (ACIP) and Recommendation of ACIP, supported by the Healthcare Infection Control Practices Advisory Committee (HICPAC), for Use of Tdap Among Health-Care Personnel. *MMWR* 2006;55(No. RR-17):1–33.

Farizo KM, Strebel PM, Chen RT, Kimbler A, Cleary TJ, Cochi SL. Fatal respiratory disease due to *Corynebacterium diphtheriae*: case report and review of guidelines for management, investigation, and control. *Clin Infect Dis* 1993;16:59–68.

Vitek CR, Wharton M. Diphtheria in the former Soviet Union: reemergence of a pandemic disease. *Emerg Infect Dis* 1998;4:539–50.

Vitek CR, Wharton M, Diphtheria toxoid. In Plotkin SA, Orenstein WA, Offit PA, eds. *Vaccines.* 5th ed. Philadelphia, PA: Saunders, 2008:139–56.

Diphtheria

Haemophilus influenzae type b

Haemophilus influenzae is a cause of bacterial infections that are often severe, particularly among infants. It was first described by Pfeiffer in 1892. During an outbreak of influenza he found the bacteria in sputum of patients and proposed a causal association between this bacterium and the clinical syndrome known as influenza. The organism was given the name *Haemophilus* by Winslow, et al. in 1920. It was not until 1933 that Smith, et al. established that influenza was caused by a virus and that *H. influenzae* was a cause of secondary infection.

In the 1930s, Margaret Pittman demonstrated that *H. influenzae* could be isolated in encapsulated and unencapsulated forms. She identified six capsular types (a–f), and observed that virtually all isolates from cerebrospinal fluid (CSF) and blood were of the capsular type b.

Before the introduction of effective vaccines, *H. influenzae* type b (Hib) was the leading cause of bacterial meningitis and other invasive bacterial disease among children younger than 5 years of age; approximately one in 200 children in this age group developed invasive Hib disease. Nearly all Hib infections occurred among children younger than 5 years of age, and approximately two-thirds of all cases occurred among children younger than 18 months of age.

Haemophilus influenzae

Haemophilus influenzae is a gram-negative coccobacillus. It is generally aerobic but can grow as a facultative anaerobe. In vitro growth requires accessory growth factors, including "X" factor (hemin) and "V" factor (nicotinamide adenine dinucleotide [NAD]).

Chocolate agar media are used for isolation. *H. influenzae* will generally not grow on blood agar, which lacks NAD.

The outermost structure of *H. influenzae* is composed of polyribosyl-ribitol phosphate (PRP), a polysaccharide that is responsible for virulence and immunity. Six antigenically and biochemically distinct capsular polysaccharide serotypes have been described; these are designated types a through f. In the prevaccine era, type b organisms accounted for 95% of all strains that caused invasive disease.

Pathogenesis

The organism enters the body through the nasopharynx. Organisms colonize the nasopharynx and may remain only transiently or for several months in the absence of symptoms (asymptomatic carrier). In the prevaccine era, Hib could be

---

6

Haemophilus influenzae type b

- Severe bacterial infection, particularly among infants
- During late 19th century believed to cause influenza
- Immunology and microbiology clarified in 1930s

Haemophilus influenzae

- Aerobic gram-negative bacteria
- Polysaccharide capsule
- Six different serotypes (a-f) of polysaccharide capsule
- 95% of invasive disease caused by type b

Haemophilus influenzae type b Pathogenesis

- Organism colonizes nasopharynx
- In some persons organism invades bloodstream and causes infection at distant site
- Antecedent upper respiratory tract infection may be a contributing factor

isolated from the nasopharynx of 0.5%–3% of normal infants and children but was not common in adults. Nontypeable (unencapsulated) strains are also frequent inhabitants of the human respiratory tract.

In some persons, the organism causes an invasive infection. The exact mode of invasion to the bloodstream is unknown. Antecedent viral or mycoplasma infection of the upper respiratory tract may be a contributing factor. The bacteria spread in the bloodstream to distant sites in the body. Meninges are especially likely to be affected.

The most striking feature of Hib disease is age-dependent susceptibility. Hib disease is not common beyond 5 years of age. Passive protection of some infants is provided by transplacentally acquired maternal IgG antibodies and breastfeeding during the first 6 months of life. In the prevaccine era peak attack rates occurred at 6–7 months of age, declining thereafter. The presumed reason for this age distribution is the acquisition of immunity to Hib with increasing age.

Antibodies to Hib capsular polysaccharide are protective. The precise level of antibody required for protection against invasive disease is not clearly established. However, a titer of 1 μg/mL 3 weeks postvaccination correlated with protection in studies following vaccination with unconjugated purified polyribosylribitol phosphate (PRP) vaccine and suggested long-term protection from invasive disease.

Acquisition of both anticapsular and serum bactericidal antibody is inversely related to the age-specific incidence of Hib disease.

In the prevaccine era, most children acquired immunity by 5–6 years of age through asymptomatic infection by Hib bacteria. Since only a relatively small proportion of children carry Hib at any time, it has been postulated that exposure to organisms that share common antigenic structures with the capsule of Hib (so-called "cross-reacting organisms") may also stimulate the development of anticapsular antibodies against Hib. Natural exposure to Hib also induces antibodies to outer membrane proteins, lipopolysaccharides, and other antigens on the surface of the bacterium.

The genetic constitution of the host may also be important in susceptibility to infection with Hib. Risk for Hib disease has been associated with a number of genetic markers, but the mechanism of these associations is unknown. No single genetic relationship regulating susceptibility or immune responses to polysaccharide antigens has yet been convincingly demonstrated.

Clinical Features

Invasive disease caused by *H. influenzae* type b can affect many organ systems. The most common types of invasive disease are meningitis, epiglottitis, pneumonia, arthritis, and cellulitis.

Meningitis is infection of the membranes covering the brain and is the most common clinical manifestation of invasive Hib disease, accounting for 50%–65% of cases in the prevaccine era. Hallmarks of Hib meningitis are fever, decreased mental status, and stiff neck (these symptoms also occur with meningitis caused by other bacteria). Hearing impairment or other neurologic sequelae occur in 15%–30% of survivors. The case-fatality rate is 2%–5%, despite appropriate antimicrobial therapy.

Epiglottitis is an infection and swelling of the epiglottis, the tissue in the throat that covers and protects the larynx during swallowing. Epiglottitis may cause life-threatening airway obstruction.

Septic arthritis (joint infection), cellulitis (rapidly progressing skin infection which usually involves face, head, or neck), and pneumonia (which can be mild focal or severe empyema) are common manifestations of invasive disease.

Osteomyelitis (bone infection) and pericarditis (infection of the sac covering the heart) are less common forms of invasive disease. Otitis media and acute bronchitis due to *H. influenzae* are generally caused by nontypeable strains. Hib strains account for only 5%–10% of *H. influenzae* causing otitis media.

Nontypeable (unencapsulated) strains may cause invasive disease but are generally less virulent than encapsulated strains. Nontypeable strains are rare causes of serious infection among children but are a common cause of ear infections in children and bronchitis in adults.

Laboratory Diagnosis

A Gram stain of an infected body fluid may demonstrate small gram-negative coccobacilli suggestive of invasive *Haemophilus* disease. CSF, blood, pleural fluid, joint fluid, and middle ear aspirates should be cultured on appropriate media. A positive culture for *H. influenzae* establishes the diagnosis.

All isolates of *H. influenzae* should be serotyped. This is an extremely important laboratory procedure that should be performed on every isolate of *H. influenzae*, especially those obtained from children younger than 15 years of age. This test determines whether an isolate is type b, which is the only type that is potentially vaccine preventable. Serotyping

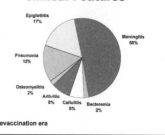

Haemophilus influenzae type b Clinical Features*

Epiglottitis 17%
Meningitis 50%
Pneumonia 15%
Osteomyelitis 2%
Arthritis 8%
Cellulitis 6%
Bacteremia 2%

*prevaccination era

Haemophilus influenzae type b Meningitis

- Accounted for approximately 50%-65% of cases in the prevaccine era
- Hearing impairment or neurologic sequelae in 15%-30%
- Case-fatality rate 2%-5% despite appropriate antimicrobial therapy

6

6

is usually done by either the state health department laboratory or a reference laboratory.

Antigen detection may be used as an adjunct to culture, particularly in diagnosing *H. influenzae* infection in patients who have been partially treated with antimicrobial agents, in which case the organism may not be viable on culture. Two tests are available. Latex agglutination is a rapid, sensitive, and specific method to detect Hib capsular polysaccharide antigen in CSF, but a negative test does not exclude the diagnosis, and false-positive tests have been reported. Antigen testing of serum and urine is not recommended. Counterimmunoelectrophoresis is similar to latex agglutination but is less sensitive, takes longer, and is more difficult to perform.

Medical Management

Hospitalization is generally required for invasive Hib disease. Antimicrobial therapy with an effective third-generation cephalosporin (cefotaxime or ceftriaxone), or chloramphenicol in combination with ampicillin should be begun immediately. The treatment course is usually 10 days. Ampicillin-resistant strains of Hib are now common throughout the United States. Children with life-threatening illness in which Hib may be the etiologic agent should not receive ampicillin alone as initial empiric therapy.

Epidemiology

Occurrence
Hib disease occurs worldwide.

Reservoir
Humans (asymptomatic carriers) are the only known reservoir. Hib does not survive in the environment on inanimate surfaces.

Transmission
The primary mode of Hib transmission is presumably by respiratory droplet spread, although firm evidence for this mechanism is lacking.

Temporal Pattern
Several studies in the prevaccine era described a bimodal seasonal pattern in the United States, with one peak during September through December and a second peak during March through May. The reason for this bimodal pattern is not known.

Haemophilus influenzae type b Medical Management
- Hospitalization required
- Treatment with an effective 3rd generation cephalosporin, or chloramphenicol plus ampicillin
- Ampicillin-resistant strains now common throughout the United States

Haemophilus influenzae type b Epidemiology
- Reservoir — Human Asymptomatic carriers
- Transmission — Respiratory droplets
- Temporal pattern — Peaks in Sept-Dec and March-May
- Communicability — Generally limited but higher in some circumstances

Communicability

The contagious potential of invasive Hib disease is considered to be limited. However, certain circumstances, particularly close contact with a case-patient (e.g., household, child care, or institutional setting) can lead to outbreaks or direct secondary transmission of the disease.

Secular Trends in the United States

H. influenzae infections became nationally reportable in 1991. Serotype-specific reporting continues to be incomplete.

Before the availability of national reporting data, several areas conducted active surveillance for *H. influenzae* disease, which allowed estimates of disease nationwide. In the early 1980s, it was estimated that about 20,000 cases occurred annually in the United States, primarily among children younger than 5 years of age (40–50 cases per 100,000 population). The incidence of invasive Hib disease began to decline dramatically in the late 1980s, coincident with licensure of conjugate Hib vaccines, and has declined by more than 99% compared with the prevaccine era.

From 1996 through 2000, an average of 1,247 invasive *H. influenzae* infections per year were reported to CDC in all age groups (range 1,162–1,398 per year). Of these, an average of 272 (approximately 22%) per year were among children younger than 5 years of age. Serotype was known for 76% of the invasive cases in this age group. Three-hundred forty-one (average of 68 cases per year) were due to type b.

There is evidence that Hib vaccines decrease the rate of carriage of Hib among vaccinated children, thereby decreasing the chance that unvaccinated children will be exposed.

Incidence is strikingly age-dependent. In the prevaccine era, up to 60% of invasive disease occurred before age 12 months, with a peak occurrence among children 6–11 months of age. Children 60 months of age and older account for less than 10% of invasive disease.

In 1998–2000, approximately 44% of children younger than 5 years of age with confirmed invasive Hib disease were younger than 6 months of age and too young to have completed a three-dose primary vaccination series. Fifty-six percent were age 6 months or older and were eligible to have completed the primary vaccination series. Of these age-eligible children, 68% were either incompletely vaccinated (fewer than 3 doses) or their vaccination status was unknown. Thirty-two percent of children aged 6–59 months with confirmed type b disease had received three or more doses of Hib vaccine, including 22 who had received a booster dose 14 or more days before onset of their illness. The cause of Hib vaccine failure in these children is not known.

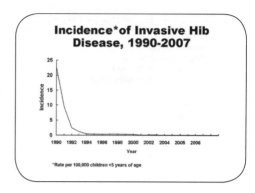

Incidence*of Invasive Hib Disease, 1990-2007

*Rate per 100,000 children <5 years of age

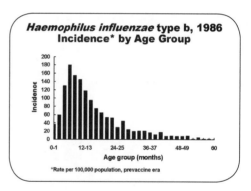

***Haemophilus influenzae* type b, 1986 Incidence* by Age Group**

*Rate per 100,000 population, prevaccine era

***Haemophilus influenzae* type b— United States, 1996-2000**

- Incidence has fallen 99% since prevaccine era
- 341 confirmed Hib cases reported during 1996-2000 (average of 68 cases per year)
- Most recent cases in unvaccinated or incompletely vaccinated children

In 2007, among children younger than 5 years of age, 22 cases of invasive disease due to Hib were reported in the United States. In addition, another 180 cases caused by unknown *H. influenzae* serotypes were reported, so the actual number of Hib cases could be between 22 and 202. Most cases were among unvaccinated or incompletely vaccinated children.

Risk factors for Hib disease include exposure factors and host factors that increase the likelihood of exposure to Hib. Exposure factors include household crowding, large household size, child care attendance, low socioeconomic status, low parental education levels, and school-aged siblings. Host factors include race/ethnicity (elevated risk among African Americans, Hispanics, Native Americans—possibly confounded by socioeconomic variables that are associated with both race/ethnicity and Hib disease), chronic disease (e.g., sickle cell anemia, antibody deficiency syndromes, malignancies, especially during chemotherapy), and possibly gender (risk is higher for males).

Protective factors (effect limited to infants younger than 6 months of age) include breastfeeding and passively acquired maternal antibody.

Secondary Hib disease is defined as illness occurring 1–60 days following contact with an ill child, and accounts for less than 5% of all invasive Hib disease. Among household contacts, six studies have found a secondary attack rate of 0.3% in the month following onset of the index case, which is about 600-fold higher than the risk for the general population. Attack rates varied substantially with age, from 3.7% among children 2 years of age and younger to 0% among contacts 6 years of age and older. In these household contacts, 64% of secondary cases occurred within the first week (excluding the first 24 hours) of disease onset in the index patient, 20% during the second week, and 16% during the third and fourth weeks.

Data are conflicting regarding the risk of secondary transmission among child care contacts. Secondary attack rates have varied from 0% to as high as 2.7%. Most studies seem to suggest that child care contacts are at relatively low risk for secondary transmission of Hib disease particularly if contacts are age-appropriately vaccinated.

Haemophilus influenzae type b Vaccines

Characteristics

A pure polysaccharide vaccine (HbPV) was licensed in the United States in 1985. The vaccine was not effective in children younger than 18 months of age. Estimates of efficacy in older children varied widely, from 88% to -69% (a negative efficacy implies greater disease risk for vaccinees

---

6

Haemophilus influenzae type b Risk Factors for Invasive Disease

- Exposure factors
  - household crowding
  - large household size
  - child care attendance
  - low socioeconomic status
  - low parental education
  - school-aged siblings
- Host factors
  - race/ethnicity
  - chronic disease

Haemophilus influenzae type b Polysaccharide Vaccine

- Available 1985-1988
- Not effective in children younger than 18 months of age
- Effectiveness in older children variable

than nonvaccinees). HbPV was used until 1988 but is no longer available in the United States.

The characteristics of the Hib polysaccharide were similar to other polysaccharide vaccines (e.g., pneumococcal, meningococcal). The response to the vaccine was typical of a T-independent antigen, most notably an age-dependent immune response, and poor immunogenicity in children 2 years of age and younger. In addition, no boost in antibody titer was observed with repeated doses, the antibody that was produced was relatively low-affinity IgM, and switching to IgG production was minimal.

Haemophilus influenzae type b Polysaccharide-Protein Conjugate Vaccines

Conjugation is the process of chemically bonding a polysaccharide (a somewhat ineffective antigen) to a protein "carrier," which is a more effective antigen. This process changes the polysaccharide from a T-independent to a T-dependent antigen and greatly improves immunogenicity, particularly in young children. In addition, repeat doses of Hib conjugate vaccines elicit booster responses and allow maturation of class-specific immunity with predominance of IgG antibody. The Hib conjugates also cause carrier priming and elicit antibody to "useful" carrier protein.

The first Hib conjugate vaccine (PRP-D, ProHIBIT) was licensed in December 1987. PRP-D is no longer available in the United States. HibTITER (HbOC) is no longer available.

Two conjugate Hib vaccines are licensed for use in infants as young as 6 weeks of age (see below). The vaccines utilize different carrier proteins. Three combination vaccines that contain Hib conjugate vaccine are also available.

Polysaccharide Vaccines

- Age-related immune response
- Not consistently immunogenic in children 2 years of age and younger
- No booster response
- Antibody with less functional activity

Polysaccharide Conjugate Vaccines

- Stimulates T-dependent immunity
- Enhanced antibody production, especially in young children
- Repeat doses elicit booster response

Haemophilus influenzae type b Conjugate Vaccines

Vaccine	Protein Carrier	Manufacturer
PRP-T (ActHIB)	Tetanus toxoid	sanofi pasteur
PRP-OMP (PedvaxHIB)	Meningococcal group B outer membrane protein	Merck

Immunogenicity and Vaccine Efficacy

Both Hib conjugate vaccines licensed for use in infants are highly immunogenic. More than 95% of infants will develop protective antibody levels after a primary series of two or three doses. Clinical efficacy has been estimated at 95% to 100%. Invasive Hib disease in a completely vaccinated infant is uncommon.

6

Hib vaccine is immunogenic in patients with increased risk for invasive disease, such as those with sickle-cell disease, leukemia, or human immunodeficiency virus (HIV) infection, and those who have had a splenectomy. However, in persons with HIV infection, immunogenicity varies with stage of infection and degree of immunocompromise. Efficacy studies have not been performed in populations with increased risk of invasive disease.

Vaccination Schedule and Use

All infants, including those born prematurely, should receive a primary series of conjugate Hib vaccine (separate or in combination), beginning at 2 months of age. The number of doses in the primary series depends on the type of vaccine used. A primary series of PRP-OMP (PedvaxHIB) vaccine is two doses; PRP-T (ActHIB) requires a three-dose primary series (see table below). A booster is recommended at 12–15 months regardless of which vaccine is used for the primary series.

ACIP-Recommended *Haemophilus influenzae* type b (Hib) Routine Vaccination Schedule

Vaccine	2 Months	4 Months	6 Months	12-15 Months
PRP-T	Dose 1	Dose 2	Dose 3	Booster
PRP-OMP	Dose 1	Dose 2		Booster

> **Haemophilus influenzae type b Vaccine**
>
> - Recommended interval 8 weeks for primary series doses
> - Minimum interval 4 weeks for primary series doses
> - Vaccination at younger than 6 weeks of age may induce immunologic tolerance to Hib antigen
> - Minimum age 6 weeks

> **Haemophilus influenzae type b Vaccine Delayed Vaccination Schedule**
>
> - Children starting late may not need entire 3 or 4 dose series
> - Number of doses child requires depends on current age
> - All children 15-59 months of age need at least 1 dose

The recommended interval between primary series doses is 8 weeks, with a minimum interval of 4 weeks. At least 8 weeks should separate the booster dose from the previous (second or third) dose. Hib vaccines may be given simultaneously with all other vaccines.

Limited data suggest that Hib conjugate vaccines given before 6 weeks of age may induce immunologic tolerance to subsequent doses of Hib vaccine. A dose given before 6 weeks of age may reduce the response to subsequent doses. As a result, Hib vaccines, including combination vaccines that contain Hib conjugate, should never be given to a child younger than 6 weeks of age.

The conjugate Hib vaccines licensed for use in infants are interchangeable. A series that includes vaccine of more than one type will induce a protective antibody level. If a child receives different brands of Hib vaccine at 2 and 4 months of age, a third dose of either brand should be administered at 6 months of age to complete the primary series. Either vaccine may be used for the booster dose, regardless of what was administered in the primary series.

Unvaccinated children 7 months of age and older may not require a full series of three or four doses. The number of doses a child needs to complete the series depends on the child's current age.

Detailed Vaccination Schedule
for *Haemophilus influenzae* type b Conjugate Vaccines

Vaccine	Age at 1st Dose (Months)	Primary Series	Booster
PRP-T (ActHIB)	2-6	3 doses, 2 months apart	12-15 months*
	7-11	2 doses, 2 months apart	12-15 months*
	12-14	1 dose	2 months later
	15-59	1 dose	—
PRP-OMP (PedvaxHIB)	2-6	2 doses, 2 months apart	12-15 months*
	7-11	2 doses, 2 months apart	12-15 months*
	12-14	1 dose	2 months later
	15-59	1 dose	—

*At least 2 months after previous dose

PRP-T (ActHIB)

Previously unvaccinated infants aged 2 through 6 months should receive three doses of vaccine administered 2 months apart, followed by a booster dose at age 12–15 months, administered at least 2 months after the last dose. Unvaccinated children aged 7 through 11 months should receive two doses of vaccine 2 months apart, followed by a booster dose at age 12–15 months, administered at least 2 months after the last dose. Unvaccinated children aged 12 through 14 months should receive two doses of vaccine, at least 2 months apart. Any previously unvaccinated child aged 15 through 59 months should receive a single dose of vaccine.

PRP-OMP (PedvaxHIB)

Unvaccinated children aged 2 through 11 months should receive two doses of vaccine 2 months apart, followed by a booster dose at 12–15 months of age, at least 2 months after the last dose. Unvaccinated children aged 12 through 14 months should receive two doses of vaccine 2 months apart. Any previously unvaccinated child 15 through 59 months of age should receive a single dose of vaccine.

Children with a lapsed Hib immunization series (i.e., children who have received one or more doses of Hib-containing vaccine but are not up-to-date for their age) may not need all the remaining doses of a three- or four-dose series. Vaccination of children with a lapsed schedule is addressed

6

in the catch-up schedule, published annually with the childhood vaccination schedule.

Hib invasive disease does not always result in development of protective anti-PRP antibody levels. Children younger than 24 months of age who develop invasive Hib disease should be considered susceptible and should receive Hib vaccine. Vaccination of these children should start as soon as possible during the convalescent phase of the illness. The schedule should be completed as recommended for the child's age.

Vaccination of Older Children and Adults

In general, Hib vaccination of persons older than 59 months of age is not recommended. The majority of older children are immune to Hib, probably from asymptomatic infection as infants. However, some older children and adults are at increased risk for invasive Hib disease and may be vaccinated if they were not vaccinated in childhood. These include those with functional or anatomic asplenia (e.g., sickle cell disease, postsplenectomy), immunodeficiency (in particular, persons with IgG2 subclass deficiency), immunosuppression from cancer chemotherapy, infection with HIV, and receipt of a hematopoietic stem cell transplant (HSCT). Previously unvaccinated persons older than 59 months of age with one of these high-risk conditions should be given at least one pediatric dose of any Hib conjugate vaccine.

Combination Vaccines

Three combination vaccines that contain *H. influenzae* type b are available in the United States—DTaP/Hib (TriHIBit, sanofi pasteur), DTaP-IPV-Hib (Pentacel, sanofi pasteur) and hepatitis B–Hib (Comvax, Merck).

TriHIBit

TriHIBit was licensed for use in the United States in September 1996. The vaccines are packaged together in separate vials, and the DTaP component (Tripedia) is used to reconstitute the Hib component (ActHIB). No other brand of DTaP and Hib vaccine may be used to produce this combination (e.g., Infanrix must not be substituted for Tripedia). In addition, when supplied as TriHIBit, the DTaP and Hib components have a single lot number. Providers should generally use only the DTaP and Hib supplied together as TriHIBit. However, it is acceptable to combine Tripedia and ActHIB that have been supplied separately (i.e., not packaged as TriHIBit). In this situation, the lot numbers of both vaccines should be recorded.

TriHIBit is not approved by the Food and Drug Administration for use as the primary series at 2, 4, or 6 months of age. It is approved only for the fourth dose of the

---

Haemophilus influenzae type b Vaccine
Vaccination Following Invasive Disease

- Children younger than 24 months may not develop protective antibody after invasive disease
- Vaccinate during convalescence
- Complete series for age

Haemophilus influenzae type b Vaccine
Use in Older Children and Adults

- Generally not recommended for persons older than 59 months of age
- Consider for high-risk persons: asplenia, immunodeficiency, HIV infection, HSCT
- One pediatric dose of any conjugate vaccine

Combination Vaccines Containing Hib

- DTaP/Hib
  - TriHIBit
- DTaP-IPV/Hib
  - Pentacel
- Hib-Hep B
  - Comvax

TriHIBit

- ActHIB reconstituted with Tripedia
- Not approved for the primary series at 2, 4, or 6 months of age
- Approved for the fourth dose of the DTaP and Hib series only
- Primary series Hib doses given as TriHIBit should be disregarded

DTaP and Hib series. If TriHIBit is administered as one or more doses of the primary series at 2, 4, or 6 months of age, the Hib doses should be disregarded, and the child should be revaccinated as age-appropriate for Hib. The DTaP doses may be counted as valid and do not need to be repeated.

Although TriHIBit cannot be used in the primary series at 2, 4, or 6 months of age, it may be used as the booster (final) dose following a series of single-antigen Hib vaccine or combination hepatitis B–Hib vaccine (Comvax). Therefore, TriHIBit can be used if the child is 12 months of age or older and has received at least one prior dose of Hib vaccine 2 or more months earlier and TriHIBit will be the last dose in the Hib series. For example, TriHIBit can be used for the booster dose at 12 through 15 months of age in a child who has received Comvax or PedvaxHib at 2 and 4 months of age, or three prior doses of HibTiter or ActHib. TriHIBit can also be used at 15 through 59 months of age in a child who has received at least one prior dose of any Hib-containing vaccine. TriHIBit should not be used if the child has received no prior Hib doses.

TriHIBit
• May be used as the booster dose of the Hib series at 12 months of age or older following any Hib vaccine series*
• Should not be used if child has receive no prior Hib doses
*booster dose should follow prior dose by at least 2 months

Comvax

Comvax is a combination hepatitis B–Hib vaccine, licensed in October 1996. The vaccine contains a standard dose of PRP-OMP (PedvaxHIB), and 5 mcg (pediatric dose) of Merck's hepatitis B vaccine. Comvax is licensed for use when either or both antigens are indicated. However, because of the potential of immune tolerance to the Hib antigen, Comvax should not be used in infants younger than 6 weeks of age (i.e., the birth dose of hepatitis B, or a dose at 1 month of age, if the infant is on a 0-1-6-month schedule). Comvax is not licensed for infants whose mothers are known to be hepatitis B surface antigen positive (i.e., acute or chronic infection with hepatitis B virus). However, the vaccine contains the same dose of Merck's hepatitis B vaccine recommended for these infants, so response to the hepatitis B component of Comvax should be adequate. The Advisory Committee on Immunization Practices (ACIP) has approved off-label use of Comvax in children whose mother is HBsAg positive or whose HBsAg status is unknown. See http://www.cdc.gov/vaccines/programs/vfc/downloads/resolutions/1003hepb.pdf.

COMVAX
• Hib-Hep B combination
• Use when either antigen is indicated
• Cannot use before 6 weeks of age
• May be used in infants whose mothers are HBsAg positive or status is unknown

Recommendations for spacing and timing of Comvax are the same as those for the individual antigens. In particular, the third dose must be given at 12 months of age or older and at least 2 months after the second dose, as recommended for PRP-OMP.

6

Pentacel Vaccine

- Contains lyophilized Hib (ActHIB) vaccine that is reconstituted with a liquid DTaP-IPV solution
- Approved for doses 1 through 4 among children 6 weeks through 4 years of age
- The DTaP-IPV solution should not be used separately (i.e., only use to reconstitute the Hib component)

Haemophilus influenzae type b Vaccine
Contraindications and Precautions

- Severe allergic reaction to vaccine component or following a prior dose
- Moderate or severe acute illness
- Age younger than 6 weeks

Haemophilus influenzae type b Vaccine
Adverse Reactions

- Swelling, redness, or pain in 5%-30% of recipients
- Systemic reactions infrequent
- Serious adverse reactions rare

Pentacel

Pentacel is a combination vaccine that contains lyophilized Hib (ActHIB) vaccine that is reconstituted with a liquid DTaP-IPV solution. The vaccine was licensed by FDA in June 2008. Pentacel is licensed by FDA for doses 1 through 4 of the DTaP series among children 6 weeks through 4 years of age. Pentacel should not be used for the fifth dose of the DTaP series, or for children 5 years or older regardless of the number of prior doses of the component vaccines. The DTaP-IPV solution is licensed only for use as the diluent for the lyophilized Hib component and should not be used separately.

Contraindications and Precautions to Vaccination

Vaccination with Hib conjugate vaccine is contraindicated for persons known to have experienced a severe allergic reaction (anaphylaxis) to a vaccine component or following a prior dose of that vaccine. Vaccination should be delayed for children with moderate or severe acute illnesses. Minor illnesses (e.g., mild upper respiratory infection) are not contraindications to vaccination. Hib conjugate vaccines are contraindicated for children younger than 6 weeks of age because of the potential for development of immunologic tolerance.

Contraindications and precautions for the use of TriHIBit, Pentacel, and Comvax are the same as those for its individual component vaccines (i.e., DTaP, Hib, IPV, and hepatitis B).

Adverse Reactions Following Vaccination

Adverse reaction following Hib conjugate vaccines are not common. Swelling, redness, or pain have been reported in 5%–30% of recipients and usually resolve within 12–24 hours. Systemic reactions such as fever and irritability are infrequent. Serious adverse reactions are rare. Available information on adverse reactions suggests that the risks for local and systemic reactions following TriHIBit administration are similar to those following concurrent administration of its individual component vaccines, and are probably due to the DTaP vaccine.

All serious adverse events that occur after receipt of any vaccine should be reported to the Vaccine Adverse Event Reporting System (VAERS) (http://vaers.hhs.gov/).

Vaccine Storage and Handling

All Hib conjugate vaccines should be shipped in insulated containers to prevent freezing. Unreconstituted or liquid vaccine should be stored at refrigerator temperature ($35°$–$46°$F [$2°$–$8°$C]). Hib vaccine must not be frozen.

ActHIB should be used within 24 hours of reconstitution and TriHIBit should be used immediately (within 30 minutes).

Surveillance and Reporting of Hib Disease

Invasive Hib disease is a reportable condition in most states. All healthcare personnel should report any case of invasive Hib disease to local and state health departments.

Selected References

American Academy of Pediatrics. *Haemophilus influenzae* infections. In: Pickering L, Baker C, Long S, McMillan J, eds. *Red Book: 2006 Report of the Committee on Infectious Diseases*. 27th ed. Elk Grove Village, IL: American Academy of Pediatrics, 2006:310–8.

Bisgard KM, Kao A, Leake J, et al. *Haemophilus influenzae* invasive disease in the United States, 1994–1995: near disappearance of a vaccine-preventable childhood disease. *Emerg Infect Dis* 1998;4:229–37.

CDC. *Haemophilus b* conjugate vaccines for prevention of *Haemophilus influenzae* type b disease among infants and children two months of age and older: recommendations of the Advisory Committee on Immunization Practices (ACIP). *MMWR* 1991;40(No. RR-1):1–7.

CDC. Progress toward elimination of *Haemophilus influenzae* type b disease among infants and children—United States, 1998–2000. *MMWR* 2002;51:234–37.

CDC. *Haemophilus influenzae* invasive disease among children aged <5 years—California, 1990–1996. *MMWR* 1998;47:737–40.

Decker MD, Edwards KM. *Haemophilus influenzae* type b vaccines: history, choice and comparisons. *Pediatr Infect Dis* J 1998;17:S113–16.

Orenstein WA, Hadler S, Wharton M. Trends in vaccine-preventable diseases. *Semin Pediatr Infect Dis* 1997;8:23–33.

6

6

Hepatitis A

The first descriptions of hepatitis (epidemic jaundice) are generally attributed to Hippocrates. Outbreaks of jaundice, probably hepatitis A, were reported in the 17th and 18th centuries, particularly in association with military campaigns. Hepatitis A (formerly called infectious hepatitis) was first differentiated epidemiologically from hepatitis B, which has a long incubation period, in the 1940s. Development of serologic tests allowed definitive diagnosis of hepatitis B. In the 1970s, identification of the virus, and development of serologic tests helped differentiate hepatitis A from other types of non-B hepatitis.

Until 2004, hepatitis A was the most frequently reported type of hepatitis in the United States. In the prevaccine era, the primary methods used for preventing hepatitis A were hygienic measures and passive protection with immune globulin (IG). Hepatitis A vaccines were licensed in 1995 and 1996. These vaccines provide long-term protection against hepatitis A virus (HAV) infection. The similarities between the epidemiology of hepatitis A and poliomyelitis suggest that widespread vaccination of appropriate susceptible populations can substantially lower disease incidence, eliminate virus transmission, and ultimately, eliminate HAV infection.

Hepatitis A Virus

Hepatitis A is caused by infection with HAV, a nonenveloped RNA virus that is classified as a picornavirus. It was first isolated in 1979. Humans are the only natural host, although several nonhuman primates have been infected in laboratory conditions. Depending on conditions, HAV can be stable in the environment for months. The virus is relatively stable at low pH levels and moderate temperatures but can be inactivated by high temperature (185°F [85°C] or higher), formalin, and chlorine.

Pathogenesis

HAV is acquired by mouth (through fecal-oral transmission) and replicates in the liver. After 10–12 days, virus is present in blood and is excreted via the biliary system into the feces. Peak titers occur during the 2 weeks before onset of illness. Although virus is present in serum, its concentration is several orders of magnitude less than in feces. Virus excretion begins to decline at the onset of clinical illness, and has decreased significantly by 7–10 days after onset of symptoms. Most infected persons no longer excrete virus in the feces by the third week of illness. Children may excrete virus longer than adults.

Hepatitis A

- Epidemic jaundice described by Hippocrates
- Differentiated from hepatitis B in 1940s
- Serologic tests developed in 1970s
- Vaccines licensed in 1995 and 1996

Hepatitis A Virus

- Picornavirus (RNA)
- Humans are only natural host
- Stable at low pH
- Inactivated by high temperature (185°F or higher), formalin, chlorine

Hepatitis A Pathogenesis

- Entry into mouth
- Viral replication in the liver
- Virus present in blood and feces 10-12 days after infection
- Virus excretion may continue for up to 3 weeks after onset of symptoms

7

Hepatitis A Clinical Features

- Incubation period 28 days (range 15-50 days)
- Illness not specific for hepatitis A
- Likelihood of symptomatic illness directly related to age
- Children generally asymptomatic, adults symptomatic

Clinical Features

The incubation period of hepatitis A is approximately 28 days (range 15–50 days). The clinical course of acute hepatitis A is indistinguishable from that of other types of acute viral hepatitis. The illness typically has an abrupt onset of fever, malaise, anorexia, nausea, abdominal discomfort, dark urine and jaundice. Clinical illness usually does not last longer than 2 months, although 10%–15% of persons have prolonged or relapsing signs and symptoms for up to 6 months. Virus may be excreted during a relapse.

The likelihood of symptomatic illness from HAV infection is directly related to age. In children younger than 6 years of age, most (70%) infections are asymptomatic. In older children and adults, infection is usually symptomatic, with jaundice occurring in more than 70% of patients. HAV infection occasionally produces fulminant hepatitis A.

Complications

In the prevaccine era, fulminant hepatitis A caused about 100 deaths per year in the United States. The case-fatality rate among persons of all ages with reported cases was approximately 0.3% but could be higher among older persons (approximately 2% among persons 40 years of age and older).

Hepatitis A results in substantial morbidity, with associated costs caused by medical care and work loss. Hospitalization rates for hepatitis A are 11%–22%. Adults who become ill lose an average of 27 work days per illness, and health departments incur the costs of postexposure prophylaxis for an average of 11 contacts per case. Average direct and indirect costs of hepatitis A range from $1,817 to $2,459 per adult case and $433 to $1,492 per pediatric case. In 1989, the estimated annual U.S. total cost of hepatitis A was more than $200 million.

Laboratory Diagnosis

Hepatitis A cannot be distinguished from other types of viral hepatitis on the basis of clinical or epidemiologic features alone. Serologic testing is required to confirm the diagnosis. Virtually all patients with acute hepatitis A have detectable IgM anti-HAV. Acute HAV infection is confirmed during the acute or early convalescent phase of infection by the presence of IgM anti-HAV in serum. IgM generally becomes detectable 5–10 days before the onset of symptoms and can persist for up to 6 months.

IgG anti-HAV appears in the convalescent phase of infection, remains present in serum for the lifetime of the person, and confers enduring protection against disease.

The antibody test for total anti-HAV measures both IgG anti-HAV and IgM anti-HAV. Persons who are total anti-HAV positive and IgM anti-HAV negative have serologic markers indicating immunity consistent with either past infection or vaccination.

Molecular virology methods such as polymerase chain reaction (PCR)-based assays can be used to amplify and sequence viral genomes. These assays are helpful to investigate common-source outbreaks of hepatitis A. Providers with questions about molecular virology methods should consult with their state health department or the CDC Division of Viral Hepatitis.

Medical Management

There is no specific treatment for hepatitis A virus infection. Treatment and management of HAV infection are supportive.

Epidemiology

Occurrence

Hepatitis A occurs throughout the world. It is highly endemic in some areas, particularly Central and South America, Africa, the Middle East, Asia, and the Western Pacific.

Reservoir

Humans are the only natural reservoir of the virus. There are no insect or animal vectors. A chronic HAV carrier state has not been reported.

Transmission

HAV infection is acquired primarily by the fecal-oral route by either person-to-person contact or ingestion of contaminated food or water. Because the virus is present in blood during the illness prodrome, HAV has been transmitted on rare occasions by transfusion. Although HAV may be present in saliva, transmission by saliva has not been demonstrated. Waterborne outbreaks are infrequent and are usually associated with sewage-contaminated or inadequately treated water.

Temporal Pattern

There is no appreciable seasonal variation in hepatitis A incidence.

Communicability

Viral shedding persists for 1 to 3 weeks. Infected persons are most likely to transmit HAV 1 to 2 weeks before the onset of

---

Hepatitis A Epidemiology

- Reservoir   Human
- Transmission   Fecal-oral
- Temporal pattern   None
- Communicability   2 weeks before to 1 week after onset

7

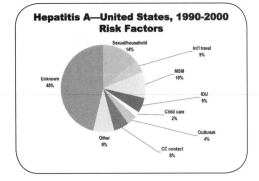

Hepatitis A—United States, 1990-2000 Risk Factors

Sexual/household 14%
Int'l travel 5%
MSM 10%
Unknown 45%
IDU 6%
Child care 2%
Outbreak 4%
CC contact 6%
Other 8%

illness, when HAV concentration in stool is highest. The risk then decreases and is minimal the week after the onset of jaundice.

Risk Factors

From 1990 through 2000, the most frequently reported source of infection was personal contact (sexual or household) with an infected person (14%). Two percent of cases involved a child or employee in child care; 6% occurred in a contact of a child or employee in child care; 5% occurred among persons reporting recent international travel; and 4% occurred in the context of a recognized foodborne outbreak. Injection-drug use was a reported risk factor in 6% of cases; men who have sex with men represented 10% of cases. Forty-five percent of reported hepatitis A case-patients could not identify a risk factor for their infection.

Groups at increased risk for hepatitis A or its complications include international travelers, men who have sex with men, and users of illegal drugs. Outbreaks of hepatitis A have also been reported among persons working with hepatitis A–infected primates. This is the only occupational group known to be at increased risk for hepatitis A.

Persons with chronic liver disease are not at increased risk of infection but are at increased risk of acquiring fulminant hepatitis A. Persons with clotting factor disorders may be at increased risk of HAV because of administration of solvent/detergent-treated factor VIII and IX concentrates.

Foodhandlers are not at increased risk for hepatitis A because of their occupation, but are noteworthy because of their critical role in common-source foodborne HAV transmission. Healthcare personnel do not have an increased prevalence of HAV infections, and nosocomial HAV transmission is rare. Nonetheless, outbreaks have been observed in neonatal intensive care units and in association with adult fecal incontinence. Institutions for persons with developmental disabilities previously were sites of high HAV endemicity. But as fewer children have been institutionalized and conditions within these institutions have improved, HAV incidence and prevalence have decreased. However, sporadic outbreaks can occur. Schools are not common sites for HAV transmission. Multiple cases among children at a school require investigation of a common source. Workers exposed to sewage have not reported any work-related HAV infection in the United States, but serologic data are not available.

Children play an important role in HAV transmission. Children generally have asymptomatic or unrecognized illnesses, so they may serve as a source of infection, particularly for household or other close contacts.

7

Secular Trends in the United States

In the United States, hepatitis A has occurred in large nationwide epidemics approximately every 10 years, with the last increase in cases in 1989. However, between epidemics HAV infection continues to occur at relatively high rates. Hepatitis A became nationally reportable as a distinct entity in 1966. The largest number of cases reported in one year (59,606) was in 1971. A total of 5,970 cases was reported in 2004. After adjusting for under-reporting, 20,000 infections are estimated to have occurred in 2004, approximately half of which were symptomatic. Hepatitis A rates have been declining since 1995, and since 1998 have been at historically low levels. A total of 2,979 cases was reported in 2007. The wider use of vaccine is probably contributing to this marked decrease in hepatitis A rates in the United States.

Historically, children 2 through 18 years of age have had the highest rates of hepatitis A (15 to 20 cases per 100,000 population in the early to mid-1990s). Since 2002, rates among children have declined and the incidence of hepatitis A is now similar in all age groups.

Based on testing from phase 1 of the Third National Health and Nutrition Examination Survey (NHANES III) conducted during 1988 through 1994, the prevalence of total antibody to HAV (anti-HAV) among the general U.S. population is 33%. Seroprevalence of HAV antibody increases with age, from 9% among 6- to 11-year-olds to 75% among persons 70 years of age and older. Anti-HAV prevalence is highest among Mexican-Americans (70%), compared with blacks (39%) and whites (23%). Anti-HAV prevalence is inversely related to income.

Prior to 2000, the incidence of reported hepatitis A was substantially higher in the western United States than in other parts of the country. From 1987 to 1997, 11 mostly western states (Arizona, Alaska, Oregon, New Mexico, Utah, Washington, Oklahoma, South Dakota, Idaho, Nevada, California) accounted for 50% of all reported cases but only 22% of the U.S. population. Many of these high-incidence states began routine hepatitis A vaccination programs for children in the late 1990s. Since 2002, rates have been similar in all parts of the country.

Many hepatitis A cases in the United States occur in the context of communitywide epidemics. Communities that experience such epidemics can be classified as high-rate and intermediate-rate communities. High-rate communities typically have epidemics every 5 to 10 years that may last for several years with substantial rates of disease (as high as 700 cases per 100,000 population annually

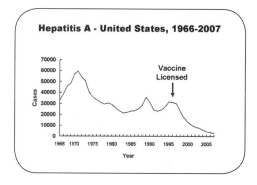

Hepatitis A - United States, 1966-2007

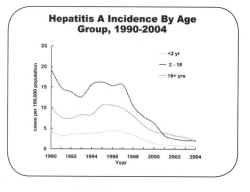

Hepatitis A Incidence By Age Group, 1990-2004

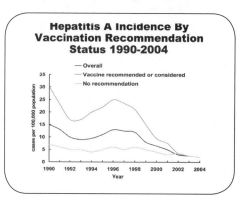

Hepatitis A Incidence By Vaccination Recommendation Status 1990-2004

during outbreaks) but few cases among persons 15 years of age and older. These communities often are relatively well-defined either geographically or ethnically and include Native American, Alaska Native, Pacific Islander, and selected Hispanic communities and certain religious communities. Experience with hepatitis A vaccination programs in these high-rate communities has shown that when relatively high (65% to 80%) first-dose vaccination coverage of preschool and school-age children is achieved and routine vaccination of young children is sustained, ongoing outbreaks of hepatitis A could be interrupted. In these areas, sustained reduction in HAV incidence has been achieved and subsequent outbreaks have been prevented.

Case Definition

The case definition for hepatitis A was approved by the Council of State and Territorial Epidemiologists (CSTE) in 1997. It reflects a clinical diagnosis of hepatitis and, because HAV cannot be differentiated from other types of viral hepatitis on clinical or epidemiologic features alone, serologic evidence of HAV-specific IgM antibody is necessary.

The clinical case definition for hepatitis A is an acute illness with discrete onset of symptoms, and jaundice or elevated serum aminotransferase levels. The laboratory criterion for diagnosis is a positive IgM anti-HAV.

Hepatitis A Vaccine

Characteristics

Two inactivated whole-virus hepatitis A vaccines are available: HAVRIX (GlaxoSmithKline) and VAQTA (Merck). To produce each vaccine, cell culture–adapted virus is propagated in human fibroblasts, purified from cell lysates, inactivated with formalin, and adsorbed to an aluminum hydroxide adjuvant. HAVRIX is prepared with a preservative (2-phenoxyathanol); VAQTA does not contain a preservative. Both vaccines are available in both pediatric and adult formulations. The pediatric formulations of both vaccines are approved for persons 12 months through 18 years. The adult formulations are approved for persons 19 years and older.

Immunogenicity and Vaccine Efficacy

Both vaccines are highly immunogenic. More than 95% of adults will develop protective antibody within 4 weeks of a single dose of either vaccine, and nearly 100% will seroconvert after receiving two doses. Among children and adolescents, more than 97% will be seropositive within a

---

Hepatitis A Vaccines

- Inactivated whole virus vaccines
- Pediatric and adult formulations
  - pediatric formulations approved for persons 12 months through 18 years
  - adult formulations approved for persons 19 years and older

---

Hepatitis A Vaccine Immunogenicity

Adults
- >95% seropositive after one dose
- 100% seropositive after two doses

Children (>12 months) and Adolescents
- >97% seropositive after one
- 100% seropositive after 2 doses

month of the first dose. In clinical trials, all recipients had protective levels of antibody after two doses.

Both vaccines are highly effective in preventing clinical hepatitis A. The efficacy of HAVRIX in protecting against clinical hepatitis A was 94% among 40,000 Thai children 1 to 16 years of age who received two doses 1 month apart while living in villages with high HAV disease rates. The efficacy of VAQTA in protecting against clinical hepatitis A was 100% among 1,000 New York children 2 to 16 years of age who received one dose while living in a community with a high HAV disease rate.

Data concerning the long-term persistence of antibody and immune memory are limited because the current vaccines have been available only since 1995 and 1996. Estimates of antibody persistence derived from kinetic models of antibody decline indicate that protective levels of anti-HAV could be present for 20 years or longer. Other mechanisms (e.g., cellular) may contribute to long-term protection, but this is unknown. The need for booster doses will be determined by postmarketing surveillance studies.

Vaccination Schedule and Use

Following its introduction in 1995, hepatitis A vaccine was primarily targeted to persons at increased risk for HAV infection, particularly international travelers. While this strategy prevented infection in this group and in other vaccinated individuals, it had little or no impact on the incidence of HAV infection in the United States.

As a result of successful vaccination programs in areas with a high incidence of HAV infection, the Advisory Committee on Immunization Practices (ACIP) in 1999 recommended that routine vaccination of children 2 years of age and older with hepatitis A vaccine be implemented in states, counties or communities where the average annual incidence of hepatitis A during 1987 through 1997 was 20 cases per 100,000 population or higher (i.e., at least twice the U.S. average of 10 cases per 100,000 population). ACIP also recommended that routine vaccination be considered for states, counties or communities where the average annual incidence of hepatitis A during 1987 through 1997 was 10 or more cases but less than 20 cases per 100,000 population. These strategies appear to have significantly reduced the incidence of hepatitis A in these areas.

Based on the successful implementation of childhood hepatitis A vaccination programs in high incidence areas, ACIP recommended in 2005 that all children should receive hepatitis A vaccine at 12 through 23 months of age. Vaccination should be integrated into the routine

---

Hepatitis A Vaccine Efficacy

HAVRIX
- 40,000 Thai children 1-16 years of age
- vaccine efficacy 94%

VAQTA
- 1,000 New York children 2-16 years of age
- vaccine efficacy 100%

7

ACIP Recommendation for Routine Hepatitis A Vaccination of Children

- All children should receive hepatitis A vaccine at 12-23 months of age
- Vaccination should be integrated into the routine childhood vaccination schedule
- Children who are not vaccinated by 2 years of age can be vaccinated at subsequent visits

MMWR 2006;55(No.RR-7):1-23

ACIP Recommendation for Routine Hepatitis A Vaccination of Children

- States, counties, and communities with existing hepatitis A vaccination programs for children 2 through 18 years of age should maintain these programs
- New efforts focused on routine vaccination of children 12 months of age should enhance, not replace ongoing vaccination programs for older children

MMWR 2006;55(No.RR-7):1-23

7

childhood vaccination schedule. Children who are not vaccinated by 2 years of age can be vaccinated at subsequent visits. ACIP encourages states, counties, and communities with existing hepatitis A vaccination programs for children 2 through 18 years of age to maintain these programs.

Persons at increased risk for HAV infection, or who are at increased risk for complications of HAV infection, should continue to be routinely vaccinated.

HAVRIX is available in two formulations: pediatric (720 ELISA units [EL.U.] per 0.5-mL dose) and adult (1,440 EL.U. per 1.0-mL dose). Children 1 through 18 years of age should receive a single primary dose of the pediatric formulation followed by a booster dose 6 to 12 months later. Adults 19 years of age and older receive one dose of the adult formulation followed by a booster 6 to 12 months later. The vaccine should be administered intramuscularly into the deltoid muscle. A needle length appropriate for the vaccinee's age and size (minimum of 1 inch) should be used.

Recommended Doses of Havrix® Hepatitis A Vaccine					
Group	Age	Dose (EL.U.)	Volume	No. Doses	Schedule*
Children and Adolescents	1-18 years	720	0.5 mL	2	0, 6-12
Adults	≥ 19 years	1,440	1.0 mL	2	0, 6-12

*Months: 0 months represents timing of the initial dose; subsequent number(s) represent months after the initial dose.

VAQTA is quantified in units (U) of antigen and is available in pediatric and adult formulations. Children 1 through 18 years of age should receive one dose of pediatric formulation (25 U per dose) with a booster dose 6 to 18 months later. Adults 19 years of age and older should receive one dose of adult formulation (50 U per dose) with a booster dose 6 to 18 months after the first dose. The vaccine should be administered intramuscularly into the deltoid muscle. A needle length appropriate for the vaccinee's age and size should be used (minimum of 1 inch).

Recommended Doses of VAQTA® Hepatitis A Vaccine					
Group	Age	Dose (U)	Volume	No. Doses	Schedule*
Children and Adolescents	1-18 years	25	0.5 mL	2	0, 6-18
Adults	≥ 19 years	50	1.0 mL	2	0, 6-18

*Months: 0 months represents timing of the initial dose; subsequent number(s) represent months after the initial dose.

Limited data indicate that vaccines from different manufacturers are interchangeable. Completion of the series with the same product is preferable. However, if the originally used product is not available or not known, vaccination with either product is acceptable.

For both vaccines, the booster dose given should be based on the person's age at the time of the booster dose, not the age when the first dose was given. For example, if a person received the first dose of the pediatric formulation of VAQTA at 18 years of age, and returns for the booster dose at age 19 years, the booster dose should be the adult formulation, not the pediatric formulation.

The minimum interval between the first and booster doses of hepatitis A vaccine is 6 calendar months. If the interval between the first and booster doses of hepatitis A vaccine extends beyond 18 months, it is not necessary to repeat the first dose.

Combination Hepatitis A and Hepatitis B Vaccine

In 2001, the Food and Drug Administration approved a combination hepatitis A and hepatitis B vaccine (Twinrix, GlaxoSmithKline). Each dose of Twinrix contains 720 EL.U. of hepatitis A vaccine (equivalent to a pediatric dose of HAVRIX), and 20 mcg of hepatitis B surface antigen protein (equivalent to an adult dose of Engerix-B). The vaccine is administered in a three-dose series at 0, 1, and 6 months. Appropriate spacing of the doses must be maintained to assure long-term protection from both vaccines. The first and second doses should be separated by at least 4 weeks, and the second and third doses should be separated by at least 5 months. Twinrix is approved for persons aged 18 years and older and can be used in persons in this age group with indications for both hepatitis A and hepatitis B vaccines.

In 2007 FDA approved an alternative schedule for Twinrix with doses at 0,7, and 21 through 30 days and a booster dose 12 months after the first dose.

Because the hepatitis B component of Twinrix is equivalent to a standard dose of hepatitis B vaccine, the schedule is the same whether Twinrix or single-antigen hepatitis B vaccine is used.

Single-antigen hepatitis A vaccine may be used to complete a series begun with Twinrix and vice versa. A person 19 years of age or older who receives one dose of Twinrix may complete the hepatitis A series with two doses of adult formulation hepatitis A vaccine separated by at least 5 months. A person who receives two doses of Twinrix may complete the hepatitis A series with one dose of adult formulation hepatitis A vaccine or Twinrix 5 months after the second dose. A person who begins the hepatitis A series

Hepatitis A Vaccines

Formulation	HAVRIX	VAQTA
Pediatric		
age	1-18 yrs	1-18 yrs
dose	0.5 ml	0.5 ml
Adult		
age	≥19 yrs	≥19 yrs
dose	1.0 ml	1.0 ml

7

Twinrix

- Combination hepatitis A vaccine (pediatric dose) and hepatitis B (adult dose)
- Schedule: 0, 1, 6 months
- Approved for persons 18 years of age and older

with single-antigen hepatitis A vaccine may complete the series with two doses of Twinrix or one dose of adult formulation hepatitis A vaccine. An 18-year-old should follow the same schedule using the pediatric formulation.

Persons at Increased Risk for Hepatitis A or Severe Outcomes of Infection

Persons at increased risk for hepatitis A should be identified and vaccinated. Hepatitis A vaccine should be strongly considered for persons 1 year of age and older who are traveling to or working in countries where they would have a high or intermediate risk of hepatitis A virus infection. These areas include all areas of the world except Canada, Western Europe and Scandinavia, Japan, New Zealand, and Australia.

The first dose of hepatitis A vaccine should be administered as soon as travel is considered. For healthy persons 40 years of age or younger, 1 dose of single antigen vaccine administered at any time before departure can provide adequate protection.

Unvaccinated adults older than 40 years of age, immuno-compromised persons, and persons with chronic liver disease planning to travel in 2 weeks or sooner should receive the first dose of vaccine and also can receive immune globulin at the same visit. Vaccine and IG should be administered with separate syringes at different anatomic sites.

Travelers who choose not to receive vaccine should receive a single dose of IG (0.02 mL/kg), which provides protection against HAV infection for up to 3 months. Persons whose travel period is more than 2 months should be administered IG at 0.06 mL/kg. IG should be repeated in 5 months for prolonged travel.

Other groups that should be offered vaccine include men who have sex with other men, persons who use illegal drugs, persons who have clotting factor disorders, and persons with occupational risk of infection. Persons with occupational risk include only those who work with hepatitis A-infected primates or with hepatitis A virus in a laboratory setting. No other groups have been shown to be at increased risk of hepatitis A infection due to occupational exposure.

Persons with chronic liver disease are not at increased risk for HAV infection because of their liver disease alone. However, these persons are at increased risk for fulminant hepatitis A should they become infected. Susceptible persons who have chronic liver disease should be vaccinated. Susceptible persons who either are awaiting or have received liver transplants should be vaccinated.

**Hepatitis A
Vaccine Recommendations**

- International travelers
- Men who have sex with men
- Persons who use illegal drugs
- Persons who have clotting factor disorders
- Persons with occupational risk
- Persons with chronic liver disease

Hepatitis A vaccination is not routinely recommended for healthcare personnel, persons attending or working in child care centers, or persons who work in liquid or solid waste management (e.g., sewer workers or plumbers). These groups have not been shown to be at increased risk for hepatitis A infection. ACIP does not recommend routine hepatitis A vaccination for food service workers, but vaccination may be considered based on local epidemiology.

Prevaccination Serologic Testing

HAV infection produces lifelong immunity to hepatitis A, so there is no benefit of vaccinating someone with serologic evidence of past HAV infection. The risk for adverse events following vaccination of such persons is not higher than the risk for serologically negative persons. As a result, the decision to conduct prevaccination testing should be based chiefly on the prevalence of immunity, the cost of testing and vaccinating (including office visit costs), and the likelihood that testing will interfere with initiating vaccination.

Testing of children is not indicated because of their expected low prevalence of infection. Persons for whom prevaccination serologic testing will likely be most cost-effective include adults who were either born in or lived for extensive periods in geographic areas that have a high endemicity of HAV infection (e.g., Central and South America, Africa, Asia); older adolescents and adults in certain populations (i.e., Native Americans, Alaska Natives, and Hispanics); adults in certain groups that have a high prevalence of infection (see above); and adults 40 years of age and older.

Commercially available tests for total anti-HAV should be used for prevaccination testing.

Postvaccination Serologic Testing

Postvaccination testing is not indicated because of the high rate of vaccine response among adults and children. Testing methods sufficiently sensitive to detect low anti-HAV concentrations after vaccination are not approved for routine diagnostic use in the United States.

Contraindications and Precautions to Vaccination

Hepatitis A vaccine should not be administered to persons with a history of a severe allergic reaction (anaphylaxis) to a vaccine component or following a prior dose of hepatitis A vaccine, hypersensitivity to alum or, in the case of HAVRIX, to the preservative 2-phenoxyethanol. Vaccination of persons with moderate or severe acute illnesses should be deferred until the person's condition has improved.

Hepatitis A Vaccine Recommendations

- Healthcare personnel not routinely recommended
- Child care centers: not routinely recommended
- Sewer workers or plumbers: not routinely recommended
- Food handlers: may be considered based on local circumstances

7

Hepatitis A Serologic Testing

Prevaccination
- not indicated for children
- may be considered for some adults and older adolescents

Postvaccination
- not indicated

Hepatitis A Vaccine Contraindications and Precautions

- Severe allergic reaction to a vaccine component or following a prior dose
- Moderate or severe acute illness

7

The safety of hepatitis A vaccination during pregnancy has not been determined. However, because it is an inactivated vaccine, the theoretical risk to the fetus is low. The risk associated with vaccination should be weighed against the risk for HAV infection. Because hepatitis A vaccine is inactivated, no special precautions are needed when vaccinating immunocompromised persons, although response to the vaccine may be suboptimal.

**Hepatitis A
Vaccine Adverse Reactions**

- Pain at injection site
- Systemic reactions not common
- No serious adverse reactions reported

Adverse Reactions Following Vaccination

For both vaccines, the most commonly reported adverse reaction following vaccination is a local reaction at the site of injection. Injection site pain, erythema, or swelling is reported by 20% to 50% of recipients. These symptoms are generally mild and self-limited. Mild systemic complaints (e.g., malaise, fatigue, low-grade fever) are reported by fewer than 10% of recipients. No serious adverse reactions have been reported.

Vaccine Storage and Handling

Hepatitis A vaccine should be stored and shipped at temperatures of 35°–46°F (2°–8°C) and should not be frozen. However, the reactogenicity and immunogenicity are not altered by storage for 1 week at 98.6°F (37°C).

Postexposure Prophylaxis

Immune globulin (IG) is typically used for postexposure prophylaxis of hepatitis A in susceptible persons. Hepatitis A vaccine may be used for postexposure prophylaxis in healthy persons 12 months through 40 years of age. Immune globulin is preferred for persons older than 40 years of age, children younger than 12 months of age, immunocompromised persons, and persons with chronic liver disease. See *MMWR* 2007;54(No.41):1080-84 (October 19, 2007) for details.

Selected References

Fiore AE, Feinstone SM, and Bell BP. Hepatitis A Vaccine. In: Plotkin SA, Orenstein, WA, and Offit PA, eds. *Vaccines*. 5th ed. Philadelphia: Saunders Company; 2008:175–203.

CDC. Update: prevention of hepatitis A virus after exposure to hepatitis A virus in international travelers. Updated recommendations of the Advisory Committee on Immunization Practices (ACIP). *MMWR* 2007;56 (No. 41):1080–84.

CDC. Prevention of hepatitis A through active or passive immunization: recommendations of the Advisory Committee on Immunization Practices (ACIP). *MMWR* 2006;55(No. RR-7):1–23.

CDC. Hepatitis A outbreak associated with green onions at a restaurant—Monaca, Pennsylvania, 2003. *MMWR* 2003;52:1155–7.

Margolis HS, Alter MJ, Hadler SC. Viral hepatitis. In: Evans AS, Kaslow, RA, eds. *Viral Infections of Humans*. Epidemiology and Control. 4th ed. New York, NY: Plenum Medical Book Company; 1997:363–418.

7

7

Hepatitis B

Viral hepatitis is a term commonly used for several clinically similar yet etiologically and epidemiologically distinct diseases. Hepatitis A (formerly called infectious hepatitis) and hepatitis B (formerly called serum hepatitis) have been recognized as separate entities since the early 1940s and can be diagnosed with specific serologic tests. Delta hepatitis is an infection dependent on the hepatitis B virus (HBV). It may occur as a coinfection with acute HBV infection or as superinfection of an HBV carrier.

Epidemic jaundice was described by Hippocrates in the 5th century BCE. The first recorded cases of "serum hepatitis," or hepatitis B, are thought to be those that followed the administration of smallpox vaccine containing human lymph to shipyard workers in Germany in l883. In the early and middle parts of the 20th century, serum hepatitis was repeatedly observed following the use of contaminated needles and syringes. The role of blood as a vehicle for virus transmission was further emphasized in 1943, when Beeson described jaundice that had occurred in seven recipients of blood transfusions. Australia antigen, later called hepatitis B surface antigen (HBsAg), was first described in 1965, and the Dane particle (complete hepatitis B virion) was identified in 1970. Identification of serologic markers for HBV infection followed, which helped clarify the natural history of the disease. Ultimately, HBsAg was prepared in quantity and now comprises the immunogen in highly effective vaccines for prevention of HBV infection.

Hepatitis B Virus

HBV is a small, double-shelled virus in the family Hepadnaviridae. Other Hepadnaviridae include duck hepatitis virus, ground squirrel hepatitis virus, and woodchuck hepatitis virus. The virus has a small circular DNA genome that is partially double-stranded. HBV contains numerous antigenic components, including HBsAg, hepatitis B core antigen (HBcAg), and hepatitis B e antigen (HBeAg). Humans are the only known host for HBV, although some nonhuman primates have been infected in laboratory conditions. HBV is relatively resilient and, in some instances, has been shown to remain infectious on environmental surfaces for more than 7 days at room temperature.

An estimated 2 billion persons worldwide have been infected with HBV, and more than 350 million persons have chronic, lifelong infections. HBV infection is an established cause of acute and chronic hepatitis and cirrhosis. It is the cause of up to 80% of hepatocellular carcinomas. The World Health Organization estimated that more than 600,000 persons died worldwide in 2002 of hepatitis B-associated acute and chronic liver disease.

Hepatitis B

- Epidemic jaundice described by Hippocrates in 5th century BCE
- Jaundice reported among recipients of human serum and yellow fever vaccines in 1930s and 1940s
- Australia antigen described in 1965
- Serologic tests developed in 1970s

8

Hepatitis B Virus

- Hepadnaviridae family (DNA)
- Numerous antigenic components
- Humans are only known host
- May retain infectivity for more than 7 days at room temperature

Hepatitis B Virus Infection

- More than 350 million chronically infected worldwide
- Established cause of chronic hepatitis and cirrhosis
- Human carcinogen—cause of up to 80% of hepatocellular carcinomas

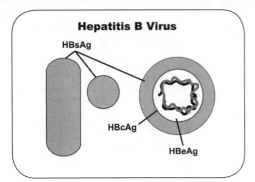

Hepatitis B Virus

HBsAg

HBcAg

HBeAg

8

Several well-defined antigen–antibody systems are associated with HBV infection. HBsAg, formerly called Australia antigen or hepatitis-associated antigen, is an antigenic determinant found on the surface of the virus. It also makes up subviral 22-nm spherical and tubular particles. HBsAg can be identified in serum 30 to 60 days after exposure to HBV and persists for variable periods. HBsAg is not infectious. Only the complete virus (Dane particle) is infectious. However, when HBsAg is present in the blood, complete virus is also present, and the person may transmit the virus. During replication, HBV produces HBsAg in excess of that needed for production of Dane particles.

HBcAg is the nucleocapsid protein core of HBV. HBcAg is not detectable in serum by conventional techniques, but it can be detected in liver tissue of persons with acute or chronic HBV infection. HBeAg, a soluble protein, is also contained in the core of HBV. HBeAg is detected in the serum of persons with high virus titers and indicates high infectivity. Antibody to HBsAg (anti-HBs) develops during convalescence after acute HBV infection or following hepatitis B vaccination. The presence of anti-HBs indicates immunity to HBV. (Anti-HBs is sometimes referred to as HBsAb, but use of this term is discouraged because of potential confusion with HBsAg.) Antibody to HBcAg (anti-HBc) indicates infection with HBV at an undefined time in the past. IgM class antibody to HBcAg (IgM anti-HBc) indicates recent infection with HBV. Antibody to HBeAg (anti-HBe) becomes detectable when HBeAg is lost and is associated with low infectivity of serum.

Clinical Features

The clinical course of acute hepatitis B is indistinguishable from that of other types of acute viral hepatitis. The incubation period ranges from 60 to 150 days (average, 90 days). Clinical signs and symptoms occur more often in adults than in infants or children, who usually have an asymptomatic acute course. However, approximately 50% of adults who have acute infections are asymptomatic.

The preicteric, or prodromal phase from initial symptoms to onset of jaundice usually lasts from 3 to l0 days. It is nonspecific and is characterized by insidious onset of malaise, anorexia, nausea, vomiting, right upper quadrant abdominal pain, fever, headache, myalgia, skin rashes, arthralgia and arthritis, and dark urine, beginning 1 to 2 days before the onset of jaundice. The icteric phase is variable but usually lasts from l to 3 weeks and is characterized by jaundice, light or gray stools, hepatic tenderness and hepatomegaly (splenomegaly is less common). During convalescence, malaise and fatigue may persist for weeks or months, while jaundice, anorexia, and other symptoms disappear.

Hepatitis B Clinical Features

• Incubation period 60-150 days (average 90 days)

• Nonspecific prodrome of malaise, fever, headache, myalgia

• Illness not specific for hepatitis B

• At least 50% of infections asymptomatic

Most acute HBV infections in adults result in complete recovery with elimination of HBsAg from the blood and the production of anti-HBs, creating immunity to future infection.

Complications

While most acute HBV infections in adults result in complete recovery, fulminant hepatitis occurs in about 1% to 2% of acutely infected persons. About 200 to 300 Americans die of fulminant disease each year (case-fatality rate 63% to 93%). Although the consequences of acute HBV infection can be severe, most of the serious complications associated with HBV infection are due to chronic infection.

Chronic HBV Infection

Approximately 5% of all acute HBV infections progress to chronic infection, with the risk of chronic HBV infection decreasing with age. As many as 90% of infants who acquire HBV infection from their mothers at birth become chronically infected. Of children who become infected with HBV between 1 year and 5 years of age, 30% to 50% become chronically infected. By adulthood, the risk of acquiring chronic HBV infection is approximately 5%.

Persons with chronic infection are often asymptomatic and may not be aware that they are infected; however, they are capable of infecting others and have been referred to as carriers. Chronic infection is responsible for most HBV-related morbidity and mortality, including chronic hepatitis, cirrhosis, liver failure, and hepatocellular carcinoma. Approximately 25% of persons with chronic HBV infection die prematurely from cirrhosis or liver cancer. Chronic active hepatitis develops in more than 25% of carriers and often results in cirrhosis. An estimated 3,000 to 4,000 persons die of hepatitis B-related cirrhosis each year in the United States. Persons with chronic HBV infection are at 12 to 300 times higher risk of hepatocellular carcinoma than noncarriers. An estimated 1,000 to 1,500 persons die each year in the United States of hepatitis B-related liver cancer.

Laboratory Diagnosis

Diagnosis is based on clinical, laboratory, and epidemiologic findings. HBV infection cannot be differentiated on the basis of clinical symptoms alone, and definitive diagnosis depends on the results of serologic testing. Serologic markers of HBV infection vary depending on whether the infection is acute or chronic.

HBsAg is the most commonly used test for diagnosing acute HBV infections or detecting carriers. HBsAg can be detected as early as 1 or 2 weeks and as late as 11 or 12

Hepatitis B Complications

- Fulminant hepatitis
- Hospitalization
- Cirrhosis
- Hepatocellular carcinoma
- Death

Chronic Hepatitis B Virus Infection

- Chronic viremia
- Responsible for most mortality
- Overall risk 5%
- Higher risk with early infection

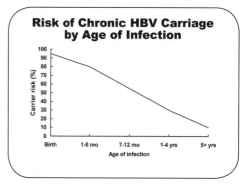

Risk of Chronic HBV Carriage by Age of Infection

weeks after exposure to HBV when sensitive assays are used. The presence of HBsAg indicates that a person is infectious, regardless of whether the infection is acute or chronic.

Anti-HBc (core antibody) develops in all HBV infections, appears shortly after HBsAg in acute disease, and indicates HBV infection at some undefined time in the past. Anti-HBc only occurs after HBV infection and does not develop in persons whose immunity to HBV is from vaccine. Anti-HBc generally persists for life and is not a serologic marker for acute infection.

IgM anti-HBc appears in persons with acute disease about the time of illness onset and indicates recent infection with HBV. IgM anti-HBc is generally detectable 4 to 6 months after onset of illness and is the best serologic marker of acute HBV infection. A negative test for IgM-anti-HBc together with a positive test for HBsAg in a single blood sample identifies a chronic HBV infection.

Interpretation of Hepatitis B Serologic Tests

Tests	Results	Interpretation
HBsAg .... Negative anti-HBc .... Negative anti-HBs .... Negative		Susceptible
HBsAg .... Negative anti-HBc .... Negative anti-HBs .... Positive with ≥10mIU/mL*		Immune due to vaccination
HBsAg .... Negative anti-HBc .... Positive anti-HBs .... Positive		Immune due to natural infection
HBsAg .... Positive anti-HBc .... Positive IgM anti-HBc .... Positive anti-HBs .... Negative		Acutely infected
HBsAg .... Positive anti-HBc .... Positive IgM anti-HBc .... Negative anti-HBs .... Negative		Chronically infected
HBsAg .... Negative anti-HBc .... Positive anti-HBs .... Negative		Four interpretations possible[†]

*Postvaccination testing, when it is recommended, should be performed 1-2 months following dose #3.

[†] 1. May be recovering from acute HBV infection.
2. May be distantly immune and the test is not sensitive enough to detect a very low level of anti-HBs in serum.
3. May be susceptible with a false positive anti-HBc.
4. May be chronically infected and have an undetectable level of HBsAg present in the serum.

HBeAg is a useful marker associated strongly with the number of infective HBV particles in the serum and a higher risk of infectivity.

Anti-HBs (surface antibody) is a protective, neutralizing antibody. The presence of anti-HBs following acute HBV infection generally indicates recovery and immunity against reinfection. Anti-HBs can also be acquired as an immune response to hepatitis B vaccine or passively transferred by administration of hepatitis B immune globulin (HBIG). When using radioimmunoassay (RIA), a minimum of 10 sample ratio units should be used to designate immunity. With enzyme immunoassay (EIA), the manufacturer's recommended positive should be considered an appropriate measure of immunity. The level of anti-HBs may also be expressed in milli-international units/mL (mIU/mL). Ten mIU/mL is considered to indicate a protective level of immunity.

Medical Management

There is no specific therapy for acute HBV infection. Treatment is supportive. Interferon is the most effective treatment for chronic HBV infection and is successful in 25% to 50% of cases.

Persons with acute or chronic HBV infections should prevent their blood and other potentially infective body fluids from contacting other persons. They should not donate blood or share toothbrushes or razors with household members.

In the hospital setting, patients with HBV infection should be managed with standard precautions.

Epidemiology

Reservoir

Although other primates have been infected in laboratory conditions, HBV infection affects only humans. No animal or insect hosts or vectors are known to exist.

Transmission

The virus is transmitted by parenteral or mucosal exposure to HBsAg-positive body fluids from persons who have acute or chronic HBV infection. The highest concentrations of virus are in blood and serous fluids; lower titers are found in other fluids, such as saliva and semen. Saliva can be a vehicle of transmission through bites; however, other types of exposure to saliva, including kissing, are unlikely modes of transmission. There appears to be no transmission of HBV via tears, sweat, urine, stool, or droplet nuclei.

Hepatitis B Epidemiology

• Reservoir	Human
• Transmission	Bloodborne Subclinical cases transmit
• Communicability	1-2 months before and after onset of symptoms Chronic carriers

In the United States, the most important route of transmission is by sexual contact, either heterosexual or homosexual, with an infected person. Fecal-oral transmission does not appear to occur. However, transmission occurs among men who have sex with men, possibly via contamination from asymptomatic rectal mucosal lesions.

Direct percutaneous inoculation of HBV by needles during injection-drug use is an important mode of transmission. Transmission of HBV may also occur by other percutaneous exposure, including tattooing, ear piercing, and acupuncture, as well as needlesticks or other injuries from sharp instruments sustained by medical personnel. These exposures account for only a small proportion of reported cases in the United States. Breaks in the skin without overt needle puncture, such as fresh cutaneous scratches, abrasions, burns, or other lesions, may also serve as routes for entry.

Contamination of mucosal surfaces with infective serum or plasma may occur during mouth pipetting, eye splashes, or other direct contact with mucous membranes of the eyes or mouth, such as hand-to-mouth or hand-to-eye contact when hands are contaminated with infective blood or serum. Transfer of infective material to skin lesions or mucous membranes via inanimate environmental surfaces may occur by touching surfaces of various types of hospital equipment. Contamination of mucosal surfaces with infective secretions other than serum or plasma could occur with contact involving semen.

Perinatal transmission from mother to infant at birth is very efficient. If the mother is positive for both HBsAg and HBeAg, 70%–90% of infants will become infected in the absence of postexposure prophylaxis. The risk of perinatal transmission is about 10% if the mother is positive only for HBsAg. As many as 90% of these infected infants will become chronically infected with HBV.

The frequency of infection and patterns of transmission vary in different parts of the world. Approximately 45% of the global population live in areas with a high prevalence of chronic HBV infection (8% or more of the population is HBsAg positive), 43% in areas with a moderate prevalence (2% to 7% of the population is HBsAg positive), and 12% in areas with a low prevalence (less than 2% of the population is HBsAg positive).

In China, Southeast Asia, most of Africa, most Pacific Islands, parts of the Middle East, and the Amazon Basin, 8% to l5% of the population carry the virus. The lifetime risk of HBV infection is greater than 60%, and most infections are acquired at birth or during early childhood, when the risk of developing chronic infections is greatest. In these areas, because most infections are asymptomatic, very little acute

---

Hepatitis B Perinatal Transmission*

- If mother positive for HBsAg and HBeAg
  - —70%-90% of infants infected
  - —90% of infected infants become chronically infected
- If positive for HBsAg only
  - —10% of infants infected
  - —90% of infected infants become chronically infected

*In the absence of postexposure prophylaxis

Global Patterns of Chronic HBV Infection

- High (≥8%): 45% of global population
  - —lifetime risk of infection >60%
  - —early childhood infections common
- Intermediate (2%-7%): 43% of global population
  - —lifetime risk of infection 20%-60%
  - —infections occur in all age groups
- Low (<2%): 12% of global population
  - —lifetime risk of infection <20%
  - —most infections occur in adult risk groups

disease related to HBV occurs, but rates of chronic liver disease and liver cancer among adults are very high. In the United States, Western Europe, and Australia, HBV infection is a disease of low endemicity. Infection occurs primarily during adulthood, and only 0.1% to 0.5% of the population are chronic carriers. Lifetime risk of HBV infection is less than 20% in low prevalence areas.

Communicability

Persons with either acute or chronic HBV infection should be considered infectious any time that HBsAg is present in the blood. When symptoms are present in persons with acute HBV infection, HBsAg can be found in blood and body fluids for 1–2 months before and after the onset of symptoms.

Secular Trends in the United States

Hepatitis has been reportable in the United States for many years. Hepatitis B became reportable as a distinct entity during the 1970s, after serologic tests to differentiate different types of hepatitis became widely available.

The incidence of reported hepatitis B peaked in the mid-1980s, with about 26,000 cases reported each year. Reported cases have declined since that time, and fell below 10,000 cases for the first time in 1996. The decline in cases during the 1980s and early 1990s is generally attributed to reduction of transmission among men who have sex with men and injection-drug users as a result of HIV prevention efforts.

During 1990–2004, incidence of acute hepatitis B in the United States declined 75%. The greatest decline (94%) occurred among children and adolescents, coincident with an increase in hepatitis B vaccine coverage. A total of 4,519 cases of hepatitis B were reported in 2007.

Reported cases of HBV infection represent only a fraction of cases that actually occur. In 2001, a total of 7,844 cases of acute hepatitis B were reported to CDC. Based on these reports, CDC estimates that 22,000 acute cases of hepatitis B resulted from an estimated 78,000 new infections. An estimated 1–1.25 million persons in the United States are chronically infected with HBV, and an additional 5,000–8,000 persons become chronically infected each year.

Before routine childhood hepatitis B vaccination was recommended, more than 80% of acute HBV infections occurred among adults. Adolescents accounted for approximately 8% of infections, and children and infants infected through perinatal transmission accounted for approximately 4% each. Perinatal transmission accounted for a disproportionate 24% of chronic infections.

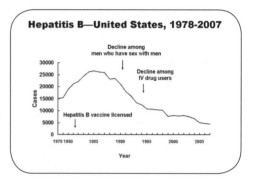

Hepatitis B—United States, 1978-2007

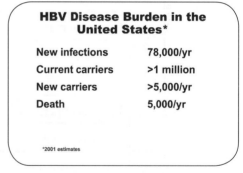

HBV Disease Burden in the United States*

New infections	78,000/yr
Current carriers	>1 million
New carriers	>5,000/yr
Death	5,000/yr

*2001 estimates

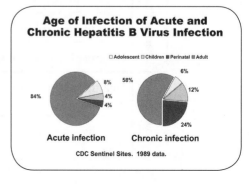

Age of Infection of Acute and Chronic Hepatitis B Virus Infection

Acute infection   Chronic infection

CDC Sentinel Sites. 1989 data.

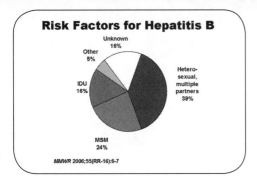

Risk Factors for Hepatitis B

Unknown 16%
Other 5%
IDU 16%
Heterosexual, multiple partners 39%
MSM 24%

MMWR 2006;55(RR-16):6-7

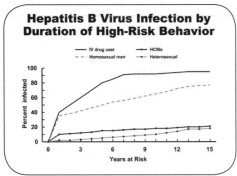

Hepatitis B Virus Infection by Duration of High-Risk Behavior

— IV drug user — HCWs
--- Homosexual men —•— Heterosexual

Percent infected
Years at Risk

In the United States in 2005, the highest incidence of acute hepatitis B was among adults aged 25–45 years. Approximately 79% of persons with newly acquired hepatitis B infection are known to engage in high-risk sexual activity or injection-drug use. Other known exposures (i.e., occupational, household, travel, and healthcare-related) together account for 5% of new infections. Approximately 16% of persons deny a specific risk factor for infection.

Although HBV infection is uncommon among adults in the general population (the lifetime risk of infection is less than 20%), it is highly prevalent in certain groups. Risk for infection varies with occupation, lifestyle, or environment (see table). Generally, the highest risk for HBV infection is associated with lifestyles, occupations, or environments in which contact with blood from infected persons is frequent. In addition, the prevalence of HBV markers for acute or chronic infection increases with increasing number of years of high-risk behavior. For instance, an estimated 40% of injection-drug users become infected with HBV after 1 year of drug use, while more than 80% are infected after 10 years.

Prevalence of Hepatitis B in Various Population Groups

	Population Group	Prevalence of Serologic Markers of HBV Infection	
		HBsAg (%)	All Markers (%)
High-Risk	Immigrants/refugees from areas of high HBV endemicity.	13	70-85
	Clients in mental health institutions.	10-20	35-80
	Users of illicit parenteral drugs.	7	60-80
	Homosexually active men.	6	35-80
	Patients of hemodialysis units.	3-10	20-80
	Household contacts of HBV carriers.	3-6	30-60
Intermediate-Risk	Prisoners (male).	1-8	10-80
	Healthcare providers – frequent blood contact.	1-2	15-30
	Staff of mental health institutions.	1	10-25
	Heterosexuals with multiple partners.	0.5	5-20
Low-Risk	Healthcare providers – no or infrequent blood contact.	0.3	3-10
	Healthy adults (first-time volunteer blood donors).	0.3	3-5

Hepatitis B Prevention Strategies

Hepatitis B vaccines have been available in the United States since 1981. However, the impact of vaccine on HBV disease has been less than optimal.

The apparent lack of impact from the vaccine can be attributed to several factors. From 1981 until 1991, vaccination was targeted to persons in groups at high risk of acquiring HBV infection. A large proportion of persons with HBV infection (25% to 30%) deny having any risk factors for the disease. These persons would not be identified by a targeted risk factor screening approach.

The three major risk groups (heterosexuals with contact with infected persons or multiple partners, injection-drug users, and men who have sex with men) are not reached effectively by targeted programs. Deterrents to immunization of these groups include lack of awareness of the risk of disease and its consequences, lack of effective public or private sector programs, and vaccine cost. Difficulty in gaining access to these populations is also a problem. Further, success in providing vaccine to persons in high-risk groups has been limited because of rapid acquisition of infection after beginning high-risk behaviors, low initial vaccine acceptance, and low rates of completion of vaccinations.

A comprehensive strategy to eliminate hepatitis B virus transmission was recommended in 1991; it includes prenatal testing of pregnant women for HBsAg to identify newborns who require immunoprophylaxis for prevention of perinatal infection and to identify household contacts who should be vaccinated, routine vaccination of infants, vaccination of adolescents, and vaccination of adults at high risk for infection. Recommendations to further enhance vaccination of adults at increased risk of HBV infection were published in 2006.

Hepatitis B Vaccine

Characteristics

A plasma-derived vaccine was licensed in the United States in 1981. It was produced from 22-nm HBsAg particles purified from the plasma of chronically infected humans. The vaccine was safe and effective but was not well accepted, possibly because of unsubstantiated fears of transmission of live HBV and other bloodborne pathogens (e.g., human immunodeficiency virus). This vaccine was removed from the U.S. market in 1992.

Recombinant hepatitis B vaccine was licensed in the United States in July 1986. A second, similar vaccine was licensed in August 1989.

Strategy to Eliminate Hepatitis B Virus Transmission—United States
- Prevent perinatal HBV transmission
- Routine vaccination of all infants
- Vaccination of children in high-risk groups
- Vaccination of adolescents
- Vaccination of adults in high-risk groups

Hepatitis B Vaccine

1965	Discovery of Australian antigen
1973	Successful HBV infection of chimpanzees
1981	Licensure of plasma-derived vaccine
1986	Licensure of recombinant vaccine
1991	Universal infant vaccination
1996	Universal adolescent vaccination

Hepatitis B Vaccine

- Composition   Recombinant HBsAg

- Efficacy   95% (Range, 80%-100%)

- Duration of
  Immunity   at least 20 years

- Schedule   3 Doses

- Booster doses not routinely recommended

Hepatitis B Vaccine Formulations

- **Recombivax HB (Merck)**
  - 5 mcg/0.5 mL (pediatric)
  - 10 mcg/1 mL (adult)
  - 40 mcg/1 mL (dialysis)

- **Engerix-B (GSK)**
  - 10 mcg/0.5 mL (pediatric)
  - 20 mcg/1 mL (adult)

Recombinant vaccine is produced by inserting a plasmid containing the gene for HBsAg into common baker's yeast (*Saccharomyces cerevisiae*). Yeast cells then produce HBsAg, which is harvested and purified. The recombinant vaccine contains more than 95% HBsAg protein (5 to 40 mcg/mL); yeast-derived proteins may constitute up to 5% of the final product, but no yeast DNA is detectable in the vaccine. HBV infection cannot result from use of the recombinant vaccine, since no potentially infectious viral DNA or complete viral particles are produced in the recombinant system. Vaccine HBsAg is adsorbed to aluminum hydroxide.

Hepatitis B vaccine is produced by two manufacturers in the United States, Merck (Recombivax HB) and GlaxoSmithKline Pharmaceuticals (Engerix-B). Both vaccines are available in both pediatric and adult formulations. Although the antigen content of the vaccines differs, vaccines made by different manufacturers are interchangeable, except for the two-dose schedule for adolescents aged 11 through 15 years. Only Merck vaccine is approved for this schedule. Providers must always follow the manufacturer's dosage recommendations.

Both the pediatric and adult formulations of Recombivax HB are approved for use in any age group. For example, the adult formulation of Recombivax HB may be used in children (0.5 mL) and adolescents (0.5 mL). However, pediatric Engerix-B is approved for use only in children and adolescents younger than 20 years of age. The adult formulation of Engerix-B is not approved for use in infants and children but may be used in both adolescents (11 through 19 years of age) and adults.

Engerix-B contains aluminum hydroxide as an adjuvant. It does not contain thimerosal as a preservative but contains a trace of thimerosal as residual from the manufacturing process. The vaccine is supplied in single-dose vials and syringes. Recombivax HB contains aluminum hydroxyphosphate sulfate as an adjuvant. None of the formulations of Recombivax HB contain thimerosal or any other preservative. The vaccine is supplied in single-dose vials.

Immunogenicity and Vaccine Efficacy

After three intramuscular doses of hepatitis B vaccine, more than 90% of healthy adults and more than 95% of infants, children, and adolescents (from birth to 19 years of age) develop adequate antibody responses. However, there is an age-specific decline in immunogenicity. After age 40 years, approximately 90% of recipients respond to a three-dose series, and by 60 years, only 75% of vaccinees develop protective antibody titers. The proportion of recipients who respond to each dose varies by age (see table).

Protection* by Age Group and Dose

Dose	Infants[†]	Teens and Adults[§]
1	16% - 40%	20% - 30%
2	80% - 95%	75% - 80%
3	98% - 100%	90% - 95%

*Anti-HBs antibody titer of 10 mIU/mL or higher

[†]Preterm infants less than 2kg have been shown to respond to vaccination less often

[§]Factors that may lower vaccine response rates are age 40 years or older, male gender, smoking, obesity, and immune deficiency

The vaccine is 80% to 100% effective in preventing infection or clinical hepatitis in those who receive the complete course of vaccine. Larger vaccine doses (2 to 4 times the normal adult dose) or an increased number of doses are required to induce protective antibody in a high proportion of hemodialysis patients and may also be necessary in other immunocompromised persons.

The recommended dosage of vaccine differs depending on the age of the recipient and type of vaccine (see table). Hemodialysis patients should receive a 40-mcg dose in a series of three or four doses. Recombivax HB has a special dialysis patient formulation that contains 40 mcg/mL.

Recommended doses of currently licensed formulations of hepatitis B vaccine, by age group and vaccine type

	Single-Antigen Vaccine				Combination Vaccine					
	Recombivax HB		Engerix-B		Comvax		Pediarix		Twinrix	
Age Group	Dose (µg)*	Volume (mL)	Dose (µg)*	Volume (mL)	Dose (µg)*	Volume (mL)	Dose (µg)*	Volume (mL)	Dose (µg)*	Volume (mL)
Infants (<1 yr)	5	0.5	10	0.5	5	0.5	10	0.5	N/A**	N/A
Children (1-10 yrs)	5	0.5	10	0.5	5	0.5	10	0.5	N/A	N/A
Adolescents										
11-15 yrs	10[†]	1.0	N/A	N/A	N/A	N/A	N/A	N/A	N/A	N/A
11-19 yrs	5	0.5	10	0.5	N/A	N/A	N/A	N/A	N/A	N/A
Adults (≥20 yrs)	10	1.0	20	1.0	N/A	N/A	N/A	N/A	20	1.0
Hemodialysis patients and other immunocompromised persons										
<20 yrs[§]	5	0.5	10	0.5	N/A	N/A	N/A	N/A	N/A	N/A
≥20 yrs	40[¶]	1.0	40[‡]	2.0	N/A	N/A	N/A	N/A	N/A	N/A

*   Recombinant hepatitis B surface antigen protein dose.
†   Adult formulation administered on a 2-dose schedule.
§   Higher doses might be more immunogenic, but no specific recommendations have been made.
¶   Dialysis formulation administered on a 3-dose schedule at 0, 1, and 6 months.
‡   Two 1.0 mL doses administered at one site, on a 4-dose schedule at 0, 1, 2, and 6 months.
** Not applicable.

The deltoid muscle is the recommended site for hepatitis B vaccination in adults and children, while the antero-lateral thigh is recommended for infants and neonates. Immunogenicity of vaccine in adults is lower when injections are given in the gluteus. Hepatitis B vaccine should be administered to infants using a needle of at least 7/8 inch length and to older children and adults of at least 1 inch length. Hepatitis B vaccine administered by any route or site other than intramuscularly in the anterolateral thigh or deltoid muscle should not be counted as valid and should be repeated unless serologic testing indicates that an adequate response has been achieved.

Available data show that vaccine-induced antibody levels decline with time. However, immune memory remains intact for more than 20 years following immunization, and both adults and children with declining antibody levels are still protected against significant HBV infection (i.e., clinical disease, HBsAg antigenemia, or significant elevation of liver enzymes). Exposure to HBV results in an anamnestic anti-HBs response that prevents clinically significant HBV infection. Chronic HBV infection has only rarely been documented among vaccine responders.

For adults and children with normal immune status, booster doses of vaccine are not recommended. Routine serologic testing to assess immune status of vaccinees is not recommended. The need for booster doses after longer intervals will continue to be assessed as additional information becomes available.

For hemodialysis patients, the need for booster doses should be assessed by annual testing of vaccinees for antibody levels, and booster doses should be provided when antibody levels decline below 10 mIU/mL.

Vaccination Schedule and Use

Infants and Children

Hepatitis B vaccination is recommended for all infants soon after birth and before hospital discharge. Infants and children younger than 11 years of age should receive 0.5 mL (5 mcg) of pediatric or adult formulation Recombivax HB (Merck) or 0.5 mL (10 mcg) of pediatric Engerix-B (GlaxoSmithKline). Primary vaccination consists of three intramuscular doses of vaccine. The usual schedule is 0, 1 to 2, and 6 to 18 months. Infants whose mothers are HBsAg positive or whose HBsAg status is unknown should receive the last (third or fourth) dose by 6 months of age (12 to 15 months if Comvax is used).

Because the highest titers of anti-HBs are achieved when the last two doses of vaccine are spaced at least 4 months apart, schedules that achieve this spacing are preferable.

Hepatitis B Vaccine Long-Term Efficacy

- Immunologic memory established following vaccination
- Exposure to HBV results in anamnestic anti-HBs response
- Chronic infection rarely documented among vaccine responders

---

Hepatitis B Vaccine

Routine booster doses are <u>NOT</u> routinely recommended for any group

---

Hepatitis B Vaccine Routine Infant Schedule

Dose	Usual Age	Minimum Interval
Primary 1	Birth	- - -
Primary 2	1- 2 months	4 weeks
Primary 3	6-18 months*	8 weeks**

* infants who mothers are HBsAg+ or whose HBsAg status is unknown should receive the third dose at 6 months of age
** at least 16 weeks after the first dose

However, schedules with 2-month intervals between doses, which conform to schedules for other childhood vaccines, have been shown to produce good antibody responses and may be appropriate in populations in which it is difficult to ensure that infants will be brought back for all their vaccinations. However, the third dose must be administered at least 8 weeks after the second dose, and should follow the first dose by at least 16 weeks. For infants, the third dose should not be given earlier than 24 weeks of age. It is not necessary to add doses or restart the series if the interval between doses is longer than recommended.

Preterm infants born to HBsAg-positive women and women with unknown HBsAg status must receive immunoprophylaxis with hepatitis B vaccine and hepatitis B immune globulin (HBIG) within 12 hours of birth. See the section on Postexposure Prophylaxis for additional information. Preterm infants with low birthweight (i.e., less than 2,000 grams) have a decreased response to hepatitis B vaccine administered before 1 month of age. However, by chronologic age 1 month, preterm infants, regardless of initial birthweight or gestational age, are as likely to respond as adequately as full-term infants. Preterm infants of low birthweight whose mothers are HBsAg negative can receive the first dose of the hepatitis B vaccine series at chronologic age 1 month. Preterm infants discharged from the hospital before chronologic age 1 month can also be administered hepatitis B vaccine at discharge if they are medically stable and have gained weight consistently. The full recommended dose should be used. Divided or reduced doses are not recommended.

Comvax

Hepatitis B vaccine is available in combination with *Haemophilus influenzae* type b (Hib) vaccine as Comvax (Merck). Each dose of Comvax contains 7.5 mcg of PRP-OMP Hib vaccine (PedvaxHIB), and 5 mcg of hepatitis B surface antigen. The dose of hepatitis B surface antigen is the same as that contained in Merck's pediatric formulation. The immunogenicity of the combination vaccine is equivalent to that of the individual antigens administered at separate sites.

Comvax is licensed for use at 2, 4, and 12 through 15 months of age. It may be used whenever either antigen is indicated and the other antigen is not contraindicated. However, the vaccine must not be administered to infants younger than 6 weeks of age because of potential suppression of the immune response to the Hib component (see Chapter 6, *Haemophilus influenzae* type b, for more details). Comvax must not be used for doses at birth or 1 month of age for a child on a 0, 1, 6 month hepatitis B vaccine schedule. Although it is not labeled for this indication by FDA, ACIP recommends that Comvax may be used in infants whose mothers are HBsAg positive or whose HBsAg status is unknown.

Third Dose of Hepatitis B Vaccine
- Minimum of 8 weeks after second dose, and
- At least 16 weeks after first dose, and
- For infants, at least 24 weeks of age

Preterm Infants
- Birth dose and HBIG if mother HBsAg positive
- Preterm infants <2,000 grams have a decreased response to vaccine administered before 1 month of age
- Delay first dose until chronologic age 1 month if mother HBsAg negative

COMVAX
- Hepatitis B-Hib combination
- Use when either antigen is indicated
- Cannot use before 6 weeks of age
- May be used in infants whose mothers are HBsAg positive or status is unknown

Pediarix

- DTaP – Hep B – IPV combination
- Approved for 3 doses at 2, 4 and 6 months
- Not approved for booster doses
- Licensed for children 6 weeks to 7 years of age

8

Pediarix

- May be used interchangeably with other pertussis-containing vaccines if necessary
- Can be given at 2, 4, and 6 months to infants who received a birth dose of hepatitis B vaccine (total of 4 doses)
- May be used in infants whose mothers are HBsAg positive or status unknown

Hepatitis B Vaccine Adolescent Vaccination

- Routine vaccination recommended through age 18 years
- Integrate into routine adolescent immunization visit
- Flexible schedules

Pediarix

In 2002, the Food and Drug Administration approved Pediarix (GlaxoSmithKline), the first pentavalent (5-component) combination vaccine licensed in the United States. Pediarix contains DTaP (Infanrix), hepatitis B (Engerix-B), and inactivated polio vaccines. In prelicensure studies, the proportion of children who developed a protective level of antibody, and the titer of antibody, were at least as high among children receiving the vaccine antigens given together as Pediarix as among children who received separate vaccines.

The minimum age for the first dose of Pediarix is 6 weeks, so it cannot be used for the birth dose of the hepatitis B series. Pediarix is approved for the first three doses of the DTaP and IPV series, which are usually given at about 2, 4, and 6 months of age; it is not approved for fourth or fifth (booster) doses of the DTaP or IPV series. However, Pediarix is approved for use through 6 years of age. A child who is behind schedule can still receive Pediarix as long as it is given for doses 1, 2, or 3 of the series, and the child is younger than 7 years of age.

A dose of Pediarix inadvertently administered as the fourth or fifth dose of the DTaP or IPV series does not need to be repeated.

Pediarix may be used interchangeably with other pertussis-containing vaccines if necessary (although ACIP prefers the use of the same brand of DTaP for all doses of the series, if possible). It can be given at 2, 4, and 6 months to infants who received a birth dose of hepatitis B vaccine (total of 4 doses of hepatitis B vaccine). Although not labeled for this indication by FDA, Pediarix may be used in infants whose mothers are HBsAg positive or whose HBsAg status is unknown.

Adolescents

Routine hepatitis B vaccination is recommended for all children and adolescents through age 18 years. All children not previously vaccinated with hepatitis B vaccine should be vaccinated at 11 or 12 years of age with the age-appropriate dose of vaccine. When adolescent vaccination programs are being considered, local data should be considered to determine the ideal age group to vaccinate (i.e., preadolescents, young adolescents) to achieve the highest vaccination rates. The vaccination schedule should be flexible and should take into account the feasibility of delivering three doses of vaccine to this age group. Unvaccinated older adolescents should be vaccinated whenever possible. Those in groups at risk for HBV infection (e.g., Asian and Pacific Islanders, sexually active) should be identified and vaccinated in settings serving this age group (i.e., schools, sexually transmitted disease clinics, detention facilities, drug treatment centers).

Persons younger than 20 years of age should receive 0.5 mL (5 mcg) of pediatric or adult formulation Recombivax HB (Merck) or 0.5 mL (10 mcg) of pediatric formulation Engerix-B (GlaxoSmithKline). The adult formulation of Engerix-B may be used in adolescents, but the approved dose is 1 mL (20 mcg).

The usual schedule for adolescents is two doses separated by no less than 4 weeks, and a third dose 4 to 6 months after the second dose. If an accelerated schedule is needed, the minimum interval between the first two doses is 4 weeks, and the minimum interval between the second and third doses is 8 weeks. However, the first and third doses should be separated by no less than 16 weeks. Doses given at less than these minimum intervals should not be counted as part of the vaccination series.

In 1999, the Food and Drug Administration approved an alternative hepatitis B vaccination schedule for adolescents 11 through 15 years of age. This alternative schedule is for two 1.0-mL (10 mcg) doses of Recombivax HB separated by 4 to 6 months. Seroconversion rates and postvaccination anti-HBs antibody titers were similar using this schedule or the standard schedule of three 5-mcg doses of RecombivaxHB. This alternative schedule is approved only for adolescents 11 through 15 years of age, and for Merck's hepatitis B vaccine. The 2-dose schedule should be completed by age 16 years.

Adults (20 Years of Age and Older)

Routine preexposure vaccination should be considered for groups of adults who are at increased risk of HBV infection. Adults 20 years of age and older should receive 1 mL (10 mcg) of pediatric or adult formulation Recombivax HB (Merck) or 1 mL (20 mcg) of adult formulation Engerix-B (GlaxoSmithKline). The pediatric formulation of Engerix-B is not approved for use in adults.

The usual schedule for adults is two doses separated by no less than 4 weeks, and a third dose 4 to 6 months after the second dose. If an accelerated schedule is needed, the minimum interval between the first two doses is 4 weeks, and the minimum interval between the second and third doses is 8 weeks. However, the first and third doses should be separated by no less than 16 weeks. Doses given at less than these minimum intervals should not be counted as part of the vaccination series. It is not necessary to restart the series or add doses because of an extended interval between doses.

Hepatitis B Vaccine Adolescent and Adult Schedule

Dose	Usual Interval	Minimum Interval
Primary 1	---	- - -
Primary 2	1 month	4 weeks
Primary 3	5 months	8 weeks*

*third dose must be separated from first dose by at least 16 weeks

Alternative Adolescent Vaccination Schedule

- Two 1.0-mL (10 mcg) doses of Recombivax HB separated by 4-6 months
- Approved only for adolescents 11-15 years of age
- Only applies to Merck hepatitis B vaccine

8

Adults at Risk for HBV Infection

• Sexual exposure

 —sex partners of HBsAg-positive persons

 —sexually active persons not in a long-term, mutually monogamous relationship*

 —persons seeking evaluation or treatment for a sexually transmitted disease

 —men who have sex with men

 *persons with more than one sex partner during the previous 6 months

Adults at Risk for HBV Infection

• Percutaneous or mucosal exposure to blood

 —current or recent IDU

 —household contacts of HBsAg-positive persons

 —residents and staff of facilities for developmentally disabled persons

 —healthcare and public safety workers with risk for exposure to blood or blood-contaminated body fluids

 —persons with end-stage renal disease

Adults at Risk for HBV Infection

• Others groups

 —international travelers to regions with high or intermediate levels (HBsAg prevalence of 2% or higher) of endemic HBV infection

 —persons with HIV infection

Hepatitis B vaccination is recommended for all unvaccinated adults at risk for HBV infection and for all adults requesting protection from HBV infection. Acknowledgment of a specific risk factor should not be a requirement for vaccination.

Persons at risk for infection by sexual exposure include sex partners of HBsAg-positive persons, sexually active persons who are not in a long-term, mutually monogamous relationship (e.g., persons with more than one sex partner during the previous 6 months), persons seeking evaluation or treatment for a sexually transmitted disease, and men who have sex with men.

Persons at risk for infection by percutaneous or mucosal exposure to blood include current or recent injection-drug users, household contacts of HBsAg-positive persons, residents and staff of facilities for developmentally disabled persons, healthcare and public safety workers with risk for exposure to blood or blood-contaminated body fluids and persons with end-stage renal disease, including predialysis, hemodialysis, peritoneal dialysis, and home dialysis patients. Persons with chronic liver disease are not at increased risk for HBV infection unless they have percutaneous or mucosal exposure to infectious blood or body fluids

Others groups at risk include international travelers to regions with high or intermediate levels (HBsAg prevalence of 2% or higher) of endemic HBV infection and persons with HIV infection.

In settings in which a high proportion of adults have risks for HBV infection (e.g., sexually transmitted disease/human immunodeficiency virus testing and treatment facilities, drug-abuse treatment and prevention settings, healthcare settings targeting services to IDUs, healthcare settings targeting services to MSM, and correctional facilities), ACIP recommends universal hepatitis B vaccination for all unvaccinated adults. In other primary care and specialty medical settings in which adults at risk for HBV infection receive care, healthcare providers should inform all patients about the health benefits of vaccination, including risks for HBV infection and persons for whom vaccination is recommended, and vaccinate adults who report risks for HBV infection and any adults requesting protection from HBV infection. To promote vaccination in all settings, healthcare providers should implement standing orders to identify adults recommended for hepatitis B vaccination and administer vaccination as part of routine clinical services, not require acknowledgment of an HBV infection risk factor for adults to receive vaccine, and use available reimbursement mechanisms to remove financial barriers to hepatitis B vaccination. Additional details about these strategies are available in the December 2006 ACIP statement on hepatitis B vaccine (see reference list).

8

Twinrix

In 2001, the Food and Drug Administration approved a combination hepatitis A and hepatitis B vaccine (Twinrix, GlaxoSmithKline). Each dose of Twinrix contains 720 ELISA units of hepatitis A vaccine (equivalent to a pediatric dose of Havrix), and 20 mcg of hepatitis B surface antigen protein (equivalent to an adult dose of Engerix-B). The vaccine is administered in a three-dose series at 0, 1, and 6 months. Appropriate spacing of the doses must be maintained to assure long-term protection from both vaccines. The first and third doses of Twinrix should be separated by at least 6 months. The first and second doses should be separated by at least 4 weeks, and the second and third doses should be separated by at least 5 months. In 2007, the FDA approved an alternative Twinrix schedule of doses at 0, 7, and 21–31 days and a booster dose 12 months after the first dose. It is not necessary to restart the series or add doses if the interval between doses is longer than the recommended interval.

Twinrix is approved for persons aged 18 years and older, and can be used in persons in this age group with indications for both hepatitis A and hepatitis B vaccines. Because the hepatitis B component of Twinrix is equivalent to a standard dose of hepatitis B vaccine, the schedule is the same whether Twinrix or single-antigen hepatitis B vaccine is used. Single-antigen hepatitis A vaccine can be used to complete a series begun with Twinrix and vice versa. See the Chapter 7, Hepatitis A, for details.

Serologic Testing of Vaccine Recipients

Prevaccination Serologic Testing

The decision to screen potential vaccine recipients for prior infection depends on the cost of vaccination, the cost of testing for susceptibility, and the expected prevalence of immune persons in the population being screened. Prevaccination testing is recommended for all foreign-born persons (including immigrants, refugees, asylum seekers, and internationally adopted children) born in Africa, Asia, the Pacific Islands, and other regions with high endemicity of HBV infection (HBsAg prevalence of 8% or higher); for household, sex, and needle-sharing contacts of HBsAg-positive persons; and for HIV-infected persons. Screening is usually cost-effective, and should be considered for groups with a high risk of HBV infection (prevalence of HBV markers 20% or higher), such as men who have sex with men, injection-drug users, and incarcerated persons. Screening is usually not cost-effective for groups with a low expected prevalence of HBV serologic markers, such as health professionals in their training years.

Prevaccination Serologic Testing

- Not indicated before routine vaccination of infants or children
- Recommended for
  - all persons born in Africa, Asia, the Pacific Islands, and other regions with HBsAg prevalence of 8% or higher
  - household, sex, and needle-sharing contacts of HBsAg-positive persons
  - HIV-infected persons
- Consider for
  - groups with high risk of HBV infection (MSM, IDU, incarcerated persons)

Serologic testing is not recommended before routine vaccination of infants and children.

Postvaccination Serologic Testing

Testing for immunity following vaccination is not recommended routinely but should be considered for persons whose subsequent management depends on knowledge of their immune status, such as chronic hemodialysis patients, other immunocompromised persons and persons with HIV infection. Testing is also recommended for sex partners of HBsAg-positive persons. When necessary, postvaccination testing should be performed 1 to 2 months after completion of the vaccine series.

Infants born to HBsAg-positive women should be tested for HBsAg and antibody to HBsAg (anti-HBs) after completion of at least 3 doses of the hepatitis B vaccine series, at age 9 through 18 months (generally at the next well-child visit). If HBsAg is not present and anti-HBs antibody is present, children can be considered to be protected.

Healthcare personnel who have contact with patients or blood and are at ongoing risk for injuries with sharp instruments or needlesticks should be routinely tested for antibody after 1 to 2 months after completion of the 3-dose series. However, a catch-up program of serologic testing for healthcare personnel vaccinated prior to December 1997 is not recommended. These persons should be tested as necessary if they have a significant exposure to HBV (see postexposure prophylaxis section below).

Routine postvaccination testing is not recommended for persons at low risk of exposure, such as public safety workers and healthcare personnel without direct patient contact.

Vaccine Nonresponse

Several factors have been associated with nonresponse to hepatitis B vaccine. These include vaccine factors (e.g., dose, schedule, injection site) and host factors. Older age (40 years and older), male sex, obesity, smoking, and chronic illness have been independently associated with nonresponse to hepatitis B vaccine. Further vaccination of persons who fail to respond to a primary vaccination series administered in the deltoid muscle produces adequate response in 15% to 25% of vaccinees after one additional dose and in 30% to 50% after three additional doses.

Persons who do not respond to the first series of hepatitis B vaccine should complete a second three-dose vaccine series. The second vaccine series should be given on the usual 0, 1, 6-month schedule. A 0, 1, 4-month accelerated schedule

---

Postvaccination Serologic Testing

- Not routinely recommended following vaccination of infants, children, adolescents, or most adults
- Recommended for:
  - chronic hemodialysis patients
  - other immunocompromised persons
  - persons with HIV infection
  - sex partners of HBsAg+ person
  - infants born to HBsAg+ women
  - certain healthcare workers

Postvaccination Serologic Testing

Healthcare personnel who have contact with patients or blood should be tested for anti-HBs (antibody to hepatitis B surface antigen) 1 to 2 months after completion of the 3-dose series

---

Management of Nonresponse to Hepatitis B Vaccine

- Complete a second series of three doses
- Should be given on the usual schedule of 0, 1 and 6 months
- Retest 1-2 months after completing the second series

may also be used. Revaccinated healthcare personnel and others for whom postvaccination serologic testing is recommended should be retested 1 to 2 months after completion of the second vaccine series.

Fewer than 5% of persons receiving six doses of hepatitis B vaccine administered by the appropriate schedule in the deltoid muscle fail to develop detectable anti-HBs antibody. Some persons who are anti-HBs negative following six doses may have a low level of antibody that is not detected by routine serologic testing ("hyporesponder"). However, one reason for persistent nonresponse to hepatitis B vaccine is that the person is chronically infected with HBV. Persons who fail to develop detectable anti-HBs after six doses should be tested for HBsAg. Persons who are found to be HBsAg positive should be counseled accordingly. Persons who fail to respond to two appropriately administered three-dose series, and who are HBsAg negative should be considered susceptible to HBV infection and should be counseled regarding precautions to prevent HBV infection and the need to obtain HBIG prophylaxis for any known or probable parenteral exposure to HBsAg-positive blood (see the postexposure prophylaxis table in this chapter).

It is difficult to interpret the meaning of a negative anti-HBs serologic response in a person who received hepatitis B in the past and was not tested after vaccination. Without postvaccination testing 1 to 2 months after completion of the series, it is not possible to determine if persons testing negative years after vaccination represent true vaccine failure (i.e., no initial response), or have anti-HBs antibody that has waned to below a level detectable by the test. The latter is the most likely explanation, because up to 60% of vaccinated people lose detectable antibody (but not protection) 9 to 15 years after vaccination.

One management option is to assume true vaccine failure and administer a second series to these persons. Serologic testing for anti-HBs antibody should be repeated 1 to 2 months after the sixth dose.

A second, probably less expensive option is to administer a single dose of hepatitis B vaccine and test for hepatitis B surface antibody in 4 to 6 weeks. If the person is anti-HBs antibody positive, this most likely indicates a booster response in a previous responder, and no further vaccination (or serologic testing) is needed. If the person is anti-HBs antibody negative after this "booster" dose, a second series should be completed (i.e., two more doses). If the person is still seronegative after six total doses, he or she should be managed as a nonresponder (see Postexposure Management, on the next page).

Persistent Nonresponse to Hepatitis B Vaccine

- <5% of vaccinees do not develop anti-HBsAg after 6 valid doses
- May be nonresponder or "hyporesponder"
- Check HBsAg status
- If exposed, treat as nonresponder with postexposure prophylaxis

8

8

Postexposure Management

Hepatitis B vaccine is recommended as part of the therapy used to prevent hepatitis B infection following exposure to HBV. Depending on the exposure circumstance, the hepatitis B vaccine series may be started at the same time as treatment with hepatitis B immune globulin (HBIG).

HBIG is prepared by cold ethanol fraction of plasma from selected donors with high anti-HBs titers; it contains an anti-HBs titer of at least 1:100,000, by RIA. It is used for passive immunization for accidental (percutaneous, mucous membrane) exposure, sexual exposure to an HBsAg-positive person, perinatal exposure of an infant, or household exposure of an infant younger than 12 months old to a primary caregiver with acute hepatitis B. Most candidates for HBIG are, by definition, in a high-risk category and should therefore be considered for vaccine as well.

Immune globulin (IG) is prepared by cold ethanol fractionation of pooled plasma and contains low titers of anti-HBs. Because titers are relatively low, IG has no valid current use for HBV disease unless hepatitis B immune globulin is unavailable.

Infants born to women who are HBsAg-positive (i.e., acutely or chronically infected with HBV) are at extremely high risk of HBV transmission and chronic HBV infection. Hepatitis B vaccination and one dose of HBIG administered within 24 hours after birth are 85%–95% effective in preventing both acute HBV infection and chronic infection. Hepatitis B vaccine administered alone beginning within 24 hours after birth is 70%–95% effective in preventing perinatal HBV infection.

HBIG (0.5 mL) should be given intramuscularly (IM), preferably within 12 hours of birth. Hepatitis B vaccine should be given IM in three doses. The first dose should be given at the same time as HBIG, but at a different site. If vaccine is not immediately available, the first injection should be given within 7 days of birth. The second and third doses should be given 1 to 2 months and 6 months, respectively, after the first. Testing for HBsAg and anti-HBs is recommended at 9 to 18 months of age (3 to 12 months after the third dose) to monitor the success of therapy. If the mother's HBsAg status is not known at the time of birth, the infant should be vaccinated within 12 hours of birth.

HBIG given at birth does not interfere with the administration of other vaccines administered at 2 months of age. Subsequent doses of hepatitis B vaccine do not interfere with the routine pediatric vaccine schedule.

Infants born to HBsAg-positive women and who weigh less than 2,000 grams at birth should receive postexposure prophylaxis as described above. However, the initial vaccine dose (at birth) should not be counted in the 3-dose schedule. The next dose in the series should be administered when the infant is chronologic age 1 month. The third dose should be given 1 to 2 months after the second, and the fourth dose should be given at 6 months of age. These infants should be tested for HBsAg and anti-HBs at 9 to 18 months of age.

Women admitted for delivery whose HBsAg status is unknown should have blood drawn for testing. While test results are pending, the infant should receive the first dose of hepatitis B vaccine (without HBIG) within 12 hours of birth. If the mother is found to be HBsAg positive, the infant should receive HBIG as soon as possible but not later than 7 days of age. If the infant does not receive HBIG, it is important that the second dose of vaccine be administered at 1 or 2 months of age.

Preterm infants (less than 2,000 grams birthweight) whose mother's HBsAg status is unknown should receive hepatitis B vaccine within 12 hours of birth. If the maternal HBsAg status cannot be determined within 12 hours of birth HBIG should also be administered because of the immune response is less reliable in preterm infants weighing less than 2,000 grams. As described above, the vaccine dose administered at birth should not be counted as part of the series, and the infant should receive three additional doses beginning at age 1 month.The vaccine series should be completed by 6 months of age.

Few data are available on the use of Comvax or Pediarix in infants born to women who have acute or chronic infection with hepatitis B virus (i.e., HBsAg-positive). Neither vaccine is licensed for infants whose mothers are known to be acutely or chronically infected with HBV. However, ACIP has approved off-label use of Comvax and Pediarix in children whose mothers are HBsAg positive, or whose HBsAg status is unknown. Comvax and Pediarix should never be used in infants younger than 6 weeks of age. Either vaccine may be administered at the same time as other childhood vaccines given at 6 weeks of age or older.

After a percutaneous (needle stick, laceration, bite) or permucosal exposure that contains or might contain HBV, blood should be obtained from the person who was the source of the exposure to determine their HBsAg status. Management of the exposed person depends on the HBsAg status of the source and the vaccination and anti-HBs response status of the exposed person. Recommended postexposure prophylaxis is described in the table below.

Prevention of Perinatal Hepatitis B Virus Infection

- Begin treatment within 12 hours of birth
- Hepatitis B vaccine (first dose) and HBIG at different sites
- Complete vaccination series at 6 months of age
- Test for response at 9-18 months of age

8

Recommended Postexposure Prophylaxis for Occupational Exposure to Hepatitis B Virus

Vaccination and antibody status of exposed person*		Treatment		
		Source HBsAg** Positive	Source HBsAg** Negative	Source unknown or not available for testing
Unvaccinated		HBIG† X 1 and initiate HB vaccine series	Initiate HB vaccine series	Initiate HB vaccine series
Previously Vaccinated	Known Responder §	No treatment	No treatment	No treatment
	Known nonresponder ‡	HBIG X 1 and initiate revaccination or HBIG X 2 ††	No treatment	If known high-risk source, treat as if source were HBsAg positive
	Antibody response unknown	Test exposed person for anti-HBs¶ – If adequate §, no treatment is necessary – If inadequate ‡, administer HBIG X 1 and vaccine booster	No treatment	Test exposed person for anti-HBs¶ – If adequate §, no treatment is necessary – If inadequate ‡, administer vaccine booster and recheck titer in 1-2 months

* Persons who have previously been infected with HBV are immune to reinfection and do not require postexposure prophylaxis

** Hepatitis B surface antigen

† Hepatitis B immune globulin; dose is 0.06 mL/kg administered intramuscularly

§ A responder is a person with adequate levels of serum antibody to HBsAg (i.e., anti-HBs $\geq$10 mIU/mL)

‡ A nonresponder is a person with inadequate response to vaccination (i.e., serum anti-HBs <10 mIU/mL)

†† The option of giving one dose of HBIG and reinitiating the vaccine series is preferred for nonresponders who have not completed a second 3-dose vaccine series. For persons who previously completed a second vaccine series but failed to respond, two doses of HBIG are preferred.

¶ Antibody to HBsAg

Source: *MMWR* 2001; 50(RR-11) pg 22

Non-Occupational Exposure to an HBsAg-Positive Source

Persons who have written documentation of a complete hepatitis B vaccine series and who did not receive postvaccination testing should receive a single vaccine booster dose. Persons who are in the process of being vaccinated but who have not completed the vaccine series should receive the appropriate dose of HBIG and should complete the vaccine series. Unvaccinated persons should receive both HBIG and hepatitis B vaccine as soon as possible after exposure (preferably within 24 hours). Hepatitis B vaccine may be administered simultaneously with HBIG in a separate injection site.

Household, sex, and needle-sharing contacts of HBsAg-positive persons should be identified. Unvaccinated sex partners and household and needle-sharing contacts should be tested for susceptibility to HBV infection and should receive the first dose of hepatitis B vaccine immediately after collection of blood for serologic testing. Susceptible persons should complete the vaccine series using an age-appropriate vaccine dose and schedule. Persons who are not fully vaccinated should complete the vaccine series.

8

Non-Occupational Exposure to a Source with Unknown HBsAg Status

Persons with written documentation of a complete hepatitis B vaccine series require no further treatment. Persons who are not fully vaccinated should complete the vaccine series. Unvaccinated persons should receive the hepatitis B vaccine series with the first dose administered as soon as possible after exposure, preferably within 24 hours.

Contraindications and Precautions to Vaccination

A severe allergic reaction (anaphylaxis) to a vaccine component or following a prior dose of hepatitis B vaccine is a contraindication to further doses of vaccine. Such allergic reactions are rare.

Persons with moderate or severe acute illness should not be vaccinated until their condition improves. However, a minor illness, such as an upper respiratory infection, is not a contraindication to vaccination.

Specific studies of the safety of hepatitis B vaccine in pregnant women have not been performed. However, more than 20 years of experience with inadvertent administration to pregnant women have not identified vaccine safety issues for either the woman or the fetus. In contrast, if a pregnant woman acquires HBV infection, it may cause severe disease in the mother and chronic infection in the newborn baby. Therefore, hepatitis B vaccine may be administered to a pregnant woman who is otherwise eligible for it.

Hepatitis B vaccine does not contain live virus, so it may be used in persons with immunodeficiency. However, response to vaccination in such persons may be suboptimal.

Adverse Reactions Following Vaccination

The most common adverse reaction following hepatitis B vaccine is pain at the site of injection, reported in 13%–29% of adults and 3%–9% of children. Mild systemic complaints, such as fatigue, headache, and irritability, have been reported in 11% to 17% of adults and 0% to 20% of children. Fever (up to 99.9°F [37.7°C]) has been reported in 1% of adults and 0.4% to 6.4% of children. Serious systemic adverse reactions and allergic reactions are rarely reported following hepatitis B vaccine. There is no evidence that administration of hepatitis B vaccine at or shortly after birth increases the number of febrile episodes, sepsis evaluations, or allergic or neurologic events in the newborn period.

Hepatitis B vaccine has been alleged to cause or exacerbate multiple sclerosis (MS). A 2004 retrospective study in a

Hepatitis B Vaccine Contraindications and Precautions

- Severe allergic reaction to a vaccine component or following a prior dose
- Moderate or severe acute illness

Hepatitis B Vaccine Adverse Reactions

	Adults	Infants and Children
Pain at injection site	13%-29%	3%-9%
Mild systemic complaints (fatigue, headache)	11%-17%	0%-20%
Temperature ≤99.9°F (37.7°C)	1%	0.4%-6%
Severe systemic reactions	rare	rare

British population found a slight increase in risk of MS among hepatitis B vaccine recipients. However, large population-based studies have shown no association between receipt of hepatitis B vaccine and either the development of MS or exacerbation of the course of MS is persons already diagnosed with the disease.

Vaccine Storage and Handling

Hepatitis B vaccines should be stored refrigerated at 35°–46°F (2°–8°C), but not frozen. Exposure to freezing temperature destroys the potency of the vaccine.

Selected References

Ascherio A, Zhang SM, Hernan MA, et al. Hepatitis B vaccination and the risk of multiple sclerosis. *N Engl J Med* 2001;344:327–32.

CDC. A comprehensive immunization strategy to eliminate transmission of hepatitis B virus infection in the United States: recommendations of the Advisory Committee on Immunization Practices (ACIP). Part 1: Immunization of infants, children, and adolescents. *MMWR* 2005;54(No. RR-16):1–32.

CDC. A comprehensive immunization strategy to eliminate transmission of hepatitis B virus nfection in the United States. Recommendations of the Advisory Committee on Immunization Practices (ACIP) Part II: Immunization of Adults. *MMWR* 2006;55(No. RR-16):1–33.

CDC. Updated U.S. Public Health Service guidelines for the management of occupational exposures to HBV, HCV, and HIV and recommendations for postexposure prophylaxis. *MMWR* 2001;50(No. RR-11):1–42.

Confavreux C, Suissa S, Saddier P, et al. Vaccinations and the risk of relapse in multiple sclerosis. *N Engl J Med* 2001;344:319–26.

Lewis E, Shinefield HR, Woodruff BA, et al. Safety of neonatal hepatitis B vaccine administration. *Pediatr Infect Dis J* 2001;20:1049–54.

Mast E, Ward J. Hepatitis B vaccine. In: Plotkin SA, Orenstein WA, Offit P, eds. *Vaccines*. 5th edition. Philadelphia, PA: Saunders; 2008:205–41.

Poland GA, Jacobson RM. Clinical practice: prevention of hepatitis B with the hepatitis B vaccine. *N Engl J Med* 2004;351:2832–8.

8

Human Papillomavirus

Human papillomavirus (HPV) is the most common sexually transmitted infection in the United States. The relationship of cervical cancer and sexual behavior was suspected for more than 100 years and was established by epidemiologic studies in the 1960s. In the early 1980s, cervical cancer cells were demonstrated to contain HPV DNA. Epidemiologic studies showing a consistent association between HPV and cervical cancer were published in the 1990s. The first vaccine to prevent infection with four types of HPV was licensed in 2006.

Human Papillomavirus

Human papillomaviruses are small, double-stranded DNA viruses that infect the epithelium. More than 100 HPV types have been identified; they are differentiated by the genetic sequence of the outer capsid protein L1. Most HPV types infect the cutaneous epithelium and cause common skin warts. About 40 types infect the mucosal epithelium; these are categorized according to their epidemiologic association with cervical cancer. Infection with low-risk, or nononcogenic types, such as types 6 and 11, can cause benign or low-grade cervical cell abnormalities, genital warts and laryngeal papillomas. High-risk, or oncogenic, HPV types act as carcinogens in the development of cervical cancer and other anogenital cancers. High-risk types (currently including types 16, 18, 31, 33, 35, 39, 45, 51, 52, 56, 58, 59, 68, 69, 73, 82) can cause low-grade cervical cell abnormalities, high-grade cervical cell abnormalities that are precursors to cancer, and anogenital cancers. High-risk HPV types are detected in 99% of cervical cancers. Type 16 is the cause of approximately 50% of cervical cancers worldwide, and types 16 and 18 together account for about 70% of cervical cancers. Infection with a high-risk HPV type is considered necessary for the development of cervical cancer, but by itself it is not sufficient to cause cancer because the vast majority of women with HPV infection do not develop cancer.

In addition to cervical cancer, HPV infection is also associated with anogenital cancers less common than cervical cancer, such as cancer of the vulva, vagina, penis and anus. The association of genital types of HPV with non-genital cancers is less well established, but studies support a role for these HPV types in a subset of oral cavity and pharyngeal cancers.

Pathogenesis

HPV infection occurs at the basal epithelium. Although the incidence of infection is high, most infections resolve spontaneously. A small proportion of infected persons become persistently infected; persistent infection is the most

Human Papillomavirus (HPV)

- Small DNA virus
- More than 100 types identified based on the genetic sequence of the outer capsid protein L1
- 40 types infect the mucosal epithelium

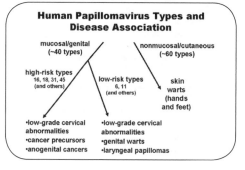

Human Papillomavirus Types and Disease Association

HPV-Associated Disease

Type	Women	Men
16/18	70% of cervical cancers	70% of anal cancers
	70% of anal/genital cancers	Transmission to women
6/11	90% of genital warts	90% of genital warts
	90% of RRP* lesions	90% of RRP lesions
		Transmission to women

* RRP = recurrent respiratory papillomatosis

Human Papillomavirus

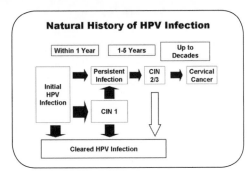

Natural History of HPV Infection

Within 1 Year	1-5 Years	Up to Decades

Initial HPV Infection → Persistent Infection → CIN 2/3 → Cervical Cancer

Initial HPV Infection → CIN 1

Cleared HPV Infection

HPV Clinical Features

- Most HPV infections are asymptomatic and result in no clinical disease
- Clinical manifestations of HPV infection include:
  - anogenital warts
  - recurrent respiratory papillomatosis
  - cervical cancer precursors (cervical intraepithelial neoplasia)
  - cancer (cervical, anal, vaginal, vulvar, penile, and some head and neck cancer)

---

important risk factor for the development of cervical cancer precursor lesions. The most common clinically significant manifestation of persistent genital HPV infection is cervical intraepithelial neoplasia, or CIN. Within a few years of infection, low-grade CIN—called CIN 1—may develop, which may spontaneously resolve and the infection clear.

Persistent HPV infection, however, may progress directly to high-grade CIN, called CIN2 or CIN3. High-grade abnormalities are at risk of progression to cancer and so are considered cancer precursors. A small proportion of high-grade abnormalities spontaneously regress. If left undetected and untreated, years or decades later CIN2 or 3 can progress to cervical cancer.

Infection with one type of HPV does not prevent infection with another type. Of persons infected with mucosal HPV, 5% to 30% are infected with multiple types of the virus.

Clinical Features

Most HPV infections are asymptomatic and result in no clinical disease. Clinical manifestations of HPV infection include anogenital warts, recurrent respiratory papillomatosis, cervical cancer precursors (cervical intraepithelial neoplasia), and cancers, including cervical, anal, vaginal, vulvar, penile, and some head and neck cancer.

Laboratory Diagnosis

HPV has not been isolated in culture. Infection is identified by detection of HPV DNA from clinical samples. Assays for HPV detection differ considerably in their sensitivity and type specificity, and detection is also affected by the anatomic region sampled as well as the method of specimen collection.

Currently, only the Digene Hybrid Capture® 2 (hc2) High-Risk HPV DNA Test is approved by the Food and Drug Administration for clinical use The hc2 uses liquid nucleic acid hybridization and detects 13 high-risk types (HPV 16, 18, 31, 33, 35, 39, 45, 51, 52, 56, 58, 59, 68). Results are reported as positive or negative and are not type-specific. The hc2 test is approved for triage of women with equivocal Papanicolaou (Pap) test results (ASC-US, atypical cells of undetermined significance) and in combination with the Pap test for cervical cancer screening in women 30 years of age and older. The test is not clinically indicated nor approved for use in men.

Epidemiologic and basic research studies of HPV generally use nucleic acid amplification methods that generate type-specific results. The PCR assays used most commonly in epidemiologic studies target genetically conserved regions in the L1 gene.

The most frequently used HPV serologic assays are VLP-based enzyme immunoassays. However, laboratory reagents used for these assays are not standardized and there are no standards for setting a threshold for a positive result.

Medical Management

There is no specific treatment for HPV infection. Medical management depends on treatment of the specific clinical manifestation of the infection (such as genital warts or abnormal cervical cell cytology).

Epidemiology

Occurrence

HPV infection occurs throughout the world.

Reservoir

Viruses in the papillomavirus family affect other species (notably rabbits and cows). However, humans are the only natural reservoir of HPV.

Transmission

HPV is transmitted by direct contact, usually sexual, with an infected person. Transmission occurs most frequently with sexual intercourse but can occur following nonpenetrative sexual activity.

Studies of newly acquired HPV infection demonstrate that infection occurs soon after onset of sexual activity. In a prospective study of college women, the cumulative incidence of infection was 40% by 24 months after first sexual intercourse. HPV 16 accounted for 10.4% of infections.

Genital HPV infection also may be transmitted by nonsexual routes, but this appears to be uncommon. Nonsexual routes of genital HPV transmission include transmission from a woman to a newborn infant at the time of birth.

Temporal Pattern

There is no known seasonal variation in HPV infection.

Communicability

HPV is presumably communicable during the acute infection and during persistent infection. This issue is difficult to study because of the inability to culture the virus. Communicability can presumed to be high because of the large number of new infections estimated to occur each year.

HPV Epidemiology	
• Reservoir	Human
• Transmission	Direct contact, usually sexual
• Temporal pattern	None
• Communicability	Presumed to be high

9

9

HPV Disease Burden in the United States

- Anogenital HPV is the most common sexually transmitted infection in the US
  - estimated 20 million currently infected
  - 6.2 million new infections/year
- Common among adolescents and young adults
- More than 80% of sexually active women will have been infected by age 50
- Infection also common in men

Cervical Cancer Disease Burden In the United States

- The American Cancer Society estimates that in 2008
  - 11,070 new cervical cancer cases
  - 3,870 cervical cancer deaths
- Almost 100% of these cervical cancer cases will be caused by one of the 40 HPV types that infect the mucosa

Risk Factors

Risk factors for HPV infection are related to sexual behavior, including the number of sex partners, lifetime history of sex partners, and the partners' sexual history. Most studies suggest that young age (less than 25 years) is a risk factor for infection. Results of epidemiologic studies are less consistent for other risk factors, including young age at sexual initiation, inconsistent condom use, number of pregnancies, genetic factors, smoking, lack of circumcision of male partner, and oral contraceptive use

Disease Burden in the United States

Anogenital HPV infection is believed to be the most common sexually transmitted infection in the United States. An estimated 20 million persons are currently infected, and an estimated 6.2 million new HPV infections occur annually. HPV infection is common among adolescents and young adults. Prevalence among adolescent girls is as high as 64%. Up to 75% of new infections occur among persons 15–24 years of age. Modeling estimates suggest that more than 80% of sexually active women will have been infected by age 50.

HPV infection is also common in men. Among heterosexual men in clinic-based studies, prevalence of genital HPV infection is often greater than 20%. Prevalence is highly dependent on the anatomic sites sampled and method of specimen collection.

The two most common types of cervical cancer worldwide, squamous cell carcinoma followed by adenocarcinoma, are both caused by HPV. The American Cancer Society estimates that in 2008 about 11,070 new cases of cervical cancer will be diagnosed in the United States. Approximately 3,870 women will die as a result of cervical cancer. HPV is believed to be responsible for nearly all of these cases of cervical cancer. HPV types 16 and 18 are associated with 70% of these cancers.

In addition to cervical cancer, HPV is believed to be responsible for 90% of anal cancers, 40% of vulvar, vaginal, or penile cancers, and 12% of oral and pharyngeal cancers.

Population-based estimates, primarily from clinics treating persons with sexually transmitted infections, indicate that about 1% of the sexually active adolescent and adult population in the United States have clinically apparent genital warts. More than 90% of cases of anogenital warts are associated with the low-risk HPV types 6 and 11.

About 4 billion dollars are spent annually on management of sequelae of HPV infections, primarily for the management of abnormal cervical cytology and treatment of cervical neoplasia. This exceeds the economic burden of any other sexually transmitted infection except human immuno-deficiency virus.

Prevention

HPV Infection

HPV transmission can be reduced but not eliminated with the use of physical barriers such as condoms. Recent studies demonstrated a significant reduction in HPV infection among young women after initiation of sexual activity when their partners used condoms consistently and correctly. Abstaining from sexual activity (i.e., refraining from any genital contact with another individual) is the surest way to prevent genital HPV infection. For those who choose to be sexually active, a monogamous relationship with an uninfected partner is the strategy most likely to prevent future genital HPV infections.

Cervical Cancer Screening

Most cases and deaths from cervical cancer can be prevented through detection of precancerous changes within the cervix by cervical cytology using the Pap test. Currently available Pap test screening can be done by a conventional Pap or a liquid-based cytology. CDC does not issue recommendations for cervical cancer screening, but various professional groups have published recommendations. The American College of Obstetricians and Gynecologists (ACOG), the American Cancer Society (ACS), and the U.S. Preventive Services Task Force (USPSTF) guidelines recommend that all women should have a Pap test for cervical cancer screening within 3 years of beginning sexual activity or by age 21, whichever occurs first. While the USPSTF recommends a conventional Pap test at least every 3 years regardless of age, ACS and ACOG recommend annual or biennial screening of women younger than age 30, depending on use of conventional or liquid–based cytology. According to these national organizations, women over age 30 with three normal consecutive Pap tests should be screened every 2 to 3 years.

The use of HPV vaccine does not eliminate the need for continued Pap test screening, since 30% of cervical cancers are caused by HPV types not included in the vaccine.

Human Papillomavirus Vaccine

Characteristics

The currently licensed vaccine is a quadrivalent HPV vaccine (Gardasil, Merck) approved by the Food and Drug Administration in June 2006. The vaccine antigen is the L1 major capsid protein of HPV, produced by using recombinant DNA technology. The L1 protein is expressed

Cervical Cancer Screening

- Cervical cancer screening – no change
  - 30% of cervical cancers caused by HPV types not prevented by the quadrivalent HPV vaccine
  - vaccinated females could subsequently be infected with non-vaccine HPV types
  - sexually active females could have been infected prior to vaccination
- Providers should educate women about the importance of cervical cancer screening

9

Human Papillomavirus

Human Papillomavirus Vaccine

- HPV L1 major capsid protein of the virus is antigen used for immunization
- L1 protein expressed in yeast cells using recombinant technology
- L1 proteins self-assemble into virus-like particles (VLP)
- Noninfectious and nononcogenic

HPV Vaccine Efficacy*

Endpoint	Efficacy
HPV 16/18-related CIN2/3 or AIS	100
HPV 6/11/16/18 related CIN	95
HPV 6/11/16/18 related genital warts	99

*Among 16-26 year old females. CIN – cervical intraepithelial neoplasia; AIS – adenocarcinoma *in situ*

in *Saccharomyces cerevisiae* (yeast) cells, and the protein self-assembles into noninfectious, nononcogenic virus-like-particles (VLP). Each 0.5-mL dose contains 20 µg HPV 6 L1 protein, 40 µg HPV 11 L1 protein, 40 µg HPV 16 L1 protein, and 20 µg HPV 18 L1 protein. The VLPs are adsorbed on 225 µg alum adjuvant. The vaccine also includes sodium chloride, L-histidine, polysorbate 80, sodium borate, and water for injection. The quadrivalent HPV vaccine contains no thimerosal or antibiotics. The vaccine is supplied in single-dose vials and syringes.

Immunogenicity and Vaccine Efficacy

The immunogenicity of the quadrivalent HPV vaccine has been measured by detection of IgG antibody to the HPV L1 by a type-specific immunoassay developed by the manufacturer. In all studies conducted to date, more than 99.5% of participants developed an antibody response to all four HPV types in the vaccine 1 month after completing the three-dose series. At that time interval, antibody titers against HPV types 6, 11, 16, and 18 were higher than those that developed after natural HPV infection.

There is no known serologic correlative of immunity and no known minimal titer determined to be protective. The high efficacy found in the clinical trials to date has precluded identification of a minimum protective antibody titer. Further follow-up of vaccinated cohorts may allow determination of serologic correlates of immunity in the future.

HPV vaccine has been found to have high efficacy for prevention of HPV vaccine type–related persistent infection, vaccine type–related CIN, CIN2/3, and external genital lesions in women 16–26 years of age. Clinical efficacy against cervical disease was determined in two double-blind, placebo-controlled trials, using various endpoints. Vaccine efficacy was 100% for prevention of HPV 16 or 18–related CIN 2/3 or adenocarcinoma in-situ (AIS). Efficacy against any CIN due to HPV 6, 11, 16, or 18 was 95%. Efficacy against HPV 6, 11, 16 or 18–related genital warts was 99%.

Although high efficacy among females without evidence of infection with vaccine HPV types was demonstrated in clinical trials, there was no evidence of efficacy against disease caused by vaccine types with which participants were infected at the time of vaccination. Participants infected with one or more vaccine HPV types prior to vaccination were protected against disease caused by the other vaccine types. However, prior infection with one HPV type did not diminish efficacy of the vaccine against other vaccine HPV types.

There is no evidence that the vaccine protects against disease due to non-vaccine HPV types or provides a therapeutic effect against cervical disease or genital warts present at the time of vaccination.

A subset of participants in the phase II HPV vaccine study has been followed for 60 months post-dose 1 with no evidence of waning protection. Study populations will continue to be followed for any evidence of waning immunity.

HPV vaccine has been shown to be immunogenic and safe in males. However, no clinical efficacy data are available for males. These studies are in progress.

Vaccination Schedule and Use

Quadrivalent HPV vaccine is licensed by the Food and Drug Administration for use among females 9 through 26 years of age. The recommended age for routine vaccination in the United States is 11 or 12 years. The vaccine can be given as young as 9 years of age at the discretion of the clinician. The vaccine should be given at the same visit as other vaccines recommended for persons of this age (e.g., Tdap, meningo-coccal conjugate, hepatitis B).

At the beginning of a vaccination program, there will be females older than 12 years of age who did not have the opportunity to receive vaccine at age 11 or 12 years. Catch-up vaccination is recommended for females 13 through 26 years of age who have not been previously vaccinated or who have not completed the full series. Ideally, vaccine should be administered before potential exposure to HPV through sexual contact; however, females who may have already been exposed to HPV should be vaccinated. Sexually active females who have not been infected with any of the HPV vaccine types will receive full benefit from vaccination. Vaccination will provide less benefit to females if they have already been infected with one or more of the four HPV vaccine types. However, it is not possible for a clinician to assess the extent to which sexually active females would benefit from vaccination, and the risk of HPV infection may continue as long as persons are sexually active. Pap testing or screening for HPV DNA or HPV antibody is not recommended prior to vaccination at any age.

HPV vaccine is administered in a three-dose series of intra-muscular injections. The second and third doses should be administered 2 and 6 months after the first dose. The third dose should follow the first dose by at least 24 weeks. An accelerated schedule for HPV vaccine is not recommended.

There is no maximum interval between doses. If the HPV vaccine schedule is interrupted, the vaccine series does

---

HPV Vaccine Efficacy

- High efficacy among females without evidence of infection with vaccine HPV types
- No evidence of efficacy against disease caused by vaccine types with which participants were infected at the time of vaccination
- Prior infection with one HPV type did not diminish efficacy of the vaccine against other vaccine HPV types

9

Routine HPV Vaccination Recommendations

- ACIP recommends routine vaccination of females 11 or 12 years of age
- The vaccination series can be started as young as 9 years of age at the clinician's discretion
- Catch-up vaccination recommended for females 13 through 26 years of age

9

HPV Vaccination Schedule

- Routine schedule is 0, 2, 6 months
- Third dose should follow the first dose by at least 24 weeks
- An accelerated schedule using minimum intervals is not recommended
- Series does not need to be restarted if the schedule is interrupted

Human Papillomavirus Vaccine

- Quadrivalent HPV vaccine is not currently approved for males, or for females younger than 9 years or older than 26 years
- Off-label use is not recommended
- Studies of safety and efficacy among males and females older than 26 years are ongoing

not need to be restarted. If the series is interrupted after the first dose, the second dose should be given as soon as possible, and the second and third doses should be separated by an interval of at least 12 weeks. If only the third dose is delayed, it should be administered as soon as possible.

HPV vaccine should be administered at the same visit as other age-appropriate vaccines, such as Tdap and quadrivalent meningococcal conjugate (MCV4) vaccines. Administering all indicated vaccines at a single visit increases the likelihood that adolescents and young adults will receive each of the vaccines on schedule. Each vaccine should be administered using a separate syringe at a different anatomic site.

The duration of protection from HPV vaccine is not known. Studies to investigate this issue are in progress. Booster doses are not recommended at this time.

HPV vaccine is not currently approved for use among males or among females younger than 9 years or older than 26 years of age. Use of the vaccine in males or females younger than 9 years or older than 26 years is not recommended. Studies among males and females older than 26 years of age are ongoing.

Females who have an equivocal or abnormal Pap test could be infected with any of more than 40 high-risk or low-risk genital HPV types. It is unlikely that such females would be infected with all four HPV vaccine types, and they may not be infected with any HPV vaccine type. Women younger than 27 years with a previously abnormal Pap test may be vaccinated. Women should be advised that data do not indicate the vaccine will have any thera-peutic effect on existing HPV infection or cervical lesions.

Females who have a positive HPV DNA test (Hybrid Capture 2®) done in conjunction with a Pap test could be infected with any of 13 high-risk types. This assay does not identify specific HPV types, and testing for specific HPV types is not done routinely in clinical practice. Women younger than 27 years with a positive HPV DNA test may be vaccinated. HPV DNA testing is not a prerequisite for vaccination. Women should be advised that the vaccine will not have a therapeutic effect on existing HPV infection or cervical lesions.

A history of genital warts or clinically evident genital warts indicate infection with HPV, most often type 6 or 11. However, these females may be infected with HPV types other than the vaccine types, and therefore they may receive HPV vaccine if they are in the recommended age group. Women with a history of genital warts should be advised that data do not indicate the vaccine will have any therapeutic effect on existing HPV infection or genital warts.

Because quadrivalent HPV vaccine is a subunit vaccine, it can be administered to females who are immunosuppressed because of disease or medications. However, the immune response and vaccine efficacy might be less than that in persons who are immunocompetent. Women who are breastfeeding may receive HPV vaccine.

Contraindications and Precautions to Vaccination

A severe allergic reaction (anaphylaxis) to a vaccine component or following a prior dose of HPV vaccine is a contraindication to receipt of HPV vaccine. A moderate or severe acute illness is a precaution to vaccination, and vaccination should be deferred until symptoms of the acute illness improve. A minor acute illness (e.g., diarrhea or mild upper respiratory tract infection, with or without fever) is not a reason to defer vaccination.

HPV vaccine is not recommended for use during pregnancy. The vaccine has not been associated with adverse pregnancy outcomes or with adverse effects on the developing fetus. However, data on vaccination during pregnancy are limited. Initiation of the vaccine series should be delayed until after completion of the pregnancy. If a woman is found to be pregnant after initiating the vaccination series, the remainder of the three-dose regimen should be delayed until after completion of the pregnancy. If a vaccine dose has been administered during pregnancy, no intervention is indicated. A vaccine in pregnancy registry has been established; patients and healthcare providers are urged to report any exposure to quadrivalent HPV vaccine during pregnancy by calling (800) 986-8999.

Adverse Reactions Following Vaccination

The most common adverse reactions reported during clinical trials of HPV vaccine were local reactions at the site of injection. These were most commonly pain (84%), swelling (25%), and erythema (25%). The majority of injection-site adverse experiences reported by recipients of quadrivalent HPV vaccine were mild to moderate in intensity. Fever was reported within 15 days of vaccination by 10% of vaccine recipients and 9% of placebo recipients. No serious adverse reactions have been reported.

A variety of systemic adverse reactions were reported by vaccine recipients, including nausea, dizziness, myalgia and

---

**HPV Vaccine
Special Situations**

- Vaccine can be administered
  - equivocal or abnormal Pap Test
  - positive HPV DNA test
  - genital warts
  - immunosuppression
  - breastfeeding

**HPV Vaccine
Contraindications and Precautions**

- Contraindication
  - severe allergic reaction to a vaccine component or following a prior dose
- Precaution
  - moderate or severe acute illnesses (defer until symptoms improve)

9

**Vaccination During Pregnancy
Provisional Recommendation**

- Initiation of the vaccine series should be delayed until after completion of pregnancy
- If a woman is found to be pregnant after initiating the vaccination series, remaining doses should be delayed until after the pregnancy
- If a vaccine dose has been administered during pregnancy, there is no indication for intervention
- Women vaccinated during pregnancy should be reported to Merck registry (800.986.8999)

**HPV Vaccine
Adverse Reactions**

- Local reactions   84%
  (pain, swelling)
- Fever   10%*
- No serious adverse reactions reported

*similar to reports in placebo recipients (9%)

malaise. However, these symptoms occurred with equal frequency among both vaccine and placebo recipients.

Syncope has been reported among adolescents who received HPV and other vaccines recommended for this age group (Tdap, MCV). Recipients should always be seated during vaccine administration. Clinicians should consider observing persons for 15–20 minutes after vaccination.

Vaccine Storage and Handling

HPV vaccine should be stored continuously at 35°–46°F (2°–8°C) and should be protected from light. The vaccine should be removed from refrigeration immediately before administration. The vaccine must not be exposed to freezing temperature. Vaccine exposed to freezing temperature should never be administered.

**HPV Vaccine
Storage and Handling**

- Store at 35°– 46°F (2°– 8°C)
- Protect from light
- Administer immediately after removing from refrigeration
- Do not expose to freezing temperature

9

Selected References

American College of Obstetricians and Gynecologists. Human papillomavirus vaccination. ACOG committee opinion No. 344. *Obstet Gynecol* 2006;108:699–705.

CDC. Quadrivalent human papillomavirus vaccine. Recommendations of the Advisory Committee on Immunization Practices (ACIP). *MMWR* 2007;56(No. RR-2):1–24.

Dunne E, Markowitz L. Genital human papillomavirus infection. *Clin Infect Dis* 2006;43:624–9.

Koutsky LA, Kiviat NB. Genital human papillomavirus. In: Holmes KK, Sparling PF, Mardh PA, et al, eds. *Sexually Transmitted Diseases*. 3rd ed. New York: McGraw-Hill; 1999:347–59.

Schiller JT, Frazer IH, Lowy DR. Human papillomavirus vaccines. In: Plotkin SA, Orenstein WA, Offit PA, eds. *Vaccines*. 5th ed. Philadelphia, PA: Saunders 2008:243–57.

Trottier H, Franco E. The epidemiology of genital human papillomavirus infection. *Vaccine 2006*;24(suppl1):51–15.

Parkin DM. The global health burden of infection-associated cancers in the year 2002. *Int J Cancer*. 2006;118:3030–44

Weinstock H, Berman S, Cates W, Jr. Sexually transmitted diseases among American youth: incidence and prevalence estimates, 2000. *Perspect Sex Reprod Health*. 2004;36:6–10.

Winer R, Hughes J, Feng Q, et al. Condom use and the risk of genital human papillomavirus infection in young women. *N Engl J Med* 2006;354:2645–54.

Winer R, Lee S, Hughes J, et al. Genital human papilloma-virus infection incidence and risk factors in a cohort of female university students. *Am J Epidemiol* 2003;157:218-26.

Human Papillomavirus

9

Influenza

Influenza is a highly infectious viral illness. The name "influenza" originated in 15th century Italy, from an epidemic attributed to "influence of the stars." The first pandemic, or worldwide epidemic, that clearly fits the description of influenza was in 1580. At least four pandemics of influenza occurred in the 19th century, and three occurred in the 20th century. The pandemic of "Spanish" influenza in 1918–1919 caused an estimated 21 million deaths worldwide.

Smith, Andrews, and Laidlaw isolated influenza A virus in ferrets in 1933, and Francis isolated influenza B virus in 1936. In 1936, Burnet discovered that influenza virus could be grown in embryonated hens' eggs. This led to the study of the characteristics of the virus and the development of inactivated vaccines. The protective efficacy of these inactivated vaccines was determined in the 1950s. The first live attenuated influenza vaccine was licensed in 2003.

Influenza Virus

Influenza is a single-stranded, helically shaped, RNA virus of the orthomyxovirus family. Basic antigen types A, B, and C are determined by the nuclear material. Type A influenza has subtypes that are determined by the surface antigens hemagglutinin (H) and neuraminidase (N). Three types of hemagglutinin in humans (H1, H2, and H3) have a role in virus attachment to cells. Two types of neuraminidase (N1 and N2) have a role in virus penetration into cells.

Influenza A causes moderate to severe illness and affects all age groups. The virus infects humans and other animals. Influenza A viruses are perpetuated in nature by wild birds, predominantly waterfowl. Most of these viruses are not pathogenic to their natural hosts and do not change or evolve. Influenza B generally causes milder disease than type A and primarily affects children. Influenza B is more stable than influenza A, with less antigenic drift and consequent immunologic stability. It affects only humans. Influenza C is rarely reported as a cause of human illness, probably because most cases are subclinical. It has not been associated with epidemic disease.

The nomenclature to describe the type of influenza virus is expressed in this order: 1) virus type, 2) geographic site where it was first isolated, 3) strain number, 4) year of isolation, and 5) virus subtype.

Antigenic Changes

Hemagglutinin and neuraminidase periodically change, apparently due to sequential evolution within immune or partially immune populations. Antigenic mutants emerge and are selected as the predominant virus to the extent that

---

Influenza

- Highly infectious viral illness
- First pandemic in 1580
- At least 4 pandemics in 19th century
- Estimated 21 million deaths worldwide in pandemic of 1918-1919
- Virus first isolated in 1933

10

Influenza Virus

- Single-stranded RNA virus
- Orthomyxoviridae family
- 3 types: A, B, C
- Subtypes of type A determined by hemagglutinin and neuraminidase

Influenza Virus Strains

- **Type A**
  - moderate to severe illness
  - all age groups
  - humans and other animals

- **Type B**
  - milder disease
  - primarily affects children
  - humans only

- **Type C**
  - rarely reported in humans
  - no epidemics

Influenza Virus

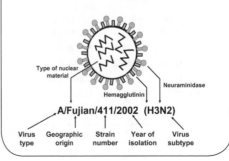

A/Fujian/411/2002 (H3N2)

| Virus type | Geographic origin | Strain number | Year of isolation | Virus subtype |

Influenza

Influenza Antigenic Changes

- Hemagglutinin and neuraminidase antigens change with time
- Changes occur as a result of point mutations in the virus gene, or due to exchange of a gene segment with another subtype of influenza virus
- Impact of antigenic changes depend on extent of change (more change usually means larger impact)

Influenza Antigenic Changes

- Antigenic Shift
  - major change, new subtype
  - caused by exchange of gene segments
  - may result in pandemic
- Example of antigenic shift
  - H2N2 virus circulated in 1957-1967
  - H3N2 virus appeared in 1968 and completely replaced H2N2 virus

10

Influenza Antigenic Changes

- Antigenic Drift
  - minor change, same subtype
  - caused by point mutations in gene
  - may result in epidemic
- Example of antigenic drift
  - in 2002-2003, A/Panama/2007/99 (H3N2) virus was dominant
  - A/Fujian/411/2002 (H3N2) appeared in late 2003 and caused widespread illness in 2003-2004

Influenza Type A Antigenic Shifts

Year	Subtype	Severity of Pandemic
1889	H3N2	Moderate
1918	H1N1	Severe
1957	H2N2	Severe
1968	H3N2	Moderate
1977	H1N1	Mild

they differ from the antecedent virus, which is suppressed by specific antibody arising in the population as a result of infection. This cycle repeats continuously. In interpandemic periods, mutants arise by serial point mutations in the RNA coding for hemagglutinin. At irregular intervals of 10 to 40 years, viruses showing major antigenic differences from prevalent subtypes appear and, because the population does not have protective antibody against these new antigens, cause pandemic disease in all age groups.

Antigenic shift is a major change in one or both surface antigens (H or N) that occurs at varying intervals. Antigenic shifts are probably due to genetic recombination (an exchange of a gene segment) between influenza A viruses, usually those that affect humans and birds. An antigenic shift may result in a worldwide pandemic if the virus is efficiently transmitted from person to person. The last major antigenic shift occurred in 1968 when H3N2 (Hong Kong) influenza appeared. It completely replaced the type A strain (H2N2, or Asian influenza) that had circulated throughout the world for the prior 10 years. There is concern among some influenza experts that the increasingly wide geographic distribution of a highly pathogenic avian virus (H5N1) could increase the chance of another antigenic shift. Although H5N1 virus is known to infect humans who are in contact with infected poultry, the virus is not efficiently transmitted from one human to another. Efficient person-to-person transmission is a necessary characteristic of an influenza virus with pandemic potential.

Antigenic drift is a minor change in surface antigens that results from point mutations in a gene segment. Antigenic drift may result in an epidemic, since the protection that remains from past exposures to similar viruses is incomplete. Drift occurs in all three types of influenza virus (A,B,C). For instance, during most of the 1997–1998 influenza season, A/Wuhan/359/95 (H3N2) was the predominant influenza strain isolated in the United States. A/Wuhan was a drifted distant relative of the 1968 Hong Kong H3N2 strain. In the last half of the 1997–1998 influenza season, a drifted variant of A/Wuhan appeared. This virus, named A/Sydney/5/97, was different enough from A/Wuhan (which had been included in the 1997–1998 vaccine) that the vaccine did not provide much protection. Both A/Wuhan and A/Sydney circulated late in the 1997–1998 influenza season. A/Sydney became the predominant strain during the 1998–1999 influenza season and was included in the 1998–1999 vaccine.

Since the late 19th century, four occurrences of antigenic shifts have led to major pandemics (1889–1891, 1918–1920, 1957–1958, and 1968–1969). A pandemic starts from a single focus and spreads along routes of travel. Typically, there are high attack rates involving all age groups, and mortality is usually markedly increased. Severity is generally not greater in the individual patient (except for the 1918–1919 strain), but because large numbers of persons are infected, the number, if not the proportion, of severe and fatal cases will be large. Onset may occur in any season of the year. Secondary and tertiary waves may occur every period of 1–2 years, usually in the winter.

Typically in an epidemic, influenza attack rates are lower than in pandemics. There is usually a rise in excess mortality. The major impact is observed in morbidity, with high attack rates and excess rates of hospitalization, especially for adults with respiratory disease. Absenteeism from work and school is high, and visits to healthcare providers increase. In the Northern Hemisphere, epidemics usually occur in late fall and continue through early spring. In the Southern Hemisphere, epidemics usually occur 6 months before or after those in the Northern Hemisphere.

Sporadic outbreaks can occasionally be localized to families, schools, and isolated communities.

Pathogenesis

Following respiratory transmission, the virus attaches to and penetrates respiratory epithelial cells in the trachea and bronchi. Viral replication occurs, which results in the destruction of the host cell. Viremia has rarely been documented. Virus is shed in respiratory secretions for 5–10 days.

Clinical Features

The incubation period for influenza is usually 2 days, but can vary from 1 to 4 days. The severity of influenza illness depends on the prior immunologic experience with antigenically related virus variants. In general, only about 50% of infected persons will develop the classic clinical symptoms of influenza.

"Classic" influenza disease is characterized by the abrupt onset of fever, myalgia, sore throat, nonproductive cough, and headache. The fever is usually 101°–102°F, and accompanied by prostration. The onset of fever is often so abrupt that the exact hour is recalled by the patient. Myalgias mainly affect the back muscles. Cough is believed to be a result of tracheal epithelial destruction. Additional symptoms may include rhinorrhea (runny nose), headache, substernal chest burning and ocular symptoms (e.g., eye pain and sensitivity to light).

Systemic symptoms and fever usually last from 2 to 3 days, rarely more than 5 days. They may be decreased by such medications as aspirin or acetaminophen. Aspirin should not be used for infants, children, or teenagers because they may be at risk for contracting Reye syndrome following an influenza infection. Recovery is usually rapid, but some

10

Influenza Pathogenesis

- **Respiratory transmission of virus**
- **Replication in respiratory epithelium with subsequent destruction of cells**
- **Viremia rarely documented**
- **Viral shedding in respiratory secretions for 5-10 days**

Influenza Clinical Features

- **Incubation period 2 days (range 1-4 days)**
- **Severity of illness depends on prior experience with related variants**
- **Abrupt onset of fever, myalgia, sore throat, nonproductive cough, headache**

patients may have lingering depression and asthenia (lack of strength or energy) for several weeks.

Complications

The most frequent complication of influenza is pneumonia, most commonly secondary bacterial pneumonia (e.g., *Streptococcus pneumoniae, Haemophilus influenzae,* or *Staphylococcus aureus*). Primary influenza viral pneumonia is an uncommon complication with a high fatality rate. Reye syndrome is a complication that occurs almost exclusively in children taking aspirin, primarily in association with influenza B (or varicella zoster), and presents with severe vomiting and confusion, which may progress to coma due to swelling of the brain.

Other complications include myocarditis (inflammation of the heart) and worsening of chronic bronchitis and other chronic pulmonary diseases. Death is reported in 0.5–1 per 1,000 cases. The majority of deaths occur among persons 65 years of age and older.

Impact of Influenza

An increase in mortality typically accompanies an influenza epidemic. Increased mortality results not only from influenza and pneumonia but also from cardiopulmonary and other chronic diseases that can be exacerbated by influenza.

In a study of influenza epidemics, approximately 19,000 influenza-associated pulmonary and circulatory deaths per influenza season occurred during 1976–1990, compared with approximately 36,000 deaths during 1990–1999. Persons 65 years of age and older account for more than 90% of deaths attributed to pneumonia and influenza. In the United States, the number of influenza-associated deaths might be increasing, in part because the number of older persons is increasing. In addition, influenza seasons in which influenza A (H3N2) viruses predominate are associated with higher mortality.

The risk for complications and hospitalizations from influenza are higher among persons 65 years of age and older, young children, and persons of any age with certain underlying medical conditions. An average of more than 200,000 hospitalizations per year are related to influenza, more than 57% of which are among persons younger than 65 years. A greater number of hospitalizations occur during years that influenza A (H3N2) is predominant. In nursing homes, attack rates may be as high as 60%, with fatality rates as high as 30%. The cost of a severe epidemic has been estimated to be $12 billion.

Among children 0–4 years of age, hospitalization rates have varied from 100 per 100,000 healthy children to as high

---

Influenza Complications

- Pneumonia
  - secondary bacterial
  - primary influenza viral
- Reye syndrome
- Myocarditis
- Death 0.5-1 per 1,000 cases

10

Impact of Influenza

- ~36,000 excess deaths per year
- >90% of deaths among persons ≥65 years of age
- Higher mortality during seasons when influenza type A (H3N2) viruses predominate

Impact of Influenza

- Highest rates of complications and hospitalization among young children and person ≥65 years
- Average of >200,000 influenza-related excess hospitalizations
- 57% of hospitalizations among persons <65 years of age
- Greater number of hospitalizations during type A (H3N2) epidemics

as 500 per 100,000 for children with underlying medical conditions. Hospitalization rates for children 24 months of age and younger are comparable to rates for persons 65 and older. Children 24-59 months of age are at less risk of hospitalization from influenza than are younger children, but are at increased risk for influenza-associated clinic and emergency department visits.

Healthy children 5 through 18 years of age are not at increased risk of complications of influenza. However, children typically have the highest attack rates during community outbreaks of influenza. They also serve as a major source of transmission of influenza within communities. Influenza has a substantial impact among school-aged children and their contacts. These impacts include school absenteeism, medical care visits, and parental work loss. Studies have documented 5 to 7 influenza-related outpatient visits per 100 children annually, and these children frequently receive antibiotics.

An influenza pandemic could affect up to 200 million people and result in up to 400,000 deaths. The 1918–1919 influenza pandemic is believed to have resulted in the death of at least 500,000 Americans in less than a year. Planning for pandemic influenza is a critical component of public health preparedness activities and should be conducted by all local and state public health agencies. The federal pandemic plan is available on the Department of Health and Human Services website at http://www.hhs.gov/pandemicflu/plan/

Laboratory Diagnosis

The diagnosis of influenza is usually suspected on the basis of characteristic clinical findings, particularly if influenza has been reported in the community.

Virus can be isolated from throat and nasopharyngeal swabs obtained within 3 days of onset of illness. Culture is performed by inoculation of the amniotic or allantoic sac of chick embryos or certain cell cultures that support viral replication. A minimum of 48 hours is required to demonstrate virus, and 1 to 2 additional days to identify the virus type. As a result, culture is helpful in defining the etiology of local epidemics, but not in individual case management.

Serologic confirmation of influenza requires demonstration of a significant rise in influenza IgG. The acute-phase specimen should be taken less than 5 days from onset, and a convalescent specimen taken 10–21 days (preferably 21 days) following onset. Complement fixation (CF) and hemagglutination inhibition (HI) are the serologic tests most commonly used. The key test is HI, which depends on the ability of the virus to agglutinate human or chicken erythrocytes and inhibition of

Hospitalization Rates for Influenza By Age and Risk Group*

Age Group	Rate** (high-risk)	Rate** (not high-risk)
0-11 mos	1900	496-1038
1-2 yrs	800	186
3-4 yrs	320	86
5-14 yrs	92	41
15-44 yrs	56-110	23-25
45-64 yrs	392-635	13-23
≥65 yrs	399-518	125-228

* Data from several studies 1972 - 1995
** Hospitalizations per 100,000 population

Influenza Among School-Aged Children

- School-aged children
  - typically have the highest attack rates during community outbreaks of influenza
  - serve as a major source of transmission of influenza within communities

Influenza Diagnosis

- Clinical and epidemiological characteristics
- Isolation of influenza virus from clinical specimen (e.g., nasopharynx, throat, sputum)
- Significant rise in influenza IgG by serologic assay
- Direct antigen testing for type A virus

10

10

this process by specific antibody. Diagnosis requires at least a fourfold rise in antibody titer. Rapid diagnostic testing for influenza antigen permits those in office and clinic settings to assess the need for antiviral use in a more timely manner.

Details about the laboratory diagnosis of influenza are available on the CDC influenza website at http://www.cdc.gov/flu/professionals/diagnosis/index.htm

Epidemiology

Occurrence
Influenza occurs throughout the world.

Reservoir
Humans are the only known reservoir of influenza types B and C. Influenza A may infect both humans and animals. There is no chronic carrier state.

Transmission
Influenza is primarily transmitted from person to person via large virus-laden droplets (particles more than 5 microns in diameter) that are generated when infected persons cough or sneeze. These large droplets can then settle on the mucosal surfaces of the upper respiratory tracts of susceptible persons who are near (within 3 feet) infected persons. Transmission may also occur through direct contact or indirect contact with respiratory secretions such as when touching surfaces contaminated with influenza virus and then touching the eyes, nose or mouth.

Temporal Pattern
Influenza activity peaks from December to March in temperate climates, but may occur earlier or later. During 1976–2008, peak influenza activity in the United States occurred most frequently in January (19% of seasons) and February (47% of seasons). However, peak influenza activity occurred in March, April, or May in 19% of seasons. Influenza occurs throughout the year in tropical areas.

Communicability
Adults can transmit influenza from the day before symptom onset to approximately 5 days after symptoms begin. Children can transmit influenza to others for 10 or more days.

Secular Trends in the United States
There is a documented association between influenza and increased morbidity in high-risk adult populations.

Influenza Epidemiology

- **Reservoir** — Human, animals (type A only)
- **Transmission** — Respiratory Probably airborne
- **Temporal pattern** — Peak December – March in temperate climate May occur earlier or later
- **Communicability** — 1 day before to 5 days after onset (adults)

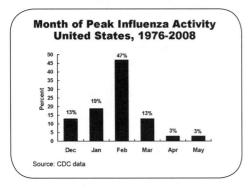

Month of Peak Influenza Activity United States, 1976-2008

Dec 13%, Jan 19%, Feb 47%, Mar 13%, Apr 3%, May 3%

Source: CDC data

Hospitalization for adults with high-risk medical conditions increases two- to fivefold during major epidemics.

The impact of influenza in the United States is quantified by measuring pneumonia and influenza (P and I) deaths. Death certificate data are collected from 122 U.S. cities with populations of more than 100,000 (total of approximately 70,000,000). P and I deaths include all deaths for which pneumonia is listed as a primary or underlying cause or for which influenza is listed on the death certificate.

An expected ratio of deaths due to P and I compared with all deaths for a given period of time is determined. The epidemic threshold for influenza seasons is generally estimated at 1.645 standard deviations above observed P and I deaths for the previous 5-year period excluding periods during influenza outbreaks. Influenza epidemic activity is signaled when the ratio of deaths due to P and I exceeds the threshold ratio for 2 consecutive weeks.

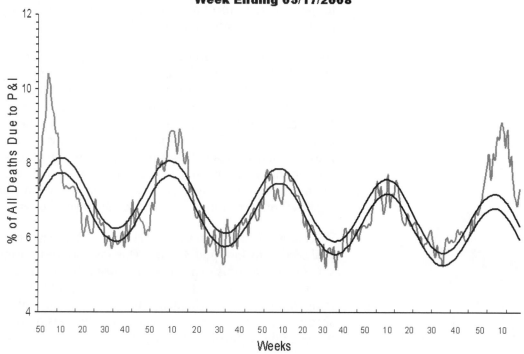

Pneumonia and Influenza Mortality for 122 U.S. Cities
Week Ending 05/17/2008

Influenza Vaccine

Characteristics

Two types of influenza vaccine are available in the United States. Trivalent inactivated influenza vaccine (TIV) has been available since the 1940s. TIV is administered by the intramuscular route and currently contains three inactivated

Influenza Vaccines

- Inactivated subunit (TIV)
  - intramuscular
  - trivalent
- Live attenuated vaccine (LAIV)
  - intranasal
  - trivalent

10

viruses: type A (H1N1), type A (H3N2), and type B. Only split-virus and subunit inactivated vaccines are available in the United States. Vaccine viruses are grown in chicken eggs, and the final product contains residual egg protein. The vaccine is available in both pediatric (0.25-mL dose) and adult (0.5-mL dose) formulations. TIV is available with thimerosal as a preservative (in multidose vials), and in reduced and preservative free formulations.

For the 2008–2009 influenza season four manufacturers provided TIV. Fluzone (sanofi pasteur) was available in multidose vials, in a thimerosal-free pediatric formulation (0.25 mL) in single-dose syringes, and in a thimerosal-free adult formulation in single-dose syringes and vials. Fluzone is the only TIV currently approved for use among children younger than 48 months. Fluvirin (Novartis) was available in multidose vials. Fluvirin is approved only for persons 4 years of age and older. Fluarix (GlaxoSmithKline) was available in a reduced-thimerosal ("preservative free") single-dose syringe for persons 18 years of age and older. FluLaval (GlaxoSmithKline) was available in a multidose vial for persons 18 years of age and older. Afluria (CSL Biotherapies) was available in a single-dose syringe and multidose vial for persons 18 years of age and older. All TIV supplied in multidose vials contains thimerosal as a preservative.

Live attenuated influenza vaccine (LAIV) was approved for use in the United States in 2003. It contains the same three influenza viruses as TIV. The viruses are cold-adapted, and replicate effectively in the mucosa of the nasopharynx. The vaccine viruses are grown in chicken eggs, and the final product contains residual egg protein. The vaccine is provided in a single-dose sprayer unit; half of the dose is sprayed into each nostril. LAIV does not contain thimerosal or any other preservative. LAIV is approved for use only in healthy, nonpregnant persons 2 through 49 years of age.

Vaccinated children can shed vaccine viruses in nasopharyngeal secretions for up to 3 weeks. One instance of transmission of vaccine virus to a contact has been documented. The transmitted virus retained its attenuated, cold-adapted, temperature-sensitive characteristics. The frequency of shedding of vaccine strains by persons 5–49 years of age has not been determined.

Immunogenicity and Vaccine Efficacy

TIV

For practical purposes, immunity following inactivated influenza vaccination is less than 1 year because of waning of vaccine-induced antibody and antigenic drift of circulating influenza viruses. Influenza vaccine efficacy varies by the similarity of the vaccine strain(s) to the circulating strain

---

Transmission of LAIV Virus

- LAIV replicates in the nasopharyngeal mucosa
- Mean shedding of virus 7.6 days – longer in children
- One instance of transmission of vaccine virus documented in a child care setting
- Transmitted virus retained attenuated, cold-adapted, temperature-sensitive characteristics
- No transmission of LAIV reported in the U.S.

Inactivated Influenza Vaccine Efficacy

- 70%-90% effective among healthy persons <65 years of age
- 30%-40% effective among frail elderly persons
- 50%-60% effective in preventing hospitalization
- 80% effective in preventing death

and the age and health status of the recipient. Vaccines are effective in protecting up to 90% of healthy vaccinees younger than 65 years of age from illness when the vaccine strain is similar to the circulating strain. However, the vaccine is only 30%–40% effective in preventing illness among persons 65 years of age and older.

Although the vaccine is not highly effective in preventing clinical illness among the elderly, it is effective in preventing complications and death. Among elderly persons, the vaccine is 50%–60% effective in preventing hospitalization and 80% effective in preventing death. During a 1982–1983 influenza outbreak in Genesee County, Michigan, unvaccinated nursing home residents were four times more likely to die than were vaccinated residents.

LAIV

LAIV has been tested in groups of both healthy children and healthy adults. A randomized, double-blind, placebo-controlled trial among healthy children 60–84 months of age assessed the efficacy of the trivalent LAIV against culture-confirmed influenza during two influenza seasons. In year 1, when vaccine and circulating virus strains were well matched, efficacy was 87% against culture-confirmed influenza. In year 2, when the type A component was not well matched between vaccine and circulating virus strains, efficacy was also 87%. Other results from this trial included a 27% reduction in febrile otitis media and a 28% reduction in otitis media with concomitant antibiotic use. Receipt of LAIV also resulted in decreased fever and otitis media in vaccine recipients who developed influenza.

A randomized, double-blind, placebo-controlled trial among 3,920 healthy working adults aged 18–49 years assessed several endpoints and documented reductions in illness, absenteeism, healthcare visits, and medication use during influenza outbreak periods. This study was conducted during the 1997–98 influenza season, when the vaccine and circulating type A strains were not well matched. This study did not include laboratory virus testing of cases. Three studies among children have demonstrated greater efficacy for LAIV compared to TIV. There is no evidence in adults that efficacy of LAIV is greater than that of TIV.

Vaccination Schedule and Use

TIV

Influenza activity peaks in temperate areas between late December and early March. TIV is most effective when it precedes exposure by no more than 2 to 4 months. It should be offered annually, beginning in September for routine patient visits. The optimal time for vaccination efforts is

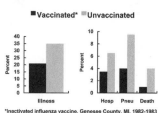

Influenza and Complications Among Nursing Home Residents

■Vaccinated* ▓Unvaccinated

*Inactivated influenza vaccine. Genesee County, MI, 1982-1983

10

LAIV Efficacy in Healthy Children

- 87% effective against culture-confirmed influenza in children 5-7 years old
- 27% reduction in febrile otitis media (OM)
- 28% reduction in OM with accompanying antibiotic use
- Decreased fever and OM in vaccine recipients who developed influenza

---

LAIV Efficacy in Healthy Adults

- 20% fewer severe febrile illness episodes
- 24% fewer febrile upper respiratory illness episodes
- 27% fewer lost work days due to febrile upper respiratory illness
- 18%-37% fewer days of healthcare provider visits due to febrile illness
- 41%-45% fewer days of antibiotic use

Timing of Inactivated Influenza Vaccine Programs

- Actively target vaccine available in September and October to persons at increase risk of influenza complications, children <9 years, and healthcare personnel
- Vaccination of all other groups should begin in November
- Continue vaccinating through December and later, as long as vaccine is available

usually during October and November. In October vaccination in provider-based settings should start or continue for all patients,-both high risk and healthy-and extend through November. Vaccination of children aged 6 months through 8 years of age who are receiving vaccine for the first time should also begin in October, if not done earlier, because those children need a second dose 4 weeks after the initial dose. Organized vaccination campaigns should be scheduled no earlier than mid-October. Vaccine may be given up to and even after influenza activity is documented in a region. Although most influenza vaccination activities should be completed by December (particularly for high-risk groups), providers should continue to provide vaccine throughout influenza season.

One dose of TIV may be administered annually for persons 9 years of age or older. Children 6 months to 9 years of age receiving influenza vaccine for the first time should receive two doses administered at least 1 month apart.

Inactivated Influenza Vaccine Dosage, by Age Group – United States

Age Group	Dosage	Number of Doses	Route
6-35 months	0.25 mL	1* or 2	IM
3-8 years	0.50 mL	1* or 2	IM
≥9 years	0.50 mL	1	IM

*Only one dose is needed if the child received two doses of influenza vaccine during a previous influenza season.

Inactivated Influenza Vaccine Recommendations

- All persons 50 years of age or older
- Healthy children 6 months through 18 years of age
- Residents of long-term care facilities
- Pregnant women
- Persons 6 months through 18 years receiving chronic aspirin therapy
- Persons 6 months of age and older with chronic illness

Inactivated Influenza Vaccine Recommendations

- Persons with the following chronic illnesses should be considered for inactivated influenza vaccine:
  - pulmonary (e.g., asthma, COPD)
  - cardiovascular (e.g., CHF)
  - metabolic (e.g., diabetes)
  - renal dysfunction
  - hemoglobinopathy
  - immunosuppression, including HIV infection
  - any condition that can compromise respiratory function or the handling of respiratory secretions

Inactivated influenza vaccine should be given by the intramuscular (IM) route. Other methods, such as intradermal, subcutaneous, topical, or mucosal should not be used unless approved by the Food and Drug Administration or recommended by ACIP.

TIV is recommended for all persons 50 years of age or older and all children 6 months through 18 years of age, regardless of the presence of chronic illness. Other groups targeted for TIV include residents of long-term care facilities, pregnant women, and persons 6 months through 18 years of age receiving chronic aspirin therapy (because of the risk of Reye syndrome following influenza infection).

Persons 6 months of age and older with a chronic illness should receive TIV annually. These chronic illnesses include the following:

■ pulmonary illnesses, such as emphysema, chronic bronchitis, or asthma

■ cardiovascular illnesses, such as congestive heart failure

- metabolic diseases, including diabetes mellitus

- renal dysfunction

- hemoglobinopathy, such as sickle cell disease

- immunosuppression, including human immunodeficiency virus (HIV) infection

- any condition (e.g., cognitive dysfunction, spinal cord injury, seizure disorder, or other neuromuscular disorder) that can compromise respiratory function or the handling of respiratory secretions

Case reports and limited studies suggest that pregnant women may be at increased risk for serious medical complications of influenza as a result of increases in heart rate, stroke volume and oxygen consumption; decreases in lung capacity; and changes in immunologic function. A study found that the risk of hospitalization for influenza-related complications was more than four times higher for women in the second or third trimester of pregnancy than for nonpregnant women. The risk of complications for these pregnant women was comparable to that for nonpregnant women with high-risk medical conditions, for whom influenza vaccine has been traditionally recommended.

ACIP recommends vaccination of women who will be pregnant during influenza season. Vaccination can occur during any trimester. Influenza season in the United States generally occurs in December through March. Only TIV should be administered to pregnant women.

Available data suggest that persons with HIV infection may have prolonged influenza illnesses and are at increased risk of complications of influenza. Many persons with HIV infection will develop protective antibody titers following inactivated influenza vaccine. In persons who have advanced HIV disease and low CD4+ T-lymphocyte cell counts, TIV vaccine may not induce protective antibody titers. A second dose of vaccine does not improve the immune response in these persons.

Some studies have demonstrated a transient increase in viral titer in the blood of vaccinated persons infected with HIV. There is no evidence of deterioration in CD4 counts or progression of clinical HIV disease. Because influenza can result in serious illness and complications and because influenza vaccination may result in protective antibody titers, ACIP believes that influenza vaccination will benefit many persons with HIV infection. LAIV should not be administered to persons with HIV infection.

10

Pregnancy and Inactivated Influenza Vaccine

- Risk of hospitalization 4 times higher than nonpregnant women
- Risk of complications comparable to nonpregnant women with high-risk medical conditions
- Vaccination (with TIV) recommended if pregnant during influenza season
- Vaccination can occur during any trimester

HIV Infection and Inactivated Influenza Vaccine

- Persons with HIV at increased risk of complications of influenza
- TIV induces protective antibody titers in many HIV-infected persons
- Transient increase in HIV replication reported
- TIV will benefit many HIV-infected persons

Persons who have contact with high-risk persons should receive TIV. These include healthcare personnel, employees of long-term care facilities, and household contacts of high-risk persons. These individuals may be younger and healthier and more likely to be protected from illness than are elderly persons. All healthcare providers should receive annual inactivated influenza vaccine. Groups that should be targeted include physicians, nurses, and other personnel in hospitals and outpatient settings who have contact with high-risk patients in all age groups, and providers of home care to high-risk persons (e.g., visiting nurses, volunteers). LAIV may be administered to healthy healthcare personnel 49 years of age or younger, except those who have contact with severely immunosuppressed persons who require hospitalization and care in a protective environment (i.e., in isolation because of severe immunosuppression).

Persons who provide essential community services and students or others in institutional settings (e.g., schools and colleges) may be considered for vaccination to minimize disruption of routine activities during outbreaks. Persons traveling outside the United States should consider influenza vaccination. The risk of exposure to influenza during foreign travel varies, depending on season of travel, the mode of travel (e.g., increased risk during cruises), and destination. Influenza can occur throughout the year in the tropics. In the Southern Hemisphere, influenza activity peaks in April–September. If not vaccinated the previous fall/winter, persons (especially those in high-risk groups) preparing to travel to the tropics at any time of the year or to the Southern Hemisphere during April–September should be considered for influenza vaccination before travel. Any person who wishes to lessen his/her chance of acquiring influenza infection may be vaccinated.

In 2005, the ACIP recommended routine vaccination of all children 6 through 59 months of age because of the increased risk of influenza-related hospitalization and physician visits in this age group. Household contacts and other caregivers of children younger than 59 months of age are also encouraged to receive annual influenza vaccination.

LAIV

LAIV is approved for healthy, nonpregnant persons 2 through 49 years of age. The vaccine can be administered to eligible persons as soon as it becomes available in the late summer or fall. Vaccination can continue throughout influenza season. One dose of LAIV may be administered by the intranasal route to persons 9 through 49 years of age. Children 2 through 8 years of age receiving influenza

10

Influenza Vaccine Recommendations

- Healthcare personnel, including home care*
- Employees of long-term care facilities
- Household contacts of high-risk persons

*LAIV should not be administered to healthcare workers who have contact with severely immunosuppressed persons who require hospitalization and care in a protective environment

Influenza Vaccine Recommendations*

- Providers of essential community services
- Students
- Persons traveling outside the U.S.
- Anyone who wishes to reduce the likelihood of becoming ill from influenza

*these groups may receive TIV, and some may be eligible for LAIV

vaccine for the first time should receive two doses administered at least 4 weeks apart.

Live Attenuated Influenza Vaccine Dosage, by Age Group – United States

Age Group	Number of Doses	Route
2-8 years, no previous influenza vaccine	2 (separated by 4 weeks)	Intranasal
5-8 years, previous influenza vaccine*	1[†] or 2	Intranasal
9-49 years	1	Intranasal

*LAIV or inactivated vaccine

[†]Only one dose is needed if the child received two doses of influenza vaccine during a previous influenza season.

Close contacts of persons at high risk for complications from influenza should receive influenza vaccine. This reduces the risk of transmission of wild-type influenza viruses to high-risk persons. Contacts of persons at high risk of complications of influenza may receive LAIV if they are otherwise eligible (i.e., 2 through 49 years of age, healthy and not pregnant). Persons in close contact with severely immunosuppressed persons who are hospitalized and receiving care in a protected environment should not receive LAIV.

Inactivated vaccines do not interfere with the immune response to live vaccines. Inactivated vaccines, such as tetanus and diphtheria toxoids, can be administered either simultaneously or at any time before or after LAIV. Other live vaccines can be administered on the same day as LAIV. Live vaccines not administered on the same day should be administered at least 4 weeks apart when possible.

Contraindications and Precautions to Vaccination

TIV

Persons with a severe allergic reaction (anaphylaxis) to a vaccine component or following a prior dose of inactivated influenza vaccine should not receive TIV. Persons with a moderate or severe acute illness normally should not be vaccinated until their symptoms have decreased. Pregnancy, breastfeeding, and immunosuppression are not contraindications to inactivated influenza vaccination.

LAIV

Persons who should not receive LAIV include children younger than 2 years of age; persons 50 years of age and older; persons with chronic medical conditions, including asthma, a recent wheezing episode, reactive airways disease or other chronic pulmonary or cardiovascular conditions,

---

Simultaneous Administration of LAIV and Other Vaccines

- Inactivated vaccines can be administered either simultaneously or at any time before or after LAIV
- Other live vaccines can be administered on the same day as LAIV
- Live vaccines not administered on the same day should be administered ≥4 weeks apart

---

Inactivated Influenza Vaccine Contraindications and Precautions

- Severe allergic reaction to a vaccine component (e.g., egg) or following a prior dose of vaccine
- Moderate or severe acute illness

Live Attenuated Influenza Vaccine Contraindications and Precautions

- Children <2 years of age*
- Persons ≥50 years of age*
- Persons with chronic medical conditions*
- Children and adolescents receiving long-term aspirin therapy*

*These persons should receive inactivated influenza vaccine

metabolic disease such as diabetes, renal disease, or hemoglobinopathy, such as sickle cell disease; and children or adolescents receiving long-term therapy with aspirin or other salicylates, because of the association of Reye syndrome with wild-type influenza infection. Persons in these groups should receive inactivated influenza vaccine.

As with other live-virus vaccines, LAIV should not be given to persons who are immunosuppressed because of disease, including HIV, or who are receiving immunosuppressive therapy. Pregnant women should not receive LAIV. Immunosuppressed persons and pregnant women should receive inactivated influenza vaccine. Since LAIV contains residual egg protein, it should not be administered to persons with a history of severe allergy to egg or any other vaccine component. The manufacturer recommends that LAIV not be administered to a person with a history of Guillain-Barré syndrome.

As with all vaccines, LAIV should be deferred for persons with a moderate or severe acute illness. If clinical judgment indicates that nasal congestion might impede delivery of the vaccine to the nasopharyngeal mucosa, deferral of administration should be considered until the condition has improved.

The effect on safety and efficacy of LAIV coadministration with influenza antiviral medications has not been studied. However, because influenza antiviral agents reduce replication of influenza viruses, LAIV should not be administered until 48 hours after cessation of influenza antiviral therapy, and influenza antiviral medications should not be administered for 2 weeks after receipt of LAIV.

Adverse Reactions Following Vaccination

TIV

Local reactions are the most common adverse reactions following vaccination with TIV. Local reactions include soreness, erythema, and induration at the site of injection. These reactions are transient, generally lasting 1 to 2 days. Local reactions are reported in 15%–20% of vaccinees.

Nonspecific systemic symptoms, including fever, chills, malaise, and myalgia, are reported in fewer than 1% of TIV recipients. These symptoms usually occur in those with no previous exposure to the viral antigens in the vaccine. They usually occur within 6–12 hours of TIV vaccination and last 1–2 days. Recent reports indicate that these systemic symptoms are no more common than in persons given a placebo injection.

Rarely, immediate hypersensitivity, presumably allergic, reactions (such as hives, angioedema, allergic asthma, or

---

Live Attenuated Influenza Vaccine Contraindications and Precautions

- Immunosuppression from any cause
- Pregnant women*
- Severe (anaphylactic) allergy to egg or other vaccine components
- History of Guillian-Barré syndrome
- Moderate or severe acute illness

*These persons should receive inactivated influenza vaccine

10

Inactivated Influenza Vaccine Adverse Reactions

Local reactions	15%-20%
Fever, malaise	not common
Allergic reactions	rare
Neurological reactions	very rare

systemic anaphylaxis) occur after vaccination with TIV. These reactions probably result from hypersensitivity to a vaccine component. The majority are most likely related to residual egg protein. Although current influenza vaccines contain only a small quantity of egg protein, this protein may induce immediate allergic reactions in persons with severe egg allergy. Persons who have developed hives, had swelling of the lips or tongue, or have experienced acute respiratory distress or collapse after eating eggs should consult a physician for appropriate evaluation to assist in determining whether influenza vaccination may proceed or should be deferred. Persons with documented immunoglobulin E (IgE)-mediated hypersensitivity to eggs—including those who have had occupational asthma or other allergic responses from exposure to egg protein—may also be at increased risk for reactions from influenza vaccines, and similar consultation should be considered. Protocols have been published for influenza vaccination of patients who have egg allergies and medical conditions that place them at increased risk for influenza infection or its complications.

The potential exists for hypersensitivity reactions to any vaccine component. Although exposure to vaccines containing thimerosal can lead to induction of hypersensitivity, most patients do not develop reactions to thimerosal administered as a component of vaccines, even when patch or intradermal tests for thimerosal indicate hypersensitivity. When it has been reported, hypersensitivity to thimerosal has usually consisted of local delayed-type hypersensitivity reactions.

Unlike the 1976 swine influenza vaccine, subsequent inactivated vaccines prepared from other virus strains have not been clearly associated with an increased frequency of Guillain-Barré syndrome (GBS). However, obtaining a precise estimate of a small increase in risk is difficult for a rare condition such as GBS, which has an annual background incidence of only one to two cases per 100,000 adult population. Among persons who received the swine influenza vaccine in 1976, the rate of GBS exceeded the background rate by less than one case per 100,000 vaccinations. Even if GBS were a true adverse reaction in subsequent years, the estimated risk for GBS was much lower than one per 100,000. Further, the risk is substantially less than that for severe influenza or its complications, which could be prevented by vaccination, especially for persons aged 65 years or older and those with a medical indication for influenza vaccine.

Although the incidence of GBS in the general population is very low, persons with a history of GBS have a substantially greater likelihood of subsequently developing GBS than do persons without such a history, irrespective of vaccination. As a result, the likelihood of coincidentally developing GBS

10

after influenza vaccination is expected to be greater among persons with a history of GBS than among persons with no history of GBS. Whether influenza vaccination might be causally associated with this risk for recurrence is not known. It seems prudent for persons known to have developed GBS within 6 weeks of a previous influenza vaccination to avoid subsequent influenza vaccination. For most persons with a history of GBS who are at high risk for severe complications from influenza, the established benefits of influenza vaccination justify yearly vaccination.

LAIV

Among children the most common adverse reactions are runny nose and headaches. However, there have been no significant differences between LAIV and placebo recipients in the proportion with these symptoms. In a clinical trial, children 6–23 months of age had an increased risk of wheezing. An increased risk of wheezing was not reported in older children.

Among healthy adults, a significantly increased rate of cough, runny nose, nasal congestion, sore throat, and chills was reported among vaccine recipients. These symptoms were reported in 10%–40% of vaccine recipients, a rate 3%–10% higher than reported for placebo recipients. There was no increase in the occurrence of fever among vaccine recipients. No serious adverse reactions have been identified in LAIV recipients, either children or adults.

No instances of Guillain-Barré syndrome have been reported among LAIV recipients. However the number of persons vaccinated to date is too small to identify such a rare vaccine adverse reaction.

Few data are available concerning the safety of LAIV among persons at high risk for development of complications of influenza, such as immunosuppressed persons or those with chronic pulmonary or cardiac disease. Until additional data are available, persons at high risk of complications of influenza should not receive LAIV. These persons should continue to receive inactivated influenza vaccine.

Vaccine Storage and Handling

TIV

Inactivated influenza vaccine is generally shipped in an insulated container with coolant packs. Although some brands of TIV vaccine can tolerate room temperature for a few days, CDC recommends that the vaccine be stored at refrigerator temperature (35°–46°F [2°–8°C]). Inactivated influenza vaccine must not be frozen. Opened multidose vials may be used until the expiration date printed on the package if no visible contamination is present.

Live Attenuated Influenza Vaccine Adverse Reactions

- **Children**
  - no significant increase in URI symptoms, fever, or other systemic symptoms
  - significantly increased risk of asthma or reactive airways disease in children 12-59 months of age
- **Adults**
  - significantly increased rate of cough, runny nose, nasal congestion, sore throat, and chills reported among vaccine recipients
  - no increase in the occurrence of fever
- **No serious adverse reactions identified**

10

LAIV

LAIV should be stored at refridgerator temperature (35°– 46° F [2°–8°C]). LAIV inadvertently exposed to freezing temperature should be placed at refrigerator temperature and used as soon as possible.

LAIV is intended for intranasal administration only and should never be administered by injection. LAIV is supplied in a prefilled single-use sprayer containing 0.2 mL of vaccine. Approximately 0.1 mL (i.e., half of the total sprayer contents) is sprayed into the first nostril while the recipient is in the upright position. An attached dose-divider clip is removed from the sprayer to administer the second half of the dose into the other nostril. If the vaccine recipient sneezes after administration, the dose should not be repeated.

Year 2010 Objectives and Coverage Levels

Year 2010 objectives are to increase influenza vaccination levels to 60% or higher among high-risk populations (90% in residents of long-term care facilities) and to reduce epidemic-related pneumonia and influenza-related deaths among persons 65 years of age and older. In 2006–2007, 66% of persons 65 years of age and older reported receiving influenza vaccine in the previous year. Vaccination levels were lower among black and Hispanic persons than among non-Hispanic white persons.

Strategies for Improving Influenza Vaccine Coverage

On average, fewer than 20% of persons in high-risk groups receive influenza vaccine each year. This points to the need for more effective strategies for delivering vaccine to high-risk persons, their healthcare providers, and household contacts. Persons for whom the vaccine is recommended can be identified and immunized in a variety of settings.

In physicians' offices and outpatient clinics, persons who should receive inactivated influenza vaccine should be identified and their charts marked. TIV use should be promoted, encouraged and recommended beginning in October and continuing through the influenza season. Those without regularly scheduled visits should receive reminders.

In nursing homes and other residential long-term care facilities, immunization with TIV should be routinely provided to all residents at one period of time immediately preceding the influenza season; consent should be obtained at the time of admission.

In acute care hospitals and continuing care centers, persons

10

Influenza Vaccine Strategies to Improve Coverage

- Ensure systematic and automatic offering of TIV to high-risk groups
- Educate healthcare providers and patients
- Address concerns about adverse events
- Emphasize physician recommendation

10

for whom vaccine is recommended who are hospitalized from October through March should be vaccinated prior to discharge. In outpatient facilities providing continuing care to high-risk patients (e.g., hemodialysis centers, hospital specialty-care clinics, outpatient rehabilitation programs), all patients should be offered TIV shortly before the onset of the influenza season.

Visiting nurses and others providing home care to high-risk persons should identify high-risk patients and administer TIV in the home, if necessary.

In facilities providing services to persons 50 years of age and older (e.g., retirement communities, recreation centers), inactivated influenza vaccine should be offered to all unvaccinated residents or attendees on site. Education and publicity programs should also be conducted in conjunction with other interventions.

For travelers, indications for influenza vaccine should be reviewed prior to travel and vaccine offered, if appropriate.

Administrators of all of the above facilities and organizations should arrange for influenza vaccine to be offered to all personnel before the influenza season. Additionally, household members of high-risk persons and others with whom they will be in contact should receive written information about why they should receive the vaccine and where to obtain it.

Antiviral Agents for Influenza

In the United States, four antiviral agents are approved for preventing or treating influenza: amantadine, rimantadine, zanamivir, and oseltamivir.

Testing of influenza A isolates from the United States and Canada has demonstrated that many of these viruses are resistant to amantadine and rimantadine. The ACIP recommends that neither amantadine nor rimantadine be used for the treatment or chemoprophylaxis of influenza A in the United States until susceptibility to these antiviral drugs has been re-established.

Zanamivir and oseltamivir are members of a new class of drugs called neuraminidase inhibitors and are active against both influenza type A and type B. Zanamivir is provided as a dry powder that is administered by inhalation. It is approved for treatment of uncomplicated acute influenza A or B in persons 7 years of age and older who have been symptomatic for no more than 48 hours. Oseltamivir is provided as an oral capsule. It is approved for the treatment of uncomplicated influenza A or B in persons 1 year of age and older who have been symptomatic for no more than 48 hours. Zanamivir is approved for prophylaxis of influenza

---

Influenza Antiviral Agents*

- **Amantadine and rimantadine**
  - Not recommended because of documented resistance in U.S. influenza isolates
- **Zanamivir and oseltamivir**
  - neuraminidase inhibitors
  - effective against influenza A and B
  - oseltamivir approved for prophylaxis

*see influenza ACIP statement or CDC influenza website for details

in persons 5 years and older. Oseltamivir is approved for prophylaxis of influenza infection among persons 1 year of age and older.

In 2007-08, a significant increase in the prevalence of oseltamivir resistance was reported among influenza A (H1N1) viruses worldwide. During the 2007-08 influenza season, 10.9% of H1N1 viruses tested in the U.S. were resistant to oseltamivir. During 2008 more than 90% of H1N1 viruses were resistant to oseltamivir. For the 2008-09 influenza season CDC recommends that persons who test positive for influenza A should receive only zanamivir if treatment is indicated. Oseltamivir should be used alone only if recent local surveillance data indicate that circulating viruses are likely to be influenza A (H3N2) or influenza B viruses, which have not been found to be resistant to oseltamivir. Additional information about influenza antiviral treatment is available on the CDC influenza website.

Antiviral agents for influenza are an adjunct to vaccine and are not a substitute for vaccine. Vaccination remains the principal means for preventing influenza-related morbidity and mortality. Additional information on the use of influenza antiviral drugs can be found in the current ACIP statement on influenza vaccine and on the CDC influenza website at http://www.cdc.gov/flu.

Nosocomial Influenza Control

Many patients in general hospitals, and especially in referral centers, are likely to be at high risk for complications of influenza. Hospitalized susceptible patients may acquire influenza from patients, hospital employees, or visitors. The preferred method of control is to administer inactivated influenza vaccine to high-risk patients and medical personnel prior to the outbreak.

During community influenza A activity, the use of antiviral prophylaxis may be considered for high-risk patients who were not immunized or were immunized too recently to have protective antibody levels. Antiviral agents may also be considered for unimmunized hospital personnel. Other measures include restricting visitors with respiratory illness, cohorting patients with influenza for 5 days following onset of illness, and postponing elective admission of patients with uncomplicated illness.

Influenza Surveillance

Influenza surveillance is intended to monitor the prevalence of circulating strains and detect new strains necessary for vaccine formulation; estimate influenza-related impact on morbidity, mortality, and economic loss; rapidly detect outbreaks; and assist disease control through rapid preven-

10

Influenza Surveillance

- Monitor prevalence of circulating strains and detect new strains

- Estimate influenza-related morbidity, mortality and economic loss

- Rapidly detect outbreaks

- Assist disease control through rapid preventive action

tive action (e.g., chemoprophylaxis of unvaccinated high-risk patients).

CDC receives weekly surveillance reports from the states showing the extent of influenza activity. Reports are classified into four categories: no cases, sporadic, regional (cases occurring in counties collectively contributing less than 50% of a state's population), widespread (cases occurring in counties collectively contributing 50% or more of a state's population).

Weekly surveillance reports are available at http://www.cdc.gov/flu/weekly/fluactivity.htm

Selected References

A special issue of *Emerging Infectious Diseases* (January 2006) focused on influenza. The issue is available on the CDC website at http://www.cdc.gov/ncidod/EID/index.htm

Belshe RB, Mendelman PM, Treanor J, et al. Efficacy of live attenuated, cold-adapted trivalent, intranasal influenza virus vaccine in children. *N Engl J Med* 1998;338:1405–12.

Bhat N, Wright JG, Broder KR, et al. Influenza-associated deaths among children in the United States, 2003–2004. *N Engl J Med.* 2005;353:2559–67.

CDC. Notice to readers: expansion of use of live attenuated influenza vaccine (FluMist) to children aged 2–4 years and other FluMist changes for the 2007–08 influenza season. *MMWR* 2007;56(No.46);1217–19.

CDC. Prevention and control of influenza: recommendations of the Advisory Committee on Immunization Practices (ACIP). *MMWR* 2008;57(No. RR-7):1–60. Note: ACIP recommendations for influenza vaccine are revised annually.

CDC. Influenza vaccination of healthcare personnel. Recommendations of the Healthcare Infection Control Practices Advisory Committee (HICPAC) and the Advisory Committee on Immunization Practices (ACIP). *MMWR* 2006; 55(No. RR-2):1–16.

Fedson DS, Houck P, Bratzler D. Hospital-based influenza and pneumococcal vaccination: Sutton's law applied to prevention. *Infect Control Hosp Epidemiol* 2000;21:692–9.

Glezen WP, Couch RB. Influenza viruses. In: Evans AS, Kaslow RA, eds. Viral Infections of Humans. *Epidemiology and Control.* 4th edition. New York, NY: Plenum Medical Book Company; 1997:473–505.

Murphy KR, Strunk RC. Safe administration of influenza vaccine in asthmatic children hypersensitive to egg protein. *J Pediatr* 1985;106:931–3.

Neuzil KM, Zhu Y, Griffin MR, et al. Burden of interpandemic influenza in children younger than 5 years: a 25 year prospective study. *J Infect Dis* 2002;185:147–52.

Nichol KL, Lind A, Margolis KL, et al. The effectiveness of vaccination against influenza in healthy, working adults. *N Engl J Med* 1995;333:889–93.

Saxen H, Virtanen M. Randomized, placebo-controlled double blind study on the efficacy of influenza immunization on absenteeism of healthcare workers. *Pediatr Infect Dis J* 1999;18:779–83.

Thompson WW, Shay DK, Weintraub E, et al. Mortality associated with influenza and respiratory syncytial virus in the United States. *JAMA* 2003;289:179–86

Thompson WW, Shay DK, Weintraub E, et al. Influenza-associated hospitalizations in the United States. *JAMA* 2004;292:1333–40.

10

Influenza

Measles

Measles is an acute viral infectious disease. References to measles can be found from as early as the 7th century. The disease was described by the Persian physician Rhazes in the 10th century as "more dreaded than smallpox."

In 1846, Peter Panum described the incubation period of measles and lifelong immunity after recovery from the disease. Enders and Peebles isolated the virus in human and monkey kidney tissue culture in 1954. The first live attenuated vaccine was licensed for use in the United States in 1963 (Edmonston B strain).

Before a vaccine was available, infection with measles virus was nearly universal during childhood, and more than 90% of persons were immune by age 15 years. Measles is still a common and often fatal disease in developing countries. The World Health Organization estimates there were more than 20 million cases and 242,000 deaths from measles in 2006.

Measles Virus

The measles virus is a paramyxovirus, genus *Morbillivirus*. It is 100–200 nm in diameter, with a core of single-stranded RNA, and is closely related to the rinderpest and canine distemper viruses. Two membrane envelope proteins are important in pathogenesis. They are the F (fusion) protein, which is responsible for fusion of virus and host cell membranes, viral penetration, and hemolysis, and the H (hemagglutinin) protein, which is responsible for adsorption of virus to cells.

There is only one antigenic type of measles virus. Although studies have documented changes in the H glycoprotein, these changes do not appear to be epidemiologically important (i.e., no change in vaccine efficacy has been observed).

Measles virus is rapidly inactivated by heat, light, acidic pH, ether, and trypsin. It has a short survival time (less than 2 hours) in the air or on objects and surfaces.

Pathogenesis

Measles is a systemic infection. The primary site of infection is the respiratory epithelium of the nasopharynx. Two to three days after invasion and replication in the respiratory epithelium and regional lymph nodes, a primary viremia occurs with subsequent infection of the reticuloendothelial system. Following further viral replication in regional and distal reticuloendothelial sites, a second viremia occurs 5–7 days after initial infection. During this viremia, there may be infection of the respiratory tract and other organs. Measles virus is shed from the nasopharynx beginning with the prodrome until 3–4 days after rash onset.

Measles

- Highly contagious viral illness
- First described in 7th century
- Near universal infection of childhood in prevaccination era
- Common and often fatal in developing countries

11

Measles Virus

- Paramyxovirus (RNA)
- Hemagglutinin important surface antigen
- One antigenic type
- Rapidly inactivated by heat and light

Measles Pathogenesis

- Respiratory transmission of virus
- Replication in nasopharynx and regional lymph nodes
- Primary viremia 2-3 days after exposure
- Secondary viremia 5-7 days after exposure with spread to tissues

11

Clinical Features

The incubation period of measles, from exposure to prodrome averages 10–12 days. From exposure to rash onset averages 14 days (range, 7–18 days).

The prodrome lasts 2–4 days (range 1–7 days). It is characterized by fever, which increases in stepwise fashion, often peaking as high as 103°–105°F. This is followed by the onset of cough, coryza (runny nose), or conjunctivitis.

Koplik spots, a rash (enanthem) present on mucous membranes, is considered to be pathognomonic for measles. It occurs 1–2 days before the rash to 1–2 days after the rash, and appears as punctate blue-white spots on the bright red background of the buccal mucosa.

The measles rash is a maculopapular eruption that usually lasts 5–6 days. It begins at the hairline, then involves the face and upper neck. During the next 3 days, the rash gradually proceeds downward and outward, reaching the hands and feet. The maculopapular lesions are generally discrete, but may become confluent, particularly on the upper body. Initially, lesions blanch with fingertip pressure. By 3–4 days, most do not blanch with pressure. Fine desquamation occurs over more severely involved areas. The rash fades in the same order that it appears, from head to extremities.

Other symptoms of measles include anorexia, diarrhea, especially in infants, and generalized lymphadenopathy.

Complications

Approximately 30% of reported measles cases have one or more complications. Complications of measles are more common among children younger than 5 years of age and adults 20 years of age and older.

From 1985 through 1992, diarrhea was reported in 8% of measles cases, making this the most commonly reported complication of measles. Otitis media was reported in 7% of cases and occurs almost exclusively in children. Pneumonia (in 6% of reported cases) may be viral or superimposed bacterial, and is the most common cause of death.

Acute encephalitis occurs in approximately 0.1% of reported cases. Onset generally occurs 6 days after rash onset (range 1–15 days) and is characterized by fever, headache, vomiting, stiff neck, meningeal irritation, drowsiness, convulsions, and coma. Cerebrospinal fluid shows pleocytosis and elevated protein. The case-fatality rate is approximately 15%. Some form of residual neurologic damage occurs in as many as 25% of cases. Seizures (with or without fever) are reported in 0.6%–0.7% of cases.

Death from measles was reported in approximately 0.2% of the cases in the United States from 1985 through 1992. As with other complications of measles, the risk of death is higher among young children and adults. Pneumonia accounts for about 60% of deaths. The most common causes of death are pneumonia in children and acute encephalitis in adults. Since 1995, an average of 1 measles-related death per year has been reported.

Subacute sclerosing panencephalitis (SSPE) is a rare degenerative central nervous system disease believed to be due to persistent measles virus infection of the brain. Onset occurs an average of 7 years after measles (range 1 month–27 years), and occurs in five to ten cases per million reported measles cases. The onset is insidious, with progressive deterioration of behavior and intellect, followed by ataxia (awkwardness), myoclonic seizures, and eventually death. SSPE has been extremely rare since the early 1980s.

Measles illness during pregnancy results in a higher risk of premature labor, spontaneous abortion, and low-birthweight infants. Birth defects (with no definable pattern of malformation) have been reported rarely, without confirmation that measles was the cause.

Atypical measles occurs only in persons who received inactivated ("killed") measles vaccine (KMV) and are subsequently exposed to wild-type measles virus. An estimated 600,000 to 900,000 persons received KMV in the United States from 1963 to 1967. KMV sensitizes the recipient to measles virus antigens without providing protection. Subsequent infection with measles virus leads to signs of hypersensitivity polyserositis. The illness is characterized by fever, pneumonia, pleural effusions, and edema. The rash is usually maculopapular or petechial, but may have urticarial, purpuric, or vesicular components. It appears first on the wrists or ankles. Atypical measles may be prevented by revaccinating with live measles vaccine. Moderate to severe local reactions with or without fever may follow vaccination; these reactions are less severe than with infection with wild measles virus.

Modified measles occurs primarily in patients who received immune globulin (IG) as postexposure prophylaxis and in young infants who have some residual maternal antibody. It is usually characterized by a prolonged incubation period, mild prodrome, and sparse, discrete rash of short duration. Similar mild illness has been reported among previously vaccinated persons.

Rarely reported in the United States, hemorrhagic measles is characterized by high fever (105°–106°F), seizures, delirium, respiratory distress, and hemorrhage into the skin and mucous membranes.

11

Measles in an immunocompromised person may be severe with a prolonged course. It is reported almost exclusively in persons with T-cell deficiencies (certain leukemias, lymphomas, and acquired immunodeficiency syndrome [AIDS]). It may occur without the typical rash, and a patient may shed virus for several weeks after the acute illness.

Measles in developing countries has resulted in high attack rates among children younger than 12 months of age. Measles is more severe in malnourished children, particularly those with vitamin A deficiency. Complications include diarrhea, dehydration, stomatitis, inability to feed, and bacterial infections (skin and elsewhere). The case-fatality rate may be as high as 25%. Measles is also a leading cause of blindness in African children.

11

Measles Laboratory Diagnosis

- Isolation of measles virus from a clinical specimen (e.g., urine, nasopharynx)
- Significant rise in measles IgG by any standard serologic assay (e.g., EIA, HA)
- Positive serologic test for measles IgM antibody

Laboratory Diagnosis

Isolation of measles virus is not recommended as a routine method to diagnose measles. However, virus isolates are extremely important for molecular epidemiologic surveillance to help determine the geographic origin of the virus and the viral strains circulating in the United States.

Measles virus can be isolated from urine, nasopharyngeal aspirates, heparinized blood, or throat swabs. Specimens for virus culture should be obtained from every person with a clinically suspected case of measles and should be shipped to the state public health laboratory or CDC, at the direction of the state health department. Clinical specimens for viral isolation should be collected at the same time as samples taken for serologic testing. Because the virus is more likely to be isolated when the specimens are collected within 3 days of rash onset, collection of specimens for virus isolation should not be delayed until serologic confirmation is obtained. Clinical specimens should be obtained within 7 days, and not more than 10 days, after rash onset. A detailed protocol for collection of specimens for viral isolation is available on the CDC website at http://www.cdc.gov/ ncidod/dvrd/revb/measles/viral_isolation.htm.

Serologic testing, most commonly by enzyme-linked immunoassay (ELISA or EIA), is widely available and may be diagnostic if done at the appropriate time. Generally, a previously susceptible person exposed to either vaccine or wild-type measles virus will first mount an IgM response and then an IgG response. The IgM response will be transient (1–2 months), and the IgG response should persist for many years. Uninfected persons should be IgM negative and will be either IgG negative or IgG positive, depending upon their previous infection history.

ELISA for IgM antibody requires only a single serum specimen and is diagnostic if positive. The preferred reference test is a capture IgM test developed by CDC. This test should be used to confirm every case of measles that is reported to have some other type of laboratory confirmation. IgM capture tests for measles are often positive on the day of rash onset. However, in the first 72 hours after rash onset, up to 20% of tests for IgM may give false-negative results. Tests that are negative in the first 72 hours after rash onset should be repeated. IgM is detectable for at least 28 days after rash onset and frequently longer.

A variety of tests for IgG antibodies to measles are available and include ELISA, hemagglutination inhibition (HI), indirect fluorescent antibody tests, microneutralization, and plaque reduction neutralization. Complement fixation, while widely used in the past, is no longer recommended.

IgG testing for acute measles requires demonstration of a rise in titer of antibody against measles virus, so two serum specimens are always required. The first specimen should be drawn as soon after rash onset as possible. The second specimen should be drawn 10–30 days later. The tests for IgG antibody should be conducted on both specimens at the same time. The same type of test should be used on both specimens. The specific criteria for documenting an increase in titer depend on the test.

Tests for IgG antibody require two serum specimens, and a confirmed diagnosis cannot be made until the second specimen is obtained. As a result, IgM tests are generally preferred to confirm the diagnosis of measles.

Epidemiology

Occurrence

Measles occurs throughout the world. However, interruption of indigenous transmission of measles has been achieved in the United States and other parts of the Western Hemisphere.

Reservoir

Measles is a human disease. There is no known animal reservoir, and an asymptomatic carrier state has not been documented.

Transmission

Measles transmission is primarily person to person via large respiratory droplets. Airborne transmission via aerosolized droplet nuclei has been documented in closed areas (e.g., office examination room) for up to 2 hours after a person with measles occupied the area.

11

Measles Epidemiology

- **Reservoir**   Human

- **Transmission**   Respiratory
  Airborne

- **Temporal pattern**   Peak in late winter–spring

- **Communicability**   4 days before to 4 days after
  rash onset

11

Temporal Pattern

In temperate areas, measles disease occurs primarily in late winter and spring.

Communicability

Measles is highly communicable, with greater than 90% secondary attack rates among susceptible persons. Measles may be transmitted from 4 days before to 4 days after rash onset. Maximum communicability occurs from onset of prodrome through the first 3–4 days of rash.

Secular Trends in the United States

Before 1963, approximately 500,000 cases and 500 deaths were reported annually, with epidemic cycles every 2–3 years. However, the actual number of cases was estimated at 3–4 million annually. More than 50% of persons had measles by age 6, and more than 90% had measles by age 15. The highest incidence was among 5–9-year-olds, who generally accounted for more than 50% of reported cases.

Following licensure of vaccine in 1963, the incidence of measles decreased by more than 98%, and 2–3-year epidemic cycles no longer occurred. Because of this success, a 1978 Measles Elimination Program set a goal to eliminate indigenous measles by October 1, 1982 (26,871 cases were reported in 1978). The 1982 elimination goal was not met, but in 1983, only 1,497 cases were reported (0.6 cases per 100,000 population), the lowest annual total ever reported up to that time.

During 1980–1988, a median of 57% of reported cases were among school-aged persons (5–19 years of age), and a median of 29% were among children younger than 5 years of age. A median of 8% of cases were among infants younger than 1 year of age.

From 1985 through 1988, 42% of cases occurred in persons who were vaccinated on or after their first birthday. During these years, 68% of cases in school-aged children (5–19 years) occurred among those who had been appropriately vaccinated. The occurrence of measles among previously vaccinated children (i.e., vaccine failure) led to the recommendation for a second dose in this age group.

Measles Resurgence in 1989–1991

From 1989 through 1991, a dramatic increase in cases occurred. During these 3 years a total of 55,622 cases were reported (18,193 in 1989; 27,786 in 1990; 9,643 in 1991). In addition to the increased number of cases, a change occurred in their age distribution. Prior to the resurgence, school-aged children had accounted for the largest proportion of

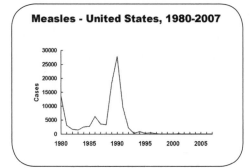

Measles - United States, 1950-2007

Measles - United States, 1980-2007

Measles Resurgence— United States, 1989-1991

- Cases   55,622
- Age group affected   Children <5 yrs
- Deaths   123

reported cases. During the resurgence, 45% of all reported cases were in children younger than 5 years of age. In 1990, 48% of patients were in this age group, the first time that the proportion of cases in children younger than 5 years of age exceeded the proportion of cases in 5–19-year-olds (35%).

Overall incidence rates were highest for Hispanics and blacks and lowest for non-Hispanic whites. Among children younger than 5 years of age, the incidence of measles among blacks and Hispanics was four to seven times higher than among non-Hispanic whites.

A total of 123 measles-associated deaths were reported (death-to-case ratio of 2.2 per 1,000 cases). Forty-nine percent of deaths were among children younger than 5 years of age. Ninety percent of fatal cases occurred among persons with no history of vaccination. Sixty-four deaths were reported in 1990, the largest annual number of deaths from measles since 1971.

The most important cause of the measles resurgence of 1989–1991 was low vaccination coverage. Measles vaccine coverage was low in many cities, including some that experienced large outbreaks among preschool-aged children throughout the early to mid-1980s. Surveys in areas experiencing outbreaks among preschool-aged children indicated that as few as 50% of children had been vaccinated against measles by their second birthday, and that black and Hispanic children were less likely to be age-appropriately vaccinated than were white children.

In addition, measles susceptibility of infants younger than 1 year of age may have increased. During the 1989–1991 measles resurgence, incidence rates for infants were more than twice as high as those in any other age group. The mothers of many infants who developed measles were young, and their measles immunity was most often due to vaccination rather than infection with wild virus. As a result, a smaller amount of antibody was transferred across the placenta to the fetus, compared with antibody transfer from mothers who had higher antibody titers resulting from wild-virus infection. The lower quantity of antibody resulted in immunity that waned more rapidly, making infants susceptible at a younger age than in the past.

The increase in measles in 1989–1991 was not limited to the United States. Large outbreaks of measles were reported by many other countries of North and Central America, including Canada, El Salvador, Guatemala, Honduras, Jamaica, Mexico, and Nicaragua.

11

Measles

Measles 1993-2007

- Endemic transmission interrupted
- Record low annual total in 2004 (37 total cases)
- Many cases among adults
- Most cases imported or linked to importation

Measles Since 1993

Reported cases of measles declined rapidly after the 1989–1991 resurgence. This decline was due primarily to intensive efforts to vaccinate preschool-aged children. Measles vaccination levels among 2-year-old children increased from 70% in 1990 to 91% in 1997.

Since 1993, fewer than 500 cases have been reported annually, and fewer than 200 cases per year have been reported since 1997. A record low annual total of 37 cases was reported in 2004. Available epidemiologic and virologic data indicate that measles transmission in the United States has been interrupted. The majority of cases are now imported from other countries or linked to imported cases. Most imported cases originate in Asia and Europe and occur both among U.S. citizens traveling abroad and persons visiting the United States from other countries. An aggressive measles vaccination program by the Pan American Health Organization has resulted in record low measles incidence in Latin America and the Caribbean, and the interruption of indigenous measles transmission in the Americas. Measles elimination from the Americas was achieved in 2002 and has been sustained since then, with only imported and importation-related measles cases occuring in the region.

Since the mid-1990s, no age group has predominated among reported cases of measles. Relative to earlier decades, an increased proportion of cases now occur among adults. In 1973, persons 20 years of age and older accounted for only about 3% of cases. In 1994, adults accounted for 24% of cases, and in 2001, for 48% of all reported cases.

The size and makeup of measles outbreaks has changed since the 1980s. Prior to 1989, the majority of outbreaks occurred among middle, high school and college student populations. As many as 95% of persons infected during these outbreaks had received one prior dose of measles vaccine. A second dose of measles vaccine was recommended for school-aged children in 1989, and all states now require two doses of measles vaccine for school-aged children. As a result, measles outbreaks in school settings are now uncommon.

In 2008 a provisional total of 132 measles cases was reported, the largest annual total since 1997. Eighty nine percent of these cases were imported from or associated with importations from other countries, particularly countries in Europe where several outbreaks are ongoing. Persons younger than 20 years of age accounted for 76% of the cases; 91% were in persons who were unvaccinated (most because of personal or religious beliefs) or of unknown vaccination status. The increase in the number of cases of measles in 2008 was not a result of a greater number of imported measles cases. It was the result of more measles transmission after the virus was imported. The importation-associated cases occurred largely among school-aged children who were eligible for vaccination but whose parents chose not to have them vaccinated. Many of these children were home-schooled and not subject to school entry vaccination requirements.

Classification of Measles Cases

Clinical Classification of Measles Cases

A suspect case is defined as a febrile illness accompanied by a generalized maculopapular rash.

A probable case meets the measles case definition of generalized maculopapular rash lasting 3 days or longer, with fever (101°F [38.3°C] or higher), which is accompanied by cough, coryza, or conjunctivitis and has no or noncontributory serologic or virologic testing and is not epidemiologically linked to a confirmed case. A confirmed case meets the case definition and is epidemiologically linked to another confirmed or probable case or is laboratory confirmed. A laboratory-confirmed case does not need to meet the clinical case definition.

Only confirmed cases should be reported to CDC, but both confirmed and probable cases should be reported as soon as possible to the local or state health department.

Epidemiologic Classification

An international imported case has its source outside the country, rash onset occurs within 21 days after entering the country, and illness cannot be linked to local transmission.

An indigenous case is any case that cannot be proved to be imported. Subclasses of indigenous cases exist; for more information, see CDC Manual for Surveillance of Vaccine-Preventable Diseases (available on the CDC website at http://www.cdc.gov/pubs/surv-manual/default.htm).

Measles Vaccine

Measles virus was first isolated by John Enders in 1954. The first measles vaccines were licensed in 1963. In that year, both an inactivated ("killed") and a live attenuated vaccine (Edmonston B strain) were licensed for use in the United States. The inactivated vaccine was withdrawn in 1967 because it did not protect against measles virus infection. Furthermore, recipients of inactivated measles vaccine frequently developed a unique syndrome, atypical measles, if they were infected with wild-type measles virus (see Atypical Measles, above). The original Edmonston B vaccine was withdrawn in 1975 because of a relatively high

11

Measles Clinical Case Definition

- Generalized rash lasting 3 days or longer, and
- Temperature 101°F (38.3°C) or higher, and
- Cough or coryza or conjunctivitis

Measles Vaccines

1963	Killed and live attenuated vaccines
1965	Live further attenuated vaccine
1967	Killed vaccine withdrawn
1968	Live further attenuated vaccine (Edmonston-Enders strain)
1971	Licensure of combined measles-mumps-rubella vaccine
1989	Two-dose schedule
2005	Licensure of combined measles-mumps-rubella-varicella vaccine

frequency of fever and rash in recipients. A live, further attenuated vaccine (Schwarz strain) was first introduced in 1965 but also is no longer used in the United States. Another live, further attenuated strain vaccine (Edmonston-Enders strain) was licensed in 1968. These further attenuated vaccines caused fewer reactions than the original Edmonston B vaccine.

Characteristics

The only measles virus vaccine now available in the United States is a live, more attenuated Edmonston-Enders strain (formerly called "Moraten"). The vaccine is available combined with mumps and rubella vaccines as MMR, or combined with mumps, rubella, and varicella vaccine as MMRV (ProQuad). The Advisory Committee on Immunization Practices (ACIP) recommends that MMR be used when any of the individual components is indicated. Use of single-antigen measles vaccine is not recommended.

Measles vaccine is prepared in chick embryo fibroblast tissue culture. MMR and MMRV are supplied as a lyophilized (freeze-dried) powder and are reconstituted with sterile, preservative-free water. The vaccines contain a small amount of human albumin, neomycin, sorbitol, and gelatin.

Immunogenicity and Vaccine Efficacy

Measles vaccine produces an inapparent or mild, noncommunicable infection. Measles antibodies develop in approximately 95% of children vaccinated at 12 months of age and 98% of children vaccinated at 15 months of age. Seroconversion rates are similar for single-antigen measles vaccine, MMR, and MMRV. Approximately 2%–5% of children who receive only one dose of MMR vaccine fail to respond to it (i.e., primary vaccine failure). MMR vaccine failure may occur because of passive antibody in the vaccine recipient, damaged vaccine, incorrect records, or possibly other reasons. Most persons who fail to respond to the first dose will respond to a second dose. Studies indicate that more than 99% of persons who receive two doses of measles vaccine (with the first dose administered no earlier than the first birthday) develop serologic evidence of measles immunity.

Although the titer of vaccine-induced antibodies is lower than that following natural disease, both serologic and epidemiologic evidence indicate that vaccine-induced immunity appears to be long-term and probably lifelong in most persons. Most vaccinated persons who appear to lose antibody show an anamnestic immune response upon revaccination, indicating that they are probably still immune. Although revaccination can increase antibody

11

Measles Vaccine

- Composition   Live virus
- Efficacy   95% (range, 90%-98%)
- Duration of Immunity   Lifelong
- Schedule   2 doses
- Should be administered with mumps and rubella as MMR or with mumps, rubella and varicella as MMRV

MMR Vaccine Failure

- Measles, mumps, or rubella disease (or lack of immunity) in a previously vaccinated person
- 2%-5% of recipients do not respond to the first dose
- Caused by antibody, damaged vaccine, incorrect records
- Most persons with vaccine failure will respond to second dose

titer in some persons, available data indicate that the increased titer may not be sustained. Some studies indicate that secondary vaccine failure (waning immunity) may occur after successful vaccination, but this appears to occur rarely and to play only a minor role in measles transmission and outbreaks.

Vaccination Schedule and Use

Two doses of measles vaccine, as combination MMR, separated by at least 4 weeks, are routinely recommended for all children. All persons born during or after 1957 should have documentation of at least one dose of MMR or other evidence of measles immunity (see below). Certain adolescents and adults should receive two doses of MMR.

The first dose of MMR should be given on or after the first birthday. Any dose of measles-containing vaccine given before 12 months of age should not be counted as part of the series. Children vaccinated with measles-containing vaccine before 12 months of age should be revaccinated with two doses of MMR vaccine, the first of which should be administered when the child is at least 12 months of age.

A second dose of MMR is recommended to produce immunity in those who failed to respond to the first dose. The second dose of MMR vaccine should routinely be given at age 4–6 years, before a child enters kindergarten or first grade. The recommended visit at age 11 or 12 years can serve as a catch-up opportunity to verify vaccination status and administer MMR vaccine to those children who have not yet received two doses of MMR.

The second dose of MMR may be administered as soon as 1 month (i.e., minimum of 28 days) after the first dose. Children who have already received two doses of MMR vaccine at least 4 weeks apart, with the first dose administered no earlier than the first birthday, do not need an additional dose when they enter school. Children without documentation of adequate vaccination against measles, mumps, and rubella or other acceptable evidence of immunity to these diseases when they enter school should be admitted after receipt of the first dose of MMR. A second dose should be administered as soon as possible, but no less than 4 weeks after the first dose.

Only doses of vaccine with written documentation of the date of receipt should be accepted as valid. Self-reported doses or a parental report of vaccination is not considered adequate documentation. A healthcare provider should not provide an immunization record for a patient unless that healthcare provider has administered the vaccine or has seen a record that documents vaccination. Persons who lack adequate documentation of vaccination or other acceptable evidence of immunity should be vaccinated. Vaccination

Measles (MMR) Vaccine Indications

- All children 12 months of age and older
- Susceptible adolescents and adults without documented evidence of immunity

11

Measles-Mumps-Rubella Vaccine

- 12 months is the recommended and minimum age
- MMR given before 12 months should not be counted as a valid dose
- Revaccinate at 12 months of age or older

Second Dose of Measles Vaccine

- Intended to produce measles immunity in persons who failed to respond to the first dose (primary vaccine failure)
- May boost antibody titers in some persons

Second Dose of Measles Vaccine

- First dose of MMR at 12-15 months
- Second dose of MMR at 4-6 years
- Second dose may be given any time at least 4 weeks after the first dose

status and receipt of all vaccinations should be documented in the patient's permanent medical record and in a vaccination record held by the individual.

MMRV is approved by the Food and Drug Administration for children 12 months through 12 years of age (that is, until the 13th birthday). MMRV should not be administered to persons 13 years of age or older.

Vaccination of Adults

Adults born in 1957 or later who do not have a medical contraindication should receive at least one dose of MMR vaccine unless they have documentation of vaccination with at least one dose of measles-, mumps- and rubella-containing vaccine or other acceptable evidence of immunity to these three diseases. With the exception of women who might become pregnant (see Chapter 18, Rubella) and persons who work in medical facilities, birth before 1957 generally can be considered acceptable evidence of immunity to measles, mumps, and rubella.

Certain groups of adults may be at increased risk for exposure to measles and should receive special consideration for vaccination. These include persons attending colleges and other post-high school educational institutions, persons working in medical facilities, and international travelers.

Colleges and other post-high school educational institutions are potential high- risk areas for measles, mumps, and rubella transmission because of large concentrations of susceptible persons. Prematriculation vaccination requirements for measles immunity have been shown to significantly decrease the risk of measles outbreaks on college campuses where they are implemented and enforced. Colleges, universities, technical and vocational schools, and other institutions for post-high school education should require documentation of two doses of MMR vaccine or other acceptable evidence of measles, mumps, and rubella immunity before entry.

Students who have no documentation of live measles, mumps, or rubella vaccination or other acceptable evidence of measles, mumps, and rubella immunity at the time of enrollment should be admitted to classes only after receiving the first dose of MMR. A second dose of MMR should be administered no less than 4 weeks (i.e., minimum of 28 days) later. Students with evidence of prior receipt of only one dose of MMR or other measles-containing vaccine on or after their first birthday should receive a second dose of MMR, provided at least 4 weeks have elapsed since their previous dose.

Persons who work in medical facilities are at higher risk for exposure to measles than the general population. All persons who work within medical facilities should have evidence of immunity to measles, mumps, and rubella. Because any

---

Adults at Increased Risk of Measles

- College students
- International travelers
- Healthcare personnel

11

Measles Immunity in Healthcare Personnel

- All persons who work within medical facilities should have evidence of immunity to measles

healthcare personnel (i.e., medical or nonmedical, paid or volunteer, full time or part time, student or nonstudent, with or without patient-care responsibilities) who is susceptible to measles or rubella can contract and transmit these diseases, all medical facilities (i.e., inpatient and outpatient, private and public) should ensure measles and rubella immunity among those who work within their facilities. (A possible exception might be a facility that treats only elderly patients considered at low risk for measles and rubella and their complications.)

Adequate vaccination for measles, mumps, and rubella for healthcare personnel born during or after 1957 consists of two doses of a live measles- and mumps-containing vaccine and at least one dose of a live rubella-containing vaccine. Healthcare personnel needing a second dose of measles-containing vaccine should be revaccinated at least 4 weeks after their first dose.

Although birth before 1957 is generally considered acceptable evidence of measles, mumps, and rubella immunity, medical facilities should consider recommending a dose of MMR vaccine to unvaccinated personnel born before 1957 who do not have a history of prior measles disease or laboratory evidence of measles immunity, and to those without laboratory evidence of rubella immunity.

Serologic screening need not be done before vaccinating for measles and rubella unless the medical facility considers it cost-effective. Serologic testing is appropriate only if tracking systems are used to ensure that tested persons who are identified as susceptible are subsequently vaccinated in a timely manner. Serologic testing for immunity to measles and rubella is not necessary for persons documented to be appropriately vaccinated or who have other acceptable evidence of immunity. If the return and timely vaccination of those screened cannot be assured, serologic testing before vaccination should not be done.

Persons who travel outside the United States are at increased risk of exposure to measles. Measles is endemic or epidemic in many countries throughout the world. Although proof of immunization is not required for entry into the United States or any other country, persons traveling or living abroad should have evidence of measles immunity. Adequate vaccination of persons who travel outside the United States is two doses of MMR.

Revaccination

Revaccination is recommended for certain persons. The following groups should be considered unvaccinated and should receive at least one dose of measles vaccine: persons 1) vaccinated before the first birthday, 2) vaccinated with killed measles vaccine (KMV), 3) vaccinated with KMV followed by live vaccine less than 4 months after the last

11

Measles Vaccine Indications for Revaccination

- Vaccinated before the first birthday
- Vaccinated with killed measles vaccine
- Vaccinated prior to 1968 with an unknown type of vaccine
- Vaccinated with IG in addition to a further attenuated strain or vaccine of unknown type

dose of KMV, 4) vaccinated before 1968 with an unknown type of vaccine (the vaccine may have been KMV), or 5) vaccinated with IG in addition to a further attenuated strain or vaccine of unknown type. (Revaccination is not necessary if IG was given with Edmonston B vaccine.)

Postexposure Prophylaxis

Live measles vaccine provides permanent protection and may prevent disease if given within 72 hours of exposure. Immune globulin (IG) may prevent or modify disease and provide temporary protection if given within 6 days of exposure. The dose is 0.25 mL/kg body weight, with a maximum of 15 mL intramuscularly. The recommended dose of IG for immunocompromised persons is 0.5mL/kg of body weight (maximum 15 mL) intramuscularly. IG may be especially indicated for susceptible household contacts of measles patients, particularly contacts younger than 1 year of age (for whom the risk of complications is highest). If the child is 12 months of age or older, live measles vaccine should be given about 5 months later when the passive measles antibodies have waned. IG should not be used to control measles outbreaks.

Contraindications and Precautions to Vaccination

Persons who have experienced a severe allergic reaction (anaphylaxis) to a vaccine component or following a prior dose of measles vaccine should generally not be vaccinated with MMR.

In the past, persons with a history of anaphylactic reactions following egg ingestion were considered to be at increased risk for serious reactions after receipt of measles- or mumps-containing vaccines, which are produced in chick embryo fibroblasts. However, data suggest that anaphylactic reactions to measles- and mumps-containing vaccines are not associated with hypersensitivity to egg antigens but to other components of the vaccines (such as gelatin). The risk for serious allergic reactions following receipt of these vaccines by egg-allergic persons is extremely low, and skin-testing with vaccine is not predictive of allergic reaction to vaccination. Therefore, MMR may be administered to egg-allergic children without prior routine skin testing or the use of special protocols.

MMR vaccine does not contain penicillin. A history of penicillin allergy is not a contraindication to vaccination with MMR or any other U.S. vaccine.

Women known to be pregnant should not receive measles vaccine. Pregnancy should be avoided for 4 weeks following MMR vaccine. Close contact with a pregnant

MMR Vaccine Contraindications and Precautions
- Severe allergic reaction to vaccine component or following prior dose
- Pregnancy
- Immunosuppression
- Moderate or severe acute illness
- Recent blood product

Measles and Mumps Vaccines and Egg Allergy
- Measles and mumps viruses grown in chick embryo fibroblast culture
- Studies have demonstrated safety of MMR in egg-allergic children
- Vaccinate without testing

11

woman is NOT a contraindication to MMR vaccination of the contact. Breastfeeding is NOT a contraindication to vaccination of either the woman or the breastfeeding child.

Replication of vaccine viruses can be prolonged in persons who are immunosuppressed or immunodeficient. Severe immunosuppression can be due to a variety of conditions, including congenital immunodeficiency, HIV infection, leukemia, lymphoma, generalized malignancy, or therapy with alkylating agents, antimetabolites, radiation, or large doses of corticosteroids. Evidence based on case reports has linked measles vaccine virus infection to subsequent death in at least six severely immunocompromised persons. For this reason, patients who are severely immunocompromised for any reason should not be given MMR vaccine. Healthy susceptible close contacts of severely immunocompromised persons should be vaccinated.

In general, persons receiving large daily doses of corticosteroids (2 mg/kg or more per day, or 20 mg or more per day of prednisone) for 14 days or more should not receive MMR vaccine because of concern about vaccine safety. MMR and its component vaccines should be avoided for at least 1 month after cessation of high-dose therapy. Persons receiving low-dose or short-course (less than 14 days) therapy, alternate-day treatment, maintenance physiologic doses, or topical, aerosol, intra-articular, bursal, or tendon injections may be vaccinated. Although persons receiving high doses of systemic corticosteroids daily or on alternate days during an interval of less than 14 days generally can receive MMR or its component vaccines immediately after cessation of treatment, some experts prefer waiting until 2 weeks after completion of therapy.

Patients with leukemia in remission who have not received chemotherapy for at least 3 months may receive MMR or its component vaccines.

Measles disease may be severe in persons with HIV infection. Available data indicate that vaccination with MMR has not been associated with severe or unusual adverse reactions in HIV-infected persons without evidence of severe immunosuppression, although antibody responses have been variable. MMR vaccine is recommended for all asymptomatic HIV-infected persons and should be considered for symptomatic persons who are not severely immunosuppressed. Asymptomatic children do not need to be evaluated and tested for HIV infection before MMR or other measles-containing vaccines are administered. A theoretical risk of an increase (probably transient) in HIV viral load following MMR vaccination exists because such an effect has been observed with other vaccines. The clinical significance of such an increase is not known.

11

Measles Vaccine and HIV Infection

- MMR recommended for persons with asymptomatic and mildly symptomatic HIV infection

- NOT recommended for those with evidence of severe immunosuppression

- Prevaccination HIV testing not recommended

MMR and other measles-containing vaccines are not recommended for HIV-infected persons with evidence of severe immunosuppression (see table). MMRV is not approved for and should not be administered to a person known to be infected with HIV.

Persons with moderate or severe acute illness should not be vaccinated until the illness has improved. This precaution

Age-specific CD4+ T-lymphocyte count and percent of total lymphocytes as criteria for severe immunosuppression in HIV-infected persons.

Criteria	age <12 months	age 1-5 years	age 6-12 years	age ≥13 years
Total CD4+ T-lymphocytes	<750 per µL	<500 per µL	<200 per µL	<200 per µL
OR	OR	OR	OR	OR
CD4+ T-lymphocytes (as % of total lymphocytes)	<15%	<15%	<15%	<14%

is intended to prevent complicating the management of an ill patient with a potential vaccine adverse reaction, such as fever. Minor illness (e.g., otitis media, mild upper respiratory infections), concurrent antibiotic therapy, and exposure to or recovery from other illness are not contraindications to measles vaccination.

Receipt of antibody-containing blood products (e.g., immune globulin, whole blood or packed red blood cells, intravenous immune globulin) may interfere with sero-conversion after measles vaccine. The length of time that such passively acquired antibody persists depends on the concentration and quantity of blood product received. For instance, it is recommended that vaccination be delayed for 3 months following receipt of immune globulin for prophy-laxis of hepatitis A; a 7 to 11 month delay is recommended following administration of intravenous immune globulin, depending on the dose. For more information, see Chapter 2, General Recommendations on Immunization, and the table in Appendix A.

Persons who have a history of thrombocytopenic purpura or thrombocytopenia (low platelet count) may be at increased risk for developing clinically significant thrombocytopenia after MMR vaccination. No deaths have been reported as a direct consequence of vaccine-induced thrombocytopenia. The decision to vaccinate with MMR depends on the benefits of immunity to measles, mumps, and rubella and the risks for recurrence or exacerbation of thrombocytopenia after vaccination or during natural infection with measles or rubella. The benefits of immunization are usually greater than the potential risks, and administration of MMR vaccine is justified because of the even greater risk for thrombocytopenia after measles or rubella disease. However, deferring a subsequent dose of MMR vaccine may be prudent if the previous episode of thrombocytopenia occurred within 6 weeks after the previous dose of the vaccine. Serologic evidence of measles immunity in such persons may be sought in lieu of MMR vaccination.

Tuberculin skin testing (TST) is not a prerequisite for vaccination with MMR or other measles-containing vaccine. TST has no effect on the response to MMR vaccination. However, measles vaccine (and possibly mumps, rubella, and varicella vaccines) may transiently suppress the response to TST in a person infected with *Mycobacterium tuberculosis*. If tuberculin skin testing is needed at the same time as administration of measles-containing vaccine, TST and vaccine can be administered at the same visit. Simultaneously administering TST and measles-containing vaccine does not interfere with reading the TST result at 48–72 hours and ensures that the person has received measles vaccine. If the measles-containing vaccine has been administered recently, TST screening should be delayed at least 4 weeks after vaccination. A delay in administering TST will remove the concern of any theoretical suppression of TST reactivity from the vaccine. TST screening can be performed and read before administering the measles-containing vaccine. This option is the least favored because it will delay receipt of the vaccine.

Adverse Reactions Following Vaccination

Adverse reactions following measles vaccine (except allergic reactions) represent replication of measles vaccine virus with subsequent mild illness. These events occur 5 to 12 days postvaccination and only in persons who are susceptible to infection. There is no evidence of increased risk of adverse reactions following MMR vaccination in persons who are already immune to the diseases.

Fever is the most common adverse reaction following MMR vaccination. Although measles, mumps, and rubella vaccines may cause fever after vaccination, the measles component of MMR vaccine is most often associated with this adverse reaction. After MMR vaccination, 5% to 15% of susceptible persons develop a temperature of 103°F (39.4°C) or higher, usually occurring 7 to 12 days after vaccination and generally lasting 1 or 2 days. Most persons with fever are otherwise asymptomatic.

Measles- and rubella-containing vaccines, including MMR, may cause a transient rash. Rashes, usually appearing 7 to 10 days after MMR or measles vaccination, have been reported in approximately 5% of vaccinees.

Rarely, MMR vaccine may cause thrombocytopenia within 2 months after vaccination. Estimates of the frequency of

Tuberculin Skin Testing (TST)* and Measles Vaccine

- Apply TST at same visit as MMR
- Delay TST at least 4 weeks if MMR given first
- Apply TST first and administer MMR when skin test read (least favored option because receipt of MMR is delayed)

*previously called PPD

11

MMR Adverse Reactions

• Fever	5%-15%
• Rash	5%
• Joint symptoms	25%
• Thrombocytopenia	<1/30,000 doses
• Parotitis	rare
• Deafness	rare
• Encephalopathy	<1/1,000,000 doses

clinically apparent thrombocytopenia from Europe are one case per 30,000–40,000 vaccinated susceptible persons, with a temporal clustering of cases occurring 2 to 3 weeks after vaccination. The clinical course of these cases was usually transient and benign, although hemorrhage occurred rarely. The risk for thrombocytopenia during rubella or measles infection is much greater than the risk after vaccination. Based on case reports, the risk for MMR-associated thrombocytopenia may be higher for persons who have previously had immune thrombocytopenic purpura, particularly for those who had thrombocytopenic purpura after an earlier dose of MMR vaccine.

Transient lymphadenopathy sometimes occurs following receipt of MMR or other rubella-containing vaccine, and parotitis has been reported rarely following receipt of MMR or other mumps-containing vaccine.

Arthralgias and other joint symptoms are reported in up to 25% of susceptible adult women given MMR vaccine. This adverse reaction is associated with the rubella component (see Chapter 18, Rubella, for more details). Allergic reactions following the administration of MMR or any of its component vaccines are rare. Most of these reactions are minor and consist of a wheal and flare or urticaria at the injection site. Immediate, anaphylactic reactions to MMR or its component vaccines are extremely rare. Allergic reactions including rash, pruritus, and purpura have been temporally associated with mumps vaccination, but these are uncommon and usually mild and of brief duration.

To date there is no convincing evidence that any vaccine causes autism or autism spectrum disorder. Concern has been raised about a possible relation between MMR vaccine and autism by some parents of children with autism. Symptoms of autism are often noticed by parents during the second year of life, and may follow administration of MMR by weeks or months. Two independent nongovernmental groups, the Institute of Medicine (IOM) and the American Academy of Pediatrics (AAP), have reviewed the evidence regarding a potential link between autism and MMR vaccine. Both groups independently concluded that available evidence does not support an association, and that the United States should continue its current MMR vaccination policy. Additional research on the cause of autism is needed.

Vaccine Storage and Handling

Measles vaccine and MMR must be shipped with refrigerant to maintain a temperature of 50°F (10°C) or less at all times. Vaccine must be refrigerated immediately on arrival and protected from light at all times. The vaccine must be stored at refrigerator temperature (35°–46°F [2°–8°C]), but may be frozen. Diluent may be stored at refrigerator temperature or at room temperature. MMRV must be shipped to maintain a

11

temperature of -4°F (-20°C) or less at all times. MMRV must be stored at an average temperature of 5°F (-15°C) or less at all times.

After reconstitution, measles and MMR vaccines must be stored at refrigerator temperature and protected from light. Reconstituted vaccine should be used immediately. If reconstituted vaccine is not used within 8 hours, it must be discarded. MMRV must be administered within 30 minutes of reconstitution.

Selected References

American Academy of Pediatrics. Measles. In: Pickering L, Baker C, Long S, McMillan J, eds. *Red Book: 2006 Report of the Committee on Infectious Diseases*. 27th ed. Elk Grove Village, IL: American Academy of Pediatrics, 2006:441–52.

Atkinson WL, Orenstein WA, Krugman S. The resurgence of measles in the United States, 1989–1990. *Ann Rev Med* 1992;43:451–63.

Bellini WJ, Rota PA. Genetic diversity of wild-type measles viruses: implications for global measles elimination programs. *Emerg Infect Dis* 1998;4:29–35.

Bellini WJ, Rota JS, Lowe LE, et al. Subacute sclerosing panencephalitis: more cases of this fatal disease are prevented by measles immunization than was previously recognized. *J Infect Dis* 2005;192:1686–93.

CDC. Measles, mumps, and rubella—vaccine use and strategies for elimination of measles, rubella, and congenital rubella syndrome and control of mumps: recommendations of the Advisory Committee on Immunization Practices (ACIP). *MMWR* 1998;47(No. RR-8):1–57.

CDC. Immunization of health-care workers: recommendations of the Advisory Committee on Immunization Practices (ACIP) and the Hospital Infection Control Practices Advisory Committee (HICPAC). *MMWR* 1997;46(No. RR-18):1–42.

Update: Measles — United States, January–July 2008. *MMWR* 2008;57(No.33):893–6.

CDC. Update: global measles control and mortality reduction—worldwide, 1991–2001. *MMWR* 2003;52:471–5.

Gerber JS, Offit PA. Vaccines and autism: a tale of shifting hypotheses. *Clin Infect Dis* 2009;48:456–61.

Halsey NA, Hyman SL, Conference Writing Panel. Measles-mumps-rubella vaccine and autistic spectrum disorder: report from the New Challenges in Childhood Immunizations Conference convened in Oak Brook, IL, June 12–13, 2000. *Pediatrics* 2001;107(5).

11

Institute of Medicine. *Institute of Medicine immunization safety review: vaccines and autism*. Washington DC: National Academy Press, 2004.

Vitek CR, Aduddel, M, Brinton MJ. Increased protection during a measles outbreak of children previously vaccinated with a second dose of measles-mumps-rubella vaccine. *Pediatr Infect Dis J* 1999;18:620–3.

11

Meningococcal Disease

Meningococcal disease is an acute, potentially severe illness caused by the bacterium *Neisseria meningitidis*. Illness believed to be meningococcal disease was first reported in the 16th century. The first definitive description of the disease was by Vieusseux in Switzerland in 1805. The bacterium was first identified in the spinal fluid of patients by Weichselbaum in 1887.

Neisseria meningitidis is a leading cause of bacterial meningitis and sepsis in the United States. It can also cause focal disease, such as pneumonia and arthritis. *N. meningitidis* is also a cause of epidemics of meningitis and bacteremia in sub-Saharan Africa. The World Health Organization has estimated that meningococcal disease was the cause of 171,000 deaths worldwide in 2000.

The first monovalent (group C) polysaccharide vaccine was licensed in the United States in 1974. A quadrivalent polysaccharide vaccine was licensed in 1978. Meningococcal conjugate vaccine has been licensed in United Kingdom since 1999 and has had a major impact on the incidence of type C meningococcal disease. A quadrivalent conjugate vaccine was first licensed in the United States in 2005.

Neisseria meningitidis

N. meningitidis, or meningococcus, is an aerobic, gram-negative diplococcus, closely related to *N. gonorrhoeae*, and to several nonpathogenic *Neisseria* species, such as *N. lactamica*. The organism has both an inner (cytoplasmic) and outer membrane, separated by a cell wall. The outer membrane contains several protein structures that enable the bacteria to interact with the host cells as well as perform other functions.

The outer membrane is surrounded by a polysaccharide capsule that is necessary for pathogenicity because it helps the bacteria resist phagocytosis and complement-mediated lysis. The outer membrane proteins and the capsular polysaccharide make up the main surface antigens of the organism.

Meningococci are classified by using serologic methods based on the structure of the polysaccharide capsule. Thirteen antigenically and chemically distinct polysaccharide capsules have been described. Some strains, often those found to cause asymptomatic nasopharyngeal carriage, are not groupable and do not have a capsule. Almost all invasive disease is caused by one of five serogroups: A, B, C, Y, and W-135. The relative importance of each serogroup depends on geographic location, as well as other factors, such as age. For instance, serogroup A is a major cause of

---

Neisseria meningitidis

- Severe acute bacterial infection
- Cause of meningitis, sepsis, and focal infections
- Epidemic disease in sub-Saharan Africa
- Current polysaccharide vaccine licensed in 1978
- Conjugate vaccine licensed in 2005

12

Neisseria meningitidis

- Aerobic gram-negative bacteria
- At least 13 serogroups based on characteristics of the polysaccharide capsule
- Most invasive disease caused by serogroups A, B, C, Y, and W-135
- Relative importance of serogroups depends on geographic location and other factors (e.g. age)

12

Meningococcal Disease Pathogenesis

- Organism colonizes nasopharynx
- In some persons organism invades bloodstream and causes infection at distant site
- Antecedent URI may be a contributing factor

Neisseria meningitidis Clinical Manifestations*

Bacteremia 43.3%
Pneumonia 6.0%
Arthritis 2.0%
Otitis media 1.0%
Meningitis 47.3%
Epiglottitis 0.3%

*1992-1996 data

Meningococcal Meningitis

- Most common pathologic presentation
- Result of hematogenous dissemination
- Clinical findings
  —fever
  —headache
  —stiff neck

Meningococcemia

- Bloodstream infection
- May occur with or without meningitis
- Clinical findings
  —fever
  —petechial or purpuric rash
  —hypotension
  —multiorgan failure

disease in sub-Saharan Africa but is rarely isolated in the United States.

Meningococci are further classified on the basis of certain outer membrane proteins. Molecular subtyping using specialized laboratory techniques (e.g., pulsed-field gel electrophoresis) can provide useful epidemiologic information.

Pathogenesis

Meningococci are transmitted by droplet aerosol or secretions from the nasopharynx of colonized persons. The bacteria attach to and multiply on the mucosal cells of the nasopharynx. In a small proportion (less than 1%) of colonized persons, the organism penetrates the mucosal cells and enters the bloodstream. The bacteria spread by way of the blood to many organs. In about 50% of bacteremic persons, the organism crosses the blood–brain barrier into the cerebrospinal fluid and causes purulent meningitis. An antecedent upper respiratory infection may be a contributing factor.

Clinical Features

The incubation period of meningococcal disease is 3 to 4 days, with a range of 2 to 10 days.

Meningitis is the most common presentation of invasive meningococcal disease and results from hematogenous dissemination of the organism. Meningeal infection is similar to other forms of acute purulent meningitis, with sudden onset of fever, headache, and stiff neck, often accompanied by other symptoms, such as nausea, vomiting, photophobia (eye sensitivity to light), and altered mental status. Meningococci can be isolated from the blood in up to 75% of persons with meningitis.

Meningococcal sepsis (bloodstream infection or meningococcemia) occurs without meningitis in 5% to 20% of invasive meningococcal infections. This condition is characterized by abrupt onset of fever and a petechial or purpuric rash, often associated with hypotension, shock, acute adrenal hemorrhage, and multiorgan failure.

Less common presentations of meningococcal disease include pneumonia (5% to 15% of cases), arthritis (2%), otitis media (1%), and epiglottitis (less than 1%).

The case-fatality rate of invasive meningococcal disease is 9% to 12%, even with appropriate antibiotic therapy. The fatality rate of meningococcemia is up to 40%. As many as 20% of survivors have permanent sequelae, such as hearing loss, neurologic damage, or loss of a limb.

Risk factors for the development of meningococcal disease include deficiencies in the terminal common complement pathway and functional or anatomic asplenia. Persons with HIV infection are probably at increased risk for meningococcal disease. Certain genetic factors (such as polymorphisms in the genes for mannose-binding lectin and tumor necrosis factor) may also be risk factors.

Family members of an infected person are at increased risk for meningococcal disease. Antecedent upper respiratory tract infection, household crowding, and both active and passive smoking also are also associated with increased risk. In the United States, African Americans and persons of low socioeconomic status have been consistently at higher risk; however, race and low socioeconomic status are likely markers for differences in factors such as household crowding rather than risk factors. During outbreaks, bar or nightclub patronage and alcohol use have also been associated with higher risk for disease.

Cases of invasive meningococcal disease, including at least two fatal cases, have been reported among microbiologists. These persons have worked with *N. meningitidis* isolates rather than patient specimens.

Studies have shown that college freshmen living in dormitories are at modestly increased risk of meningococcal disease. However, U.S. college students are not at higher risk for meningococcal disease than other persons of similar age.

Laboratory Diagnosis

Invasive meningococcal disease is typically diagnosed by isolation of *N. meningitidis* from a normally sterile site. However, sensitivity of bacterial culture may be low, particularly when performed after initiation of antibiotic therapy. A Gram stain of cerebrospinal fluid showing gram-negative diplococci strongly suggests meningococcal meningitis.

Kits to detect polysaccharide antigen in cerebrospinal fluid are rapid and specific, but false-negative results are common, particularly in serogroup B disease. Antigen tests of urine or serum are unreliable.

Serologic testing (e.g., enzyme immunoassay) for antibodies to polysaccharide may be used as part of the evaluation if meningococcal disease is suspected but should not be used to establish the diagnosis.

Medical Management

The clinical presentation of meningococcal meningitis is similar to other forms of bacterial meningitis. Consequently, empiric therapy with broad-spectrum antibiotics (e.g., third-generation cephalosporin, vancomycin) should be started promptly after appropriate cultures have been obtained.

Neisseria meningitidis
Risk Factors for Invasive Disease

- Host factors
  - terminal complement pathway deficiency
  - asplenia
  - genetic risk factors
- Exposure factors
  - household exposure
  - concurrent upper respiratory tract infection
  - demographic and socioeconomic factors and crowding
  - active and passive smoking

12

Meningococcal Disease Among Young Adults, United States, 1998-1999

•18-23 years old	1.4 /100,000
•18-23 years old not college student	1.4 /100,000
•Freshmen	1.9 /100,000
•Freshmen in dorm	5.1 /100,000

Bruce et al, *JAMA* 2001;286:688-93

Meningococcal Disease
Laboratory Diagnosis

- Bacterial culture
- Gram stain
- Non-culture methods
  - antigen detection in CSF
  - serology

Neisseria meningitidis
Medical Management

- Initial empiric antibiotic treatment after appropriate cultures are obtained
- Treatment with penicillin alone recommended after confirmation of *N. meningitidis*

Many antibiotics are effective for *N. meningitidis* infection, including penicillin. Few penicillin-resistant strains of meningococcus have been reported in the United States. Once *N. meningitidis* infection has been confirmed, penicillin alone is recommended.

Epidemiology

Occurrence

Meningococcal disease occurs worldwide in both endemic and epidemic form.

Reservoir

Humans are the only natural reservoir of meningococcus. As many as 10% of adolescents and adults are asymptomatic transient carriers of *N. meningitidis*, most strains of which are not pathogenic (i.e., strains that are not groupable).

Transmission

Primary mode is by respiratory droplet spread or by direct contact.

Temporal Pattern

Meningococcal disease occurs throughout the year, However, the incidence is highest in the late winter and early spring.

Communicability

The communicability of *N. meningitidis* is generally limited. In studies of households in which a case of meningococcal disease has occurred, only 3%–4% of households had secondary cases. Most households had only one secondary case. Estimates of the risk of secondary transmission are generally 2–4 cases per 1,000 household members at risk. However, this risk is 500–800 times that in the general population.

Secular Trends in the United States

Approximately 1,000 to 3,000 cases of meningococcal disease are reported each year in the United States (0.4–1.3 cases per 100,000 population). In 2004, an estimated 125 deaths due to meningococcal disease occurred in the United States. Infants younger than 12 months of age have the highest rates of disease. Incidence of disease declines in early childhood, increases during adolescence and early adulthood, then declines among older adults. The rate of invasive disease among persons 17–20 years of age is approximately twice that of the overall U.S. population. Although incidence is relatively low, more cases occur in

Meningococcal Disease Epidemiology

- Reservoir — Human
- Transmission — Respiratory droplets
- Temporal pattern — Peaks in late winter and early spring
- Communicability — Generally limited

12

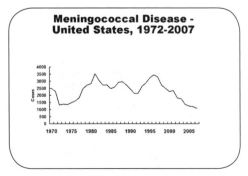

Meningococcal Disease - United States, 1972-2007

persons 23–64 years of age than in any other age group. The proportion of cases among adolescents and young adults has increased in recent years. During 1992–1998, 28% of reported case-patients were 12–29 years of age.

The proportion of disease caused by different serogroups has changed during the last 15 years. From 1988 to 1991, most cases of meningococcal disease in the United States were due to either serogroup C or B, and serogroup Y accounted for only 2% of cases. However, during 1996–2001, serogroup Y accounted for 21% of cases, with serogroups B and C accounting for 31% and 42%, respectively. Nongroupable strains accounted for 5% of cases. The proportion of cases caused by each serogroup also varies by age group. In 2001, 65% of cases among infants aged less than 1 year were caused by serogroup B, for which no vaccine is available in the United States. Among persons 18–34 years of age, 41% of cases were due to serogroup B, and 25% and 14% were due to serogroups C and Y, respectively.

In the United States, meningococcal outbreaks account for less than 5% of reported cases (95%–97% of cases are sporadic). However, since 1991, the frequency of localized outbreaks has increased. Most of these outbreaks have been caused by serogroup C. Since 1997, localized outbreaks caused by serogroups Y and B have also been reported. See http://www.cdc.gov/mmwr/PDF/rr/rr4605.pdf for additional information on the evaluation and management of meningococcal outbreaks.

Large outbreaks of serogroup A meningococcal disease occur in the African "meningitis belt," an area that extends from Ethiopia to Senegal. Rates of endemic meningococcal disease in this area are several times higher than in industrialized countries. In addition, outbreaks occur every 8–12 years with attack rates of 500–1000 cases per 100,000 population.

Meningococcal Vaccines

Characteristics

Meningococcal Polysaccharide Vaccine (MPSV4)
The first meningococcal polysaccharide vaccine was licensed in the United States in 1974. The current quadrivalent A, C, Y, W-135 polysaccharide vaccine (Menomune, sanofi pasteur) was licensed in 1978. Each dose consists of 50 mcg of each of the four purified bacterial capsular polysaccharides. The vaccine contains lactose as a stabilizer.

MPSV4 is administered by subcutaneous injection. The vaccine is available in single-dose and 10-dose vials. Fifty-dose vials are no longer available. Diluent for the

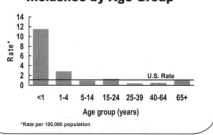

Meningococcal Disease, 1998 Incidence by Age Group

*Rate per 100,000 population

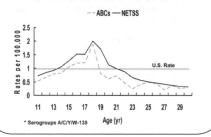

Rates of Meningococcal Disease* by Age, United States, 1991-2002

* Serogroups A/C/Y/W-135

Meningococcal Disease in the United States

- Distribution of cases by serogroup varies by time and age group
- In 1996-2001:
  - 21% serogroup Y
  - 31% serogroup B
  - 42% serogroup C
  - 65% of cases among children <1 year of age due to serogroup B

Meningococcal Outbreaks in the United States

- Outbreaks account for <5% of reported cases
- Frequency of localized outbreaks has increased since 1991
- Most recent outbreaks caused by serogroup C
- Since 1997 outbreaks caused by serogroup Y and B organisms have also been reported

Meningococcal Polysaccharide Vaccine (MPSV4)

- Menomune (sanofi pasteur)
- Quadrivalent polysaccharide vaccine (A, C, Y, W-135)
- Administered by subcutaneous injection
- 10-dose vial contains thimerosal as a preservative

12

single-dose vial is sterile water without preservative. Diluent for the 10-dose vial is sterile water with thimerosal added as a preservative. After reconstitution the vaccine is a clear colorless liquid.

No vaccine is available in the United States for serogroup B.

Meningococcal Conjugate Vaccine (MCV44)

Meningococcal conjugate vaccine (Menactra, sanofi pasteur) was first licensed in the United States in 2005. The vaccine contains *N. meningitidis* serogroups A, C, Y and W-135 capsular polysaccharide antigens individually conjugated to diphtheria toxoid protein. Each 0.5-mL dose of vaccine is formulated in sodium phosphate buffered isotonic sodium chloride solution to contain 4 mcg each of meningococcal A, C, Y, and W-135 polysaccharides conjugated to approximately 48 mcg of diphtheria toxoid protein carrier.

MCV4 is administered by intramuscular injection. It is supplied as a liquid in a single-dose vial. The vaccine does not contain a preservative.

Immunogenicity and Vaccine Efficacy

Meningococcal Polysaccharide Vaccine

The characteristics of MPSV4 are similar to other polysaccharide vaccines (e.g., pneumococcal polysaccharide). The vaccine is generally not effective in children younger than 18 months of age. The response to the vaccine is typical of a T-cell independent antigen, with an age-dependent response, and poor immunogenicity in children younger than 2 years of age. In addition, little boost in antibody titer occurs with repeated doses; the antibody which is produced is relatively low-affinity IgM, and "switching" from IgM to IgG production is poor.

A protective level of antibody is usually achieved within 7–10 days of vaccination. Among infants and children younger than 5 years of age, the level of antibody against serogroup A and C polysaccharide decreases substantially during the first 3 years following a single dose of vaccine. In healthy adults, antibody levels also decrease, but antibodies are detectable as long as 10 years after vaccination. Although vaccine-induced protection likely persists in school-aged children and adults for at least 3 years, the efficacy of the group A vaccine in children younger than 5 years of age may decrease markedly within this period. In one study, efficacy declined from more than 90% to less than 10% 3 years after vaccination among children who were younger than 4 years of age when vaccinated. Efficacy was 67% among children who were older than 4 years of age at vaccination.

Meningococcal Conjugate Vaccine (MCV4)

- Menactra® (sanofi pasteur)
- Quadrivalent polysaccharide vaccine (A, C, Y, W-135) conjugated to diphtheria toxoid
- Administered by intramuscular injection
- Single-dose vials do not contain a preservative

12

Meningococcal Conjugate Vaccine

The approval of MCV4 was based on studies that compared the serologic response to a single dose to the response of persons of similar age who received a single dose of meningococcal polysaccharide vaccine. In these studies a similar proportion of recipients achieved at least a fourfold rise in serum bactericidal antibody titer assay following MCV4 as those who received MPSV4. The proportion of recipients in each group that achieved a titer of 1:128 (the titer considered to predict protection) was more than 98% in both groups.

Because the polysaccharides are conjugated to diphtheria toxoid for MCV4, it is believed that this vaccine will have a longer duration of protection than for MPSV4. In addition, MCV4 is expected to reduce asymptomatic carriage of *N. meningiditis* and produce "herd" immunity, as occurs for *Streptococcus pneumoniae* and *Haemophilus influenzae* type b following receipt of the respective conjugate vaccines. Pure polysaccharide vaccines have little or no effect on carriage of the vaccine organism.

Vaccination Schedule And Use

Meningococcal Polysaccharide Vaccine

For children 2 years of age and older and adults, MPSV4 is administered as a single 0.5-mL dose. The vaccine can be administered at the same time as other vaccines but should be given at a different anatomic site.

Routine vaccination of civilians with MPSV4 is not recommended because of its relative ineffectiveness in children younger than 2 years of age (the age group with the highest risk for sporadic disease) and because of its relatively short duration of protection. Use of MPSV4 should be limited to persons older than 55 years of age, or when MCV4 is not available.

Meningococcal Conjugate Vaccine

MCV4 is recommended for all children at 11 or 12 years of age. It is also recommended for all children 13 through 18 years of age who have not been previously vaccinated. Unvaccinated college freshmen who live in a dormitory should be vaccinated. Persons 2 through 55 years of age at increased risk of meningococcal disease should be vaccinated.

MCV4 is preferred for routine vaccination of adolescents and persons 2 through 55 years of age who are at increased risk of meningococcal disease. MPSV4 is an acceptable alternative for persons 2 through 55 years of age if MCV4 is not available.

Meningococcal vaccination is recommended for persons

12

Meningococcal Vaccine Recommendations

- Recommended for persons at increased risk of meningococcal disease:
  - microbiologists who are routinely exposed to isolates of *N. meningitidis*
  - military recruits
  - persons who travel to and U.S. citizens who reside in countries in which *N. meningitidis* is hyperendemic or epidemic
  - terminal complement component deficiency
  - functional or anatomic asplenia

  MMWR 2005; 54(RR-7);1-21

Meningococcal Endemic Areas 2004

Meningitis Belt, 2004
Areas Outside the Meningitis Belt With Epidemics of Meningococcal Meningitis, 2000-2004

Meningococcal Vaccine Recommendations

- Both MCV4 and MPSV4 recommended for control of outbreaks caused by vaccine-preventable serogroups
- Outbreak definition:
  - 3 or more confirmed or probable primary cases
  - period ≤3 months
  - primary attack rate ≥10 cases per 100,000 population*

*Population-based rates should be used rather than age-specific attack rates

at increased risk for meningococcal disease, including microbiologists who are routinely exposed to isolates of *N. meningitidis*, military recruits, persons who travel to and U.S. citizens who reside in countries in which *N. meningitidis* is hyperendemic or epidemic, persons with terminal complement component deficiency, and persons with functional or anatomic asplenia.

For travelers, vaccination is especially recommended for those visiting countries in the sub-Saharan Africa "meningitis belt" (Ethiopia in the east to Senegal in the west). Epidemics in the meningitis belt usually occur during the dry season (i.e., from December to June). Vaccination is recommended for travelers visiting the region during this time. Vaccination is required by the government of Saudi Arabia for all travelers to Mecca during the annual Hajj. Information concerning geographic areas for which vaccination is recommended can be obtained from the CDC Travelers Health website at http://www.cdc.gov/travel.

MCV4 can be administered at the same visit as other indicated vaccines. All vaccines should be given at separate sites with separate syringes.

Both MCV4 and MPSV4 are recommended for use in control of meningococcal outbreaks caused by vaccine-preventable serogroups (A, C, Y, and W-135). An outbreak is defined by the occurrence of at least three confirmed or probable primary cases of serogroup C meningococcal disease during a period of 3 months or less, with a resulting primary attack rate of 10 or more cases per 100,000 population. For calculation of this threshold, population-based rates are used, and not age-specific attack rates, as have been calculated for college students. These recommendations are based on experience with serogroup C meningococcal outbreaks, but these principles may be applicable to outbreaks caused by the other vaccine-preventable meningococcal serogroups.

Revaccination

Revaccination may be indicated for persons previously vaccinated with MPSV4 who remain at increased risk for infection (e.g., persons residing in areas in which disease is epidemic), particularly for children who were first vaccinated when they were younger than 4 years of age. Such children should be considered for revaccination after 3 years if they remain at high risk. Although the need for revaccination of older children and adults after receiving MPSV4 has not been determined, antibody levels rapidly decline in 2–3 years, and if indications still exist for vaccination, revaccination may be considered 5 years after receipt of the first dose. MCV4 is recommended for revaccination of persons 2 through 55 years of age. However, use of MPSV4 is acceptable.

12

The Advisory Committee on Immunization Practices (ACIP) expects that MCV4 will provide longer protection than MPSV4. However, studies are needed to confirm this assumption. More data will likely become available within the next 5 years to guide recommendations on revaccination for persons who were previously vaccinated with MCV4. At the present time, revaccination after receipt of MCV4 is not recommended.

Contraindications and Precautions to Vaccination

For both MCV4 and MPSV4, a severe allergic (anaphylactic) reaction to a vaccine component or following a prior dose of either vaccine is a contraindication to receipt of further doses. A moderate or severe acute illness is reason to defer routine vaccination, but a minor illness is not. Breastfeeding and immunosuppression are not contraindications to vaccination. Studies of vaccination with MPSV4 during pregnancy have not documented adverse effects among either pregnant women or newborns. No data are available on the safety of MCV4 during pregnancy. However, pregnancy is not considered to be a contraindication to either MPSV4 or MCV4.

Adverse Reactions Following Vaccination

Meningococcal Polysaccharide Vaccine

Adverse reactions to MPSV4 are generally mild. The most frequent are local reactions, such as pain and redness at the injection site. These reactions last for 1 or 2 days, and occur in up to 48% of recipients. Fever (100°–103°F) within 7 days of vaccination is reported for up to 3% of recipients. Systemic reactions, such as headache and malaise, within 7 days of vaccination are reported for up to 60% of recipients. Fewer than 3% of recipients reported these systemic reactions as severe.

Meningococcal Conjugate Vaccine

Reported adverse reactions following MCV4 are similar to those reported after MPSV4. The most frequent are local reactions, which are reported in up to 59% of recipients. Fever (100°–103°F) within 7 days of vaccination is reported for up to 5% of recipients. Systemic reactions, such as headache and malaise are reported in up to 60% of recipients with 7 days of vaccination. Less than 3% of recipients reported these systemic reactions as severe.

As of December 31, 2008 the Vaccine Adverse Event Reporting System (VAERS) received 33 confirmed case reports of Guillain-Barré syndrome (GBS) after receipt of MCV4.

**Meningococcal Vaccines
Contraindications and Precautions**

- Severe allergic reaction to vaccine component or following a prior dose of vaccine
- Moderate or severe acute illness

12

**Meningococcal Vaccines
Adverse Reactions**

	MCV4	MPSV4
• Local reactions for 1-2 days	4%-48%	11%-59%
• Fever ≥100°F	3%	5%
• Systemic reactions (headache, malaise fatigue)	3%-60%	4%-62%

Symptom onset occurred 2 to 33 days after vaccination. Data are not sufficient to determine at this time if MCV4 increases the risk of GBS in persons who receive the vaccine. GBS is a rare illness, and the expected background population rates of GBS are not precisely known. Because ongoing known risk for serious meningococcal disease exists, CDC recommends continuation of current vaccination strategies. Whether receipt of MCV4 vaccine might increase the risk for recurrence of GBS is unknown. Until this issue is clarified, persons with a history of GBS who are not in a high-risk group for invasive meningococcal disease should not receive MCV4.

All severe adverse events that occur after receipt of any vaccine should be reported to VAERS. For information on reporting, see the VAERS website at http://www.vaers.hhs.gov.

Vaccine Storage and Handling

Both MPSV4 and MCV4 should be shipped in insulated containers to prevent exposure to freezing temperature. Vaccine should be stored at refrigerator temperature (35°–46° F, [2°–8° C]). The vaccines must not be exposed to freezing temperature, and any vaccine exposed to freezing temperature should not be used.

Single-dose vials of MPSV4 must be used within 30 minutes of reconstitution, and multidose vials must be discarded 10 days after reconstitution. MCV4 should not be drawn into a syringe until immediately before use.

Surveillance and Reporting of Meningococcal Disease

Invasive meningococcal disease is a reportable condition in most states. All healthcare personnel should report any case of invasive meningococcal disease to local and state health departments.

Antimicrobial Chemoprophylaxis

In the United States, the primary means for prevention of sporadic meningococcal disease is antimicrobial chemoprophylaxis of close contacts of infected persons. Close contacts include household members, child care center contacts, and anyone directly exposed to the patient's oral secretions (e.g., through kissing, mouth-to-mouth resuscitation, endotracheal intubation, or endotracheal tube management).

For travelers, antimicrobial chemoprophylaxis should be considered for any passenger who had direct contact with respiratory secretions from an index patient or for anyone seated directly next to an index patient on a prolonged flight (i.e., one lasting more than 8 hours). The attack rate for household contacts exposed to patients who have sporadic

12

meningococcal disease was estimated to be four cases per 1,000 persons exposed, which is 500–800 times greater than the rate for the total population. In the United Kingdom, the attack rate among healthcare personnel exposed to patients with meningococcal disease was determined to be 25 times higher than among the general population.

Because the rate of secondary disease for close contacts is highest immediately after onset of disease in the index patient, antimicrobial chemoprophylaxis should be administered as soon as possible, ideally less than 24 hours after identification of the index patient. Conversely, chemoprophylaxis administered more than 14 days after onset of illness in the index patient is probably of limited or no value. Oropharyngeal or nasopharyngeal cultures are not helpful in determining the need for chemoprophylaxis and might unnecessarily delay institution of this preventive measure.

Rifampin, ciprofloxacin, and ceftriaxone are 90%–95% effective in reducing nasopharyngeal carriage of *N. meningitidis* and are all acceptable antimicrobial agents for chemoprophylaxis. Systemic antimicrobial therapy for meningococcal disease with agents other than ceftriaxone or other third-generation cephalosporins might not reliably eradicate nasopharyngeal carriage of *N. meningitidis*. If other agents have been used for treatment, the index patient should receive chemoprophylactic antibiotics for eradication of nasopharyngeal carriage before being discharged from the hospital.

12

Selected References

CDC. Active Bacterial Core surveillance (ABCs) 2005 provisional meningococcal surveillance report. Available at http://www.cdc.gov/ncidod/dbmd/abcs/survreports/mening05prelim.htm.

CDC. Prevention and control of meningococcal disease: recommendations of the Advisory Committee on Immunization Practices (ACIP). *MMWR* 2005;54(No. RR-7):1–21.

CDC. Recommendation fom the Advisory Committee on Immunization Practices (ACIP) for use of quadrivalent meningococcal vaccine (MCV44) in children aged 2–10 years at increased risk for invasive meningococcal disease. *MMWR* 2007;56(48):1265–6.

CDC. Update: Guillain-Barré Syndrome among recipients of Menactra® meningococcal conjugate vaccine—United States, June 2005–September 2006. *MMWR* 2006;55:1120–4.

Granoff DM, Harrison L, Borrow R. Meningococcal vaccine. In: Plotkin SA, Orenstein WA, Offit PA, eds. *Vaccines*. 5th ed.

Philadelphia, PA: Saunders; 2008: 399–434.

Harrison LH, Pass MA, Mendelsohn AB, et al. Invasive meningococcal disease in adolescents and young adults. *JAMA* 2001;286:694–9.

Jodar L, Feavers IM, Salisbury D, Granoff DM. Development of vaccines against meningococcal disease. *Lancet* 2002;359(9316):1499–1508.

Rosenstein NE, Perkins BA, Stephens DS, et al. Meningococcal disease. *N Engl J Med* 2001;344:1378–88.

Shepard CW, Ortega-Sanchez IR, Scott RD, Rosenstein NE; ABCs Team. Cost-effectiveness of conjugate meningococcal vaccination strategies in the United States. *Pediatrics* 2005;115:1220–32.

Sejvar JJ, Johnson D, Popovic T, et al. Assessing the risk of laboratory-acquired meningococcal disease. *J Clin Microbiolol* 2005;43:4811–4.

12

Mumps

Mumps is an acute viral illness. Parotitis and orchitis were described by Hippocrates in the 5th century BCE. In 1934, Johnson and Goodpasture showed that mumps could be transmitted from infected patients to rhesus monkeys and demonstrated that mumps was caused by a filterable agent present in saliva. This agent was later shown to be a virus. Mumps was a frequent cause of outbreaks among military personnel in the prevaccine era, and was one of the most common causes of aseptic meningitis and sensorineural deafness in childhood. During World War I, only influenza and gonorrhea were more common causes of hospitalization among soldiers. A multistate mumps outbreak in 2006 resulted in more than 6,000 reported cases.

Mumps Virus

Mumps virus is a paramyxovirus in the same group as parainfluenza and Newcastle disease virus. Parainfluenza and Newcastle disease viruses produce antibodies that cross-react with mumps virus. The virus has a single-stranded RNA genome.

The virus can be isolated or propagated in cultures of various human and monkey tissues and in embryonated eggs. It has been recovered from the saliva, cerebrospinal fluid, urine, blood, milk, and infected tissues of patients with mumps.

Mumps virus is rapidly inactivated by formalin, ether, chloroform, heat, and ultraviolet light.

Pathogenesis

The virus is acquired by respiratory droplets. It replicates in the nasopharynx and regional lymph nodes. After 12 to 25 days a viremia occurs, which lasts from 3 to 5 days. During the viremia, the virus spreads to multiple tissues, including the meninges, and glands such as the salivary, pancreas, testes, and ovaries. Inflammation in infected tissues leads to characteristic symptoms of parotitis and aseptic meningitis.

Clinical Features

The incubation period of mumps is 14 to 18 days (range, 14 to 25 days). The prodromal symptoms are nonspecific, and include myalgia, anorexia, malaise, headache, and low-grade fever.

Parotitis is the most common manifestation and occurs in 30% to 40% of infected persons. Parotitis may be unilateral or bilateral, and any combination of single or multiple salivary glands may be affected. Parotitis tends to occur within the first 2 days and may first be noted as earache and tenderness on palpation of the angle of the jaw. Symptoms tend to decrease after 1 week and usually resolve after 10 days.

Mumps

- Acute viral illness
- Parotitis and orchitis described by Hippocrates in 5th century BCE
- Viral etiology described by Johnson and Goodpasture in 1934
- Frequent cause of outbreaks among military personnel in prevaccine era

Mumps Virus

- Paramyxovirus
- RNA virus
- One antigenic type
- Rapidly inactivated by chemical agents, heat, and ultraviolet light

13

Mumps Pathogenesis

- Respiratory transmission of virus
- Replication in nasopharynx and regional lymph nodes
- Viremia 12-25 days after exposure with spread to tissues
- Multiple tissues infected during viremia

Mumps Clinical Features

- Incubation period 14-18 days
- Nonspecific prodrome of myalgia, malaise, headache, low-grade fever
- Parotitis in 30%-40%
- Up to 20% of infections asymptomatic

Mumps

As many as 20% of mumps infections are asymptomatic. An additional 40% to 50% may have only nonspecific or primarily respiratory symptoms.

Complications

Central nervous system (CNS) involvement in the form of aseptic meningitis (inflammatory cells in cerebrospinal fluid) is common, occurring asymptomatically in 50% to 60% of patients. Symptomatic meningitis (headache, stiff neck) occurs in up to 15% of patients and resolves without sequelae in 3 to 10 days. Adults are at higher risk for this complication than are children, and boys are more commonly affected than girls (3:1 ratio). Parotitis may be absent in as many as 50% of such patients. Encephalitis is rare (less than 2 per 100,000 mumps cases).

Orchitis (testicular inflammation) is the most common complication in postpubertal males. It occurs in as many as 50% of postpubertal males, usually after parotitis, but it may precede it, begin simultaneously, or occur alone. It is bilateral in approximately 30% of affected males. There is usually abrupt onset of testicular swelling, tenderness, nausea, vomiting, and fever. Pain and swelling may subside in 1 week, but tenderness may last for weeks. Approximately 50% of patients with orchitis have some degree of testicular atrophy, but sterility is rare.

Oophoritis (ovarian inflammation) occurs in 5% of postpubertal females. It may mimic appendicitis. There is no relationship to impaired fertility.

Pancreatitis is infrequent, but occasionally occurs without parotitis; the hyperglycemia is transient and is reversible. Although single instances of diabetes mellitus have been reported, a causal relationship with mumps virus infection has yet to be conclusively demonstrated; many cases of temporal association have been described both in siblings and individuals, and outbreaks of diabetes have been reported a few months or years after outbreaks of mumps.

Deafness caused by mumps virus occurs in approximately 1 per 20,000 reported cases. Hearing loss is unilateral in approximately 80% of cases and may be associated with vestibular reactions. Onset is usually sudden and results in permanent hearing impairment.

Electrocardiogram changes compatible with myocarditis are seen in 3%–15% of patients with mumps, but symptomatic involvement is rare. Complete recovery is the rule, but deaths have been reported.

Other less common complications of mumps include arthralgia, arthritis, and nephritis. An average of one death from mumps per year was reported during 1980–1999.

Mumps Complications

CNS involvement	15% of clinical cases
Orchitis	20%-50% in post-pubertal males
Pancreatitis	2%-5%
Deafness	1/20,000
Death	Average 1 per year (1980 – 1999)

Laboratory Diagnosis

The diagnosis of mumps is usually suspected based on clinical manifestations, in particular the presence of parotitis.

Mumps virus can be isolated from clinical specimens. The preferred sample for viral isolation is a swab from the parotid duct, or the duct of another affected salivary gland. Collection of viral samples from persons suspected of having mumps is strongly recommended. Mumps virus can also be detected by polymerase chain reaction (PCR).

Serology is the simplest method for confirming mumps virus infection and enzyme immunoassay (EIA), is the most commonly used test. EIA is widely available and is more sensitive than other serologic tests. It is available for both IgM and IgG. IgM antibodies usually become detectable during the first few days of illness and reach a peak about a week after onset. However, as with measles and rubella, mumps IgM may be transient or missing in persons who have had any doses of mumps-containing vaccine. Sera should be collected as soon as possible after symptom onset for IgM testing or as the acute-phase specimen for IgG seroconversion. Convalescent-phase sera should be collected 2 weeks later. A negative serologic test, especially in a vaccinated person, should not be used to rule out a mumps diagnosis because the tests are not sensitive enough to detect infection in all persons with clinical illness. In the absence of another diagnosis, a person meeting the clinical case definition should be reported as a mumps case.

Epidemiology

Occurrence
Mumps occurs worldwide.

Reservoir
Mumps is a human disease. Although persons with asymptomatic or nonclassical infection can transmit the virus, no carrier state is known to exist.

Transmission
Mumps is spread through airborne transmission or by direct contact with infected droplet nuclei or saliva.

Temporal Pattern
Mumps incidence peaks predominantly in late winter and spring, but the disease has been reported throughout the year.

Mumps Laboratory Diagnosis

- Isolation of mumps virus
- Detection of mumps antigen by PCR
- Serologic testing
  - positive IgM antibody
  - significant increase in IgG antibody between acute and convalescent specimens

Mumps Epidemiology

Reservoir	Human. Asymptomatic infections may transmit
Transmission	Respiratory drop nuclei
Temporal pattern	Peak in late winter and spring
Communicability	3 days before to 4 days after onset of active disease

13

Communicability

Contagiousness is similar to that of influenza and rubella, but is less than that for measles or varicella. The infectious period is considered to be from 3 days before to the 4th day of active disease; virus has been isolated from saliva 7 days before to 9 days after onset of parotitis.

Secular Trends in the United States

Mumps became a nationally reportable disease in the United States in 1968. However, an estimated 212,000 cases occurred in the United States in 1964. Following vaccine licensure, reported mumps decreased rapidly. Approximately 3,000 cases were reported annually in 1983–1985 (1.3–1.55 cases per 100,000 population).

In 1986 and 1987, there was a relative resurgence of mumps, which peaked in 1987, when 12,848 cases were reported. The highest incidence of mumps during the resurgence was among older school-age and college-age youth (10–19 years of age), who were born before routine mumps vaccination was recommended. Mumps incidence in this period correlated with the absence of comprehensive state requirements for mumps immunization. Several mumps outbreaks among highly vaccinated school populations were reported, indicating that high coverage with a single dose of mumps vaccine did not always prevent disease transmission, probably because of vaccine failure.

Since 1989, the number of reported mumps cases has steadily declined, from 5,712 cases to a total of 258 cases in 2004. In 2006 a multistate mumps outbreak resulted in more than 6,000 reported cases. Eight states in the Midwest reported the majority of cases. The outbreak peaked in mid-April. The median age of persons reported with mumps was 22 years. Many cases occurred among college students, many of whom had received one or two doses of MMR vaccine.

Before vaccine licensure in 1967, and during the early years of vaccine use, most reported cases occurred in the 5–9-year age group; 90% of cases occurred among children 15 years of age and younger. In the late 1980s, there was a shift towards older children. Since 1990, persons age 15 years and older have accounted for 30% to 40% of cases per year (42% in 2002). Males and females are affected equally.

Eighty percent or more of adults in urban and suburban areas with or without a history of mumps have serologic evidence of immunity.

Case Definition

The clinical case definition of mumps is an acute onset of unilateral or bilateral tender, self-limited swelling of the

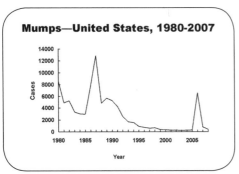

Mumps—United States, 1968-2007

Mumps—United States, 1980-2007

13

Mumps Clinical Case Definition

- Acute onset of unilateral or bilateral tender, self-limited swelling of the parotid or other salivary gland lasting more than 2 days and without other apparent cause

parotid or other salivary gland lasting more than 2 days and without other apparent cause.

Mumps Vaccine

Characteristics

Mumps virus was isolated in 1945, and an inactivated vaccine was developed in 1948. This vaccine produced only short-lasting immunity, and its use was discontinued in the mid-1970s. The currently used Jeryl Lynn strain of live attenuated mumps virus vaccine was licensed in December 1967.

Mumps vaccine is available combined with measles and rubella vaccines (as MMR), or combined with measles, rubella, and varicella vaccine as MMRV (ProQuad). The Advisory Committee on Immunization Practices (ACIP) recommends that MMR be used when any of the individual components is indicated. Use of single-antigen mumps vaccine is not recommended.

Mumps vaccine is prepared in chick embryo fibroblast tissue culture. MMR and MMRV are supplied as a lyophilized (freeze-dried) powder and are reconstituted with sterile, preservative-free water. The vaccine contains small amounts of human albumin, neomycin, sorbitol, and gelatin.

Immunogenicity and Vaccine Efficacy

Mumps vaccine produces an inapparent, or mild, noncommunicable infection. More than 97% of recipients of a single dose develop measurable antibody. Seroconversion rates are similar for single antigen mumps vaccine, MMR, and MMRV. Postlicensure studies conducted in the United States during 1973–1989 determined that one dose of mumps or MMR vaccine was 75%–91% effective. A study from the United Kingdom documented vaccine effectiveness of 88% with two doses. The duration of vaccine-induced immunity is believed to be greater than 25 years, and is probably lifelong in most vaccine recipients.

Vaccination Schedule and Use

One dose of mumps-containing vaccine is routinely recommended for all preschool-age children 12 months of age and older and for persons born during or after 1957 not at high risk of mumps exposure. The first dose of mumps-containing vaccine should be given on or after the first birthday. Mumps-containing vaccine given before 12 months of age should not be counted as part of the series. Children vaccinated with mumps-containing vaccine before 12 months of age should be revaccinated with two doses of MMR vaccine, the first of which should be administered when the child is at least 12 months of age.

Mumps Vaccine

- **Composition**   Live virus (Jeryl Lynn strain)
- **Efficacy**   95% (Range, 90%-97%)
- **Duration of Immunity**   Lifelong
- **Schedule**   At least 1 dose
- Should be administered with measles and rubella (MMR) or with measles, rubella and varicella (MMRV)

13

Mumps (MMR) Vaccine Indications

- One dose (as MMR) for preschool-age children 12 months of age and older and persons born during or after 1957 not at high risk of mumps exposure
- Second dose (as MMR) for school-age children and adults at high risk of mumps exposure (i.e., healthcare personnel, international travelers and students at post-high school educational institutions

In 2006, ACIP recommended a second dose of mumps vaccine for school-age children and for adults at high risk of mumps exposure (i.e., healthcare personnel, international travelers, and students at post-high school educational institutions).The combined MMR vaccine is recommended for both doses to ensure immunity to all three viruses.

The second dose of MMR vaccine should be given routinely at age 4 through 6 years, before a child enters kindergarten or first grade. The recommended health visit at age 11 or 12 years can serve as a catch-up opportunity to verify vaccination status and administer MMR vaccine to those children who have not yet received two doses of MMR. The second dose of MMR may be administered as soon as 4 weeks (i.e., 28 days) after the first dose.

Only doses of vaccine with written documentation of the date of receipt should be accepted as valid. Self-reported doses or a parental report of vaccination is not considered adequate documentation. A clinician should not provide an immunization record for a patient unless that clinician has administered the vaccine or has seen a record that documents vaccination. Persons who lack adequate documentation of vaccination or other acceptable evidence of immunity should be vaccinated. Vaccination status and receipt of all vaccinations should be documented in the patient's permanent medical record and in a vaccination record held by the individual.

MMRV is approved by the Food and Drug Administration for children 12 months through 12 years of age (that is, until the 13th birthday). MMRV should not be administered to persons 13 years of age or older.

Mumps Immunity

Generally, persons can be considered immune to mumps if they were born before 1957, have serologic evidence of mumps immunity, have documentation of physician-diagnosed mumps, or have documentation of vaccination with at least one dose of live mumps vaccine on or after their first birthday. Demonstration of mumps IgG antibody by any commonly used serologic assay is acceptable evidence of mumps immunity. Persons who have an "equivocal" serologic test result should be considered susceptible to mumps.

Although persons born before 1957 can generally be considered to be immune to mumps, ACIP recommends that healthcare facilities should strongly consider recommending one dose of mumps-containing vaccine to unvaccinated healthcare personnel born before 1957 who do not have other evidence of mumps immunity, such as laboratory evidence of immunity.

Mumps Immunity

- Born before 1957
- Serologic evidence of mumps immunity
- Documentation of physician-diagnosed mumps
- Documentation of adequate vaccination

Mumps Immunity

- Healthcare facilities should strongly consider recommending 1 dose of mumps-containing vaccine to unvaccinated personnel born before 1957 who do not have other evidence of mumps immunity

13

Postexposure Prophylaxis

Neither mumps immune globulin nor immune globulin (IG) is effective postexposure prophylaxis. Vaccination after exposure is not harmful and may possibly avert later disease.

Contraindications and Precautions to Vaccination

Persons who have experienced a severe allergic reaction (anaphylaxis) to a vaccine component or following a prior close of mumps vaccine should generally not be vaccinated with MMR.

In the past, persons with a history of anaphylactic reactions following egg ingestion were considered to be at increased risk of serious reactions after receipt of measles- or mumps-containing vaccines, which are produced in chick embryo fibroblasts. However, data suggest that most anaphylactic reactions to measles- and mumps-containing vaccines are not associated with hypersensitivity to egg antigens but to other components of the vaccines (such as gelatin). The risk for serious allergic reactions such as anaphylaxis following receipt of these vaccines by egg-allergic persons is extremely low, and skin-testing with vaccine is not predictive of allergic reaction to vaccination. As a result, MMR may be administered to egg-allergic children without prior routine skin-testing or the use of special protocols.

MMR vaccine does not contain penicillin. A history of penicillin allergy is not a contraindication to MMR vaccination.

Pregnant women should not receive mumps vaccine, although the risk in this situation is theoretic. There is no evidence that mumps vaccine virus causes fetal damage. Pregnancy should be avoided for 4 weeks after vaccination with MMR vaccine.

Persons with immunodeficiency or immunosuppression resulting from leukemia, lymphoma, generalized malignancy, immune deficiency disease, or immunosuppressive therapy should not be vaccinated. However, treatment with low-dose (less than 2 mg/kg/day), alternate-day, topical, or aerosolized steroid preparations is not a contraindication to mumps vaccination. Persons whose immunosuppressive therapy with steroids has been discontinued for 1 month (3 months for chemotherapy) may be vaccinated. See Chapter 11, Measles, for additional details on vaccination of immunosuppressed persons, including those with human immunodeficiency virus infection.

Persons with moderate or severe acute illness should not be vaccinated until the illness has improved. Minor illness (e.g., otitis media, mild upper respiratory infections), concurrent

---

**MMR Vaccine
Contraindications and Precautions**

- Severe allergic reaction to vaccine component or following a prior dose
- Pregnancy
- Immunosuppression
- Moderate or severe acute illness
- Recent blood product

Measles and Mumps Vaccines and Egg Allergy

- Measles and mumps viruses grown in chick embryo fibroblast culture
- Studies have demonstrated safety of MMR in egg allergic children
- Vaccinate without testing

13

antibiotic therapy, and exposure or recovery from other illnesses are not contraindications to mumps vaccination.

Receipt of antibody-containing blood products (e.g., immune globulin, whole blood or packed red blood cells, intravenous immune globulin) may interfere with sero-conversion following mumps vaccination. Vaccine should be given 2 weeks before, or deferred for at least 3 months following, administration of an antibody-containing blood product. See Chapter 2, General Recommendations on Immunization, for details.

A family history of diabetes is not a contraindication for vaccination.

Adverse Reactions Following Vaccination

Mumps vaccine is very safe. Most adverse events reported following MMR vaccine (such as fever, rash, and joint symptoms) are attributable to the measles or rubella components. No adverse reactions were reported in large-scale field trials. Subsequently, parotitis and fever have been reported rarely. A few cases of orchitis (all suspect) also have been reported.

Rare cases of CNS dysfunction, including cases of deafness, within 2 months of mumps vaccination have been reported. The calculated incidence of CNS reactions is approximately one per 800,000 doses of Jeryl Lynn strain of mumps vaccine virus. The Institute of Medicine (1993) concluded that evidence is inadequate to accept or reject a causal relation-ship between the Jeryl Lynn strain of mumps vaccine and aseptic meningitis, encephalitis, sensorineural deafness, or orchitis.

Allergic reactions, including rash, pruritus, and purpura, have been temporally associated with vaccination, but these are transient and generally mild.

Vaccine Storage and Handling

MMR vaccine must be shipped with refrigerant to maintain a temperature of 50°F (10°C) or less at all times. Vaccine must be refrigerated immediately on arrival and protected from light at all times. The vaccine must be stored at refrigerator temperature (35°–46°F [2°–8°C]), but may be frozen. Diluent may be stored at refrigerator temperature or at room temperature. MMRV must be shipped to maintain a tempera-ture of -4°F (-20°C) or less at all times. It must be stored at an average temperature of 5°F (-15°C) or less at all times.

After reconstitution, MMR vaccines must be stored at refrig-erator temperature and protected from light. Reconstituted vaccine should be used immediately. If reconstituted vaccine

---

13

MMR Adverse Reactions	
• Fever	5%-15%
• Rash	5%
• Joint symptoms	25%
• Thrombocytopenia	<1/30,000 doses
• Parotitis	rare
• Deafness	rare
• Encephalopathy	<1/1,000,000 doses

is not used within 8 hours, it must be discarded. MMRV must be administered within 30 minutes of reconstitution.

Selected References

CDC. Brief report: Update: Mumps activity—United States, January 1–October 7, 2006. *MMWR* 2006;55:1152–3.

CDC. Update: Multistate outbreak of mumps—United States, January 1–May 2, 2006. *MMWR* 2006;55:559–63.

CDC. Notice to readers: Updated recommendations of the Advisory Committee on Immunization Practices (ACIP) for the control and elimination of mumps. *MMWR* 2006;55:629–30.

CDC. Measles, mumps, and rubella—vaccine use and strategies for elimination of measles, rubella, and congenital rubella syndrome and control of mumps. Recommendations of the Advisory Committee on Immunization Practices (ACIP). *MMWR* 1998;47(No. RR-8):1–57.

Dayan GH and Rubin S. Mumps outbreaks in unvaccinated populations: are available mumps vaccines effective enough to prevent outbreaks? *Clin Infect Dis* 2008;47:1458-67.

Hirsh BS, Fine PEM, Kent WK, et al. Mumps outbreak in a highly vaccinated population. *J Pediatr* 1991;119:187–93.

Orenstein WA, Hadler S, Wharton M. Trends in vaccine-preventable diseases. *Semin Pediatr Infect Dis* 1997;8:23–33.

Plotkin SA, Rubin SA. Mumps vaccine. In: Plotkin SA, Orenstein, WA, Offit PA, eds. *Vaccines*. 5th ed. Philadelphia, PA: Saunders;2008:435–65.

Van Loon FPL, Holmes SJ, Sirotkin BI, et al. Mumps surveillance—United States, 1988–1993. In: CDC Surveillance Summaries, August 11, 1995. *MMWR* 1995;44(No. SS-3):1-14.

13

Mumps

Pertussis

Pertussis, or whooping cough, is an acute infectious disease caused by the bacterium *Bordetella pertussis*. Outbreaks of pertussis were first described in the 16th century, and the organism was first isolated in 1906.

In the 20th century, pertussis was one of the most common childhood diseases and a major cause of childhood mortality in the United States. Before the availability of pertussis vaccine in the 1940s, more than 200,000 cases of pertussis were reported annually. Since widespread use of the vaccine began, incidence has decreased more than 80% compared with the prevaccine era.

Pertussis remains a major health problem among children in developing countries, with 294,000 deaths resulting from the disease in 2002 (World Health Organization estimate).

Bordetella pertussis

B. pertussis is a small, aerobic gram-negative rod. It is fastidious and requires special media for isolation (see Laboratory Diagnosis).

B. pertussis produces multiple antigenic and biologically active products, including pertussis toxin, filamentous hemagglutinin, agglutinogens, adenylate cyclase, pertactin, and tracheal cytotoxin. These products are responsible for the clinical features of pertussis disease, and an immune response to one or more produces immunity following infection. Immunity following *B. pertussis* infection does not appear to be permanent.

Pathogenesis

Pertussis is primarily a toxin-mediated disease. The bacteria attach to the cilia of the respiratory epithelial cells, produce toxins that paralyze the cilia, and cause inflammation of the respiratory tract, which interferes with the clearing of pulmonary secretions. Pertussis antigens appear to allow the organism to evade host defenses, in that lymphocytosis is promoted but chemotaxis is impaired. Until recently it was thought that *B. pertussis* did not invade the tissues. However, recent studies have shown the bacteria to be present in alveolar macrophages.

Clinical Features

The incubation period of pertussis is commonly 7–10 days, with a range of 4–21 days, and rarely may be as long as 42 days. The clinical course of the illness is divided into three stages.

Pertussis

- Highly contagious respiratory infection caused by *Bordetella pertussis*
- Outbreaks first described in 16th century
- *Bordetella pertussis* isolated in 1906
- Estimated 294,000 deaths worldwide in 2002

14

Bordetella pertussis

- Fastidious gram-negative bacteria
- Antigenic and biologically active components:
  – pertussis toxin (PT)
  – filamentous hemagglutinin (FHA)
  – agglutinogens
  – adenylate cyclase
  – pertactin
  – tracheal cytotoxin

Pertussis Pathogenesis

- Primarily a toxin-mediated disease
- Bacteria attach to cilia of respiratory epithelial cells
- Inflammation occurs which interferes with clearance of pulmonary secretions
- Pertussis antigens allow evasion of host defenses (lymphocytosis promoted but impaired chemotaxis)

Pertussis Clinical Features

- Incubation period 7-10 days (range 4-21 days)
- Insidious onset, similar to minor upper respiratory infection with nonspecific cough
- Fever usually minimal throughout course of illness

Pertussis Clinical Features

- Catarrhal stage   1-2 weeks

- Paroxysmal cough stage   1-6 weeks

- Convalescence   Weeks to months

Pertussis Among Adolescents and Adults

- **Disease often milder than in infants and children**
- **Infection may be asymptomatic, or may present as classic pertussis**
- **Persons with mild disease may transmit the infection**
- **Older persons often source of infection for children**

Pertussis Complications*

Condition	Percent reported
Pneumonia	5.2
Seizures	0.8
Encephalopathy	0.1
Hospitalization	20
Death	0.2

*Cases reported to CDC 1997-2000 (N=28,187)

The first stage, the catarrhal stage, is characterized by the insidious onset of coryza (runny nose), sneezing, low-grade fever, and a mild, occasional cough, similar to the common cold. The cough gradually becomes more severe, and after 1–2 weeks, the second, or paroxysmal stage, begins. Fever is generally minimal throughout the course of the illness.

It is during the paroxysmal stage that the diagnosis of pertussis is usually suspected. Characteristically, the patient has bursts, or paroxysms, of numerous, rapid coughs, apparently due to difficulty expelling thick mucus from the tracheobronchial tree. At the end of the paroxysm, a long inspiratory effort is usually accompanied by a characteristic high-pitched whoop. During such an attack, the patient may become cyanotic (turn blue). Children and young infants, especially, appear very ill and distressed. Vomiting and exhaustion commonly follow the episode. The person does not appear to be ill between attacks.

Paroxysmal attacks occur more frequently at night, with an average of 15 attacks per 24 hours. During the first 1 or 2 weeks of this stage, the attacks increase in frequency, remain at the same level for 2 to 3 weeks, and then gradually decrease. The paroxysmal stage usually lasts 1 to 6 weeks but may persist for up to 10 weeks. Infants younger than 6 months of age may not have the strength to have a whoop, but they do have paroxysms of coughing.

In the convalescent stage, recovery is gradual. The cough becomes less paroxysmal and disappears in 2 to 3 weeks. However, paroxysms often recur with subsequent respiratory infections for many months after the onset of pertussis.

Adolescents and adults and children partially protected by the vaccine may become infected with *B. pertussis* but may have milder disease than infants and young children. Pertussis infection in these persons may be asymptomatic, or present as illness ranging from a mild cough illness to classic pertussis with persistent cough (i.e., lasting more than 7 days). Inspiratory whoop is not common.

Even though the disease may be milder in older persons, those who are infected may transmit the disease to other susceptible persons, including unimmunized or incompletely immunized infants. Older persons are often found to have the first case in a household with multiple pertussis cases, and are often the source of infection for children.

Complications

The most common complication, and the cause of most pertussis-related deaths, is secondary bacterial pneumonia. Young infants are at highest risk for acquiring pertussis-associated complications. Data from 1997–2000 indicate that pneumonia occurred in 5.2% of all reported pertussis cases, and among 11.8% of infants younger than 6 months of age.

Neurologic complications such as seizures and encephalopathy (a diffuse disorder of the brain) may occur as a result of hypoxia (reduction of oxygen supply) from coughing, or possibly from toxin. Neurologic complications of pertussis are more common among infants. Other less serious complications of pertussis include otitis media, anorexia, and dehydration. Complications resulting from pressure effects of severe paroxysms include pneumothorax, epistaxis, subdural hematomas, hernias, and rectal prolapse.

In 2004 through 2006 a total of 82 deaths from pertussis were reported to the CDC. Children 3 months of age or younger accounted for 69 (84%) of these deaths.

Adolescents and adults may also develop complications of pertussis, such as difficulty sleeping, urinary incontinence, pneumonia, and rib fracture.

Laboratory Diagnosis

The diagnosis of pertussis is based on a characteristic clinical history (cough for more than 2 weeks with whoop, paroxysms, or posttussive vomiting) as well as a variety of laboratory tests (culture, polymerase chain reaction [PCR], direct fluorescent antibody [DFA] and serology).

Culture is considered the gold standard laboratory test and is the most specific of the laboratory tests for pertussis. However, fastidious growth requirements make *B. pertussis* difficult to culture. The yield of culture can be affected by specimen collection, transportation, and isolation techniques. Specimens from the posterior nasopharynx, not the throat, should be obtained using Dacron® or calcium alginate (not cotton) swabs. Isolation rates are highest during the first 3 to 4 weeks of illness (catarrhal and early paroxysmal stages). Cultures are variably positive (30%–50%) and may take as long as 2 weeks, so results may be too late for clinical usefulness. Cultures are less likely to be positive if performed later in the course of illness (more than 2 weeks after cough onset) or on specimens from persons who have received antibiotics or have been vaccinated. Since adolescents and adults have often been coughing for several weeks before they seek medical attention, it is often too late for culture to be useful.

Because of the increased sensitivity and faster reporting of results of PCR, many laboratories are now using this method exclusively. PCR should be used in addition to, and not as a replacement for culture. No PCR product has been approved by the Food and Drug Administration (FDA), and there are no standardized protocols, reagents, or reporting

Pertussis Complications by Age
■ Pneumonia ■ Hospitalization

*Cases reported to CDC 1997-2000 (N=28,187)

Pertussis Deaths in the United States, 2004-2006

	Age at onset ≤3 mos	>3 mos	Total
2004	24	3	27
2005	32	7	39
2006	13	3	16
Total	69	13	82
	(84%)	(16%)	

CDC, unpublished data, 2007

14

14

formats for pertussis PCR testing. Consequently, PCR assays vary widely among laboratories. Specificity can be poor, with high rates of false-positive results in some laboratories. Like culture, PCR is also affected by specimen collection. An inappropriately obtained nasopharyngeal swab will likely be negative by both culture and PCR. PCR is less affected by prior antibiotic therapy, since the organism does not need to be viable to be positive by PCR. Continued use of culture is essential for confirmation of PCR results.

DFA testing of nasopharyngeal specimens may be useful as a rapid screening test for pertussis. Use of the monoclonal DFA test has improved the specificity, but DFA still has a low sensitivity and should not be relied upon as a criterion for laboratory confirmation.

Serologic testing could be useful for adults and adolescents who present late in the course of their illness, when both culture and PCR are likely to be negative. However, there is no FDA-approved diagnostic test. The currently available serologic tests measure antibodies that could result from either infection or vaccination, so a positive serologic response simply means that the person has been exposed to pertussis by either recent or remote infection or by recent or remote vaccination. Since vaccination can induce both IgM and IgA antibodies (in addition to IgG antibodies), use of such serologic assays cannot differentiate infection from vaccine response. At this time, serologic test results should not be relied upon for case confirmation of pertussis infection.

An elevated white blood cell count with a lymphocytosis is usually present in classical disease of infants. The absolute lymphocyte count often reaches 20,000 or greater. However, there may be no lymphocytosis in some infants and children or in persons with mild or modified cases of pertussis. More information on the laboratory diagnosis of pertussis is available at http://www.cdc.gov/vaccines/pubs/surv-manual/default.pdf

Medical Management

The medical management of pertussis cases is primarily supportive, although antibiotics are of some value. Erythromycin is the drug of choice. This therapy eradicates the organism from secretions, thereby decreasing communicability and, if initiated early, may modify the course of the illness.

An antibiotic effective against pertussis (such as azithromycin, erythromycin or trimethoprim-sulfamethoxazole) should be administered to all close contacts of persons with pertussis, regardless of age and vaccination status. Revised treatment and postexposure prophylaxis recommendations were published in December 2005 (see reference list). All close contacts younger than 7 years of age who have not completed the four-dose primary series should complete the series with the minimal intervals. (see table in Appendix A). Close contacts who are 4–6 years of age and who have not yet received the second booster dose (usually the fifth dose of DTaP) should be vaccinated. The administration of Tdap to persons 10 through 64 years of age who have been exposed to a person with pertussis is not contraindicated, but the efficacy of postexposure use of Tdap is unknown.

Epidemiology

Occurrence
Pertussis occurs worldwide.

Reservoir
Pertussis is a human disease. No animal or insect source or vector is known to exist. Adolescents and adults are an important reservoir for *B. pertussis* and are often the source of infection for infants.

Transmission
Transmission most commonly occurs by the respiratory route through contact with respiratory droplets, or by contact with airborne droplets of respiratory secretions. Transmission occurs less frequently by contact with freshly contaminated articles of an infected person.

Temporal Pattern
Pertussis has no distinct seasonal pattern, but it may increase in the summer and fall.

Communicability
Pertussis is highly communicable, as evidenced by secondary attack rates of 80% among susceptible household contacts. Persons with pertussis are most infectious during the catarrhal period and the first 2 weeks after cough onset (i.e., approximately 21 days).

Secular Trends in the United States
Before the availability of vaccine, pertussis was a common cause of morbidity and mortality among children. During the 6-year period from 1940 through 1945, more than 1 million cases of pertussis were reported, an average of 175,000 cases per year (incidence of approximately 150 cases per 100,000 population).

Following introduction of whole-cell pertussis vaccine in the 1940s, pertussis incidence gradually declined, reaching

Pertussis Epidemiology

- Reservoir   Human
                  Adolescents and adults

- Transmission   Respiratory droplets

- Communicability   Maximum in catarrhal stage
                      Secondary attack rate
                      up to 80%

14

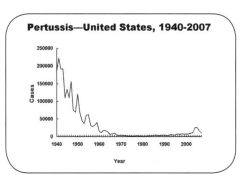

Pertussis—United States, 1940-2007

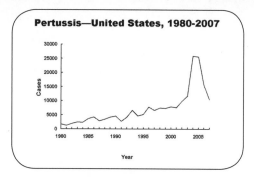

Pertussis—United States, 1980-2007

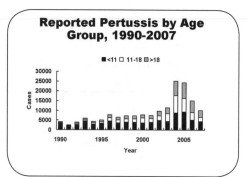

Reported Pertussis by Age Group, 1990-2007

■ <11 ☐ 11-18 ▨ >18

15,000 reported cases in 1960 (approximately 8 per 100,000 population). By 1970, annual incidence was fewer than 5,000 cases per year, and during 1980–1990, an average of 2,900 cases per year were reported (approximately 1 per 100,000 population).

Pertussis incidence has been gradually increasing since the early 1980s. A total of 25,827 cases was reported in 2004, the largest number since 1959. The reasons for the increase are not clear.

During 2001–2003, the highest average annual pertussis incidence was among infants younger than 1 year of age (55.2 cases per 100,000 population), and particularly among children younger than 6 months of age (98.2 per 100,000 population). In 2002, 24% of all reported cases were in this age group. However, in recent years, adolescents (11–18 years of age) and adults (19 years and older) have accounted for an increasing proportion of cases. During 2001–2003, the annual incidence of pertussis among persons aged 10–19 years increased from 5.5 per 100,000 in 2001, to 6.7 in 2002, and 10.9 in 2003. In 2004 and 2005, approximately 60% of reported cases were among persons 11 years of age and older. Increased recognition and diagnosis of pertussis in older age groups probably contributed to this increase of reported cases among adolescents and adults.

Of the 10,650 children 3 months to 4 years of age with reported pertussis during 1990–1996 and known vaccination status, 54% were not age-appropriately vaccinated with DTaP.

Pertussis Surveillance

Pertussis cases are reported to CDC via two systems. States provide information about cases of pertussis, including demographic information, through the National Electronic Transmittal System for Surveillance. More detailed information is reported to CDC through the Supplementary Pertussis Surveillance System. Although many pertussis cases are not reported, the surveillance system is useful for monitoring epidemiologic trends. For instance, although the highest incidence of pertussis occurs in infancy, the age group at greatest risk for severe illness and complications, in recent years, the surveillance system has reflected an increase in the incidence of pertussis in all age groups, most notably among adolescents and adults.

Guidelines on pertussis surveillance and outbreak control are available at http://www.cdc.gov/vaccines/pubs/pertussis-guide/guide.htm.

Case Definition

The current case definition for pertussis was developed and adopted by the Council of State and Territorial Epidemiologists (CSTE) and CDC. It defines a clinical case of pertussis as an acute cough illness lasting at least 2 weeks with either paroxysms of coughing, inspiratory "whoop," or posttussive vomiting without other apparent cause (as reported by a health professional).

Case Classification

Probable—Meets the clinical case definition, but is not laboratory confirmed and is not epidemiologically linked to a laboratory-confirmed case.

Confirmed—A clinically compatible case that is laboratory confirmed or epidemiologically linked to a laboratory-confirmed case.

The clinical case definition above is appropriate for endemic or sporadic cases. In outbreak settings, including household exposures, a case can be defined as an acute cough illness lasting at least 2 weeks without other symptoms. See the pertussis chapter of the Manual for the Surveillance of Vaccine-Preventable Diseases (available at http://www.cdc.gov/vaccines/pubs/surv-manual/default.htm) for more information on case classification.

Pertussis Vaccines

Whole-Cell Pertussis Vaccine

Whole-cell pertussis vaccine is composed of a suspension of formalin-inactivated *B. pertussis* cells. It was developed in the 1930s and used widely in clinical practice by the mid-1940s.

Based on controlled efficacy trials conducted in the 1940s and on subsequent observational efficacy studies, a primary series of four doses of whole-cell DTP vaccine was 70%–90% effective in preventing serious pertussis disease. Protection decreased with time, resulting in little or no protection 5 to 10 years following the last dose. Local reactions such as redness, swelling, and pain at the injection site occurred following up to half of doses of whole-cell DTP vaccines. Fever and other mild systemic events were also common. Concerns about safety led to the development of more purified (acellular) pertussis vaccines that are associated with a lower frequency of adverse reactions. Whole-cell pertussis vaccines are no longer available in the United States but are still used in many other countries.

Acellular Pertussis Vaccine

Characteristics

Acellular pertussis vaccines are subunit vaccines that contain purified, inactivated components of *B. pertussis* cells.

14

Whole-Cell Pertussis Vaccine

- Developed in mid-1930s and combined as DTP in mid-1940s
- 70%-90% efficacy after 3 doses
- Protection for 5-10 years
- Local adverse reactions common

Several acellular pertussis vaccines have been developed for different age groups; these contain different pertussis components in varying concentrations. Acellular pertussis vaccines are available only as combinations with tetanus and diphtheria toxoids.

Pediatric Formulation (DTaP)

Three pediatric acellular pertussis vaccines are currently available for use in the United States. All three vaccines are combined with diphtheria and tetanus toxoids as DTaP and are approved for children 6 weeks through 6 years of age (to age 7 years). Infanrix (GlaxoSmithKline) contains three antigens, mostly pertussis toxin (PT) and FHA. Tripedia (sanofi pasteur) contains two components, FHA and PT, in equal amounts. Daptacel (sanofi pasteur) contains five components, PT, FHA, pertactin, and fimbriae types 2 and 3. None of the available DTaP vaccines contains thimerosal as a preservative, although Infanrix and Daptacel contain 2-phenoxyethanol as a preservative. Tripedia does not contain a preservative. All three vaccines are supplied in single-dose vials or syringes.

Adolescent and Adult Formulation (Tdap)

Acellular pertussis–containing vaccines were first licensed for adolescents and adults in 2005. Two vaccines are currently available. Both vaccines are combined with tetanus toxoid and a reduced amount of diphtheria toxoid compared with pediatric DTaP (that is, similar quantities of tetanus and diphtheria toxoid to adult formulation Td). Boostrix (GlaxoSmithKline) is approved for persons 10 through 64 years of age, and contains three pertussis antigens (PT, FHA, and pertactin) in a reduced quantity compared with the GlaxoSmithKline pediatric formulation. The vaccine contains aluminum hydroxide as an adjuvant and does not contain a preservative. Adacel (sanofi pasteur) is approved for persons 11 through 64 years of age. It contains the same five pertussis components as Daptacel but with a reduced quantity of PT. Adacel contains aluminum phosphate as an adjuvant and does not contain a preservative. Both vaccines are supplied in single-dose vials or syringes.

Immunogenicity and Vaccine Efficacy

DTaP

Since 1991, several studies conducted in Europe and Africa have evaluated the efficacy of DTaP vaccines administered to infants. These studies varied in type and number of vaccines, design, case definition, and laboratory method used to confirm the diagnosis of pertussis, so comparison among studies must b e made with caution. Point estimates of vaccine efficacy ranged from 80% to 85% for vaccines

Pertussis-containing Vaccines

- DTaP (pediatric)
  - approved for children 6 weeks through 6 years (to age 7 years)

- Tdap (adolescent and adult)
  - approved for persons 10 through 64 years (Boostrix) and 11 through 64 years (Adacel)

14

Composition* of Acellular Pertussis Vaccines

Product	PT	FHA	PERT	FIM
Daptacel	10	5	3	5
Infanrix	25	25	8	--
Tripedia	23	23	--	--
Boostrix	8	8	2.5	--
Adacel	2.5	5	3	5

*mcg per dose

DTaP Clinical Trials

Product	Location	VE (95% CI)
Daptacel	Sweden	85% (80-89)
Tripedia	Germany	80% (59-90)
Infanrix	Italy	84% (76-89)

currently licensed in the United States. Confidence intervals for vaccine efficacy overlap, suggesting that none of the vaccines is significantly more effective than the others. When studied, the acellular pertussis vaccine was significantly more effective than whole-cell DTP. Mild local and systemic adverse reactions and more serious adverse reactions (such as high fever, persistent crying, hypotonic hyporesponsive episodes, and seizures) occurred less frequently among infants vaccinated with acellular pertussis vaccines than among those vaccinated with whole-cell DTP.

Tdap

Adolescent and adult formulation Tdap vaccines were licensed on the basis of noninferiority of the serologic response to the various components compared with each company's pediatric DTaP formulation (Infanrix and Daptacel) among persons who had received pediatric DTaP or DTP in childhood. For both vaccines, the antibody response to a single dose of Tdap was similar to that following three doses of DTaP in infants. This type of study is known as "bridging." The new vaccines are assumed to have similar clinical efficacy as DTaP vaccine since a similar level of antibody to the components was achieved.

Vaccination Schedule and Use

DTaP

The primary series of DTaP vaccine consists of four doses, the first three doses given at 4- to 8-week intervals (minimum of 4 weeks), beginning at 6 weeks to 2 months of age. The fourth dose is given 6–12 months after the third to maintain adequate immunity for the ensuing preschool years. DTaP should be administered simultaneously with all other indicated vaccines.

The fourth dose of all brands of DTaP is licensed, and recommended by ACIP, to be administered at 15–18 months of age (17–20 months for Daptacel). However, ACIP recommends that in certain circumstances the fourth dose be given earlier than 15 months of age. The fourth dose of DTaP may be given if the child is at least 12 months of age, and at least 6 months have elapsed since the third dose of pertussis vaccine was given, and, in the opinion of the immunization provider, the child is unlikely to return for an additional visit at 15–18 months of age. All three of these criteria should be met in order to administer the fourth dose of DTaP at 12–14 months of age.

Children who received all four primary doses before the fourth birthday should receive a fifth (booster) dose of DTaP before entering school. This booster dose is not necessary (but may be given) if the fourth dose in the primary series

Routine DTaP Primary Vaccination Schedule

Dose	Age	Minimum Interval
Primary 1	2 months	---
Primary 2	4 months	4 weeks
Primary 3	6 months	4 weeks
Primary 4	15-18 months	6 months

DTaP Fourth Dose

- Recommended at 15-18 months*
- May be given earlier if:
  - child is 12 months of age, and
  - 6 months since DTaP3, and
  - unlikely to return at 15-18 months

  *17-20 months for Daptacel

14

was given on or after the fourth birthday. The booster dose increases antibody levels and may decrease the risk of school-age children transmitting the disease to younger siblings who are not fully vaccinated.

For children who started the vaccination series with whole-cell DTP, DTaP should be substituted for any remaining doses of the pertussis series.

ACIP recommends that the series be completed with the same brand of DTaP vaccine if possible. However, limited data suggest that "mix and match" DTaP schedules do not adversely affect safety and immunogenicity. If the vaccine provider does not know or have available the type of DTaP vaccine previously administered to a child, any available DTaP vaccine should be used to continue or complete the vaccination series. Unavailability of the vaccine used for earlier doses is not a reason for missing the opportunity to administer a dose of acellular pertussis vaccine for which the child is eligible.

Interruption of the recommended schedule or delayed doses does not lead to a reduction in the level of immunity reached on completion of the primary series. There is no need to restart a series regardless of the time that has elapsed between doses.

Tdap

Both Tdap vaccines are approved by the Food and Drug Administration for a single (booster) dose for persons who have completed the recommended childhood DTP/DTaP vaccination series. Boostrix is approved for persons 10 through 64 years of age; Adacel is approved for persons 11 through 64 years of age.

ACIP recommends that adolescents 11 or 12 years of age should receive a single dose of Tdap instead of Td. Adolescents 13 through 18 years who have not received Tdap should receive a single dose of Tdap as their catch-up booster instead of Td if they have completed the recommended childhood DTaP/DTP vaccination series, and have not yet received a Td booster.

A 5-year interval between Td and Tdap is encouraged to reduce the risk of local and systemic adverse reactions. However, ACIP did not define an absolute minimum interval between Td and Tdap. The interval between Td and Tdap may be shorter than 5 years if protection from pertussis needed. The decision whether to administer Tdap when less than 5 years has elapsed since the last dose of Td should be based on whether the benefit of pertussis immunity outweighs the risk of a local adverse reaction. An interval of less than 5 years can be considered in situations

Interchangeability of Different Brands of DTaP Vaccine

- Series should be completed with same brand of vaccine if possible
- Limited data suggest that "mix and match" DTaP schedules do not adversely affect safety and immunogenicity
- Use different brand of DTaP if necessary

Tdap Vaccines

- Boostrix (GlaxoSmithKline)
  - approved for persons 10 through 64 years of age
- Adacel (sanofi pasteur)
  - approved for persons 11 through 64 years of age

Recommendations for Tdap Vaccination of Adolescents

- Adolescents 11 or 12 years of age should receive a single dose of Tdap instead of Td*
- Adolescents 13 through 18 years who have not received Tdap should receive a single dose of Tdap as their catch-up booster instead of Td*

*if the person has completed the recommended childhood DTaP/DTP vaccination series, and has not yet received a Td booster

MMWR 2006;55(RR-3):1-43.

of increased risk of pertussis, such as during a pertussis outbreak, or if protection is needed because of household or other close contact with an infant younger than 12 months of age or a young child who has not been vaccinated against pertussis.

ACIP recommends that adults 19 through 64 years of age receive a single dose of Tdap to replace a single dose of Td for booster immunization against tetanus, diphtheria and pertussis. Tdap may be given at an interval less than 10 years since receipt of the last tetanus toxoid-containing vaccine to protect against pertussis. Special emphasis should be placed on Tdap vaccination of adults who have close contact with infants, such as childcare and healthcare personnel, and parents. Ideally, Tdap should be given at least 1 month before beginning close contact with the infant.

Any woman who might become pregnant is encouraged to receive a single dose of Tdap if she has not already received a dose. Women who have not received Tdap (including women who are breastfeeding) should receive a dose in the immediate postpartum period, before discharge from the hospital or birthing center, if 2 years or more have elapsed since the last Td. Shorter intervals since the last Td can be used if necessary. If Tdap cannot be administered before discharge, it should be given as soon as feasible. The dose of Tdap replaces the next routine dose of Td.

ACIP recommends Td when tetanus and diphtheria protection is required during pregnancy. However, pregnancy is not a contraindication for use of Tdap. A clinician may choose to administer Tdap to a pregnant woman in certain circumstances, such as during a community pertussis outbreak. When Td or Tdap is administered during pregnancy, the second or third trimester is preferred to avoid coincidental association of vaccination and spontaneous termination of a pregnancy, which is more common in the first trimester. Clinicians can choose to administer Tdap instead of Td to pregnant adolescents for routine or "catch-up" vaccination because the incidence of pertussis is high among adolescents. Others for whom Tdap might be considered during pregnancy are pregnant healthcare personnel and child care providers (to prevent transmission to infants younger than 12 months of age and to other vulnerable persons) and pregnant women employed in an institution or living in a community with increased pertussis activity.

Healthcare personnel who work in hospitals or ambulatory care settings and have direct patient contact should receive a single dose of Tdap as soon as feasible. Priority should be given to vaccination of healthcare personnel who have direct contact with infants 12 months of age and younger. An interval as short as 2 years (or less) from the last dose of Td is recommended for the Tdap dose.

Minimum Interval Between Td and Tdap

- A 5-year interval since the last Td dose is encouraged to reduce the chance of a local reaction
- ACIP did not define an absolute minimum interval between Td and Tdap
- Interval between Td and Tdap may be shorter if protection from pertussis needed
- Decision to administer Tdap based on whether the benefit of pertussis immunity outweighs the risk of a local adverse reaction

MMWR 2006;55(RR-3):1-43.

Tdap Vaccination of Adults 19 Through 64 Years of Age

- Single dose of Tdap to replace a single dose of Td
- May be given at an interval less than 10 years since receipt of last tetanus toxoid-containing vaccine
- Special emphasis on adults with close contact with infants (e.g., childcare and healthcare personnel, and parents)

MMWR 2006;55(RR-17):1-37.

14

Use of Tdap Among Pregnant Women

- Any woman who might become pregnant is encouraged to receive a single dose of Tdap
- Women who have not received Tdap should receive a dose in the immediate postpartum period
- ACIP recommends Td when tetanus and diphtheria protection is required during pregnancy
- Pregnancy is not a contraindication for Tdap
- Clinician may choose to administer Tdap to a pregnant woman in certain circumstances (such as during a community pertussis outbreak)

MMWR 2008; 57(RR-4): 1–37

Tdap Vaccine and Healthcare Personnel

- Healthcare personnel who work in hospitals or ambulatory care settings and have direct patient contact should receive a single dose of Tdap as soon as feasible*
- Priority should be given to vaccination of healthcare personnel who have direct contact with infants 12 months of age and younger
- An interval as short as 2 years (or less) from the last dose of Td is recommended for the Tdap dose

*if they have not previously received Tdap.
MMWR 2006;55(RR-17):1-37.

Tdap vaccine may be given at the same visit, or any time before or after any other vaccine.

Immunity following pertussis is not permanent. Persons with a history of pertussis should receive a single dose of Tdap if it is otherwise indicated.

All adolescents and adults should have documentation of having received a primary series of at least three doses of tetanus and diphtheria toxoids during their lifetime. A person without such documentation should receive a series of three doses of tetanus- and diphtheria-containing vaccine. One of these doses, preferably the first, should be Tdap if the person is at least 10 years of age (the minimum age approved for one of the two available Tdap products). The remaining two doses should be adult formulation Td.

No pertussis vaccine is approved for children 7–9 years of age or for persons older than 64 years. ACIP does not recommend the use of Tdap in persons in these age groups.

Combination Vaccines Containing DTaP

TriHIBit

Two combination vaccines that contain DTap are currently licensed in the United States. TriHIBit (sanofi pasteur) contains DTaP and Hib (*Haemophilus influenzae* type b) vaccine. The vaccines are provided in separate vials, and the DTaP component (Tripedia) is used to reconstitute the Hib component (ActHIB). No other brand of DTaP and Hib vaccine may be used to produce this combination (e.g., Infanrix must not be substituted for Tripedia). In addition, when supplied as TriHIBit, the DTaP and Hib components have a single lot number. Providers should generally use only the DTaP and Hib supplied together as TriHIBit. However, it is acceptable to combine Tripedia and ActHIB that have been supplied separately (i.e., not packaged as TriHIBit). In this situation, the lot numbers of both vaccines should be recorded in the child's chart.

TriHIBit is not approved by the Food and Drug Administration for use as the primary series at 2, 4, or 6 months of age. It is approved only for the fourth dose of the DTaP and Hib series. If TriHIBit is administered as one or more doses of the primary series at 2, 4, or 6 months of age, the Hib doses should not be counted, and the child should be revaccinated as age-appropriate for Hib. The DTaP doses may be counted as valid and do not need to be repeated.

Although TriHIBit cannot be used in the primary series at

Tdap For Persons Without A History of DTP or DTaP

- All adolescents and adults should have documentation of having received a series of DTaP, DTP, DT, or Td
- Persons without documentation should receive a series of 3 vaccinations
- Preferred schedule:
  - single dose of Tdap*
  - Td at least 4 weeks after the Tdap dose
  - second dose of Td at least 6 months after the Td dose

*off-label recommendation. *MMWR* 2006;55(RR-3):1-43

TriHIBit

- DTaP/Hib combination

- Do not use for primary immunization at 2, 4, or 6 months of age

- May be used as the booster dose of the Hib series at 12 months of age or older following any Hib vaccine*

*booster dose should follow prior dose by at least 2 months

14

2, 4, or 6 months of age, it may be used as the booster (final) dose following a series of single-antigen Hib vaccine or combination hepatitis B–Hib vaccine (Comvax). TriHIBit can be used if the child is 12 months of age or older, has received at least one prior dose of Hib vaccine 2 or more months earlier, and TriHIBit will be the last dose in the Hib series. For example, TriHIBit can be used for the booster dose at 12–15 months of age in a child who has received Comvax or PedvaxHib at 2 and 4 months of age, or three prior doses of HibTiter or ActHib. TriHIBit can also be used at 15 through 59 months of age in a child who has received at least one prior dose of any Hib-containing vaccine. TriHIBit should not be used if the child has received no prior Hib doses.

Pediarix

In 2002, the FDA approved Pediarix (GlaxoSmithKline), the first pentavalent (5 component) combination vaccine licensed in the United States. Pediarix contains DTaP (Infanrix), hepatitis B (Engerix-B), and inactivated polio vaccines. In prelicensure studies, the proportion of children who developed a protective level of antibody and the titer of antibody were at least as high when the vaccine antigens were given together as Pediarix as when children received separate vaccines.

The minimum age for the first dose of Pediarix is 6 weeks, so it cannot be used for the birth dose of the hepatitis B series. Pediarix is approved for the first three doses of the DTaP and inactivated polio vaccine (IPV) series, which are usually given at about 2, 4, and 6 months of age; it is not approved for fourth or fifth (booster) doses of the DTaP or IPV series. However, Pediarix is approved for use through 6 years of age. A child who is behind schedule can receive Pediarix as long as it is given for doses 1, 2, or 3 of the series, and the child is younger than 7 years of age.

A dose of Pediarix inadvertently administered as the fourth or fifth dose of the DTaP or IPV series does not need to be repeated.

Pediarix may be used interchangeably with other pertussis-containing vaccines if necessary (although ACIP prefers the use of the same brand of DTaP for all doses of the series, if possible). It can be given at 2, 4, and 6 months to infants who received a birth dose of hepatitis B vaccine (total of four doses of hepatitis B vaccine). Although not labeled for this indication by FDA, Pediarix may be used in infants whose mothers are HBsAg positive or whose HBsAg status is not known.

Pediarix

- DTaP–Hep B–IPV combination
- Minimum age 6 weeks
- Approved for 3 doses at 2, 4 and 6 months
- Not approved for booster doses
- Licensed for children 6 weeks through 6 years of age

14

Pediarix

- May be used interchangeably with other pertussis-containing vaccines if necessary
- Can be given at 2, 4, and 6 months to infants who received a birth dose of hepatitis B vaccine (total of 4 doses)
- May be used in infants whose mothers are HBsAg positive or status is not known*

*off-label recommendation

Pentacel

Pentacel is a combination vaccine that contains lyophilized Hib (ActHIB) vaccine that is reconstituted with a liquid DTaP-IPV solution. The vaccine was licensed by FDA in June 2008. Pentacel is licensed by FDA for doses 1 through 4 of the DTaP series among children 6 weeks through 4 years of age. The minimum intervals for Pentacel are determined by the DTaP component. The first three doses must be separated by at least 4 weeks. The fourth dose must be separated from the third by at least 6 calendar months, and not administered before 12 months of age. Pentacel should not be used for the fifth dose of the DTaP series, or for children 5 years or older regardless of the number of prior doses of the component vaccines.

The DTaP-IPV solution is licensed only for use as the diluent for the lyophilized Hib component and should not be used separately.

Other DTaP Issues

In certain circumstances, vaccination with DTaP vaccine should be delayed until a child with a known or suspected neurologic condition has been evaluated, treatment initiated, and the condition stabilized. These conditions include the presence of an evolving neurologic disorder (e.g., uncontrolled epilepsy, infantile spasms, and progressive encephalopathy), a history of seizures that has not been evaluated, or a neurologic event that occurs between doses of pertussis vaccine.

A family history of seizures or other neurologic diseases, or stable or resolved neurologic conditions (e.g., controlled idiopathic epilepsy, cerebral palsy, developmental delay) are not contraindications to pertussis vaccination. Acetaminophen or ibuprofen may be administered to children with such histories or conditions at the time of DTaP vaccination and for 24 hours thereafter to reduce the possibility of postvaccination fever, which could cause a febrile seizure.

Reducing the dose of whole-cell DTP or DTaP vaccine or giving the full dose in multiple smaller doses may result in an altered immune response and inadequate protection. Furthermore, there is no evidence that the chance of a significant vaccine reaction is likely to be reduced by this practice. The use of multiple reduced doses that together equal a full immunizing dose, or the use of smaller, divided doses is not endorsed or recommended. Any vaccination using less than the standard dose should not be counted, and the person should be revaccinated according to age.

14

Pentacel Vaccine

- Contains lyophilized Hib (ActHIB) vaccine that is reconstituted with a liquid DTaP-IPV solution
- Approved for doses 1 through 4 among children 6 weeks through 4 years of age
- The DTaP-IPV solution should not be used separately (i.e., only use to reconstitute the Hib component)

Pertussis Vaccine Use in Children with Underlying Neurologic Disorders

Underlying Condition	Recommendation
Prior seizure	Delay and assess*
Suspected neurologic disorder	Delay and assess*
Neurologic event between doses	Delay and assess*
Stable/resolved neurologic condition	Vaccinate

*vaccinate after treatment initiated and condition stabilized

---

Pertussis Vaccination of Children Who Have Recovered From Pertussis

- If documented disease, do not need additional doses of pediatric pertussis vaccine*
- Satisfactory documentation of disease:
  - recovery of *B. pertussis* on culture, or
  - typical symptoms and clinical course when epidemiologically linked to a culture-confirmed case

*Tdap is recommended when the child is age eligible

Children who have recovered from documented pertussis do not need additional doses of pediatric pertussis vaccine. However, Tdap vaccine is recommended when the child becomes age eligible. Satisfactory documentation includes recovery of *B. pertussis* on culture or typical symptoms and clinical course when these are epidemiologically linked to a culture-confirmed case, as may occur during outbreaks. When such confirmation of diagnosis is lacking, vaccination should be completed because cough illness may be caused by other *Bordetella* species, other bacteria, or certain viruses.

Contraindications and Precautions to Vaccination

DTaP

Contraindications to further vaccination with DTaP are a severe allergic reaction (anaphylaxis) to a vaccine component or following prior dose of vaccine, and encephalopathy not due to another identifiable cause occurring within 7 days after vaccination.

Moderate or severe acute illness is a precaution to vaccination. Children with mild illness, such as otitis media or upper respiratory infection, should be vaccinated. Children for whom vaccination is deferred because of moderate or severe acute illness should be vaccinated when their condition improves.

Certain infrequent adverse reactions following DTaP vaccination are considered to be precautions for subsequent doses of pediatric pertussis vaccine. These adverse reactions are a temperature of 105°F (40.5°C) or higher within 48 hours that is not due to another identifiable cause; collapse or shock-like state (hypotonic hyporesponsive episode) within 48 hours; persistent, inconsolable crying lasting 3 hours or longer, occurring within 48 hours; and convulsions with or without fever occurring within 3 days.

There are circumstances (e.g., during a communitywide outbreak of pertussis) in which the benefit of vaccination outweighs the risk, even if one of the four precautionary adverse reactions occurred following a prior dose. In these circumstances, one or more additional doses of pertussis vaccine should be considered. DTaP should be used in these circumstances.

Tdap

Tdap is contraindicated for persons with a history of a severe allergic reaction to a vaccine component or following a prior dose of vaccine. Tdap is also contraindicated for persons with a history of encephalopathy not due to

14

DTaP Contraindications

- Severe allergic reaction to vaccine component or following a prior dose
- Encephalopathy not due to another identifiable cause occurring within 7 days after vaccination

DTaP Precautions*

- Moderate or severe acute illness
- Temperature 105°F (40.5°C) or higher within 48 hours with no other identifiable cause
- Collapse or shock-like state (hypotonic hyporesponsive episode) within 48 hours
- Persistent, inconsolable crying lasting 3 hours or longer, occurring within 48 hours
- Convulsions with or without fever occurring within 3 days

*may consider use in outbreaks

Tdap Contraindications

- Severe allergic reaction to vaccine component or following a prior dose
- Encephalopathy not due to another identifiable cause occurring within 7 days after vaccination with a pertussis-containing vaccine

another identifiable cause occurring within 7 days after administration of a pertussis-containing vaccine.

Precautions to Tdap include a history of Guillain-Barré syndrome within 6 weeks after a previous dose of tetanus toxoid-containing vaccine and a progressive neurologic disorder (such as uncontrolled epilepsy or progressive encephalopathy) until the condition has stabilized. Persons with a history of a severe local reaction (Arthus reaction) following a prior dose of a tetanus and/or diphtheria toxoid-containing vaccine should generally not receive Tdap or Td vaccination until at least 10 years have elapsed after the last Td-containing vaccine. Moderate or severe acute illness is a precaution to vaccination. Persons for whom vaccination is deferred because of moderate or severe acute illness should be vaccinated when their condition improves.

As noted above, certain conditions following DTaP vaccine, such as temperature of 105°F or higher, collapse or shock-like state, persistent crying, or convulsions with or without fever are a precaution to subsequent doses of DTaP. However, occurrence of one of these adverse reactions following DTaP vaccine in childhood is not a contraindication or precaution to administration of Tdap to an adolescent or adult. A history of extensive limb swelling following DTaP is not a contra- indication to Tdap vaccination. A stable neurologic disorder (such as controlled seizures or cerebral palsy), pregnancy, breastfeeding, and immunosuppression are not contraindications or precautions to administration of Tdap.

Adverse Reactions Following Vaccination

DTaP

As with all injected vaccines, administration of DTaP may cause local reactions, such as pain, redness, or swelling. Local reactions have been reported in 20%–40% of children after the first three doses. Local reactions appear to be more frequent after the fourth and/or fifth doses. Mild systemic reactions such as drowsiness, fretfulness, and low-grade fever may also occur. Temperature of 101°F or higher is reported in 3%–5% of DTaP recipients. These reactions are self-limited and can be managed with symptomatic treatment with acetaminophen or ibuprofen. Moderate or severe systemic reactions (such as fever [105°F or higher], febrile seizures, persistent crying lasting 3 hours or longer, and hypotonic hyporesponsive episodes) have been reported after administration of DTaP but occur less frequently than among children who received whole-cell DTP. Rates of these less common reactions vary by symptom and vaccine but generally occur in fewer than 1 in 10,000 doses. See

---

Tdap Precautions

- History of Guillain-Barré syndrome within 6 weeks after a previous dose of tetanus toxoid-containing vaccine
- Progressive neurologic disorder until the condition has stabilized
- History of a severe local reaction (Arthus reaction) following a prior dose of a tetanus and/or diphtheria toxoid-containing vaccine
- Moderate or severe acute illness

14

DTaP Adverse Reactions

- Local reactions 20%-40% (pain, redness, swelling)
- Temp of 101°F 3%-5% or higher
- More severe adverse reactions not common
- Local reactions more common following 4th and 5th doses

---

the pertussis chapter in the textbook Vaccines (Plotkin and Orenstein, eds., 2008) for a comprehensive review of DTaP adverse event data.

Information on adverse reactions following a full series of DTaP is also limited. Available data suggest a substantial increase in the frequency and magnitude of local reactions after the fourth and fifth doses. For example, swelling at the site of injection occurred in 2% of patients after the first dose of Tripedia, and in 29% following the fourth dose. Increases in the frequency of fever after the fourth dose have also been reported, although the increased frequencies of other systemic reactions (e.g., fretfulness, drowsiness, or decreased appetite) have not been observed. Further details on this issue can be found in a supplemental ACIP statement published in 2000 (*MMWR* 2000;49(No RR-13):1–8).

Swelling involving the entire thigh or upper arm has been reported after booster doses of certain acellular pertussis vaccines. The limb swelling may be accompanied by erythema, pain and fever. Although the swelling may interfere with walking, most children have no limitation of activity. The pathogenesis and frequency of substantial local reactions and limb swelling are not known, but these conditions appear to be self-limited and resolve without sequelae.

ACIP recommends that a fifth dose of DTaP be administered before a child enters school. It is not known whether children who experience entire limb swelling after a fourth dose of DTaP are at increased risk for this reaction after the fifth dose. Because of the importance of this dose in protecting a child during school years, ACIP recommends that a history of extensive swelling after the fourth dose should not be considered a contraindication to receipt of a fifth dose at school entry. Parents should be informed of the increase in reactogenicity that has been reported following the fourth and fifth doses of DTaP.

Tdap

The safety of Tdap vaccines was evaluated as part of prelicensure studies. The most common adverse reaction following both brands of Tdap vaccine is a local reaction, such as pain (66%), redness (25%) or swelling (21%) at the site of injection. Temperature of 100.4°F or higher was reported by 1.4% of Tdap recipients and 1.1% of Td recipients. Tdap recipients also reported a variety of nonspecific systemic events, such as headache, fatigue and gastrointestinal symptoms. Local reactions, fever, and nonspecific systemic symptoms occurred at approximately the same rate in recipients of Tdap and the comparison group that received Td without acellular pertussis vaccine. No serious adverse events have been attributed to Tdap.

Adverse Reactions Following the 4th and 5th DTaP Dose

• Local adverse reactions and fever increased with 4th and 5th doses of DTaP

• Reports of swelling of entire limb

• Extensive swelling after 4th dose NOT a contraindication to 5th dose

---

14

Tdap Adverse Reactions

• Local reactions   21%-66%
  (pain, redness, swelling)

• Temp of 100.4°F   1.4%
  or higher

• Adverse reactions occur at approximately the same rate as Td alone (without acellular pertussis vaccine)

Pertussis

Pertussis-Containing Vaccines Storage and Handling

- Stored at 35°–46°F (2°–8°C) at all times
- Must never be frozen
- Vaccine exposed to freezing temperature must not be administered and should be discarded
- Should not be used after the expiration date printed on the box or label

Vaccine Storage and Handling

DTaP, Td and Tdap vaccines should be stored at 35°–46°F (2°–8°C) at all times. The vaccines must never be frozen. Vaccine exposed to freezing temperature must not be administered and should be discarded. DTaP, Td and Tdap should not be used after the expiration date printed on the box or label.

Selected References

American Academy of Pediatrics. Pertussis. In: Pickering L, Baker CJ, Long SS, McMillan JA,eds Red Book: *2006 Report of the Committee on Infectious Diseases*. 27th ed. Elk Grove Village, IL: American Academy of Pediatrics, 2006:498–520.

CDC. Pertussis vaccination: use of acellular pertussis vaccines among infants and young children. Recommendations of the Advisory Committee on Immunization Practices (ACIP). *MMWR* 1997;46(No. RR-7):1–25.

CDC. Recommended antimicrobial agents for the treatment and postexposure prophylaxis of pertussis. 2005 CDC Guidelines. *MMWR* 2005;54(No. RR-14):1–16.

CDC. Preventing tetanus, diphtheria, and pertussis among adolescents: use of tetanus toxoid, reduced diphtheria toxoid and acellular pertussis vaccine: recommendations of the Advisory Committee on Immunization Practices (ACIP). *MMWR* 2006;55(No. RR-3):1–43.

CDC. Preventing tetanus, diphtheria, and pertussis among adults: use of tetanus toxoid, reduced diphtheria toxoid and acellular pertussis vaccine: recommendations of the Advisory Committee on Immunization Practices (ACIP). *MMWR* 2006;55(No. RR-17):1–33.

CDC. Pertussis—United States, 2001–2003. *MMWR* 2005;54:1283–6.

Cherry JD, The epidemiology of pertussis: a comparison of the epidemiology of the disease pertussis with the epidemiology of *Bordetella pertussis* infection. *Pediatrics* 2005;115:1422–7.

Edwards KM, Decker MD. Pertussis vaccines. In: Plotkin SA, Orenstein WA, Offit PA, eds. *Vaccines*. 5th edition. Philadelphia: Saunders; 2008:467–517.

Greenberg DP. Pertussis in adolescents: increasing incidence brings attention to the need for booster immunization of adolescents. *Pediatr Infect Dis J* 2005;24:721–8.

Ward JI, Cherry JD, Chang SJ, et al. Efficacy of an acellular pertussis vaccine among adolescents and adults. *N Engl J Med* 2005;353:1555–63.

Woo EJ, Burwen DR, Gatumu SNM, et al. Extensive limb swelling after immunization: Reports to the Vaccine Adverse Event Reporting System. *Clin Infect Dis* 2003;37:351–8.

14

Pneumococcal Disease

Streptococcus pneumoniae causes an acute bacterial infection. The bacterium, also called pneumococcus, was first isolated by Pasteur in 1881 from the saliva of a patient with rabies. The association between the pneumococcus bacterium and lobar pneumonia was first described by Friedlander and Talamon in 1883, but pneumococcal pneumonia was confused with other types of pneumonia until the discovery of the Gram stain in 1884. From 1915 to 1945, the chemical structure and antigenicity of the pneumococcal capsular polysaccharide, its association with virulence, and the role of bacterial polysaccharides in human disease were explained. More than 80 serotypes of pneumococci had been described by 1940.

Efforts to develop effective pneumococcal vaccines began as early as 1911. However, with the advent of penicillin in the 1940s, interest in the vaccine declined, until it was observed that many patients still died despite antibiotic treatment. By the late 1960s, efforts were again being made to develop a polyvalent pneumococcal vaccine. The first pneumococcal vaccine was licensed in the United States in 1977. The first conjugate pneumococcal vaccine was licensed in 2000.

Streptococcus pneumoniae

Streptococcus pneumoniae bacteria are lancet-shaped, gram-positive, facultative anaerobic organisms. They are typically observed in pairs (diplococci) but may also occur singularly or in short chains. Some pneumococci are encapsulated, their surfaces composed of complex polysaccharides. Encapsulated organisms are pathogenic for humans and experimental animals, whereas organisms without capsular polysaccharides are not. Capsular polysaccharides are the primary basis for the pathogenicity of the organism. They are antigenic and form the basis for classifying pneumococci by serotypes. Ninety serotypes have been identified, based on their reaction with type-specific antisera. Type-specific antibody to capsular polysaccharide is protective. These antibodies and complement interact to opsonize pneumococci, which facilitates phagocytosis and clearance of the organism. Antibodies to some pneumococcal capsular polysaccharides may cross-react with related types as well as with other bacteria, providing protection against additional serotypes.

Most *S. pneumoniae* serotypes have been shown to cause serious disease, but only a few serotypes produce the majority of pneumococcal infections. The 10 most common serotypes are estimated to account for about 62% of invasive disease worldwide. The ranking and serotype prevalence differ by patient age group and geographic area. In the United States, the seven most common serotypes isolated from blood or cerebrospinal fluid (CSF) of children younger

Pneumococcal Disease

- *S. pneumoniae* first isolated by Pasteur in 1881
- Confused with other causes of pneumonia until discovery of Gram stain in 1884
- More than 80 serotypes described by 1940
- First U.S. vaccine in 1977

15

Streptococcus pneumoniae

- Gram-positive bacteria
- 90 known serotypes
- Polysaccharide capsule important virulence factor
- Type-specific antibody is protective

than 6 years of age account for 80% of infections. These seven serotypes account for only about 50% of isolates from older children and adults.

Pneumococci are common inhabitants of the respiratory tract and may be isolated from the nasopharynx of 5% to 70% of healthy adults. Rates of asymptomatic carriage vary with age, environment, and the presence of upper respiratory infections. Only 5%–10% of adults without children are carriers. In schools and orphanages, 27%–58% of students and residents may be carriers. On military installations, as many as 50%–60% of service personnel may be carriers. The duration of carriage varies and is generally longer in children than adults. In addition, the relationship of carriage to the development of natural immunity is poorly understood.

Clinical Features

The major clinical syndromes of pneumococcal disease are pneumonia, bacteremia, and meningitis. The immunologic mechanism that allows disease to occur in a carrier is not clearly understood. However, disease most often occurs when a predisposing condition exists, particularly pulmonary disease.

Pneumococcal pneumonia is the most common clinical presentation of pneumococcal disease among adults, although pneumonia alone is not considered to be "invasive" disease. The incubation period of pneumococcal pneumonia is short, about 1 to 3 days. Symptoms generally include an abrupt onset of fever and chills or rigors. Typically there is a single rigor, and repeated shaking chills are uncommon. Other common symptoms include pleuritic chest pain, cough productive of mucopurulent, rusty sputum, dyspnea (shortness of breath), tachypnea (rapid breathing), hypoxia (poor oxygenation), tachycardia (rapid heart rate), malaise, and weakness. Nausea, vomiting, and headaches occur less frequently.

As many as 175,000 hospitalizations from pneumococcal pneumonia are estimated to occur annually in the United States. Pneumococci account for up to 36% of adult community-acquired pneumonia and 50% of hospital-acquired pneumonia. Pneumonia is a common bacterial complication of influenza and measles. The case-fatality rate is 5%–7% and may be much higher among elderly persons. Complications of pneumococcal pneumonia include empyema (i.e., infection of the pleural space), pericarditis (inflammation of the sac surrounding the heart), and endobronchial obstruction, with atelectasis and lung abscess formation.

More than 50,000 cases of pneumococcal bacteremia occur each year. Bacteremia occurs in about 25%–30% of patients

15

Pneumococcal Pneumonia Clinical Features

- Abrupt onset
- Fever
- Shaking chills
- Pleuritic chest pain
- Productive cough
- Dyspnea, tachypnea, hypoxia

Pneumococcal Pneumonia

- Estimated 175,000 hospitalizations per year in the United States
- Up to 36% of adult community-acquired pneumonia and 50% of hospital-acquired pneumonia
- Common bacterial complication of influenza and measles
- Case-fatality rate 5%-7%, higher in elderly

Pneumococcal Bacteremia

- More than 50,000 cases per year in the United States
- Rates higher among elderly and very young infants
- Case-fatality rate ~20%; up to 60% among the elderly

with pneumococcal pneumonia. The overall case-fatality rate for bacteremia is about 20% but may be as high as 60% among elderly patients. Patients with asplenia who develop bacteremia may experience a fulminant clinical course.

Pneumococci cause 13%–19% of all cases of bacterial meningitis in the United States. An estimated 3,000 to 6,000 cases of pneumococcal meningitis occur each year. One-fourth of patients with pneumococcal meningitis also have pneumonia. The clinical symptoms, CSF profile and neurologic complications are similar to other forms of purulent bacterial meningitis. Symptoms may include headache, lethargy, vomiting, irritability, fever, nuchal rigidity, cranial nerve signs, seizures and coma. The case-fatality rate of pneumococcal meningitis is about 30% but may be as high as 80% among elderly persons. Neurologic sequelae are common among survivors. Persons with a cochlear implant appear to be at increased risk of pneumococcal meningitis.

Conditions that increase the risk of invasive pneumococcal disease include decreased immune function from disease or drugs, functional or anatomic asplenia, chronic heart, pulmonary including asthma, liver, or renal disease, smoking cigarettes, and cerebrospinal fluid, or CSF leak.

Pneumococcal Disease in Children

Bacteremia without a known site of infection is the most common invasive clinical presentation of pneumococcal infection among children 2 years of age and younger, accounting for approximately 70% of invasive disease in this age group. Bacteremic pneumonia accounts for 12%–16% of invasive pneumococcal disease among children 2 years of age and younger. With the decline of invasive Hib disease, *S. pneumoniae* has become the leading cause of bacterial meningitis among children younger than 5 years of age in the United States. Before routine use of pneumococcal conjugate vaccine, children younger than 1 year had the highest rates of pneumococcal meningitis, approximately 10 cases per 100,000 population.

Pneumococci are a common cause of acute otitis media, and are detected in 28%–55% of middle ear aspirates. By age 12 months, more than 60% of children have had at least one episode of acute otitis media. Middle ear infections are the most frequent reasons for pediatric office visits in the United States, resulting in more than 20 million visits annually. Complications of pneumococcal otitis media may include mastoiditis and meningitis.

Before routine use of pneumococcal conjugate vaccine, the burden of pneumococcal disease among children younger than 5 years of age was significant. An estimated 17,000 cases of invasive disease occurred each year, of which 13,000

Pneumococcal Meningitis

- Estimated 3,000 - 6,000 cases per year in the United States
- Case-fatality rate ~30%, up to 80% in the elderly
- Neurologic sequelae common among survivors
- Increased risk after cochlear implant

Conditions That Increase Risk for Invasive Pneumococcal Disease

- Decreased immune function
- Asplenia (functional or anatomic)
- Chronic heart, pulmonary, liver or renal disease
- Cigarette smoking
- Cerebrospinal fluid (CSF) leak

15

Pneumococcal Disease in Children

- Bacteremia without known site of infection most common clinical presentation
- *S. pneumoniae* leading cause of bacterial meningitis among children <5 years of age
- Common cause of acute otitis media

Burden of Pneumococcal Disease in Children*

Syndrome	Cases
Bacteremia	13,000
Meningitis	700
Death	200
Otitis media	5,000,000

*Prior to routine use of pneumococcal conjugate vaccine

were bacteremia without a known site of infection and about 700 were meningitis. An estimated 200 children died every year as a result of invasive pneumococcal disease. Although not considered invasive disease, an estimated 5 million cases of acute otitis media occured each year among children younger than 5 years of age.

Children with functional or anatomic asplenia, particularly those with sickle cell disease, and children with human immunodeficiency virus (HIV) infection are at very high risk for invasive disease, with rates in some studies more than 50 times higher than those among children of the same age without these conditions (i.e., incidence rates of 5,000–9,000 per 100,000 population). Rates are also increased among children of certain racial and ethnic groups, in particular those of Alaska Native, African American, and certain American Indian groups (Arizona, New Mexico, and Navajo populations in Colorado and Utah). The reason for this increased risk by race and ethnicity is not known with certainty but was also noted for invasive *Haemophilus influenzae* infection (also an encapsulated bacterium). Attendance at a child care center has also been shown to increase the risk of invasive pneumococcal disease and acute otitis media 2–3-fold among children younger than 59 months of age. Children with a cochlear implant are at increased risk for pneumococcal meningitis.

Children at Increased Risk of Invasive Pneumococcal Disease

- Functional or anatomic asplenia, especially sickle cell disease
- HIV infection
- Alaska Native, African American, American Indian
- Child care attendance
- Cochlear implant

Laboratory Diagnosis

A definitive diagnosis of infection with *S. pneumoniae* generally relies on isolation of the organism from blood or other normally sterile body sites. Tests are also available to detect capsular polysaccharide antigen in body fluids.

The appearance of lancet-shaped diplococci on Gram stain is suggestive of pneumococcal infection, but interpretation of stained sputum specimens may be difficult because of the presence of normal nasopharyngeal bacteria. The suggested criteria for obtaining a diagnosis of pneumococcal pneumonia using Gram stained sputnum includes more than 25 white blood cells and fewer than 10 epithelial cells per 100-power field, and a predominance of gram-positive diplococci.

The quellung reaction (capsular swelling; capsular precipitation reaction) is a test that provides rapid identification of pneumococci in clinical specimens, including spinal fluid, sputum, and exudates. The procedure involves mixing loopfuls of bacteria in suspension, pneumococcal antiserum, and methylene blue on the surface of a glass slide and examining under oil immersion. If the reaction is positive, the organism will be surrounded by a large capsule.

15

Several rapid tests for detection of pneumococcal polysaccharide antigen in CSF and other body fluids are available. These tests generally lack sufficient sensitivity or specificity to assist in the diagnosis of invasive pneumococcal disease.

Medical Management

Resistance to penicillin and other antibiotics is common. In some areas of the United States, up to 40% of invasive pneumococcal isolates are resistant to penicillin. Treatment will usually include a broad-spectrum cephalosporin, and often vancomycin, until results of antibiotic sensitivity testing are available.

Epidemiology

Occurrence

Pneumococcal disease occurs throughout the world.

Reservoir

S. pneumoniae is a human pathogen. The reservoir for pneumococci is presumably the nasopharynx of asymptomatic human carriers. There is no animal or insect vector.

Transmission

Transmission of *S. pneumoniae* occurs as the result of direct person-to-person contact via respiratory droplets and by autoinoculation in persons carrying the bacteria in their upper respiratory tract. The pneumococcal serotypes most often responsible for causing infection are those most frequently found in carriers. The spread of the organism within a family or household is influenced by such factors as crowding, season, and the presence of upper respiratory infections or pneumococcal disease such as pneumonia or otitis media. The spread of pneumococcal disease is usually associated with increased carriage rates. However, high carriage rates do not appear to increase the risk of disease transmission in households.

Temporal Pattern

Pneumococcal infections are more common during the winter and in early spring when respiratory diseases are more prevalent.

Communicability

The period of communicability for pneumococcal disease is unknown, but presumably transmission can occur as long as the organism appears in respiratory secretions.

Pneumococcal Disease Epidemiology	
• Reservoir	Human carriers
• Transmission	Respiratory Autoinoculation
• Temporal pattern	Winter and early spring
• Communicability	Unknown Probably as long as organism in respiratory secretions

15

Secular Trends in the United States

Estimates of the incidence of pneumococcal disease have been made from a variety of population-based studies. More than 40,000 cases and more than 4,400 deaths from invasive pneumococcal disease (bacteremia and meningitis) are estimated to have occurred in the United States in 2007. More than half of these cases occurred in adults who had an indication for pneumococcal polysaccharide vaccine. In addition, there are thousands of cases of nonbacteremic pneumonia, and millions of cases of otitis media, which are considered noninvasive infections.

The overall incidence of invasive pneumococcal disease (bacteremia, meningitis, or other infection of a normally sterile site) in the United States in 1998–1999 was estimated to be approximately 24 cases per 100,000 population. However, incidence rates vary greatly by age group. The highest rates of invasive pneumococcal disease occur among young children, especially those younger than 2 years of age. In 1998, the rate of invasive disease in this age group was estimated to be 188 per 100,000 population; this age group accounted for 20% of all cases of invasive pneumococcal disease. Incidence was lowest among persons 5–17 years of age, and increased to 61 per 100,000 population among persons 65 years of age and older.

Data from the Active Bacterial Core surveillance (ABCs) system suggest that the use of pneumococcal conjugate vaccine is having an impact on the incidence of invasive disease among young children. Data from 2006 indicate that rates of invasive disease due to vaccine serotypes have declined more than 95% among children younger than 5 years of age, compared with 1998–1999 (prior to licensure of the vaccine).

Community-acquired pneumococcal pneumonia is usually a sporadic disease in carriers who have a breakdown in their pulmonary defense mechanisms. Outbreaks of pneumococcal pneumonia are not common. When outbreaks occur, they are usually in crowded environments, such as correctional facilities and nursing homes. During outbreaks, persons with invasive disease often have underlying illness and may have a high fatality rate.

Pneumococcal Vaccines

Characteristics

Pneumococcal Polysaccharide Vaccine

Pneumococcal polysaccharide vaccine is composed of purified preparations of pneumococcal capsular polysaccharide. The first polysaccharide pneumococcal vaccine was licensed in the United States in 1977. It contained purified capsular polysaccharide antigen from 14 different types of pneumococcal bacteria. In 1983, a 23-valent polysaccharide

---

Invasive Pneumococcal Disease Incidence by Age Group—1998

*Rate per 100,000 population
Source: Active Bacterial Core surveillance/EIP Network

Rate (per 100,000) of Invasive Pneumococcal Disease (IPD) Among Children Younger Than 5 Years of Age

	Before Vaccine	2006
All IPD	100	24
Vaccine serotypes	80	0.5

Source. Active Bacteria Core Surveillance/EIP Network

Pneumococcal Disease Outbreaks

- Outbreaks not common
- Generally occur in crowded environments (jails, nursing homes)
- Persons with invasive disease often have underlying illness
- May have high fatality rate

Pneumococcal Vaccines

1977	14-valent polysaccharide vaccine licensed
1983	23-valent polysaccharide vaccine licensed (PPSV23)
2000	7-valent polysaccharide conjugate vaccine licensed (PCV7)

15

vaccine (PPSV23) was licensed and replaced the 14-valent vaccine, which is no longer produced. PPSV23 contains polysaccharide antigen from 23 types of pneumococcal bacteria that cause 88% of bacteremic pneumococcal disease. In addition, cross-reactivity occurs for several capsular types that account for an additional 8% of bacteremic disease.

The polysaccharide vaccine currently available in the United States (Pneumovax 23, Merck) contains 25 mcg of each antigen per dose and contains 0.25% phenol as a preservative. The vaccine is available in a single-dose vial or syringe, and in a 5-dose vial. Pneumococcal vaccine is given by injection and may be administered either intramuscularly or subcutaneously.

Pneumococcal Conjugate Vaccine

The first pneumococcal conjugate vaccine (PCV7) was licensed in the United States in 2000. It includes purified capsular polysaccharide of seven serotypes of *S. pneumoniae* (4, 9V, 14, 19F, 23F, 18C, and 6B) conjugated to a nontoxic variant of diphtheria toxin known as CRM197. The serotypes included in PCV7 accounted for 86% of bacteremia, 83% of meningitis, and 65% of acute otitis media among children younger than 6 years of age in the United States during 1978–1994. Additional pneumococcal polysaccharide conjugate vaccines containing 9 and 11 serotypes of *S. pneumoniae* are being developed. The vaccine is administered intramuscularly. It does not contain thimerosal as a preservative, and is available only in single-dose vials.

Immunogenicity and Vaccine Efficacy

Pneumococcal Polysaccharide Vaccine

More than 80% of healthy adults who receive PPSV23 develop antibodies against the serotypes contained in the vaccine, usually within 2 to 3 weeks after vaccination. Older adults, and persons with some chronic illnesses or immunodeficiency may not respond as well, if at all. In children younger than 2 years of age, antibody response to most serotypes is generally poor. Elevated antibody levels persist for at least 5 years in healthy adults but decline more quickly in persons with certain underlying illnesses.

PPSV23 vaccine efficacy studies have resulted in various estimates of clinical effectiveness. Overall, the vaccine is 60%–70% effective in preventing invasive disease. The vaccine may be less effective in preventing pneumococcal infection in some groups, particularly those with significant underlying illness. Although the vaccine may not be as effective in some persons, especially those who do not have normal resistance to infection, it is still recommended for such persons because they are at high risk of developing

---

Pneumococcal Polysaccharide Vaccine

- Purified capsular polysaccharide antigen from 23 types of pneumococcus
- Account for 88% of bacteremic pneumococcal disease
- Cross-react with types causing additional 8% of disease

Pneumococcal Conjugate Vaccine

- Pneumococcal polysaccharide conjugated to nontoxic diphtheria toxin (7 serotypes)
- Vaccine serotypes account for 86% of bacteremia and 83% of meningitis among children <6 years of age

---

15

Pneumococcal Polysaccharide Vaccine

- Purified pneumococcal polysaccharide (23 types)
- Not effective in children <2 years
- 60%-70% against invasive disease
- Less effective in preventing pneumococcal pneumonia

severe disease. PPSV23 has not been demonstrated to provide protection against pneumococcal pneumonia. For this reason, providers should avoid referring to PPSV23 as "pneumonia vaccine."

Studies comparing patterns of pneumococcal carriage before and after PPSV23 vaccination have not shown clinically significant decreases in carrier rates among vaccinees. In addition, no change in the distribution of vaccine-type and non–vaccine-type organisms has been observed as the result of vaccination.

Pneumococcal Conjugate Vaccine

After four doses of PCV7 vaccine, more than 90% of healthy infants develop antibody to all seven serotypes contained in the vaccine. PCV7 has been shown to be immunogenic in infants and children, including those with sickle cell disease and HIV infection. In a large clinical trial, PCV7 was shown to reduce invasive disease caused by vaccine serotypes by 97%, and reduce invasive disease caused by all serotypes, including serotypes not in the vaccine, by 89%. Efficacy against pneumonia varied depending on the specificity of the diagnosis. The vaccine reduced clinically diagnosed pneumonia by 11%, but reduced pneumonia confirmed by x-ray with consolidation of 2.5 or more centimeters by 73%. Children who received PCV7 had 7% fewer episodes of acute otitis media and underwent 20% fewer tympanostomy tube placements than did unvaccinated children. The duration of protection following PCV7 is currently not known. There is evidence that PCV7 reduces nasopharyngeal carriage of pneumococcal serotypes included in the vaccine.

Vaccination Schedule and Use

Pneumococcal Polysaccharide Vaccine

Pneumococcal polysaccharide vaccine should be administered routinely to all adults 65 years of age and older. The vaccine is also indicated for persons 2 years of age and older with a normal immune system who have a chronic illness, including cardiovascular disease, pulmonary disease, diabetes, alcoholism, cirrhosis, cerebrospinal fluid leak, or a cochlear implant.

Immunocompromised persons 2 years of age and older who are at increased risk of pneumococcal disease or its complications should also be vaccinated. This group includes persons with splenic dysfunction or absence (either from disease or surgical removal), Hodgkin disease, lymphoma, multiple myeloma, chronic renal failure, nephrotic syndrome (a type of kidney disease), or conditions such as organ transplantation associated with immunosuppression. Persons immunosuppressed from chemotherapy

Pneumococcal Conjugate Vaccine

- Highly immunogenic in infants and young children, including those with high-risk medical conditions
- >90% effective against invasive disease
- Less effective against pneumonia and acute otitis media

Pneumococcal Polysaccharide Vaccine Recommendations

- Adults 65 years of age or older
- Persons 2 years of age or older with
  —chronic illness
  —anatomic or functional asplenia
  —immunocompromised (disease, chemotherapy, steroids)
  —HIV infection
  —environments or settings with increased risk
  —cochlear implant

15

or high-dose corticosteroid therapy (14 days or longer) should be vaccinated. Persons 2 years of age and older with asymptomatic or symptomatic HIV infection should be vaccinated. Pneumococcal vaccine should be considered for persons living in special environments or social settings with an identified increased risk of pneumococcal disease or its complications, such as certain Native American (i.e., Alaska Native, Navajo, and Apache) populations.

In 2008 ACIP added two new indications for pneumococcal polysaccharide vaccine for adults 19 years of age and older. These new indications are asthma and cigarette smoking. These groups were added because of evidence of an increased risk of invasive pneumococcal disease. Available data do NOT support asthma or cigarette smoking as indications for PPSV23 among persons younger than 19 years.

If elective splenectomy or cochlear implant is being considered, the vaccine should be given at least 2 weeks before the procedure. If vaccination prior to the procedure is not feasible, the vaccine should be given as soon as possible after surgery. Similarly, there should also be a 2-week interval between vaccination and initiation of cancer chemotherapy or other immunosuppressive therapy, if possible.

Providers should not withhold vaccination in the absence of an immunization record or complete record. The patient's verbal history may be used to determine vaccination status. Persons with uncertain or unknown vaccination status should be vaccinated.

The target groups for pneumococcal polysaccharide vaccine and influenza vaccine overlap. These vaccines should be given at the same time at different sites if indicated, although most recipients need only a single lifetime dose of PPSV23 (see Revaccination).

Pneumococcal Conjugate Vaccine

All children younger than 24 months of age and children age 24–59 months with a high-risk medical condition should be routinely vaccinated with PCV7. The primary series beginning in infancy consists of three doses routinely given at 2, 4, and 6 months of age. A fourth (booster) dose is recommended at 12–15 months of age. PCV7 should be administered at the same time as other routine childhood immunizations, using a separate syringe and injection site. For children vaccinated at younger than 12 months of age, the minimum interval between doses is 4 weeks. Doses given at 12 months of age and older should be separated by at least 8 weeks.

Unvaccinated children 7 months of age and older do not require a full series of four doses. The number of doses a

15

> ### Pneumococcal Conjugate Vaccine
>
> - Routine vaccination of children age <24 months and children 24-59 months with a high-risk medical condition
> - Doses at 2, 4, 6, months of age, booster dose at 12-15 months of age
> - Unvaccinated children >7 months of age require fewer doses

> ### Pneumococcal Conjugate Vaccine
>
> - Children aged 24-59 months at high risk and previously vaccinated with PPV23 should receive 2 doses of PCV7
> - Children at high risk who previously received PCV7 should receive PPV23 at age >2 years

child needs to complete the series depends on the child's current age. Unvaccinated children aged 7 through 11 months should receive two doses of vaccine at least 4 weeks apart, followed by a booster dose at age 12 thorugh 15 months. Unvaccinated children aged 12 through 23 months should receive two doses of vaccine, at least 8 weeks apart. Previously unvaccinated healthy children 24 through 59 months of age should receive a single dose of PCV7. Unvaccinated children 24 through 59 months of age with sickle cell disease, asplenia, HIV infection, chronic illness, cochlear implant, or immunocompromising conditions should receive two doses of PCV7 separated by at least 8 weeks.

PCV7 is not routinely recommended for persons older than 59 months of age.

Few data are available on the use of PCV7 among children previously vaccinated with PPSV23. Children 24 through 59 months of age who have already received PPSV23 and who are at high risk of invasive pneumococcal disease (sickle cell disease, asplenia, cochlear implant, HIV infection or other immunocompromising conditions or chronic diseases) could benefit from the immunologic priming induced by PPSV23. ACIP recommends that these children receive two doses of PCV7 separated by at least 8 weeks. The first dose of PCV7 should be given no sooner than 2 months after PPSV23. Similarly, children 24 through 59 months of age who have already received one or more doses of PCV7 and who are at high risk of invasive pneumococcal disease will benefit from the additional serotypes included in PPSV23. Vaccination with PPSV23 should be considered for these high-risk children. PPSV23 should be given no sooner than 2 months after the last dose of PCV7. Routine administration of PPSV23 to healthy children 24 through 59 months of age is not recommended.

Revaccination

Pneumococcal Polysaccharide Vaccine
Following vaccination with PPSV23, antibody levels decline after 5–10 years and decrease more rapidly in some groups than others. However, the relationship between antibody titer and protection from invasive disease is not certain (i.e., higher antibody level does not necessarily mean better protection), so the ability to define the need for revaccination based only on serology is limited. In addition, currently available pneumococcal polysaccharide vaccines elicit a T-cell-independent response, and do not produce a sustained increase ("boost") in antibody titers. Available data do not indicate a substantial increase in protection in the majority of revaccinated persons.

Pneumococcal Polysaccharide Vaccine Revaccination

- Routine revaccination of immunocompetent persons is not recommended
- Revaccination recommended for persons age >2 years at highest risk of serious pneumococcal infection
- Single revaccination dose >5 years after first dose

Because of the lack of evidence of improved protection with multiple doses of pneumococcal vaccine, routine revaccination of immunocompetent persons previously vaccinated with 23-valent polysaccharide vaccine is not recommended. However, revaccination is recommended for persons 2 years of age and older who are at highest risk for serious pneumococcal infection and for those who are likely to have a rapid decline in pneumococcal antibody levels. Only one PPSV23 revaccination dose is recommended for high-risk persons. The second dose should be administered 5 or more years after the first dose. Revaccination 3 years after the previous dose may be considered for children at highest risk for severe pneumococcal infection who would be 10 years of age or less at the time of revaccination, including children who received PCV7.

Persons at highest risk include all persons 2 years of age and older with functional or anatomic asplenia (e.g., from sickle cell disease or splenectomy), HIV infection, leukemia, lymphoma, Hodgkin disease, multiple myeloma, generalized malignancy, chronic renal failure, nephrotic syndrome, or other conditions associated with immunosuppression (e.g., organ or bone marrow transplantation) and those receiving immunosuppressive chemotherapy, including long-term corticosteroids. Persons aged 65 years and older should be administered a second dose of pneumococcal vaccine if they received the vaccine more than 5 years previously, and were younger than 65 years of age at the time of the first dose.

Pneumococcal Conjugate Vaccine

Revaccination after an age-appropriate primary series with PCV7 is not currently recommended.

Contraindications and Precautions to Vaccination

For both pneumococcal polysaccharide and conjugate vaccines, a severe allergic reaction (anaphylaxis) to a vaccine component or following a prior dose is a contraindication to further doses of vaccine. Such allergic reactions are rare. Persons with moderate or severe acute illness should not be vaccinated until their condition improves. However, minor illnesses, such as upper respiratory infections, are not a contraindication to vaccination.

The safety of PPSV23 vaccine for pregnant women has not been studied, although no adverse consequences have been reported among newborns whose mothers were inadvertently vaccinated during pregnancy. Women who are at high risk of pneumococcal disease and who are candidates for pneumococcal vaccine should be vaccinated before pregnancy, if possible.

Pneumococcal Polysaccharide Vaccine Candidates for Revaccination

- Persons ≥2 years of age with:
  - functional or anatomic asplenia
  - immunosuppression
  - transplant
  - chronic renal failure
  - nephrotic syndrome
- Persons vaccinated at <65 years of age

15

Pneumococcal Vaccines Contraindications and Precautions

- Severe allergic reaction to vaccine component or following prior dose of vaccine
- Moderate or severe acute illness

> **Pneumococcal Vaccines Adverse Reactions**
>
> - Local reactions
>   - polysaccharide   30%-50%
>   - conjugate   10%-20%
> - Fever, myalgia
>   - polysaccharide   <1%
>   - conjugate   15%-24%
> - Severe adverse reactions   rare

Adverse Reactions Following Vaccination

Pneumococcal Polysaccharide Vaccine

The most common adverse reactions following either pneumococcal polysaccharide or conjugate vaccine are local reactions. For PPSV23, 30%–50% of vaccinees report pain, swelling, or erythema at the site of injection. These reactions usually persist for less than 48 hours.

Local reactions are reported more frequently following a second dose of PPSV23 vaccine than following the first dose. Moderate systemic reactions (such as fever and myalgia) are not common (fewer than 1% of vaccinees), and more severe systemic adverse reactions are rare.

A transient increase in HIV replication has been reported following PPSV23 vaccine. No clinical or immunologic deterioration has been reported in these persons.

Pneumococcal Conjugate Vaccine

Local reactions following PCV7 occur in 10%–20% of recipients. Fewer than 3% of local reactions are considered to be severe (e.g., tenderness that interferes with limb movement). Local reactions are more common with the fourth dose than with the first three doses. In clinical trials of pneumococcal conjugate vaccine, fever (higher than 100.4°F [38°C]) within 48 hours of any dose of the primary series was reported for 15%–24% of children. However, in these studies, whole-cell pertussis vaccine was administered simultaneously with each dose, and some or most of the reported febrile episodes may be attributable to the DTP. In one study, acellular pertussis vaccine (DTaP) was given at the same visit as the booster dose of PCV7. In this study, 11% of recipients had a temperature higher than 102.2°F (39°C). No severe adverse events attributable to PCV7 have been reported.

Vaccine Storage and Handling

Pneumococcal polysaccharide vaccine should be shipped in an insulated container with coolant packs. Although pneumococcal polysaccharide vaccine can tolerate room temperature for a few days, CDC recommends that the vaccine be stored at refrigerator temperature (35°–46°F [2°–8°C]).

Pneumococcal conjugate vaccine should be stored at refrigerator temperature. Pneumococcal vaccines must not be frozen.

Opened multidose vials may be used until the expiration date printed on the package if they are not visibly contaminated.

Goals and Coverage Levels

The *Healthy People 2010* goal is to achieve at least 90% coverage for pneumococcal polysaccharide vaccine among persons 65 years of age and older. Data from the 2003 Behavioral Risk Factor Surveillance System (BRFSS, a population-based, random-digit-dialed telephone survey of the noninstitutionalized U.S. population 18 years of age and older) estimate that 64% of persons 65 years of age or older had ever received pneumococcal polysaccharide. Vaccination coverage levels were lower among persons 18–64 years of age with a chronic illness.

Opportunities to vaccinate high-risk persons are missed both at the time of hospital discharge and during visits to clinicians' offices. Effective programs for vaccine delivery are needed, including offering the vaccine in hospitals at discharge and in clinicians' offices, nursing homes, and other long-term care facilities.

More than 65% of the persons who have been hospitalized with severe pneumococcal disease had been admitted to a hospital in the preceding 3–5 years, yet few had received pneumococcal vaccine. In addition, persons who frequently visit physicians and who have chronic conditions are more likely to be at high risk of pneumococcal infection than those who require infrequent visits. Screening and subsequent immunization of hospitalized persons found to be at high risk could have a significant impact on reducing complications and death associated with pneumococcal disease.

Pneumococcal Polysaccharide Vaccine Coverage

- Healthy People 2010 goal: 90% coverage for persons ≥65 years
- 2003 BRFSS: 64% of persons ≥65 years of age ever vaccinated
- Vaccination coverage levels were lower among persons 18-64 years of age with a chronic illness

---

Pneumococcal Polysaccharide Vaccine Missed Opportunities

- >65% of patients with severe pneumococcal disease had been hospitalized within preceding 3-5 years yet few had received vaccine
- May be administered simultaneously with influenza vaccine

15

Selected References

Black S, Shinefield HR, Fireman B, et al. Efficacy, safety and immunogenicity of heptavalent pneumococcal conjugate vaccine in children. *Pediatr Infect Dis J* 2000;19:187–95.

CDC. Active Bacterial Core surveillance. Available at http://www.cdc.gov/ncidod/dbmd/abcs/.

CDC. Pneumococcal vaccination for cochlear implant candidates and recipients: updated recommendations of the Advisory Committee on Immunization Practices. MMWR 2003;52(31):739-40.

CDC. Prevention of pneumococcal disease among infants and young children using a pneumococcal conjugate vaccine. Recommendations of the Advisory Committee on Immunization Practices (ACIP). *MMWR* 2000;49(No. RR-9):1–35.

CDC. Prevention of pneumococcal disease. Recommendations of the Advisory Committee on Immunization Practices (ACIP). *MMWR* 1997;46(No. RR-8):1–24.

CDC. Public health and aging: influenza vaccination coverage among adults aged >50 years and pneumococcal vaccination coverage among adults aged >65 years—United States, 2002. *MMWR* 2003;52:987–92.

Jackson LA, Benson P, Sneller VP, et al. Safety of revaccination with pneumococcal polysaccharide vaccine. *JAMA* 1999;281:243–8.

Robinson KA, Baughman W, Rothrock G. Epidemiology of invasive *Streptococcus pneumoniae* infections in the United States, 1995–1998. Opportunities for prevention in the conjugate vaccine era. *JAMA* 2001;285:1729–35.

Whitney CG. The potential of pneumococcal conjugate vaccines for children. Pediatr Infect Dis J 2002;21:961–70.

Whitney CG, Farley MM, Hadler J, et al. Decline in invasive pneumococcal disease after introduction of protein-polysaccharide conjugate vaccine. *N Engl J Med* 2003;348:1737–46.

Whitney CG, Shaffner W, Butler JC. Rethinking recommendations for use of pneumococcal vaccines in adults. *Clin Infect Dis* 2001;33:662–75.

Whitney CG. Impact of conjugate pneumococcal vaccines. *Pediatr Infect Dis J* 2005;24:729–30.

15

Poliomyelitis

The words polio (grey) and myelon (marrow, indicating the spinal cord) are derived from the Greek. It is the effect of poliomyelitis virus on the spinal cord that leads to the classic manifestation of paralysis.

Records from antiquity mention crippling diseases compatible with poliomyelitis. Michael Underwood first described a debility of the lower extremities in children that was recognizable as poliomyelitis in England in 1789. The first outbreaks in Europe were reported in the early 19th century, and outbreaks were first reported in the United States in 1843. For the next hundred years, epidemics of polio were reported from developed countries in the Northern Hemisphere each summer and fall. These epidemics became increasingly severe, and the average age of persons affected rose. The increasingly older age of persons with primary infection increased both the disease severity and number of deaths from polio. Polio reached a peak in the United States in 1952, with more than 21,000 paralytic cases. However, following introduction of effective vaccines, polio incidence declined rapidly. The last case of wild-virus polio acquired in the United States was in 1979, and global polio eradication may be achieved within the next decade.

Poliovirus

Poliovirus is a member of the enterovirus subgroup, family Picornaviridae. Enteroviruses are transient inhabitants of the gastrointestinal tract, and are stable at acid pH. Picornaviruses are small, ether-insensitive viruses with an RNA genome.

There are three poliovirus serotypes (P1, P2, and P3). There is minimal heterotypic immunity between the three serotypes. That is, immunity to one serotype does not produce significant immunity to the other serotypes.

The poliovirus is rapidly inactivated by heat, formaldehyde, chlorine, and ultraviolet light.

Pathogenesis

The virus enters through the mouth, and primary multiplication of the virus occurs at the site of implantation in the pharynx and gastrointestinal tract. The virus is usually present in the throat and in the stool before the onset of illness. One week after onset there is less virus in the throat, but virus continues to be excreted in the stool for several weeks. The virus invades local lymphoid tissue, enters the bloodstream, and then may infect cells of the central nervous system. Replication of poliovirus in motor neurons of the anterior horn and brain stem results in cell destruction and causes the typical manifestations of poliomyelitis.

Poliomyelitis
- First described by Michael Underwood in 1789
- First outbreak described in U.S. in 1843
- More than 21,000 paralytic cases reported in the U.S. in 1952
- Global eradication within next decade

Poliovirus
- Enterovirus (RNA)
- Three serotypes: 1, 2, 3
- Minimal heterotypic immunity between serotypes
- Rapidly inactivated by heat, formaldehyde, chlorine, ultraviolet light

Poliomyelitis Pathogenesis
- Entry into mouth
- Replication in pharynx, GI tract, local lymphatics
- Hematologic spread to lymphatics and central nervous system
- Viral spread along nerve fibers
- Destruction of motor neurons

16

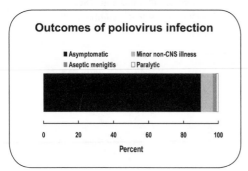

Outcomes of poliovirus infection

- Asymptomatic
- Aseptic menigitis
- Minor non-CNS illness
- Paralytic

Percent

Clinical Features

The incubation period for poliomyelitis is commonly 6 to 20 days with a range of 3 to 35 days.

The response to poliovirus infection is highly variable and has been categorized on the basis of the severity of clinical presentation.

Up to 95% of all polio infections are inapparent or asymptomatic. Estimates of the ratio of inapparent to paralytic illness vary from 50:1 to 1,000:1 (usually 200:1). Infected persons without symptoms shed virus in the stool and are able to transmit the virus to others.

Approximately 4%–8% of polio infections consist of a minor, nonspecific illness without clinical or laboratory evidence of central nervous system invasion. This clinical presentation is known as abortive poliomyelitis, and is characterized by complete recovery in less than a week. Three syndromes observed with this form of poliovirus infection are upper respiratory tract infection (sore throat and fever), gastrointestinal disturbances (nausea, vomiting, abdominal pain, constipation or, rarely, diarrhea), and influenza-like illness. These syndromes are indistinguishable from other viral illnesses.

Nonparalytic aseptic meningitis (symptoms of stiffness of the neck, back, and/or legs), usually following several days after a prodrome similar to that of minor illness, occurs in 1%–2% of polio infections. Increased or abnormal sensations can also occur. Typically these symptoms will last from 2 to 10 days, followed by complete recovery.

Fewer than 1% of all polio infections result in flaccid paralysis. Paralytic symptoms generally begin 1 to 10 days after prodromal symptoms and progress for 2 to 3 days. Generally, no further paralysis occurs after the temperature returns to normal. The prodrome may be biphasic, especially in children, with initial minor symptoms separated by a 1- to 7-day period from more major symptoms. Additional prodromal signs and symptoms can include a loss of superficial reflexes, initially increased deep tendon reflexes and severe muscle aches and spasms in the limbs or back. The illness progresses to flaccid paralysis with diminished deep tendon reflexes, reaches a plateau without change for days to weeks, and is usually asymmetrical. Strength then begins to return. Patients do not experience sensory losses or changes in cognition.

Many persons with paralytic poliomyelitis recover completely and, in most, muscle function returns to some degree. Weakness or paralysis still present 12 months after onset is usually permanent.

Paralytic polio is classified into three types, depending on

16

the level of involvement. Spinal polio is most common, and during 1969–1979, accounted for 79% of paralytic cases. It is characterized by asymmetric paralysis that most often involves the legs. Bulbar polio leads to weakness of muscles innervated by cranial nerves and accounted for 2% of cases during this period. Bulbospinal polio, a combination of bulbar and spinal paralysis, accounted for 19% of cases.

The death-to-case ratio for paralytic polio is generally 2%–5% among children and up to 15%–30% for adults (depending on age). It increases to 25%–75% with bulbar involvement.

Laboratory Diagnosis

Viral Isolation

Poliovirus may be recovered from the stool or pharynx of a person with poliomyelitis. Isolation of virus from the cerebrospinal fluid (CSF) is diagnostic, but is rarely accomplished.

If poliovirus is isolated from a person with acute flaccid paralysis, it must be tested further, using oligonucleotide mapping (fingerprinting) or genomic sequencing, to determine if the virus is "wild type" (that is, the virus that causes polio disease) or vaccine type (virus that could derive from a vaccine strain).

Serology

Neutralizing antibodies appear early and may be at high levels by the time the patient is hospitalized; therefore, a fourfold rise in antibody titer may not be demonstrated.

Cerebrospinal Fluid

In poliovirus infection, the CSF usually contains an increased number of white blood cells (10–200 cells/mm3, primarily lymphocytes) and a mildly elevated protein (40–50 mg/100 mL).

Epidemiology

Occurrence

At one time poliovirus infection occurred throughout the world. Transmission of wild poliovirus was interrupted in the United States in 1979, or possibly earlier. A polio eradication program conducted by the Pan American Health Organization led to elimination of polio in the Western Hemisphere in 1991. The Global Polio Eradication Program has dramatically reduced poliovirus transmission throughout the world. In 2008, only 1,655 confirmed cases of polio were reported globally and polio was endemic in four countries.

16

Poliomyelitis

Reservoir
Humans are the only known reservoir of poliovirus, which is transmitted most frequently by persons with inapparent infections. There is no asymptomatic carrier state except in immune deficient persons.

Transmission
Person-to-person spread of poliovirus via the fecal-oral route is the most important route of transmission, although the oral-oral route may account for some cases.

Temporal Pattern
Poliovirus infection typically peaks in the summer months in temperate climates. There is no seasonal pattern in tropical climates.

Communicability
Poliovirus is highly infectious, with seroconversion rates among susceptible household contacts of children nearly 100%, and greater than 90% among susceptible household contacts of adults. Persons infected with poliovirus are most infectious from 7 to 10 days before and after the onset of symptoms, but poliovirus may be present in the stool from 3 to 6 weeks.

Secular Trends in the United States
Before the 18th century, polioviruses probably circulated widely. Initial infections with at least one type probably occurred in early infancy, when transplacentally acquired maternal antibodies were high. Exposure throughout life probably provided continual boosting of immunity, and paralytic infections were probably rare. (This view has been recently challenged based on data from lameness studies in developing countries.)

In the immediate prevaccine era, improved sanitation allowed less frequent exposure and increased the age of primary infection. Boosting of immunity from natural exposure became more infrequent and the number of susceptible persons accumulated, ultimately resulting in the occurrence of epidemics, with 13,000 to 20,000 paralytic cases reported annually.

In the early vaccine era, the incidence dramatically decreased after the introduction of inactivated polio vaccine (IPV) in 1955. The decline continued following oral polio vaccine (OPV) introduction in 1961. In 1960, a total of 2,525 paralytic cases were reported, compared with 61 in 1965.

The last cases of paralytic poliomyelitis caused by endemic transmission of wild virus in the United States were in

Poliovirus Epidemiology

- Reservoir — Human
- Transmission — Fecal-oral; Oral-oral possible
- Communicability — 7 to 10 days before onset; Virus present in stool 3 to 6 weeks

16

1979, when an outbreak occurred among the Amish in several Midwest states. The virus was imported from the Netherlands.

From 1980 through 1999, a total of 152 confirmed cases of paralytic poliomyelitis were reported, an average of 8 cases per year. Six cases were acquired outside the United States and imported. The last imported case was reported in 1993. Two cases were classified as indeterminant (no poliovirus isolated from samples obtained from the patients, and patients had no history of recent vaccination or direct contact with a vaccine recipient). The remaining 144 (95%) cases were vaccine-associated paralytic polio (VAPP) caused by live oral polio vaccine.

In order to eliminate VAPP from the United States, ACIP recommended in 2000 that IPV be used exclusively in the United States. The last case of VAPP acquired in the United States was reported in 1999. In 2005, an unvaccinated U.S. resident was infected with polio vaccine virus in Costa Rica and subsequently developed VAPP. Also in 2005, several asymptomatic infections with a vaccine-derived poliovirus were detected in unvaccinated children in Minnesota. The source of the vaccine virus has not been determined, but it appeared to have been circulating among humans for at least 2 years based on genetic changes in the virus. No VAPP has been reported from this virus.

Poliovirus Vaccines

Inactivated poliovirus vaccine (IPV) was licensed in 1955 and was used extensively from that time until the early 1960s. In 1961, type 1 and 2 monovalent oral poliovirus vaccine (MOPV) was licensed, and in 1962, type 3 MOPV was licensed. In 1963, trivalent OPV was licensed and largely replaced IPV use. Trivalent OPV was the vaccine of choice in the United States and most other countries of the world after its introduction in 1963. An enhanced-potency IPV was licensed in November 1987 and first became available in 1988. Use of OPV was discontinued in the United States in 2000.

Characteristics

Inactivated poliovirus vaccine

Two enhanced forms of inactivated poliovirus vaccine are currently licensed in the United States, but only one vaccine (IPOL, sanofi pasteur) is actually distributed. This vaccine contains all three serotypes of polio vaccine virus. The viruses are grown in a type of monkey kidney tissue culture (Vero cell line) and inactivated with formaldehyde. The vaccine contains 2-phenoxyethanol as a preservative, and trace amounts of neomycin, streptomycin, and polymyxin B. It is supplied in a single-dose prefilled syringe and should

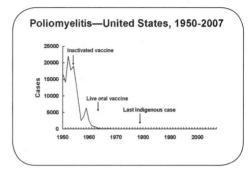

Poliomyelitis—United States, 1950-2007

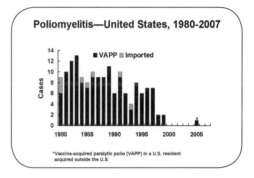

Poliomyelitis—United States, 1980-2007

16

Poliovirus Vaccine

- 1955 Inactivated vaccine
- 1961 Types 1 and 2 monovalent OPV
- 1962 Type 3 monovalent OPV
- 1963 Trivalent OPV
- 1987 Enhanced-potency IPV (IPV)

Inactivated Polio Vaccine

- Contains 3 serotypes of vaccine virus
- Grown on monkey kidney (Vero) cells
- Inactivated with formaldehyde
- Contains 2-phenoxyethanol, neomycin, streptomycin, polymyxin B

be administered by either subcutaneous or intramuscular injection.

Oral poliovirus vaccine

Trivalent OPV contains live attenuated strains of all three serotypes of poliovirus in a 10:1:3 ratio. The vaccine viruses are grown in monkey kidney tissue culture (Vero cell line). The vaccine is supplied as a single 0.5-mL dose in a plastic dispenser. The vaccine contains trace amounts of neomycin and streptomycin. OPV does not contain a preservative.

Live attenuated polioviruses replicate in the intestinal mucosa and lymphoid cells and in lymph nodes that drain the intestine. Vaccine viruses are excreted in the stool of the vaccinated person for up to 6 weeks after a dose. Maximum viral shedding occurs in the first 1–2 weeks after vaccination, particularly after the first dose.

Vaccine viruses may spread from the recipient to contacts. Persons coming in contact with fecal material of a vaccinated person may be exposed and infected with vaccine virus.

Immunogenicity and Vaccine Efficacy

Inactivated poliovirus vaccine

IPV is highly effective in producing immunity to poliovirus and protection from paralytic poliomyelitis. Ninety percent or more of vaccine recipients develop protective antibody to all three poliovirus types after two doses, and at least 99% are immune following three doses. Protection against paralytic disease correlates with the presence of antibody.

IPV appears to produce less local gastrointestinal immunity than does OPV, so persons who receive IPV are more readily infected with wild poliovirus than OPV recipients.

The duration of immunity with IPV is not known with certainty, although it probably provides protection for many years after a complete series.

Oral poliovirus vaccine

OPV is highly effective in producing immunity to poliovirus. A single dose of OPV produces immunity to all three vaccine viruses in approximately 50% of recipients. Three doses produce immunity to all three poliovirus types in more than 95% of recipients. As with other live-virus vaccines, immunity from oral poliovirus vaccine is probably lifelong. OPV produces excellent intestinal immunity, which helps prevent infection with wild virus.

Serologic studies have shown that seroconversion following three doses of either IPV or OPV is nearly 100% to all three

---

Oral Polio Vaccine

- Contains 3 serotypes of vaccine virus
- Grown on monkey kidney (Vero) cells
- Contains neomycin and streptomycin
- Shed in stool for up to 6 weeks following vaccination

16

Inactivated Polio Vaccine

- Highly effective in producing immunity to poliovirus
- 90% or more immune after 2 doses
- At least 99% immune after 3 doses
- Duration of immunity not known with certainty

Oral Polio Vaccine

- Highly effective in producing immunity to poliovirus
- Approximately 50% immune after 1 dose
- More than 95% immune after 3 doses
- Immunity probably lifelong

vaccine viruses. However, seroconversion rates after three doses of a combination of IPV and OPV are lower, particularly to type 3 vaccine virus (as low as 85% in one study). A fourth dose (most studies used OPV as the fourth dose) usually produces seroconversion rates similar to three doses of either IPV or OPV.

Vaccination Schedule and Use

Trivalent OPV was the vaccine of choice in the United States (and most other countries of the world) since it was licensed in 1963. The nearly exclusive use of OPV led to elimination of wild-type poliovirus from the United States in less than 20 years. However, one case of VAPP occurred for every 2 to 3 million doses of OPV administered, which resulted in 8 to 10 cases of VAPP each year in the United States (see Adverse Reactions section for more details on VAPP). From 1980 through 1999, VAPP accounted for 95% of all cases of paralytic poliomyelitis reported in the United States.

In 1996, ACIP recommended an increase in use of IPV through a sequential schedule of IPV followed by OPV. This recommendation was intended to *reduce* the occurrence of vaccine-associated paralytic polio. The sequential schedule was expected to eliminate VAPP among vaccine recipients by producing humoral immunity to polio vaccine viruses with inactivated polio vaccine prior to exposure to live vaccine virus. Since OPV was still used for the third and fourth doses of the polio vaccination schedule, a risk of VAPP would continue to exist among contacts of vaccinees, who were exposed to live vaccine virus in the stool of vaccine recipients.

The sequential IPV–OPV polio vaccination schedule was widely accepted by both providers and parents. Fewer cases of VAPP were reported in 1998 and 1999, suggesting an impact of the increased use of IPV. However, only the complete discontinuation of use of OPV would lead to complete elimination of VAPP. To further the goal of complete elimination of paralytic polio in the United States, ACIP recommended in July 1999 that inactivated polio vaccine be used exclusively in the United States beginning in 2000. OPV is no longer routinely available in the United States. Exclusive use of IPV eliminated the shedding of live vaccine virus, and eliminated any indigenous VAPP.

A primary series of IPV consists of three doses. In infancy, these primary doses are integrated with the administration of other routinely administered vaccines. The first dose may be given as early as 6 weeks of age but is usually given at 2 months of age, with a second dose at 4 months of age. The third dose should be given at 6–18 months of age. The first and second doses of IPV are necessary to induce a primary immune response, and the third dose of IPV ensures

Polio Vaccination Recommendations, 1996-1999

- Increased use of IPV (sequential IPV-OPV schedule) recommended in 1996
- Intended to *reduce* the risk of vaccine-associated paralytic polio (VAPP)
- Continued risk of VAPP for contacts of OPV recipients

16

Polio Vaccination Recommendations

- Exclusive use of IPV recommended in 2000
- OPV no longer routinely available in the United States
- Indigenous VAPP eliminated

Polio Vaccination Schedule

Age	Vaccine	Minimum Interval
2 months	IPV	---
4 months	IPV	4 weeks
6-18 months	IPV	4 weeks
4-6 years*	IPV	4 weeks

*the fourth dose of IPV may be given as early as 18 weeks of age

"boosting" of antibody titers to high levels. The preferred interval between the second and third doses of IPV is 2–8 months. However, if accelerated protection is needed, the minimum interval between all doses of IPV is 4 weeks, and the minimum age for the fourth dose is 18 weeks. Children who receive three doses of IPV before the fourth birthday should receive a fourth dose before or at school entry. The fourth dose is not needed if the third dose is given on or after the fourth birthday. If all four IPV doses are administered after 6 weeks of age and are all separated by at least 4 weeks, a fifth dose is not needed, even if the fourth dose was administered before 4 years of age (except if a specific state school entry requirement mandates a dose of polio vaccine on or after the fourth birthday). It is not necessary to repeat or add doses if the interval between doses is prolonged.

Only IPV is available for routine polio vaccination of children in the United States. A polio vaccination schedule begun with OPV should be completed with IPV. If a child receives both types of vaccine, four doses of any combination of IPV or OPV by 4–6 years of age is considered a complete poliovirus vaccination series. A minimum interval of 4 weeks should separate all doses of the series.

There are three combination vaccines that contain inactivated polio vaccine. Pediarix is produced by GlaxoSmithKline and contains DTaP, hepatitis B and IPV vaccines. Pediarix is licensed for the first 3 doses of the DTaP series among children 6 weeks through 6 years of age. Kinrix is also produced by GSK and contains DTaP and IPV. Kinrix is licensed only for the fifth dose of DTaP and fourth dose of IPV among children 4 through 6 years of age. Pentacel is produced by sanofi pasteur and contains DTaP, Hib and IPV. It is licensed for the first four doses of the component vaccines among children 6 weeks through 4 years of age. Pentacel is not licensed for children 5 years or older. Additional information about these combination vaccines is in the pertussis chapter of this book.

Polio Vaccination of Adults

Routine vaccination of adults (18 years of age and older) who reside in the United States is not necessary or recommended because most adults are already immune and have a very small risk of exposure to wild poliovirus in the United States.

Some adults, however, are at increased risk of infection with poliovirus. These include travelers to areas where poliomyelitis is endemic or epidemic (currently limited to South Asia, the eastern Mediterranean, and Africa), laboratory workers handling specimens that may contain polioviruses, and healthcare personnel in close contact with patients who may be excreting wild polioviruses. In addition, members of specific population groups with a current disease caused

---

Schedules That Include Both IPV and OPV

- Only IPV is available in the United States
- Schedule begun with OPV should be completed with IPV
- Any combination of 4 doses of IPV and OPV by 4-6 years of age constitutes a complete series

16

Combination Vaccines That Contain IPV

- Pediarix
  - DTaP, Hepatitis B and IPV
- Kinrix
  - DTaP and IPV
- Pentacel
  - DTaP, Hib and IPV

Polio Vaccination of Adults

- Routine vaccination of U.S. residents 18 years of age and older not necessary or recommended
- May consider vaccination of travelers to polio-endemic countries and selected laboratory workers

by wild polioviruses (e.g., during an outbreak) are also at increased risk.

Recommendations for poliovirus vaccination of adults in the above categories depend upon the previous vaccination history and the time available before protection is required.

■ For unvaccinated adults (including adults without a written record of prior polio vaccination) at increased risk of exposure to poliomyelitis, primary immunization with IPV is recommended. The recommended schedule is two doses separated by 1 to 2 months, and a third dose given 6 to 12 months after the second dose.

In some circumstances time will not allow completion of this schedule. If 8 weeks or more are available before protection is needed, three doses of IPV should be given at least 4 weeks apart. If 4 to 8 weeks are available before protection is needed, two doses of IPV should be given at least 4 weeks apart. If less than 4 weeks are available before protection is needed, a single dose of IPV is recommended. In all instances, the remaining doses of vaccine should be given later, at the recommended intervals, if the person remains at increased risk.

■ Adults who have previously completed a primary series of 3 or more doses and who are at increased risk of exposure to poliomyelitis should be given one dose of IPV. The need for further supplementary doses has not been established. Only one supplemental dose of polio vaccine is recommended for adults who have received a complete series (i.e., it is not necessary to administer additional doses for subsequent travel to a polio endemic country).

■ Adults who have previously received less than a full primary course of OPV or IPV and who are at increased risk of exposure to poliomyelitis should be given the remaining doses of IPV, regardless of the interval since the last dose and type of vaccine previously received. It is not necessary to restart the series of either vaccine if the schedule has been interrupted.

Contraindications And Precautions To Vaccination

Severe allergic reaction (anaphylaxis) to a vaccine component, or following a prior dose of vaccine, is a contraindication to further doses of that vaccine. Since IPV contains trace amounts of streptomycin, neomycin, and polymyxin B, there is a possibility of allergic reactions in persons sensitive to these antibiotics. Persons with allergies that are not anaphylactic, such as skin contact sensitivity, may be vaccinated.

Moderate or severe acute illness is a precaution for IPV.

Polio Vaccination of Unvaccinated Adults

• IPV

• Use standard IPV schedule if possible (0, 1-2 months, 6-12 months)

• May separate doses by 4 weeks if accelerated schedule needed

---

16

Polio Vaccination of Previously Vaccinated Adults

• Previously complete series
  —administer one dose of IPV

• Incomplete series
  —administer remaining doses in series
  —no need to restart series

Polio Vaccine Contraindications and Precautions

• Severe allergic reaction to a vaccine component or following a prior dose of vaccine

• Moderate or severe acute illness

Breastfeeding does not interfere with successful immunization against poliomyelitis with IPV. IPV may be administered to a child with diarrhea. Minor upper respiratory illnesses with or without fever, mild to moderate local reactions to a prior dose of vaccine, current antimicrobial therapy, and the convalescent phase of an acute illness are not contraindications for vaccination with IPV.

Contraindications to combination vaccines that contain IPV are the same as the contraindications to the individual components (e.g., DTaP, hepatitis B).

Adverse Reactions Following Vaccination

Minor local reactions (pain, redness) may occur following IPV. No serious adverse reactions to IPV have been documented. Because IPV contains trace amounts of streptomycin, polymyxin B, and neomycin, allergic reactions may occur in persons sensitive to these antibiotics.

Vaccine-Associated Paralytic Poliomyelitis

Vaccine-associated paralytic polio is a rare adverse reaction following live oral poliovirus vaccine. Inactivated poliovirus vaccine does not contain live virus, so it cannot cause VAPP. The mechanism of VAPP is believed to be a mutation, or reversion, of the vaccine virus to a more neurotropic form. These mutated viruses are called revertants. Reversion is believed to occur in almost all vaccine recipients, but it only rarely results in paralytic disease. The paralysis that results is identical to that caused by wild virus, and may be permanent.

VAPP is more likely to occur in persons 18 years of age and older than in children, and is much more likely to occur in immunodeficient children than in those who are immunocompetent. Compared with immunocompetent children, the risk of VAPP is almost 7,000 times higher for persons with certain types of immunodeficiencies, particularly B-lymphocyte disorders (e.g., agammaglobulinemia and hypogammaglobulinemia), which reduce the synthesis of immune globulins. There is no procedure available for identifying persons at risk of paralytic disease, except excluding older persons and screening for immunodeficiency.

From 1980 through 1998, 152 cases of paralytic polio were reported in the United States; 144 (95%) of these cases were VAPP, and the remaining eight were in persons who acquired documented or presumed wild-virus polio outside the United States. Of the 144 VAPP cases, 59 (41%) occurred in healthy vaccine recipients (average age 3 months). Forty-four (31%) occurred in healthy contacts of vaccine recipients (average age 26 years), and 7 (5%) were community acquired (i.e.,

---

Polio Vaccine Adverse Reactions

- Rare local reactions (IPV)
- No serious reactions to IPV have been documented
- Paralytic poliomyelitis (OPV)

16

Vaccine-Associated Paralytic Polio

- Increased risk in persons 18 years and older
- Increased risk in persons with immunodeficiency
- No procedure available for identifying persons at risk of paralytic disease
- 5-10 cases per year with exclusive use of OPV
- Most cases in healthy children and their household contacts

---

Vaccine-Associated Paralytic Polio (VAPP) 1980-1998

- Healthy recipients of OPV — 41%
- Healthy contacts of OPV recipients — 31%
- Community acquired — 5%
- Immunodeficient — 24%

vaccine virus was recovered but there was no known contact with a vaccine recipient). Thirty-four (24%) of VAPP cases occurred in persons with immunologic abnormalities (27 in vaccine recipients and 7 in contacts of vaccine recipients). None of the vaccine recipients were known to be immunologically abnormal prior to vaccination.

The risk of VAPP is not equal for all OPV doses in the vaccination series. The risk of VAPP is 7 to 21 times higher for the first dose than for any other dose in the OPV series. From 1980 through 1994, 303 million doses of OPV were distributed and 125 cases of VAPP were reported, for an overall risk of VAPP of one case per 2.4 million doses. Forty-nine paralytic cases were reported among immunocompetent recipients of OPV during this period. The overall risk to these recipients was one VAPP case per 6.2 million OPV doses. However, 40 (82%) of these 49 cases occurred following receipt of the first dose, making the risk of VAPP one case per 1.4 million first doses. The risk for all other doses was one per 27.2 million doses. The reason for this difference by dose is not known with certainty, but it is probably because the vaccine virus is able to replicate longer in a completely nonimmune infant. This prolonged replication increases the chance of the emergence of a revertant virus that may cause paralysis. The situation is similar for contacts. A nonimmune child may shed virus longer, increasing the chance of exposure of a contact.

The last case of VAPP acquired in the United States was reported in 1999. As noted previously, a U.S. resident with VAPP was reported in 2005, but the vaccine virus infection was acquired in Costa Rica.

Vaccine Storage and Handling

IPV may be shipped without refrigeration provided it is delivered within 4 days. It should be maintained at 35°–46°F (2°–8°C). The vaccine should be clear and colorless. Any vaccine showing particulate matter, turbidity, or change in color should be discarded.

Outbreak Investigation and Control

Collect preliminary clinical and epidemiologic information (including vaccine history and contact with OPV vaccines) on any suspected case of paralytic polio. Notify CDC, (404-639-8255) after appropriate local and state health authorities have been notified. Intensify field investigation to verify information and collect appropriate specimens for viral isolation and serology.

A single case of paralytic poliomyelitis demands immediate attention. If the evidence indicates vaccine-associated disease, no outbreak control program is needed. If, however, evidence indicates wild virus (for example, two cases in a

16

community), all unvaccinated persons in the epidemic area who are 6 weeks of age and older and whose vaccine histories are uncertain should be vaccinated.

Polio Eradication

Following the widespread use of poliovirus vaccine in the mid-1950s, the incidence of poliomyelitis declined rapidly in many industrialized countries. In the United States, the number of cases of paralytic poliomyelitis reported annually declined from more than 20,000 cases in 1952 to fewer than 100 cases in the mid-1960s. The last documented indigenous transmission of wild poliovirus in the United States was in 1979.

In 1985, the member countries of the Pan American Health Organization adopted the goal of eliminating poliomyelitis from the Western Hemisphere by 1990. The strategy to achieve this goal included increasing vaccination coverage; enhancing surveillance for suspected cases (i.e., surveillance for acute flaccid paralysis); and using supplemental immunization strategies such as national immunization days, house-to-house vaccination, and containment activities. Since 1991, when the last wild-virus–associated indigenous case was reported from Peru, no additional cases of poliomyelitis have been confirmed despite intensive surveillance. In September 1994, an international commission certified the Western Hemisphere to be free of indigenous wild poliovirus. The commission based its judgment on detailed reports from national certification commissions that had been convened in every country in the region.

In 1988, the World Health Assembly (the governing body of the World Health Organization) adopted the goal of global eradication of poliovirus by the year 2000. Although this goal was not achieved, substantial progress has been made. One type of poliovirus appears to have already been eradicated. In 1988, an estimated 350,000 cases of paralytic polio occurred, and the disease was endemic in more than 125 countries. By 2006, fewer than 2,000 cases were reported globally—a reduction of more than 99% from 1988—and polio remained endemic in only four countries. In addition, one type of poliovirus appears to have already been eradicated. The last isolation of type 2 virus was in India in October 1999.

The polio eradication initiative is led by a coalition of international organizations that includes WHO, the United Nations Children's Fund (UNICEF), CDC, and Rotary International. Other bilateral and multilateral organizations also support the initiative. Rotary International has contributed more than $600 million to support the eradication initiative. Current information on the status of the global polio eradication initiative is available on the World Health Organization website at www.polioeradication.org/.

Polio Eradication

- Last case in United States in 1979
- Western Hemisphere certified polio free in 1994
- Last isolate of type 2 poliovirus in India in October 1999
- Global eradication goal

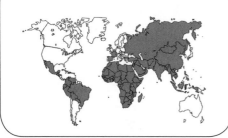

Wild Poliovirus 1988

Wild Poliovirus 2008

16

Postpolio Syndrome

After an interval of 30–40 years, 25%–40% of persons who contracted paralytic poliomyelitis in childhood experience new muscle pain and exacerbation of existing weakness, or develop new weakness or paralysis. This disease entity is referred to as postpolio syndrome. Factors that increase the risk of postpolio syndrome include increasing length of time since acute poliovirus infection, presence of permanent residual impairment after recovery from the acute illness, and female sex. The pathogenesis of postpolio syndrome is thought to involve the failure of oversized motor units created during the recovery process of paralytic poliomyelitis. Postpolio syndrome is not an infectious process, and persons experiencing the syndrome do not shed poliovirus.

For more information, or for support for persons with postpolio syndrome and their families, contact:

Post-Polio Health International
4207 Lindell Boulevard #110
St. Louis, MO 63108-2915
314-534-0475

www.post-polio.org

Selected References

CDC. Imported vaccine-associated paralytic poliomyelitis—United States, 2005. *MMWR* 2006;55:97–9.

CDC. Progress toward interruption of wild poliovirus transmission—worldwide, 2008. *MMWR* 2009;58:308–12.

CDC. Poliomyelitis prevention in the United States: updated recommendations of the Advisory Committee on Immunization Practices. (ACIP). *MMWR* 2000;49 (No. RR-5):1–22.

CDC. Apparent global interruption of wild poliovirus type 2 transmission. *MMWR* 2001;50:222–4.

16

Poliomyelitis

Rotavirus

Diarrheal disease has been recognized in humans since antiquity.Until the early 1970s, a bacterial, viral, or parasitic etiology of diarrheal disease in children could be detected in fewer than 30% of cases. In 1973, Bishop and colleagues observed a virus particle in the intestinal tissue of children with diarrhea by using electron micrography. This virus was subsequently called "rotavirus" because of its similarity in appearance to a wheel (*rota* is Latin for wheel). By 1980, rotavirus was recognized as the most common cause of severe gastroenteritis in infants and young children in the United States. It is now known that infection with rotavirus is nearly universal, with almost all children infected by 5 years of age. Rotavirus is responsible for 20–60 deaths per year in the United States and up to 500,000 deaths from diarrhea worldwide. A vaccine to prevent rotavirus gastroenteritis was first licensed in August 1998 but was withdrawn in 1999 because of its association with intussusception. Second-generation vaccines were licensed in 2006 and 2008.

Rotavirus

Rotavirus is a double-stranded RNA virus of the family *Reoviridae*. The virus is composed of three concentric shells that enclose 11 gene segments. The outermost shell contains two important proteins—VP7, or G-protein, and VP4, or P-protein. VP7 and VP4 define the serotype of the virus and induce neutralizing antibody that is probably involved in immune protection. From 1996 through 2005, five strains of rotavirus (G1–4, G9) accounted for 90% of isolates from children younger than 5 years in the United States. Of these, the G1 strain accounted for more than 75% of isolates.

Rotavirus is very stable and may remain viable in the environment for weeks or months if not disinfected.

Rotaviruses cause infection in many species of mammals, including cows and monkeys. These animal strains are antigenically distinct from those causing human infection, and they rarely cause infection in humans.

Pathogenesis

The virus enters the body through the mouth. Viral replication occurs in the villous epithelium of the small intestine. Replication outside the small intestine and systemic spread of the virus (viremia) are believed to be uncommon in immunocompetent persons. Infection may result in decreased intestinal absorption of sodium, glucose, and water, and decreased levels of intestinal lactase, alkaline phosphatase, and sucrase activity, and may lead to isotonic diarrhea.

The immune correlates of protection from rotavirus are poorly understood. Serum and mucosal antibodies against

---

Rotavirus

- First identified as cause of diarrhea in 1973
- Most common cause of severe gastroenteritis in infants and children
- Nearly universal infection by 5 years of age
- Responsible for up to 500,000 diarrheal deaths each year worldwide

Rotavirus

- Reovirus (RNA)
- VP7 and VP4 proteins define virus serotype and induce neutralizing antibody
- 5 predominant strains in U.S. (G1-G4, G9) and accounted for 90% of isolates
- G1 strain accounts for 75% of infections
- Very stable and may remain viable for weeks or months if not disinfected

17

Rotavirus Pathogenesis

- Entry through mouth
- Replication in epithelium of small intestine
- Replication outside intestine and viremia uncommon
- Infection leads to isotonic diarrhea

Rotavirus

Rotavirus Immunity

- Antibody against VP7 and VP4 probably important for protection
- First infection usually does not lead to permanent immunity
- Reinfection can occur at any age
- Subsequent infections generally less severe

Rotavirus Clinical Features

- Short incubation period (usually less than 48 hours)
- First infection after age 3 months generally most severe
- May be asymptomatic or result in severe dehydrating diarrhea with fever and vomiting
- Gastrointestinal symptoms generally resolve in 3 to 7 days

17

Rotavirus Complications

- Severe diarrhea
- Dehydration
- Electrolyte imbalance
- Metabolic acidosis
- Immunodeficient children may have more severe or prolonged disease

VP7 and VP4 are probably important for protection from disease. Cell-mediated immunity probably plays a role in recovery from infection and in protection.

Recovery from a first rotavirus infection usually does not lead to permanent immunity. After a single natural infection, 38% of children are protected against any subsequent rotavirus infection, 77% are protected against rotavirus diarrhea, and 87% are protected against severe diarrhea. Reinfection can occur at any age. Subsequent infections confer progressively greater protection and are generally less severe than the first. Recurrent rotavirus infections affect persons of all ages. Recurrent infections are usually asymptomatic or result in mild diarrhea that may be preceded or accompanied by vomiting and low-grade fever.

Clinical Features

The incubation period for rotavirus diarrhea is short, usually less than 48 hours. The clinical manifestations of infection vary and depend on whether it is the first infection or reinfection. The first infection after 3 months of age is generally the most severe. Infection may be asymptomatic, may cause self-limited watery diarrhea, or may result in severe dehydrating diarrhea with fever and vomiting. Up to one-third of infected children may have a temperature greater than 102°F (39°C). The gastrointestinal symptoms generally resolve in 3 to 7 days.

The clinical features and stool characteristics of rotavirus diarrhea are nonspecific, and similar illness may be caused by other pathogens. As a result, confirmation of a diarrheal illness as rotavirus requires laboratory testing.

Complications

Rotavirus infection in infants and young children can lead to severe diarrhea, dehydration, electrolyte imbalance, and metabolic acidosis. Children who are immunocompromised because of congenital immunodeficiency or because of bone marrow or solid organ transplantation may experience severe or prolonged rotavirus gastroenteritis and may have evidence of abnormalities in multiple organ systems, particularly the kidney and liver.

Laboratory Diagnosis

The most widely available method for confirmation of rotavirus infection is detection of rotavirus antigen in stool by enzyme immunoassay (EIA). Several commercial test kits are available that detect an antigen common to human rotaviruses. These kits are simple to use, inexpensive, and very sensitive. Other techniques (such as electron microscopy, reverse transcription polymerase chain reaction, nucleic acid hybridization, sequence analysis, and culture) are used primarily in research settings. Rotavirus antigen has also been identified in the serum of patients 3–7 days after disease onset, but at present, routine diagnostic testing is based primarily on testing of fecal specimens.

Epidemiology

Occurrence

Rotavirus occurs throughout the world. The prevalence of rotavirus strains varies by geographic area, and strains not included in the vaccine are present in some parts of the world.

Reservoir

The reservoir of rotavirus is the gastrointestinal tract and stool of infected humans. Although rotavirus infection occurs in many nonhuman mammals, transmission of animal rotaviruses to humans is believed to be rare and probably does not lead to clinical illness. Although immuno-deficient persons may shed rotavirus for a prolonged period, a true carrier state has not been described.

Transmission

Rotaviruses are shed in high concentration in the stool of infected persons. Transmission is by fecal-oral spread, both through close person-to-person contact and by fomites (such as toys and other environmental surfaces contaminated by stool). Rotaviruses are also probably transmitted by other modes such as fecally contaminated food and water and respiratory droplets.

Temporal Pattern

In temperate climates, disease is more prevalent during fall and winter. In the United States, annual epidemic peaks usually progress from the Southwest during November and December and spread to the Northeast by April and May. The reason for this seasonal pattern is unknown. In tropical climates, the disease is less seasonal than in temperate areas.

Communicability

Rotavirus is highly communicable, as evidenced by the nearly universal infection of children by age 5 years. Infected persons shed large quantities of virus in their stool beginning 2 days before the onset of diarrhea and for up to 10 days after onset of symptoms. Rotavirus may be detected in the stool of immunodeficient persons for more than 30 days after infection. Spread within families, institutions, hospitals, and child care settings is common.

Rotavirus Epidemiology

- Reservoir — Human
- Transmission — Fecal-oral, fomites
- Temporal pattern — Fall and winter (temperate areas)
- Communicability — 2 days before to 10 days after onset

17

Rotavirus Disease in the United States

- Estimated 3 million cases per year*
- 95% of children infected by 5 years of age
- Highest incidence among children 3 to 35 months of age
- Responsible for 5% to 10% of all gastroenteritis episodes among children younger than 5 years of age

*Prevaccine era

Rotavirus Disease in the United States

- Annually*responsible for:
  - more than 400,000 physician visits
  - more than 200,000 emergency department visits
  - 55,000-70,000 hospitalizations
  - 20-60 deaths
- Annual direct and indirect costs estimated at approximately $1 billion

*Prevaccine era

Risk Groups for Rotavirus Infection

- Groups with increased exposure to virus
  - children in child care centers
  - children in hospital wards (nosocomial rotavirus)
  - caretakers, parents of these children
  - children, adults with immuno-deficiency-related diseases (e.g., severe combined immunodeficiency, HIV, bone marrow transplant)

Secular Trends in the United States

Rotavirus infection is not nationally notifiable in the United States. Estimates of incidence and disease burden are based on special surveys, cohort studies, and hospital discharge data.

Rotavirus infection is nearly universal. In the prevaccine era an estimated 3 million rotavirus infections occurred every year in the United States and 95% of children experienced at least one rotavirus infection by age 5 years. The incidence of rotavirus is similar in developed and developing countries, suggesting that improved sanitation alone is not sufficient to prevent the infection.

Infants younger than 3 months of age have relatively low rates of rotavirus infection, probably because of passive maternal antibody, and possibly breastfeeding. The incidence of clinical illness is highest among children 3 to 35 months of age. Rotavirus infection of adults is usually asymptomatic but may cause diarrheal illness.

In the United States, rotaviruses are responsible for 5% to 10% of all gastroenteritis episodes among children younger than 5 years of age. However, they are the most common cause of severe diarrheal disease and account for a higher proportion of severe episodes leading to clinic or hospital visits. Rotavirus accounts for 30% to 50% of all hospitalizations for gastroenteritis among U.S. children younger than 5 years of age, and more than 70% of hospitalizations for gastroenteritis during the seasonal peaks.

In the prevaccine era rotavirus infection was responsible for more than 400,000 physician visits, more than 200,000 emergency department (ED) visits, 55,000 to 70,000 hospitalizations each year, and 20 to 60 deaths. Annual direct and indirect costs were estimated at approximately $1 billion, primarily due to the cost of time lost from work to care for an ill child.

Groups at increased risk for rotavirus infection are those with increased exposure to virus. These include children who attend child care centers, children in hospital wards (nosocomial rotavirus), caretakers and parents of children in child care or hospitals, and children and adults with immuno-deficiency-related diseases (e.g., severe combined immunode-ficiency disease (SCID), HIV, bone marrow transplant).

Rotavirus Vaccines

The first rotavirus vaccines were derived from either bovine (cow) or rhesus (monkey) origin. Studies demonstrated that these live oral vaccines could prevent rotavirus diarrhea in young children, but efficacy varied widely. Because immunity to G (VP7) or P (VP4) proteins was associated with disease protection and recovery, new live virus vaccines were developed that incorporated G proteins or both G and P proteins for each of the predominant serotypes.

In 1998, a rhesus-based tetravalent rotavirus vaccine (RRV-TV, Rotashield) was licensed and recommended for routine immunization of U.S. infants. However, RRV-TV was withdrawn from the U.S. market within 1 year of its introduction because of its association with intussusception. The risk of intussusception was most elevated (more than a 20-fold increase) within 3 to 14 days after receipt of the first dose of RRV-TV, with a smaller (approximately 5-fold) increase in risk within 3 to 14 days after the second dose. Overall, the risk associated with the first dose of RRV-TV was estimated to be about one case per 10,000 vaccine recipients. Some researchers have suggested that the risk of intussusception associated with RRV-TV was age-dependent and that the absolute number of intussusception events, and possibly the relative risk of intussusception associated with the first dose of RRV-TV, increased with increasing age at vaccination.

Characteristics

There are currently two rotavirus vaccines licensed for use in the United States. RV5 (RotaTeq) is a live oral vaccine manufactured by Merck and licensed by the Food and Drug Administration in February 2006. RV5 contains five reassortant rotaviruses developed from human and bovine parent rotavirus strains. Each 2-mL vial of vaccine contains approximately 2×10^6 infectious units of each of the five reassortant strains. The vaccine viruses are suspended in a buffer solution that contains sucrose, sodium citrate, sodium phosphate monobasic monohydrate, sodium hydroxide, polysorbate 80, and tissue culture media. Trace amounts of fetal bovine serum might be present. The vaccine contains no preservatives or thimerosal.

Fecal shedding of vaccine virus was evaluated in a subset of persons enrolled in the phase III trials. Vaccine virus was shed by 9% of 360 infants after dose 1, but none of 249 and 385 infants after doses 2 and 3, respectively. Shedding was observed as early as 1 day and as late as 15 days after a dose. The potential for transmission of vaccine virus was not assessed.

RV1 (Rotarix), a live oral vaccine manufactured by GlaxoSmithKline, was licensed by the FDA in April 2008. RV1 contains one strain of live attenuated human strain 89-12 (type G1P1A[8]) rotavirus. RV1 is provided as a lyophilized powder that is reconstituted before administration. Each 1-mL dose of reconstituted vaccine contains at least 10^6 median cell culture infective units of virus. The vaccine contains amino acids, dextran, Dulbecco's modified Eagle medium, sorbitol and sucrose. The diluent contains calcium

Rotavirus Vaccines

- RV5 (RotaTeq)
  - contains five reassortant rotaviruses developed from human and bovine parent rotavirus strains
  - vaccine viruses suspended in a buffer solution
  - contains no preservatives or thimerosal

17

Rotavirus Vaccines

- RV1 (Rotarix)
  - contains one strain of live attenuated human rotavirus (type G1P1A[8])
  - provided as a lyophilized powder that is reconstituted before administration
  - contains no preservatives or thimerosal

carbonate, sterile water and xanthan. The vaccine contains no preservatives or thimerosal.

Fecal shedding of rotavirus antigen was evaluated in all or a subset of infants from seven studies in various countries. After dose 1, rotavirus antigen shedding was detected by ELISA in 50% to 80% (depending on the study) of infants at approximately day 7 and 0 to 24% at approximately day 30. After dose 2, rotavirus antigen shedding was detected in 4% to 18% of infants at approximately day 7, and 0 to 1.2% at approximately day 30. The potential for transmission of vaccine virus to others was not assessed.

Vaccine Effectiveness

Phase III clinical trials of RV5 (Rotateq) efficacy have involved more than 70,000 infants 6 through 12 weeks of age in 11 countries.

After completion of a three-dose RV5 regimen, the efficacy of rotavirus vaccine against rotavirus gastroenteritis of any severity was 74%, and against severe rotavirus gastroenteritis (defined by severity of fever, vomiting, diarrhea and changes in behavior) was 98%. Vaccine efficacy varied by rotavirus serotype.

In a large study, the efficacy of RV5 vaccine against rotavirus gastroenteritis requiring office visits was evaluated among 5,673 children, and efficacy against rotavirus gastroenteritis requiring ED visits and hospitalizations was evaluated among 68,038 children during the first 2 years of life. RV5 vaccine reduced the incidence of office visits by 86%, ED visits by 94%, and hospitalizations for rotavirus gastroenteritis by 96%. The efficacy of fewer than three doses is not known.

Phase III clinical trials of RV1 (Rotarix) efficacy have involved more than 21,000 infants 6 through 12 weeks of age, primarily in two studies in Latin America and Europe.

After completion of a two-dose RV1 regimen, the efficacy of rotavirus vaccine against severe rotavirus gastroenteritis (Latin America study) was 85%, and against any rotavirus gastroenteritis (Europe study) was 87%. RV1 reduced hospitalization for rotavirus gastroenteritis by 85% to 100% (depending on the study). The efficacy of fewer than two doses is not known.

Duration of Immunity

The duration of immunity from rotavirus vaccine is not known. Efficacy through 2 rotavirus seasons has been studied for both vaccines. In general efficacy is lower in the second season than in the first.

Rotavirus Vaccine Effectiveness

Condition	Effectiveness
Any rotavirus gastroenteritis	74%-87%
Severe gastroenteritis	85%-98%

Both vaccines significantly reduced physician visits for diarrhea, and reduced rotavirus-related hospitalization

17

Vaccination Schedule and Use

Revised ACIP recommendations for the use of rotavirus vaccine were published in *MMWR* in February 2009. Because of similar estimates of efficacy and safety, neither The Advisory Committee on Immunization Practices (ACIP) nor the Academies of Pediatrics or Family Physicians state a preference for one vaccine versus the other.

ACIP recommends routine rotavirus vaccination of all infants without a contraindication. The vaccine should be administered as a series of either two or three oral doses, for RV1 and RV5, respectively, beginning at 2 months of age. The vaccination series for both vaccines may be started as early as 6 weeks of age. Subsequent doses in the series should be separated from the previous dose by 1 to 2 months. Rotavirus vaccine should be given at the same visit as other vaccines given at these ages.

The maximum age for any dose of RV1 approved by the FDA is 24 weeks, while the maximum FDA-approved age for any dose of RV5 is 32 weeks. This difference, as well as the different number of doses in the series could complicate decisions by clinicians who encounter children who received a brand of rotavirus vaccine other than the brand the clinician has in stock. There are currently no data on schedules that include both RV1 and RV5.

The ACIP developed age recommendations that vary from those of the manufacturers. ACIP recommendations state that the maximum age for the first dose of both vaccines is 14 weeks 6 days. This is an off-label recommendation for RV5 since the approved maximum age for the first dose of that vaccine is 12 weeks. The minimum interval between doses of both rotavirus vaccines is 4 weeks. The maximum age for any dose of either rotavirus vaccine is 8 months 0 days. No rotavirus vaccine should be administered to infants older than 8 months 0 days of age. This is an off-label recommendation for both vaccines, because the labeled maximum age for RV1 is 24 weeks, and the labeled maximum age for RV5 is 32 weeks.

ACIP did NOT define a maximum interval between doses. It is preferable to adhere to the recommended interval of 8 weeks. But if the interval is prolonged, the infant can still receive the vaccine as long as it can be given on or before the 8-month birthday. It is not necessary to restart the series or add doses because of a prolonged interval between doses.

There are few data on the safety or efficacy of giving more than one dose, even partial doses, close together. ACIP recommends that providers not repeat the dose if the infant spits out or regurgitates the vaccine. Any remaining doses should be administered on schedule. Doses of rotavirus vaccine should be separated by at least 4 weeks.

Rotavirus Vaccine Recommendations

- Routine vaccination of all infants without a contraindication
- 2 (RV1) or 3 (RV5) oral doses beginning at 2 months of age
- Subsequent doses in the series should be separated from the previous dose by 1 to 2 months

MMWR 2009;58:(RR-2)

Rotavirus Vaccine Recommendations

- For both rotavirus vaccines
  - maximum age for first dose is 14 weeks 6 days
  - minimum interval between doses is 4 weeks
  - maximum age for any dose is 8 months 0 days

MMWR 2009;58:(RR-2)

Rotavirus Vaccine Recommendations

- ACIP did not define a maximum interval between doses
- If the interval between doses is prolonged, the infant can still receive the vaccine as long as it can be given on or before the infant's 8-month birthday
- It is not necessary to restart the series or add doses because of a prolonged interval between doses

MMWR 2009;58:(RR-2)

Rotavirus Vaccine

- ACIP recommends that providers not repeat the dose if the infant spits out or regurgitates the vaccine
- Any remaining doses should be administered on schedule
- Doses of rotavirus vaccine should be separated by at least 4 weeks.

17

Rotavirus Vaccine Recommendations

- Complete the series with the same product whenever possible
- If product used for a prior dose or doses is not available or not known, continue or complete the series with the product that is available
- If any dose in the series was RV5 (RotaTeq) or the vaccine brand used for any prior dose is not known, a total of 3 doses of rotavirus vaccine should be administered

MMWR 2009;58:(RR-2)

Rotavirus Vaccine Recommendations

- Infants documented to have had rotavirus gastroenteritis before receiving the full course of rotavirus vaccinations should still begin or complete the 2- or 3-dose schedule

MMWR 2009;58:(RR-2)

Rotavirus Vaccine Contraindications

- Severe allergic reaction to a vaccine component (including latex) or following a prior dose of vaccine
  - latex rubber is contained in the RV1 oral applicator

Rotavirus Vaccine Precautions*

- Altered immunocompetence
- Acute, moderate or severe gastroenteritis or other acute illness
- History of intussusception

*The decision to vaccinate if a precaution is present should be made on a case-by-case risk and benefit basis.

17

ACIP recommends that the rotavirus vaccine series should be completed with the same product whenever possible. However, vaccination should not be deferred if the product used for a prior dose or doses is not available or is not known. In this situation, the provider should continue or complete the series with the product that is available. If any dose in the series was RV5 (RotaTeq) or the vaccine brand used for any prior dose in the series is not known, a total of three doses of rotavirus vaccine should be administered.

Breastfeeding does not appear to diminish immune response to rotavirus vaccine. Infants who are being breastfed should be vaccinated on schedule.

There are at least 5 serotypes of rotavirus that may cause diarrheal disease in the United States. In addition, infants may experience multiple episodes of rotavirus diarrhea because the initial infection may provide only partial immunity. Infants documented to have had rotavirus gastroenteritis before receiving the full course of rotavirus vaccinations should still begin or complete the 2- or 3-dose schedule.

Contraindications and Precautions to Vaccination

Rotavirus vaccine is contraindicated for infants who are known to have had a severe allergic reaction (anaphylactic) to a vaccine component or following a prior dose of vaccine. Latex rubber is contained in the RV1 oral applicator, so infants with a severe allergy to latex should not receive RV1. The RV5 dosing tube is latex free.

Precaution conditions are those that may increase the chance of a vaccine adverse reaction or reduce the efficacy of the vaccine. In general, infants with precautions to vaccination, described below, should not receive the vaccine until the condition improves unless the benefit of vaccination outweighs the risk of an adverse reaction. However, clinicians may consider use of the vaccine on a case-by-case basis.

Children who are immunocompromised because of congenital immunodeficiency, or hematopoietic stem cell or solid organ transplantation sometimes experience severe, prolonged, and even fatal rotavirus gastroenteritis. However, no safety or efficacy data are available regarding administration of rotavirus vaccine to infants who are, or are potentially immunocompromised due to either disease or drugs. Clinicians will need to use their judgment in this situation.

There are no data on the use of rotavirus vaccine among infants who are exposed to or infected with HIV. However, two considerations support vaccination of these infants.

First, the HIV diagnosis might not be established in infants born to HIV-infected mothers by the time they reach the age of the first rotavirus vaccine dose. Only 3% percent or less of HIV-exposed infants in the United States will be determined to be HIV infected. Second, vaccine strains of rotavirus are considerably attenuated, and exposure to an attenuated rotavirus is preferable to exposure to wild-type rotavirus.

Rotavirus vaccine should generally not be administered to infants with acute, moderate or severe gastroenteritis, or other acute illness until the condition improves. However, infants with mild acute gastroenteritis or other mild acute illness can be vaccinated, particularly if the delay in vaccination will delay the first dose of vaccine beyond 15 weeks 0 days of age.

Available data suggest that infants with a history of intussusception might be at higher risk for a repeat episode than other infants. Until postlicensure data on the safety of rotavirus vaccine are available, the risks for and the benefits of vaccination should be considered when vaccinating infants with a previous episode of intussusception.

No data are available on the immune response to rotavirus vaccine in infants who have recently received a blood product. In theory, infants who have recently received an antibody-containing blood product might have a reduced immunologic response to a dose of oral rotavirus vaccine. However, 2 or 3 doses of vaccine are administered in the full rotavirus vaccine series, and no increased risk for adverse events is expected. ACIP now recommends that rotavirus vaccine may be administered at any time before, concurrent with, or after administration of any blood product.

Available data suggest that preterm infants (i.e., infants born at less than 37 weeks' gestation) are at increased risk for hospitalization from rotavirus during the first 1 to 2 years of life. In clinical trials, rotavirus vaccine appeared to be generally well tolerated in preterm infants, although a relatively small number of preterm infants have been evaluated. ACIP considers the benefits of rotavirus vaccination of preterm infants to outweigh the risks of adverse events. ACIP supports vaccination of a preterm infant according to the same schedule and precautions as a full-term infant, provided the following conditions are met: the infant's chronological age is at least 6 weeks, the infant is clinically stable, and the vaccine is administered at the time of discharge or after discharge from the neonatal intensive care unit or nursery. Although the lower level of maternal antibody to rotavirus in very preterm infants theoretically could increase the risk for adverse reactions from rotavirus vaccine, ACIP believes the benefits of vaccinating the infant when age eligible, clinically stable, and no longer in the hospital outweigh the theoretic risks.

Rotavirus Vaccine - Conditions Not Considered to be Precautions

- Pre-existing chronic gastrointestinal conditions
  - no data available
  - ACIP considers the benefits of vaccination to outweigh the theoretic risks
- Recent receipt of an antibody-containing blood product
  - no data available
  - ACIP recommends that rotavirus vaccine may be administered at any time before, concurrent with, or after administration of any blood product

17

Rotavirus Vaccine and Preterm Infants

- ACIP supports vaccination of a preterm infant if:
  - chronological age is at least 6 weeks
  - clinically stable; and
  - vaccine is administered at time of discharge or after discharge from neonatal intensive care unit or nursery

Vaccine strains of rotavirus are shed in the feces of vaccinated infants. So if an infant were to be vaccinated with rotavirus vaccine while still needing care in the hospital, a theoretic risk exists for vaccine virus being transmitted to infants in the same unit who are acutely ill, and to preterm infants who are not age eligible for vaccine. ACIP considers that, in usual circumstances, the risk from shedding outweighs the benefit of vaccinating an infant who will remain in the hospital and recommends that these infants not be vaccinated until they meet the conditions described above.

Although rotavirus is shed in the feces of vaccinated infants transmission of vaccine virus has not been documented. Infants living in households with persons who have or are suspected of having an immunodeficiency disorder or impaired immune status can be vaccinated. ACIP believes that the indirect protection of the immunocompromised household member provided by vaccinating the infant in the household, and thereby preventing wild-type rotavirus disease, outweighs the small risk for transmitting vaccine virus to the immunocompromised household member.

Infants living in households with pregnant women should be vaccinated according to the same schedule as infants in households without pregnant women. Because the majority of women of childbearing age have preexisting immunity to rotavirus, the risk for infection by the attenuated vaccine virus is considered to be very low. Although transmission of vaccine virus has not been documented, it is prudent for all members of the household to employ measures such as good hand washing after changing a diaper or otherwise coming in contact with the feces of the vaccinated infant.

Adverse Reactions Following Vaccination

Intussusception

The phase 3 clinical trials of both vaccines were very large, primarily to be able to study the occurrence of intussusception in both vaccine and placebo recipients. The RV1 trials included more than 63,000 infants, of whom half received vaccine and half received a placebo. In the 30 days following either vaccine dose there were 7 cases of intussusception among the vaccine recipients and 7 cases diagnosed among the placebo recipients. The RV5 clinical trials included more than 69,000 infants, of whom half received vaccine and half received a placebo. In the 42 days after vaccination 6 cases of intussusception were diagnosed among the vaccinated infants and 5 cases were diagnosed among the placebo recipients.

These data indicate the background incidence of intussusception in infants, as evidenced by its occurrence in

---

Immunosuppressed Household Contacts of Rotavirus Vaccine Recipients

- Infants living in households with persons who have or are suspected of having an immunodeficiency disorder or impaired immune status can be vaccinated
- Protection provided by vaccinating the infant outweighs the small risk of transmitting vaccine virus

---

Pregnant Household Contacts of Rotavirus Vaccine Recipients

- Infants living in households with pregnant women should be vaccinated
  - majority of women of childbearing age have pre-existing immunity to rotavirus
  - risk for infection by vaccine virus is considered to be very low

---

Rotavirus Vaccine and Intussusception*

	No. of Infants	Vaccine Recipients	Placebo Recipients
RV1	63,225	7 cases	7 cases
RV5	69,625	6 cases	5 cases

*RV1- 0-30 days after either dose
RV5- 0-42 days after any dose

infants who received a placebo. They also show that while intussusception is to be expected in recipients of rotavirus vaccine, the risk is no higher than among children who are not vaccinated.

Other Adverse Events

A variety of other adverse reactions were reported during the 7 or 8 days after rotavirus vaccination in the clinical trials, including vomiting in 15% to 18%, diarrhea in 9% to 24%, irritability in 13% to 62%, and fever in 40% to 43%. However, the rate of these symptoms in vaccinated children was similar to the rate in unvaccinated children. No serious adverse reactions attributable to rotavirus vaccine have been reported.

Vaccine Storage and Handling

Both rotavirus vaccines must be stored at refrigerator temperatures (35°–46°F [2°–8°C]) and protected from light. RV1 diluent may be stored at room temperature. The vaccines must not be frozen. The shelf life of properly stored vaccine is 24 months. RV5 should be administered as soon as possible after being removed from refrigeration. RV1 should be administered within 24 hours of reconstitution. Reconstituted RV1 may be stored at refrigerator or room temperature.

Healthcare personnel may be concerned about exposure to vaccine virus during administration of rotavirus vaccine or contact with vaccinated infants. Hand hygiene using soap and water or alcohol-based hand cleaners should already be standard practice wherever vaccines are being administered. This practice should minimize the risk of transmission of rotavirus vaccine virus during administration. Therefore, there are no restrictions on immunosuppressed or pregnant healthcare personnel administering the vaccine.

Rotavirus Surveillance

Rotavirus gastroenteritis is not a reportable disease in the United States, and testing for rotavirus infection is not always performed when a child seeks medical care for acute gastroenteritis. Rotavirus disease surveillance systems need to be adequately sensitive and specific to document the effectiveness of the vaccination program. Methods of surveillance for rotavirus disease at the national level include review of national hospital discharge databases for rotavirus-specific or rotavirus-compatible diagnoses, surveillance for rotavirus disease at three sites that participate in the New Vaccine Surveillance Network, and reports of rotavirus detection from a sentinel system of laboratories. At the state and local levels, surveillance efforts at sentinel hospitals or by review of hospital discharge databases can

---

Rotavirus Vaccine Adverse Reactions

- Vomiting   15%-18%
- Diarrhea   9%-24%
- Irritability   13%-62%
- Fever   40%-43%
- Serious adverse   None
  reactions

Rotavirus Vaccine Storage and Handling

- Store at 35°- 46° F (2°-8° C) and protect from light
- RV1 diluent may be stored at room temperature
- Do not freeze vaccines
- Administer RV5 as soon as possible after being removed from refrigeration
- RV1 should be administered within 24 hours of reconstitution

17

be used to monitor the impact of the vaccine program. Special studies (e.g., case-control studies and retrospective cohort studies) will be used to measure the effectiveness of rotavirus vaccine under routine use in the United States. CDC has established a national strain surveillance system of sentinel laboratories to monitor circulating rotavirus strains before and after the introduction of rotavirus vaccine. This system is designed to detect new or unusual strains causing gastroenteritis that might not be prevented effectively by vaccination, which might affect the success of the vaccination program.

Selected References

American Academy of Pediatrics. Rotavirus infections. In:Pickering LK, Baker CJ, Long SS, McMilliam JA, eds. RedBook: *2006 Report of the Committee on Infectious Diseases*. 27th ed. Elk Grove Village, IL: American Academy of Pediatrics, 2006:572–4.

CDC. Prevention of rotavirus gastroenteritis among infants and children. Recommendations of the Advisory Committee on Immunization Practices (ACIP). *MMWR* 2009;58(No. RR-2):1–24.

Fischer TK, Viboud C, Parashar U, et al. Hospitalizations and deaths from diarrhea and rotavirus among children <5 years of age in the United States, 1993-2003. *J Infect Dis* 2007;195:1117–25.

Murphy TV, Gargiullo PM, Massoudi MS, et al. Intussusception among infants given an oral rotavirus vaccine. *N Engl J Med* 2001;344:564–72.

Parashar UD, Hummelman EG, Bresee JS, et al. Global illness and deaths caused by rotavirus disease in children. *Emerg Infect Dis* 2003;9:565–72.

Vesikari T, Matson DO, Dennehy P, et al. Safety and efficacy of a pentavalent human–bovine (WC3) reassortant rotavirus vaccine. *N Engl J Med* 2006;354:23–33.

Vesikari T, Karvonen A, Prymula R, et al. Efficacy of human rotavirus vaccine against rotavirus gastroenteritis during the first 2 years of life in European infants: randomized, double-blind controlled study. *Lancet* 2007;370:1757-63.

17

Rubella

The name rubella is derived from Latin, meaning "little red." Rubella was initially considered to be a variant of measles or scarlet fever and was called "third disease." It was not until 1814 that it was first described as a separate disease in the German medical literature, hence the common name "German measles." In 1914, Hess postulated a viral etiology based on his work with monkeys. Hiro and Tosaka in 1938 confirmed the viral etiology by passing the disease to children using filtered nasal washings from persons with acute cases.

Following a widespread epidemic of rubella infection in 1940, Norman Gregg, an Australian ophthalmologist, reported in 1941 the occurrence of congenital cataracts among 78 infants born following maternal rubella infection in early pregnancy. This was the first published recognition of congenital rubella syndrome (CRS). Rubella virus was first isolated in 1962 by Parkman and Weller. The first rubella vaccines were licensed in 1969.

Rubella Virus

Rubella virus is classified as a togavirus, genus *Rubivirus*. It is most closely related to group A arboviruses, such as eastern and western equine encephalitis viruses. It is an enveloped RNA virus, with a single antigenic type that does not cross-react with other members of the togavirus group. Rubella virus is relatively unstable and is inactivated by lipid solvents, trypsin, formalin, ultraviolet light, low pH, heat, and amantadine.

Pathogenesis

Following respiratory transmission of rubella virus, replication of the virus is thought to occur in the nasopharynx and regional lymph nodes. A viremia occurs 5 to 7 days after exposure with spread of the virus throughout the body. Transplacental infection of the fetus occurs during viremia. Fetal damage occurs through destruction of cells as well as mitotic arrest.

Clinical Features

Acquired Rubella

The incubation period of rubella is 14 days, with a range of 12 to 23 days. Symptoms are often mild, and up to 50% of infections may be subclinical or inapparent. In children, rash is usually the first manifestation and a prodrome is rare. In older children and adults, there is often a 1 to 5 day prodrome with low-grade fever, malaise, lymphadenopathy, and upper respiratory symptoms preceding the rash. The rash of rubella is maculopapular and occurs 14 to 17 days after exposure. The rash usually occurs initially on the

Rubella
- From Latin meaning "little red"
- Discovered in 18th century - thought to be variant of measles
- First described as distinct clinical entity in German literature
- Congenital rubella syndrome (CRS) described by Gregg in 1941

Rubella Virus
- Togavirus
- RNA virus
- One antigenic type
- Rapidly inactivated by chemical agents, ultraviolet light, low pH, and heat

18

Rubella Pathogenesis
- Respiratory transmission of virus
- Replication in nasopharynx and regional lymph nodes
- Viremia 5-7 days after exposure with spread to tissues
- Placenta and fetus infected during viremia

Rubella Clinical Features
- Incubation period 14 days (range 12-23 days)
- Prodrome of low-grade fever
- Maculopapular rash 14-17 days after exposure
- Lymphadenopathy in second week

face and then progresses from head to foot. It lasts about 3 days and is occasionally pruritic. The rash is fainter than measles rash and does not coalesce. The rash is often more prominent after a hot shower or bath. Lymphadenopathy may begin a week before the rash and last several weeks. Postauricular, posterior cervical, and suboccipital nodes are commonly involved.

Arthralgia and arthritis occur so frequently in adults that they are considered by many to be an integral part of the illness rather than a complication. Other symptoms of rubella include conjunctivitis, testalgia, or orchitis. Forschheimer spots may be noted on the soft palate but are not diagnostic for rubella.

Complications

Complications of rubella are not common, but they generally occur more often in adults than in children.

Arthralgia or arthritis may occur in up to 70% of adult women who contract rubella, but it is rare in children and adult males. Fingers, wrists, and knees are often affected. Joint symptoms tend to occur about the same time or shortly after appearance of the rash and may last for up to 1 month; chronic arthritis is rare.

Encephalitis occurs in one in 6,000 cases, more frequently in adults (especially in females) than in children. Mortality estimates vary from 0 to 50%.

Hemorrhagic manifestations occur in approximately one per 3,000 cases, occurring more often in children than in adults. These manifestations may be secondary to low platelets and vascular damage, with thrombocytopenic purpura being the most common manifestation. Gastrointestinal, cerebral, or intrarenal hemorrhage may occur. Effects may last from days to months, and most patients recover.

Additional complications include orchitis, neuritis, and a rare late syndrome of progressive panencephalitis.

Congenital Rubella Syndrome

Prevention of CRS is the main objective of rubella vaccination programs in the United States.

A rubella epidemic in the United States in 1964–1965 resulted in 12.5 million cases of rubella infection and about 20,000 newborns with CRS. The estimated cost of the epidemic was $840 million. This does not include the emotional toll on the families involved.

Infection with rubella virus is most severe in early gestation. The virus may affect all organs and cause a variety

---

Rubella Complications

Arthralgia or arthritis
adult female	up to 70%
children	rare

Thrombocytopenic
purpura	1/3,000 cases
Encephalitis	1/6,000 cases
Neuritis	rare
Orchitis	rare

18

Epidemic Rubella – United States, 1964-1965

- 12.5 million rubella cases
- 2,000 encephalitis cases
- 11,250 abortions (surgical/spontaneous)
- 2,100 neonatal deaths
- 20,000 CRS cases
  - deaf - 11,600
  - blind - 3,580
  - mentally retarded - 1,800

of congenital defects. Infection may lead to fetal death, spontaneous abortion, or premature delivery. The severity of the effects of rubella virus on the fetus depends largely on the time of gestation at which infection occurs. As many as 85% of infants infected in the first trimester of pregnancy will be found to be affected if followed after birth. While fetal infection may occur throughout pregnancy, defects are rare when infection occurs after the 20th week of gestation. The overall risk of defects during the third trimester is probably no greater than that associated with uncomplicated pregnancies.

Congenital infection with rubella virus can affect virtually all organ systems. Deafness is the most common and often the sole manifestation of congenital rubella infection, especially after the fourth month of gestation. Eye defects, including cataracts, glaucoma, retinopathy, and microphthalmia may occur. Cardiac defects such as patent ductus arteriosus, ventricular septal defect, pulmonic stenosis, and coarctation of the aorta are possible. Neurologic abnormalities, including microcephaly and mental retardation, and other abnormalities, including bone lesions, splenomegaly, hepatitis, and thrombocytopenia with purpura may occur.

Manifestations of CRS may be delayed from 2 to 4 years. Diabetes mellitus appearing in later childhood occurs frequently in children with CRS. In addition, progressive encephalopathy resembling subacute sclerosing panencephalitis has been observed in some older children with CRS. Children with CRS have a higher than expected incidence of autism.

Infants with CRS may have low titers by hemagglutination inhibition (HI) but may have high titers of neutralizing antibody that may persist for years. Reinfection may occur. Impaired cell-mediated immunity has been demonstrated in some children with CRS.

Laboratory Diagnosis

Many rash illnesses can mimic rubella infection, and as many as 50% of rubella infections may be subclinical. The only reliable evidence of acute rubella infection is a positive viral culture for rubella or detection of rubella virus by polymerase chain reaction, the presence of rubella-specific IgM antibody, or demonstration of a significant rise in IgG antibody from paired acute- and convalescent-phase sera.

Rubella virus can be isolated from nasal, blood, throat, urine and cerebrospinal fluid specimens from rubella and CRS patients. Virus may be isolated from the pharynx 1 week before and until 2 weeks after rash onset. Although isolation of the virus is diagnostic of rubella infection, viral cultures are labor intensive, and therefore not done in many laboratories; they are generally not used for routine diagnosis of

---

Congenital Rubella Syndrome

- Infection may affect all organs

- May lead to fetal death or premature delivery

- Severity of damage to fetus depends on gestational age

- Up to 85% of infants affected if infected during first trimester

---

Congenital Rubella Syndrome

- Deafness
- Cataracts
- Heart defects
- Microcephaly
- Mental retardation
- Bone alterations
- Liver and spleen damage

18

Rubella Laboratory Diagnosis

- Isolation of rubella virus from clinical specimen (e.g., nasopharynx, urine)

- Positive serologic test for rubella IgM antibody

- Significant rise in rubella IgG by any standard serologic assay (e.g., enzyme immunoassay)

rubella. Viral isolation is an extremely valuable epidemiologic tool and should be attempted for all suspected cases of rubella or CRS. Information about rubella virus isolation can be found on the CDC website at http://www.cdc.gov/ncidod/dvrd/revb/measles/surv_rubellavirus.htm.

Serology is the most common method of confirming the diagnosis of rubella. Acute rubella infection can be serologically confirmed by a significant rise in rubella antibody titer in acute- and convalescent-phase serum specimens or by the presence of serum rubella IgM. Serum should be collected as early as possible (within 7–10 days) after onset of illness, and again 14–21 days (minimum of 7) days later.

False-positive serum rubella IgM tests have occurred in persons with parvovirus infections, with a positive heterophile test for infectious mononucleosis, or with a positive rheumatoid factor.

The serologic tests available for laboratory confirmation of rubella infections vary among laboratories. The state health department can provide guidance on available laboratory services and preferred tests.

Enzyme-linked immunosorbent assay (ELISA). ELISA is sensitive, widely available, and relatively easy to perform. It can also be modified to measure IgM antibodies. Most of the diagnostic testing done for rubella antibodies uses some variation of ELISA.

Epidemiology

Occurrence
Rubella occurs worldwide.

Reservoir
Rubella is a human disease. There is no known animal reservoir. Although infants with CRS may shed rubella virus for an extended period, a true carrier state has not been described.

Transmission
Rubella is spread from person to person via airborne transmission or droplets shed from the respiratory secretions of infected persons. There is no evidence of insect transmission.

Rubella may be transmitted by persons with subclinical or asymptomatic cases (up to 50% of all rubella virus infections).

Temporal Pattern
In temperate areas, incidence is usually highest in late winter and early spring.

Rubella Epidemiology

• Reservoir	Human
• Transmission	Respiratory
	Subclinical cases may transmit
• Temporal pattern	Peak in late winter and spring
• Communicability	7 days before to 5-7 days after rash onset
	Infants with CRS may shed virus for a year or more

18

Communicability

Rubella is only moderately contagious. The disease is most contagious when the rash first appears, but virus may be shed from 7 days before to 5–7 days or more after rash onset.

Infants with CRS shed large quantities of virus from body secretions for up to 1 year and can therefore transmit rubella to persons caring for them who are susceptible to the disease.

Secular Trends in the United States

Rubella and congenital rubella syndrome became nationally notifiable diseases in 1966. The largest annual total of cases of rubella in the United States was in 1969, when 57,686 cases were reported (58 cases per 100,000 population). Following vaccine licensure in 1969, rubella incidence declined rapidly. By 1983, fewer than 1,000 cases per year were reported (less than 0.5 cases per 100,000 population). A moderate resurgence of rubella occurred in 1990–1991, primarily due to outbreaks in California (1990) and among the Amish in Pennsylvania (1991). In 2003, a record low annual total of seven cases was reported. In October 2004, CDC convened an independent expert panel to review available rubella and CRS data. After a careful review, the panel unanimously agreed that rubella was no longer endemic in the United States.

Until recently, there was no predominant age group for rubella cases. From 1982 through 1992, approximately 30% of cases occurred in each of three age groups: younger than 5, 5–14, and 15–39 years. Adults 40 years of age and older typically accounted for less than 10% of cases. However, since 1993, persons 15–39 years of age have accounted for more than half the cases. In 2003, this age group accounted for 71% of all reported cases.

Most reported rubella in the United States since the mid-1990s has occurred among Hispanic young adults who were born in areas where rubella vaccine is routinely not given.

CRS surveillance is maintained through the National Congenital Rubella Registry, which is managed by the National Center for Immunization and Respiratory Diseases. The largest annual total of reported CRS cases to the registry was in 1970 (67 cases). An average of 5–6 CRS cases have been reported annually since 1980. Although reported rubella activity has consistently and significantly decreased since vaccine has been used in the United States, the incidence of CRS has paralleled the decrease in rubella cases only since the mid-1970s. The decline in CRS since the mid-1970s was due to an increased effort to vaccinate

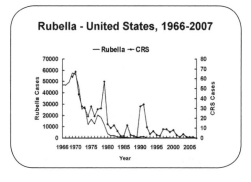

Rubella - United States, 1966-2007

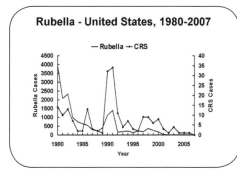

Rubella - United States, 1980-2007

18

18

susceptible adolescents and young adults, especially women. Rubella outbreaks are almost always followed by an increase in CRS.

Rubella outbreaks in California and Pennsylvania in 1990–1991 resulted in 25 cases of CRS in 1990 and 33 cases in 1991. Two CRS cases were reported in 2001, and in 2004, no cases were reported. Since 1997, the mothers of the majority of infants with CRS were Hispanic women, many of whom were born in Latin American or Caribbean countries where rubella vaccine is routinely not used or has only recently begun to be used.

Classification of Rubella Cases

Clinical Case Definition of Acquired Rubella

A clinical case of rubella is defined as an illness with all of the following characteristics: 1) acute onset of generalized maculopapular rash; 2) a temperature higher than 99°F (37.2°C), if measured; and 3) arthralgia or arthritis, lymphadenopathy, or conjunctivitis. Cases meeting the measles case definition are excluded. Also excluded are cases with serology compatible with recent measles virus infection.

Case Classification of Acquired Rubella

A suspected case is any generalized rash illness of acute onset. A probable case meets the clinical case definition, has noncontributory or no serologic or virologic test results, and is not epidemiologically linked to a laboratory-confirmed case. A confirmed case is laboratory confirmed or meets the clinical case definition and is epidemiologically linked to a laboratory-confirmed case.

Clinical Case Definition of Congenital Rubella Syndrome

The clinical case definition of CRS is an illness, usually manifesting in infancy, resulting from rubella infection in utero and characterized by symptoms from the following categories:

A. Cataracts, congenital glaucoma, congenital heart disease (most commonly patent ductus arteriosus or peripheral pulmonary artery stenosis), loss of hearing, pigmentary retinopathy

B. Purpura, hepatosplenomegaly, jaundice, microcephaly, developmental delay, meningoencephalitis, radiolucent bone disease

Case Classification of Congenital Rubella Syndrome

An infection-only case is one with laboratory evidence of infection but without any clinical symptoms or signs. A suspected case has some compatible clinical findings, but does not meet the criteria for a probable case. A probable case is one that is not laboratory confirmed, has any two complications listed in category A above or one complication from category A and one from B, and lacks evidence of any other etiology. A confirmed case is a clinically consistent case that is laboratory confirmed. In probable cases, either or both of the eye-related findings (cataracts and congenital glaucoma) count as a single complication. In cases classified as infection only, if any compatible signs or symptoms (e.g., hearing loss) are identified later, the case is reclassified as confirmed.

Rubella Vaccine

Three rubella vaccines were licensed in the United States in 1969: HPV-77:DE-5 (duck embryo), HPV-77:DK-12 (dog kidney), and GMK-3:RK53 Cendevax (rabbit kidney) strains. HPV-77:DK-12 was later removed from the market because there was a higher rate of joint complaints following vaccination with this strain. In 1979, the RA 27/3 (human diploid fibroblast) strain (Meruvax-II, Merck) was licensed and all other strains were discontinued.

Characteristics

The RA 27/3 rubella vaccine is a live attenuated virus. It was first isolated in 1965 at the Wistar Institute from a rubella-infected aborted fetus. The virus was attenuated by 25–30 passages in tissue culture, using human diploid fibroblasts. It does not contain duck, chicken or egg protein.

Vaccine virus is not communicable except in the setting of breastfeeding (see Contraindications, below), even though virus may be cultured from the nasopharynx of vaccinees.

Rubella vaccine is available combined with measles and mumps vaccines as MMR, or combined with mumps, measles, and varicella vaccine as MMRV (ProQuad). The Advisory Committee on Immunization Practices (ACIP) recommends that combined measles-mumps-rubella vaccine (MMR) be used when any of the individual components is indicated. Use of single-antigen rubella vaccine is not recommended.

MMR and MMRV are supplied as a lyophylized (freeze-dried) powder and are reconstituted with sterile, preservative-free water. The vaccines contains a small amount of human albumin, neomycin, sorbitol, and gelatin.

Rubella Vaccine

Vaccine	Trade Name	Licensure
HPV-77:DE5	Meruvax	1969
HPV-77:DK12	Rubelogen	1969
GMK-3:RK53	Cendevax	1969
RA 27/3*	Meruvax II	1979

*Only vaccine currently licensed in U.S.

Rubella Vaccine

- Composition — Live virus (RA 27/3 strain)
- Efficacy — 95% (Range, 90%-97%)
- Duration of Immunity — Lifelong
- Schedule — At least 1 dose
- Should be administered with measles and mumps as MMR or with measles, mumps and varicella as MMRV

18

Immunogenicity and Vaccine Efficacy

RA 27/3 rubella vaccine is safe and more immunogenic than rubella vaccines used previously. In clinical trials, 95% or more of vaccinees aged 12 months and older developed serologic evidence of rubella immunity after a single dose. More than 90% of vaccinated persons have protection against both clinical rubella and viremia for at least 15 years. Follow-up studies indicate that one dose of vaccine confers long-term, probably lifelong, protection. Seroconversion rates are similar for single-antigen rubella vaccine, MMR, and MMRV.

Several reports indicate that viremic reinfection following exposure may occur in vaccinated persons who have low levels of detectable antibody. The frequency and consequences of this phenomenon are unknown, but it is believed to be uncommon. Rarely, clinical reinfection and fetal infection have been reported among women with vaccine-induced immunity. Rare cases of CRS have occurred among infants born to women who had documented serologic evidence of rubella immunity before they became pregnant.

Vaccination Schedule and Use

At least one dose of rubella-containing vaccine, as combination MMR (or MMRV) vaccine, is routinely recommended for all children 12 months of age or older. All persons born during or after 1957 should have documentation of at least one dose of MMR. The first dose of MMR should be given on or after the first birthday. Any dose of rubella-containing vaccine given before 12 months of age should not be counted as part of the series. Children vaccinated with rubella-containing vaccine before 12 months of age should be revaccinated when the child is at least 12 months of age.

A second dose of MMR is recommended to produce immunity to measles and mumps in those who failed to respond to the first dose. Data indicate that almost all persons who do not respond to the measles component of the first dose will respond to a second dose of MMR. Few data on the immune response to the rubella and mumps components of a second dose of MMR are available. However, most persons who do not respond to the rubella or mumps component of the first MMR dose would be expected to respond to the second dose. The second dose is not generally considered a booster dose because a primary immune response to the first dose provides long-term protection. Although a second dose of vaccine may increase antibody titers in some persons who responded to the first dose, available data indicate that these increased antibody titers are not sustained. The combined

---

Rubella Vaccine (MMR) Indications

- All infants 12 months of age and older
- Susceptible adolescents and adults without documented evidence of rubella immunity
- Emphasis on nonpregnant women of childbearing age, particularly those born outside the U.S.

18

MMR vaccine is recommended for both doses to ensure immunity to all three viruses.

The second dose of MMR vaccine should routinely be given at age 4 through 6 years, before a child enters kindergarten or first grade. The recommended health visit at age 11 or 12 years can serve as a catch-up opportunity to verify vaccination status and administer MMR vaccine to those children who have not yet received two doses of MMR (with the first dose administered no earlier than the first birthday). The second dose of MMR may be administered as soon as 1 month (i.e., minimum of 28 days) after the first dose. The minimum interval between doses of MMRV is 3 months.

All older children not previously immunized should receive at least one dose of rubella vaccine as MMR or MMRV if 12 years of age or younger.

Adults born in 1957 or later who do not have a medical contraindication should receive at least one dose of MMR vaccine unless they have documentation of vaccination with at least one dose of measles-, mumps-, and rubella-containing vaccine or other acceptable evidence of immunity to these three diseases. Some adults at high risk of measles and mumps exposure may require a second dose. This second dose should be administered as combined MMR vaccine (see Measles chapter for details). Efforts should be made to identify and vaccinate susceptible adolescents and adults, particularly women of childbearing age who are not pregnant. Particular emphasis should be placed on vaccinating both males and females in colleges, places of employment, and healthcare settings.

Only doses of vaccine with written documentation of the date of receipt should be accepted as valid. Self-reported doses or a parental report of vaccination is not considered adequate documentation. A healthcare provider should not provide an immunization record for a patient unless that healthcare provider has administered the vaccine or has seen a record that documents vaccination. Persons who lack adequate documentation of vaccination or other acceptable evidence of immunity should be vaccinated. Vaccination status and receipt of all vaccinations should be documented in the patient's permanent medical record and in a vaccination record held by the individual.

MMRV is approved by the Food and Drug Administration for children 12 months through 12 years of age (that is, until the 13th birthday). MMRV should not be administered to persons 13 years or older.

18

Rubella

Rubella Immunity

- Documentation of one dose of rubella-containing vaccine on or after the first birthday

- Serologic evidence of immunity

- Birth before 1957 (except women of childbearing age)

Rubella Immunity

- Birth before 1957 is not acceptable evidence of rubella immunity for women who might become pregnant

- Only serology or documented vaccination should be accepted

18

Rubella Immunity

Persons generally can be considered immune to rubella if they have documentation of vaccination with at least one dose of MMR (or MMRV) or other live rubella-containing vaccine administered on or after their first birthday, have serologic evidence of rubella immunity, or were born before 1957. Persons who have an "equivocal" serologic test result should be considered rubella-susceptible. Although only one dose of rubella-containing vaccine is required as acceptable evidence of immunity to rubella, children should receive two doses of MMR vaccine according to the routine childhood vaccination schedule.

Birth before 1957 provides only presumptive evidence of rubella immunity; it does not guarantee that a person is immune to rubella. Because rubella can occur in some unvaccinated persons born before 1957 and because congenital rubella and congenital rubella syndrome can occur in the offspring of women infected with rubella during pregnancy, birth before 1957 is not acceptable evidence of rubella immunity for women who might become pregnant. Only a positive serologic test for rubella antibody or documentation of appropriate vaccination should be accepted for women who may become pregnant.

Healthcare personnel born before 1957 also should not be presumed to be immune. Medical facilities should consider recommending at least one dose of MMR vaccine to unvaccinated healthcare personnel born before 1957 who do not have laboratory evidence of rubella immunity. Rubella vaccination or laboratory evidence of rubella immunity is particularly important for healthcare personnel who could become pregnant, including those born before 1957. This recommendation is based on serologic studies which indicate that among hospital personnel born before 1957, 5% to 9% had no detectable measles antibody.

Clinical diagnosis of rubella is unreliable and should not be considered in assessing immune status. Because many rash illnesses may mimic rubella infection and many rubella infections are unrecognized, the only reliable evidence of previous rubella infection is the presence of serum rubella IgG antibody. Laboratories that regularly perform antibody testing are generally the most reliable because their reagents and procedures are strictly standardized.

Occasionally, a person with a history of documented rubella vaccination is found to have a negative serum IgG by ELISA. Such persons may be given a dose of MMR vaccine and do not need to be retested for serologic evidence of rubella immunity.

Serologic screening need not be done before vaccinating for measles and rubella unless the medical facility considers it cost-effective. Serologic testing is appropriate only if tracking systems are used to ensure that tested persons who are identified as susceptible are subsequently vaccinated in a timely manner. If the return and timely vaccination of those screened cannot be assured, vaccination should be done without prior testing. Serologic testing for immunity to measles and rubella is not necessary for persons documented to be appropriately vaccinated or who have other acceptable evidence of immunity.

Neither rubella vaccine nor immune globulin is effective for postexposure prophylaxis of rubella. Vaccination after exposure is not harmful and may possibly avert later disease.

Contraindications and Precautions to Vaccination

Persons who have experienced a severe allergic reaction (anaphylaxis) to a vaccine compnent or following a prior dose of rubella vaccine should generally not be vaccinated with MMR.

Women known to be pregnant or attempting to become pregnant should not receive rubella vaccine. Although there is no evidence that rubella vaccine virus causes fetal damage, pregnancy should be avoided for 4 weeks (28 days) after rubella or MMR vaccination.

Persons with immunodeficiency or immunosuppression, resulting from leukemia, lymphoma, generalized malignancy, immune deficiency disease, or immunosuppressive therapy should not be vaccinated. However, treatment with low-dose (less than 2 mg/kg/day), alternate-day, topical, or aerosolized steroid preparations is not a contraindication to rubella vaccination. Persons whose immunosuppressive therapy with steroids has been discontinued for 1 month (3 months for chemotherapy) may be vaccinated. Rubella vaccine should be considered for persons with asymptomatic or mildly symptomatic HIV infection.

Persons with moderate or severe acute illness should not be vaccinated until the illness has improved. Minor illness (e.g., otitis media, mild upper respiratory infections), concurrent antibiotic therapy, and exposure or recovery from other illnesses are not contraindications to rubella vaccination.

Receipt of antibody-containing blood products (e.g., immune globulin, whole blood or packed red blood cells, intravenous immune globulin) may interfere with seroconversion to rubella vaccine. Vaccine should be given 2 weeks before, or deferred for at least 3 months following

MMR Vaccine Contraindications and Precautions
- Severe allergic reaction to vaccine component or following a prior dose
- Pregnancy
- Immunosuppression
- Moderate or severe acute illness
- Recent blood product

18

administration of an antibody-containing blood product. If rubella vaccine is given as combined MMR, a longer delay may be necessary before vaccination. For more information, see Chapter 2, General Recommendations on Immunization.

Previous administration of human anti-Rho(D) immune globulin (RhoGam) does not generally interfere with an immune response to rubella vaccine and is not a contraindication to postpartum vaccination. However, women who have received anti-Rho immune globulin should be serologically tested 6–8 weeks after vaccination to ensure that seroconversion has occurred.

Although vaccine virus may be isolated from the pharynx, vaccinees do not transmit rubella to others, except occasionally in the case of the vaccinated breastfeeding woman. In this situation, the infant may be infected, presumably through breast milk, and may develop a mild rash illness, but serious effects have not been reported. Infants infected through breastfeeding have been shown to respond normally to rubella vaccination at 12–15 months of age. Breastfeeding is not a contraindication to rubella vaccination and does not alter rubella vaccination recommendations.

Adverse Reactions Following Vaccination

Rubella vaccine is very safe. Most adverse reactions reported following MMR vaccination (such as fever and rash) are attributable to the measles component. The most common complaints following rubella vaccination are fever, lymphadenopathy, and arthralgia. These adverse reactions only occur in susceptible persons and are more common in adults, especially in women.

Joint symptoms, such as arthralgia (joint pain) and arthritis (joint redness and/or swelling), are associated with the rubella component of MMR. Arthralgia and transient arthritis occur more frequently in susceptible adults than in children and more frequently in susceptible women than in men. Acute arthralgia or arthritis is rare following vaccination of children with RA 27/3 vaccine. By contrast, approximately 25% of susceptible postpubertal females develop acute arthralgia following RA 27/3 vaccination, and approximately 10% have been reported to have acute arthritis-like signs and symptoms. Rarely, transient peripheral neuritic complaints, such as paresthesias and pain in the arms and legs, have been reported.

When acute joint symptoms occur, or when pain or paresthesias not associated with joints occur, the symptoms generally begin 1–3 weeks after vaccination, persist for 1 day to 3 weeks, and rarely recur. Adults with acute joint symptoms following rubella vaccination rarely have had to

18

MMR Adverse Reactions

- Fever   5%-15%
- Rash   5%
- Joint symptoms   25%
- Thrombocytopenia   <1/30,000 doses
- Parotitis   rare
- Deafness   rare
- Encephalopathy   <1/1,000,000 doses

Rubella Vaccine Arthropathy

- Acute arthralgia in about 25% of vaccinated, susceptible adult women
- Acute arthritis-like signs and symptoms occurs in about 10% of recipients
- Rare reports of chronic or persistent symptoms
- Population-based studies have not confirmed an association with rubella vaccine

disrupt work activities.

Data from studies in the United States and experience from other countries using the RA 27/3 strain rubella vaccine have not supported an association between the vaccine and chronic arthritis. One study among 958 seronegative immunized and 932 seronegative unimmunized women aged 15–39 years found no association between rubella vaccination and development of recurrent joint symptoms, neuropathy, or collagen disease.

The ACIP continues to recommend the vaccination of all adult women who do not have evidence of rubella immunity.

Rubella Vaccination of Women of Childbearing Age

Women who are pregnant or who intend to become pregnant within 4 weeks should not receive rubella vaccine. ACIP recommends that vaccine providers ask a woman if she is pregnant or likely to become pregnant in the next 4 weeks. Those who are pregnant or intend to become pregnant should not be vaccinated. All other women should be vaccinated after being informed of the theoretical risks of vaccination during pregnancy and the importance of not becoming pregnant during the 4 weeks following vaccination. ACIP does not recommend routine pregnancy screening of women before rubella vaccination.

If a pregnant woman is inadvertently vaccinated or if she becomes pregnant within 4 weeks after vaccination, she should be counseled about the concern for the fetus (see below), but MMR vaccination during pregnancy should not ordinarily be a reason to consider termination of the pregnancy.

When rubella vaccine was licensed, concern existed about women being inadvertently vaccinated while they were pregnant or shortly before conception. This concern came from the known teratogenicity of the wild-virus strain. To determine whether CRS would occur in infants of such mothers, CDC maintained a registry from 1971 to 1989 of women vaccinated during pregnancy. This was called the Vaccine in Pregnancy (VIP) Registry.

Although subclinical fetal infection has been detected serologically in approximately 1%–2% of infants born to susceptible vaccinees, regardless of the vaccine strain, the data collected by CDC in the VIP Registry showed no evidence of CRS occurring in offspring of the 321 susceptible women who received rubella vaccine and who continued pregnancy to term. The observed risk of vaccine-induced malformation was 0%, with a maximum theoretical risk of

Vaccination of Women of Childbearing Age

- Ask if pregnant or likely to become so in next 4 weeks

- Exclude those who say "yes"

- For others
  – explain theoretical risks
  – vaccinate

18

Vaccination in Pregnancy Study 1971-1989

- 321 women vaccinated

- 324 live births

- No observed CRS

- 95% confidence limits 0%-1.2%

1.6%, based on 95% confidence limits (1.2% for all types of rubella vaccine). Since the risk of the vaccine to the fetus appears to be extremely low, if it exists at all, routine termination of pregnancy is not recommended. Individual counseling for these women is recommended. As of April 30, 1989, CDC discontinued the VIP registry.

The ACIP continues to state that because of the small theoretical risk to the fetus of a vaccinated woman, pregnant women should not be vaccinated.

Vaccine Storage and Handling

MMR and MMRV vaccines must be shipped with refrigerant to maintain a temperature of 50°F (10°C) or less at all times. Vaccine must be refrigerated immediately on arrival and protected from light at all times. The vaccine must be stored at refrigerator temperature (35°–46°F [2°–8°C]), but may be frozen. Diluent may be stored at refrigerator temperature or at room temperature. MMRV must be shipped to maintain a temperature of -4°F (-20°C) or colder at all times. MMRV must be stored at an average temperature of 5°F (-15°C) or colder at all times.

After reconstitution, MMR vaccines must be stored at refrigerator temperature and protected from light. Reconstituted vaccine should be used immediately. If reconstituted vaccine is not used within 8 hours, it must be discarded. MMRV must be administered within 30 minutes of reconstitution.

Strategies to Decrease Rubella and CRS

Vaccination of Susceptible Postpubertal Females

Elimination of indigenous rubella and CRS can be maintained by continuing efforts to vaccinate susceptible adolescents and young adults of childbearing age, particularly those born outside the United States. These efforts should include vaccinating in family planning clinics, sexually transmitted disease (STD) clinics, and as part of routine gynecologic care; maximizing use of premarital serology results; emphasizing immunization for college students; vaccinating women postpartum and postabortion; immunizing prison staff and, when possible, prison inmates, especially women inmates; offering vaccination to at-risk women through the special supplemental program for Women, Infants and Children (WIC); and implementing vaccination programs in the workplace, particularly those employing persons born outside the United States.

Hospital Rubella Programs

Emphasis should be placed on vaccinating susceptible hospital personnel, both male and female (e.g., volunteers, trainees, nurses, physicians.) Ideally, all hospital employees should be immune. It is important to note that screening programs alone are not adequate. Vaccination of susceptible staff must follow.

Selected References

American Academy of Pediatrics. Rubella. In: Pickering L, Baker C, Long S, McMillan S, eds. *Red Book: 2006 Report of the Committee on Infectious Diseases.* 27th ed. Elk Grove Village, IL: American Academy of Pediatrics, 2006:574–9.

CDC. Measles, mumps, and rubella—vaccine use and strategies for elimination of measles, rubella, and congenital rubella syndrome and control of mumps. Recommendations of the Advisory Committee on Immunization Practices (ACIP). *MMWR* 1998;47(No. RR-8):1–57.

CDC. Immunization of health-care workers. Recommendations of the Advisory Committee on Immunization Practices (ACIP) and the Hospital Infection Control Advisory Committee (HICPAC). *MMWR* 1997;46(No. RR-18):1–42.

CDC. Control and prevention of rubella: evaluation and management of suspected outbreaks, rubella in pregnant women, and surveillance for congenital rubella syndrome. *MMWR* 2001;50(No. RR-12):1–30.

CDC. Rubella vaccination during pregnancy—United States, 1971–1988. *MMWR* 1989;38:289–93.

CDC. Notice to readers. Revised ACIP recommendations for avoiding pregnancy after receiving rubella-containing vaccine. *MMWR* 2001;50:1117.

Frenkel LM, Nielsen K, Garakian A, et al. A search for persistent rubella virus infection in persons with chronic symptoms after rubella and rubella immunization and in patients with juvenile rheumatoid arthritis. *Clin Infect Dis* 1996;22:287–94.

Mellinger AK, Cragan JD, Atkinson WL, et al. High incidence of congenital rubella syndrome after a rubella outbreak. *Pediatr Infect Dis J* 1995;14:573–78.

Orenstein WA, Hadler S, Wharton M. Trends in vaccine-preventable diseases. *Semin Pediatr Infect Dis* 1997;8:23–33.

Reef SE, Frey TK, Theall K, et al. The changing epidemiology of rubella in the 1990s. *JAMA* 2002;287:464–72.

18

Rubella

Tetanus

Tetanus is an acute, often fatal, disease caused by an exotoxin produced by the bacterium *Clostridium tetani*. It is characterized by generalized rigidity and convulsive spasms of skeletal muscles. The muscle stiffness usually involves the jaw (lockjaw) and neck and then becomes generalized.

Although records from antiquity (5th century BCE) contain clinical descriptions of tetanus, it was Carle and Rattone in 1884 who first produced tetanus in animals by injecting them with pus from a fatal human tetanus case. During the same year, Nicolaier produced tetanus in animals by injecting them with samples of soil. In 1889, Kitasato isolated the organism from a human victim, showed that it produced disease when injected into animals, and reported that the toxin could be neutralized by specific antibodies. In 1897, Nocard demonstrated the protective effect of passively transferred antitoxin, and passive immunization in humans was used for treatment and prophylaxis during World War I. Tetanus toxoid was developed by Descombey in 1924. It was first widely used during World War II.

Clostridium tetani

C. tetani is a slender, gram-positive, anaerobic rod that may develop a terminal spore, giving it a drumstick appearance. The organism is sensitive to heat and cannot survive in the presence of oxygen. The spores, in contrast, are very resistant to heat and the usual antiseptics. They can survive autoclaving at 249.8°F (121°C) for 10–15 minutes. The spores are also relatively resistant to phenol and other chemical agents.

The spores are widely distributed in soil and in the intestines and feces of horses, sheep, cattle, dogs, cats, rats, guinea pigs, and chickens. Manure-treated soil may contain large numbers of spores. In agricultural areas, a significant number of human adults may harbor the organism. The spores can also be found on skin surfaces and in contaminated heroin.

C. tetani produces two exotoxins, tetanolysin and tetanospasmin. The function of tetanolysin is not known with certainty. Tetanospasmin is a neurotoxin and causes the clinical manifestations of tetanus. On the basis of weight, tetanospasmin is one of the most potent toxins known. The estimated minimum human lethal dose is 2.5 nanograms per kilogram of body weight (a nanogram is one billionth of a gram), or 175 nanograms for a 70-kg (154lb) human.

Tetanus

- First described by Hippocrates
- Etiology discovered in 1884 by Carle and Rattone
- Passive immunization used for treatment and prophylaxis during World War I
- Tetanus toxoid first widely used during World War II

Clostridium tetani

- Anaerobic gram-positive, spore-forming bacteria
- Spores found in soil, animal feces; may persist for months to years
- Multiple toxins produced with growth of bacteria
- Tetanospasmin estimated human lethal dose = 2.5 ng/kg

19

19

Pathogenesis

C. tetani usually enters the body through a wound. In the presence of anaerobic (low oxygen) conditions, the spores germinate. Toxins are produced and disseminated via blood and lymphatics. Toxins act at several sites within the central nervous system, including peripheral motor end plates, spinal cord, and brain, and in the sympathetic nervous system. The typical clinical manifestations of tetanus are caused when tetanus toxin interferes with release of neurotransmitters, blocking inhibitor impulses. This leads to unopposed muscle contraction and spasm. Seizures may occur, and the autonomic nervous system may also be affected.

Clinical Features

The incubation period ranges from 3 to 21 days, usually about 8 days. In general the further the injury site is from the central nervous system, the longer the incubation period. The shorter the incubation period, the higher the chance of death. In neonatal tetanus, symptoms usually appear from 4 to 14 days after birth, averaging about 7 days.

On the basis of clinical findings, three different forms of tetanus have been described.

Local tetanus is an uncommon form of the disease, in which patients have persistent contraction of muscles in the same anatomic area as the injury. These contractions may persist for many weeks before gradually subsiding. Local tetanus may precede the onset of generalized tetanus but is generally milder. Only about 1% of cases are fatal.

Cephalic tetanus is a rare form of the disease, occasionally occurring with otitis media (ear infections) in which *C. tetani* is present in the flora of the middle ear, or following injuries to the head. There is involvement of the cranial nerves, especially in the facial area.

The most common type (about 80%) of reported tetanus is generalized tetanus. The disease usually presents with a descending pattern. The first sign is trismus or lockjaw, followed by stiffness of the neck, difficulty in swallowing, and rigidity of abdominal muscles. Other symptoms include elevated temperature, sweating, elevated blood pressure, and episodic rapid heart rate. Spasms may occur frequently and last for several minutes. Spasms continue for 3–4 weeks. Complete recovery may take months.

Neonatal tetanus is a form of generalized tetanus that occurs in newborn infants. Neonatal tetanus occurs in infants born without protective passive immunity, because the mother is not immune. It usually occurs through infection of the unhealed umbilical stump, particularly when the stump is cut with an unsterile instrument. Neonatal tetanus is common in some developing countries (estimated more than 257,000 annual deaths worldwide in 2000-2003), but very rare in the United States.

Complications

Laryngospasm (spasm of the vocal cords) and/or spasm of the muscles of respiration leads to interference with breathing. Fractures of the spine or long bones may result from sustained contractions and convulsions. Hyperactivity of the autonomic nervous system may lead to hypertension and/or an abnormal heart rhythm.

Nosocomial infections are common because of prolonged hospitalization. Secondary infections may include sepsis from indwelling catheters, hospital-acquired pneumonias, and decubitus ulcers. Pulmonary embolism is particularly a problem in drug users and elderly patients. Aspiration pneumonia is a common late complication of tetanus, found in 50%–70% of autopsied cases. In recent years, tetanus has been fatal in approximately 11% of reported cases. Cases most likely to be fatal are those occurring in persons 60 years of age and older (18%) and unvaccinated persons (22%). In about 20% of tetanus deaths, no obvious pathology is identified and death is attributed to the direct effects of tetanus toxin.

Laboratory Diagnosis

There are no laboratory findings characteristic of tetanus. The diagnosis is entirely clinical and does not depend upon bacteriologic confirmation. *C. tetani* is recovered from the wound in only 30% of cases and can be isolated from patients who do not have tetanus. Laboratory identification of the organism depends most importantly on the demonstration of toxin production in mice.

Medical Management

All wounds should be cleaned. Necrotic tissue and foreign material should be removed. If tetanic spasms are occurring, supportive therapy and maintenance of an adequate airway are critical.

Tetanus immune globulin (TIG) is recommended for persons with tetanus. TIG can only help remove unbound tetanus toxin. It cannot affect toxin bound to nerve endings. A single intramuscular dose of 3,000 to 5,000 units is generally recommended for children and adults, with part of the dose infiltrated around the wound if it can be identified. Intravenous immune globulin (IVIG) contains tetanus antitoxin and may be used if TIG is not available.

Tetanus Complications

- Laryngospasm
- Fractures
- Hypertension
- Nosocomial infections
- Pulmonary embolism
- Aspiration pneumonia
- Death

19

Because of the extreme potency of the toxin, tetanus disease does not result in tetanus immunity. Active immunization with tetanus toxoid should begin or continue as soon as the person's condition has stabilized.

Wound Management

Antibiotic prophylaxis against tetanus is neither practical nor useful in managing wounds; proper immunization plays the more important role. The need for active immunization, with or without passive immunization, depends on the condition of the wound and the patient's immunization history (see *MMWR* 2006;55[RR-17] for details). Rarely have cases of tetanus occurred in persons with a documented primary series of tetanus toxoid.

Persons with wounds that are neither clean nor minor, and who have had 0–2 prior doses of tetanus toxoid or have an uncertain history of prior doses should receive TIG as well as Td or Tdap. This is because early doses of toxoid may not induce immunity, but only prime the immune system. The TIG provides temporary immunity by directly providing antitoxin. This ensures that protective levels of antitoxin are achieved even if an immune response has not yet occurred.

Epidemiology

Occurrence

Tetanus occurs worldwide but is most frequently encountered in densely populated regions in hot, damp climates with soil rich in organic matter.

Reservoir

Organisms are found primarily in the soil and intestinal tracts of animals and humans.

Mode of Transmission

Transmission is primarily by contaminated wounds (apparent and inapparent). The wound may be major or minor. In recent years, however, a higher proportion of patients had minor wounds, probably because severe wounds are more likely to be properly managed. Tetanus may follow elective surgery, burns, deep puncture wounds, crush wounds, otitis media (ear infections), dental infection, animal bites, abortion, and pregnancy.

Communicability

Tetanus is not contagious from person to person. It is the only vaccine-preventable disease that is infectious but not contagious.

Tetanus Wound Management

Vaccination History	Clean, minor wounds Td*	Clean, minor wounds TIG	All other wounds Td*	All other wounds TIG
Unknown or less than 3 doses	Yes	No	Yes	Yes
3 or more doses	No+	No	No**	No

* Tdap may be substituted for Td if the person has not previously received Tdap and is 10 years or older
+ Yes, if more than 10 years since last dose
** Yes, if more than 5 years since last dose

19

Tetanus Epidemiology

- Reservoir — Soil and intestine of animals and humans
- Transmission — Contaminated wounds Tissue injury
- Temporal pattern — Peak in summer or wet season
- Communicability — Not contagious

Secular Trends in the United States

A marked decrease in mortality from tetanus occurred from the early 1900s to the late 1940s. In the late 1940s, tetanus toxoid was introduced into routine childhood immunization and tetanus became nationally notifiable. At that time, 500–600 cases (approximately 0.4 cases per 100,000 population) were reported per year.

After the 1940s, reported tetanus incidence rates declined steadily. Since the mid-1970s, 50–100 cases (~0.05 cases per 100,000) have been reported annually. From 2000 through 2007 an average of 31 cases were reported per year. The death-to-case ratio has declined from 30% to approximately 10% in recent years. An all-time low of 20 cases (0.01 cases per 100,000) was reported in 2003.

From 1980 through 2000, 70% of reported cases of tetanus were among persons 40 years of age or older. From 1980 through 1990, a median of 21% of reported cases were among persons younger than 40 years of age. The age distribution of reported cases shifted to a younger age group in the last half of the 1990s. Persons younger than 40 years accounted for 28% of cases during 1991–1995, increasing to 42% of cases during 1996–2000. This change in age distribution is a result of both an increase in cases in persons younger than 40 years and a decrease in cases in older people. The increase in cases among younger persons is related in part to an increased number of cases among young injection-drug users in California in the late 1990s.

Almost all reported cases of tetanus are in persons who have either never been vaccinated, or who completed a primary series but have not had a booster in the preceding 10 years.

Heroin users, particularly persons who inject themselves subcutaneously, appear to be at high risk for tetanus. Quinine is used to dilute heroin and may support the growth of *C. tetani*.

Neonatal tetanus is rare in the United States, with only two cases reported since 1989. Neither of the infants' mothers had ever received tetanus toxoid.

During 1998–2000 (the most recent years for which data are available), acute injuries or wounds preceded tetanus in 94 (73%) of the 129 cases for which information was available. Among the most frequent wound types were puncture wounds (50%), lacerations (33%), and abrasions (9%). The most common puncture wound was from stepping on a nail (15 cases). Other puncture wounds involved barbed wire, splinters, animal or insect bites, self-piercing, and self-performed tattoos. The environment in which acute injuries occurred was indoors or at home in 45%, in the yard, garden, or farm in 31%, and other outdoor locations in 23%.

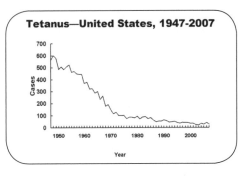

Tetanus—United States, 1947-2007

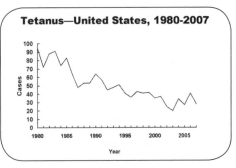

Tetanus—United States, 1980-2007

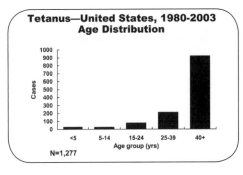

Tetanus—United States, 1980-2003
Age Distribution

N=1,277

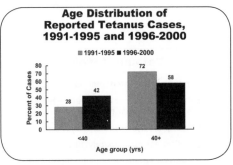

Age Distribution of Reported Tetanus Cases, 1991-1995 and 1996-2000

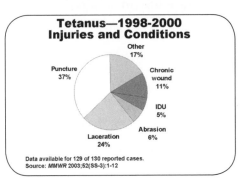

Tetanus—1998-2000
Injuries and Conditions

Data available for 129 of 130 reported cases.
Source: *MMWR* 2003;52(SS-3):1-12

19

Five percent of reported case-patients were intravenous drug users without other known injury, and 11% had chronic wounds. Twenty patients were reported to have received at least a primary series of tetanus toxoid; 18 had an outcome reported. Among these 18 patients, one (6%) death occurred; the death was in an injection-drug user whose last dose of tetanus toxoid was 11 years before the onset of tetanus. A total of 110 patients reported fewer than three doses of tetanus toxoid or had an unknown vaccination history; 95 of these patients had an outcome reported. Nineteen (20%) deaths occurred among these 95 patients.

Tetanus Toxoid

Characteristics

Tetanus toxoid was first produced in 1924, and tetanus toxoid immunizations were used extensively in the armed services during World War II. Tetanus cases among this population declined from 70 in World War I (13.4/100,000 wounds and injuries) to 12 in World War II (0.44/100,000). Of the 12 case-patients, half had received no prior toxoid.

Tetanus toxoid consists of a formaldehyde-treated toxin. The toxoid is standardized for potency in animal tests according to Food and Drug Administration (FDA) regulations. Occasionally, potency is mistakenly equated with Lf units, which are a measure of the quantity of toxoid, not its potency in inducing protection.

There are two types of toxoid available—adsorbed (aluminum salt precipitated) toxoid and fluid toxoid. Although the rates of seroconversion are about equal, the adsorbed toxoid is preferred because the antitoxin response reaches higher titers and is longer lasting than that following the fluid toxoid.

Tetanus toxoid is available as a single-antigen preparation, combined with diphtheria toxoid as pediatric diphtheria-tetanus toxoid (DT) or adult tetanus-diphtheria (Td), and with both diphtheria toxoid and acellular pertussis vaccine as DTaP or Tdap. Tetanus toxoid is also available as combined DTaP-HepB-IPV (Pediarix) and DTaP-IPV/Hib (Pentacel—see Chapter 14 for more information). Pediatric formulations (DT and DTaP) contain a similar amount of tetanus toxoid as adult Td, but contain 3 to 4 times as much diphtheria toxoid. Children younger than 7 years of age should receive either DTaP or pediatric DT. Persons 7 years of age or older should receive the adult formulation (adult Td), even if they have not completed a series of DTaP or pediatric DT. The use of single-antigen tetanus toxoid is not recommended. Tetanus toxoid should be given in combination with diphtheria toxoid, since periodic boosting is needed for both antigens. Two brands of Tdap are available: Boostrix (approved for

---

DTaP, DT, Td and Tdap

	Diphtheria	Tetanus
DTaP, DT	7-8 Lf units	5-12.5 Lf units
Td, Tdap (adult)	2-2.5 Lf units	5 Lf units

DTaP and pediatric DT used through age 6 years. Adult Td for persons 7 years and older. Tdap for persons 10-18 years (Boostrix) or 10-64 years (Adacel)

19

Tetanus Toxoid

- Formalin-inactivated tetanus toxin
- Schedule   Three or four doses + booster
  Booster every 10 years
- Efficacy   Approximately 100%
- Duration   Approximately 10 years
- Should be administered with diphtheria toxoid as DTaP, DT, Td, or Tdap

persons 10 through 64 years of age) and Adacel (approved for persons 11 through 64 years of age). DTaP and Tdap vaccines do not contain thimerosal as a preservative.

Immunogenicity and Vaccine Efficacy

After a primary series (three properly spaced doses of tetanus toxoid in persons 7 years of age and older, and four doses in children younger than 7 years of age) essentially all recipients achieve antitoxin levels considerably greater than the protective level of 0.1 IU/mL.

Efficacy of the toxoid has never been studied in a vaccine trial. It can be inferred from protective antitoxin levels that a complete tetanus toxoid series has a clinical efficacy of virtually 100%; cases of tetanus occurring in fully immunized persons whose last dose was within the last 10 years are extremely rare.

Antitoxin levels decrease with time. While some persons may be protected for life, by 10 years after the last dose, most persons have antitoxin levels that only approach the minimal protective level. As a result, routine boosters are recommended every 10 years.

In a small percentage of individuals, antitoxin levels fall below the minimal protective level before 10 years have elapsed. To ensure adequate protective antitoxin levels, persons who sustain a wound that is other than clean and minor should receive a tetanus booster if more than 5 years have elapsed since their last dose. (See Wound Management for details on persons who previously received fewer than three doses.)

Vaccination Schedule and Use

DTaP (diphtheria and tetanus toxoids and acellular pertussis vaccine) is the vaccine of choice for children 6 weeks through 6 years of age. The usual schedule is a primary series of four doses at 2, 4, 6, and 15–18 months of age. The first, second, and third doses of DTaP should be separated by a minimum of 4 weeks. The fourth dose should follow the third dose by no less than 6 months and should not be administered before 12 months of age.

If a child has a valid contraindication to pertussis vaccine, pediatric DT should be used to complete the vaccination series. If the child was younger than 12 months old when the first dose of DT was administered (as DTaP or DT), the child should receive a total of four primary DT doses. If the child was 12 months of age or older at the time that the first dose of DT was administered, three doses (third dose 6–12 months after the second) completes the primary DT series.

19

Routine DTaP Primary Vaccination Schedule

Dose	Age	Interval
Primary 1	2 months	---
Primary 2	4 months	4 weeks
Primary 3	6 months	4 weeks
Primary 4	15-18 months	6 months

Children Who Receive DT

- The number of doses of DT needed to complete the series depends on the child's age at the first dose:
  - if first dose given at younger than 12 months of age, 4 doses are recommended
  - if first dose given at 12 months or older, 3 doses complete the primary series

If the fourth dose of DTaP, DTP, or DT is administered before the fourth birthday, a booster dose is recommended at 4–6 years of age. The fifth dose is not required if the fourth dose was given on or after the fourth birthday.

Because of waning antitoxin titers, most persons have antitoxin levels below the optimal level 10 years after the last dose of DTaP, DTP, DT, or Td. Additional booster doses of tetanus and diphtheria toxoids are required every 10 years to maintain protective antitoxin titers. The first booster dose of Td may be given at 11 or 12 years of age if at least 5 years have elapsed since the last dose of DTaP, DTP, or DT. The Advisory Committee on Immunization Practices (ACIP) recommends that this dose be administered as Tdap. If a dose is given sooner as part of wound management, the next booster is not needed for 10 years thereafter. More frequent boosters are not indicated and have been reported to result in an increased incidence and severity of local adverse reactions.

Td is the vaccine of choice for children 7 years and older and for adults. A primary series is three or four doses, depending on whether the person has received prior doses of diphtheria-containing vaccine and the age these doses were administered. The number of doses recommended for children who received one or more doses of DTP, DTaP, or DT before age 7 years is discussed above. For unvaccinated persons 7 years and older (including persons who cannot document prior vaccination), the primary series is three doses. The first two doses should be separated by at least 4 weeks, and the third dose given 6 to 12 months after the second. ACIP recommends that *one* of these doses (preferably the first) be administered as Tdap. A booster dose of Td should be given every 10 years. Tdap is approved for a single dose at this time (i.e., it should not be used for all the doses of Td in a previously unvaccinated person 7 years or older). Refer to the pertussis chapter for more information about Tdap.

Interruption of the recommended schedule or delay of subsequent doses does not reduce the response to the vaccine when the series is finally completed. There is no need to restart a series regardless of the time elapsed between doses.

Tetanus disease does not confer immunity because of the very small amount of toxin required to produce illness. Persons recovering from tetanus should begin or complete active immunization with tetanus toxoid (Td) during convalescence.

Contraindications and Precautions to Vaccination

A severe allergic reaction (anaphylaxis) to a vaccine component or following a prior dose of tetanus toxoid is a contraindication to receipt of tetanus toxoid. If a generalized reaction is suspected to represent allergy, it may be

---

Routine DTaP Schedule Children Younger Than 7 years of Age

Booster Doses
- 4 through 6 years of age, before entering school
- 11 or 12 years of age if 5 years since last dose (Tdap)
- Every 10 years thereafter (Td)

Routine Td Schedule Unvaccinated Persons 7 Years of Age or Older

Dose*	Interval
Primary 1	---
Primary 2	4 weeks
Primary 3	6 to 12 months

Booster dose every 10 years

*ACIP recommends that <u>one</u> of these doses (preferably the first) be administered as Tdap

---

Diphtheria and Tetanus Toxoids Contraindications and Precautions

- Severe allergic reaction to vaccine component or following a prior dose
- Moderate or severe acute illness

19

useful to refer an individual for appropriate skin testing before discontinuing tetanus toxoid immunization. A moderate or severe acute illness is reason to defer routine vaccination, but a minor illness is not.

If a contraindication to using tetanus toxoid-containing preparations exists, passive immunization with tetanus immune globulin (TIG) should be considered whenever an injury other than a clean minor wound is sustained.

See Chapter 14, Pertussis, for additional information on contraindications and precautions to Tdap.

Adverse Reactions Following Vaccination

Local adverse reactions (e.g., erythema, induration, pain at the injection site) are common but are usually self-limited and require no therapy. A nodule may be palpable at the injection site of adsorbed products for several weeks. Abscess at the site of injection has been reported. Fever and other systemic symptoms are not common.

Exaggerated local (Arthus-like) reactions are occasionally reported following receipt of a diphtheria- or tetanus-containing vaccine. These reactions present as extensive painful swelling, often from shoulder to elbow. They generally begin from 2 to 8 hours after injections and are reported most often in adults, particularly those who have received frequent doses of diphtheria or tetanus toxoid. Persons experiencing these severe reactions usually have very high serum antitoxin levels; they should not be given further routine or emergency booster doses of Td more frequently than every 10 years. Less severe local reactions may occur in persons who have multiple prior boosters.

Severe systemic reactions such as generalized urticaria (hives), anaphylaxis, or neurologic complications have been reported after receipt of tetanus toxoid. A few cases of peripheral neuropathy and Guillain-Barré syndrome (GBS) have been reported following tetanus toxoid administration. The Institute of Medicine has concluded that the available evidence favors a causal relationship between tetanus toxoid and both brachial neuritis and GBS, although these reactions are very rare.

Vaccine Storage and Handling

All tetanus-toxoid-containing vaccines should be stored at 35°–46°F (2°–8°C). Freezing reduces the potency of the tetanus component. Vaccine exposed to freezing temperature should never be administered.

> **Diphtheria and Tetanus Toxoids Adverse Reactions**
>
> - Local reactions (erythema, induration)
> - Fever and systemic symptoms not common
> - Exaggerated local reactions (Arthus-type)
> - Severe systemic reactions rare

19

Selected References

CDC. Diphtheria, tetanus, and pertussis: Recommendations for vaccine use and other preventive measures. Recommendations of the Advisory Committee on Immunization Practices (ACIP). *MMWR* 1991;40 (No. RR-10):1–28.

CDC. Pertussis vaccination: use of acellular pertussis vaccines among infants and young children. Recommendations of the Advisory Committee on Immunization Practices (ACIP). *MMWR* 1997;46(No. RR-7):1–25.

CDC. Preventing tetanus, diphtheria, and pertussis among adolescents: use of tetanus toxoid, reduced diphtheria toxoid and acellular pertussis vaccines. Recommendations of the Advisory Committee on Immunization Practices (ACIP). *MMWR* 2006;55(No. RR-3):1–34.

CDC. Preventing tetanus, diphtheria, and pertussis among adults: use of tetanus toxoid, reduced diphtheria toxoid and acellular pertussis vaccines. Recommendations of the Advisory Committee on Immunization Practices (ACIP) and Recommendation of ACIP, supported by the Healthcare Infection Control Practices Advisory Committee (HICPAC), for Use of Tdap Among Health-Care Personnel. *MMWR* 2006;55(No. RR-17):1–33.

CDC. Tetanus surveillance—United States, 1998–2000. *MMWR* 2003;52(No. SS-3):1–12.

Wassilak SGF, Roper MH, Kretsinger K, Orenstein WA. Tetanus toxoid. In: Plotkin SA, Orenstein WA, Offit PA, eds. *Vaccines*. 5th ed. Philadelphia, PA: Saunders, 2008:805–39.

World Health Organization. The "high-risk" approach: the WHO-recommended strategy to accelerate elimination of neonatal tetanus. *Wlky Epidemiol Rec* 1996;71:33–36.

19

Varicella

Varicella is an acute infectious disease caused by varicella zoster virus (VZV). The recurrent infection (herpes zoster, also known as shingles) has been recognized since ancient times. Primary varicella infection (chickenpox) was not reliably distinguished from smallpox until the end of the 19th century. In 1875, Steiner demonstrated that chickenpox was caused by an infectious agent by inoculating volunteers with the vesicular fluid from a patient with acute varicella. Clinical observations of the relationship between varicella and herpes zoster were made in 1888 by von Bokay, when children without evidence of varicella immunity acquired varicella after contact with herpes zoster. VZV was isolated from vesicular fluid of both chickenpox and zoster lesions in cell culture by Thomas Weller in 1954. Subsequent laboratory studies of the virus led to the development of a live attenuated varicella vaccine in Japan in the 1970s. The vaccine was licensed for use in the United States in March 1995. The first vaccine to reduce the risk of herpes zoster was licensed in May 2006.

Varicella Zoster Virus

VZV is a DNA virus and is a member of the herpesvirus group. Like other herpesviruses, VZV has the capacity to persist in the body after the primary (first) infection as a latent infection. VZV persists in sensory nerve ganglia. Primary infection with VZV results in chickenpox. Herpes zoster (shingles) is the result of recurrent infection. The virus is believed to have a short survival time in the environment.

Pathogenesis

VZV enters through the respiratory tract and conjunctiva. The virus is believed to replicate at the site of entry in the nasopharynx and in regional lymph nodes. A primary viremia occurs 4 to 6 days after infection and disseminates the virus to other organs, such as the liver, spleen, and sensory ganglia. Further replication occurs in the viscera, followed by a secondary viremia, with viral infection of the skin. Virus can be cultured from mononuclear cells of an infected person from 5 days before to 1 or 2 days after the appearance of the rash.

Clinical Features

The incubation period is 14 to 16 days after exposure, with a range of 10 to 21 days. The incubation period may be prolonged in immunocompromised patients and those who have received postexposure treatment with a varicella antibody–containing product.

Varicella Zoster Virus

- Herpesvirus (DNA)
- Primary infection results in varicella (chickenpox)
- Recurrent infection results in herpes zoster (shingles)
- Short survival in environment

20

Varicella Pathogenesis

- Respiratory transmission of virus
- Replication in nasopharynx and regional lymph nodes
- Repeated episodes of viremia
- Multiple tissues, including sensory ganglia, infected during viremia

Varicella Clinical Features

- Incubation period 14-16 days (range 10-21 days)
- Mild prodrome for 1-2 days
- Rash generally appears first on head; most concentrated on trunk
- Successive crops over several days with lesions present in several stages of development

Primary Infection (Chickenpox)

A mild prodrome may precede the onset of a rash. Adults may have 1 to 2 days of fever and malaise prior to rash onset, but in children the rash is often the first sign of disease.

The rash is generalized and pruritic and progresses rapidly from macules to papules to vesicular lesions before crusting. The rash usually appears first on the head, then on the trunk, and then the extremities; the highest concentration of lesions is on the trunk (centripetal distribution). Lesions also can occur on mucous membranes of the oropharynx, respiratory tract, vagina, conjunctiva, and the cornea. Lesions are usually 1 to 4 mm in diameter. The vesicles are superficial and delicate and contain clear fluid on an erythematous base. Vesicles may rupture or become purulent before they dry and crust. Successive crops appear over several days, with lesions present in several stages of development. For example, macular lesions may be observed in the same area of skin as mature vesicles. Healthy children usually have 200 to 500 lesions in 2 to 4 successive crops.

The clinical course in healthy children is generally mild, with malaise, pruritus (itching), and temperature up to 102°F for 2 to 3 days. Adults may have more severe disease and have a higher incidence of complications. Respiratory and gastrointestinal symptoms are absent. Children with lymphoma and leukemia may develop a severe progressive form of varicella characterized by high fever, extensive vesicular eruption, and high complication rates. Children infected with human immunodeficiency virus also may have severe, prolonged illness.

Recovery from primary varicella infection usually results in lifetime immunity. In otherwise healthy persons, a second occurrence of chickenpox is not common, but it can happen, particularly in immunocompromised persons. As with other viral diseases, reexposure to natural (wild) varicella may lead to reinfection that boosts antibody titers without causing clinical illness or detectable viremia.

Recurrent Disease (Herpes Zoster)

Herpes zoster, or shingles, occurs when latent VZV reactivates and causes recurrent disease. The immunologic mechanism that controls latency of VZV is not well understood. However, factors associated with recurrent disease include aging, immunosuppression, intrauterine exposure to VZV, and having had varicella at a young age (younger than 18 months). In immunocompromised persons, zoster may disseminate, causing generalized skin lesions and central nervous system, pulmonary, and hepatic involvement.

The vesicular eruption of zoster generally occurs unilaterally in the distribution of a sensory nerve. Most often,

Herpes Zoster (Shingles)

- Reactivation of varicella zoster virus
- Associated with:
  - aging
  - immunosuppression
  - intrauterine exposure
  - varicella at younger than 18 months of age

20

this involves the trunk or the fifth cranial nerve. Two to four days prior to the eruption, there may be pain and paresthesia in the involved area. There are few systemic symptoms.

Complications

Varicella

Acute varicella is generally mild and self-limited, but it may be associated with complications. Secondary bacterial infections of skin lesions with *Staphylococcus* or *Streptococcus* are the most common cause of hospitalization and outpatient medical visits. Secondary infection with invasive group A streptococci may cause serious illness and lead to hospitalization or death. Pneumonia following varicella is usually viral but may be bacterial. Secondary bacterial pneumonia is more common in children younger than 1 year of age. Central nervous system manifestations of varicella range from aseptic meningitis to encephalitis. Involvement of the cerebellum, with resulting cerebellar ataxia, is the most common and generally has a good outcome. Encephalitis is an infrequent complication of varicella (estimated 1.8 per 10,000 cases) and may lead to seizures and coma. Diffuse cerebral involvement is more common in adults than in children. Reye syndrome is an unusual complication of varicella and influenza and occurs almost exclusively in children who take aspirin during the acute illness. The etiology of Reye syndrome is unknown. There has been a dramatic decrease in the incidence of Reye syndrome during the past decade, presumably related to decreased use of aspirin by children.

Rare complications of varicella include aseptic meningitis, transverse myelitis, Guillain-Barré syndrome, thrombocytopenia, hemorrhagic varicella, purpura fulminans, glomerulonephritis, myocarditis, arthritis, orchitis, uveitis, iritis, and hepatitis.

In the prevaccine era, approximately 11,000 persons with varicella required hospitalization each year. Hospitalization rates were approximately 2–3 per 1,000 cases among healthy children and 8 per 1,000 cases among adults. Death occurred in approximately 1 in 60,000 cases. From 1990 through 1996, an average of 103 deaths from varicella were reported each year. Most deaths occur in immunocompetent children and adults. Since 1996, the number of hospitalizations and deaths from varicella has declined more than 90%.

The risk of complications from varicella varies with age. Complications are infrequent among healthy children. They occur much more frequently in persons older than 15 years of age and infants younger than 1 year of age. For instance, among children 1–14 years of age, the fatality rate of vari-

Varicella Complications

- Bacterial infection of skin lesions
- Pneumonia (viral or bacterial)
- Central nervous system manifestations
- Reye syndrome
- Hospitalization: 2-3 per 1,000 cases
- Death: 1 per 60,000 cases
- Postherpetic neuraligia (complication of zoster)

20

Groups at Increased Risk of Complications of Varicella

- Persons older than 15 years
- Infants younger than 1 year
- Immunocompromised persons
- Newborns of women with rash onset within 5 days before to 2 days after delivery

Varicella Fatality Rate-United States, 1990-1994

*Deaths per 100,000 cases. Meyer et al, *J Infect Dis* 2000;182:383-90

cella is approximately 1 per 100,000 cases, among persons 15–19 years, it is 2.7 per 100,000 cases, and among adults 30–49 years of age, 25.2 per 100,000 cases. Adults account for only 5% of reported cases of varicella but approximately 35% of mortality.

Immunocompromised persons have a high risk of disseminated disease (up to 36% in one report). These persons may have multiple organ system involvement, and the disease may become fulminant and hemorrhagic. The most frequent complications in immunocompromised persons are pneumonia and encephalitis. Children with HIV infection are at increased risk for morbidity from varicella and herpes zoster.

The onset of maternal varicella from 5 days before to 2 days after delivery may result in overwhelming infection of the neonate and a fatality rate as high as 30%. This severe disease is believed to result from fetal exposure to varicella virus without the benefit of passive maternal antibody. Infants born to mothers with onset of maternal varicella 5 days or more prior to delivery usually have a benign course, presumably due to passive transfer of maternal antibody across the placenta.

Herpes Zoster

Postherpetic neuralgia, or pain in the area of the ocurrence that persists after the lesions have resolved, is a distressing complication of zoster. There is currently no adequate therapy available. Postherpetic neuralgia may last a year or longer after the episode of zoster. Ocular nerve and other organ involvement with zoster can occur, often with severe sequelae.

Congenital VZV Infection

Primary maternal varicella infection in the first 20 weeks of gestation is occasionally associated with a variety of abnormalities in the newborn, including low birth weight, hypoplasia of an extremity, skin scarring, localized muscular atrophy, encephalitis, cortical atrophy, chorioretinitis, and microcephaly. This constellation of abnormalities, collectively known as congenital varicella syndrome, was first recognized in 1947. The risk of congenital abnormalities from primary maternal varicella infection appears to be very low (less than 2%). Rare reports of congenital birth defects following maternal zoster exist, but virologic confirmation of maternal lesions is lacking.

Laboratory Diagnosis

Laboratory diagnosis is not routinely required, but is useful if confirmation of the diagnosis or determination of susceptibility is necessary. Varicella incidence has declined

Congenital Varicella Syndrome

- Results from maternal infection during pregnancy
- Low birth weight, atrophy of extremity with skin scarring, eye and neurologic abnormalities
- Risk appears to be low (less than 2%)
- Period of risk may extend through first 20 weeks of pregnancy

20

dramatically as a result of routine varicella immunization in the United States. This has had the combined effect of increasing the number of atypical cases (either vaccine adverse events or breakthrough wild-type infection in immunized persons) and of reducing physicians' experience in diagnosing varicella. As a result, the need for laboratory confirmation of varicella has increased.

Varicella zoster virus may be isolated in tissue culture. The most frequent source of isolation is vesicular fluid. Laboratory techniques allow differentiation of wild-type and vaccine strains of VZV.

Rapid varicella virus identification techniques are indicated for a case with severe or unusual disease to initiate specific antiviral therapy. VZV polymerase chain reaction (PCR) is the method of choice for rapid clinical diagnosis. Real-time PCR methods are widely available and are the most sensitive and specific method of the available tests. Results are available within several hours. If real-time PCR is unavailable, the direct fluorescent antibody (DFA) method can be used, although it is less sensitive than PCR and requires more meticulous specimen collection and handling.

Specimens are best collected by unroofing a vesicle, preferably a fresh fluid-filled vesicle, and then rubbing the base of a skin lesion with a polyester swab. Crusts from lesions are also excellent specimens for PCR. Other specimen sources such as nasopharyngeal secretions, saliva, blood, urine, bronchial washings, and cerebrospinal fluid are considered less desirable sources than skin lesions because positive test results from such specimens are much less likely. Because viral proteins persist after cessation of viral replication, PCR and DFA may be positive when viral cultures are negative. Additional information concerning virus isolation and strain differentiation can be found at http://www.cdc.gov/vaccines/pubs/surv-manual/downloads/chpt17_varicella.pdf

A reliable history of chickenpox has been found to be a valid measure of immunity to varicella because the rash is distinctive and subclinical cases are unusual. As a result, serologic testing of children is generally not necessary. However, serologic testing may be useful in adult vaccination programs. A variety of serologic tests for varicella antibody are available. Available tests include complement fixation (CF), indirect fluorescent antibody (IFA), fluorescent antibody to membrane antigen (FAMA), neutralization, indirect hemagglutination (IHA), immune adherence hemagglutination (IAHA), radioimmunoassay (RIA), latex agglutination (LA), and enzyme-linked immunosorbent assay (ELISA). ELISA is sensitive and specific, simple to perform, and widely available commercially. A commercially available LA is sensitive, simple, and rapid to perform. LA is generally more sensitive than commercial ELISAs, although it can

Varicella Laboratory Diagnosis

- Isolation of varicella virus from clinical specimen
- Rapid varicella virus identification using PCR (preferred, if available) or DFA
- Significant rise in varicella IgG by any standard serologic assay (e.g., enzyme immunoassay)

20

result in false-positive results, leading to failure to identify persons without evidence of varicella immunity. This latter concern can be minimized by performing LA as a dilution series. Either of these tests would be useful for screening for varicella immunity.

Antibody resulting from vaccination is generally of lower titer than antibody resulting from varicella disease. Commercial antibody assays, particularly the LA test, may not be sensitive enough to detect vaccine-induced antibody in some recipients. Because of the potential for false-negative serologic tests, routine postvaccination serologic testing is not recommended. For diagnosis of acute varicella infection, serologic confirmation would include a significant rise in varicella IgG by any standard serologic assay. Testing using commercial kits for IgM antibody is not recommended since available methods lack sensitivity and specificity; false-positive IgM results are common in the presence of high IgG levels. The National VZV Laboratory at CDC has developed a reliable IgM capture assay. Call 404-639-0066, 404-639-3667, or e-mail vzvlab@cdc.gov for details about collecting and submitting specimens for testing.

Epidemiology

Occurrence
Varicella and herpes zoster occur worldwide. Some data suggest that in tropical areas, varicella infection occurs more commonly among adults than children. The reason(s) for this difference in age distribution are not known with certainty, but may be related to lack of childhood varicella infection in rural populations.

Reservoir
Varicella is a human disease. No animal or insect source or vector is known to exist.

Transmission
Infection with VZV occurs through the respiratory tract. The most common mode of transmission of VZV is believed to be person to person from infected respiratory tract secretions. Transmission may also occur by respiratory contact with airborne droplets or by direct contact or inhalation of aerosols from vesicular fluid of skin lesions of acute varicella or zoster.

Temporal Pattern
In temperate areas, varicella has a distinct seasonal fluctuation, with the highest incidence occurring in winter and early spring. In the United States, incidence is highest

Varicella Epidemiology

- Reservoir — Human
- Transmission — Airborne droplet
  Direct contact with lesions
- Temporal pattern — Peak in winter and early spring (U.S.)
- Communicability — 1-2 days before to 4-5 days after onset of rash
  May be longer in immunocompromised

20

between March and May and lowest between September and November. Less seasonality is reported in tropical areas. Herpes zoster has no seasonal variation and occurs throughout the year.

Communicability

The period of communicability extends from 1 to 2 days before the onset of rash through the first 4 to 5 days, or until lesions have formed crusts. Immunocompromised patients with varicella are probably contagious during the entire period new lesions are appearing. The virus has not been isolated from crusted lesions.

Varicella is highly contagious. It is less contagious than measles, but more so than mumps and rubella. Secondary attack rates among susceptible household contacts of persons with varicella are as high as 90% (that is, 9 of 10 susceptible household contacts of persons with varicella will become infected).

Secular Trends in the United States

Varicella

In the prevaccine era, varicella was endemic in the United States, and virtually all persons acquired varicella by adulthood. As a result, the number of cases occurring annually was estimated to approximate the birth cohort, or approximately 4 million per year. Varicella was removed from the list of nationally notifiable conditions in 1981, but some states continued to report cases to CDC. The majority of cases (approximately 85%) occurred among children younger than 15 years of age. The highest age-specific incidence of varicella was among children 1–4 years of age, who accounted for 39% of all cases. This age distribution was probably a result of earlier exposure to VZV in preschool and child care settings. Children 5–9 years of age accounted for 38% of cases. Adults 20 years of age and older accounted for only 7% of cases (National Health Interview Survey data, 1990–1994).

Data from three active varicella surveillance areas indicate that the incidence of varicella, as well as varicella-related hospitalizations, has decreased significantly since licensure of vaccine in 1995. In 2004, varicella vaccination coverage among children 19–35 months in two of the active surveillance areas was estimated to be 89% and 90%. Compared with 1995, varicella cases declined 83%–93% by 2004. Cases declined most among children aged 1–4 and 5–9 years, but a decline occurred in all age groups including infants and adults, indicating reduced transmission of the virus in these groups. The reduction of varicella cases is the result of the increasing use of varicella vaccine. Varicella vaccine

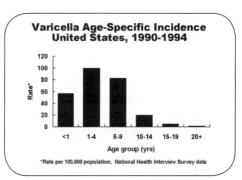

Varicella Age-Specific Incidence United States, 1990-1994

*Rate per 100,000 population. National Health Interview Survey data

Varicella Cases by Month Antelope Valley, CA, 1995–2004

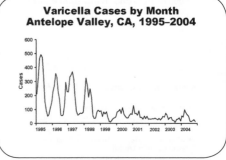

Reduction in Age-Specific Varicella Incidence Rate Varicella Active Surveillance Project Sites, 1995 to 2004

Age group	Antelope Valley, CA* (%)	West Philadelphia (%)
< 1	83	77
1-4	94	89
5-9	83	95
10-14	49	98
15-19	65	78
20+	81	67
Total	83	93

*2003 population used for rate calculations

coverage among 19–35-month-old children was estimated by the National Immunization Survey to be 90% in 2007.

Despite high one-dose vaccination coverage and success of the vaccination program in reducing varicella morbidity and mortality, varicella surveillance indicates that the number of reported varicella cases appears to have plateaued. An increasing proportion of cases represent breakthrough infection (chickenpox occurring in a previously vaccinated person). In 2001–2005, outbreaks were reported in schools with high varicella vaccination coverage (96%–100%). These outbreaks had many similarities: all occurred in elementary schools; vaccine effectiveness was within the expected range (72%–85%); the highest attack rates occurred among the younger students; each outbreak lasted about 2 months; and persons with breakthrough infection transmitted the virus although the breakthrough disease was mild. Overall attack rates among vaccinated children were 11%–17%, with attack rates in some classrooms as high as 40%. These data indicate that even in settings where almost everyone was vaccinated and vaccine performed as expected, varicella outbreaks could not be prevented with the current one-dose vaccination policy. These observations led to the recommendation in 2006 for a second routine dose of varicella vaccine.

Herpes Zoster

Herpes zoster is not a notifiable condition. An estimated 500,000 to 1 million episodes of zoster occur annually in the United States. The lifetime risk of zoster is estimated to be at least 32%. Increasing age and cellular immunosuppression are the most important risk factors; 50% of persons living until age 85 years will develop zoster.

Vaccines Containing Varicella Virus

Three varicella-containing vaccines are now approved for use in the United States: varicella vaccine (Varivax), combination measles-mumps-rubella-varicella (MMRV) vaccine (ProQuad), and herpes zoster vaccine (Zostavax).

Characteristics

Varicella Vaccine

Varicella vaccine (Varivax, Merck) is a live attenuated viral vaccine, derived from the Oka strain of VZV. The vaccine virus was isolated by Takahashi in the early 1970s from vesicular fluid from an otherwise healthy child with varicella disease. Varicella vaccine was licensed for general use in Japan and Korea in 1988. It was licensed in the United States in 1995 for persons 12 months of age and older. The virus was attenuated by sequential passage in human embryonic lung cell culture, embryonic guinea pig fibroblasts, and

---

Varicella in the United States

- Increasing proportion of cases are a result of breakthrough infection
- Outbreaks reported in schools with high varicella vaccination coverage
- Persons with breakthrough infection may transmit virus

Herpes Zoster

- 500,000 to 1 million episodes occur annually in the United States
- Lifetime risk of zoster estimated to be 32%
- 50% of persons living until age 85 years will develop zoster

20

Varicella-Containing Vaccines

- Varicella vaccine (Varivax)
  - approved for persons 12 months and older
- Measles-mumps-rubella-varicella vaccine (ProQuad)
  - approved for children 12 months through 12 years
- Herpes zoster vaccine (Zostavax)
  - approved for persons 60 years and older

in WI-38 human diploid cells. The Oka/Merck vaccine has undergone further passage through MRC-5 human diploid cell cultures for a total of 31 passages. The reconstituted vaccine contains small amounts of sucrose, processed porcine gelatin, sodium chloride, monosodium L-glutamate, sodium diphosphate, potassium phosphate, and potassium chloride, and trace quantities of residual components of MRC-5 cells (DNA and protein), EDTA, neomycin, and fetal bovine serum. The vaccine is reconstituted with sterile water and contains no preservative.

Measles-Mumps-Rubella-Varicella Vaccine

In September 2005, the Food and Drug Administration (FDA) licensed a combined live attenuated measles-mumps-rubella and varicella vaccine (ProQuad, Merck) for use in persons 12 months through 12 years of age. The attenuated measles, mumps, and rubella vaccine viruses in MMRV are identical and of equal titer to those in the measles-mumps-rubella (MMR) vaccine. The titer of Oka/Merck varicella zoster virus is higher in MMRV vaccine than in single-antigen varicella vaccine, a minimum of 9,772 (3.99 $\log^{10}$) plaque-forming units (PFU) versus 1,350 PFU (~3.13 $\log^{10}$), respectively. Each 0.5-mL dose contains a small quantity of sucrose, hydrolyzed gelatin, sodium chloride, sorbitol, monosodium L-glutamate, sodium phosphate dibasic, human albumin, sodium bicarbonate, potassium phosphate monobasic, potassium chloride; potassium phosphate dibasic; residual components of MRC-5 cells (DNA and protein) neomycin, bovine calf serum, and other buffer and media ingredients. The vaccine is reconstituted with sterile water and contains no preservative.

Herpes Zoster Vaccine

In May 2006, the FDA approved herpes zoster vaccine (Zostavax, Merck) for use in persons 60 years of age and older. The vaccine contains the same Oka/Merck varicella zoster virus used in varicella and MMRV vaccines but at a much higher titer (a minimum of 19,400 PFU versus 1,350 PFU in varicella vaccine). Each 0.65-mL dose contains a small amount of sucrose, hydrolyzed porcine gelatin, sodium chloride, monosodium L-glutamate, sodium phosphate dibasic, potassium phosphate monobasic, potassium chloride; residual components of MRC-5 cells including (DNA and protein); neomycin and bovine calf serum. The vaccine is reconstituted with sterile water and contains no preservative.

Immunogenicity and Vaccine Efficacy

Varicella Vaccine

After one dose of single-antigen varicella vaccine, 97% of children 12 months to 12 years of age develop detectable antibody titers. More than 90% of vaccine responders

20

Varicella Vaccine Immunogenicity and Efficacy

- Detectable antibody
  - 97% of children 12 months-12 years following 1 dose
  - 99% of persons 13 years and older after 2 doses
- 70%-90% effective against any varicella disease
- 95%-100% effective against severe varicella disease

maintain antibody for at least 6 years. In Japanese studies, 97% of children had antibody 7 to 10 years after vaccination. Vaccine efficacy is estimated to be 70% to 90% against infection, and 90% to 100% against moderate or severe disease.

Among healthy adolescents and adults 13 years of age and older, an average of 78% develop antibody after one dose, and 99% develop antibody after a second dose given 4 to 8 weeks later. Antibody persisted for at least 1 year in 97% of vaccinees after the second dose given 4 to 8 weeks after the first dose.

Immunity appears to be long-lasting, and is probably permanent in the majority of vaccinees. Breakthrough infection is significantly milder, with fewer lesions (generally fewer than 50), many of which are maculopapular rather than vesicular. Most persons with breakthrough infection do not have fever.

Although findings of some studies have suggested otherwise, most investigations have not identified time since vaccination as a risk factor for breakthrough varicella. Some, but not all, recent investigations have identified the presence of asthma, use of steroids, and vaccination at younger than 15 months of age as risk factors for breakthrough varicella. Breakthrough varicella infection could be a result of several factors, including interference of vaccine virus replication by circulating antibody, impotent vaccine resulting from storage or handling errors, or inaccurate recordkeeping.

Interference from live viral vaccine administered before varicella vaccine could also reduce vaccine effectiveness. A study of 115,000 children in two health maintenance organizations during 1995–1999 found that children who received varicella vaccine less than 30 days after MMR vaccination had a 2.5-fold increased risk of breakthrough varicella compared with those who received varicella vaccine before, simultaneously with, or more than 30 days after MMR.

Studies have shown that a second dose of varicella vaccine boosts immunity and reduces breakthrough disease in children.

MMRV Vaccine

MMRV vaccine was licensed on the basis of equivalence of immunogenicity of the antigenic components rather than the clinical efficacy. Clinical studies involving healthy children age 12–23 months indicated that those who received a single dose of MMRV vaccine developed similar levels of antibody to measles, mumps, rubella and varicella as children who received MMR and varicella vaccines concomitantly at separate injection sites.

Varicella Breakthrough Infection

- Immunity appears to be long-lasting for most recipients
- Breakthrough disease much milder than in unvaccinated persons
- No consistent evidence that risk of breakthrough infection increases with time since vaccination

---

Varicella Breakthrough Infection

- Retrospective cohort study of 115,000 children vaccinated in 2 HMOs (January 1995 through December 1999)
- Risk of breakthrough varicella 2.5 times higher if varicella vaccine administered less than 30 days following MMR
- No increased risk if varicella vaccine given simultaneously or more than 30 days after MMR

MMWR 2001;50(47):1058-61

20

Herpes Zoster Vaccine

The primary clinical trial for zoster vaccine included more than 38,000 adults 60 to 80 years of age with no history of prior shingles. Participants were followed for a median of 3.1 years after a single dose of vaccine. Compared with the placebo group, the vaccine group had 51% fewer episodes of zoster. Efficacy was highest for persons 60–69 years of age (64%) and declined with increasing age. Efficacy was 18% for participants 80 years or older. Vaccine recipients who developed zoster generally had less severe disease. Vaccine recipients also had about 66% less postherpetic neuralgia, the pain that can persist long after the shingles rash has resolved. The duration of reduction of risk of zoster is not known.

Vaccination Schedule and Use

Varicella Vaccine

Varicella virus vaccine is recommended for all children without contraindications at 12 through15 months of age. The vaccine may be given to all children at this age regardless of prior history of varicella.

A second dose of varicella vaccine should be administered at 4 through 6 years of age, at the same visit as the second dose of MMR vaccine. The second dose may be administered earlier than 4 through 6 years of age if at least 3 months have elapsed following the first dose (i.e., the minimum interval between doses of varicella vaccine for children younger than 13 years is 3 months). However, if the second dose is administered at least 28 days following the first dose, the second dose does not need to be repeated. A second dose of varicella vaccine is also recommended for persons older than 4 through 6 years of age who have received only one dose. Varicella vaccine doses administered to persons 13 years or older should be separated by 4 to 8 weeks.

All varicella-containing vaccines should be administered by the subcutaneous route. Varicella vaccine has been shown to be safe and effective in healthy children when administered at the same time as MMR vaccine at separate sites and with separate syringes. If varicella and MMR vaccines are not administered at the same visit, they should be separated by at least 28 days. Varicella vaccine may also be administered simultaneously (but at separate sites with separate syringes) with all other childhood vaccines. ACIP strongly recommends that varicella vaccine be administered simultaneously with all other vaccines recommended at 12 through 15 months of age.

Children with a clinician-diagnosed or verified history of typical chickenpox can be assumed to be immune to varicella. Serologic testing of such children prior to vaccination

---

Herpes Zoster Vaccine Efficacy

- Compared with placebo group vaccine group had:
    - —51% fewer episodes of zoster
    - —lower efficacy for older recipients
    - —less severe disease
    - —66% less postherpetic neuralgia

NEJM 2005;352(22):2271-84.

Varicella Vaccine Recommendations Children

- Routine vaccination at 12-15 months of age
- Routine second dose at 4-6 years of age
- Minimum interval between doses of varicella vaccine for children younger than 13 years of age is 3 months

---

20

is not warranted because the majority of children between 12 months and 12 years of age without a clinical history of chickenpox are not immune. Prior history of chickenpox is not a contraindication to varicella vaccination.

Varicella vaccine should be administered to all adolescents and adults 13 years of age and older who do not have evidence of varicella immunity (see Varicella Immunity section). Persons 13 years of age and older should receive two doses of varicella vaccine separated by at least 4 weeks. If there is a lapse of more than 4 weeks after the first dose, the second dose may be administered at any time without repeating the first dose.

Assessment of varicella immunity status of all adolescents and adults and vaccination of those who lack evidence of varicella immunity are desirable to protect these individuals from the higher risk of complications from acquired varicella. Vaccination may be offered at the time of routine healthcare visits. However, specific assessment efforts should be focused on adolescents and adults who are at highest risk of exposure and those most likely to transmit varicella to others.

The ACIP recommends that all healthcare personnel be immune to varicella. In healthcare settings, serologic screening of personnel who are uncertain of their varicella history, or who claim not to have had the disease is likely to be cost-effective. Testing for varicella immunity following two doses of vaccine is not necessary because 99% of persons are seropositive after the second dose. Moreover, available commercial assays are not sensitive enough to detect antibody following vaccination in all instances.

Seroconversion does not always result in full protection against disease, although no data regarding correlates of protection are available for adults. If a vaccinated healthcare provider is exposed to VZV, the employee should be monitored daily from day 10 to day 21 after exposure through the employee health or infection control program to determine clinical status (screen for fever, skin lesions, and systemic symptoms). Persons with varicella may be infectious starting 2 days before rash onset. In addition, the healthcare providershould be instructed to immediately report fever, headache, or other constitutional symptoms and any skin lesions (which may be atypical). The person should be placed on sick leave immediately if symptoms occur.

The risk of transmission of vaccine virus from a vaccinated person to a susceptible contact appears to be very low (see Transmission of Varicella Vaccine Virus section), and the benefits of vaccinating susceptible healthcare providers clearly outweigh this potential risk. Transmission of vaccine virus appears to occur primarily if and when the vaccinee develops a vaccine-associated rash. As a safeguard, medical

---

**Varicella Vaccine Recommendations
Adolescents and Adults**

- All persons 13 years of age and older without evidence of varicella immunity
- Two doses separated by at least 4 weeks
- Do not repeat first dose because of extended interval between doses

---

**Varicella Vaccine Recommendations
Healthcare Personnel**

- Recommended for all susceptible healthcare personnel
- Prevaccination serologic screening probably cost-effective
- Postvaccination testing not necessary or recommended

20

facilities may wish to consider protocols for personnel who develop a rash following vaccination (e.g., avoidance of contact with persons at high risk of serious complications, such as immunosuppressed persons who do not have evidence of varicella immunity).

MMRV Vaccine

MMRV vaccine is indicated for vaccination against measles, mumps, rubella and varicella in children 12 months through 12 years of age. Persons 13 years of age and older should not receive MMRV. When used, MMRV vaccine should be administered on or after the first birthday, preferably as soon as the child becomes eligible for vaccination. MMRV may be used for both the first and second doses of MMR and varicella in children younger than 13 years. The minimum interval between doses of MMRV is 3 months. However, if the second dose is administered at least 28 days following the first dose, the second dose does not need to be repeated.

Herpes Zoster Vaccine

Zoster vaccine is approved by FDA for persons 60 years and older. ACIP recommends a single dose of zoster vaccine for adults 60 years of age and older whether or not they report a prior episode of herpes zoster. Persons with a chronic medical condition may be vaccinated unless a contraindication or precaution exists for the condition (see Conraindications and Precautions to Vaccination).

Postexposure Prophylaxis

Varicella Vaccine

Data from the United States and Japan in a variety of settings indicate that varicella vaccine is 70% to 100% effective in preventing illness or modifying the severity of illness if used within 3 days, and possibly up to 5 days, after exposure. ACIP recommends the vaccine for use in persons who do not have evidence of varicella immunity following exposure to varicella. If exposure to varicella does not cause infection, postexposure vaccination should induce protection against subsequent exposure. If the exposure results in infection, there is no evidence that administration of varicella vaccine during the incubation period or prodromal stage of illness increases the risk for vaccine-associated adverse reactions. Although postexposure use of varicella vaccine has potential applications in hospital settings, preexposure vaccination of all healthcare workers without evidence of varicella immunity is the recommended and preferred method for preventing varicella in healthcare settings.

MMRV Vaccine

- Approved for children 12 months through 12 years of age (to age 13 years)
- Do not use for persons 13 years and older
- May be used for both first and second doses of MMR and varicella vaccines
- Minimum interval between doses is 3 months

Herpes Zoster Vaccine

- ACIP recommends a single dose among persons 60 years and older
- May vaccinate regardless of prior history of herpes zoster (shingles)
- Persons with a chronic medical condition may be vaccinated unless a contraindication or precaution exists for the condition

MMWR 2008;57(No. RR-5)

20

Varicella Vaccine Postexposure Prophylaxis

- Varicella vaccine is recommended for use in persons without evidence of varicella immunity after exposure to varicella
  - 70%-100% effective if given within 72 hours of exposure
  - not effective if administered more than 5 days after exposure but will produce immunity if not infected

Varicella outbreaks in some settings (e.g., child care facilities and schools) can persist up to 6 months. Varicella vaccine has been used successfully to control these outbreaks. The ACIP recommends a second dose of varicella vaccine for outbreak control. During a varicella outbreak, persons who have received one dose of varicella vaccine should receive a second dose, provided the appropriate vaccination interval has elapsed since the first dose (3 months for persons aged 12 months to 12 years and at least 4 weeks for persons aged 13 years of age and older).

MMRV Vaccine

MMRV vaccine may be used as described for varicella vaccine, and for measles as described in Chapter 11, Measles.

Herpes Zoster Vaccine

Exposure to a person with either primary varicella (chickenpox) or herpes zoster does not cause zoster in the exposed person. Herpes zoster vaccine has no role in the postexposure management of either chickenpox or zoster and should not be used for this purpose.

Varicella Immunity

In 2007, the ACIP published a revised definition for evidence of immunity to varicella. Evidence of immunity to varicella includes any of the following:

■ Documentation of age-appropriate vaccination:

– Preschool-aged children 12 months of age or older: one dose

– School-aged children, adolescents, and adults: two doses

■ Laboratory evidence of immunity or laboratory confirmation of disease. Commercial assays can be used to assess disease -induced immunity, but they lack adequate sensitivity to reliably detect vaccine-induced immunity (i.e., they may yield false-negative results).

■ Born in the United States before 1980. For healthcare providers and pregnant women, birth before 1980 should not be considered evidence of immunity. Persons born outside the United States should meet one of the other criteria for varicella immunity.

■ A healthcare provider diagnosis or verification of varicella disease. Verification of history or diagnosis of typical disease can be done by any healthcare provider (e.g., school or occupational clinic nurse, nurse practitioner, physician assistant, physician). For persons reporting a history of or presenting with atypical and/or mild

---

Varicella Immunity

- Written documentation of age-appropriate vaccination
- Laboratory evidence of immunity or laboratory confirmation of disease
- Born in the United States before 1980*
- Healthcare provider diagnosis or verification of varicella disease
- History of herpes zoster based on healthcare provider diagnosis

*except healthcare personnel and pregnant women.
MMWR 2007;56(No. RR-4)

20

cases, assessment by a physician or designee is recommended, and one of the following should be sought: a) an epidemiologic link to a typical varicella case, or b) evidence of laboratory confirmation if laboratory testing was performed at the time of acute disease. When such documentation is lacking, a person should not be considered as having a valid history of disease, because other diseases may mimic mild atypical varicella.

■ History of herpes zoster based on healthcare provider diagnosis.

Contraindications and Precautions to Vaccination

Varicella and MMRV Vaccines
Contraindications and precautions are similar for all varicella-containing vaccines. Persons with a severe allergic reaction (anaphylaxis) to a vaccine component or following a prior dose of vaccine should not receive varicella vaccine. Varicella, MMRV, and zoster vaccines all contain minute amounts of neomycin and hydrolyzed gelatin but do not contain egg protein or preservative.

Persons with immunosuppression due to leukemia, lymphoma, generalized malignancy, immune deficiency disease, or immunosuppressive therapy should not be vaccinated with a varicella-containing vaccine. However, treatment with low-dose (less than 2 mg/kg/day), alternate-day, topical, replacement, or aerosolized steroid preparations is not a contraindication to vaccination. Persons whose immunosuppressive therapy with steroids has been discontinued for 1 month (3 months for chemotherapy) may be vaccinated.

Single-antigen varicella vaccine may be administered to persons with impaired humoral immunity (e.g., hypogammaglobulinemia). However, the blood products used to treat humoral immunodeficiency may interfere with the response to vaccination. Recommended spacing between administration of the blood product and receipt of varicella vaccine should be observed (see Chapter 2, General Recommendations on Immunization, for details).

Persons with moderate or severe cellular immunodeficiency resulting from infection with human immunodeficiency virus (HIV), including persons diagnosed with acquired immunodeficiency syndrome (AIDS) should not receive varicella vaccine. HIV-infected children with CD4 T-lymphocyte percentage of 15% or higher, and older children and adults with a CD4 count of 200 per microliter or higher may be considered for vaccination. These persons may receive MMR and single-antigen varicella vaccines, but should not receive MMRV.

Varicella-Containing Vaccines Contraindications and Precautions

- Severe allergic reaction to vaccine component or following a prior dose
- Immunosuppression
- Pregnancy
- Moderate or severe acute illness
- Recent blood product (except herpes zoster vaccine)

Varicella Vaccine Use in Immunocompromised Persons
- MMRV not approved for use in persons with HIV infection
- Do not administer zoster vaccine to immunosuppressed persons

20

Women known to be pregnant or attempting to become pregnant should not receive a varicella-containing vaccine. To date, no adverse outcomes of pregnancy or in a fetus have been reported among women who inadvertently received varicella vaccine shortly before or during pregnancy. Although the manufacturer's package insert states otherwise, ACIP recommends that pregnancy be avoided for 1 month following receipt of varicella vaccine.

The ACIP recommends prenatal assessment and postpartum vaccination for varicella. Women should be assessed during a prenatal healthcare visit for evidence of varicella immunity. Upon completion or termination of pregnancy, women who do not have evidence of varicella immunity should receive the first dose of varicella vaccine before discharge from the healthcare facility. The second dose should be administered at least 4 weeks later at the postpartum or other healthcare visit. Standing orders are recommended for healthcare settings where completion or termination of pregnancy occurs to ensure administration of varicella vaccine.

The manufacturer, in collaboration with CDC, has established a Varicella Vaccination in Pregnancy registry to monitor the maternal–fetal outcomes of pregnant women inadvertently given varicella vaccine. The telephone number for the Registry is 800-986-8999.

Vaccination of persons with moderate or severe acute illnesses should be postponed until the condition has improved. This precaution is intended to prevent complicating the management of an ill patient with a potential vaccine adverse event, such as fever. Minor illness, such as otitis media and upper respiratory infections, concurrent antibiotic therapy, and exposure or recovery from other illnesses are not contraindications to varicella vaccine. Although there is no evidence that either varicella or varicella vaccine exacerbates tuberculosis, vaccination is not recommended for persons known to have untreated active tuberculosis. Tuberculosis skin testing is not a prerequisite for varicella vaccination.

The effect of the administration of antibody-containing blood products (e.g., immune globulin, whole blood or packed red blood cells, or intravenous immune globulin) on the response to varicella vaccine virus is unknown. Because of the potential inhibition of the response to varicella vaccination by passively transferred antibodies, varicella or MMRV vaccine should not be administered for 3–11 months after receipt of antibody-containing blood products. ACIP recommends applying the same intervals used to separate antibody-containing products and MMR to varicella vaccine (see chapter 2, General Recommendations on Immunization, and Appendix A for additional details). Immune globulin should not be given for 3 weeks following vaccination unless the benefits exceed those

Varicella Vaccination in Pregnancy Registry

800.986.8999

20

of the vaccine. In such cases, the vaccinees should either be revaccinated or tested for immunity at least 3 months later (depending on the antibody-containing product administered) and revaccinated if seronegative.

No adverse events following varicella vaccination related to the use of salicylates (e.g., aspirin) have been reported to date. However, the manufacturer recommends that vaccine recipients avoid the use of salicylates for 6 weeks after receiving varicella or MMRV vaccine because of the association between aspirin use and Reye syndrome following chickenpox.

Zoster Vaccine

As with all vaccines, a severe allergic reaction to a vaccine component or following a prior dose is a contraindication to zoster vaccination. As with other live virus vaccines, pregnancy or planned pregnancy within 4 weeks and immunosuppression are contraindications to zoster vaccination.

Zoster vaccine should not be administered to persons with primary or acquired immunodeficiency. This includes persons with leukemia, lymphomas, or other malignant neoplasms affecting the bone marrow or lymphatic system. The package insert implies that zoster vaccine should not be administered to anyone who has ever had leukemia or lymphoma. However, ACIP recommends that persons whose leukemia or lymphoma is in remission and who have not received chemotherapy or radiation for at least 3 months can be vaccinated. Other immunosuppressive conditions that contraindicate zoster vaccine include AIDS or other clinical manifestation of HIV. This includes CD4 T-lymphocyte values less than 200 per mm or less than 15% of total lymphocytes.

Persons receiving high-dose corticosteroid therapy should not be vaccinated. High dose is defined as 20 milligrams or more per day of prednisone or equivalent lasting two or more weeks. Zoster vaccination should be deferred for at least 1 month after discontinuation of therapy. As with other live viral vaccines, persons receiving lower doses of corticosteroids may be vaccinated. Topical, inhaled or intra-articular steroids, or long-term alternate-day treatment with low to moderate doses of short-acting systemic corticosteroids are not considered to be sufficiently immunosuppressive to contraindicate zoster vaccine.

Low doses of drugs used for the treatment of rheumatoid arthritis, inflammatory bowel disease, and other conditions, such as methotrexate, azathioprine, or 6-mercaptopurine, are also not considered sufficiently immunosuppressive to create safety concerns for zoster vaccine. Low-dose therapy with these drugs is NOT a contraindication for administration of zoster vaccine.

Zoster Vaccine Contraindications and Precautions
- Severe allergic reaction to a vaccine component or following a prior dose
- Pregnancy or planned pregnancy within 4 weeks
- Immunosuppression from any cause

Zoster Vaccine Contraindications Immunosuppression
- Leukemia, lymphoma or other malignant neoplasm affecting the bone marrow or lymphatic system
- AIDS or other clinical manifestation of HIV infection
- High-dose corticosteroid therapy
- Recombinant human immune mediators and immune modulators

Zoster Vaccine Precautions
- Moderate or severe acute illness
- Current treatment with an antiviral drug active against herpesviruses
- Recent receipt of a blood product is NOT a precaution

20

The experience of hematopoietic stem cell transplant recipients with varicella-containing vaccines, including zoster vaccine is limited. Physicians should assess the immune status of the recipient on a case-by-case basis to determine the relevant risks. If a decision is made to vaccinate with zoster vaccine, the vaccine should be administered at least 24 months after transplantation.

The safety and efficacy of zoster vaccine administered concurrently with recombinant human immune mediators and immune modulators (such as the anti–tumor necrosis factor agents adalimumab, infliximab, and etanercept) is not known. It is preferable to administer zoster vaccine before treatment with these drugs. If it is not possible to administer zoster vaccine to patients before initiation of treatment, physicians should assess the immune status of the recipient on a case-by-case basis to determine the relevant risks and benefits. Otherwise, vaccination with zoster vaccine should be deferred for at least 1 month after discontinuation of treatment.

As with all vaccines, moderate or severe acute illness is a precaution to vaccination. Current treatment with an antiviral drug active against herpesviruses, such as acyclovir, famciclovir, or valacyclovir, is a precaution to vaccination. These drugs can interfere with replication of the vaccine virus. Persons taking these drugs should discontinue them at least 24 hours before administration of zoster vaccine, and the drugs should not be taken for at least 14 days after vaccination.

Persons with a history of varicella are immune and generally maintain a high level of antibody to varicella zoster virus, a level comparable to that found in donated blood and antibody-containing blood products. Receiving an antibody-containing blood product will not change the amount of antibody in the person's blood. As a result, unlike most other live virus vaccines, recent receipt of a blood product is not a precaution for zoster vaccine. Zoster vaccine can be administered at any time before, concurrent with, or after receiving blood or other antibody-containing blood products.

Adverse Reactions Following Vaccination

Varicella Vaccine

The most common adverse reactions following varicella vaccine are local reactions, such as pain, soreness, erythema, and swelling. Based on information from the manufacturer's clinical trials of varicella vaccine, local reactions are reported by 19% of children and by 24% of adolescents and adults (33% following the second dose). These local adverse

---

Varicella Vaccine Adverse Reactions

- Local reactions (pain, erythema)
  - 19% (children)
  - 24% (adolescents and adults)
- Generalized rash – 4%-6%
  - may be maculopapular rather than vesicular
  - average 5 lesions
- Systemic reactions not common
- Adverse reactions similar for MMRV

20

reactions are generally mild and self-limited. A varicella-like rash at injection site is reported by 3% of children and by 1% of adolescents and adults following the second dose. In both circumstances, a median of two lesions have been present. These lesions generally occur within 2 weeks, and are most commonly maculopapular rather than vesicular. A generalized varicella-like rash is reported by 4%–6% of recipients of varicella vaccine (1% after the second dose in adolescents and adults), with an average of five lesions. Most of these generalized rashes occur within 3 weeks and most are maculopapular.

Systemic reactions are not common. Fever within 42 days of vaccination is reported by 15% of children and 10% of adolescents and adults. The majority of these episodes of fever have been attributed to concurrent illness rather than to the vaccine.

Varicella vaccine is a live virus vaccine and may result in a latent infection, similar to that caused by wild varicella virus. Consequently, zoster caused by the vaccine virus has been reported, mostly among vaccinated children. Not all these cases have been confirmed as having been caused by vaccine virus. The risk of zoster following vaccination appears to be less than that following infection with wild-type virus. The majority of cases of zoster following vaccine have been mild and have not been associated with complications such as postherpetic neuralgia.

MMRV Vaccine

The clinical trial of MMRV compared events that occurred within 42 days of receiving either MMRV or MMR and varicella vaccine separately in different anatomic sites. The frequencies of local reactions and generalized varicella-like rash were similar to those described for varicella vaccine. A temperature of 102°F or higher within 42 days of vaccination was more common in the MMRV group (22%) than in the group that received MMR and varicella vaccine at different sites (15%). A measles-like rash also occurred more frequently in MMRV recipients (3%) than in the group receiving separate injections (2.1%). Both fever and measles-like rash usually occurred 5–12 days following vaccination.

Herpes Zoster Vaccine

In the largest clinical trial of zoster vaccine, local reactions (erythema, pain or tenderness, and swelling) were the most common adverse reaction reported by vaccine recipients (34%), and were reported more commonly than by placebo recipients (6%). A temperature of 101°F or higher within 42 days of vaccination occurred at a similar frequency among both vaccine (0.8%) and placebo (0.9%) recipients. No serious adverse reactions were identified during the trial.

Zoster Following Vaccination

- Most cases in children
- Not all cases caused by vaccine virus
- Risk from vaccine virus less than from wild-type virus
- Usually a mild illness without complications such as postherpetic neuralgia

---

20

Herpes Zoster Vaccine Adverse Reactions

- Local reactions – 34% (pain, erythema)
- No increased risk of fever
- No serious adverse reactions identified

Transmission of Varicella Vaccine Virus

Available data suggest that transmission of varicella vaccine virus is a rare event. Instances of suspected secondary transmission of vaccine virus have been reported, but in few instances has the secondary clinical illness been shown to be caused by vaccine virus. Several cases of suspected secondary transmission have been determined to have been caused by wild varicella virus. In studies of household contacts, several instances of asymptomatic seroconversion have been observed. It appears that transmission occurs mainly, and perhaps only, when the vaccinee develops a rash. If a vaccinated child develops a rash, it is recommended that close contact with persons who do not have evidence of varicella immunity and who are at high risk of complications of varicella, such as immunocompromised persons, be avoided until the rash has resolved.

Transmission of varicella vaccine virus from recipients of zoster vaccine has not been reported.

Vaccine Storage and Handling

Varicella vaccine is very fragile, and all vaccines that contain it must be handled with extreme care. To maintain potency, all varicella-containing vaccines must be stored frozen at an average temperature of 5°F (-15°C). Household freezers, including frost-free models, manufactured since the mid-1990s are acceptable for storage of these vaccines. Refrigerators with ice compartments that are not tightly enclosed or are enclosed with unsealed, uninsulated doors (i.e., small dormitory-style refrigerator/freezer combinations) are not capable of maintaining the required storage temperature. Regardless of the type of freezer, providers should check the adequacy of their freezer storage before obtaining vaccine by monitoring and verifying the temperature of their freezer.

The vaccine diluent should be stored separately at room temperature or in the refrigerator. The vaccine should be reconstituted according to the directions in the package insert and only with the diluent supplied (or with the diluent supplied for MMR vaccine), which does not contain preservative or other antiviral substances that might inactivate the vaccine virus. Once reconstituted, all varicella-containing vaccines must be used immediately to minimize loss of potency. The vaccine must be discarded if not used within 30 minutes of reconstitution.

Single-antigen varicella may be stored at refrigerator temperature for up to 72 hours. Vaccine stored in the refrigerator cannot be refrozen and must be discarded after 72 hours at this temperature.

Mishandled varicella vaccine should be clearly marked and replaced in the freezer separate from properly handled

---

Varicella-Containing Vaccine Storage and Handling

- Store frozen at 5°F (-15°C) or lower at all times
- Store diluent at room temperature or refrigerate
- Discard if not used within 30 minutes of reconstitution

20

vaccine. The manufacturer must be contacted for recommendations before any mishandled vaccine is used. The Merck Vaccine Division varicella information telephone number is 800-9VARIVAX (800-982-7482).

Zoster vaccine cannot be stored at refrigerator temperature at any time.

Because of the lability of varicella vaccine, transport of the vaccine from a central clinic or storage area to an off-site clinic can be difficult. If off-site transport is attempted, a properly insulated container should be used, the vaccine should be transported on dry ice, and the temperature should be monitored continuously, to ensure that the appropriate storage temperature is maintained (see Appendix C).

Varicella Zoster Immune Globulin

In 2004, the only U.S.-licensed manufacturer of varicella zoster immune globulin (VZIG) (Massachusetts Public Health Biologic Laboratories, Boston, Massachusetts) discontinued production of VZIG. The supply of the licensed VZIG product was depleted in early 2006. In February 2006, an investigational (not licensed) VZIG product, VariZIG (Cangene Corporation, Winnipeg, Canada) became available under an investigational new drug application (IND) submitted to the FDA. This product can be requested from the sole authorized U.S. distributor, FFF Enterprises (Temecula, California), for patients who have been exposed to varicella and who are at increased risk for severe disease and complications.

The investigational VariZIG, similar to licensed VZIG, is a purified human immune globulin preparation made from plasma containing high levels of anti-varicella antibodies (immunoglobulin class G [IgG]). Unlike the previous product, the investigational product is lyophilized. When properly reconstituted, VariZIG is approximately a 5% solution of IgG that can be administered intramuscularly. As with any product used under IND, patients must be informed of potential risks and benefits and must give informed consent before receiving the product.

Patients without evidence of immunity to varicella (i.e., without history of disease or age-appropriate vaccination) who are at high risk for severe disease and complications, who have been exposed to varicella, and from whom informed consent has been obtained, are eligible to receive the IND application product under an expanded access protocol. The patient groups recommended by ACIP to receive VariZIG include the following:

- Immunocompromised patients
- Neonates whose mothers have signs and symptoms of varicella around the time of delivery (i.e., 5 days before to 2 days after)

Varicella Vaccine Information

800-9VARIVAX

20

- Preterm infants born at 28 weeks gestation or later who are exposed during the neonatal period and whose mothers do not have evidence of immunity

- Preterm infants born earlier than 28 weeks' gestation or who weigh 1,000g or less at birth and were exposed during the neonatal period, regardless of maternal history of varicella disease or vaccination

- Pregnant women

Addition information concerning the acquisition and use of this product is available in the March 3, 2006, edition of *Morbidity and Mortality Weekly Report*, available at http://www.cdc.gov/*MMWR*/preview/*MMWR*html/mm5508a5.htm

Selected References

CDC. Prevention of varicella: recommendations of the Advisory Committee on Immunization Practices (ACIP). *MMWR* 2007;56(No. RR-4):1–40.

CDC. Notice to readers. Licensure of a combined live attenuated measles, mumps, rubella, and varicella vaccine. *MMWR* 2005;54:1212.

CDC. Prevention of herpes zoster. Recommendations of the Advisory Committee on Immunization Practices. *MMWR* 2008;57(No.RR-5).

Davis MM, Patel MS, Gebremariam A. Decline in varicella-related hospitalizations and expenditures for children and adults after introduction of varicella vaccine in the United States. *Pediatrics* 2004;114:786–92.

Kuter B, Matthews H, Shinefield H, et al. Ten year follow-up of healthy children who received one or two injections of varicella vaccine. *Pediatr Infect Dis J* 2004;23:132–7.

Seward JF, Watson BM, Peterson CL, et al. Varicella disease after introduction of varicella vaccine in the United States, 1995–2000. *JAMA* 2002;287:606–11.

Seward JF, Zhang JX, Maupin TJ, Mascola L, Jumaan AO. Contagiousness of varicella in vaccinated cases: a household contact study. *JAMA* 2004;292:704–8.

Shields KE, Galil K, Seward J, et al. Varicella vaccine exposure during pregnancy: data from the first 5 years of the pregnancy registry. *Obstet Gynecol* 2001; 98:14–19.

Vazquez M, LaRuissa PS, Gershon AA, et al. Effectiveness over time of varicella vaccine. *JAMA* 2004;291:851–92.

20

APPENDIX A
Schedules and Recommendations

A

Appendix A

A

Immunization Schedules on the Web

Childhood and Adolescent Immunization Schedule Schedule:

www.cdc.gov/vaccines/recs/schedules/child-schedule.htm

Contains:
- English and Spanish versions
- Color and black & white versions
- 4-page, 2-page, and pocket-size versions
- Palm OS and Pocket PC Handheld versions
- Screenreader accessible version
- Downloadable files for office printing or commercial printing
- Link to past years' schedules
- Interactive childhood vaccine scheduler
- more . . .

Adult Immunization Schedule Schedule:

www.cdc.gov/vaccines/recs/schedules/adult-schedule.htm

Contains:
- Color and black & white versions
- 4-page, 2-page, and pocket-size versions
- Downloadable files for office printing or commercial printing
- Screenreader accessible version
- Summary of changes since last year's version
- Adult vaccination screening form
- Adult and adolescent vaccine "quiz"
- more . . .

A

Recommended Immunization Schedule for Persons Aged 0 Through 6 Years—United States • 2009
For those who fall behind or start late, see the catch-up schedule

Vaccine ▼ Age ▶	Birth	1 month	2 months	4 months	6 months	12 months	15 months	18 months	19–23 months	2–3 years	4–6 years
Hepatitis B[1]	HepB	HepB		see footnote 1		HepB					
Rotavirus[2]			RV	RV	RV[2]						
Diphtheria, Tetanus, Pertussis[3]			DTaP	DTaP	DTaP	see footnote 3	DTaP				DTaP
Haemophilus influenzae type b[4]			Hib	Hib	Hib[4]	Hib					
Pneumococcal[5]			PCV	PCV	PCV	PCV				PPSV	
Inactivated Poliovirus			IPV	IPV		IPV					IPV
Influenza[6]						Influenza (Yearly)					
Measles, Mumps, Rubella[7]						MMR		see footnote 7			MMR
Varicella[8]						Varicella		see footnote 8			Varicella
Hepatitis A[9]						HepA (2 doses)				HepA Series	
Meningococcal[10]										MCV	

Range of recommended ages

Certain high-risk groups

This schedule indicates the recommended ages for routine administration of currently licensed vaccines, as of December 1, 2008, for children aged 0 through 6 years. Any dose not administered at the recommended age should be administered at a subsequent visit, when indicated and feasible. Licensed combination vaccines may be used whenever any component of the combination is indicated and other components are not contraindicated and if approved by the Food and Drug Administration for that dose of the series. Providers should consult the relevant Advisory Committee on Immunization Practices statement for detailed recommendations, including high-risk conditions: http://www.cdc.gov/vaccines/pubs/acip-list.htm. Clinically significant adverse events that follow immunization should be reported to the Vaccine Adverse Event Reporting System (VAERS). Guidance about how to obtain and complete a VAERS form is available at http://www.vaers.hhs.gov or by telephone, 800-822-7967.

1. Hepatitis B vaccine (HepB). *(Minimum age: birth)*
At birth:
- Administer monovalent HepB to all newborns before hospital discharge.
- If mother is hepatitis B surface antigen (HBsAg)-positive, administer HepB and 0.5 mL of hepatitis B immune globulin (HBIG) within 12 hours of birth.
- If mother's HBsAg status is unknown, administer HepB within 12 hours of birth. Determine mother's HBsAg status as soon as possible and, if HBsAg-positive, administer HBIG (no later than age 1 week).

After the birth dose:
- The HepB series should be completed with either monovalent HepB or a combination vaccine containing HepB. The second dose should be administered at age 1 or 2 months. The final dose should be administered no earlier than age 24 weeks.
- Infants born to HBsAg-positive mothers should be tested for HBsAg and antibody to HBsAg (anti-HBs) after completion of at least 3 doses of the HepB series, at age 9 through 18 months (generally at the next well-child visit).

4-month dose:
- Administration of 4 doses of HepB to infants is permissible when combination vaccines containing HepB are administered after the birth dose.

2. Rotavirus vaccine (RV). *(Minimum age: 6 weeks)*
- Administer the first dose at age 6 through 14 weeks (maximum age: 14 weeks 6 days). Vaccination should not be initiated for infants aged 15 weeks or older (i.e., 15 weeks 0 days or older).
- Administer the final dose in the series by age 8 months 0 days.
- If Rotarix® is administered at ages 2 and 4 months, a dose at 6 months is not indicated.

3. Diphtheria and tetanus toxoids and acellular pertussis vaccine (DTaP). *(Minimum age: 6 weeks)*
- The fourth dose may be administered as early as age 12 months, provided at least 6 months have elapsed since the third dose.
- Administer the final dose in the series at age 4 through 6 years.

4. Haemophilus influenzae type b conjugate vaccine (Hib). *(Minimum age: 6 weeks)*
- If PRP-OMP (PedvaxHIB® or Comvax® [HepB-Hib]) is administered at ages 2 and 4 months, a dose at age 6 months is not indicated.
- TriHiBit® (DTaP/Hib) should not be used for doses at ages 2, 4, or 6 months but can be used as the final dose in children aged 12 months or older.

5. Pneumococcal vaccine. *(Minimum age: 6 weeks for pneumococcal conjugate vaccine [PCV]; 2 years for pneumococcal polysaccharide vaccine [PPSV])*
- PCV is recommended for all children aged younger than 5 years. Administer 1 dose of PCV to all healthy children aged 24 through 59 months who are not completely vaccinated for their age.
- Administer PPSV to children aged 2 years or older with certain underlying medical conditions (see *MMWR* 2000;49[No. RR-9]), including a cochlear implant.

6. Influenza vaccine. *(Minimum age: 6 months for trivalent inactivated influenza vaccine [TIV]; 2 years for live, attenuated influenza vaccine [LAIV])*
- Administer annually to children aged 6 months through 18 years.
- For healthy nonpregnant persons (i.e., those who do not have underlying medical conditions that predispose them to influenza complications) aged 2 through 49 years, either LAIV or TIV may be used.
- Children receiving TIV should receive 0.25 mL if aged 6 through 35 months or 0.5 mL if aged 3 years or older.
- Administer 2 doses (separated by at least 4 weeks) to children aged younger than 9 years who are receiving influenza vaccine for the first time or who were vaccinated for the first time during the previous influenza season but only received 1 dose.

7. Measles, mumps, and rubella vaccine (MMR). *(Minimum age: 12 months)*
- Administer the second dose at age 4 through 6 years. However, the second dose may be administered before age 4, provided at least 28 days have elapsed since the first dose.

8. Varicella vaccine. *(Minimum age: 12 months)*
- Administer the second dose at age 4 through 6 years. However, the second dose may be administered before age 4, provided at least 3 months have elapsed since the first dose.
- For children aged 12 months through 12 years the minimum interval between doses is 3 months. However, if the second dose was administered at least 28 days after the first dose, it can be accepted as valid.

9. Hepatitis A vaccine (HepA). *(Minimum age: 12 months)*
- Administer to all children aged 1 year (i.e., aged 12 through 23 months). Administer 2 doses at least 6 months apart.
- Children not fully vaccinated by age 2 years can be vaccinated at subsequent visits.
- HepA also is recommended for children older than 1 year who live in areas where vaccination programs target older children or who are at increased risk of infection. See *MMWR* 2006;55(No. RR-7).

10. Meningococcal vaccine. *(Minimum age: 2 years for meningococcal conjugate vaccine [MCV] and for meningococcal polysaccharide vaccine [MPSV])*
- Administer MCV to children aged 2 through 10 years with terminal complement component deficiency, anatomic or functional asplenia, and certain other high-risk groups. See *MMWR* 2005;54(No. RR-7).
- Persons who received MPSV 3 or more years previously and who remain at increased risk for meningococcal disease should be revaccinated with MCV.

The Recommended Immunization Schedules for Persons Aged 0 Through 18 Years are approved by the Advisory Committee on Immunization Practices (www.cdc.gov/vaccines/recs/acip), the American Academy of Pediatrics (http://www.aap.org), and the American Academy of Family Physicians (http://www.aafp.org).
DEPARTMENT OF HEALTH AND HUMAN SERVICES • CENTERS FOR DISEASE CONTROL AND PREVENTION

CS103164

Recommended Immunization Schedule for Persons Aged 7 Through 18 Years—United States • 2009
For those who fall behind or start late, see the schedule below and the catch-up schedule

Vaccine ▼ Age ▶	7–10 years	11–12 years	13–18 years
Tetanus, Diphtheria, Pertussis[1]	see footnote 1	Tdap	Tdap
Human Papillomavirus[2]	see footnote 2	HPV (3 doses)	HPV Series
Meningococcal[3]	MCV	MCV	MCV
Influenza[4]	Influenza (Yearly)		
Pneumococcal[5]	PPSV		
Hepatitis A[6]	HepA Series		
Hepatitis B[7]	HepB Series		
Inactivated Poliovirus[8]	IPV Series		
Measles, Mumps, Rubella[9]	MMR Series		
Varicella[10]	Varicella Series		

Legend:
- Range of recommended ages
- Catch-up immunization
- Certain high-risk groups

This schedule indicates the recommended ages for routine administration of currently licensed vaccines, as of December 1, 2008, for children aged 7 through 18 years. Any dose not administered at the recommended age should be administered at a subsequent visit, when indicated and feasible. Licensed combination vaccines may be used whenever any component of the combination is indicated and other components are not contraindicated and if approved by the Food and Drug Administration for that dose of the series. Providers should consult the relevant Advisory Committee on Immunization Practices statement for detailed recommendations, including high-risk conditions: http://www.cdc.gov/vaccines/pubs/acip-list.htm. Clinically significant adverse events that follow immunization should be reported to the Vaccine Adverse Event Reporting System (VAERS). Guidance about how to obtain and complete a VAERS form is available at http://www.vaers.hhs.gov or by telephone, 800-822-7967.

1. **Tetanus and diphtheria toxoids and acellular pertussis vaccine (Tdap).** *(Minimum age: 10 years for BOOSTRIX® and 11 years for ADACEL®)*
   - Administer at age 11 or 12 years for those who have completed the recommended childhood DTP/DTaP vaccination series and have not received a tetanus and diphtheria toxoid (Td) booster dose.
   - Persons aged 13 through 18 years who have not received Tdap should receive a dose.
   - A 5-year interval from the last Td dose is encouraged when Tdap is used as a booster dose; however, a shorter interval may be used if pertussis immunity is needed.

2. **Human papillomavirus vaccine (HPV).** *(Minimum age: 9 years)*
   - Administer the first dose to females at age 11 or 12 years.
   - Administer the second dose 2 months after the first dose and the third dose 6 months after the first dose (at least 24 weeks after the first dose).
   - Administer the series to females at age 13 through 18 years if not previously vaccinated.

3. **Meningococcal conjugate vaccine (MCV).**
   - Administer at age 11 or 12 years, or at age 13 through 18 years if not previously vaccinated.
   - Administer to previously unvaccinated college freshmen living in a dormitory.
   - MCV is recommended for children aged 2 through 10 years with terminal complement component deficiency, anatomic or functional asplenia, and certain other groups at high risk. See *MMWR* 2005;54(No. RR-7).
   - Persons who received MPSV 5 or more years previously and remain at increased risk for meningococcal disease should be revaccinated with MCV.

4. **Influenza vaccine.**
   - Administer annually to children aged 6 months through 18 years.
   - For healthy nonpregnant persons (i.e., those who do not have underlying medical conditions that predispose them to influenza complications) aged 2 through 49 years, either LAIV or TIV may be used.
   - Administer 2 doses (separated by at least 4 weeks) to children younger than 9 years who are receiving influenza vaccine for the first time or who were vaccinated for the first time during the previous influenza season but only received 1 dose.

5. **Pneumococcal polysaccharide vaccine (PPSV).**
   - Administer to children with certain underlying medical conditions (see *MMWR* 1997;46[No. RR-8]), including a cochlear implant. A single revaccination should be administered to children with functional or anatomic asplenia or other immunocompromising condition after 5 years.

6. **Hepatitis A vaccine (HepA).**
   - Administer 2 doses at least 6 months apart.
   - HepA is recommended for children older than 1 year who live in areas where vaccination programs target older children or who are at increased risk of infection. See *MMWR* 2006;55(No. RR-7).

7. **Hepatitis B vaccine (HepB).**
   - Administer the 3-dose series to those not previously vaccinated.
   - A 2-dose series (separated by at least 4 months) of adult formulation Recombivax HB® is licensed for children aged 11 through 15 years.

8. **Inactivated poliovirus vaccine (IPV).**
   - For children who received an all-IPV or all-oral poliovirus (OPV) series, a fourth dose is not necessary if the third dose was administered at age 4 years or older.
   - If both OPV and IPV were administered as part of a series, a total of 4 doses should be administered, regardless of the child's current age.

9. **Measles, mumps, and rubella vaccine (MMR).**
   - If not previously vaccinated, administer 2 doses or the second dose for those who have received only 1 dose, with at least 28 days between doses.

10. **Varicella vaccine.**
    - For persons aged 7 through 18 years without evidence of immunity (see *MMWR* 2007;56[No. RR-4]), administer 2 doses if not previously vaccinated or the second dose if they have received only 1 dose.
    - For persons aged 7 through 12 years, the minimum interval between doses is 3 months. However, if the second dose was administered at least 28 days after the first dose, it can be accepted as valid.
    - For persons aged 13 years and older, the minimum interval between doses is 28 days.

The Recommended Immunization Schedules for Persons Aged 0 Through 18 Years are approved by the Advisory Committee on Immunization Practices (www.cdc.gov/vaccines/recs/acip), the American Academy of Pediatrics (http://www.aap.org), and the American Academy of Family Physicians (http://www.aafp.org).
DEPARTMENT OF HEALTH AND HUMAN SERVICES • CENTERS FOR DISEASE CONTROL AND PREVENTION

CS103164

Catch-up Immunization Schedule for Persons Aged 4 Months Through 18 Years Who Start Late or Who Are More Than 1 Month Behind—United States • 2009

The table below provides catch-up schedules and minimum intervals between doses for children whose vaccinations have been delayed. A vaccine series does not need to be restarted, regardless of the time that has elapsed between doses. Use the section appropriate for the child's age.

CATCH-UP SCHEDULE FOR PERSONS AGED 4 MONTHS THROUGH 6 YEARS

Vaccine	Minimum Age for Dose 1	Minimum Interval Between Doses			
		Dose 1 to Dose 2	Dose 2 to Dose 3	Dose 3 to Dose 4	Dose 4 to Dose 5
Hepatitis B[1]	Birth	4 weeks	8 weeks (and at least 16 weeks after first dose)		
Rotavirus[2]	6 wks	4 weeks	4 weeks[2]		
Diphtheria, Tetanus, Pertussis[3]	6 wks	4 weeks	4 weeks	6 months	6 months[3]
Haemophilus influenzae type b[4]	6 wks	4 weeks if first dose administered at younger than age 12 months / 8 weeks (as final dose) if first dose administered at age 12-14 months / No further doses needed if first dose administered at age 15 months or older	4 weeks[4] if current age is younger than 12 months / 8 weeks (as final dose)[4] if current age is 12 months or older and second dose administered at younger than age 15 months / No further doses needed if previous dose administered at age 15 months or older	8 weeks (as final dose) This dose only necessary for children aged 12 months through 59 months who received 3 doses before age 12 months	
Pneumococcal[5]	6 wks	4 weeks if first dose administered at younger than age 12 months / 8 weeks (as final dose for healthy children) if first dose administered at age 12 months or older or current age 24 through 59 months / No further doses needed for healthy children if first dose administered at age 24 months or older	4 weeks if current age is younger than 12 months / 8 weeks (as final dose for healthy children) if current age is 12 months or older / No further doses needed for healthy children if previous dose administered at age 24 months or older	8 weeks (as final dose) This dose only necessary for children aged 12 months through 59 months who received 3 doses before 12 months or for high-risk children who received 3 doses at any age	
Inactivated Poliovirus[6]	6 wks	4 weeks	4 weeks	4 weeks[6]	
Measles, Mumps, Rubella[7]	12 mos	4 weeks			
Varicella[8]	12 mos	3 months			
Hepatitis A[9]	12 mos	6 months			

CATCH-UP SCHEDULE FOR PERSONS AGED 7 THROUGH 18 YEARS

Vaccine	Minimum Age for Dose 1	Minimum Interval Between Doses			
Tetanus, Diphtheria/ Tetanus, Diphtheria, Pertussis[10]	7 yrs[10]	4 weeks	4 weeks if first dose administered at younger than age 12 months / 6 months if first dose administered at age 12 months or older	6 months if first dose administered at younger than age 12 months	
Human Papillomavirus[11]	9 yrs	Routine dosing intervals are recommended[11]			
Hepatitis A[9]	12 mos	6 months			
Hepatitis B[1]	Birth	4 weeks	8 weeks (and at least 16 weeks after first dose)		
Inactivated Poliovirus[6]	6 wks	4 weeks	4 weeks	4 weeks[6]	
Measles, Mumps, Rubella[7]	12 mos	4 weeks			
Varicella[8]	12 mos	3 months if the person is younger than age 13 years / 4 weeks if the person is aged 13 years or older			

1. Hepatitis B vaccine (HepB).
- Administer the 3-dose series to those not previously vaccinated.
- A 2-dose series (separated by at least 4 months) of adult formulation Recombivax HB® is licensed for children aged 11 through 15 years.

2. Rotavirus vaccine (RV).
- The maximum age for the first dose is 14 weeks 6 days. Vaccination should not be initiated for infants aged 15 weeks or older (i.e., 15 weeks 0 days or older).
- Administer the final dose in the series by age 8 months 0 days.
- If Rotarix® was administered for the first and second doses, a third dose is not indicated.

3. Diphtheria and tetanus toxoids and acellular pertussis vaccine (DTaP).
- The fifth dose is not necessary if the fourth dose was administered at age 4 years or older.

4. Haemophilus influenzae type b conjugate vaccine (Hib).
- Hib vaccine is not generally recommended for persons aged 5 years or older. No efficacy data are available on which to base a recommendation concerning use of Hib vaccine for older children and adults. However, studies suggest good immunogenicity in persons who have sickle cell disease, leukemia, or HIV infection, or who have had a splenectomy; administering 1 dose of Hib vaccine to these persons is not contraindicated.
- If the first 2 doses were PRP-OMP (PedvaxHIB® or Comvax®), and administered at age 11 months or younger, the third (and final) dose should be administered at age 12 through 15 months and at least 8 weeks after the second dose.
- If the first dose was administered at age 7 through 11 months, administer 2 doses separated by 4 weeks and a final dose at age 12 through 15 months.

5. Pneumococcal vaccine.
- Administer 1 dose of pneumococcal conjugate vaccine (PCV) to all healthy children aged 24 through 59 months who have not received at least 1 dose of PCV on or after age 12 months.
- For children aged 24 through 59 months with underlying medical conditions, administer 1 dose of PCV if 3 doses were received previously or administer 2 doses of PCV at least 8 weeks apart if fewer than 3 doses were received previously.
- Administer pneumococcal polysaccharide vaccine (PPSV) to children aged 2 years or older with certain underlying medical conditions (see MMWR 2000;49[No. RR-9]), including a cochlear implant, at least 8 weeks after the last dose of PCV.

6. Inactivated poliovirus vaccine (IPV).
- For children who received an all-IPV or all-oral poliovirus (OPV) series, a fourth dose is not necessary if the third dose was administered at age 4 years or older.
- If both OPV and IPV were administered as part of a series, a total of 4 doses should be administered, regardless of the child's current age.

7. Measles, mumps, and rubella vaccine (MMR).
- Administer the second dose at age 4 through 6 years. However, the second dose may be administered before age 4, provided at least 28 days have elapsed since the first dose.
- If not previously vaccinated, administer 2 doses with at least 28 days between doses.

8. Varicella vaccine.
- Administer the second dose at age 4 through 6 years. However, the second dose may be administered before age 4, provided at least 3 months have elapsed since the first dose.
- For persons aged 12 months through 12 years, the minimum interval between doses is 3 months. However, if the second dose was administered at least 28 days after the first dose, it can be accepted as valid.
- For persons aged 13 years and older, the minimum interval between doses is 28 days.

9. Hepatitis A vaccine (HepA).
- HepA is recommended for children older than 1 year who live in areas where vaccination programs target older children or who are at increased risk of infection. See MMWR 2006;55(No. RR-7).

10. Tetanus and diphtheria toxoids vaccine (Td) and tetanus and diphtheria toxoids and acellular pertussis vaccine (Tdap).
- Doses of DTaP are counted as part of the Td/Tdap series
- Tdap should be substituted for a single dose of Td in the catch-up series or as a booster for children aged 10 through 18 years; use Td for other doses.

11. Human papillomavirus vaccine (HPV).
- Administer the series to females at age 13 through 18 years if not previously vaccinated.
- Use recommended routine dosing intervals for series catch-up (i.e., the second and third doses should be administered at 2 and 6 months after the first dose). However, the minimum interval between the first and second doses is 4 weeks. The minimum interval between the second and third doses is 12 weeks, and the third dose should be given at least 24 weeks after the first dose.

Recommended Adult Immunization Schedule
UNITED STATES · 2009

Note: These recommendations *must* be read with the footnotes that follow containing number of doses, intervals between doses, and other important information.

Figure 1. Recommended adult immunization schedule, by vaccine and age group

VACCINE ▼ / AGE GROUP ▶	19–26 years	27–49 years	50–59 years	60–64 years	≥65 years
Tetanus, diphtheria, pertussis (Td/Tdap)[1,*]	Substitute 1-time dose of Tdap for Td booster; then boost with Td every 10 yrs				Td booster every 10 yrs
Human papillomavirus (HPV)[2,*]	3 doses (females)				
Varicella[3,*]	2 doses				
Zoster[4]				1 dose	1 dose
Measles, mumps, rubella (MMR)[5,*]	1 or 2 doses		1 dose		
Influenza[6,*]	1 dose annually				
Pneumococcal (polysaccharide)[7,8]	1 or 2 doses				1 dose
Hepatitis A[9,*]	2 doses				
Hepatitis B[10,*]	3 doses				
Meningococcal[11,*]	1 or more doses				

*Covered by the Vaccine Injury Compensation Program.

Legend:

For all persons in this category who meet the age requirements and who lack evidence of immunity (e.g., lack documentation of vaccination or have no evidence of prior infection)

Recommended if some other risk factor is present (e.g., on the basis of medical, occupational, lifestyle, or other indications)

No recommendation

Report all clinically significant postvaccination reactions to the Vaccine Adverse Event Reporting System (VAERS). Reporting forms and instructions on filing a VAERS report are available at www.vaers.hhs.gov or by telephone, 800-822-7967.

Information on how to file a Vaccine Injury Compensation Program claim is available at www.hrsa.gov/vaccinecompensation or by telephone, 800-338-2382. To file a claim for vaccine injury, contact the U.S. Court of Federal Claims, 717 Madison Place, N.W., Washington, D.C. 20005; telephone, 202-357-6400.

Additional information about the vaccines in this schedule, extent of available data, and contraindications for vaccination is also available at www.cdc.gov/vaccines or from the CDC-INFO Contact Center at 800-CDC-INFO (800-232-4636) in English and Spanish, 24 hours a day, 7 days a week.

Use of trade names and commercial sources is for identification only and does not imply endorsement by the U.S. Department of Health and Human Services.

A

Figure 2. Vaccines that might be indicated for adults based on medical and other indications

VACCINE ▼ / INDICATION ▶	Pregnancy	Immuno-compromising conditions (excluding human immunodeficiency virus [HIV])[13]	HIV infection[3,12,13] CD4+ T lymphocyte count <200 cells/µL	HIV infection[3,12,13] CD4+ T lymphocyte count ≥200 cells/µL	Diabetes, heart disease, chronic lung disease, chronic alcoholism	Asplenia[12] (including elective splenectomy and terminal complement component deficiencies)	Chronic liver disease	Kidney failure, end-stage renal disease, receipt of hemodialysis	Health-care personnel
Tetanus, diphtheria, pertussis (Td/Tdap)[1,*]	Td	Substitute 1-time dose of Tdap for Td booster; then boost with Td every 10 yrs							
Human papillomavirus (HPV)[2,*]		3 doses for females through age 26 yrs							
Varicella[3,*]	Contraindicated		Contraindicated		2 doses				
Zoster[4]	Contraindicated		Contraindicated		1 dose				
Measles, mumps, rubella (MMR)[5,*]	Contraindicated		Contraindicated		1 or 2 doses				
Influenza[6,*]			1 dose TIV annually		1 dose TIV annually				1 dose TIV or LAIV annually
Pneumococcal (polysaccharide)[7,8]					1 or 2 doses				
Hepatitis A[9,*]					2 doses				
Hepatitis B[10,*]					3 doses				
Meningococcal[11,*]					1 or more doses				

*Covered by the Vaccine Injury Compensation Program.

Legend:
- For all persons in this category who meet the age requirements and who lack evidence of immunity (e.g., lack documentation of vaccination or have no evidence of prior infection)
- Recommended if some other risk factor is present (e.g., on the basis of medical, occupational, lifestyle, or other indications)
- No recommendation

These schedules indicate the recommended age groups and medical indications for which administration of currently licensed vaccines is commonly indicated for adults ages 19 years and older, as of January 1, 2009. Licensed combination vaccines may be used whenever any components of the combination are indicated and when the vaccine's other components are not contraindicated. For detailed recommendations on all vaccines, including those used primarily for travelers or that are issued during the year, consult the manufacturers' package inserts and the complete statements from the Advisory Committee on Immunization Practices (www.cdc.gov/vaccines/pubs/acip-list.htm).

The recommendations in this schedule were approved by the Centers for Disease Control and Prevention's (CDC) Advisory Committee on Immunization Practices (ACIP), the American Academy of Family Physicians (AAFP), the American College of Obstetricians and Gynecologists (ACOG), and the American College of Physicians (ACP).

CS200484-A

DEPARTMENT OF HEALTH AND HUMAN SERVICES
CENTERS FOR DISEASE CONTROL AND PREVENTION

CDC

Footnotes

Recommended Adult Immunization Schedule—UNITED STATES · 2009

For complete statements by the Advisory Committee on Immunization Practices (ACIP), visit www.cdc.gov/vaccines/pubs/ACIP-list.htm.

1. Tetanus, diphtheria, and acellular pertussis (Td/Tdap) vaccination

Tdap should replace a single dose of Td for adults aged 19 through 64 years who have not received a dose of Tdap previously.

Adults with uncertain or incomplete history of primary vaccination series with tetanus and diphtheria toxoid-containing vaccines should begin or complete a primary vaccination series. A primary series for adults is 3 doses of tetanus and diphtheria toxoid-containing vaccines; administer the first 2 doses at least 4 weeks apart and the third dose 6–12 months after the second. However, Tdap can substitute for any one of the doses of Td in the 3-dose primary series. The booster dose of tetanus and diphtheria toxoid-containing vaccine should be administered to adults who have completed a primary series and if the last vaccination was received 10 or more years previously. Tdap or Td vaccine may be used, as indicated.

If a woman is pregnant and received the last Td vaccination 10 or more years previously, administer Td during the second or third trimester. If the woman received the last Td vaccination less than 10 years previously, administer Tdap during the immediate postpartum period. A dose of Tdap is recommended for postpartum women, close contacts of infants aged less than 12 months, and all health-care personnel with direct patient contact if they have not previously received Tdap. An interval as short as 2 years from the last Td is suggested; shorter intervals can be used. Td may be deferred during pregnancy and Tdap substituted in the immediate postpartum period, or Tdap may be administered instead of Td to a pregnant woman after an informed discussion with the woman.

Consult the ACIP statement for recommendations for administering Td as prophylaxis in wound management.

2. Human papillomavirus (HPV) vaccination

HPV vaccination is recommended for all females aged 11 through 26 years (and may begin at 9 years) who have not completed the vaccine series. History of genital warts, abnormal Papanicolaou test, or positive HPV DNA test is not evidence of prior infection with all vaccine HPV types; HPV vaccination is recommended for persons with such histories.

Ideally, vaccine should be administered before potential exposure to HPV through sexual activity; however, females who are sexually active should still be vaccinated consistent with age-based recommendations. Sexually active females who have not been infected with any of the four HPV vaccine types receive the full benefit of the vaccination. Vaccination is less beneficial for females who have already been infected with one or more of the HPV vaccine types.

A complete series consists of 3 doses. The second dose should be administered 2 months after the first dose; the third dose should be administered 6 months after the first dose.

HPV vaccination is not specifically recommended for females with the medical indications described in Figure 2, "Vaccines that might be indicated for adults based on medical and other indications." Because HPV vaccine is not a live-virus vaccine, it may be administered to persons with the medical indications described in Figure 2. However, the immune response and vaccine efficacy might be less for persons with the medical indications described in Figure 2 than in persons who do not have the medical indications described or who are immunocompetent. Health-care personnel are not at increased risk because of occupational exposure, and should be vaccinated consistent with age-based recommendations.

3. Varicella vaccination

All adults without evidence of immunity to varicella should receive 2 doses of single-antigen varicella vaccine if not previously vaccinated or the second dose if they have received only one dose unless they have a medical contraindication. Special consideration should be given to those who 1) have close contact with persons at high risk for severe disease (e.g., health-care personnel and family contacts of persons with immunocompromising conditions) or 2) are at high risk for exposure or transmission (e.g., teachers; child care employees; residents and staff members of institutional settings, including correctional institutions; college students; military personnel; adolescents and adults living in households with children; nonpregnant women of childbearing age; and international travelers).

Evidence of immunity to varicella in adults includes any of the following: 1) documentation of 2 doses of varicella vaccine at least 4 weeks apart; 2) U.S.-born before 1980 (although for health-care personnel and pregnant women, birth before 1980 should not be considered evidence of immunity); 3) history of varicella based on diagnosis or verification of varicella by a health-care provider (for a patient reporting a history of or presenting with an atypical case, a mild case, or both, health-care providers should seek either an epidemiologic link with a typical varicella case or to a laboratory-confirmed case or evidence of laboratory confirmation, if it was performed at the time of acute disease); 4) history of herpes zoster based on health-care provider diagnosis or verification of herpes zoster by a health-care provider; or 5) laboratory evidence of immunity or laboratory confirmation of disease.

Pregnant women should be assessed for evidence of varicella immunity. Women who do not have evidence of immunity should receive the first dose of varicella vaccine upon completion or termination of pregnancy and before discharge from the health-care facility. The second dose should be administered 4–8 weeks after the first dose.

4. Herpes zoster vaccination

A single dose of zoster vaccine is recommended for adults aged 60 years and older regardless of whether they report a prior episode of herpes zoster. Persons with chronic medical conditions may be vaccinated unless their condition constitutes a contraindication.

5. Measles, mumps, rubella (MMR) vaccination

Measles component: Adults born before 1957 generally are considered immune to measles. Adults born during or after 1957 should receive 1 or more doses of MMR unless they have a medical contraindication, documentation of 1 or more doses, history of measles based on health-care provider diagnosis, or laboratory evidence of immunity.

A second dose of MMR is recommended for adults who 1) have been recently exposed to measles or are in an outbreak setting; 2) have been vaccinated previously with killed measles vaccine; 3) have been vaccinated with an unknown type of measles vaccine during 1963–1967; 4) are students in postsecondary educational institutions; 5) work in a health-care facility; or 6) plan to travel internationally.

Mumps component: Adults born before 1957 generally are considered immune to mumps. Adults born during or after 1957 should receive 1 dose of MMR unless they have a medical contraindication, history of mumps based on health-care provider diagnosis, or laboratory evidence of immunity.

A second dose of MMR is recommended for adults who 1) live in a community experiencing a mumps outbreak and are in an affected age group; 2) are students in postsecondary educational institutions; 3) work in a health-care facility; or 4) plan to travel internationally. For unvaccinated health-care personnel born before 1957 who do not have other evidence of mumps immunity, administering 1 dose on a routine basis should be considered and administering a second dose during an outbreak should be strongly considered.

Rubella component: 1 dose of MMR vaccine is recommended for women whose rubella vaccination history is unreliable or who lack laboratory evidence of immunity. For women of childbearing age, regardless of birth year, rubella immunity should be determined and women should be counseled regarding congenital rubella syndrome. Women who do not have evidence of immunity should receive MMR upon completion or termination of pregnancy and before discharge from the health-care facility.

6. Influenza vaccination

Medical indications: Chronic disorders of the cardiovascular or pulmonary systems, including asthma; chronic metabolic diseases, including diabetes mellitus, renal or hepatic dysfunction, hemoglobinopathies, or immunocompromising conditions (including immunocompromising conditions caused by medications or human immunodeficiency virus [HIV]); any condition that compromises respiratory function or the handling of respiratory secretions or that can increase the risk of aspiration (e.g., cognitive dysfunction, spinal cord injury, or seizure disorder or other neuromuscular disorder); and pregnancy during the influenza season. No data exist on the risk for severe or complicated influenza disease among persons with asplenia; however, influenza is a risk factor for secondary bacterial infections that can cause severe disease among persons with asplenia.

Occupational indications: All health-care personnel, including those employed by long-term care and assisted-living facilities, and caregivers of children less than 5 years old.

Other indications: Residents of nursing homes and other long-term care and assisted-living facilities; persons likely to transmit influenza to persons at high risk (e.g., in-home household contacts and caregivers of children aged less than 5 years old, persons 65 years old and older and persons of all ages with high-risk condition[s]); and anyone who would like to decrease their risk of getting influenza. Healthy, nonpregnant adults aged less than 50 years without high-risk medical conditions who are not contacts of severely immunocompromised persons in special care units can receive either intranasally administered live, attenuated influenza vaccine (FluMist®) or inactivated vaccine. Other persons should receive the inactivated vaccine.

7. Pneumococcal polysaccharide (PPSV) vaccination

Medical indications: Chronic lung disease (including asthma); chronic cardiovascular diseases; diabetes mellitus; chronic liver diseases, cirrhosis; chronic alcoholism, chronic renal failure or nephrotic syndrome; functional or anatomic asplenia (e.g., sickle cell disease or splenectomy [if elective splenectomy is planned, vaccinate at least 2 weeks before surgery]); immunocompromising conditions; and cochlear implants and cerebrospinal fluid leaks. Vaccinate as close to HIV diagnosis as possible.

Other indications: Residents of nursing homes or long-term care facilities and persons who smoke cigarettes. Routine use of PPSV is not recommended for Alaska Native or American Indian persons younger than 65 years unless they have underlying medical conditions that are PPSV indications. However public health authorities may consider recommending PPSV for Alaska Natives and American Indians aged 50 through 64 years who are living in areas in which the risk of invasive pneumococcal disease is increased.

8. Revaccination with PPSV

One-time revaccination after 5 years for persons with chronic renal failure or nephrotic syndrome; functional or anatomic asplenia (e.g., sickle cell disease or splenectomy); and for persons with immunocompromising conditions. For persons aged 65 years and older, one-time revaccination if they were vaccinated 5 or more years previously and were aged less than 65 years at the time of primary vaccination.

9. Hepatitis A vaccination

Medical indications: Persons with chronic liver disease and persons who receive clotting factor concentrates.

Behavioral indications: Men who have sex with men and persons who use illegal drugs.

Occupational indications: Persons working with hepatitis A virus (HAV)-infected primates or with HAV in a research laboratory setting.

Other indications: Persons traveling to or working in countries that have high or intermediate endemicity of hepatitis A (a list of countries is available at wwwn.cdc.gov/travel/contentdiseases.aspx) and any person seeking protection from HAV infection.

Single-antigen vaccine formulations should be administered in a 2-dose schedule at either 0 and 6–12 months (Havrix®), or 0 and 6–18 months (Vaqta®). If the combined hepatitis A and hepatitis B vaccine (Twinrix®) is used, administer 3 doses at 0, 1, and 6 months; alternatively, a 4-dose schedule, administered on days 0, 7 and 21 to 30 followed by a booster dose at month 12 may be used.

10. Hepatitis B vaccination

Medical indications: Persons with end-stage renal disease, including patients receiving hemodialysis; persons with HIV infection; and persons with chronic liver disease.

Occupational indications: Health-care personnel and public-safety workers who are exposed to blood or other potentially infectious body fluids.

Behavioral indications: Sexually active persons who are not in a long-term, mutually monogamous relationship (e.g., persons with more than 1 sex partner during the previous 6 months); persons seeking evaluation or treatment for a sexually transmitted disease; current or recent injection-drug users; and men who have sex with men.

Other indications: Household contacts and sex partners of persons with chronic hepatitis B virus (HBV) infection; clients and staff members of institutions for persons with developmental disabilities; international travelers to countries with high or intermediate prevalence of chronic HBV infection (a list of countries is available at wwwn.cdc.gov/travel/contentdiseases.aspx); and any adult seeking protection from HBV infection.

Hepatitis B vaccination is recommended for all adults in the following settings: STD treatment facilities; HIV testing and treatment facilities; facilities providing drug-abuse treatment and prevention services; health-care settings targeting services to injection-drug users or men who have sex with men; correctional facilities; end-stage renal disease programs and facilities for chronic hemodialysis patients; and institutions and nonresidential daycare facilities for persons with developmental disabilities.

If the combined hepatitis A and hepatitis B vaccine (Twinrix®) is used, administer 3 doses at 0, 1, and 6 months; alternatively, a 4-dose schedule, administered on days 0, 7 and 21 to 30 followed by a booster dose at month 12 may be used.

Special formulation indications: For adult patients receiving hemodialysis or with other immunocompromising conditions, 1 dose of 40 μg/mL (Recombivax HB®) administered on a 3-dose schedule or 2 doses of 20 μg/mL (Engerix-B®) administered simultaneously on a 4-dose schedule at 0, 1, 2 and 6 months.

11. Meningococcal vaccination

Medical indications: Adults with anatomic or functional asplenia, or terminal complement component deficiencies.

Other indications: First-year college students living in dormitories; microbiologists who are routinely exposed to isolates of *Neisseria meningitidis*; military recruits; and persons who travel to or live in countries in which meningococcal disease is hyperendemic or epidemic (e.g., the "meningitis belt" of sub-Saharan Africa during the dry season [December–June]), particularly if their contact with local populations will be prolonged. Vaccination is required by the government of Saudi Arabia for all travelers to Mecca during the annual Hajj.

Meningococcal conjugate (MCV) vaccine is preferred for adults with any of the preceding indications who are aged 55 years or younger, although meningococcal polysaccharide vaccine (MPSV) is an acceptable alternative. Revaccination with MCV after 5 years might be indicated for adults previously vaccinated with MPSV who remain at increased risk for infection (e.g., persons residing in areas in which disease is epidemic).

12. Selected conditions for which *Haemophilus influenzae* type b (Hib) vaccine may be used

Hib vaccine generally is not recommended for persons aged 5 years and older. No efficacy data are available on which to base a recommendation concerning use of Hib vaccine for older children and adults. However, studies suggest good immunogenicity in persons who have sickle cell disease, leukemia, or HIV infection or who have had a splenectomy; administering 1 dose of vaccine to these persons is not contraindicated.

13. Immunocompromising conditions

Inactivated vaccines generally are acceptable (e.g., pneumococcal, meningococcal, and influenza [trivalent inactivated influenza vaccine]), and live vaccines generally are avoided in persons with immune deficiencies or immunocompromising conditions. Information on specific conditions is available at www.cdc.gov/vaccines/pubs/acip-list.htm.

Recommended and Minimum Ages and Intervals Between Doses of Routinely Recommended Vaccines[1]

Vaccine and dose number	Recommended age for this dose	Minimum age for this dose	Recommended interval to next dose	Minimum interval to next dose
Hepatitis B (HepB)-1[2]	Birth	Birth	1-4 months	4 weeks
HepB-2	1-2 months	4 weeks	2-17 months	8 weeks
HepB-3[3]	6-18 months	24 weeks	–	–
Diphtheria-tetanus-acellular pertussis (DTaP)-1[2]	2 months	6 weeks	2 months	4 weeks
DTaP-2	4 months	10 weeks	2 months	4 weeks
DTaP-3	6 months	14 weeks	6-12 months[4]	6 months[4,5]
DTaP-4	15-18 months	12 months	3 years	6 months[4]
DTaP-5	4-6 years	4 years	–	–
Haemophilus influenzae type b (Hib)-1[2,6]	2 months	6 weeks	2 months	4 weeks
Hib-2	4 months	10 weeks	2 months	4 weeks
Hib-3[7]	6 months	14 weeks	6-9 months[4]	8 weeks
Hib-4	12-15 months	12 months	–	–
Inactivated poliovirus (IPV)-1[2]	2 months	6 weeks	2 months	4 weeks
IPV-2	4 months	10 weeks	2-14 months	4 weeks
IPV-3	6-18 months	14 weeks	3-5 years	4 weeks
IPV-4	4-6 years	18 weeks	–	–
Pneumococcal conjugate (PCV)-1[6]	2 months	6 weeks	2 months	4 weeks
PCV-2	4 months	10 weeks	2 months	4 weeks
PCV-3	6 months	14 weeks	6 months	8 weeks
PCV-4	12-15 months	12 months	–	–
Measles-mumps-rubella (MMR)-1[8]	12-15 months	12 months	3-5 years	4 weeks
MMR-2[8]	4-6 years	13 months	–	–
Varicella (Var)-1[8]	12-15 months	12 months	3-5 years	12 weeks [9]
Var-2[8]	4-6 years	15 months	–	–
Hepatitis A (HepA)-1[2]	12-23 months	12 months	6-18 months[4]	6 months[4]
HepA-2	18-41 months	18 months	–	–
Influenza, Inactivated (TIV)[10]	6-59 months	6 months[11]	1 month	4 weeks
Influenza, Live attenuated (LAIV)[10]	–	2 years	1 month	4 weeks
Meningococcal Conjugate (MCV)	11-12 years	2 years	–	–
Meningococcal Polysaccharide (MPSV)-1	–	2 years	5 years[12]	5 years[12]
MPSV-2[13]	–	7 years	–	–
Tetanus-diphtheria (Td)	11-12 years	7 years	10 years	5 years
Tetanus-diphtheria-acellular pertussis (Tdap)[14]	≥11 years	10 years	–	–
Pneumococcal polysaccharide (PPSV)-1	–	2 years	5 years	5 years
PPSV-2[15]	–	7 years	–	–

A

Vaccine and dose number	Recommended age for this dose	Minimum age for this dose	Recommended interval to next dose	Minimum interval to next dose
Human papillomavirus (HPV)-1[16]	11-12 years	9 years	2 months	4 weeks
HPV-2	11-12 years (+2 months)	109 months	4 months	12 weeks
HPV-3[17]	11-12 years (+6 months)	114 months	–	–
Rotavirus (RV)-1[18]	2 months	6 weeks	2 months	4 weeks
RV-2	4 months	10 weeks	2 months	4 weeks
RV-3[19]	6 months	14 weeks	–	–
Zoster[20]	60 years	60 years	–	–

1   Use of licensed combination vaccines is preferred over separate injections of their equivalent component vaccines. (CDC. Combination vaccines for childhood immunization: recommendations of the Advisory Committee on Immunization Practices [ACIP], the American Academy of Pediatrics [AAP], and the American Academy of Family Physicians [AAFP]. *MMWR* 1999;48[No. RR-5]). When administering combination vaccines, the minimum age for administration is the oldest age for any of the individual components; the minimum interval between doses is equal to the greatest interval of any of the individual components.

2   Combination vaccines containing the Hepatitis B component are available (HepB-Hib, DTaP-HepB-IPV, HepA-HepB). These vaccines should not be administered to infants younger than 6 weeks of age because of the other components (i.e., Hib, DTaP, IPV, and HepA).

3   HepB-3 should be administered at least 8 weeks after HepB-2 and at least 16 weeks after HepB-1, and it should not be administered before age 24 weeks.

4   Calendar months.

5   The minimum recommended interval between DTaP-3 and DTaP-4 is 6 months. However, DTaP-4 need not be repeated if administered at least 4 months after DTaP-3.

6   For Hib and PCV, children receiving the first dose of vaccine at age 7 months of age or older require fewer doses to complete the series (CDC. Recommended childhood and adolescent immunization schedule – United States, 2006. *MMWR* 2005; 54 [Nos. 51 & 52]:Q1-Q4).

7   If PRP-OMP (Pedvax-Hib®, Merck Vaccine Division), was administered at 2 and 4 months of age a dose at 6 months of age is not required.

8   Combination measles-mumps-rubella-varicella (MMRV) vaccine can be used for children 12 months through 12 years of age. Also see footnote 9.

9   The minimum interval from Var-1 to Var-2 for persons beginning the series at 13 years or older is 4 weeks.

10   One dose of influenza vaccine per season is recommended for most people. Children younger than 9 years of age who are receiving influenza vaccine for the first time, or received only 1 dose the previous season (if it was their first vaccination season) should receive 2 doses this season.

11   The minimum age for inactivated influenza vaccine varies by vaccine manufacturer. Only Fluzone (manufactured by sanofi pasteur) is approved for children 6-35 months of age. The minimum age for Fluvirin (manufactured by Novartis) is 4 years. For Fluarix and FluLaval (manufactured by GlaxoSmithKline) and Afluria (manufactured by CSL Ltd), the minimum age is 18 years.

12   Some experts recommend a second dose of MPSV-3 years after the first dose for people at increased risk for meningococcal disease.

13   A second dose of meningococcal vaccine is recommended for people previously vaccinated with MPSV who remain at high risk for meningococcal disease. MCV is preferred when revaccinating persons aged 2-55 years, but a second dose of MPSV is acceptable. (CDC. Prevention and Control of Meningococcal Disease Recommendations of the Advisory Committee on Immunization Practices [ACIP]. *MMWR* 2005; 54: No. RR-7.)

14   Only one dose of Tdap is recommended. Subsequent doses should be administered as Td. If vaccination to prevent tetanus and/or diphtheria disease is required for children 7 through 9 years of age, Td should be administered (minimum age for Td is 7 years). For one brand of Tdap the minimum age is 11 years. The preferred interval between Tdap and a previous dose of Td is 5 years. In persons who have received a primary series of tetanus-toxoid containing vaccine, for management of a tetanus-prone wound, the minimum interval after a previous dose of any tetanus-containing vaccine is 5 years.

15   A second dose of PPSV is recommended for persons at highest risk for serious pneumococcal infection and those who are likely to have a rapid decline in pneumococcal antibody concentration. Revaccination 3 years after the previous dose can be considered for children at highest risk for severe pneumococcal infection who would be younger than 10 years of age at the time of revaccination. (CDC. Prevention of pneumococcal disease: recommendations of the Advisory Committee on Immunization Practices [ACIP]. *MMWR* 1997;46[No. RR-8]).

16   HPV is approved only for females 9-26 years of age.

17   HPV-3 should be administered at least 12 weeks after HPV-2 and at least 24 weeks after HPV-1, and it should not be administered before 114 months of age.

18   The first dose of RV must be administered at 6-14 weeks of age. The vaccine series should not be started after a child has reached 15 weeks of age. RV may be administered on the day a child reaches his or her 8 month birthday but not later, regardless of the number of doses administered previously.

19   If Rotarix (RV1) is administered as age appropriate, a third dose is not necessary.

20   Herpes zoster vaccine is approved as a single dose for persons 60 years and older with a history of varicella.

Adapted from Table 1, ACIP General Recommendations on Immunization: *MMWR* 2006;55(No. RR-15)

March 2009

A

Appendix A

Summary of Recommendations for Childhood and Adolescent Immunization (Page 1 of 3)

Vaccine name and route	Schedule for routine vaccination and other guidelines (any vaccine can be given with another)	Schedule for catch-up vaccination and related issues	Contraindications and precautions (mild illness is not a contraindication)
Hepatitis B (HepB) *Give IM*	• Vaccinate all children age 0 through 18yrs. • Vaccinate all newborns with monovalent vaccine prior to hospital discharge. Give dose #2 at age 1–2m and the final dose at age 6–18m (the last dose in the infant series should not be given earlier than age 24wks). After the birth dose, the series may be completed using 2 doses of single-antigen vaccine or up to 3 doses of Comvax (ages 2m, 4m, 12–15m) or Pediarix (ages 2m, 4m, 6m), which may result in giving a total of 4 doses of hepatitis B vaccine. • **If mother is HBsAg-positive:** give the newborn HBIG + dose #1 within 12hrs of birth; complete series at age 6m or, if using Comvax, at age 12–15m. • **If mother's HBsAg status is unknown:** give the newborn dose #1 within 12hrs of birth. If mother is subsequently found to be HBsAg positive, give infant HBIG within 7d of birth and follow the schedule for infants born to HBsAg-positive mothers.	• Do not restart series, no matter how long since previous dose. • 3-dose series can be started at any age. • Minimum spacing between doses: 4wks between #1 and #2, 8wks between #2 and #3, and at least 16wks between #1 and #3 (e.g., 0-, 2-, 4m; 0-, 1-, 4m). **Special Notes on Hepatitis B Vaccine (HepB)** **Dosing of HepB:** Vaccine brands are interchangeable. For persons age 0 through 19yrs, give 0.5 mL of either Engerix-B or Recombivax HB. **Alternative dosing schedule for unvaccinated adolescents age 11 through 15yrs:** Give 2 doses Recombivax HB 1.0 mL (adult formulation) spaced 4–6m apart. (Engerix-B is not licensed for a 2-dose schedule.) **For preterm infants:** Consult ACIP hepatitis B recommendations (*MMWR* 2005; 54 [RR-16]).*	**Contraindication** Previous anaphylaxis to this vaccine or to any of its components. **Precaution** Moderate or severe acute illness.
DTaP, DT (Diphtheria, tetanus, acellular pertussis) *Give IM*	• Give to children at ages 2m, 4m, 6m, 15–18m, 4–6yrs. • May give dose #1 as early as age 6wks. • May give #4 as early as age 12m if 6m have elapsed since #3 and the child is unlikely to return at age 15–18m. • Do not give DTaP/DT to children age 7yrs and older. • If possible, use the same DTaP product for all doses.	• #2 and #3 may be given 4wks after previous dose. • #4 may be given 6m after #3. • If #4 is given before 4th birthday, wait at least 6m for #5 (age 4–6yrs). • If #4 is given after 4th birthday, #5 is not needed.	**Contraindications** • Previous anaphylaxis to this vaccine or to any of its components. • For DTaP/Tdap only: encephalopathy within 7d after DTP/DTaP. **Precautions** • Moderate or severe acute illness. • History of Arthus reaction following a prior dose of tetanus- and/or diphtheria-toxoid-containing vaccine, including MCV.
Td, Tdap (Tetanus, diphtheria, acellular pertussis) *Give IM*	• Give 1-time Tdap dose to adolescents age 11–12yrs if 5yrs have elapsed since last dose DTaP; then boost every 10yrs with Td. • Give 1-time dose of Tdap to all adolescents who have not received previous Tdap. Special efforts should be made to give Tdap to persons age 11yrs and older who are - in contact with infants younger than age 12m. - healthcare workers with direct patient contact. • In pregnancy, when indicated, give Td or Tdap in 2nd or 3rd trimester. If not administered during pregnancy, give Tdap in immediate postpartum period.	• If never vaccinated with tetanus- and diphtheria-containing vaccine: give Td dose #1 now, dose #2 4wks later, and dose #3 6m after #2, then give booster every 10yrs. A 1-time Tdap may be substituted for any dose in the series, preferably as dose #1. For persons who previously received a Td booster, an interval of 2yrs or less between Td and Tdap may be used.	• Guillain-Barré syndrome within 6wks after previous dose of tetanus toxoid-containing vaccine. • For DTaP/Tdap only: Any of these events following a previous dose of DTP/DTaP: 1) temperature of 105°F (40.5°C) or higher within 48hrs; 2) continuous crying for 3hrs or more within 48hrs; 3) collapse or shock-like state within 48hrs; 4) convulsion with or without fever within 3d. • For DTaP/Tdap only: Unstable neurologic disorder. **Note:** Use of Td or Tdap is not contraindicated in pregnancy. At the provider's discretion, either vaccine may be administered during the 2nd or 3rd trimester.
Polio (IPV) *Give SC or IM*	• Give to children at ages 2m, 4m, 6–18m, 4–6yrs. • May give dose #1 as early as age 6wks. • Not routinely recommended for U.S. residents age 18yrs and older (except certain travelers).	• All doses should be separated by at least 4wks. • If dose #3 is given after 4th birthday, dose #4 is not needed.	**Contraindication** Previous anaphylaxis to this vaccine or to any of its components. **Precautions** • Moderate or severe acute illness. • Pregnancy.
Human papillomavirus (HPV) *Give IM*	• Give 3-dose series to girls at age 11–12yrs on a 0, 2, 6m schedule. (May be given as early as age 9yrs.) • Vaccinate all older girls and women (through age 26yrs) who were not previously vaccinated.	• Minimum spacing between doses: 4wks between #1 and #2; 12 wks between #2 and #3. Overall, there must be at least 24wks between doses #1 and #3.	**Contraindication** Previous anaphylaxis to this vaccine or to any of its components. **Precautions** • Moderate or severe acute illness. • Pregnancy.

*This document was adapted from the recommendations of the Advisory Committee on Immunization Practices (ACIP). To obtain copies of the recommendations, call the CDC-INFO Contact Center at (800) 232-4636; visit CDC's website at www.cdc.gov/vaccines/pubs/ACIP-list.htm; or visit the Immunization Action Coalition (IAC) website at www.immunize.org/acip. This table is revised periodically. Visit IAC's website at www.immunize.org/childrules to make sure you have the most current version.

Technical content reviewed by the Centers for Disease Control and Prevention, November 2008.

Immunization Action Coalition • 1573 Selby Avenue • Saint Paul, MN 55104 • (651) 647-9009 • www.immunize.org • www.vaccineinformation.org • admin@immunize.org

www.immunize.org/catg.d/p2010.pdf • Item #P2010 (11/08)

Summary of Recommendations for Childhood and Adolescent Immunization

Vaccine name and route	Schedule for routine vaccination and other guidelines (any vaccine can be given with another)	Schedule for catch-up vaccine administration and related issues	Contraindications and precautions (mild illness is not a contraindication)
Varicella (Var) (Chickenpox) *Give SC*	• Give dose #1 at age 12–15m. • Give dose #2 at age 4–6yrs. Dose #2 may be given earlier if at least 3m since dose #1. • Give a second dose to all older children and adolescents with history of only 1 dose. • MMRV may be used in children age 12m through 12yrs.	• If younger than age 13yrs, space dose #1 and #2 at least 3m apart. If age 13yrs or older, space at least 4wks apart. • May use as postexposure prophylaxis if given within 5d. • If Var and either MMR, LAIV, and/or yellow fever vaccine are not given on the same day, space them at least 28d apart.	**Contraindications** • Previous anaphylaxis to this vaccine or to any of its components. • Pregnancy or possibility of pregnancy within 4wks. • Children on high-dose immunosuppressive therapy or who are immunocompromised because of malignancy and primary or acquired cellular immunodeficiency, including HIV/AIDS (although vaccination may be considered if CD4+ T-lymphocyte percentages are either 15% or greater in children ages 1 through 8yrs or 200 cells/mL or greater in children age 9yrs or older). **Precautions** • Moderate or severe acute illness. • If blood, plasma, and/or immune globulin (IG or VZIG) were given in past 11m, see ACIP statement *General Recommendations on Immunization** regarding time to wait before vaccinating. **Note:** For patients with humoral immunodeficiency or leukemia, see ACIP recommendations*.
MMR (Measles, mumps, rubella) *Give SC*	• Give dose #1 at age 12–15m. • Give dose #2 at age 4–6yrs. Dose #2 may be given earlier if at least 4wks since dose #1. • Give a second dose to all older children and teens with history of only 1 dose. • MMRV may be used in children age 12m through 12yrs.	• If MMR and either Var, LAIV, and/or yellow fever vaccine are not given on the same day, space them at least 28d apart. • When using MMR for both doses, minimum interval is 4wks. • When using MMRV for both doses, minimum interval is 3m. • Within 72hrs of measles exposure, give 1 dose of MMR as postexposure prophylaxis to susceptible healthy children age 12m and older.	**Contraindications** • Previous anaphylaxis to this vaccine or to any of its components. • Pregnancy or possibility of pregnancy within 4wks. • Severe immunodeficiency (e.g., hematologic and solid tumors; receiving chemotherapy; congenital immunodeficiency; long-term immunosuppressive therapy, or severely symptomatic HIV). Note: HIV infection is NOT a contraindication to MMR for children who are not severely immunocompromised (consult ACIP MMR recommendations [*MMWR* 1998;47 [RR-8] for details*). **Precautions** • Moderate or severe acute illness. • If blood, plasma, or immune globulin given in past 11m, see ACIP statement *General Recommendations on Immunization** regarding time to wait before vaccinating. • History of thrombocytopenia or thrombocytopenic purpura. **Note:** MMR is not contraindicated if a TST (tuberculosis skin test) was recently applied. If TST and MMR are not given on same day, delay TST for at least 4wks after MMR.
Influenza Trivalent inactivated influenza vaccine (TIV) *Give IM* Live attenuated influenza vaccine (LAIV) *Give intranasally*	• Vaccinate all children and teens age 6m through 18yrs, as well as all household contacts of infants and children through age 59m (4yrs 11m). • Vaccinate persons age 19yrs and older who - have a risk factor (e.g., pregnancy, heart or lung disease, renal, hepatic, hematologic, or metabolic disorder [including diabetes], immunosuppression, or have a condition that compromises respiratory function or the handling of respiratory secretions or that can increase the risk of aspiration) or live in a chronic-care facility. - live or work with at-risk people as listed above. • All other persons who want to reduce the likelihood of becoming ill with influenza or of spreading it to others. • LAIV may be given to healthy, non-pregnant persons age 2–49yrs. • Give 2 doses to first-time vaccinees age 6m through 8yrs, spaced 4wks apart. • For TIV, give 0.25 mL dose to children age 6–35m and 0.5 mL dose if age 3yrs and older.		**Contraindications** • Previous anaphylaxis to this vaccine, to any of its components, or to eggs. • For LAIV only: Pregnancy, asthma, reactive airways disease, or other chronic disorder of the pulmonary or cardiovascular systems; an underlying medical condition, including metabolic diseases such as diabetes, renal dysfunction, and hemoglobinopathies; known or suspected immune deficiency diseases or immunosuppressed states; for children younger than age 5yrs, possible reactive airways disease (e.g., recurrent wheezing or a wheezing episode within the past 12m). **Precautions** • Moderate or severe acute illness. • History of Guillain-Barré syndrome within 6wks of a previous influenza vaccination. **Note:** If LAIV and either MMR, Var, and/or yellow fever vaccine are not given on the same day, space them at least 28d apart.
Rotavirus (RV) *Give orally*	• Rotarix (RV1): give at age 2m, 4m • RotaTeq (RV5): give at age 2m, 4m, 6m • May give dose #1 as early as age 6wks. • Give dose #3 no later than age 8m 0 days.	• Do not begin series in infants older than age 15wks 0 days. • Intervals between doses may be as short as 4wks. • If prior vaccination included use of different or unknown brand(s), a total of 3 doses should be given.	**Contraindication** Previous anaphylaxis to this vaccine or to any of its components, including latex for RV1. **Precautions** • Moderate or severe acute illness. • Altered immunocompetence. • Moderate to severe acute gastroenteritis or chronic gastrointestinal disease. • History of intussusception.

A

Summary of Recommendations for Childhood and Adolescent Immunization

Vaccine name and route	Schedule for routine vaccination and other guidelines (any vaccine can be given with another)	Schedule for catch-up vaccination and related issues	Contraindications and precautions (mild illness is not a contraindication)
Hib (*Haemophilus influenzae* type b) *Give IM*	• ActHib (PRP-T): give at age 2m, 4m, 6m, 12–15m (booster dose). • PedvaxHIB or Comvax (containing PRP-OMP): give at age 2m, 4m, 12–15m (booster dose). • Dose #1 of Hib vaccine should not be given earlier than age 6wks. • The last dose (booster dose) is given no earlier than age 12m and a minimum of 8wks after the previous dose. • Hib vaccines are interchangeable; however, if different brands of Hib vaccines are administered for dose #1 and dose #2, a total of 3 doses are necessary to complete the primary series in infants. • Any Hib vaccine may be used for the booster dose. • Hib is not routinely given to children age 5yrs and older.	**All Hib vaccines:** • If #1 was given at 12–14m, give booster in 8wks. • Give only 1 dose to unvaccinated children from age 15 through 59m. **ActHib:** • #2 and #3 may be given 4wks after previous dose. • If #1 was given at age 7–11m, only 3 doses are needed; #2 is given 4–8wks after #1, then boost at age 12–15m (wait at least 8wks after dose #2). **PedvaxHIB and Comvax:** • #2 may be given 4wks after dose #1.	**Contraindications** • Previous anaphylaxis to this vaccine or to any of its components. • Age younger than 6wks. **Precaution** Moderate or severe acute illness.
Pneumo. conjugate (PCV) *Give IM*	• Give at ages 2m, 4m, 6m, 12–15m. • Dose #1 may be given as early as age 6wks. • Give 1 dose to unvaccinated healthy children age 24–59m. • For high-risk** children ages 24–59m, give 2 doses at least 8wks apart if previous vaccinations were fewer than 3 doses, or give 1 dose if previously received 3 doses. • PCV is not routinely given to children age 5yrs and older. ****High-risk:** Those with sickle cell disease; anatomic/functional asplenia; chronic cardiac, pulmonary, or renal disease; diabetes; cerebrospinal fluid leaks; HIV infection; immunosuppression; diseases associated with immunosuppressive and/or radiation therapy; or who have or will have a cochlear implant.	• For age 7–11m: If history of 0–2 doses, give additional doses 4wks apart with no more than 3 total doses by age 12m; then give booster 8wks later. • For age 12–23m: If 0–1 dose before age 12m, give 2 doses at least 8wks apart. If 2–3 doses before age 12m, give 1 dose at least 8wks after previous dose. • For age 24–59m: If patient has had no previous doses, or has a history of 1–3 doses given before age 12m but no booster dose, or has a history of only 1 dose given at age 12–23m, give 1 dose now.	**Contraindication** Previous anaphylaxis to this vaccine or to any of its components. **Precaution** Moderate or severe acute illness.
Pneumo. polysacch. (PPSV) *Give IM or SC*	• Give 1 dose at least 8wks after final dose of PCV to high-risk children age 2yrs and older. • For children who are immunocompromised or have sickle cell disease or functional or anatomic asplenia, give a 2nd dose of PPSV 5yrs after previous PPSV (consult ACIP PPSV recommendations at http://www.cdc.gov/vaccines/pubs/ACIP-list.htm*).		**Contraindication** Previous anaphylaxis to this vaccine or to any of its components. **Precaution** Moderate or severe acute illness.
Hepatitis A (HepA) *Give IM*	• Give 2 doses to all children at age 1yr (12–23m) spaced 6m apart. • Vaccinate all previously unvaccinated children and adolescents age 2 years and older who – Live in a state, county, or community with a routine vaccination program already in place for children age 2yrs and older. – Travel anywhere except U.S., W. Europe, N. Zealand, Australia, Canada, or Japan. – Wish to be protected from HAV infection. – Have chronic liver disease, clotting factor disorder, or are MSM adolescents. – Are injecting or non-injecting drug users.	• Minimum interval between doses is 6m. • Children who are not fully vaccinated by age 2yrs can be vaccinated at subsequent visits. • Consider routine vaccination of children age 2yrs and older in areas with no existing program. • Give 1 dose as postexposure prophylaxis to incompletely vaccinated children age 12m and older who have recently (during the past 2wks) been exposed to hepatitis A virus.	**Contraindication** Previous anaphylaxis to this vaccine or to any of its components. **Precautions** • Moderate or severe acute illness. • Pregnancy.
Meningo-coccal conjugate (MCV) *Give IM* **polysaccharide (MPSV)** *Give SC*	• Give 1-time dose of MCV to adolescents age 11 through 18yrs. • Vaccinate all college freshmen living in dorms who have not been vaccinated. • Vaccinate all children age 2yrs and older who have any of the following risk factors (MCV is preferable to MPSV): – Anatomic or functional asplenia, or terminal complement component deficiency. – Travel to or reside in countries in which meningococcal disease is hyperendemic or epidemic (e.g., the "meningitis belt" of Sub-Saharan Africa).	If previously vaccinated with MPSV and risk continues, give MCV 5yrs after MPSV.	**Contraindication** Previous anaphylaxis to this vaccine or to any of its components, including diphtheria toxoid (for MCV). **Precautions** • Moderate or severe acute illness. • For MCV only: history of Guillain-Barré syndrome (GBS).

A

Summary of Recommendations for Adult Immunization

Vaccine name and route	For whom vaccination is recommended	Schedule for vaccine administration (any vaccine can be given with another)	Contraindications and precautions (mild illness is not a contraindication)
Influenza Trivalent inactivated influenza vaccine (TIV) *Give IM* Live attenuated influenza vaccine (LAIV) *Give intranasally*	• All persons who want to reduce the likelihood of becoming ill with influenza or of spreading it to others. • Persons age 50yrs and older. [TIV only] • Persons with medical problems (e.g., heart or lung disease, renal, hepatic, hematologic, or metabolic disorder [including diabetes], immunosuppression). [TIV only] • Persons with any condition that compromises respiratory function or the handling of respiratory secretions or that can increase the risk of aspiration (e.g., cognitive dysfunction, spinal cord injury, seizure disorder, or other neuromuscular disorder). [TIV only] • Persons living in chronic care facilities. [TIV only] • Persons who work or live with high-risk people. • Women who will be pregnant during the influenza season (December–spring). [If currently pregnant, TIV only] • All healthcare personnel and other persons who provide direct care to high-risk people. • Household contacts and out-of-home caregivers of children age 0–59m. • Travelers at risk for complications of influenza who go to areas where influenza activity exists or who may be among people from areas of the world where there is current influenza activity (e.g., on organized tours). [TIV only] • Students or other persons in institutional settings (e.g., residents of dormitories or correctional facilities). **Note:** LAIV may not be given to some of the persons listed to the left; see contraindications listed in far right column.	• Give 1 dose every year in the fall or winter. • Begin vaccination services as soon as vaccine is available and continue until the supply is depleted. • Continue to give vaccine to unvaccinated adults throughout the influenza season (including when influenza activity is present in the community) and at other times when the risk of influenza exists. • If 2 or more of the following live virus vaccines are to be given—LAIV, MMR, Var, and/or yellow fever vaccine—they should be given on the same day. If they are not, space them by at least 28d.	**Contraindications** • Previous anaphylactic reaction to this vaccine, to any of its components, or to eggs. • For LAIV only, age 50yrs or older, pregnancy, asthma, reactive airway disease or other chronic disorder of the pulmonary or cardiovascular system; an underlying medical condition, including metabolic disease such as diabetes, renal dysfunction, and hemoglobinopathy; a known or suspected immune deficiency disease or immunosuppressed state. **Precautions** • Moderate or severe acute illness. • History of Guillain-Barré syndrome (GBS) within 6wks of previous influenza vaccination.
Pneumococcal polysaccharide (PPSV) *Give IM or SC*	• Persons age 65yrs and older. • Persons who have chronic illness or other risk factors, including chronic cardiac or pulmonary disease, chronic liver disease, alcoholism, diabetes, CSF leaks, cigarette smoking, as well as people living in special environments or social settings (including Alaska Natives and certain American Indian populations age 50 through 64 years if recommended by local public health authorities). • Those at highest risk of fatal pneumococcal infection, including persons who - have anatomic asplenia, functional asplenia, or sickle cell disease - have an immunocompromising condition, including HIV infection, leukemia, lymphoma, Hodgkin's disease, multiple myeloma, generalized malignancy, chronic renal failure, or nephrotic syndrome - are receiving immunosuppressive chemotherapy (including corticosteroids) - have received an organ or bone marrow transplant - are candidates for or recipients of cochlear implants.	• Give 1 dose if unvaccinated or if previous vaccination history is unknown. • Give a 1-time revaccination at least 5yrs after 1st dose to persons - age 65yrs and older if the 1st dose was given prior to age 65yrs - at highest risk of fatal pneumococcal infection or rapid antibody loss (see the 3rd bullet in the box to left for listings of persons at highest risk)	**Contraindication** Previous anaphylactic reaction to this vaccine or to any of its components. **Precaution** Moderate or severe acute illness.
Zoster (shingles) (Zos) *Give SC*	• Persons age 60yrs and older.	• Give 1-time dose if unvaccinated, regardless of previous history of herpes zoster (shingles) or chickenpox.	**Contraindications** • Previous anaphylactic reaction to any component of zoster vaccine (e.g., gelatin & neomycin). • Primary cellular or acquired immunodeficiency. • Pregnancy. **Precaution** Moderate or severe acute illness.

*This document was adapted from the recommendations of the Advisory Committee on Immunization Practices (ACIP). To obtain copies of these recommendations, call the CDC-INFO Contact Center at (800) 232-4636; visit CDC's website at www.cdc.gov/vaccines/pubs/ACIP-list.htm; or visit the Immunization Action Coalition (IAC) website at www.immunize.org/acip. This table is revised periodically. Visit IAC's website at www.immunize.org/adultrules to make sure you have the most current version.

Technical content reviewed by the Centers for Disease Control and Prevention, November 2008.

Immunization Action Coalition • 1573 Selby Avenue • Saint Paul, MN 55104 • (651) 647-9009 • www.immunize.org • www.vaccineinformation.org • admin@immunize.org

www.immunize.org/catg.d/p2011.pdf • Item #P2011 (11/08)

Summary of Recommendations for Adult Immunization (continued)

Vaccine name and route	For whom vaccination is recommended	Schedule for vaccine administration (any vaccine can be given with another)	Contraindications and precautions (mild illness is not a contraindication)
Hepatitis B (HepB) *Give IM* Brands may be used interchangeably.	• All persons through age 18yrs. • All adults wishing to be protected from hepatitis B virus infection. • High-risk persons, including household contacts and sex partners of HBsAg-positive persons; injecting drug users; sexually active persons not in a long-term, mutually monogamous relationship; men who have sex with men; persons with HIV; persons seeking evaluation or treatment for an STD; patients receiving hemodialysis and patients with renal disease that may result in dialysis; healthcare personnel and public safety workers who are exposed to blood; clients and staff of institutions for the developmentally disabled; inmates of long-term correctional facilities; and certain international travelers. • Persons with chronic liver disease. **Note:** Provide serologic screening for immigrants from endemic areas. If patient is chronically infected, assure appropriate disease management. Screen sex partners and household members; give HepB at the same visit if not already vaccinated.	• Give 3 doses on a 0, 1, 6m schedule. • Alternative timing options for vaccination include 0, 2, 4m and 0, 1, 4m. • There must be at least 4wks between doses #1 and #2, and at least 8wks between doses #2 and #3. Overall, there must be at least 16wks between doses #1 and #3. • **Schedule for those who have fallen behind:** If the series is delayed between doses, DO NOT start the series over. Continue from where you left off. For Twinrix® (hepatitis A and B combination vaccine [GSK]) for patients age 18yrs and older only: give 3 doses on a 0, 1, 6m schedule. There must be at least 4wks between doses #1 and #2, and at least 5m between doses #2 and #3.	**Contraindication** Previous anaphylactic reaction to this vaccine or to any of its components. **Precaution** Moderate or severe acute illness.
Hepatitis A (HepA) *Give IM* Brands may be used interchangeably.	• All persons wishing to be protected from hepatitis A virus (HAV) infection. • Persons who travel or work anywhere EXCEPT the U.S., Western Europe, New Zealand, Australia, Canada, and Japan. • Persons with chronic liver disease; injecting and non-injecting drug users; men who have sex with men; people who receive clotting-factor concentrates; persons who work with HAV in experimental lab settings (not routine medical laboratories); persons who work with HAV in experimental lab settings (not routine medical laboratories); food handlers when health authorities or private employers determine vaccination to be appropriate. • Unvaccinated adults age 40yrs or younger with recent (within 2 wks) exposure to HAV. For persons older than age 40yrs with recent (within 2 wks) exposure to HAV, immune globulin is preferred over HepA vaccine.	An alternative schedule can also be used at 0, 7d, 21–30d, and a booster at 12m. • Give 2 doses. • The minimum interval between doses #1 and #2 is 6m. • If dose #2 is delayed, do not repeat dose #1. Just give dose #2.	**Contraindication** Previous anaphylactic reaction to this vaccine or to any of its components. **Precautions** • Moderate or severe acute illness. • Safety during pregnancy has not been determined, so benefits must be weighed against potential risk.
Td, Tdap (Tetanus, diphtheria, pertussis) *Give IM*	• All adults who lack written documentation of a primary series consisting of at least 3 doses of tetanus- and diphtheria-toxoid-containing vaccine. • A booster dose of tetanus- and diphtheria-toxoid-containing vaccine may be needed for wound management as early as 5yrs after receiving a previous dose, so consult ACIP recommendations.* • Using tetanus toxoid (TT) instead of Td or Tdap is not recommended. • In pregnancy, when indicated, give Td or Tdap in 2nd or 3rd trimester. If not administered during pregnancy, give Tdap in immediate postpartum period. **For Tdap only:** • All adults younger than age 65yrs who have not already received Tdap. • Adults in contact with infants younger than age 12m (e.g., parents, grandparents younger than age 65yrs, childcare providers, healthcare personnel) who have not received a dose of Tdap should be prioritized for vaccination. • Healthcare personnel who work in hospitals or ambulatory care settings and have direct patient contact and who have not received Tdap.	• For persons who are unvaccinated or behind, complete the primary series with Td (spaced at 0, 1–2m, 6–12m intervals). One-time dose of Tdap may be used for any dose if younger than age 65yrs. • Give Td booster every 10yrs after the primary series has been completed. For adults younger than age 65yrs, a 1-time dose of Tdap is recommended to replace the next Td. • Intervals of 2yrs or less between Td and Tdap may be used. **Note:** The two Tdap products are licensed for different age groups: Adacel™ (sanofi) for use in persons age 11–64yrs and Boostrix® (GSK) for use in persons age 10–18yrs.	**Contraindications** • Previous anaphylactic reaction to this vaccine or to any of its components. • For Tdap only, history of encephalopathy within 7d following DTP/DTaP. **Precautions** • Moderate or severe acute illness. • GBS within 6wks of receiving a previous dose of tetanus-toxoid-containing vaccine. • Unstable neurologic condition. • History of Arthus reaction following a previous dose of tetanus- and/or diphtheria-toxoid-containing vaccine, including MCV. **Note:** Use of Td/Tdap is not contraindicated in pregnancy. Either vaccine may be given during trimester #2 or #3 at the provider's discretion.
Polio (IPV) *Give IM or SC*	Not routinely recommended for U.S. residents age 18yrs and older. **Note:** Adults living in the U.S. who never received or completed a primary series of polio vaccine need not be vaccinated unless they intend to travel to areas where exposure to wild-type virus is likely (i.e., India, Pakistan, Afghanistan, and Nigeria). Previously vaccinated adults can receive 1 booster dose if traveling to polio endemic areas.	• Refer to ACIP recommendations* regarding unique situations, schedules, and dosing information.	**Contraindication** Previous anaphylactic or neurologic reaction to this vaccine or to any of its components. **Precautions** • Moderate or severe acute illness. • Pregnancy.

Summary of Recommendations for Adult Immunization (continued) (Page 3 of 3)

Vaccine name and route	For whom vaccination is recommended	Schedule for vaccine administration (any vaccine can be given with another)	Contraindications and precautions (mild illness is not a contraindication)
Varicella (Var) (Chickenpox) *Give SC*	• All adults without evidence of immunity. **Note:** Evidence of immunity is defined as written documentation of 2 doses of varicella vaccine; a history of varicella disease or herpes zoster (shingles) based on healthcare-provider diagnosis; laboratory evidence of immunity; laboratory confirmation of disease; and/or birth in the U.S. before 1980, with the exceptions that follow. Healthcare personnel (HCP) and pregnant women born in the U.S. before 1980 who do not meet any of the criteria above should be tested. If they are not immune, give the first dose of varicella vaccine immediately (HCP) or postpartum and before hospital discharge (pregnant women). Give the second dose 4–8 wks later. Routine post-vaccination testing is not recommended.	• Give 2 doses. • Dose #2 is given 4–8wks after dose #1. • If the second dose is delayed, do not repeat dose #1. Just give dose #2. • If 2 or more of the following live virus vaccines are to be given—LAIV, MMR, Var, and/or yellow fever vaccine—they should be given on the same day. If they are not, space them by at least 28d. • May use as postexposure prophylaxis if given within 5d.	**Contraindications** • Previous anaphylactic reaction to this vaccine or to any of its components. • Pregnancy or possibility of pregnancy within 4wks. • Persons on high-dose immunosuppressive therapy or who are immunocompromised because of malignancy and primary or acquired cellular immunodeficiency, including HIV/AIDS (although vaccination may be considered if CD4+ T-lymphocyte counts are greater than or equal to 200 cells/µL. See *MMWR* 2007;56,RR-4). **Precautions** • Moderate or severe acute illness. • If blood, plasma, and/or immune globulin (IG or VZIG) were given in past 11m, see ACIP statement *General Recommendations on Immunization** regarding time to wait before vaccinating.
Meningococcal Conjugate vaccine (MCV) *Give IM* Polysaccharide vaccine (MPSV) *Give SC*	• All persons age 11 through 18yrs. • College freshmen living in a dormitory. • Persons with anatomic or functional asplenia or with a terminal-complement component deficiency. • Persons who travel to or reside in countries in which meningococcal disease is hyperendemic or epidemic (e.g., the "meningitis belt" of Sub-Saharan Africa). • Microbiologists routinely exposed to isolates of *N. meningitidis*.	• Give 1 dose. • If previous vaccine was MPSV, revaccinate after 3yrs if risk continues. • Revaccination after MCV is not recommended. • MCV is preferred over MPSV for persons age 55yrs and younger, although MPSV is an acceptable alternative.	**Contraindication** Previous anaphylactic or neurologic reaction to this vaccine or to any of its components, including diphtheria toxoid (for MCV). **Precautions** • Moderate or severe acute illness. • For MCV only, history of Guillain-Barré syndrome (GBS).
MMR (Measles, mumps, rubella) *Give SC*	• Persons born in 1957 or later (especially those born outside the U.S.) should receive at least 1 dose of MMR if there is no serologic proof of immunity or documentation of a dose given on or after the first birthday. • Persons in high-risk groups, such as healthcare personnel (paid, unpaid, or volunteer), students entering college and other post–high school educational institutions, and international travelers, should receive a total of 2 doses. • Persons born before 1957 are usually considered immune, but proof of immunity (serology or vaccination) may be desirable for healthcare personnel. • Women of childbearing age who do not have acceptable evidence of rubella immunity or vaccination.	• Give 1 or 2 doses (see criteria in 1st and 2nd bullets in box to left). • If dose #2 is recommended, give it no sooner than 4wks after dose #1. • If a pregnant woman is found to be rubella susceptible, give 1 dose of MMR postpartum. • If 2 or more of the following live virus vaccines are to be given—LAIV, MMR, Var, and/or yellow fever vaccine—they should be given on the same day. If they are not, space them by at least 28d. • Within 72hrs of measles exposure, give 1 dose as postexposure prophylaxis to susceptible adults.	**Contraindications** • Previous anaphylactic reaction to this vaccine or to any of its components. • Pregnancy or possibility of pregnancy within 4wks. • Severe immunodeficiency (e.g., hematologic and solid tumors; receiving chemotherapy; congenital immunodeficiency; long-term immunosuppressive therapy; or severely symptomatic HIV). **Note:** HIV infection is NOT a contraindication to MMR for those who are not severely immunocompromised (i.e., CD4+ T-lymphocyte counts greater than or equal to 200 cells/µL). **Precautions** • Moderate or severe acute illness. • If blood, plasma, and/or immune globulin were given in past 11m, see ACIP statement *General Recommendations on Immunization** regarding time to wait before vaccinating. **Note:** History of thrombocytopenia or thrombocytopenic purpura. **Note:** If TST (tuberculosis skin test) and MMR are both needed but not given on same day, delay TST for 4–6wks after MMR.
Human papillomavirus (HPV) *Give IM*	All previously unvaccinated women through age 26yrs.	• Give 3 doses on a 0, 2, 6m schedule. • There must be at least 4wks between doses #1 and #2 and at least 12wks between doses #2 and #3. Overall, there must be at least 24wks between doses #1 and #3.	**Contraindication** Previous anaphylactic reaction to this vaccine or to any of its components. **Precautions** • Moderate or severe acute illness. • Data on vaccination in pregnancy are limited. Vaccination should be delayed until after completion of the pregnancy.

Suggested intervals between administration of immune globulin preparations and measles- or varicella-containing vaccine

Product / Indication	Dose, including mg immunoglobulin G (IgG)/kg body weight	Recommended interval before measles or varicella-containing[1] vaccine administration
RSV monoclonal antibody (Synagis™)[2]	15 mg/kg intramuscularly (IM)	None
Tetanus IG (TIG)	250 units (10 mg IgG/kg) IM	3 months
Hepatitis A IG		
Contact prophylaxis	0.02 mL/kg (3.3 mg IgG/kg) IM	3 months
International travel	0.06 mL/kg (10 mg IgG/kg) IM	3 months
Hepatitis B IG (HBIG)	0.06 mL/kg (10 mg IgG/kg) IM	3 months
Rabies IG (RIG)	20 IU/kg (22 mg IgG/kg) IM	4 months
Measles prophylaxis IG		
Standard (i.e., nonimmunocompromised) contact	0.25 mL/kg (40 mg IgG/kg) IM	5 months
Immunocompromised contact	0.50 mL/kg (80 mg IgG/kg) IM	6 months
Blood tranfusion		
Red blood cells (RBCs), washed	10 mL/kg negligible IgG/kg intravenously (IV)	None
RBCs, adenine-saline added	10 mL/kg (10 mg IgG/kg) IV	3 months
Packed RBCs (Hct 65%)[3]	10 mL/kg (60 mg IgG/kg) IV	6 months
Whole blood (Hct 35%–50%)[3]	10 mL/kg (80-100 mg IgG/kg) IV	6 months
Plasma/platelet products	10 mL/kg (160 mg IgG/kg) IV	7 months
Cytomegalovirus intravenous immune globulin (IGIV)	150 mg/kg maximum	6 months
IGIV		
Replacement therapy for immune deficiencies[4]	300-400 mg/kg IV[5]	8 months
Immune thrombocytopenic purpura	400 mg/kg IV	8 months
Immune thrombocytopenic purpura	1000 mg/kg IV	10 months
Postexposure varicella prophylaxis[5]	400 mg/kg IV	8 months
Kawasaki disease	2 g/kg IV	11 months

This table is not intended for determining the correct indications and dosages for using antibody-containing products. Unvaccinated persons might not be fully protected against measles during the entire recommended interval, and additional doses of immune globulin or measles vaccine might be indicated after measles exposure. Concentrations of measles antibody in an immune globulin preparation can vary by manufacturer's lot. Rates of antibody clearance after receipt of an immune globulin preparation also might vary. Recommended intervals are extrapolated from an estimated half-life of 30 days for passively acquired antibody and an observed interference with the immune response to measles vaccine for 5 months after a dose of 80 mg IgG/kg.

1 "Varicella-containing vaccine," as used here, does not include zoster vaccine. Zoster vaccine may be given with antibody-containing blood products.

2 Contains antibody only to respiratory syncytial virus.

3 Assumes a serum IgG concentration of 16 mg/mL.

4 Measles and varicella vaccinations are recommended for children with asymptomatic or mildly symptomatic human immunodeficiency virus (HIV) infection but are contraindicated for persons with severe immunosuppression from HIV or any other immunosuppressive disorder.

5 The investigational product VariZIG, similar to licensed VZIG, is a purified human immune globulin preparation made from plasma containing high levels of anti-varicella antibodies (immunoglobulin class G [IgG]). When indicated, health-care providers should make every effort to obtain and administer VariZIG. In situations in which administration of VariZIG does not appear possible within 96 hours of exposure, administration of immune globulin intravenous (IGIV) should be considered as an alternative. IGIV also should be administered within 96 hours of exposure. Although licensed IGIV preparations are known to contain anti-varicella antibody titers, the titer of any specific lot of IGIV that might be available is uncertain because IGIV is not routinely tested for antivaricella antibodies. The recommended IGIV dose for postexposure prophylaxis of varicella is 400 mg/kg, administered once. For a pregnant woman who cannot receive VariZIG within 96 hours of exposure, clinicians can choose either to administer IGIV or closely monitor the woman for signs and symptoms of varicella and institute treatment with acyclovir if illness occurs. (CDC. A new product for postexposure prophylaxis available under an investigational new drug application expanded access protocol. *MMWR* 2006;55:209-10.)

Healthcare Personnel Vaccination Recommendations

Vaccine	Recommendations in brief
Hepatitis B	Give 3-dose series (dose #1 now, #2 in 1 month, #3 approximately 5 months after #2). Give IM. Obtain anti-HBs serologic testing 1–2 months after dose #3.
Influenza	Give 1 dose of TIV or LAIV annually. Give TIV intramuscularly or LAIV intranasally.
MMR	For healthcare personnel (HCP) born in 1957 or later without serologic evidence of immunity or prior vaccination, give 2 doses of MMR, 4 weeks apart. For HCP born prior to 1957, see below. Give SC.
Varicella (chickenpox)	For HCP who have no serologic proof of immunity, prior vaccination, or history of varicella disease, give 2 doses of varicella vaccine, 4 weeks apart. Give SC.
Tetanus, diphtheria, pertussis	Give all HCP a Td booster dose every 10 years, following the completion of the primary 3-dose series. Give a 1-time dose of Tdap to all HCP younger than age 65 years with direct patient contact. Give IM.
Meningococcal	Give 1 dose to microbiologists who are routinely exposed to isolates of *N. meningitidis*.

Hepatitis A, typhoid, and polio vaccines are not routinely recommended for HCP who may have on-the-job exposure to fecal material.

Hepatitis B

Healthcare personnel (HCP) who perform tasks that may involve exposure to blood or body fluids should receive a 3-dose series of hepatitis B vaccine at 0-, 1-, and 6-month intervals. Test for hepatitis B surface antibody (anti-HBs) to document immunity 1–2 months after dose #3.

- If anti-HBs is at least 10 mIU/mL (positive), the patient is immune. No further serologic testing or vaccination is recommended.
- If anti-HBs is less than 10 mIU/mL (negative), the patient is unprotected from hepatitis B virus (HBV) infection; revaccinate with a 3-dose series. Retest anti-HBs 1–2 months after dose #3.
  - If anti-HBs is positive, the patient is immune. No further testing or vaccination is recommended.
  - If anti-HBs is negative following 6 doses of vaccine, the patient is a non-responder.

For non-responders: HCP who are non-responders should be considered susceptible to HBV and should be counseled regarding precautions to prevent HBV infection and the need to obtain HBIG prophylaxis for any known or probable parenteral exposure to hepatitis B surface antigen (HBsAg)-positive blood.[1] It is also possible that non-responders are persons who are HBsAg positive. Testing should be considered. HCP found to be HBsAg positive should be counseled and medically evaluated.

Note: Anti-HBs testing is not recommended routinely for previously vaccinated HCP who were not tested 1–2 months after their original vaccine series. These HCP should be tested for anti-HBs when they have an exposure to blood or body fluids. If found to be anti-HBs negative, the HCP should be treated as if susceptible.[1]

Influenza

Trivalent (Inactivated) Influenza Vaccine (TIV): May give to any HCP.
Live, Attenuated Influenza Vaccine (LAIV): May give to any non-pregnant healthy HCP age 49 years and younger.

1. All HCP should receive annual influenza vaccine. Groups that should be targeted include all personnel (including volunteers) in hospitals, outpatient, and home-health settings who have any patient contact.
2. TIV is preferred over LAIV for HCP who are in close contact with severely immunosuppressed persons (e.g., stem cell transplant patients) when patients require a protective environment.

Measles, Mumps, Rubella (MMR)

HCP who work in medical facilities should be immune to measles, mumps, and rubella.

- HCP born in 1957 or later can be considered immune to measles, mumps, or rubella only if they have documentation of (a) physician-diagnosed measles or mumps disease; or (b) laboratory evidence of measles, mumps, or rubella immunity (HCP who have an "indeterminate" or "equivocal" level of immunity upon testing should be considered nonimmune); or (c) appropriate vaccination against measles, mumps, and rubella (i.e., administration on or after the first birthday of two doses of live measles and mumps vaccines separated by 28 days or more, and at least one dose of live rubella vaccine).
- Although birth before 1957 generally is considered acceptable evidence of measles, mumps, and rubella immunity, healthcare facilities should consider recommending a dose of MMR vaccine (two doses during a mumps outbreak) to unvaccinated HCP born before 1957 who are in either of the following categories: (a) do not have a history of physician-diagnosed measles and mumps disease or laboratory evidence of measles and mumps immunity and (b) do not have laboratory evidence of rubella immunity.

Varicella

It is recommended that all HCP be immune to varicella. Evidence of immunity in HCP includes documentation of 2 doses of varicella vaccine given at least 28 days apart, history of varicella or herpes zoster based on physician diagnosis, laboratory evidence of immunity, or laboratory confirmation of disease.

Tetanus/Diphtheria/Pertussis (Td/Tdap)

All adults who have completed a primary series of a tetanus/diphtheria-containing product (DTP, DTaP, DT, Td) should receive Td boosters every 10 years. As soon as feasible, HCP younger than age 65 years with direct patient contact should be given a 1-time dose of Tdap, with priority given to those having contact with infants younger than age 12 months.

Meningococcal

Vaccination is recommended for microbiologists who are routinely exposed to isolates of *N. meningitidis*. Use of MCV4 is preferred for persons younger than age 56 years; give IM. If MCV4 is unavailable, MPSV is an acceptable alternative for HCP younger than age 56 years. Use of MPSV is recommended for HCP older than age 55; give SC.

References
1. See Table 3 in "Updated U.S. Public Health Service Guidelines for the Management of Occupational Exposures to HBV, HCV, and HIV and Recommendations for Postexposure Prophylaxis," *MMWR*, June 29, 2001, Vol. 50, RR-11.

For additional specific ACIP recommendations, refer to the official ACIP statements published in *MMWR*. To obtain copies, visit CDC's website at www.cdc.gov/vaccines/pubs/ACIP-list.htm; or visit the Immunization Action Coalition (IAC) website at www.immunize.org/acip.

Adapted with thanks from the Michigan Department of Community Health

Technical content reviewed by the Centers for Disease Control and Prevention, July 2008.

www.immunize.org/catg.d/p2017.pdf • Item #P2017 (7/08)

Immunization Action Coalition • 1573 Selby Ave. • St. Paul, MN 55104 • (651) 647-9009 • www.immunize.org • www.vaccineinformation.org

A-17

Vaccination of Persons with Primary and Secondary Immune Deficiencies

PRIMARY

Category	Specific Immunodeficiency	Contraindicated Vaccines[1]	Risk-Specific Recommended Vaccines[1]	Effectiveness & Comments
B-lymphocyte (humoral)	Severe antibody deficiencies (e.g., X-linked agammaglobulinemia and common variable immunodeficiency)	OPV[2] Smallpox LAIV BCG Ty21a (live oral typhoid) Yellow Fever	Pneumococcal Influenza (TIV) Consider measles and varicella vaccination.	The effectiveness of any vaccine will be uncertain if it depends only on the humoral response; IGIV interferes with the immune response to measles vaccine and possibly varicella vaccine.
	Less severe antibody deficiencies (e.g., selective IgA deficiency and IgG subclass deficiency)	OPV[2] BCG Ty21a (live oral typhoid) Other live vaccines appear to be safe.	Pneumococcal Influenza (TIV)	All vaccines probably effective. Immune response may be attenuated.
T-lymphocyte (cell-mediated and humoral)	Complete defects (e.g., severe combined immunodeficiency [SCID] disease, complete DiGeorge syndrome)	All live vaccines [3,4]	Pneumococcal Influenza (TIV)	Vaccines may be ineffective.
	Partial defects (e.g., most patients with DiGeorge syndrome, Wiskott-Aldrich syndrome, ataxia-telangiectasia)	All live vaccines [3,4]	Pneumococcal Meningococcal Hib (if not administered in infancy) Influenza (TIV)	Effectiveness of any vaccine depends on degree of immune suppression.
Complement	Deficiency of early components (C1-C4), late components (C5-C9), properdin, factor B.	None	Pneumococcal Meningococcal Influenza (TIV)	All routine vaccines probably effective.
Phagocytic function	Chronic granulomatous disease, leukocyte adhesion defects, and myeloperoxidase deficiency.	Live bacterial vaccines[3]	Pneumococcal[5] Influenza (TIV) (to decrease secondary bacterial infection).	All inactivated vaccines safe and probably effective. Live viral vaccines probably safe and effective.

[1] Other vaccines that are not specifically contraindicated may be used if otherwise indicated.
[2] OPV is no longer licensed in the United States, and therefore is not recommended for routine use.
[3] Live bacterial vaccines: BCG, and Ty21a Salmonella typhi vaccine.
[4] Live viral vaccines: MMR, OPV, LAIV, yellow fever, varicella (including MMRV and zoster vaccine), and vaccinia (smallpox). Smallpox vaccine is not recommended for children or the general public.
[5] Pneumococcal vaccine is not indicated for children with chronic granulomatous disease.

Vaccination of Persons with Primary and Secondary Immune Deficiencies

Specific Immunodeficiency	SECONDARY		
	Contraindicated Vaccines[1]	Recommended Vaccines[1]	Effectiveness & Comments
HIV/AIDS	OPV[2] Smallpox BCG LAIV Withhold MMR and varicella in severely immunocompromised persons.	Influenza (TIV) Pneumococcal Consider Hib (if not administered in infancy) and Meningococcal vaccination.	MMR, varicella, and all inactivated vaccines, including inactivated influenza, might be effective.[3]
Malignant neoplasm, transplantation, immunosuppressive or radiation therapy	Live viral and bacterial, depending on immune status.[4,5]	Influenza (TIV) Pneumococcal	Effectiveness of any vaccine depends on degree of immune suppression.
Asplenia	None	Pneumococcal Meningococcal Hib (if not administered in infancy)	All routine vaccines probably effective.
Chronic renal disease	LAIV	Pneumococcal Influenza (TIV) Hepatitis B	All routine vaccines probably effective.

[1] Other vaccines that are not specifically contraindicated may be used if otherwise indicated.
[2] OPV is no longer licensed in the United States, and therefore is not recommended for routine use.
[3] HIV-infected children should receive IG after exposure to measles, and may receive varicella and measles vaccine if CD4+ lymphocyte count is ≥15%.
[4] Live viral vaccines: MMR, OPV, LAIV, yellow fever, varicella (including MMRV and zoster vaccine), and vaccinia (smallpox). Smallpox vaccine is not recommended for children or the general public.
[5] Live bacterial vaccines: BCG, and Ty21a *Salmonella typhi* vaccine.

AIDS: Acquired Immunodeficiency Syndrome
BCG: Bacilli Calmette-Guerin vaccine
Hib: *Haemophilus influenzae* type b vaccine
HIV: Human Immunodeficiency Virus
IGIV: Immune Globulin Intravenous

IG: Immunoglobulin
LAIV: Live, Attenuated Influenza Vaccine
MMR: Measles, Mumps, Rubella vaccine
OPV: Oral Poliovirus Vaccine (live)
TIV: Trivalent (inactivated) Influenza Vaccine

Modified from American Academy of Pediatrics. Passive Immunization. In: Pickering LK, Baker C, Long S, McMillen J, ed. *Red Book: 2006 Report of the Committee on Infectious Diseases.* 27th ed. Elk Grove Village, IL: American Academy of Pediatrics; 2006: [71-72] and CDC. General Recommendations on Immunization: Recommendations of the Advisory Committee on Immunization Practices (ACIP). *MMWR* 2006: 55 (No. RR-15).

APPENDIX B
Vaccines

Appendix B

B

U.S. Vaccines

Vaccine	Trade Name	Abbreviation	Manufacturer	Type	Route	Comments
Anthrax	BioThrax	AVA	BioPort	Inactivated Bacterial	IM	
DTaP	Daptacel	DTaP	sanofi	Inactivated Bacterial	IM	Tetanus & diphtheria toxoids and pertussis vaccine. Not licensed for 5th dose.
	Infanrix	DTaP	GlaxoSmithKline	Inactivated Bacterial	IM	Tetanus & diphtheria toxoids and pertussis vaccine.
	Tripedia	DTaP	sanofi	Inactivated Bacterial	IM	Tetanus & diphtheria toxoids and pertussis vaccine.
Diphtheria - Tetanus	(Generic)	DT	sanofi	Inactivated Bacterial Toxoids	IM	Pediatric formulation
DTaP/Hib	TriHIBit	DTaP/Hib	sanofi	Inactivated Bacterial	IM	ActHIB reconstituted with Tripedia. Licensed for 4th dose of DTaP & Hib series (not primary series).
DTaP-IPV	Kinrix	DTaP-IPV	GlaxoSmithKline	Inactivated Bacterial & Viral	IM	Licensed for 5th (DTaP) and 4th (IPV) booster at 4-6 years
DTaP-HepB-IPV	Pediarix	DTaP-HepB-IPV	GlaxoSmithKline	Inactivated Bacterial & Viral	IM	Licensed for doses at 2, 4, 6 months (through 6 years of age). Not licensed for boosters.
DTaP-IPV/Hib	Pentacel	DTaP-IPV/Hib	sanofi	Inactivated Bacterial & Viral	IM	Licensed for 4 doses at 2, 4, 6, and 15-18 months.
Haemophilus influenzae type b (Hib)	PedvaxHIB	Hib	Merck	Inactivated Bacterial	IM	PRP-OMP. Polysaccharide conjugate (mening. protein carrier). 2-dose schedule.
	ActHIB	Hib	sanofi	Inactivated Bacterial	IM	PRP-T. Polysaccharide conjugate (tetanus toxoid carrier). 3-dose schedule.
Haemophilus influenzae type b - Hepatitis B	Comvax	Hib-HepB	Merck	Inactivated Bacterial & Viral	IM	Should not be used for HepB birth dose.

B

Vaccine	Trade Name	Abbreviation	Manufacturer	Type	Route	Comments
Hepatitis A	Havrix	HepA	GlaxoSmithKline	Inactivated Viral	IM	Pediatric (≤18) and adult formulations. Pediatric = 720 EL.U., 0.5mL Adult = 1,140 EL.U., 1.0mL Minimum age = 1 year.
	Vaqta	HepA	Merck	Inactivated Viral	IM	Pediatric (≤18) and adult formulations. Pediatric = 25 U, 0.5mL Adult = 50 U, 1.0mL Minimum age = 1 year.
Hepatitis B	Engerix-B	HepB	GlaxoSmithKline	Inactivated Viral	IM	Pediatric (≤19) and adult formulations. Pediatric formulation is not licensed for adults.
	Recombivax HB	HepB	Merck	Inactivated Viral	IM	Pediatric (≤19), adult, and dialysis formulations. Two pediatric doses may be substituted for an adult dose.
Hepatitis A - Hepatitis B	Twinrix	HepA-HepB	GlaxoSmithKline	Inactivated Viral	IM	Pediatric dose of HepA + adult dose of HepB. Minimum age = 18 years. 3-dose series.
Herpes Zoster (Shingles)	Zostavax	ZOS	Merck	Live Viral	SC	Licensed for age 60 and older.
Human Papillomavirus (HPV)	Gardasil	HPV4	Merck	Inactivated Viral	IM	Quadrivalent, Types 6, 11, 16 & 18. Licensed for females 9-26 years.
	Cervarix	HPV2	GlaxoSmithKline	Inactivated viral	IM	Bivalent, Types 16 & 18. **NOT YET LICENSED IN U.S.**

Vaccine	Trade Name	Abbreviation	Manufacturer	Type	Route	Comments
	Fluarix	TIV	GlaxoSmithKline	Inactivated Viral	IM	Trivalent Types A & B. Minimum age = 18 years.
	Fluvirin	TIV	Chiron	Inactivated Viral	IM	Trivalent Types A & B Purified surface antigen. Minimum age = 4 years.
Influenza	Fluzone	TIV	sanofi	Inactivated Viral	IM	Trivalent Types A & B Subvirion. Minimum age multidose vial = 6 months. Age range 0.25ml prefilled syringe = 6-35 months. Minimum age 0.5ml prefilled syringe = 3 years.
	FluLaval	TIV	GlaxoSmithKline	Inactivated Viral	IM	Trivalent Types A & B Minimum age = 18 years.
	Afluria	TIV	CSL	Inactivated Viral	IM	Trivalent Types A & B Minimum age = 18 years.
	FluMist	LAIV	Medimmune	Live attenuated viral	Intra-nasal	Trivalent Types A & B. Age range 5-49 years.
Japanese Encephalitis	JE-Vax	JE	sanofi	Inactivated viral	SC	
	Ixiaro	JE	Novartis	Inactivated viral	IM	Licensed for age 17 and older.
MMR	M-M-R II	MMR	Merck	Live attenuated viral	SC	Measles, mumps, rubella.
MMRV	ProQuad	MMRV	Merck	Live attenuated viral	SC	Measles, mumps, rubella, varicella.
Meningococcal	Menomune	MPSV4	sanofi	Inactivated bacterial	SC	Polysaccharide, containing serogroups A, C, Y, & W-135.
	Menactra	MCV4	sanofi	Inactivated bacterial	IM	Polysaccharide conjugate (diphtheria toxoid carrier), containing serogroups A, C, Y, & W-135. Age range 2-49.

B

Vaccine	Trade Name	Abbreviation	Manufacturer	Type	Route	Comments
Pneumococcal	Pneumovax 23	PPSV23	Merck	Inactivated bacterial	SC or IM	Polysaccharide. Contains 23 strains. Minimum age = 2 yrs.
	Prevnar	PCV7	Wyeth	Inactivated bacterial, conjugate	IM	Polysaccharide conjugate (diphtheria protein carrier). Contains 7 strains. Routine age range = 2-59 months.
	PCV13	PCV13	Wyeth	Inactivated bacterial, conjugate	IM	Polysaccharide conjugate (diphtheria protein carrier). Contains 13 strains. **NOT YET LICENSED IN U.S.**
Polio	Ipol	IPV	sanofi	Inactivated viral	SC or IM	Trivalent, Types 1, 2, & 3.
Rabies	Imovax Rabies		sanofi	Inactivated viral	IM	
	RabAvert		Chiron	Inactivated viral	IM	
Rotavirus	RotaTeq	RV5	Merck	Live viral	Oral	Pentavalent. First dose between 6 weeks and 14 weeks 6 days; complete 3-dose series by 8 months 0 days.
	Rotarix	RV1	GlaxoSmithKline	Live viral	Oral	Monovalent. First dose between 6 weeks and 14 weeks 6 days; complete 2-dose series by 8 months 0 days.
Tetanus - (reduced) diphtheria	Decavac	Td	sanofi	Inactivated bacterial toxoids	IM	Tetanus/diphtheria toxoids. Adult formulation
	(Generic)	Td	Massachusetts Biological Labs	Inactivated bacterial toxoids	IM	Tetanus/diphtheria toxoids. Adult formulation
Tdap	Boostrix	Tdap	GlaxoSmithKline	Inactivated bacterial	IM	Tetanus & diphtheria toxoids & pertussis vaccine. Licensed for ages 10-64.
	Adacel	Tdap	sanofi	Inactivated bacterial	IM	Tetanus & diphtheria toxoids & pertussis vaccine. Licensed for ages 11-64.

Vaccine	Trade Name	Abbreviation	Manufacturer	Type	Route	Comments
Tetanus Toxoid	(Generic)	TT	sanofi	Inactivated bacterial toxoid	IM	Tetanus toxoid. May be used for adults or children.
Typhoid	Typhim Vi		sanofi	Inactivated bacterial	IM	Polysaccharide.
	Vivotif Berna		Berna	Live bacterial	Oral	Ty21a strain.
Varicella	Varivax	VAR	Merck	Live viral	SC	
Vaccinia (Smallpox)	ACAM2000		Acambis	Live Viral	Percu-taneous	
Yellow Fever	YF-Vax	YF	sanofi	Live viral	SC	
Zoster				(See Herpes Zoster)		

April 2009

Selected *Discontinued* U.S. Vaccines

Trade Name	Antigen(s)	Years
Acel-Imune	DTaP	1991-2001
Attenuvax-Smallpox	Measles-Smallpox	1967
b-CAPSA-1	Hib (polysaccharide)	1985-89
Biavax	Rubella-Mumps (live)	
BioRab	Rabies	1988-2007
Cendevax	Rubella (live)	1969-79
Certiva	DTaP	1998-2000
Dip-Pert-Tet	DTP	
Diptussis	Diphtheria/Pertussis	1949-55
Dryvax	Vaccinia	1944-2008
Ecolarix	Measles-Rubella (live)	
Flu Shield	Influenza	
Fluogen	Influenza	
Heptavax-B	Hepatitis B (plasma derived)	1981-90
HIB-Immune	Hib (polysaccharide)	1985-89
HibTITER	Hib (conjugate)	1990-2007
HIB-Vax	Hib (polysaccharide)	1985-89
Liovax	Smallpox	
Lirubel	Measles-Rubella (live)	1974-78
Lirugen	Measles (live)	1965-76
Lymerix	Lyme disease	1998-2002
M-Vac	Measles	1963-79
M-M-Vax	Measles-Mumps (live)	1973
Meningovax	Meningococcal	
Mevilin-L	Measles (live)	
MOPV	Polio (live, oral -monovalent, types I, II, & III)	
Mumpsvax	Mumps (live)	

Trade Name	Antigen(s)	Years
OmniHIB	Hib (conjugate)	
Orimune	Polio (live, oral)	1961-2000
Perdipigen	Diphtheria/Pertussis	1949-55
Pfizer-Vax Measles-K	Measles (inactivated)	1963-68
Pfizer-Vax Measles-L	Measles (live)	1965-70
Pnu-Imune	Pneumococcal (polysaccharide 14- or 23-valent)	1977-83
Poliovax	Polio (inactivated)	1988-91
ProHIBIT	Hib (conjugate)	1987-2000
Purivax	Polio (inactivated)	1956-65
Quadrigen	DTP-Polio	1959-68
Rabies Iradogen	Rabies	1908-57
RotaShield	Rotavirus	1998-99
Rubelogen	Rubella (live)	1969-72
Rubeovax	Measles (live)	1963-71
Serobacterin	Pertussis	1945-54
Solgen	DTP	1962-77
Tetra-Solgen	DTP-Polio	1959-68
Tetramune	DTP-Hib	
Tetravax	DTP-Polio	1959-65
Topagen	Pertussis (intranasal)	
Tri-Immunol	DTP	
Tridipigen	DTP	
Trinfagen No. 1	DT-Polio	Early 1960s
Trinivac	DTP	1952-64
Trivivac	DTP	
Wyvac	Rabies	1982-85

February 2008

Vaccine Excipient & Media Summary

This section begins with a summary of the excipients included in licensed vaccines in the United States, as of the revision date at the bottom of the page.

Excipients are inactive ingredients of a drug product necessary for production of a finished pharmaceutical formulation.

After the list of excipients is a list of culture media used in the manufacturing process of vaccines licensed in the United States.

Growth media are culture materials used to produce mass quantities of a microorganism antibody, or other immunologic agent, suitable for further processing into a finished pharmaceutical product.

All reasonable efforts have been made to ensure the accuracy of this information, but manufacturers may change product contents before that information is reflected here.

Excipients Included in US Licensed Vaccines[a]		
Excipient	Use	Vaccine
Albumin, egg (Ovalbumin)	Growth medium	Influenza (*Fluarix, FluLaval*), Rabies (*RabAvert*)
Albumin, human serum	Component of growth medium, protein stabilizer	Measles (*Attenuvax*), MMR (*MMR-II*), MMRV (*ProQuad*), Mumps (*Mumpsvax*), Rabies (*Imovax*), Rubella (*Meruvax II*)
Albumin or serum, bovine	Component of growth medium, protein stabilizer	Hepatitis A (*Havrix, Vaqta*), Measles (*Attenuvax*), MMR (*MMR-II*), MMRV (*ProQuad*), Mumps (*Mumpsvax*), Rabies (*Imovax, RabAvert*), Rotavirus (*RotaTeq*), Rubella (*Meruvax II*), Vaccinia (*Dryvax*), Varicella (*Varivax*)
Aluminum hydroxide	Adjuvant	Anthrax (*BioThrax*), DTaP (*Infanrix*), DTaP-Hep B-IPV (*Pediarix*), Td (Massachusetts), Hepatitis A (*Havrix*), Hepatitis A-Hepatitis B (*Twinrix*), Hepatitis B (*Engerix-B*), Tdap (*Boostrix*)
Aluminum hydroxyphosphate sulfate	Adjuvant	Hib (*PedvaxHIB*, Hib-Hepatitis B (*Comvax*), Hepatitis A (*Vaqta*), Hepatitis B (*Recombivax HB*), Human papillomavirus (*Gardasil*)
Aluminum phosphate	Adjuvant	DTaP (*Daptacel*), Hepatitis A-Hepatitis B (*Twinrix*), Pneumococcal (*Prevnar*), Rabies (*BioRab*), Td (*Decavac*), Td (Massachusetts), Tdap (*Adacel*)
Aluminum potassium sulfate	Adjuvant	DTaP (*Daptacel, Tripedia*), DTaP-Hib (*TriHIBit*), DT (Sanofi Pasteur)
Amino acids	Component of growth medium	Anthrax (*BioThrax*), Hepatitis A (*Havrix*), Hepatitis A-Hepatitis B (*Twinrix*), Rotavirus (*Rotarix*), Td (Aventis Pasteur), Typhoid oral (*Vivotif*)
Ammonium sulfate	Protein fractionation	DTaP-Hib (*TriHIBit*), Hib (*Act-HIB*)
Amphotericin B	Antibacterial	Rabies (*RabAvert*)
Ascorbic acid	Antioxidant	Typhoid oral (*Vivotif*)

Vaccine Excipient & Media Summary

Excipients Included in US Licensed Vaccines[a]		
Excipient	Use	Vaccine
Bactopeptone	Component of growth medium	Influenza (varies seasonally)
Beta-propiolactone	Viral inactivator	Influenza (*Fluvirin*), Rabies (*Imovax, RabAvert*)
Benzethonium chloride	Preservative	Anthrax (*BioThrax*)
Brilliant green	Dye	Vaccinia (*Dryvax-historic*)
Calcium carbonate	Antacid	Rotavirus (*Rotarix*)
Calcium chloride	Medium nutrient	Rotavirus (*Rotarix*)
Chlortetracycline	Antibacterial	Rabies (*RabAvert*), Vaccinia (*Dryvax*)
Cystine	Medium nutrient	Rotavirus (*Rotarix*)
Dextran	Medium nutrient	Rotavirus (*Rotarix*)
DNA	Manufacturing residue	Hepatitis A (*Vaqta*)
Dulbecco's Modified Eagle Medium (DMEM)	Growth medium	Rotavirus (*Rotarix*)
Ethylenediamine-tetraacetic acid sodium (EDTA)	Preservative	Rabies (*RabAvert*), Varicella (*Varivax*)
Egg protein	Manufacturing residue	Influenza (all brands), Yellow fever (*YF-Vax*)
Ferric (III) nitrate	Medium nutrient	Rotavirus (*Rotarix*)
Formaldehyde, formalin	Antimicrobial, toxin inactivator, stabilizier	Anthrax (*BioThrax*), DTaP (all brands), DTaP-Hep B-IPV (*Pediarix*), DTaP-Hib (*TriHIBit*), DT (all brands), Td (all brands), Hepatitis A (*Havrix, Vaqta*), Hepatitis A-Hepatitis B (*Twinrix*), Hib (*ActHIB*), Hib-Hepatitis B (*Comvax*), Influenza (*Fluzone, Fluarix, FluLaval*), Japanese encephalitis (*JE-Vax*), Poliovirus inactivated (*Ipol*), Tdap (*Adacel, Boostrix*)
Gelatin	Stabilizer in freeze-drying, solvent	DTaP (*Tripedia*), DTaP-Hib (*TriHIBit*), Hepatitis B (*Recombivax-HB*), Human papillomavirus (*Gardasil*), Influenza (*Fluzone*), Japanese encephalitis (*JE-Vax*), Measles (*Attenuvax*), Mumps (*Mumpsvax*), Rubella (*Meruvax II*), MMR (*MMR-II*), MMRV (*ProQuad*), Rabies (*RabAvert*), Typhoid oral (*Vivotif*), Varicella (*Varivax*), Yellow fever (*YF-Vax*), Zoster (*Zostavax*)
Gentamicin	Antibacterial	Influenza (*Fluarix, FluMist*)
Glucose	Medium nutrient	Rotavirus (*Rotarix*)
Glutamine	Medium nutrient	Rotavirus (*Rotarix*)
Glutaraldehyde	Toxin detoxifier	DTaP (*Infanrix*), DTaP-Hep B-IPV (*Pediarix*), Tdap (*Boostrix*)
Glycerin	Solvent	Vaccinia (*DryVax*)
Glycine	Protein stabilizer	DT (most brands), Td (most brands)
Histidine	Stabilizer	Human papillomavirus (*Gardasil*)
Hydrochloric acid	Adjust pH	DTaP (most brands), DT (most brands)

B

Vaccine Excipient & Media Summary

Excipients Included in US Licensed Vaccines[a]		
Excipient	Use	Vaccine
Hydrocortisone	Component of growth medium	Influenza (*Fluarix*)
Lactose	Stabilizer in freeze-drying, filling	BCG (*Tice*), Hib (some packages), Meningococcal (*Menomune*), Typhoid oral (*Vivotif*)
Magnesium stearate	Lubricant for capsule filling	Typhoid oral (*Vivotif*)
Magnesium sulfate	Medium nutrient	Rotavirus (*Rotarix*)
Monosodium glutamate	Stabilizer	Influenza (*FluMist*), MMRV (*ProQuad*), Varicella (*Varivax*), Zoster (*Zostavax*)
Mouse serum protein	Manufacturing residue	Japanese encephalitis (*JE-Vax*)
MRC-5 cellular protein	Manufacturing residue	Hepatitis A (*Havrix, Vaqta*), Hepatitis A-Hepatitis B (*Twinrix*), MMRV (*ProQuad*), Rabies (*Imovax*), Poliovirus inactivated (*Poliovax*), Varicella (*Varivax*)
Neomycin	Antibacterial	DTaP-Hep B-IPV (*Pediarix*), Hepatitis A-Hepatitis B (*Twinrix*), Influenza (*Fluvirin*), Measles (*Attenuvax*), Mumps (*Mumpsvax*), Rubella (*Meruvax II*), MMR (*MMR-II*), MMRV (*ProQuad*), Poliovirus inactivated (*Ipol*), Rabies (*Imovax, RabAvert*), Vaccinia (*DryVax*), Varicella (*Varivax*), Zoster (*Zostavax*)
Phenol	Preservative, antibacterial	Pneumococcal (*Pneumovax-23*), Typhoid inactivated (*Typhim Vi*), Vaccinia (*Dryvax*)
Phenol red (phenolsulfon-phthalein)	pH indicator, dye	Rabies (*Imovax*), Rotavirus (*Rotarix*)
2-Phenoxyethanol	Preservative, stabilizer	DTaP (*Infanrix, Daptacel*), DTaP-Heb B-IPV (*Pediarix*), Hepatitis A (*Havrix*), Hepatitis A-Hepatitis B (*Twinrix*), Poliovirus inactivated (*Ipol*), Td (Sanofi Pasteur)
Phosphate buffers (eg, disodium, monosodium, potassium, sodium dihydrogenphosphate)	Adjust pH	DTaP (most brands), DT (most brands), Hib (*Act-Hib*), Hepatitis A (*Havrix*), Hepatitis A-Hepatitis B (*Twinrix*), Hepatitis B (*Engerix-B*), Influenza (*Fluarix, FluMist, FluLaval*), Measles (*Attenuvax*), Meningococcal (*Menactra*), Mumps (*Mumpsvax*), Poliovirus inactivated (*Ipol*), Rabies (*BioRab*), Rubella (*Meruvax II*), MMR (*MMR-II*), MMRV (*ProQuad*), Rotavirus (*RotaTeq*), Typhoid inactivated (*Typhim Vi*), Varicella (*Varivax*), Zoster (*Zostavax*)
Polydimethylsilozone	Antifoaming agent	Typhoid inactivated (*Typhim Vi*)
Polymyxin B	Antibacterial	DTaP-Heb B-IPV (*Pediarix*), Influenza (*Fluvirin*), Poliovirus inactivated (*Ipol*), Vaccinia (*Dryvax*)

Vaccine Excipient & Media Summary

Excipients Included in US Licensed Vaccines[a]		
Excipient	Use	Vaccine
Polyoxyethylene9-10 nonyl phenol (Triton N-101, octoxynol 9)	Nonionic surfactant (viral inactivation)	Influenza (*Fluvirin*)
Polyoxyethylated octyl phenol (also called ethylene glycol octyl phenyl ether, octoxynol-10, octyl-phenoxypolyethoxyethanol, p-isooctyphenyl ether, Triton X-100)	Nonionic surfactant (viral inactivation)	Influenza (*Fluarix*, *Fluzone*)
Polysorbate 20	Surfactant	Hepatitis A (*Havrix*), Hepatitis A-Hepatitis B (*Twinrix*)
Polysorbate 80	Surfactant	DTaP (*Infanrix*, *Tripedia*), DTaP-Heb B-IPV (*Pediarix*), DTaP-Hib (*TriHIBit*), Human papillomavirus (*Gardasil*), Influenza (*Fluarix*), Rotavirus (*RotaTeq*), Tdap (*Adacel*, *Boostrix*)
Potassium chloride	Adjust pH, tonicity, medium nutrient	MMRV (*ProQuad*), Rotavirus (*Rotarix*), Zoster (*Zostavax*)
Potassium glutamate	Stabilizer	Rabies (*RabAvert*)
Serum, bovine calf	Component of growth medium	Zoster (*Zostavax*)
Sodium acetate	Adjust pH	DT (some brands), Td (some brands)
Sodium bicarbonate	Adjust pH	MMRV (*ProQuad*)
Sodium borate	Adjust pH	Hepatitis A (*Vaqta*), Hib-Hepatitis B (*Comvax*), Human papillomavirus (*Gardasil*)
Sodium chloride	Adjust tonicity	Most vaccines, including Anthrax, BCG, Human papillomavirus (*Gardasil*), Influenza (*Fluarix*), Measles, Meningococcal (*Menactra*), Mumps, MMR, MMRV, Pneumococcal, Polio inactivated, Rabies, Rotavirus (*Rotarix*), Rubella, Typhoid inactivated, Varicella, Yellow fever, Tdap (*Boostrix*), Zoster (*Zostavax*)
Sodium citrate	Adjust pH	Rotavirus (*RotaTeq*)
Sodium deoxycholate	Anionic surfactant (viral inactivation)	Influenza (*Fluarix*, *FluLaval*)
Sodium hydrogenocarbonate	Medium nutrient	Rotavirus (*Rotarix*)
Sodium hydroxide	Adjust pH	DT (most brands), Rotavirus (*RotaTeq*), Td (most brands)
Sodium phosphate	Medium nutrient	Rotavirus (*Rotarix*)
Sodium pyruvate	Medium nutrient	Rotavirus (*Rotarix*)
Sorbitol	Stabilizer, solvent	Measles (*Attenuvax*), Mumps (*Mumpsvax*), Rotavirus (*Rotarix*), Rubella (*Meruvax II*), MMR (*MMR-II*), MMRV (*ProQuad*), Yellow fever (*YF-Vax*)
Streptomycin	Antibacterial	Poliovirus inactivated (*Ipol*), Vaccinia (*Dryvax*)

Vaccine Excipient & Media Summary

Excipients Included in US Licensed Vaccines[a]		
Excipient	Use	Vaccine
Sucrose	Stabilizer	DTaP-Hib (*TriHIBit*), Hib (*Act-HIB*), Influenza (*FluMist*), Measles (*Attenuvax*), Mumps (*Mumpsvax*), MMR (*MMR-II*), MMRV (*ProQuad*), Rotavirus (*RotaTeq*), Typhoid oral (*Vivotif*), Varicella (*Varivax*), Zoster (*Zostavax*)
Sucrose	Medium nutrient	Rotavirus (*Rotarix*)
Thimerosal	Preservative in some multi-dose containers (see package labeling for precise content)	DTaP (some multidose containers), DTaP-Hib (*TriHIBit*), DT (some multidose containers), Td (some multidose containers), Hib (some multidose containers), Influenza (some multidose containers), Japanese encephalitis (*JE-Vax*), Meningococcal (*Menomune*), Rabies (*BioRab*). Some single-dose containers contain trace amounts of thimerosal from the production process, but substantially lower concentrations than if used as a preservative. Consult product monographs and labeling for details.
Tocopheryl hydrogen succinate	Component of growth medium	Influenza (*Fluarix*)
Tyrosine	Medium nutrient	Rotavirus (*Rotarix*)
Urea	Stabilizer	Varicella vaccine (*Varivax*, refrigerator stable)
Vitamins unspecified	Component of growth medium	Anthrax (*BioThrax*), Rabies (*Imovax*), Rotavirus (*Rotarix*), Td (Sanofi Pasteur)
Xanthan	Thickening agent	Rotavirus (*Rotarix*)
Yeast protein	Component of growth medium	DTaP-Heb B-IPV (*Pediarix*), Hepatitis A-Hepatitis B (*Twinrix*), Hepatitis B (*Engerix-B, Recombivax-HB*), Hib (*HibTiter*), Hib-Hepatitis B (*Comvax*)

a Proprietary names appear in italics.

Vaccine Excipient & Media Summary

Vaccine-Production Media[a]	
Vaccine Culture Media	Vaccine(s)
Bovine protein	DTaP-Hep B-IPV (poliovirus component, *Pediarix*), Pneumococcal (*Pneumovax-23*), Typhoid oral (*Vivotif*)
Calf skin	Vaccinia (*Dryvax*)
Chick embryo fibroblast tissue culture	Measles (*Attenuvax*), Mumps (*Mumpsvax*), combination vaccines containing them, MMRV (*ProQuad*), Rabies (*RabAvert*)
Chick kidney cells	Influenza (master viruses for *FluMist*)
Chicken embryo (fertilized egg)	Influenza (all brands), Yellow fever (*YF-Vax*)
Cohen-Wheeler, modified (pertussis components)	DTaP (alternate is Stainer-Scholte media)
Fenton media containing bovine casein	Tdap (*Boostrix*)
Human diploid tissue culture, MRC-5	Hepatitis A (*Havrix, Vaqta*), Hepatitis A-Hepatitis B (*Twinrix*), MMRV (*ProQuad*), Poliovirus inactivated (*Poliovax*), Rabies (*Imovax*), Varicella (*Varivax*), Zoster (*Zostavax*)
Human diploid tissue culture, WI-38	Rubella (*Meruvax II*), combination vaccines containing it, MMRV (*ProQuad*), Varicella (*Varivax*), Zoster (*Zostavax*)
Lathan medium derived from bovine casein	DTaP (*Infanrix*, tetanus component), DTaP-Hep B-IPV (*Pediarix*), Tdap (*Boostrix*)
Linggoud-Fenton medium containing bovine extract	DTaP (*Infanrix* diphtheria component), DTaP-Hep B-IPV (*Pediarix*), Tdap (*Boostrix*)
Medium 199 (including amino acids, vitamins, sucrose, phosphate, glutamate, human albumin, fetal bovine serum)	Measles (*Attenuvax*), Mumps (*Mumpsvax*), combination vaccines containing them
Minimum essential medium (including amino acids, vitamins, fetal bovine serum, human albumin)	Rubella (*Meruvax II*), combination vaccines containing it
Monkey kidney tissue culture, Vero (Vervet or African green monkeys)	DTaP-Hep B-IPV (poliovirus component, *Pediarix*), Poliovirus inactivated (*Ipol*), Rotavirus (*RotaTeq*)
Mouse brain culture	Japanese encephalitis (*JE-Vax*)
Mueller-Hinton agar medium	Meningococcal conjugate (*Menactra*)
Mueller-Miller medium	Diphtheria and tetanus vaccines (most brands), meningococcal conjugate (*Menactra*)
Puziss-Wright medium 1095	Anthrax (*BioThrax*)
Rhesus fetal lung tissue culture	Rabies (*BioRab*)
Stainer-Scholte medium	DTaP (*Daptacel, Infanrix*, pertussis component), DTaP-Hep B-IPV (*Pediarix*), Tdap (*Boostrix*)
Soy peptone broth	Pneumococcal (*Prevnar*)
Synthetic/semi-synthetic	Anthrax (*BioThrax*), BCG (*Tice*), DT (all brands), Td (all brands), Hib (all brands), Meningococcal (*Menomune*), Pneumococcal (*Pneumovax-23*), Typhoid inactivated (*Typhim Vi*)
Watson-Scherp medium	Meningococcal conjugate (*Menactra*)
Yeast or yeast extract (typically *Saccharomyces cerevisiae*)	Hepatitis A-Hepatitis B (*Twinrix*), Hepatitis B (*Engerix-B, Recombivax-HB*), Hib (*HibTiter, PedvaxHIB*), Hib-Hepatitis B (*Comvax*), Human papillomavirus (*Gardasil*), Medium for growing *Corynebacterium diphtheriae* strain C7 (b197) to obtain CRM$_{197}$ protein for conjugation to polysaccharides (*HibTiter, Prevnar*).

a Proprietary names appear in italics.

B

Vaccine Excipient & Media Summary

References: Canadian National Advisory Committee on Immunization. Statement on thimerosal. *Can Comm Dis Rep*. 2003;29(ACS-1):1-10.

CDC. Thimerosal in vaccines: a joint statement of the American Academy of Pediatrics and the Public Health Service. *MMWR*. 1999;48:563-565.

Fletcher MA, Hessel L, Plotkin SA. Human diploid cell strains (HDCS) viral vaccines. *Dev Biol Stand*. 1998;93:97-107.

Grabenstein JD. Immunologic necessities: Diluents, adjuvants, and excipients. *Hosp Pharm*. 1996;31:1387-92,1397-1401.

Grabenstein JD. Clinical management of hypersensitivities to vaccine components. *Hosp Pharm*. 1997;32:77-84,87.

Hayflick L. The limited in vitro lifetime of human diploid cell strains. *Exp Cell Res*. 1965;37:614-636.

Jacobs JP, Jones CM, Baille JP. Characteristics of a human diploid cell designated MRC-5. *Nature*. 1970;227(5254):168-170.

Jacobs JP. The status of human diploid cell strain MRC-5 as an approved substrate for the production of viral vaccines. *J Biol Stand*. 1976;4(2):97-99.

Offit PA, Jew RK. Addressing parents's concerns: Do vaccines contain harmful preservatives, adjuvants, additives, or residuals. *Pediatrics*. 2003;112:1394-1401.

B

Vaccine Excipient & Media Summary, Part 2
Excipients Included in U.S. Vaccines, by Vaccine

Includes vaccine ingredients (e.g., adjuvants and preservatives) as well as substances used during the manufacturing process, including vaccine-production media, that are removed from the final product and present only in trace quantities. In addition to the substances listed, most vaccines contain Sodium Chloride (table salt).

Vaccine	Contains
Anthrax (BioThrax)	Aluminum Hydroxide, Amino Acids, Benzethonium Chloride, Formaldehyde or Formalin, Inorganic Salts and Sugars, Vitamins
BCG (Tice)	Asparagine, Citric Acid, Lactose, Glycerin, Iron Ammonium Citrate, Magnesium Sulfate, Potassium Phosphate
DTaP (Daptacel)	Aluminum Phosphate, Ammonium Sulfate, Casamino Acid, Dimethyl-beta-cyclodextrin, Formaldehyde or Formalin, Glutaraldehyde, 2-Phenoxyethanol
DTaP (Infanrix)	Aluminum Hydroxide, Bovine Extract, Formaldehyde or Formalin, Glutaraldhyde, 2-Phenoxyethanol, Polysorbate 80
DTaP (Tripedia)	Aluminum Potassium Sulfate, Ammonium Sulfate, Bovine Extract, Formaldehyde or Formalin, Gelatin, Polysorbate 80, Sodium Phosphate, Thimerosal*
DTaP/Hib (TriHIBit)	Aluminum Potassium Sulfate, Ammonium Sulfate, Bovine Extract, Formaldehyde or Formalin, Gelatin, Polysorbate 80, Sucrose, Thimerosal*
DTaP-IPV (Kinrix)	Aluminum Hydroxide, Bovine Extract, Formaldehyde, Lactalbumin Hydrolysate, Monkey Kidney Tissue, Neomycin Sulfate, Polymyxin B, Polysorbate 80
DTaP-HepB-IPV (Pediarix)	Aluminum Hydroxide, Aluminum Phosphate, Bovine Protein, Lactalbumin Hydrolysate, Formaldehyde or Formalin, Glutaraldhyde, Monkey Kidney Tissue, Neomycin, 2-Phenoxyethanol, Polymyxin B, Polysorbate 80, Yeast Protein
DtaP-IPV/Hib (Pentacel)	Aluminum Phosphate, Bovine Serum Albumin, Formaldehyde, Glutaraldhyde, MRC-5 DNA and Cellular Protein, Neomycin, Polymyxin B Sulfate, Polysorbate 80, 2-Phenoxyethanol,
DT (sanofi)	Aluminum Potassium Sulfate, Bovine Extract, Formaldehyde or Formalin, Thimerosal (multi-dose) or Thimerosal* (single-dose)
DT (Massachusetts)	Aluminum Hydroxide, Formaldehyde or Formalin
Hib (ACTHib)	Ammonium Sulfate, Formaldehyde or Formalin, Sucrose
Hib (PedvaxHib)	Aluminum Hydroxyphosphate Sulfate
Hib/Hep B (Comvax)	Amino Acids, Aluminum Hydroxyphosphate Sulfate, Dextrose, Formaldehyde or Formalin, Mineral Salts, Sodium Borate, Soy Peptone, Yeast Protein
Hep A (Havrix)	Aluminum Hydroxide, Amino Acids, Formaldehyde or Formalin, MRC-5 Cellular Protein, Neomycin Sulfate, 2-Phenoxyethanol, Phosphate Buffers, Polysorbate
Hep A (Vaqta)	Aluminum Hydroxyphosphate Sulfate, Bovine Albumin or Serum, DNA, Formaldehyde or Formalin, MRC-5 Cellular Protein, Sodium Borate
Hep B (Engerix-B)	Aluminum Hydroxide, Phosphate Buffers, Thimerosal*, Yeast Protein

Vaccine	Contains
Hep B (Recombivax)	Aluminum Hydroxyphosphate Sulfate, Amino Acids, Dextrose, Formaldehyde or Formalin, Mineral Salts, Potassium Aluminum Sulfate, Soy Peptone, Yeast Protein
HepA/HepB (Twinrix)	Aluminum Hydroxide, Aluminum Phosphate, Amino Acids, Dextrose, Formaldehyde or Formalin, Inorganic Salts, MRC-5 Cellular Protein, Neomycin Sulfate, 2-Phenoxyethanol, Phosphate Buffers, Polysorbate 20, Thimerosal*, Vitamins, Yeast Protein
Human Papillomavirus (HPV) (Gardasil)	Amino Acids, Amorphous Aluminum Hydroxyphosphate Sulfate, Carbohydrates, L-histidine, Mineral Salts, Polysorbate 80, Sodium Borate, Vitamins
Influenza (Afluria)	Beta-Propiolactone, Calcium Chloride, Neomycin, Ovalbumin, Polymyxin B, Potassium Chloride, Potassium Phosphate, Sodium Phosphate, Sodium Taurodeoxychoalate.
Influenza (Fluarix)	Egg Albumin (Ovalbumin), Egg Protein, Formaldehyde or Formalin, Gentamicin, Hydrocortisone, Octoxynol-10, α-Tocopheryl Hydrogen Succinate, Polysorbate 80, Sodium Deoxycholate, Sodium Phosphate, Thimerosal*
Influenza (Flulaval)	Egg Albumin (Ovalbumin), Egg Protein, Formaldehyde or Formalin, Sodium Deoxycholate, Phosphate Buffers, Thimerosal
Influenza (Fluvirin)	Beta-Propiolactone , Egg Protein, Neomycin, Polymyxin B, Polyoxyethylene 9-10 Nonyl Phenol (Triton N-101, Octoxynol 9), Thimerosal (multidose containers), Thimerosal* (single-dose syringes)
Influenza (Fluzone)	Egg Protein, Formaldehyde or Formalin, Gelatin, Octoxinol-9 (Triton X-100), Thimerosal (multidose containers)
Influenza (FluMist)	Chick Kidney Cells, Egg Protein, Gentamicin Sulfate, Monosodium Glutamate, Sucrose Phosphate Glutamate Buffer
IPV (Ipol)	Calf Serum Protein, Formaldehyde or Formalin, Monkey Kidney Tissue, Neomycin, 2-Phenoxyethanol, Polymyxin B, Streptomycin,
Japanese Encephalitis (JE-Vax)	Formaldehyde or Formalin, Gelatin, Mouse Serum Protein, Polysorbate 80, Thimerosal
Japanese Encephalitis (Ixiaro)	Aluminum Hydroxide, Bovine Serum Albumin, Formaldehyde, Protamine Sulfate, Sodium Metabisulphite
Meningococcal (Menactra)	Formaldehyde or Formalin, Phosphate Buffers
Meningococcal (Menomune)	Lactose, Thimerosal (10-dose vials only)
MMR (MMR-II)	Amino Acid, Bovine Albumin or Serum, Chick Embryo Fibroblasts, Human Serum Albumin, Gelatin, Glutamate, Neomycin, Phosphate Buffers, Sorbitol, Sucrose, Vitamins
MMRV (ProQuad)	Bovine Albumin or Serum, Gelatin, Human Serum Albumin, Monosodium L-glutamate, MRC-5 Cellular Protein, Neomycin, Sodium Phosphate Dibasic, Sodium Bicarbonate, Sorbitol, Sucrose, Potassium Phosphate Monobasic, Potassium Chloride, Potassium Phosphate Dibasic
Pneumococcal (Pneumovax)	Bovine Protein, Phenol
Pneumococcal (Prevnar)	Aluminum Phosphate, Amino Acid, Soy Peptone, Yeast Extract

B

Vaccine	Contains
Rabies (Imovax)	Human Serum Albumin, Beta-Propiolactone, MRC-5 Cellular Protein, Neomycin, Phenol Red (Phenolsulfonphthalein), Vitamins
Rabies (RabAvert)	Amphotericin B, Beta-Propiolactone, Bovine Albumin or Serum, Chicken Protein, Chlortetracycline, Egg Albumin (Ovalbumin), Ethylenediamine-Tetraacetic Acid Sodium (EDTA), Neomycin, Potassium Glutamate
Rotavirus (RotaTeq)	Cell Culture Media, Fetal Bovine Serum, Sodium Citrate, Sodium Phosphate Monobasic Monohydrate, Sodium Hydroxide Sucrose, Polysorbate 80
Rotavirus (Rotarix)	Amino Acids, Calcium Carbonate, Calcium Chloride, D-glucose, Dextran, Ferric (III) Nitrate, L-cystine, L-tyrosine, Magnesium Sulfate, Phenol Red, Potassium Chloride, Sodium Hydrogenocarbonate, Sodium Phosphate, Sodium L-glutamine, Sodium Pyruvate, Sorbitol, Sucrose, Vitamins, Xanthan
Td (Decavac)	Aluminum Potassium Sulfate, Bovine Extract, Formaldehyde or Formalin, 2-Phenoxyethanol, Peptone, Thimerosal*
Td (Massachusetts)	Aluminum Hydroxide, Aluminum Phosphate, Formaldehyde or Formalin, Thimerosal (some multidose containers)
Tdap (Adacel)	Aluminum Phosphate, Formaldehyde or Formalin, Glutaraldehyde, 2-Phenoxyethanol
Tdap (Boostrix)	Aluminum Hydroxide, Bovine Extract, Formaldehyde or Formalin, Glutaraldehyde, Polysorbate 80
Typhoid (inactivated – Typhim Vi)	Disodium Phosphate, Monosodium Phosphate, Phenol, Polydimethylsilozone, Hexadecyltrimethylammonium Bromide
Typhoid (oral – Ty21a)	Amino Acids, Ascorbic Acid, Bovine Protein, Casein, Dextrose, Galactose, Gelatin, Lactose, Magnesium Stearate, Sucrose, Yeast Extract
Vaccinia (ACAM2000)	Glycerin, Human Serum Albumin, Mannitol, Monkey Kidney Cells, Neomycin, Phenol, Polymyxin B
Varicella (Varivax)	Bovine Albumin or Serum, Ethylenediamine-Tetraacetic Acid Sodium (EDTA), Gelatin, Monosodium L-Glutamate, MRC-5 DNA and Cellular Protein, Neomycin, Potassium Chloride, Potassium Phosphate Monobasic, Sodium Phosphate Monobasic, Sucrose
Yellow Fever (YF-Vax)	Egg Protein, Gelatin, Sorbitol
Zoster (Zostavax)	Bovine Calf Serum, Hydrolyzed Porcine Gelatin, Monosodium L-glutamate, MRC-5 DNA and Cellular Protein, Neomycin, Potassium Phosphate Monobasic, Potassium Chloride, Sodium Phosphate Dibasic, Sucrose

April 2009

*Where "thimerosal" is marked with an asterisk (*) it indicates that the product should be considered equivalent to thimerosal-free products. This vaccine may contain trace amounts (<0.3 mcg) of mercury left after post-production thimerosal removal, but these amounts have no biological effect. *JAMA* 1999;282(18) and *JAMA* 2000;283(16)

Adapted from Grabenstein JD. *ImmunoFacts: Vaccines & Immunologic Drugs.* St. Louis, MO: Wolters Kluwer Health Inc.; 2009 and individual products' package inserts.

All reasonable efforts have been made to ensure the accuracy of this information, but manufacturers may change product contents before that information is reflected here.

B

Latex in Vaccine Packaging

"If a person reports a severe (anaphylactic) allergy to latex, vaccines supplied in vials or syringes that contain natural rubber should not be administered unless the benefit of vaccination outweighs the risk for a potential allergic reaction. For latex allergies other than anaphylactic allergies (e.g., a history of contact allergy to latex gloves), vaccines supplied in vials or syringes that contain dry natural rubber or rubber latex can be administered." (ACIP *General Recommendations on Immunization.* 2006)

The following table is accurate, to the best of our knowledge, as of April 2009. If in doubt, check the package insert for the vaccine in question.

Vaccine		Latex?
Anthrax (BioThrax)		YES – Vial.
Comvax		YES – Vial
DTaP	Daptacel	YES – Vial
	Infanrix	YES – Syringe NO – Vial
	Tripedia	YES – Vial
DT (Generic)		YES – Vial
Hib	HibTITER	YES – Vial
	PedvaxHIB	Yes – Vial
	ActHIB	YES – Diluent vial NO – Lyophilized vaccine vial
Hepatitis A	Havrix	YES – Syringe NO – Vial
	Vaqta	YES – Vial YES – Syringe
Hepatitis B	Engerix-B	YES – Syringe NO – Vial
	Recombivax HB	YES – Vial
HPV (Gardasil)		NO
Influenza	Fluarix	YES – Syringe
	Fluvirin	NO
	Fluzone	NO
	FluLaval	NO
	Afluria	NO
	FluMist	NO
Japanese Encephalitis	JE-Vax	NO
	Ixiaro	NO
Kinrix		YES – Syringe NO – Vial
MMR (M-M-R II)		NO
MMRV (ProQuad)		NO
Measles (Attenuvax)		NO
Mumps (Mumpsvax)		NO
Rubella (Meruvax II)		NO
Meningococcal	Menomune	YES – Vial
	Menactra	YES – Vial NO – Syringe

Vaccine		Latex?
Pediarix		YES – Syringe NO – Vial
Pentacel		NO
Pneumococcal	Pneumovax 23	NO
	Prevnar	YES – Vial
Polio (IPOL)		YES – Syringe NO – Vial
Rabies	Imovax Rabies	NO
	RabAvert	NO
Rotavirus	RotaTeq	NO
	Rotarix	YES – Applicator NO – Vial & Transfer Adapter
Td	Decavac	NO – Vial NO – Syringe
	Generic	YES – Vial YES – Syringe
Tdap	Adacel	NO
	Boostrix	YES – Syringe NO – Vial
TriHIBit		YES – Vial
Twinrix		YES – Syringe NO – Vial
Typhoid	Typhim Vi	NO
	Vivotif Berna	N/A
Varicella (Varivax)		NO
Vaccinia (Smallpox) (ACAM2000)		NO
Yellow Fever (YF-Vax)		YES – Vial

April 2009

Vaccine	Brand Name		Manufacturer	Thimerosal Concentration[1]	Mercury mcg/0.5 ml
Anthrax	BioThrax		BioPort Corporation	0	0
DTaP	Tripedia		sanofi pasteur	*	*
	Infanrix		GlaxoSmithKline	0	0
	DAPTACEL		sanofi pasteur	0	0
DTaP-HepB-IPV	Pediarix		GlaxoSmithKline	0	0
DTaP-IPV-Hib	Pentacel		sanofi pasteur	0	0
DTaP-Hib	TriHIBit		sanofi pasteur	*	*
DTwP	All Products			.01%	25
DT	Diphtheria & Tetanus Toxoids Adsorbed USP	multi-dose	sanofi pasteur	.01%	25
		single dose		*	*
Td	DECAVAC		sanofi pasteur	*	*
	Tetanus and Diphtheria Toxoids Adsorbed		sanofi pasteur	*	*
Tdap	ADACEL		sanofi pasteur	0	0
	Boostrix		GlaxoSmithKline	0	0
Tetanus Toxoid	Tetanus Toxoid Adsorbed USP			.01%	25
	Tetanus Toxoid Adsorbed Adult Use		sanofi pasteur	.01%	25
	Booster			.01%	25
Hib	ActHIB		sanofi pasteur	0	0
	HibTITER		Wyeth-Ayerst	0	0
	PedvaxHIB liquid(2)		Merck	0	0
Hib/HepB	Comvax (3)		Merck	0	0
Hepatitis A	Havrix		GlaxoSmithKline	0	0
	Vaqta adult/pediatric		Merck	0	0
Hepatitis B	Engerix-B preservative free		GlaxoSmithKline	0	0
	Recombivax HB preservative free		Merck	0	0
Hep A-B	Twinrix		GlaxoSmithKline	0	0
HPV	Gardasil		Merck	0	0
Influenza 2008/9 Formula	Afluria	multi-dose	CSL Limited	.01%	24.5
		single dose		0	0
	Fluarix		GlaxoSmithKline		≤1
	FluLaval		GlaxoSmithKline	.01%	25
	FluMist		MedImmune	0	0
	Fluvirin		Novartis	.01%	24.5
	Fluzone	5 mL vial	sanofi pasteur	.01%	25
		No Preservative		0	0
IPV	IPOL		sanofi pasteur	0	0
Meningococcal	Menactra		sanofi pasteur	0	0
	MENOMUNE-A/C/Y/W-135	multi-dose	sanofi pasteur	.01%	25
		single dose		0	0
MMR	M-M-R II		Merck	0	0
MMR-Varicella	ProQuad		Merck	0	0
Polio	IPOL		sanofi pasteur	0	0
Pneumococcal	Prevnar		Wyeth-Ayerst	0	0
	Pneumovax 23		Merck	0	0
Rabies	RabAvert		Chiron	0	0
	IMOVAX		sanofi pasteur	0	0
Rotavirus	RotaTeq		Merck	0	0
Typhoid Fever	Typhim Vi		sanofi pasteur	0	0
	Vivotif		Berna Biotch	0	0
Varicella Zoster	Varivax		Merck	0	0
	Zostavax		Merck	0	0
Yellow Fever	YF-VAX		sanofi pasteur	0	0

1. A concentration of 1:10,000 is equivalent to a 0.01% concentration. Thimerosal is approximately 50% Hg by weight. A 1:10,000 concentration contains 25 mcg of Hg per 0.5 mL.
2. A previously marketed lyophilized preparation contained 0.005% thimerosal.
3. COMVAX is not approved for use under 6 weeks of age because of decreased response to the Hib component

* This product should be considered equivalent to thimerosal-free products. This vaccine may contain trace amounts (<0.3 mcg) of mercury left after post-production thimerosal removal; these amounts have no biological effect. JAMA 1999;282(18) and JAMA 2000;283(16).

Pediatric/VFC Vaccine Price List

Vaccine	Brandname/ Tradename	Packaging	CDC Cost/Dose	Private Sector Cost/Dose	Contract End Date	Manufacturer
DTaP [1]	Tripedia® DAPTACEL®	10 pack - 1 dose vials 10 pack - 1 dose vials	$13.25 $13.75	$22.35 $23.03	03/31/2010	Sanofi Pasteur
DTaP [1]	Infanrix®	10 pack - 1 dose vials 5 pack - 1 dose T-L syringes. No Needle	$13.75 $13.75	$20.96 $21.44	03/31/2010	GlaxoSmithKline
DTaP-IPV [2]	Kinrix®	10 pack - 1 dose vials 5 pack - 1 dose T-L syringes	$32.25 $32.25	$48.00 $48.00	03/31/2010	GlaxoSmithKline
DTaP-Hep B-IPV [4]	Pediarix®	10 pack - 1 dose vials 5 pack - 1 dose T-L syringes. No Needle	$48.75 $48.75	$70.72 $70.72	03/31/2010	GlaxoSmithKline
DTaP-IP-HI [4]	Pentacel®	5 pack - 1 dose vials	$51.49	$72.91	03/31/2010	Sanofi Pasteur
DTaP-Hib [2]	TriHIBit®	5 pack - 1 dose vials	$27.31	$44.88	03/31/2010	Sanofi Pasteur
e-IPV [5]	IPOL®	10 dose vials 10-pack – 1 dose syringes, No Needle	$11.51 $11.51	$23.90 $27.62	03/31/2010	Sanofi Pasteur
Hepatitis B-Hib [3]	COMVAX®	10 pack - 1 dose vials	$28.80	$43.56	03/31/2010	Merck
Hepatitis A Pediatric [5]	VAQTA®	10 pack - 1 dose vials	$13.00	$30.37	03/31/2010	Merck
Hepatitis A Pediatric [5]	Havrix®	10 pack - 1 dose vials 5 pack - 1 dose T-L syringes. No Needle	$12.75 $12.75	$27.41 $27.41	03/31/2010	GlaxoSmithKline
Hepatitis A-Hepatitis B 18 only [3]	Twinrix®	10 pack - 1 dose vials 5 pack - 1 dose T-L syringes, No Needle	$41.50 $41.50	$78.16 $78.42	03/31/2010	GlaxoSmithKline
Hepatitis B [5] Pediatric/Adolescent	ENGERIX B®	10 pack - 1 dose vials 5 pack - 1 dose T-L syringes, No Needle	$9.75 $9.75	$21.37 $21.37	03/31/2010	GlaxoSmithKline
Hepatitis B [5] Pediatric/Adolescent	RECOMBIVAX HB®	10 pack - 1 dose vials	$10.00	$23.20	03/31/2010	Merck

B

Hib [5]	PedvaxHIB®	10 pack - 1 dose vials	$11.29	$22.77	03/31/2010	Merck
Hib [5]	ActHIB®	5 pack - 1 dose vials	$8.66	$22.83	03/31/2010	Sanofi Pasteur
HPV - Quadrivalent Human Papillomavirus Types 6, 11, 16 and 18 Recombinant [5]	Gardasil®	10 pack – 1 dose vials	$105.58	$130.27	03/31/2010	Merck
Measles, Mumps, Rubella and Varicella (MMR-V) [2]	ProQuad®	10 pack - 1 dose vials	$82.67	$128.90	03/31/2010	Merck
Meningococcal Conjugate (Groups A, C, Y and W-135) [5]	Menactra®	5 pack - 1 dose vials	$80.13	$98.52	03/31/2010	Sanofi Pasteur
Measles, Mumps and Rubella (MMR) [1]	MMRII®	10 pack - 1 dose vials	$18.30	$48.31	03/31/2010	Merck
Pneumococcal 7-valent [5] (Pediatric)	Prevnar®	10 pack – 1 dose syringes, No Needle	$71.04	$83.88	03/31/2010	Wyeth/Lederle
Rotavirus, Live, Oral, Pentavalent [5]	RotaTeq®	10 pack - 1 dose 2mL tubes	$57.20	$69.59	03/31/2010	Merck
Rotavirus, Live, Oral, Oral [5]	Rotarix®	10 pack - 1 dose vials	$83.25	$102.50	03/31/2010	GlaxoSmithKline
Tetanus & Diphtheria Toxoids [3]	DECAVAC®	10 pack - 1 dose syringes No Needle 10 pack – 1 dose vials	$18.17 $18.17	$19.49 $19.49	03/31/2010	Sanofi Pasteur
Tetanus & Diphtheria Toxoids [3]	MassBiologics	10 pack - 1 dose vials	$15.00		03/31/2010	MassBiologics
Tetanus Toxoid, Reduced Diphtheria Toxoid and Acellular Pertussis [1]	BOOSTRIX®	10 pack - 1 dose vials 5 pack - 1 dose TL syringes, No Needle	$30.75 $30.75	$37.55 $37.55	03/31/2010	GlaxoSmithKline
Tetanus Toxoid, Reduced Diphtheria Toxoid and Acellular Pertussis [1]	ADACEL®	10 pack - 1 dose vials 5 pack - 1 dose BD Leur-Lok syringes	$30.75 $30.75	$37.43 $37.43	03/31/2010	Sanofi Pasteur
Varicella [5]	Varivax®	10 pack - 1 dose vials	$64.53	$80.58	03/31/2010	Merck

[1] Vaccine cost includes $2.25 dose Federal Excise Tax
[2] Vaccine cost includes $3.00 per dose Federal Excise Tax
[3] Vaccine cost includes $1.50 per dose Federal Excise Tax
[4] Vaccine cost includes $3.75 per dose Federal Excise Tax
[5] Vaccine cost includes $0.75 per dose Federal Excise Tax
[6] Vaccines which contain Thimerosal as a preservative

These price lists are current as of April 8, 2009
Find current Vaccine Price Lists online at www.cdc.gov/vaccines/programs/vfc/cdc-vac-price-list.htm

Adult Vaccine Price List

Vaccine	Brandname/ Tradename	Packaging	CDC Cost/ Dose	Private Sector Cost/ Dose	Contract End Date	Manufacturer
Hepatitis A Adult [5]	VAQTA®	1 dose vials 10 pack - 1 dose vials	$20.00 $19.75	$63.51 $59.99	6/30/09	Merck
Hepatitis A Adult [5]	Havrix®	10 pack - 1 dose vials 5 pack - 1 dose T-L syringes, No Needle	$18.99 $18.99	$60.69 $60.69	6/30/09	GlaxoSmithKline
Hepatitis A-Hepatitis B Adult [3]	Twinrix®	10 pack - 1 dose vials 5 pack - 1 dose T-L syringes, No Needle	$38.64 $38.64	$86.44 $86.44	6/30/09	GlaxoSmithKline
Hepatitis B-Adult [5]	RECOMBIVAX HB®	1 dose vials 10 pack - 1 dose vials 6 pack - 1 dose prefilled syringe	$23.78 $23.372 $25.30	$59.70 $59.09 $61.22	6/30/09	Merck
Hepatitis B-Adult [5]	ENGERIX-B®	10 pack - 1 dose vials 5 pack - 1 dose T-L syringes, No Needle	$24.90 $24.90	$52.50 $52.50	6/30/09	GlaxoSmithKline
Pneumococcal Polysaccharide (23 Valent)	Pneumovax®	1 pack - 5 dose vials 10 pack – single dose 0.5 mL vials	$16.26 $18.93	$32.99 $37.03	6/30/09	Merck
Tetanus & Diphtheria Toxoids [3]	Tetanus & Diphtheria Toxoids Adsorbed for Adults No Preservative	10 pack - 1 dose vials	$13.50	$18.23	6/30/09	MassBioLogics (Akorn, Inc)
Zoster Vaccine Live	Zostavax®	10 pack - 1 dose vial 1 pack-single dose 0.65mL vials	$107.67 $113.16	$153.93 $161.50	6/30/09	Merck

[1] Vaccine cost includes $2.25 dose Federal Excise Tax
[2] Vaccine cost includes $3.00 per dose Federal Excise Tax
[3] Vaccine cost includes $1.50 per dose Federal Excise Tax
[4] Vaccine cost includes $3.75 per dose Federal Excise Tax
[5] Vaccine cost includes $0.75 per dose Federal Excise Tax
[6] Vaccines which contain Thimerosal as a preservative

Pediatric Influenza Vaccine Price List

Vaccine	Brandname/ Tradename	Packaging	CDC Cost/ Dose	Private Sector Cost/ Dose	Contract End Date	Manufacturer
Influenza [5] (Age 6 months and older)	Fluzone®	10 dose vials	$9.09	$11.17	2/28/2010	Sanofi Pasteur
Influenza [5] (Age 6-35 months)	Fluzone® Pediatric dose No Preservative	10 pack - 1 dose syringes	$11.05	$13.16	2/28/2010	Sanofi Pasteur
Influenza [5] (Age 36 months and older)	Fluzone® No-Preservative	10 pack - 1 dose syringes 10 pack – 1 dose vials	$10.31 $10.31	$12.41 $12.41	2/28/2010	Sanofi Pasteur
Influenza [6] [5] (Age 4 years and older)	Fluvirin® Fluvirin® Preservative-free	10 dose vials 10 pack-1 dose syringes	$7.75 $8.50	$9.75 $11.25	2/28/2010 2/28/2010	Novartis Novartis
Influenza [5] Live, Intranasal (Age 2-49 years)	FluMist® No Preservative	10 pack – 1 dose sprayers	$15.25	$19.70	2/28/2010	MedImmune

[5] Vaccine cost includes $0.75 per dose Federal Excise Tax
[6] Vaccines which contain Thimerosal as a preservative

Foreign Language Terms

Aids to translating foreign immunization records.

Table 1: **Disease, Vaccine, and Related Terms.** This table lists terms for vaccine-preventable diseases, vaccines, and other items that might be found on an immunization record, by language.

Table 2: **Trade Names.** This table lists the names of specific vaccines that are used, or have been used, internationally, along with the manufactuer and country or region, when known.

These tables have been adapted from lists developed by
the Minnesota Department of Health Immunization Program
(now maintained by the Immunization Action Coalition)
and the
Washington State Department of Health.

See also:
http://www.immunize.org/izpractices/p5120.pdf
http://www.immunize.org/izpractices/p5121.pdf
http://www.doh.wa.gov/cfh.immunize/documents/schmanul.pdf (Appendix E)

These lists are not comprehensive and, while we have checked and rechecked sources,
we do not claim complete accuracy.

Foreign Vaccines
Table 1: Disease, Vaccine, and Related Terms

Albanian	
Difteria	Diphtheria
Fruthi	Measles
Pertusisi	Pertussis
Tetanozi	Tetanus

Arabic	
Alhasiba	Rubella
As'al	Pertussis
Athab	Mumps
Difteria	Diphtheria
El Safra	Hepatitis
Has 'ba	Measles
Shel'el	Polio

Bosnian	
Beseže	BCG
Detepe	DPT
Difterija	Diphtheria
Dječja paraliza	Polio
Gripa	Influenza
Male boginje	Rubella
Ospice	Measles
Rubeola	Rubella
Upala pluća	Pneumonia
Veliki boginje	Smallpox
Veliki kašalj	Pertussis
Zauške	Mumps
Žutica	Hepatitis

Croatian	
Beseže	BCG
Detepe	DTP
Difterija	Diphtheria
Dječja paraliza	Polio
Gripa	Influenza
Hri pavac	Pertussis
Kašalj hripavac	Pertussis
Upala pluća	Pneumonia
Veliki boginje	Smallpox
Vodene kozice	Varicella
Zapaljenje	Hepatitis
Zaušnjaci	Mumps
Žutica	Hepatitis

Czech	
Davivy Kasel	Pertussis
Difterie	Diphtheria
Hepatitida	Hepatitis

Parotitida	Mumps
Pertuse	Pertussis
Poliomyelitis	Polio
Plané Nestovice	Chickenpox
Spalnicky	Measles
Subinuira	Influenza
Zardenky	Rubella
Zaškrt	Diphtheria
Zlutá Zimnice	Yellow Fever

Danish	
Bornelammelse	Polio
Difteritis	Diphtheria
DKTP	DTP + IPV
Faaresyge (Fåresyge)	Mumps
Kighoste	Pertussis
Leverbetaendelse	Hepatitis
Meslinger	Measles
MFR	MMR
Rode Hunde	Rubella
Stivkrampe	Tetanus

Dutch	
BMR	MMR
Bof	Mumps
Difterie	Diphtheria
Gelekoorts	Yellow Fever
Gordelroos	Varicella
Griep	Influenza
Kinderverlamming	Polio
Kinkhoest	Pertussis
Longontsteking	Pneumonia
Mazelen	Measles
Pokken	Smallpox
Rode hond	Rubella
Stijfkramp	Tetanus
Tering	Tuberculosis
Waterpekkea	Chickenpox

Ethiopian (Oromiffaa)	
Cufaa	Tetanus
Difteeriyaa	Diphtheria
Gifira	Measles
Gifira farangli	Rubella
Laamsheesaa	Polio
Qakkee	Pertussis
Shimbiraa	Hepatitis

Finnish	
Hinkuyska	Pertussis

B

Jaykkakouristus	Tetanus
Kurkkumata	Diphtheria
Lapsihalvaus	Polio
Sikotauti	Mumps
Tuhkarokko	Measles
Vihurirokko	Rubella
French	
Coqueluche	Pertussis
Diphtérie	Diphtheria
DTC, DT Coq	DTP
Fievre jaune	Yellow Fever
Grippe	Influenza
l'Haemophilus b	Hib
Oreillons	Mumps
Poliomyélite	Polio
ROR	MMR
Rougeole	Measles
Rubéole	Rubella
Tétanos	Tetanus
Tuberculose	Tuberculosis
Variole	Smallpox
German	
Diphtherie	Diphtheria
FSME	Tick-borne encephalitis
Gelbfieber	Yellow Fever
Grippe	Influenza
Keuchhusten	Pertussis
Kinderlähmung	Polio
Masern	Measles
Pocken	Smallpox
Röteln	Rubella
Starrkramph	Tetanus
Tuberkulose	Tuberculosis
Wundstarrkrampf	Tetanus
Zei Genpeter	Mumps
Greek	
Διφθερίτιδα, Τέτανος και Κοκκύτης	DTP
Ο Αιμόφιλος της γρίππης τύπου B	Hib
Μηνιγγοκοκκική Ασθένεα ομάδας C	Meningococcal C
Ιλαρά - Μαγουλάδες – Ερυθρά	MMR
Πολιομυελίτιδα	Polio
Τέτανος και Διφθερίτιδα	Td
Haitian Creole	
Difteri	Diphtheria
Epatit	Hepatitis
Flou	Influenza
Koklich	Pertussis
Lawoujòl, Laroujòl	Measles
Malmouton	Mumps

Polyo	Polio
Ribeyòl	Rubella
Saranpyon	Varicella
Tetanòs	Tetanus
Hmong	
Hawb pob	Pertussis
Kabmob siab hom B	Hepatitis B
Kub cer	Diphtheria
Qhua Maj	Rubella
Qhua Pias	Measles
Qog	Mumps
Tuag tes tuag taw	Polio
Ua npuag	Tetanus
Indonesian	
Batuk rejan	Pertussis
Beguk	Mumps
Biring Peluh	Rubella
Campak	Measles
Difteri	Diphtheria
Penyakit lumpuh	Polio
Radang hati	Hepatitis
Italian	
Antipolio inattivato	IPV
Difterite	Diphtheria
Emofilo b	Hib
Epatite	Hepatitis
Febbre Giallo	Yellow Fever
Morbillo	Measles
MPR (morbillo, parotite, rosolia)	MMR
Parotite	Mumps
Pertosse	Pertussis
Poliomielite	Polio
Polmonite	Pneumonia
Rosolia	Rubella
Tetano	Tetanus
Tosse Asinina	Pertussis
Tubercolosi	Tuberculosis
Vaioloso	Smallpox
Japanese	
A 型肝炎	Hepatitis A
B 型肝炎	Hepatitis B
Fushin (風疹)	Rubella
Hashika (麻疹 or はしか)	Measles
Hashofu (破傷風)	Tetanus
Hyakaseki (百日咳)	Pertussis
Jifuteria (ジフテリア)	Diphtheria
Otafukukuaze (流行性耳下腺炎 or おたふくかぜ)	Mumps
Sh naimahi (ポリオ)	Polio

三種混合	DTaP
水痘 or みずぼうそう	Varicella
肺炎球菌	Pneumococcal
インフルエンザ菌	Hib
日本脳炎	Japanese Encephalitis
インフルエンザ	Influenza
ツベルクリン	PPD
追加接種	Booster

Malay	
Batok rejan	Pertussis
Penyaakit bengok	Mumps
Sakit champak	Measles
Sakit rengkong	Diphtheria

Norwegian	
Difteri	Diphtheria
Kikhoste	Pertussis
Kopper	Smallpox
Kusma	Mumps
Leverbetennelse	Hepatitis
Meslinger	Measles
Poliomyelitt	Polio
Røde hunder	Rubella
Stivkrampe	Tetanus
Vannkopper	Varicella

Polish	
Błonicy, Błonica, Błonnica	Diphtheria
Dyfteria	Diphtheria
Gruzlica	Tuberculosis
Grypa	Influenza
Koklusz	Pertussis
Krztuscowi, Krztusiec	Pertussis
Odra	Measles
Ospa	Smallpox
Ospa Wietrzna	Chickenpox
Paraliz dzieciecy	Polio
Pojar German	Rubella
Pojarul, Pojarului	Measles
Przypominajace	Booster
Rozyczka	Rubella
Swinka	Mumps
Tezec, Tężcowi	Tetanus
Zapalenie pluc	Pneumonia
Zapalenie watroby	Hepatitis
Zólta Goraczka	Yellow Fever

Portugese	
Cachumba (papeira)	Mumps
Coqueluche	Pertussis
Difteria	Diphtheria
Febre Amarela	Yellow Fever

Gripe	Influenza
Hepatite	Hepatitis
Paralisia infantil	Polio
Parotidite epidémica	Mumps
Poliomielite	Polio
Rúbéola	Rubella
Sarampo	Measles
Tetânica, Tétano	Tetanus
Triplice	DTP
VAHB	Hepatitis B Vaccine
VAP	Polio Vaccine
Varicela	Chickenpox
VAS	Measles Vaccine
VASPR	MMR
VAT	Tetanus Vaccine

Romanian	
AR	Measles
Difteria (Difteriei)	Diphtheria
Di Te	DT
Di-Te-Per	DTP
Febra Galbena	Yellow Fever
Gripa	Influenza
Hepatita	Hepatitis
Holera	Cholera
Oreion, Oreionului	Mumps
Pneumoniei	Pneumonia
Poliomielitic	Polio
Rubeolei, Rubeola	Rubella
Rujeola, Rujeolei	Measles
Tetanos, Tetanosul, Tetanosului	Tetanus
Tuse convulsiva, Tusei convulsive	Pertussis
Varicelă, Varicelei	Varicella
Variola, Variolei	Smallpox

Russian	
Бцж	BCG
АКДС	DTP
Дифтерит, Дифтерия	Diphtheria
Гемоифлюс инфлюзнцы типа Б	Hib
Гепатит	Hepatitis
Грипп	Influenza
Корь	Measles
Свинка, Паротит	Mumps
Коклюш	Pertussis
Воспале лёгких Пневмония	Pneumonia
Полиомиелит	Polio
Краснуха	Rubella
Оспа	Smallpox
Столбняк, Столбняка	Tetanus
Туберкулез	Tuberculosis

B

Ветрянка	Varicella
Манту	Mantoux (TB Test)
Вакцина	Vaccine
Вакцинация	Series
Ревакцинация	Booster

Samoan	
Mami	Mumps
Misela	Measles
Rupela	Rubella

Serbian	
Beseže	BCG
Detepe	DTP
Difterija	Diphtheria
Dječja paraliza	Polio
Gripa	Influenza
Hri pavac	Pertussis
Male boginje	Rubella
Pljuskavice, Kozice	Varicella
Upala pluća	Pneumonia
Veliki boginje	Smallpox
Veliki kašalj	Pertussis
Zapaljenje	Hepatitis
Zaušnjaci	Mumps
Žutica	Hepatitis

Slovak	
Chripka	Influenza
Cierny kasel	Pertussis
Diftéria	Diphtheria
DiTePe	DTP
Hepatitida	Hepatitis
Krzamak	Measles
Osypky	Measles
Parotitis	Mumps
Polyomyelitida	Polio
Priusnica	Mumps
Ruzienka	Rubella
Zápaľ plüc	Pneumonia
Záskrt	Diphtheria

Spanish	
Cólera	Cholera
Coqueluche	Pertussis
Difteria	Diphtheria
Doble Antigen	Td (Mexico)
Doble Viral	Measles-Rubella (Mexico)
Duple	DT (Cuba)
Gripe	Influenza
Hemófilo tipo b	Hib
Numonía	Pneumonia
Paperas, Parotiditis	Mumps

Poliomielitis	Polio
Pulmonía	Pneumonia
Rubéola	Rubella
Sarampión, Sarampión Comun	Measles
Sarampión Aleman	Rubella
SPR	MMR
Tetánica, Tétano	Tetanus
Tos Ferina	Pertussis
Varicela	Varicella
Viruela	Smallpox

Somali	
Bus-buska	Varicella
Cagaarshowga	Hepatitis
Cuno xanuun	Diphtheria
Dabayl	Polio
Duf	Polio
Furuq	Smallpox
Gowracato	Diphtheria
Gurra dhaabsis	Mumps
Hablobaas	Varicella
Haemophilus nooca b	Hib
Infilowense	Influenza
Jadeeco	Measles
Jadeeco been, Jadeeco jarmalka	Rubella
Joonis	Hepatitis
Kix	Pertussis
Qaamow-Qashiir	Mumps
Qaaxo-Tiibi	Tuberculosis
Qanja Barar	Mumps
Sambabaha	Pneumonia
Tallaakla Qaaxada	BCG
Taytano	Tetanus
Wareento	Pneumonia
Xiiqdheer	Pertussis

Swedish	
Difteri	Diphtheria
Duplex	DT
Gula Febern	Yellow Fever
Kikhosta	Pertussis
Kolera	Cholera
Mässling, Masslingormerly	Measles
Pässjura	Mumps
Polio	Polio
Rőda Hund	Rubella
Smittkoppor	Smallpox
Stelkramp	Tetanus
Trippel	DTP

Tagalog	
Beke	Mumps
Dipterya	Diphtheria

B

Pertusis	Pertussis
Polyo	Polio
Tetano	Tetanus
Tigdas	Measles
Turkish	
Boğmaca	Pertussis
Çocuk Felci	Polio
DBT	DPT
Difteri	Diphtheria
Erken Yaz-Beyin Iltihabı'na	Tick-borne encephalitis
Grip	Influenza
KKK	MMR
Kabakulak	Mumps
Kızamık	Measles
Kımamıkçık	Rubella
Meningekoklar	Meningococcal
Kuduz	Rabies
Pnömokoklar	Pneumococcal
Su Çiçeği	Varicella
Tetanos	Tetanus
Ukranian	
Кір	Measles
Поліо	Polio
Стовбняк	Tetanus
Vietnamese	
Bach Hâu	Diphtheria
Bai liet	Polio
Ban Đo	Rubella
Dai	Rabies
Ho Gà	Pertussis
Quai Bi	Mumps
Sài Uon Ván	Tetanus
So'i	Measles
Sot Tê Liêt	Polio
Thuong hàn	Typhoid
Uon ván	Tetanus
Viêm gan siêu vi B (VGSV B)	Hepatitis B
VNNB	Japanese encephalitis

April 2009

B

Foreign Language Terms
Table 2: Trade Names

Trade name	Antigen(s)	Manufacturer, Country
A.D.T.	Diphtheria, tetanus (adsorbed)	Commonwealth, Australia
A.K.D.S.	Diphtheria, tetanus, pertussis	UK
ACVax	Meningococcal (polysaccharide A & C)	GSK, UK
ACWYVax	Meningococcal (polysaccharide A, C, W, Y135)	GSK, UK
Acelluvax	Pertussis (acellular)	Chiron, Italy
ACTAcel	Diphtheria, tetanus, pertussis, Hib	Sanofi Pasteur, Argentina
Adifteper	Diphtheria, tetanus, pertussis	Ism, Italy
Adinvira A+B	Influenza (whole virus)	Imuna
Adiugrip	Influenza	Sanofi Pasteur
Admun	Influenza (whole virus)	Duncan
Admune GP	Influenza (whole virus)	Duncan
Agrippal	Influenza	Socopharm
AH	Hepatitis B	(Romania)
Aimmugen	Hepatitis A (inactivated)	Chemo-Sero-Therapeutic Resh Inst, Japan
Aldiana	Diphtheria (absorbed)	Sevac, Czech Republic
Alditeana	Diphtheria, tetanus (absorbed)	Sevac, Czech Republic
Alditerpera	Diphtheria, tetanus (adsorbed), pertussis	Sevac, Czech Republic
Almevax	Rubella	Evans
Alorbat	Influenza (whole virus)	Asta Pharma
Alteana Sevac	Tetanus	Institute of Sera and Vaccines
Amaril	Yellow fever	Sanofi Pasteur, France
AmBirix	Hepatitis A, Hepatitis B	GSK, Europe
AMC	Hib (polysaccharide)	Cuba
Anadifterall	Diphtheria (adsorbed)	Chiron, Italy
Anatetall	Tetanus (adsorbed)	Chiron, Italy
Anatoxal Di Te	Diphtheria, tetanus	Berna Biotech, Europe
Anatoxal Di Te Per	Diphtheria, tetanus, pertussis	Berna Biotech, Europe
AP	Polio	(Romania)
Arilvax	Yellow fever	MEDI, UK
ATPA	Tetanus Toxoid	(Romania)
AVAC-1, AVA	Anthrax	(for U.S. military use)
AVAXIM	Hepatitis A	Aventis Pasteur, France
B-Hepavac II	Hepatitis B	Merck, Singapore

Trade name	Antigen(s)	Manufacturer, Country
Begrivac	Influenza (split virus)	Chiron, Germany
Betagen	Hepatitis B	Sanofi Pasteur
Biaflu Zonale	Influenza (whole virus)	Farmabiagini, Itali
Biken-HB	Hepatitis B	Biken, Japan
Bilive	Hepatitis A/Hepatitis B (Recombinant)	Sinovac, China
Bimmugen	Hepatitis B (recombinant, adsorbed, yeast derived)	Chemo-Sero-Therapeutic Resh Inst, Japan
Biviraten Berna	Measles, mumps (live)	Berna Biotech, Switzerland
Buccopol Berna	Polio (oral)	Berna Biotech, Europe
BVAC	Botulinum antitoxin	(for U.S. military use)
B-Vaxin	Hepatitis B	Laboratorios Pablo Cassara, Argentina
C.D.T.	Diphtheria, tetanus (pediatric, adsorbed)	Commonwealth, Australia
CEF	Measles (Schwarz strain)	Chiron, Italy
Cacar	Smallpox	Indonesia
Campak Kerig	Measles	Pasteur Institute, Indonesia
Celluvax	Pertussis (acellular)	Chiron, Italy
Cinquerix	Diphtheria, tetanus, pertussis, Hib, Polio	GSK, Europe
Cocquelucheau	Pertussis (adsorbed)	Sanofi Pasteur, France
D-Immun	Diphtheria	Osterreichisches Institut, Austria
D.S.D.P.T.	Diphtheria, tetanus, pertussis (adsorbed)	Dong Shin Pharm, Korea
D.T. Bis Rudivax	Diphtheria, tetanus, rubella	Sanofi Pasteur, France
Di Anatoxal	Diphtheria	Berna Biotech, Europe
Di Te Per Pol Impfstoff	Diphtheria, tetanus, pertussis, polio	Berna Biotech, Switzerland
Di-Te-Pol SSI	Diphtheria, tetanus, polio	Statens Seruminstitut, Denmark
Dif-Tet-All	Diphtheria, tetanus	Chiron, Italy
Diftavax	Diphtheria, tetanus	Sanofi Pasteur
Ditanrix	Diphtheria, tetanus	GSK, Europe
DiTe Anatoxal	Diphtheria, tetanus (adsorbed)	Berna Biotech, Switzerland
Ditoxim	Diphtheria, tetanus (adsorbed)	Dong Shin Pharm, Korea
Double Anigen B.I.	Diphtheria, tetanus	Bengal Immunity Co, India
DT Adulte	Diphtheria, tetanus (adult)	Sanofi Pasteur, France
DT Bis	Diphtheria, tetanus (booster)	Sanofi Pasteur, France
DT Coq	Diphtheria, tetanus, pertussis	Sanofi Pasteur, France
DT Polio	Diphtheria, tetanus, polio	Sanofi Pasteur, France
DT TAB	Diphtheria, tetanus, *Salmonella typhi, Paratyphi A & B*	Sanofi Pasteur, France
DT Vax	Diphtheria, tetanus (pediatric)	Sanofi Pasteur, France

B

Trade name	Antigen(s)	Manufacturer, Country
DT Wellcovax	Diphtheria, tetanus (pediatric)	Chiron, UK
Dual Antigen Sii	Diphtheria, tetanus (adsorbed)	Serum Institute of India (Sii)
Dultavax	Diphtheria, tetanus, polio	Aventis Pasteur, France
Dupla	Diphtheria, tetanus	Instituto Butantan, Brazil
Duplex	Diphtheria, tetanus	Sweden
Ecolarix	Measles, rubella (Schwarz & RA 27/3)	GSK, Europe
Elvarix	Influenza (split virus)	VEB Sachsesches Serumwerk Dresden
Encepur	Tick-borne encephalitis	Chiron, Europe
Enivac-HB	Hepatitis B (Recombinant DNA)	Centro de Ingenieria Genetica Y Biotecnologia, Cuba
Enterovaccino	Typhoid (IM)	Isi
Enzira	Influenza	CSL
Eolarix	Measles, rubella (Schwarz & RA 27/3)	GSK, Europe
Epaxal Berna	Hepatitis A - virosomal vaccine	Berna Biotech, Switzerland
Ervax	Rubella (live)	GSK, Mexico
Ervevax RA 27/3	Rubella (live)	GSK, Belgium
Esavalenti	Diphtheria, tetanus, pertussis, polio, Hib, hepatitis B	Italy
Euvax-B	Hepatitis B (recombinant DNA)	LG Chemical, South Korea
Fendrix	Hepatitis B (dialysis formulation)	GSK, Europe
Fluad Agrippal-S1	Influenza	Chiron, Italy
Flubron	Influenza (whole virus)	Pfizer
Flugen	Influenza	UK
Fluvax	Influenza	CSL, Australia
Fluvirine	Influenza	CellTech Pharma SA
FOH-M	Polio (Inactivated)	Russia
FrocuoOke	Polio (Inactivated)	Russia
FSME-IMMUNE	Tick-borne encephalitis	Baxter, Austria
FSPD	Measles	Russia
Funed-CEME	Diphtheria, tetanus, pertussis	Belo Horizonte, Brazil
Gen H-B-Vax	Hepatitis B	Merck-Behringwerke
GenHevac B Pasteur	Hepatitis B	Sanofi Pasteur
Gene Vac-B	Hepatitis B	Serum Institute of India (Sii)
Gripax	Influenza (whole virus)	Hebrew University
Gripe	Influenza (whole virus)	Spain
Gripovax	Influenza (whole virus)	GSK
Gunevax	Rubella	Chiron, Italy

B

Trade name	Antigen(s)	Manufacturer, Country
H-Adiftal	Diphtheria	Ism, Italy
H-Adiftetal	Diphtheria, tetanus (adult)	Ism, Italy
H-Atetal	Tetanus	Ism, Italy
HarPaBreHnr B CtauOHAP	Rubella	Russia
HAVPur	Hepatitis A	Chiron, Germany
HB Vax Pro	Hepatitis B	SP
HBY	Hepatitis B (recombinant)	KGC, Japan
Heberbiovac HB	Hepatitis B	Heberbiotec, Cuba
Hepabest	Hepatitis A	Sanofi Pasteur, Mexico
Hepacare	Hepatitis B (recombinant)	Chiron, Europe
Hepaccine-B	Hepatitis B (plasma derived)	Chiel Jedang, South Korea
Hepagene	Hepatitis B	Chiron, Europe
Hepativax	Hepatitis B	LG Life Sciences, Korea
Hepavax-B	Hepatitis B (plasma derived)	Korea Green Cross, South Korea
Hepavax-Gene	Hepatitis B (recombinant DNA)	Korea Green Cross, South Korea
Hepcare	Hepatitis B	Chiron, Europe
Heprecomb	Hepatitis B (yeast derived)	Berna Biotech, Switzerland
Hevac B	Hepatitis B (plasma derived)	Sanofi Pasteur, France
Hexavac (Hexavax)	Diphtheria, tetanus, pertussis, polio, hepatitis B, Hib	Sanofi Pasteur, Europe
Hiberix	Hib conjugate	GSK
HIBest	*Haemophilus influenzae* type b	Sanoti Pasteur
Hinkuys karokoe	Pertussis (adsorbed)	Natl. Public Health Institute, Finland
HIS	Influenza	Serbian Institute, Yugoslavia
IBV	Polio (inactivated)	Statens Seruminstitut, Denmark
Immravax	Measles, mumps, rubella	Sanofi Pasteur, Europe
Immugrip	Influenza	Pierre Fabre Médicament
Immunil	Pneumococcal (polysaccharide)	Sidus
Imovax Parotiditis	Mumps	Sanofi Pasteur, Europe
Imovax Polio	Polio	Sanofi Pasteur, Europe
Imovax Sarampion	Measles	Sanofi Pasteur, Europe
Imovax D.T.	Diphtheria, tetanus (adult)	Sanofi Pasteur, Europe
Imovax Gripe	Influenza	Sanofi Pasteur, Europe
Imovax R.O.R.	Measles, rubella, mumps (live)	Sanofi Pasteur, Europe
Imovax Rubeola	Measles	Sanofi Pasteur, Europe
Imovax Mumps	Mumps	Sanofi Pasteur, Europe

B

Trade name	Antigen(s)	Manufacturer, Country
Imovax Oreillons	Mumps	Sanofi Pasteur, Europe
Imovax Rage	Rabies vaccine	Sanofi Pasteur, Europe
Imovax Tetano	Tetanus	Sanofi Pasteur, Europe
Infanrix Hexa	DTaP, polio, Hib, hepatitis B	GSK, France
Infanrix Penta	DTaP, hepatitis B, polio	GSK, Europe
Infanrix Quinta	DTaP, polio, Hib	GSK, Europe
Infanrix Tetra	DTaP, polio	GSK, Europe
Inflexal	Influenza	Swiss Serum and Vaccine Institute
Influmix	Influenza (whole virus)	Schiapparelli
Influpozzi Zonale	Influenza (whole virus)	Ivp
Influsplit SSW	Influenza (split virus)	VEB Sachsecsches Serumwerk Dresden
Influvac	Influenza	Solvay-Pharma
Influvirus	Influenza	Ism, Italy
Invirin	Influenza (whole virus)	GSK
Ipad TP	Tetanus, polio	Sanofi Pasteur, France
IPV-Virelon	Polio (inactivated)	Chiron, Europe
Isiflu Zonale	Influenza (whole virus)	Isi, Italy
Istivac	Influenza	Sanofi Pasteur, Europe
Kaksoisrokote Dubbelvaccin	Diphtheria, tetanus (pediatric)	Natl. Public Health Institute, Finland
Kikhoste-Vaksine	Pertussis	Statens Institutt for Folkehelse, Norway
Koplivac	Measles (Edmonston strain)	Philips-Duphar, Australia
Kotipa	Cholera, typhoid, paratyphoid	Perum Bio Farma, Indonesia
Krztuscowi	Pertussis	(Poland)
Ksztu	Pertussis	(Poland)
Lancy Vaxina	Smallpox	Swiss Serum and Vaccine Institute, Switzerland
Lavantuu tirokote	Typhoid	Central Pub Health La, Finland
Liomorbillo	Measles	
Liovaxs	Smallpox	Chiron, Italy
Lirugen	Measles	Sanofi Pasteur
LM - 3 RIT	Measles, mumps, rubella (live)	Dong Shin Pharm, Korea
LM - 2 RIT	Measles, mumps (live)	Dong Shin Pharm, Korea
Lteanas Imuna	Tetanus (adsorbed)	Imuna sp., Slovakia
Lyssavac N	Rabies	Berna Biotech, Europe
M-M-Rvax	Measles, mumps, rubella	Chiron, Europe
M-M-Vax	Measles, mumps	Merck, Europe
M-Vac	Measles (live)	Serum Institute of India (Sii)

Trade name	Antigen(s)	Manufacturer, Country
Masern-Impfstoff SSW	Measles (live)	Chiron, Germany
Massling	Measles	Sweden
MDPH-PA	Anthrax	
Measavac	Measles (Edmonston strain)	Pfizer, UK
Mencevax A	Meningococcal (polysaccharide) (Group A)	SmithKline/RIT, Belgium
Mencevax ACWY	Meningococcal quadravalent	GSK
Mengivax A/C	Meningococcal (conjugate) (Groups A & C)	Sanofi Pasteur, Europe
Meningitec	Meningococcal (conjugate) (Group C)	Wyeth, UK, Australia
Meningtec	Meningococcal (conjugate) (Group C)	Wyeth, Canada
Meninvact	Meningococcus (conjugate) (Group C)	Sanofi Pasteur
Menjugate	Meningococcus (conjugate) (Group C)	Socopharm
Menpovax 4	Meningococcal (polysaccharide) (Groups A, C, Y & W135)	Chiron, Europe
Menpovax A+C	Meningococcal (Groups A & C)	Chiron, Italy
MeNZB	Meningococcal B	Novartis (New Zealand)
Mesavac	Measles (Edmonston strain)	Pfizer, UK
Mevilin-L	Measles (Schwarz strain)	Chiron, UK
MFV	Influenza (whole virus)	Servier, UK
MFV-Ject	Influenza (whole virus)	Sanofi Pasteur, Europe
Miniflu	Influenza	Schiapparelli, Italy
Mo-Ru Viraten	Measles, rubella	Berna Biotech, Canada
Moniarix	Pneumococcal (polysaccharide)	GSK, Europe
Monovax / Monovac	BCG	Sanofi Pasteur, France
Mopavac	Measles, mumps (live, attenuated)	Sevac, Czech Republic
Morbilvax	Measles (live, attenuated)	Chiron, Italy
Morubel	Measles, rubella (live, attenuated)	Chiron, Italy
Moruman Berna	Measles immunoglobulin	Berna, Switzerland
Morupar	Measles, mumps, rubella (live, attenuated)	Chiron, Italy
Movivac	Measles (live, attenuated)	Sevac, Czech Republic
Mumaten	Mumps (live)	Berna Biogech, Switzerland
Munevan	Influenza (whole virus)	Medeva
Mutagrip	Influenza	Sanofi Pasteur, Germany
Nasoflu	Influenza	GSK, Europe
Neis Vac-C	Meningococcal (conjugate) (Group C)	Baxter, Europe & Canada
Neotyf	Typhoid (oral)	Chiron, Italy
Nilgrip	Influenza`	CSL
Nivgrip	Influenza (whole virus)	Nicolau Institute of Virology, Romania

B

Trade name	Antigen(s)	Manufacturer, Country
NorHOMHerHTA	Polio (Inactivated)	Russia
Nothav	Hepatitis A	Chiron, Italy
Okavax	Varicella	Sanofi Pasteur, Japan & Europe
Oral Virelon	OPV	Chiron, Germany
Pariorix	Mumps (live)	GSK, Mexico & Europe
Pavivac	Mumps (live)	Sevac, Czech Republic
Pediacel	DTaP, Hib, IPV	Europe
Penta	Diphtheria, tetanus, (acellular) pertussis, Hib, IPV	Sanofi Pasteur, Europe
PENT-HIBest	Diphtheria, tetanus, pertussis, polio, Hib	Sanofi Pasteur
Pentacel	Diphtheria, tetanus, pertussis, polio, Hib	Sanofi Pasteur, Canada
Pentacoq	Diphtheria, tetanus, pertussis, polio, Hib	Sanofi Pasteur
PentAct-HIB	Diphtheria, tetanus, pertussis, polio, Hib	Sanofi Pasteur, Europe
Pentavac	Diphtheria, tetanus, pertussis, polio, Hib	Sanofi Pasteur
Pentavalente	Diphtheria, tetanus, pertussis, hepatitis B, Hib	Mexico
Pentavalenti	Diphtheria, tetanus, pertussis, polio, Hib OR Diphtheria, tetanus, pertussis, polio, hepatitis B	Italy
Pentaxim	Diphtheria, tetanus, pertussis, polio, Hib	Aventis Pasteur, France
Pluserix	Measles, rubella	GSK, Mexico & Europe
Pneumopur	Pneumococcal (polysaccharide)	Chiron, Europe
POLIAcel	Diphtheria, tetanus, pertussis, polio, HIB	Sanofi Pasteur, Argentina
Poliomyelite	Polio (inactivated)	France
Polioral	Polio (oral)	Chiron, Germany
Polio Sabin	Polio (oral)	GSK, Europe
Poloral	Polio (oral)	Swiss Serum and Vaccine Institute
Prevenar	Pneumococcal (7-valent, conjugate)	Wyeth, France
Previgrip	Influenza	Chiron France
Primavax	Diphtheria, tetanus, hepatitis B	Sanofi Pasteur, Europe
Priorix	Measles, mumps, rubella (live)	GSK, Europe & Australia
Priorix-Tetra	Measles, mumps, rubella, varicella	GSK, Europe
Probivac-B	Hepatitis B	Probiomed, Mexico
Procomvax	Hib, hepatitis B	Merck, Sanofi Pasteur, Europe
Pulmovax	Pneumococcal (polysaccharide)	Merck
Q-Vac	Diphtheria, tetanus, pertussis, hepatitia B	Serum Institute of India (Sii)
Quadracel	Diphtheria, tetanus, pertussis, polio	Sanofi Pasteur, Mexico
QUADRAcel/Hibest	Diphtheria, tetanus, pertussis, polio, Hib	Sanofi Pasteur, Argentina
Quadravax	DTP + polio	GSK

Trade name	Antigen(s)	Manufacturer, Country
Quatro-Virelon	Diphtheria, tetanus, pertussis, polio	Chiron, Europe
Quinivax-IN	Diphtheria, tetanus, pertussis, Hib, polio	Valda Laboratori, Europe
Quintuple	Diphtheria, tetanus, pertussis, Hib, Polio	GSK, Mexico
R-HB Vaccine	Hepatitis B (recombinant)	Mitsubishi Chem Corp, Japan
R-Vac	Rubella (live)	Serum Institute of India (Sii)
Rabdomune	Rabies	Impdfstofwerke, Germany
Rabipur	Rabies	Chiron, Germany
Rabivac	Rabies	Chiron, Germany
Rasilvax	Rabies	Chiron, Italy
RDCV	Rabies	
Repevax	DTaP, IPV	Sanofi Pasteur
Revaxis	Td, IPV	Sanofi Pasteur, Europe
Rimevax	Measles (live)	GSK, Mexico & Europe
Rimparix	Measles, mumps (live)	GSK, Europe
RIT - LM-2	Measles, mumps (live)	Dong Shin Pharm, Korea
RIT - LM-3	Measles, mumps, rubella (live)	Dong Shin Pharm, Korea
Rorvax	Measles, mumps, rubella (live)	Sanofi Pasteur, Europe & Brazil
Rosovax	Rubella	Ism, Italy
Rouvax	Measles (live, attenuated)	Sanofi Pasteur, Europe
Rubavax	Rubella (live)	Sanofi Pasteur, UK
Rubeaten	Rubella (live)	Berna Biotech, Europe
Rubellovac	Rubella	Chiron, Germany
Rubilin	Rubella (live)	Chiron, UK
Rudi-Rouvax	Measles, rubella (live)	Sanofi Pasteur, France
Rudivax	Rubella (live, attenuated)	Sanofi Pasteur, Europe
Sahia	Polio (live, oral)	Multiple manufacturers
Sampar	Plague	Sanofi Pasteur, Indonesia
Sandovac	Influenza	Sandoz, Austria
Serap	Diphtheria, tetanus, pertussis	Perum Bio Farma, Indonesia
Shanvac-B	Hepatitis B	Shantha, India
SMBV	Rabies	Sanofi Pasteur, Europe
Sii Rabivax	Rabies	Serum Institute of India (Sii)
Sii Triple Antigen	Diphtheria, tetanus, pertussis	Serum Institute of India (Sii)
Stamaril	Yellow fever (live, attenuated)	Sanofi Pasteur, Europe
Streptopur	Pneumococcal (polysaccharide)	Chiron, Europe
Subinvira	Influenza (split virus)	Imuna, Czech Republic

B

Trade name	Antigen(s)	Manufacturer, Country
T. Polio	Tetanus toxoid, polio	SP (Canada)
T.A.B.	Typhoid, paratyphoid (A & B)	- Institute Pasteur, Tunisia - Egypt - Pharmaceutical Industries Corp, Burma
T-Immun	Tetanus (adsorbed)	Baxter, Germany
T-Vaccinol	Tetanus	Roehm Pharma, Germany
T-Wellcovax	Tetanus	Wellcopharm, Germany
Tanrix	Tetanus	GSK, Europe
Td-Pur	Tetanus, diphtheria	Chiron, Europe
Td-Virelon	Tetanus, diphtheria, polio	Chiron, Europe
Te Anatoxal	Tetanus	Berna Biotech, Switzerland
Telvaclptap	Tetanus	Yugoslavia
Tet-Aktiv	Tetanus	Tropon-Cutter, Germany
Tet-Tox	Tetanus	CSL Limited, Australia
Tetagrip	Tetanus, influenza	SP (France)
Tetamun SSW	Tetanus (fluid, nonadsorbed)	Veb Sachsisches Serumwerk, Germany
Tetamyn	Tetanus	Bioclon, Mexico
Tetanol	Tetanus (adsorbed)	Chiron, Sanofi Pasteur, Europe & Mexico
Tetanovac	Tetanus	Sanofi Pasteur, Mexico
Tetasorbat SSW	Tetanus (adsorbed)	Veb Sachsisches Serumwerk, Germany
Tetatox	Tetanus (adsorbed)	Berna Biotech, Italy
Tetavax	Tetanus (adsorbed)	Sanofi Pasteur, Europe
Tetracoq 05	Diphtheria, tetanus, pertussis, polio	Sanofi Pasteur, France
TetrAct-HIB	Diphtheria, tetanus, pertussis, Hib	Sanofi Pasteur, Europe
Tetravac Acellulaire	Diphtheria, tetanus, pertussis, polio	Sanofi Pasteur, Europe
Tetravalenti	Diphtheria, tetanus, pertussis, hepatitis B	Italy
Tetraxim	Tetanus, diphtheria, pertussis, polio	Sanofi Pasteur, Europe
Theracys	BCG	Aventis Pasteur, Canada
Ticovac	Tick-borne encephalitis	Baxter SA
Tifovax	Typhoid (Vi polysaccharide)	Sanofi Pasteur, Mexico
Titifica	Typhoid and para typhoid	Italy
TOPV	Trivalent oral polio vaccine	Multiple manufacturers and countries
Trenin DPT Behring	Diphtheria, tetanus, pertussis	Chiron Behring GmbH, Germany
Tresivac	Measles, mumps, rubella	Serum Institute of India (Sii)
Triacel	Diphtheria, tetanus, (acellular) pertussis	Sanofi Pasteur, Europe & Mexico
Triacelluvax	Diphtheria, tetanus, (acellular) pertussis	Chiron, Europe
Trimovax	Measles, mumps, rubella (live)	Sanofi Pasteur, Europe

B

Trade name	Antigen(s)	Manufacturer, Country
Tripacel	Diphtheria, tetanus, (acellular) pertussis	Sanofi Pasteur, Europe
Triple antigen	Diphtheria, tetanus, pertussis	- Chowgule & Co., India - CSL Limited, Australia
Triple Sabin	Polio (live, oral)	Mexico
Triple	Diphtheria, tetanus, pertussis	Cuba, Mexico
Triple Viral	Measles, mumps, rubella	Mexico Immunology Institute, Croatia
Triplice (VT)	Diphtheria, tetanus, pertussis	Instituto Butantan, Brazil
Triplice Viral (VTV)	Measles, mumps, rubella	Instituto Butantan, Brazil
Triplovax	Measles, mumps, rubella	Sanofi Pasteur, Europe & Brazil
Tritanrix	DTwP	GSK
Tritanrix-HB	DTwP/hepatitis B	GSK, Mexico
Tritanrix-HB-Hib	DTwP/hepatitis B/Hib	GSK
Trivacuna Leti	Diphtheria, tetanus (adsorbed), pertussis	Laboratory Leti, Spain
Trivax	Diphtheria, tetanus (plain), pertussis	Chiron, UK
Trivax-AD	Diphtheria, tetanus (adsorbed), pertussis	Chiron, UK
Trivax-Hib	Diphtheria, tetanus, pertussis, Hib	GSK, Europe
Trivb	Diphtheria, tetanus, pertussis	Brazil
Triviraten	Measles, mumps, rubella (live, attenuated)	Berna Biotech, Switzerland
Trivivac	Measles, mumps, rubella (live, attenuated)	Sevac, Czech Republic
Trivivax	Measles, mumps, rubella	Sanofi Pasteur, Mexico
Tussitrupin Forte	Pertussis	Staatliches Institut, Germany
Tuvax	BCG	Japan BCG Laboratory, Japan
Tyne	BCG	Sweden
Typherix	Typhoid (Vi polysaccharide)	GSK, Europe & Australia
Typhopara-typhoidique	Typhoid and para typhoid	France
Typhoral-L	Typhoid (Ty21a oral)	Berna Biotech, Germany
Typh-Vax	Typhoid	CSL Limited, Australia
Va-Diftet	Diphtheria, tetanus	Finlay Vacunas y Sueros, Cuba
Va-Mengoc-BC	Meningococcal (Groups B & C)	Finlay Vacunas y Sueros, Cuba
Vac-DPT	Diphtheria, tetanus, pertussis	Bioclon, Mexico
Vaccin Difteric Adsorbit	Diphtheria toxoid (adsorbed)	Cantacuzino Institute, Romania
Vaccin Rabique Pasteur	Rabies	Pasteur Vaccins
Vaccin Combinat Diftero-Tetanic	Diphtheria, tetanus (adsorbed)	Cantacuzino Institute, Romania
Vaccin tuberculeux attenue lyophilise	BCG	Sanofi Pasteur, France
Vaccinum Morbillorum Vivum	Measles (live)	Moscow Research Institute, Russia

B

Trade name	Antigen(s)	Manufacturer, Country
Vacina Dupla	Diphtheria, tetanus	Instituto Butantan, Brazil
Vacina Triplice	Diphtheria, tetanus, pertussis	Instituto Butantan, Brazil
Vacina Triplice Viral	Measles, mumps, rubella	Brazil
Vacunol	Tetanus	Temis-Lostato, Brazil
Vakcin Sampar	Plague	Perum Bio Farma, Indonesia
Vaksin Cacar	Smallpox	Indonesia
Vaksin Serap	Diphtheria, tetanus, pertussis	Perum Bio Farma, Indonesia
Vaksin Campak Kerig	Measles (live, attenuated)	Perum Bio Farma, Indonesia
Vaksin Kotipa	Cholera, typhoid and paratyphoid A, B & C	Perum Bio Farma (Indonesia)
Vamoavax	Measles, mumps (live)	Institute of Immunology, Croatia
Varicella-RIT	Varicella	GSK, Europe
Varicellon	Varicella zoster immunoglobulin	Behringwerke Aktiengesellschaft, Germany
Varie	Smallpox (lyophilized)	Institute of Sera and Vaccine, Czech Republic
Varilrix	Varicella (live, Oka strain)	GSK, Europe & Mexico
Vax-Tet	Tetanus	Finlay Vacunas & Sueros, Cuba
Vaxem-Hib	Hib (polysaccharide)	Chiron, Europe
Vaxicoq	Pertussis (adsorbed)	Sanofi Pasteur, France
Vaxigrip	Influenza	Sanofi Pasteur, Europe & Australia
Vaxihaler-Flu	Influenza (inhaler)	Riker, UK
Vaxipar	Mumps (live)	Chiron, Italy
VCDT	Diphtheria, tetanus (pediatric)	Cantacuzino Institute, Romania
VDA Vaccin Difteric Adsorbit	Diphtheria	Cantacuzino Institut, Romania
Verorab	Rabies (purified vero cell)	Sanofi Pasteur, France
Vibriomune	Cholera	Duncan Flockhart, UK
Viralinte	Hepatitis B	Ivax Pharmaceuticals, Mexico
Virelon C	Polio (Inactivated)	Chiron, Germany
Virelon T 20	Polio (live, oral, trivalent)	Chiron, Germany
Virivac	Measles, mumps, rubella (live)	Merck, Finland
Virovac Massling, Perotid, Rubella	Measles, mumps, rubella	Sweden
Vopix	OPV	PT Biofarma, Indonesia
VT (Vacina Triplice)	Diphtheria, tetanus, pertussis	Instituto Butantan, Brazil
VTV (Vacina Triplice Viral)	Measles, mumps, rubella	Brazil
VVR	Measles (live, attenuated)	Cantucuzino Institute, Romania
Welltrivax trivalente	Diphtheria, tetanus, pertussis	Spain

Trade name	Antigen(s)	Manufacturer, Country
X-Flu	Influenza	CSL
Zaantide	Diphtheria anti-toxin	Imunoloski Zavod, Croatia
Zaantite	Tetanus anti-toxin	Imunoloski Zavod, Croatia
Zaditeadvax	Diphtheria, tetanus	Imunoloski Zavod, Croatia
Zaditevax	Diphtheria, tetanus	Imunoloski Zavod, Croatia
Zamevax A+C	Meningococcal (polysaccharide, Groups A & C)	Imunoloski Zavod, Croatia
Zamovax	Measles (live)	Imunoloski Zavod, Croatia
Zamruvax	Measles, rubella (live)	Imunoloski Zavod, Croatia
Zapavax	Mumps	Imunoloski Zavod, Croatia
Zaruvax	Rubella (live)	Imunoloski Zavod, Croatia
Zatetravax	Diphtheria, tetanus, pertussis, parapertussis	Imunoloski Zavod, Croatia
Zatevax	Tetanus	Imunoloski Zavod, Croatia
Zatribavax	Diphtheria, tetanus, pertussis	Imunoloski Zavod, Croatia
Zatrivax	Measles, rubella, mumps (live)	Imunoloski Zavod, Croatia

April 2009

Appendix B

B

APPENDIX C
Vaccine Storage & Handling

C

VACCINE MANAGEMENT

Recommendations for Storage and Handling of Selected Biologicals

April 2009

Contents

DT: Diphtheria, Tetanus Toxoids–Pediatric

Td: Tetanus, Diphtheria Toxoids–Adult

Shipping Requirements

Should be shipped in insulated container.
Maintain temperature at 35° to 46°F (2° to 8°C). *Do not freeze or expose to freezing temperatures.*

Condition upon Arrival

Should not have been frozen or exposed to freezing temperatures. Refrigerate upon arrival.
If you have questions about the condition of the material at the time of delivery, you should 1) immediately place material in recommended storage; and 2) then follow your state health department immunization program policy and contact either the manufacturer's Quality Control office or the immunization program for guidance.

Storage Requirements

Refrigerate immediately upon arrival. Store at 35° to 46°F (2° to 8°C). *Do not freeze or expose to freezing temperatures.*

Shelf Life

Check expiration date on vial or manufacturer-filled syringe.

Instructions for Use

Inspect visually for extraneous particulate matter and/or discoloration. If these conditions exist, the vaccine should not be used. Shake vial or manufacturer-filled syringe well before use. Discard vaccine if it cannot be resuspended with thorough agitation.

Shelf Life After Opening

Single-Dose Vials: The vaccine should be administered shortly after withdrawal from the vial.
Multidose Vials: Withdraw single dose of vaccine into separate sterile needle and syringe for each immunization. The vaccine should be administered shortly after withdrawal from the vial. Unused portions of multidose vials may be refrigerated at 35° to 46°F (2° to 8°C) and used until expired, if not contaminated or unless otherwise stated in the manufacturer's product information.
Manufacturer-Filled Syringes: The vaccine should be administered shortly after the needle is attached to the syringe.

Special Instructions

Rotate stock so that the earliest dated material is used first.
Note: All vaccine materials should be disposed of using medical waste disposal procedures. Contact the state health department for details.

DTaP: Diphtheria Toxoid, Tetanus Toxoid, Acellular Pertussis Vaccine–Pediatric

DTaP/Hib: Diphtheria Toxoid, Tetanus Toxoid, Acellular Pertussis Vaccine Combined with *Haemophilus influenzae* type b Conjugate Vaccine–Pediatric (TriHIBit)

DTaP-IPV: Diphtheria Toxoid, Tetanus Toxoid, Acellular Pertussis Vaccine, Inactivated Polio Vaccine–Pediatric (Kinrix)

DTaP-IPV/Hib: Diphtheria Toxoid, Tetanus Toxoid, Acellular Pertussis Vaccine, Inactivated Polio Vaccine combined with *Haemophilus influenzae* type b Conjugate Vaccine–Pediatric (Pentacel)

DTaP-HepB-IPV: Diphtheria Toxoid, Tetanus Toxoid, Acellular Pertussis Vaccine, Hepatitis B Vaccine, Inactivated Polio Vaccine–Pediatric (Pediarix)

Tdap: Tetanus Toxoid, Diphtheria Toxoid, Acellular Pertussis Vaccine–Adult

Shipping Requirements

Should be shipped in insulated container. Maintain temperature at 35° to 46°F (2° to 8°C). *Do not freeze or expose to freezing temperatures.*

Condition upon Arrival

Should not have been frozen or exposed to freezing temperatures. Refrigerate upon arrival.

If you have questions about the condition of the material at the time of delivery, you should 1) immediately place material in recommended storage; and 2) then follow your state health department immunization program policy and contact either the manufacturer's Quality Control office or the immunization program for guidance.

Storage Requirements

Refrigerate immediately upon arrival. Store at 35° to 46°F (2° to 8°C). ***Do not freeze or expose to freezing temperatures.***

Shelf Life

Check expiration date on vial, container, or manufacturer-filled syringe.

Instructions for Reconstitution*† or Use

Inspect visually for extraneous particulate matter and/or discoloration. If these conditions exist, the vaccine should not be used. Shake vial or manufacturer-filled syringe well before use. Discard vaccine if it cannot be resuspended with thorough agitation.

Shelf Life After Reconstitution*† or Opening

Single-Dose Vials: The vaccine should be administered shortly after withdrawal from the vial.

Manufacturer-Filled Syringes: The vaccine should be administered shortly after the needle is attached to the syringe.

Special Instructions

Rotate stock so that the earliest dated material is used first.

Note: All vaccine materials should be disposed of using medical waste disposal procedures. Contact the state health department for details.

---

* DTaP/Hib (TriHIBit) is ActHIB (sanofi pasteur) reconstituted with Tripedia (sanofi pasteur). Once reconstituted, this combination vaccine must be used within 30 minutes or discarded. The only DTaP vaccine that can be used to reconstitute the ActHIB for TriHIBit is Tripedia. No other brand of DTaP is approved for this use.

† DTaP-IPV/Hib (Pentacel is ActHIB (sanofi pasteur) reconstituted with a DTaP-IPV solution. Once reconstituted, this combination vaccine must be used within 30 minutes or discarded. This combination arrives with the DTaP-IPV vials and the ActHIB vials packaged together. Do not store them separately and do not administer them separately.

Hepatitis Vaccines:
HepA: Hepatitis A, **HepB:** Hepatitis B, **HepA-HepB:** Hepatitis A/B (Twinrix), **HepB-Hib:** Hepatitis B/*Haemophilus influenzae* type b (Comvax)

Shipping Requirements
Should be shipped in insulated container. Maintain temperature at 35° to 46°F (2° to 8°C). *Do not freeze or expose to freezing temperatures.*

Condition upon Arrival
Should not have been frozen or exposed to freezing temperatures. Refrigerate upon arrival.
If you have questions about the condition of the material at the time of delivery, you should 1) immediately place material in recommended storage; and 2) then follow your state health department immunization program policy and contact either the manufacturer's Quality Control office or the immunization program for guidance.

Storage Requirements
Refrigerate immediately upon arrival. Store at 35° to 46°F (2° to 8°C). *Do not freeze or expose to freezing temperatures.*

Shelf Life
Check expiration date on vial or manufacturer-filled syringe.

Instructions for Use
Inspect visually for extraneous particulate matter and/or discoloration. If these conditions exist, the vaccine should not be used. Shake vial or manufacturer-filled syringe well before use. Discard vaccine if it cannot be resuspended with thorough agitation.

Shelf Life After Opening
Single-Dose Vials: The vaccine should be administered shortly after withdrawal from the vial.
Manufacturer-Filled Syringes: The vaccine should be administered shortly after the needle is attached to the syringe.

Special Instructions
Rotate stock so that the earliest dated material is used first.
Note: All vaccine materials should be disposed of using medical waste disposal procedures. Contact the state health department for details.

Hib: *Haemophilus influenzae* type b Conjugate Vaccine

Shipping Requirements

Should be shipped in insulated container. Maintain temperature at 35° to 46°F (2° to 8°C). *Do not freeze or expose to freezing temperatures.*

Condition upon Arrival

Should not have been frozen or exposed to freezing temperatures. Refrigerate upon arrival.

If you have questions about the condition of the material at the time of delivery, you should 1) immediately place material in recommended storage; and 2) then follow your state health department immunization program policy and contact either the manufacturer's Quality Control office or the immunization program for guidance.

Storage Requirements

Vaccine: Refrigerate immediately upon arrival. Store at 35° to 46°F (2° to 8°C). *Do not freeze or expose to freezing temperatures.*

Diluent: May be refrigerated or stored at room temperature (68° to 77°F [20° to 25°C]). *Do not freeze or expose to freezing temperatures.*

Shelf Life

Check expiration date on vial.

Instructions for Reconstitution* or Use

Inspect visually for extraneous particulate matter and/or discoloration. If these conditions exist, the vaccine should not be used. Shake vial or manufacturer-filled syringe well before use. Discard vaccine if it cannot be resuspended with thorough agitation.

Shelf Life After Opening

Single-Dose Vials: The vaccine should be administered shortly after withdrawal from the vial.

Special Instructions

Rotate stock so that the earliest dated material is used first.

Note: All vaccine materials should be disposed of using medical waste disposal procedures. Contact the state health department for details.

---

*ActHIB (sanofi pasteur) reconstituted with 0.4% sodium chloride diluent should be used within 24 hours after reconstitution. If sanofi pasteur DTaP-Tripedia is used to reconstitute ActHIB, the TriHIBit vaccine must be used within 30 minutes of reconstitution. Only sanofi pasteur DTaP-Tripedia or the diluent shipped with the product may be used to reconstitute the sanofi pasteur ActHIB product. No other brand of DTaP is licensed for use in reconstitution of ActHIB.

HPV: Human Papillomavirus Vaccine

Shipping Requirements

Should be shipped in insulated container. Maintain temperature at 35° to 46°F (2° to 8°C). *Do not freeze or expose to freezing temperatures.*

Condition upon Arrival

Should not have been frozen or exposed to freezing temperatures. Refrigerate upon arrival.
If you have questions about the condition of the material at the time of delivery, you should 1) immediately place material in recommended storage; and 2) then follow your state health department immunization program policy and contact either the manufacturer's Quality Control office or the immunization program for guidance.

Storage Requirements

Refrigerate immediately upon arrival. Store at 35° to 46°F (2° to 8°C). *Do not freeze or expose to freezing temperatures.* Protect from light at all times.

Shelf Life

Check expiration date on vial or manufacturer-filled syringe.

Instructions for Use

Inspect visually for extraneous particulate matter and/or discoloration. If these conditions exist, the vaccine should not be used. Shake vial or manufacturer-filled syringe well before use. Discard vaccine if it cannot be resuspended with thorough agitation.

Shelf Life After Opening

Single-Dose Vials: The vaccine should be administered shortly after withdrawal from the vial.
Manufacturer-Filled Syringes: The vaccine should be administered shortly after the needle is attached to the syringe.

Special Instructions

Rotate stock so that the earliest dated material is used first.
Note: All vaccine materials should be disposed of using medical waste disposal procedures. Contact the state health department for details.

IPV: Inactivated Polio Vaccine

Shipping Requirements

Should be shipped in insulated container. Maintain temperature at 35° to 46°F (2° to 8°C). *Do not freeze or expose to freezing temperatures.*

Condition upon Arrival

Should not have been frozen or exposed to freezing temperatures. Refrigerate upon arrival.
If you have questions about the condition of the material at the time of delivery, you should 1) immediately place material in recommended storage; and 2) then follow your state health department immunization program policy and contact either the manufacturer's Quality Control office or the immunization program for guidance.

Storage Requirements

Refrigerate immediately upon arrival. Store at 35° to 46°F (2° to 8°C). *Do not freeze or expose to freezing temperatures.*

Shelf Life

Check expiration date on vial or manufacturer-filled syringe.

Instructions for Use

Inspect visually for extraneous particulate matter and/or discoloration. If these conditions exist, the vaccine should not be used. Shake vial or manufacturer-filled syringe well before use. Discard vaccine if it cannot be resuspended with thorough agitation.

Shelf Life After Opening

Multidose Vials: Withdraw single dose of vaccine into separate sterile needle and syringe for each immunization. The vaccine should be administered shortly after withdrawal from the vial. Unused portions of multidose vials may be refrigerated at 35° to 46°F (2° to 8°C) and used until expired, if not contaminated or unless otherwise stated in the manufacturer's product information.
Manufacturer-Filled Syringes: The vaccine should be administered shortly after the needle is attached to the syringe.

Special Instructions

Rotate stock so that the earliest dated material is used first.
Note: All vaccine materials should be disposed of using medical waste disposal procedures. Contact the state health department for details.

TIV: Trivalent Inactivated Influenza Vaccine

Shipping Requirements

Should be shipped in insulated container. Maintain temperature at 35° to 46°F (2° to 8°C). *Do not freeze or expose to freezing temperatures.*

Condition upon Arrival

Should not have been frozen or exposed to freezing temperatures. Refrigerate upon arrival.
If you have questions about the condition of the material at the time of delivery, you should 1) immediately place material in recommended storage; and 2) then follow your state health department immunization program policy and contact either the manufacturer's Quality Control office or the immunization program for guidance.

Storage Requirements

Refrigerate immediately upon arrival. Store at 35° to 46°F (2° to 8°C). *Do not freeze or expose to freezing temperatures.* Protect **Fluarix** and **FluLaval** from light at all times by storing in original package.

Shelf Life

Formulated for use during current influenza season. Check expiration date on vial or manufacturer-filled syringe.

Instructions for Use

Inspect visually for extraneous particulate matter and/or discoloration. If these conditions exist, the vaccine should not be used. Shake vial or manufacturer-filled syringe well before use. Discard vaccine if it cannot be resuspended with thorough agitation.

Shelf Life After Opening

Single-Dose Vials: The vaccine should be administered shortly after withdrawal from the vial.
Multidose Vials: Withdraw single dose of vaccine into separate sterile needle and syringe for each immunization. The vaccine should be administered shortly after withdrawal from the vial. Unused portions of multidose vials may be refrigerated at 35° to 46°F (2° to 8°C) and used until expired, if not contaminated or unless otherwise stated in the manufacturer's product information.
Manufacturer-Filled Syringes: The vaccine should be administered shortly after the needle is attached to the syringe.

Special Instructions

Rotate stock so that the earliest dated material is used first.
Note: All vaccine materials should be disposed of using medical waste disposal procedures. Contact the state health department for details.

LAIV: Live Attenuated Influenza Vaccine

Shipping Requirements

Initially shipped to authorized distributors in the frozen state 5°F (-15°C). Shipped from the distributor to healthcare facilities in the refrigerated state at 35° to 46°F (2° to 8°C).

Condition upon Arrival

Refrigerate upon arrival.

If you have questions about the condition of the material at the time of delivery, you should 1) immediately place material in recommended storage; and 2) then follow your state health department immunization program policy and contact either the manufacturer's Quality Control office or the immunization program for guidance.

Storage Requirements

Refrigerate immediately upon arrival. Store at 35° to 46°F (2° to 8°C). *Do not freeze or expose to freezing temperatures.* If LAIV is inadvertently frozen, the vaccine should be moved immediately to the refrigerator and may be used until the expiration date printed on the package.

Shelf Life

Formulated for use during current influenza season. Check expiration date on package.

Instructions for Use

LAIV is a colorless to pale yellow liquid and is clear to slightly cloudy; some particulates may be present but do not affect the use of the product. After removal of the sprayer from the refrigerator, remove the rubber tip protector. Follow manufacturer's instructions to deliver ½ dose into one nostril. Then remove the dose-divider clip and deliver the remainder of the dose into the other nostril.

Shelf Life After Opening

Single-Dose Sprayer: The vaccine should be administered shortly after removal from the refrigerator.

Special Instructions

Rotate stock so that the earliest dated material is used first.

Note: All vaccine materials should be disposed of using medical waste disposal procedures. Contact the state health department for details.

MMR: Measles, Mumps, Rubella Vaccine

Shipping Requirements
Vaccine: Should be shipped in insulated container. Must be shipped with refrigerant. Maintain temperature at 50°F (10°C) or less. If shipped with dry ice, diluent must be shipped separately.
Diluent: May be shipped with vaccine, but do not place in container with dry ice.

Condition upon Arrival
Maintain at 50°F (10°C) or less. Do not use warm vaccine. Refrigerate upon arrival.
If you have questions about the condition of the material at the time of delivery, you should 1) immediately place material in recommended storage; and 2) then follow your state health department immunization program policy and contact either the manufacturer's Quality Control office or the immunization program for guidance.

Storage Requirements
Vaccine: Refrigerate immediately upon arrival. Store at 35° to 46°F (2° to 8°C). Protect from light at all times, since such exposure may inactivate the vaccine viruses.
Diluent: May be refrigerated or stored at room temperature (68° to 77°F [20° to 25°C]). *Do not freeze or expose to freezing temperatures.*
Note: MMR vaccine may be stored in the refrigerator or freezer.

Shelf Life
Check expiration date on vial.

Instructions for Reconstitution and Use
Reconstitute just before use according to the manufacturer's instructions. Use only the diluent supplied to reconstitute the vaccine.

Shelf Life After Reconstitution, Thawing or Opening
Single-Dose Vials: After reconstitution, use immediately or store at 35° to 46°F (2° to 8°C) and protect from light. *Discard if not used within 8 hours of reconstitution.*
Multidose Vials: Withdraw single dose of reconstituted vaccine into separate sterile needle and syringe for each immunization. The vaccine should be administered shortly after withdrawal from the vial. Unused portions of multidose vials may be refrigerated at 35° to 46°F (2° to 8°C), but must be discarded if not used within 8 hours after reconstitution.

Special Instructions
Rotate stock so that the earliest dated material is used first.
Note: All vaccine materials should be disposed of using medical waste disposal procedures. Contact the state health department for details.

MCV: Meningococcal Conjugate Vaccine

Shipping Requirements

Should be shipped in insulated container. Maintain temperature at 35° to 46°F (2° to 8°C). *Do not freeze or expose to freezing temperatures.*

Condition upon Arrival

Should not have been frozen or exposed to freezing temperatures. Refrigerate upon arrival.
If you have questions about the condition of the material at the time of delivery, you should 1) immediately place material in recommended storage; and 2) then follow your state health department immunization program policy and contact either the manufacturer's Quality Control office or the immunization program for guidance.

Storage Requirements

Refrigerate immediately upon arrival. Store at 35° to 46°F (2° to 8°C). *Do not freeze or expose to freezing temperatures.*

Shelf Life

Check expiration date on vial or manufacturer-filled syringe.

Instructions for Use

Inspect visually for extraneous particulate matter and/or discoloration. If these conditions exist, the vaccine should not be used. Shake vial or manufacturer-filled syringe well before use. Discard vaccine if it cannot be resuspended with thorough agitation.

Shelf Life After Opening

Single-Dose Vials: The vaccine should be administered shortly after withdrawal from the vial.
Manufacturer-Filled Syringes: The vaccine should be administered shortly after the needle is attached to the syringe.

Special Instructions

Rotate stock so that the earliest dated material is used first.
Note: All vaccine materials should be disposed of using medical waste disposal procedures. Contact the state health department for details.

MPSV: Meningococcal Polysaccharide Vaccine

Shipping Requirements

Should be shipped in insulated container. Maintain temperature at 35° to 46°F (2° to 8°C). *Do not freeze or expose to freezing temperatures.*

Condition upon Arrival

Should not have been frozen or exposed to freezing temperatures. Refrigerate upon arrival.
If you have questions about the condition of the material at the time of delivery, you should 1) immediately place material in recommended storage; and 2) then follow your state health department immunization program policy and contact either the manufacturer's Quality Control office or the immunization program for guidance.

Storage Requirements

Vaccine: Refrigerate immediately upon arrival. Store at 35° to 46°F (2° to 8°C). *Do not freeze or expose to freezing temperatures.*
Diluent: May be refrigerated or stored at room temperature (68° to 77°F [20° to 25°C]). *Do not freeze or expose to freezing temperatures.*

Shelf Life

Check expiration date on vial.

Instructions for Reconstitution and Use

Reconstitute just before using according to the manufacturer's instructions. Use only the diluent supplied to reconstitute the vaccine.

Shelf Life After Reconstitution or Opening

Single-Dose Vials: Use within 30 minutes of reconstitution.
Multidose Vials: Unused portions of multidose vials may be refrigerated at 35° to 46°F (2° to 8°C) and used up to 35 days after reconstruction.

Special Instructions

Rotate stock so that the earliest dated material is used first.
Note: All vaccine materials should be disposed of using medical waste disposal procedures. Contact the state health department for details.

PCV: Pneumococcal Conjugate Vaccine

Shipping Requirements

Should be shipped in insulated container. Maintain temperature at 35° to 46°F (2° to 8°C). *Do not freeze or expose to freezing temperatures.*

Condition upon Arrival

Should not have been frozen or exposed to freezing temperatures. Refrigerate upon arrival.
If you have questions about the condition of the material at the time of delivery, you should 1) immediately place material in recommended storage; and 2) then follow your state health department immunization program policy and contact either the manufacturer's Quality Control office or the immunization program for guidance.

Storage Requirements

Refrigerate immediately upon arrival. Store at 35° to 46°F (2° to 8°C). *Do not freeze or expose to freezing temperatures.*

Shelf Life

Check expiration date on vial or manufacturer-filled syringe.

Instructions for Use

Inspect visually for extraneous particulate matter and/or discoloration. If these conditions exist, the vaccine should not be used. Shake vial or manufacturer-filled syringe well before use. Discard vaccine if it cannot be resuspended with thorough agitation.

Shelf Life After Opening

Single-Dose Vials: The vaccine should be administered shortly after withdrawal from the vial.
Manufacturer-Filled Syringes: The vaccine should be administered shortly after the needle is attached to the syringe.

Special Instructions

Rotate stock so that the earliest dated material is used first.
Note: All vaccine materials should be disposed of using medical waste disposal procedures. Contact the state health department for details.

PPSV: Pneumococcal Polysaccharide Vaccine

Shipping Requirements

Should be shipped in insulated container. Maintain temperature at 35° to 46°F (2° to 8°C). *Do not freeze or expose to freezing temperatures.*

Condition upon Arrival

Should not have been frozen or exposed to freezing temperatures. Refrigerate upon arrival.
If you have questions about the condition of the material at the time of delivery, you should 1) immediately place material in recommended storage; and 2) then follow your state health department immunization program policy and contact either the manufacturer's Quality Control office or the immunization program for guidance.

Storage Requirements

Refrigerate immediately upon arrival. Store at 35° to 46°F (2° to 8°C). *Do not freeze or expose to freezing temperatures.*

Shelf Life

Check expiration date on vial.

Instructions for Use

Inspect visually for extraneous particulate matter and/or discoloration. If these conditions exist, the vaccine should not be used. Shake vial or manufacturer-filled syringe well before use. Discard vaccine if it cannot be resuspended with thorough agitation.

Shelf Life After Opening

Single-Dose Vials: The vaccine should be administered shortly after withdrawal from the vial.
Multidose Syringes: Withdraw single dose of vaccine into separate sterile needle and syringe for each immunization. The vaccine should be administered shortly after withdrawal from the vial. Unused portions of multidose vials may be refrigerated at 35° to 46°F (2° to 8°C) and used until expired, if not contaminated or unless otherwise stated in the manufacturer's product information.

Special Instructions

Rotate stock so that the earliest dated material is used first.
Note: All vaccine materials should be disposed of using medical waste disposal procedures. Contact the state health department for details.

C

Rotavirus Vaccine

Shipping Requirements

Should be shipped in insulated container. Maintain temperature at 35° to 46°F (2° to 8°C). *Do not freeze or expose to freezing temperatures.*

Condition upon Arrival

Should not have been frozen or exposed to freezing temperatures. Refrigerate upon arrival.
If you have questions about the condition of the material at the time of delivery, you should 1) immediately place material in recommended storage; and 2) then follow your state health department immunization program policy and contact either the manufacturer's Quality Control office or the immunization program for guidance.

Storage Requirements

Refrigerate immediately upon arrival. Store at 35° to 46°F (2° to 8°C). *Do not freeze or expose to freezing temperatures.* Protect from light at all times, since such exposure may inactivate the vaccine viruses.

Shelf Life

Check expiration date on package.

Instructions for Reconstitution or Use

Each dose of **RotaTeq** is supplied in a container consisting of a squeezable plastic, latex-free dosing tube with a twist-off cap, allowing for direct oral administration. The dosing tube is contained in a pouch. Remove the dosing tube from the pouch, screw the cap clockwise to puncture the tube, and screw the cap off counter-clockwise so that the liquid can be squeezed from the tube during oral administration of the vaccine.

Each dose of **Rotarix** is supplied as a vial of lyophilized vaccine. The 1mL of diluent is supplied in a prefilled oral applicator with a plunger stopper (contains latex), and a transfer adapter for reconstitution.

Shelf Life After Opening

Pouched Single-Dose Tubes: RoteTeq vaccine should be administered shortly after withdrawal from the refrigerator. The dosing tube should not be returned to the refrigerator once the screw cap has been removed.

Oral Applicator: Rotarix should be administered within 24 hours of reconstitution.

Special Instructions

Rotate stock so that the earliest dated material is used first.

Note: All vaccine materials should be disposed of using medical waste disposal procedures. Contact the state health department for details.

Varicella (Chickenpox) Vaccine

Shipping Requirements

Vaccine: Should be shipped in insulated container. Must be shipped with dry ice only, at 5°F (-15°C) or colder. Should be delivered within 2 days.

Diluent: May be shipped with vaccine, but do not place in container with dry ice.

Condition upon Arrival

Should be frozen. Vaccine should remain at 5°F (-15°C) or colder until arrival at the healthcare facility. Dry ice should still be present in the shipping container when the vaccine is delivered.

If you have questions about the condition of the material at the time of delivery, you should 1) immediately place material in recommended storage; and 2) then follow your state health department immunization program policy and contact either the manufacturer's Quality Control office or the immunization program for guidance.

Storage Requirements

Vaccine: Freeze immediately upon arrival. Maintain vaccine in a continuously frozen state at 5°F (-15°C) or colder. *No freeze/thaw cycles are allowed with this vaccine.* Vaccine should only be stored in freezers or refrigerator/freezers with separate external doors and compartments. Acceptable storage may be achieved in standard household freezers purchased in the last 10 years, and standard household refrigerator/freezers a separate, sealed freezer compartment. "Dormitory-style" units are not appropriate for the storage of varicella vaccine. *Do not store lyophilized vaccine in the refrigerator.* If lyophilized vaccine is inadvertently stored in the refrigerator, it should be used within 72 hours. Lyophilized vaccine stored at 35° to 46° F (2° to 8°C) which is not used within 72 hours should be discarded. Protect the vaccine from light at all times since such exposure may inactivate the vaccine virus.

In order to maintain temperatures of 5°F (-15°C) or colder, it will be necessary in most refrigerator/freezer models to turn the temperature dial down to the coldest setting. This may result in the refrigerator compartment temperature being lowered as well. Careful monitoring of the refrigerator temperature will be necessary to avoid freezing killed or inactivated vaccines.

Diluent: May be refrigerated or stored at room temperature (68° to 77°F [20° to 25°C]). *Do not freeze or expose to freezing temperatures.*

Shelf Life

Check expiration date on vial.

Instructions for Reconstitution and Use

Reconstitute just before use according to the manufacturer's instructions. Use only the diluent supplied to reconstitute the vaccine.

Shelf Life After Reconstitution, Thawing or Opening

Single-Dose Vials: Discard reconstituted vaccine if it is not used within *30 minutes* of reconstitution. *Do not freeze reconstituted vaccine.*

Special Instructions

Rotate stock so that the earliest dated material is used first.

If this vaccine is stored at a temperature warmer than 5°F (-15°C), it will result in a loss of potency and a reduced shelf life. If a power outage or some other situation occurs that results in the vaccine storage temperature rising above the recommended temperature, the healthcare provider should contact Merck, the vaccine manufacturer, at 1-800-9-VARIVAX for an evaluation of the product potency before using the vaccine.

Note: All vaccine materials should be disposed of using medical waste disposal procedures. Contact the state health department for details.

Zoster (Shingles) Vaccine

Shipping Requirements

Vaccine: Should be shipped in insulated container. Must be shipped with dry ice only, at 5°F (-15°C) or colder. Should be delivered within 2 days.

Diluent: May be shipped with vaccine, but do not place in container with dry ice.

Condition upon Arrival

Should be frozen. Vaccine should remain at 5°F (-15°C) or colder until arrival at the healthcare facility. Dry ice should still be present in the shipping container when the vaccine is delivered.

If you have questions about the condition of the material at the time of delivery, you should 1) immediately place material in recommended storage; and 2) then follow your state health department immunization program policy and contact either the manufacturer's Quality Control office or the immunization program for guidance.

Storage Requirements

Vaccine: Freeze immediately upon arrival. Maintain vaccine in a continuously frozen state at 5°F (-15°C) or colder. *No freeze/thaw cycles are allowed with this vaccine.* Vaccine should only be stored in freezers or refrigerator/freezers with separate external doors and compartments. Acceptable storage may be achieved in standard household freezers purchased in the last 10 years, and standard household refrigerator/freezers a separate, sealed freezer compartment. "Dormitory-style" units are not appropriate for the storage of varicella vaccine. *Do not store lyophilized vaccine in the refrigerator.* Protect the vaccine from light at all times since such exposure may inactivate the vaccine virus.

In order to maintain temperatures of 5°F (-15°C) or colder, it will be necessary in most refrigerator/freezer models to turn the temperature dial down to the coldest setting. This may result in the refrigerator compartment temperature being lowered as well. Careful monitoring of the refrigerator temperature will be necessary to avoid freezing killed or inactivated vaccines.

Diluent: May be refrigerated or stored at room temperature (68° to 77°F [20° to 25°C]). *Do not freeze or expose to freezing temperatures.*

Shelf Life

Check expiration date on vial.

Instructions for Reconstitution and Use

Reconstitute just before use according to the manufacturer's instructions. Use only the diluent supplied to reconstitute the vaccine.

Shelf Life After Reconstitution, Thawing or Opening

Single-Dose Vials: Discard reconstituted vaccine if it is not used within *30 minutes* of reconstitution. *Do not freeze reconstituted vaccine.*

Special Instructions

Rotate stock so that the earliest dated material is used first.

If this vaccine is stored at a temperature warmer than 5°F (-15°C), it will result in a loss of potency and a reduced shelf life. If a power outage or some other situation occurs that results in the vaccine storage temperature rising above the recommended temperature, the healthcare provider should contact Merck, the vaccine manufacturer, at 1-800-MERCK-90 for an evaluation of the product potency before using the vaccine.

Note: All vaccine materials should be disposed of using medical waste disposal procedures. Contact the state health department for details.

Manufacturer Quality Control Office
Telephone Numbers

Manufacturer/Distributor	Telephone Number	Product(s)
sanofi pasteur www.sanofipasteur.us	800-822-2463	DTaP, DTaP-Hib, DT, DTaP-IPV-Hib, Td, Tdap, TT, Hib, Influenza (TIV), IPV, MCV, MPSV
Talecris Biotherapeutics www.telecrisusa.com	800-520-2807	HBIG, IGIM, RIG, TIG
Centers for Disease Control & Prevention Drug Service www.cdc.gov/ncidod.srp/drugs/drug-service.html	404-639-3670	Distributor for Diphtheria antitoxin
Novartis www.novartis-vaccines.com/products/index/shtml	800-244-7668	Influenza (TIV)
GlaxoSmithKline www.gsk.com	866-475-8222 (customer support) 888-825-5249 (customer support)	DTaP, DTaP-IPV, DTaP-HepB-IPV, Tdap, HepA, HepB, HepA-HepB, Rotavirus, Influenza (TIV)
Massachusetts Biological Labs	617-474-3000 617-983-6400	Td, IGIM, TT
MedImmune, Inc. www.medimmune.com	877-633-4411	Influenza (LAIV)
Merck www.merckvaccines.com	800-637-2590	Hib, Hib-HepB, HepA, HepB, HPV, MMR, PPSV, Rotavirus, Varicella, Zoster
Nabi Biopharmaceuticals www.nabi.com	800-635-1766	HBIG
Wyeth www.wyeth.com	800-934-5556	Hib, PCV

April 2009

Checklist for Safe Vaccine Handling and Storage

Here are the 20 most important things you can do to safeguard your vaccine supply. Are you doing them all? Reviewing this list can help you improve your clinic's vaccine management practices.

Yes   No

1. We have a designated person in charge of the handling and storage of our vaccines.

2. We have a back-up person in charge of the handling and storage of our vaccines.

3. A vaccine inventory log is maintained that documents:
   _____ Vaccine name and number of doses received
   _____ Date the vaccine was received
   _____ Arrival condition of vaccine
   _____ Vaccine manufacturer and lot number
   _____ Vaccine expiration date

4. Our refrigerator for vaccines is either household-style or commercial-style, NOT dormitory-style. The freezer compartment has a separate exterior door. Alternatively, we use two storage units: a free-standing refrigerator and a separate, free-standing freezer.

5. We do NOT store any food or drink in the refrigerator or freezer.

6. We store vaccines in the middle of the refrigerator or freezer, and NOT in the door.

7. We stock and rotate our vaccine supply so that the newest vaccine of each type (with the longest expiration date) is placed behind the vaccine with the shortest expiration date.

8. We check vaccine expiration dates and we first use those that will expire soonest.

9. We post a sign on the refrigerator door showing which vaccines should be stored in the refrigerator and which should be stored in the freezer.

10. We always keep a thermometer in the refrigerator.

11. The temperature in the refrigerator is maintained at 35–46°F (2–8°C).

12. We keep extra containers of water in the refrigerator to help maintain cold temperatures.

13. We always keep a thermometer in the freezer.

14. The temperature in the freezer is maintained at +5°F (-15°C) or colder.

15. We keep ice packs and other ice-filled containers in the freezer to help maintain cold temperatures.

16. We post a temperature log on the refrigerator door on which we record the refrigerator and freezer temperatures twice a day—first thing in the morning and at clinic closing time—and we know whom to call if the temperature goes out of range.

17. We have a "Do Not Unplug" sign next to the refrigerator's electrical outlet.

18. In the event of a refrigerator failure, we take the following steps:
   _____ We assure that the vaccines are placed in a location with adequate refrigeration.
   _____ We mark exposed vaccines and separate them from undamaged vaccines.
   _____ We note the refrigerator or freezer temperature and contact the vaccine manufacturer or state health department to determine how to handle the affected vaccines.
   _____ We follow the vaccine manufacturer's or health department's instructions as to whether the affected vaccines can be used, and, if so, we mark the vials with the revised expiration date provided by the manufacturer or health department.

19. We have obtained a detailed written policy for general and emergency vaccine management from our local or state health department.

20. If all above answers are "yes," we are patting ourselves on the back. If not, we have assigned someone to implement needed changes!

Technical content reviewed by the Centers for Disease Control and Prevention, July 2008.   www.immunize.org/catg.d/p3035.pdf • Item #P3035 (7/08)

Immunization Action Coalition • 1573 Selby Ave. • St. Paul, MN 55104 • (651) 647-9009 • www.immunize.org • www.vaccineinformation.org

Vaccine Handling Tips
Outdated or improperly stored vaccines won't protect patients!

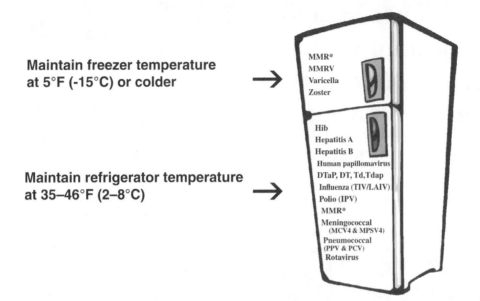

Maintain freezer temperature at 5°F (-15°C) or colder →

MMR*
MMRV
Varicella
Zoster

Maintain refrigerator temperature at 35–46°F (2–8°C) →

Hib
Hepatitis A
Hepatitis B
Human papillomavirus
DTaP, DT, Td,Tdap
Influenza (TIV/LAIV)
Polio (IPV)
MMR*
Meningococcal
(MCV4 & MPSV4)
Pneumococcal
(PPV & PCV)
Rotavirus

Order vaccine carefully.
Inventory your vaccine at least monthly and before placing an order. Expired vaccine must never be used and is money wasted!

Store vaccine correctly.†
Refrigerate or freeze immediately upon receiving shipment. Do not store vaccine in the door of the refrigerator or freezer. Inactivated vaccines should always be placed in the middle of the refrigerator far enough away from the freezer compartment to protect them from freezing.

Always use the vaccine with the earliest expiration date first.
Move vaccine with the earliest expiration date to the front and mark it to be used first. Keep vials in their boxes. Never use outdated vaccine.

Stabilize temperatures.
Store ice packs in the freezer and large jugs of water in the refrigerator along with the vaccine. This will help maintain a stable, cold temperature in case of a power failure or if the refrigerator or freezer doors are opened frequently or left open. Frequent opening of the refrigerator unit's doors can lead to temperature variations inside, which could affect vaccine efficacy. For this reason you should not store food or beverages in the refrigerator or freezer.

Safeguard the electrical supply to the refrigerator.
Make sure the refrigerator is plugged into an outlet in a protected area where it cannot be disconnected accidentally. Label the refrigerator, electrical outlets, fuses, and circuit breakers on the power circuit with information that clearly identifies the perishable nature of vaccines and the immediate steps to be taken in case of interruption of power (use DO NOT UNPLUG stickers). If your building has auxiliary power, use the outlet supplied by that system.

*MMR may be stored in either the freezer or the refrigerator.

†Refer to package insert for specific instructions on the storage of each vaccine. If you have questions about the condition of the vaccine, you should immediately place the vaccine in recommended storage and call the vaccine manufacturer(s) to determine whether the potency of the vaccine(s) has been affected. For other questions, call the immunization program at your state or local health department.

Record your health department's phone number here: _____

Adapted by the Immunization Action Coalition, courtesy of the Minnesota Department of Health

Technical content reviewed by the Centers for Disease Control and Prevention, May 2007.   www.immunize.org/catg.d/p3048.pdf • Item #P3048 (5/07)

Immunization Action Coalition • 1573 Selby Ave. • St. Paul, MN 55104 • (651) 647-9009 • www.immunize.org • www.vaccineinformation.org

WARNING

Do not unplug the refrigerator/
freezer or break circuit.
Expensive vaccine in storage.

In event of electrical problem, immediately contact:

WARNING

Do not unplug the refrigerator/
freezer or break circuit.
Expensive vaccine in storage.

In event of electrical problem, immediately contact:

WARNING

Do not unplug the refrigerator/
freezer or break circuit.
Expensive vaccine in storage.

In event of electrical problem, immediately contact:

APPENDIX D
Vaccine Administration

Vaccine Administration

Appropriate vaccine administration is critical to vaccine effectiveness. The recommended site, route and dosage for each vaccine are based on clinical trials, practical experience and theoretical considerations. The following information provides general guidelines for administration of vaccines for those who administer vaccines, as well as those in training, education and supervisory positions. This information should be used in conjunction with professional standards for medication administration, vaccine manufacturers' product guidelines, CDC's Advisory Committee on Immunization Practices (ACIP) General Recommendations on Immunization, the American Academy of Pediatrics' (AAP) Report of the Committee on Infectious Diseases *Red Book*, and state/agency-related policies and procedures. An education plan that includes competency-based training on vaccine administration should be considered for all persons who administer vaccines to children or adults (refer to "Skills Checklist for Immunization" - page D16).

Preparation

Patient Preparation - Patients should be prepared for vaccination with consideration for their age and stage of development. Parents/guardians and patients should be encouraged to take an active role before, during and after the administration of vaccines (see "Be There for Your Child During Shots" poster at http://cdlhn.com/default.htm, search for IMM674S).

- **Screening** - All patients should be screened for contraindications and precautions for each scheduled vaccine. Many state immunization programs and other organizations have developed and make available standardized screening tools. Basic screening questions can be found in Chapter 2. Sample screening forms for children and adults are available from the Immunization Action Coalition (www.immunize.org).

- **Vaccine Safety & Risk Communication** - Parents/guardians and patients are exposed through the media to information about vaccines, some of which is inaccurate or misleading. Healthcare providers should be prepared to discuss the benefits and risks of vaccines using Vaccine Information Statements (VIS) and other reliable resources. Establishing an open dialogue provides a safe, trust-building environment in which individuals can freely evaluate information, discuss vaccine concerns and make informed decisions regarding immunization (see Chapter 4 and Appendices E and F).

- **Atraumatic Care** - Vaccine safety issues and the need for multiple injections have increased the concerns and anxiety associated with immunizations. Healthcare providers need to display confidence and establish an environment that promotes a sense of security and trust for the patient and family, utilizing a variety of techniques to minimize the stress and discomfort associated with receiving injections. This is particularly important when administering vaccines to children.

  - **Positioning & Comforting Restraint** - The healthcare provider must accommodate for the patient's comfort, safety, age, activity level, and the site of administration when considering patient positioning and restraint. For a child, the parent/guardian should be encouraged to hold the child during administration. If the parent is uncomfortable, another person may assist or the patient may be positioned safely on an examination table (refer to "Comforting Restraint for Immunizations" - page D23).

- **Pain Control** - Pain is a subjective phenomenon influenced by multiple factors, including an individual's age, anxiety level, previous healthcare experiences, and culture. Consideration for these factors is important as the provider develops a planned approach to management of injection pain (see "Be There for Your Child During Shots" poster).

  - *Topical Anesthetics* or a vapocoolant spray may be applied to decrease pain at the injection site. These products should be used only for the ages recommended and as directed by the product manufacturer.

  - *Analgesic Agents* - A non-aspirin containing pain reliever may be considered to decrease discomfort and fever following vaccination. These products should be used only in age-appropriate doses.

  - *Diversionary Techniques* - Age-appropriate non pharmacologic techniques may provide distraction from pain associated with injections. Diversion can be accomplished through a variety of techniques, some of which are outlined on the "Be There for Your Child During Shots" poster.

  - *Dual Administrators* - Some providers favor the technique of two individuals simultaneously administering vaccines at separate sites. The premise is that this procedure may decrease anxiety from anticipation of the next injection(s). The effectiveness of this procedure in decreasing pain or stress associated with vaccine injections has not been evaluated.

Infection Control - Healthcare providers should follow Standard Precautions to minimize the risks of spreading disease during vaccine administration.

- **Handwashing** - The single, most effective disease prevention activity is good handwashing. Hands should be washed thoroughly with soap and water or cleansed with an alcohol-based waterless antiseptic between patients, before vaccine preparation or any time hands become soiled, e.g. diapering, cleaning excreta.

- **Gloving** - Gloves are not required to be worn when administering vaccines unless the person administering the vaccine is likely to come into contact with potentially infectious body fluids or has open lesions on the hands. It is important to remember that gloves cannot prevent needlestick injuries.

- **Needlestick Injuries** should be reported immediately to the site supervisor, with appropriate care and follow-up given as directed by state/local guidelines. Safety needles or needle-free injection devices should be used if available to reduce the risk of injury.

- **Equipment Disposal** - Used needles should not be detached from syringes, recapped or cut before disposal. All used syringe/needle devices should be placed in puncture proof containers to prevent accidental needlesticks and reuse. Empty or expired vaccine vials are considered medical waste and should be disposed of according to state regulations.

Vaccine Preparation - Proper vaccine handling and preparation is critical in maintaining the integrity of the vaccine during transfer from the manufacturer's vial to the syringe and ultimately to the patient.

• **Equipment Selection**

- **Syringe Selection** - A separate needle and syringe should be used for each injection. A parenteral vaccine may be delivered in either a 1-mL or 3-mL syringe as long as the prescribed dosage is delivered. Syringe devices with sharps engineered sharps injury protection are availble, recommended by OSHA, and required in many states to reduce the incidence of needle stick injuries and potential disease transmission. Personnel should be involved in evaluation and selection of these products. Staff should receive training with these device before using them in the clinical area.

- **Needle Selection** - Vaccine must reach the desired tissue site for optimal immune response. Therefore, needle selection should be based upon the prescribed route, size of the individual, volume and viscosity of the vaccine, and injection technique. (See Subcutaneous & Intramuscular Injections, below.) Typically, vaccines are not highly viscous, and therefore a fine gauge needle (22-25 gauge) can be used.

- **Needle-Free Injection** - A new generation of needle-free vaccine delivery devices has been developed in an effort to decrease the risks of needlestick injuries to healthcare workers and to prevent improper reuse of syringes and needles. For more information on needle-free injection technology, see the CDC website: www.cdc.gov/od/science/iso/vaxtech/nfit/.

• **Inspecting Vaccine** - Each vaccine vial should be carefully inspected for damage or contami nation prior to use. The expiration date printed on the vial or box should be checked. Vaccine can be used through the last day of the month indicated by the expiration date unless otherwise stated on the package labeling. Expired vaccine should never be used.

• **Reconstitution** - Some vaccines are prepared in a lyophilized form that requires reconstitution, which should be done according to manufacturer guidelines. Diluent solutions vary; use only the specific diluent supplied for the vaccine. Once reconstituted, the vaccine must be either administered within the time guidelines provided by the manufacturer or discarded. Changing the needle after reconstitution of the vaccine is not necessary unless the needle has become contaminated or bent. Continue with standard medication preparation guidelines.

• **Prefilling Syringes** - CDC strongly discourages filling syringes in advance, because of the increased risk of administration errors. Once the vaccine is in the syringe it is difficult to identify the type or brand of vaccine. Other problems associated with this practice are vaccine wastage, and possible bacterial growth in vaccines that do not contain a preservative. Furthermore, medication administration guidelines state that the individual who administers a medication should be the one to draw up and prepare it. An alternative to prefilling syringes is to use filled syringes supplied by the vaccine manufacturer. Syringes other than those filled by the manufacturer are designed for immediate administration, not for vaccine storage.

In certain circumstances, such as a large influenza clinic, more than one syringe can be filled. One person should prefill only a few syringes at a time, and the same person should administer them. Any syringes left at the end of the clinic day should be discarded.

Under no circumstances should MMR, varicella, or zoster vaccines ever be reconstituted and drawn prior to the immediate need for them. These live virus vaccines are unstable and begin to deteriorate as soon as they are reconstituted with diluent.

• **Labeling** - Once a vaccine is drawn into a syringe, the content should be indicated on the syringe. There are a variety of methods for identifying or labeling syringes (e.g. keep syringes with the appropriate vaccine vials, place the syringes in a labeled partitioned tray, or use color coded labels or preprinted labels).

Strategies to Prevent Immunization Administration Errors

1. When possible, involve staff in the selection of vaccine products to be used in your facility. Orient new staff to vaccines your office uses and validate their knowledge and skills about vaccine administration. Train all staff on the use and administration of new vaccines.

2. Keep current reference materials available for staff on each vaccine used in your facility. Keep reference sheets for timing and spacing, recommended sites, routes, and needle lengths posted for easy reference in your medication preparation area.

3. Rotate vaccines so that those with the shortest expiration dates are in the front of the storage unit. Use these first and frequently check the storage unit to remove and discard any expired vaccine.

4. Consider the potential for product mix-ups when storing vaccines. Do not store sound-alike and look-alike vaccines next to each other. Label storage containers or baskets with the age indications for each vaccine.

5. Administer only vaccines that you have prepared for administration. Triple-check your work before you administer a vaccine and ask other staff to do the same.

6. Counsel parents and patients on vaccines to be administered and the importance of maintaining immunization records on all family members. Educated clients may notice a potential error and help prevent it.

Administering Vaccines: Dose, Route, Site, and Needle Size

Vaccines	Dose	Route
Diphtheria, Tetanus, Pertussis (DTaP, DT, Tdap, Td)	0.5 mL	IM
Haemophilus influenzae type b (Hib)	0.5 mL	IM
Hepatitis A (HepA)	≤18 yrs: 0.5 mL ≥19 yrs: 1.0 mL	IM
Hepatitis B (HepB) *Persons 11–15 yrs may be given Recombivax HB® (Merck) 1.0 mL adult formulation on a 2-dose schedule.*	≤19 yrs: 0.5 mL* ≥20 yrs: 1.0 mL	IM
Human papillomavirus (HPV)	0.5 mL	IM
Influenza, live attenuated (LAIV)	0.2 mL	Intranasal spray
Influenza, trivalent inactivated (TIV)	6–35 mos: 0.25 mL ≥3 yrs: 0.5 mL	IM
Measles, mumps, rubella (MMR)	0.5 mL	SC
Meningococcal – conjugate (MCV)	0.5 mL	IM
Meningococcal – polysaccharide (MPSV)	0.5 mL	SC
Pneumococcal conjugate (PCV)	0.5 mL	IM
Pneumococcal polysaccharide (PPSV)	0.5 mL	IM or SC
Polio, inactivated (IPV)	0.5 mL	IM or SC
Rotavirus (RV)	2.0 mL	Oral
Varicella (Var)	0.5 mL	SC
Zoster (Zos)	0.65 mL	SC

Combination Vaccines

Vaccines	Dose	Route
DTaP+HepB+IPV (Pediarix®) DTaP+Hib+IPV (Pentacel®) DTaP+Hib (Trihibit®) DTaP+IPV (Kinrix®) Hib+HepB (Comvax®)	0.5 mL	IM
MMR+Var (ProQuad®)	≤12 yrs: 0.5 mL	SC
HepA+HepB (Twinrix®)	≥18 yrs: 1.0 mL	IM

Injection Site and Needle Size

Subcutaneous (SC) injection

Use a 23–25 gauge needle. Choose the injection site that is appropriate to the person's age and body mass.

Age	Needle Length	Injection Site
Infants (1–12 mos)	⅝"	Fatty tissue over anterolateral thigh muscle
Children 12 mos or older, adolescents, and adults	⅝"	Fatty tissue over anterolateral thigh muscle or fatty tissue over triceps

Intramuscular (IM) injection

Use a 22–25 gauge needle. Choose the injection site and needle length appropriate to the person's age and body mass.

Age	Needle Length	Injection Site
Newborns (1st 28 days)	⅝"*	Anterolateral thigh muscle
Infants (1–12 mos)	1"	Anterolateral thigh muscle
Toddlers (1–2 yrs)	1–1¼" ⅝–1"*	Anterolateral thigh muscle or deltoid muscle of arm
Children & teens (3–18 years)	⅝–1"* 1"–1¼"	Deltoid muscle of arm or anterolateral thigh muscle
Adults 19 yrs or older		
Male or female less than 130 lbs	⅝–1"*	Deltoid muscle of arm
Female 130–200 lbs Male 130–260 lbs	1–1½"	Deltoid muscle of arm
Female 200+ lbs Male 260+ lbs	1½"	Deltoid muscle of arm

A ⅝" needle may be used only if the skin is stretched tight, subcutaneous tissue is not bunched, and injection is made at a 90-degree angle.

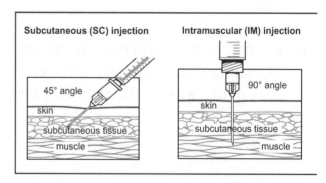

Please note: Always refer to the package insert included with each biologic for complete vaccine administration information. CDC's Advisory Committee on Immunization Practices (ACIP) recommendations for the particular vaccine should be reviewed as well.

Technical content reviewed by the Centers for Disease Control and Prevention, February 2009.   www.immunize.org/catg.d/p3085.pdf • Item #P3085 (2/09)

Immunization Action Coalition • 1573 Selby Ave. • St. Paul, MN 55104 • (651) 647-9009 • www.immunize.org • www.vaccineinformation.org

Administering Vaccines to Adults: Dose, Route, Site, Needle Size, and Preparation

Vaccine	Dose	Route	Site	Needle Size	Vaccine Preparation
Tetanus, Diphtheria (Td) with Pertussis (Tdap)	0.5 mL	IM	Deltoid muscle	22–25g, 1–1½"*	Shake vial vigorously to obtain a uniform suspension prior to withdrawing each dose. Whenever solution and container permit, inspect vaccine visually for particulate matter and/or discoloration prior to administration. If problems are noted (e.g., vaccine cannot be resuspended), the vaccine should not be administered.
Hepatitis A (HepA)	≤18 yrs.: 0.5 mL ≥19 yrs.: 1.0 mL	IM	Deltoid muscle	22–25g, 1–1½"*	
Hepatitis B (HepB)	≤19 yrs.: 0.5 mL ≥20 yrs.: 1.0 mL	IM	Deltoid muscle	22–25g, 1–1½"*	
HepA+HepB (Twinrix)	≥18 yrs.: 1.0 mL	IM	Deltoid muscle	22–25g, 1–1½"*	
Human papillomavirus (HPV)	0.5 mL	IM	Deltoid muscle	22–25g, 1–1½"*	
Influenza, trivalent inactivated (TIV)	0.5 mL	IM	Deltoid muscle	22–25g, 1–1½"*	
Pneumococcal polysaccharide (PPSV)	0.5 mL	IM	Deltoid muscle	22–25g, 1–1½"*	
		SC	Fatty tissue over triceps	23–25g, ⅝"	
Meningococcal, conjugated (MCV)	0.5 mL	IM	Deltoid muscle	22–25g, 1–1½"*	
Meningococcal, polysaccharide (MPSV)	0.5 mL	SC	Fatty tissue over triceps	23–25g, ⅝"	Reconstitute just before using. Use only the diluent supplied with the vaccine. Inject the volume of the diluent shown on the diluent label into the vial of lyophilized vaccine and gently agitate to mix thoroughly. Withdraw the entire contents and administer immediately after reconstitution. Discard single dose MPSV, varicella, and zoster vaccines if not used within 30 minutes after reconstitution. **Note:** Unused reconstituted MMR vaccine and multidose MPSV vaccine may be stored at 35–46°F (2–8°C) for a limited time. The reconstituted MPSV vaccine must be used within 35 days; the reconstituted MMR vaccine must be used within 8 hours. Do not freeze either reconstituted vaccine.
Measles, mumps, rubella (MMR)	0.5 mL	SC	Fatty tissue over triceps	23–25g, ⅝"	
Zoster (Zos)	0.65 mL	SC	Fatty tissue over triceps	23–25g, ⅝"	
Varicella (Var)	0.5 mL	SC	Fatty tissue over triceps	23–25g, ⅝"	
Influenza, live, attenuated (LAIV)	0.2 mL (0.1 mL into each nostril)	Intranasal spray	Intranasal	NA	Consult package insert.

*When giving intramuscular injections, a ⅝" needle is sufficient in adults weighing <130 lbs (<60 kg); a 1" needle is sufficient in adults weighing 130–152 lbs (60–70 kg); a 1–1½" needle is recommended in women weighing 152–200 lbs (70–90 kg) and men weighing 152–260 lbs (70–118 kg); a 1½" needle is recommended in women weighing >200 lbs (>90 kg) or men weighing >260 lbs (>118 kg). A ⅝" (16mm) needle may be used only if the skin is stretched tight, the subcutaneous tissue is not bunched, and injection is made at a 90-degree angle.

Please note: Always refer to the package insert included with each biologic for complete vaccine administration information. CDC's Advisory Committee on Immunization Practices (ACIP) recommendations for the particular vaccine should be reviewed as well. Access the ACIP recommendations at www.immunize.org/acip.

Technical content reviewed by the Centers for Disease Control and Prevention, February 2009.

www.immunize.org/catg.d/p3084.pdf • Item #P3084 (2/09)

Immunization Action Coalition • 1573 Selby Ave. • St. Paul, MN 55104 • (651) 647-9009 • www.immunize.org • www.vaccineinformation.org

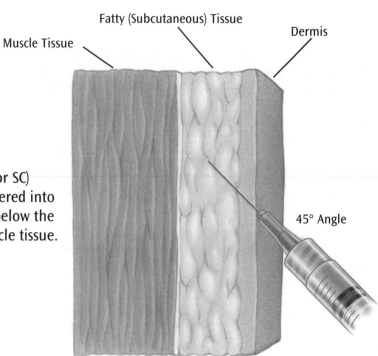

Muscle Tissue | Fatty (Subcutaneous) Tissue | Dermis

- **Subcutaneous** (Sub-Q or SC) injections are administered into the fatty tissue found below the dermis and above muscle tissue.

45° Angle

Lynne Larson, www.biovisuals.com

- **Site** - Subcutaneous tissue can be found all over the body. The usual sites for vaccine administration are the thigh (for infants <12 months of age) and the upper outer triceps of the arm (for persons ≥12 months of age). If necessary, the upper outer triceps area can be used to administer subcutaneous injections to infants.

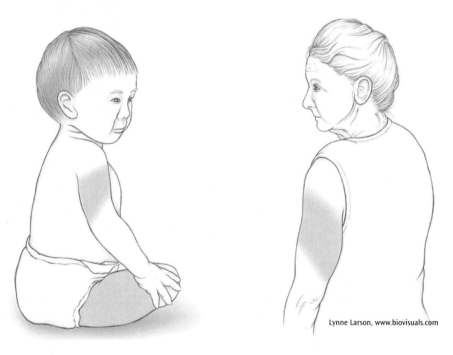

Lynne Larson, www.biovisuals.com

- **Needle Gauge & Length** - 5/8-inch, 23- to 25-gauge needle

- **Technique**

  - Follow standard medication administration guidelines for site assessment/selection and site preparation.

  - To avoid reaching the muscle, pinch up the fatty tissue, insert the needle at a 45° angle and inject the vaccine into the tissue.

  - Withdraw the needle and apply light pressure to the injection site for several seconds with a dry cotton ball or gauze.

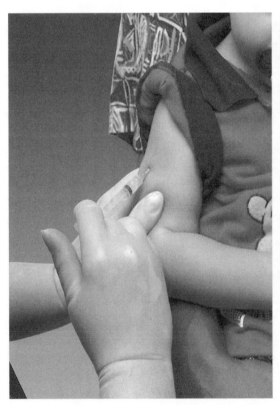 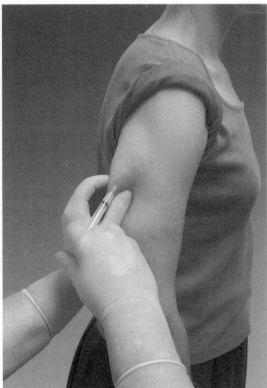

Subcutaneous Administration Techniques

Muscle Tissue

Fatty (Subcutaneous) Tissue

Dermis

- **Intramuscular** (IM) injections are administered into muscle tissue below the dermis and subcutaneous tissue.

90° Angle

Lynne Larson, www.biovisuals.com

- **Site** - Although there are several IM injection sites on the body, the recommended IM sites for vaccine administration are the vastus lateralis muscle (anterolateral thigh) and the deltoid muscle (upper arm). The site depends on the age of the individual and the degree of muscle development.

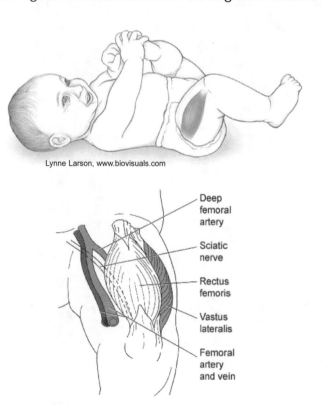

Lynne Larson, www.biovisuals.com

Deep femoral artery

Sciatic nerve

Rectus femoris

Vastus lateralis

Femoral artery and vein

The vastus lateralis muscle of the upper thigh used for intramuscular injections.

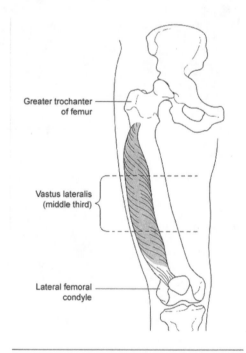

Greater trochanter of femur

Vastus lateralis (middle third)

Lateral femoral condyle

The vastus lateralis site of the right thigh, used for an intramuscular injection.

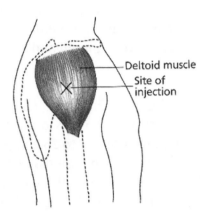

Deltoid muscle
Site of injection

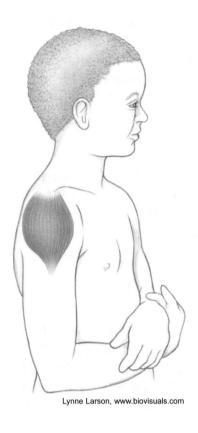

Lynne Larson, www.biovisuals.com

- **Needle Gauge** - 22- to 25-gauge needle

- **Needle Length** - For all intramuscular injections, the needle should be long enough to reach the muscle mass and prevent vaccine from seeping into subcutaneous tissue, but not so long as to involve underlying nerves, blood vessels, or bone. The vaccinator should be familiar with the anatomy of the area into which the vaccine will be injected.

Decision on needle size and site of injection must be made for each person on the basis of the size of the muscle, the thickness of adipose tissue at the injection site, the volume of the material to be administered, injection technique, and the depth below the muscle surface into which the material is to be injected

- *Infants (Younger Than 12 Months)*
  For the majority of infants, the anterolateral aspect of the thigh is the recommended site for injection because it provides a large muscle mass. The muscles of the buttock have not been used for administration of vaccines in infants and children because of concern about potential injury to the sciatic nerve, which is well documented after injection of antimicrobial agents into the buttock. If the gluteal muscle must be used, care should be taken to define the anatomic landmarks.*

*If the gluteal muscle is chosen, injection should be administered lateral and superior to a line between the posterior superior iliac spine and the greater trochanter or in the ventrogluteal site, the center of a triangle bounded by the anterior superior iliac spine, the tubercle of the iliac crest, and the upper border of the greater trochanter.

Injection technique is the most important factor to ensure efficient intramuscular vaccine delivery. If the subcutaneous and muscle tissue are bunched to minimize the chance of striking bone, a 1-inch needle is required to ensure intramuscular administration in infants. For the majority of infants, a 1-inch, 22-25-gauge needle is sufficient to penetrate muscle in an infant's thigh. For new born (first 28 days of life) and premature infants, a 5/8 inch needle usually is adequate if the skin is stretched flat between thumb and forefinger and the needle inserted at a 90-degree angle to the skin.

- *Toddlers and Older Children (12 Months through 10 Years)*
The deltoid muscle should be used if the muscle mass is adequate. The needle size for deltoid site injections can range from 22 to 25 gauge and from 5/8 to 1 inch on the basis of the size of the muscle and the thickness of adipose tissue at the injection site. A 5/8-inch needle is adequate only for the deltoid muscle and only if the skin is stretched flat between thumb and forefinger and the needle inserted at a 90° angle to the skin. For toddlers, the anterolateral thigh can be used, but the needle should be at least 1 inch in length.

- *Adolescents and Adults (11 Years or Older)*
For adults and adolescents, the deltoid muscle is recommended for routine intramuscular vaccinations. The anterolateral thigh also can be used. For men and women weighing less than 130 lbs (60 kg) a 5/8-1-inch needle is sufficient to ensure intramuscular injection. For women weighing 130-200 lbs (60-90 kg) and men 130-260 lbs (60-118kg), a 1-1½-inch needle is needed. For women weighing more than 200 lbs (90 kg) or men weighing more than 260 lbs (118 kg), a 1½-inch needle is required.

- **Technique**

  - Follow standard medication administration guidelines for site assessment/selection and site preparation.

  - To avoid injection into subcutaneous tissue, spread the skin of the selected vaccine administration site taut between the thumb and forefinger, isolating the muscle. Another technique, acceptable mostly for pediatric and geriatric patients, is to grasp the tissue and "bunch up" the muscle.

  - Insert the needle fully into the muscle at a 90° angle and inject the vaccine into the tissue.

  - Withdraw the needle and apply light pressure to the injection site for several seconds with a dry cotton ball or gauze.

• **Aspiration** - Aspiration is the process of pulling back on the plunger of the syringe prior to injection to ensure that the medication is not injected into a blood vessel. Although this practice is advocated by some experts, the procedure is not required because no large blood vessels exist at the recomended injection sites.

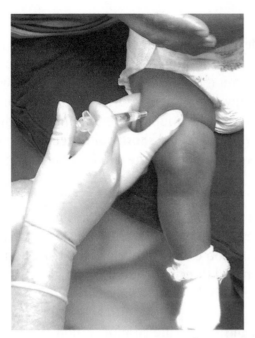 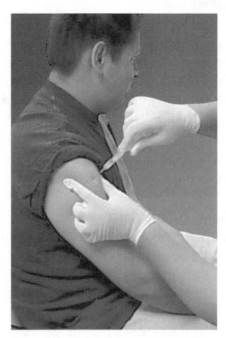

Intramuscular Administration Techniques

- **Multiple Vaccinations** - When administering multiple vaccines, NEVER mix vaccines in the same syringe unless approved for mixing by the Food and Drug Administration (FDA). If more than one vaccine must be administered in the same limb, the injection sites should be separated by 1-2 inches so that any local reactions can be differentiated. Vaccine doses range from 0.2 mL to 1 mL. The recommended maximum volume of medication for an IM site, varies among references and depends on the muscle mass of the individual. However, administering two IM vaccines into the same muscle would not exceed any suggested volume ranges for either the vastus lateralis or the deltoid muscle in any age group. The option to also administer a subcutaneous vaccine into the same limb, if necessary, is acceptable since a different tissue site is involved.

If a vaccine and an immune globulin preparation are administered simultaneously (e.g., Td/Tdap and tetanus immune globulin [TIG] or hepatitis B vaccine and hepatitis B immune globulin [HBIG]), a separate anatomic site should be used for each injection. The location of each injection should be documented in the patient's medical record.

- **Nonstandard Administration** - Deviation from the recommended route, site and dosage of vaccine is strongly discouraged and can result in inadequate protection. In situations where nonstandard administration has occurred, refer to the ACIP General Recommendation on Immunization, *MMWR* 2006; 55 (RR-15), for specific guidance.

D

Special Situations

Bleeding Disorders - Individuals with a bleeding disorder or who are receiving anticoagulant therapy may develop hematomas in IM injection sites. Prior to administration of IM vaccines the patient or family should be instructed about the risk of hematoma formation from the injection. Additionally, a physician familiar with the patient's bleeding disorder or therapy should be consulted regarding the safety of administration by this route. If the patient periodically receives hemophilia replacement factor or other similar therapy, IM vaccine administration should ideally be scheduled shortly after replacement therapy. A 23-gauge or finer needle should be used and firm pressure applied to the site for at least 2 minutes. The site should not be rubbed or massaged.

Latex Allergy - Administration of a vaccine supplied in a vial or syringe that contains natural rubber (refer to product information) should not be administered to an individual with a history of a severe (anaphylactic) allergy to latex, unless the benefit of vaccination clearly outweighs the risk of an allergic reaction. These situations are rare. Medical consultation and direction should be sought regarding vaccination. A local or contact sensitivity to latex is not a contraindication to vaccination.

Syncopal or Vasovagal Response ("fainting") may occur during vaccine administration, especially with adolescents and adults. Because individuals may fall and sustain injury as a result, the provider should have the patient sit during injection(s). A syncopal or vasovagal response is not common and is not an allergic reaction. However, if syncope develops, the provider should observe and administer supportive care until the patient is recovered.

Anaphylaxis (a life-threatening acute allergic reaction) - Each facility that administers vaccines should have a protocol, procedures and equipment to provide initial care for suspected anaphylaxis. Facility staff should be prepared to recognize and respond appropriately to this type of emergency situation. All staff should maintain current CPR certification. Emergency protocols, procedures and equipment/supplies should be reviewed periodically. For additional information on medical management of vaccine reactions in children, teens, and adults, see the 2006 ACIP General Recommendations on Immunization (p. 19), the 2006 AAP *Red Book* (pp. 64-66), and pages D28-D31 of this appendix. Although both fainting and allergic reactions are rare, vaccine providers should strongly consider observing patients for 15 minutes after they are vaccinated.

Documentation

All vaccines administered should be fully documented in the patient's permanent medical record. Documentation should include:

1. Date of administration

2. Name or common abbreviation of vaccine

3. Vaccine lot number

4. Vaccine manufacturer

5. Administration site

6. Vaccine Information Statement (VIS) edition date (found in the lower right corner of the back of the VIS).

7. Name and address of vaccine administrator. This should be the address where the record is kept. If immunizations are given in a shopping mall, for example, the address would be the clinic where the permanent record will reside.

Facilities that administer vaccines are encouraged to participate in state/local immunization information systems. The patient or parent should be provided with an immunization record that includes the vaccines administered with dates of administration.

> The California Department of Health Services' Immunization Branch
> has developed a complete package of resources on vaccine administration, available at
> http://www.eziz.org/pages/vaccineadmin.html

Skills Checklist for Immunization

IMM-694B (9/01)

The Skills Checklist is a self-assessment tool for health care staff who administer immunizations. To complete it, review the competency areas below and the clinical skills, techniques, and procedures outlined for each of them. Score yourself in the Self-Assessment column. If you check **Need to Improve** you indicate you need further study, practice or change is needed. When you check **Meets or Exceeds** you indicate you believe you are performing at the expected level of competence, or higher.

Supervisors: Use the Skills Checklist to clarify responsibilities and expectations for staff who administer vaccines. When you use it for performance reviews, give staff the opportunity to score themselves in advance. Next observe their performance as they provide immunizations to several patients and score in the Supervisor Review columns. If improvement is needed, meet with them to develop a Plan of Action (over) that will help them achieve the level of competence you expect; circle desired actions or write in others. In 30 days, observe their performance again. When all competency areas meet expectations, file the Skills Checklist in their personnel folder. At the end of the probationary period and annually thereafter, observe them again and complete the Skills Checklist.

Competency	Clinical Skills, Techniques, and Procedures	Self-Assessment		Supervisor Review		
		Need to Improve	Meets or Exceeds	Need to Improve	Meets or Exceeds	Plan of Action*
A. Patient/Parent Education	1. Welcomes patient/family, establishes rapport, and answers any questions.					
	2. Explains what vaccines will be given and which type(s) of injection will be done.					
	3. Accommodates language or literacy barriers and special needs of patient/parents to help make them feel comfortable and informed about the procedure.					
	4. Verifies patient/parents received the Vaccine Information Statements for indicated vaccines and had time to read them and ask questions.					
	5. Screens for contraindications. (MA: score NA–not applicable–if this is MD function.)					
	6. Reviews comfort measures and after care instructions with patient/parents, inviting questions.					
B. Medical Protocols	1. Identifies the location of the medical protocols (i.e. immunization protocol, emergency protocol, reference material).					
	2. Identifies the location of the epinephrine, its administration technique, and clinical situations where its use would be indicated.					
	3. Maintains up-to-date CPR certification.					
	4. Understands the need to report any needlestick injury and to maintain a sharps injury log.					
C. Vaccine Handling	1. Checks vial expiration date. Double-checks vial label and contents prior to drawing up.					
	2. Maintains aseptic technique throughout.					
	3. Selects the correct needle size. 1"-11/2" for IM (DTaP, Td, Hib, HepA, HepB, Pneumo Conj., Flu); 5/8" for SC (MMR, Var); IPV and Pneumo Poly depends on route to be used.					
	4. Shakes vaccine vial and/or reconstitutes and mixes using the diluent supplied. Inverts vial and draws up correct dose of vaccine. Rechecks vial label.					
	5. Labels each filled syringe or uses labeled tray to keep them identified.					
	6. Demonstrates knowledge of proper vaccine handling, e.g. protects MMR from light, logs refrigerator temperature.					

Competency	Clinical Skills, Techniques, and Procedures	Self-Assessment		Supervisor Review		
		Need to Improve	Meets or Exceeds	Need to Improve	Meets or Exceeds	Plan of Action*
D. Administering Immunizations	1. Rechecks the physician's order or instructions against prepared syringes.					
	2. Washes hands and if office policy puts on disposable gloves.					
	3. Demonstrates knowledge of the appropriate route for each vaccine. (IM for DTaP, Td, Hib, HepA, HepB, Pneumo Conj, Flu; SC for MMR, Var; Either SC or IM for IPV and Pneumo Poly).					
	4. Positions patient and/or restrains the child with parent's help; locates anatomic landmarks specific for IM or SC					
	5. Preps the site with an alcohol wipe using a circular motion from the center to a 2" to 3" circle. Allows alcohol to dry.					
	6. Controls the limb with the non-dominant hand; holds the needle an inch from the skin and inserts it quickly at the appropriate angle (45° for SC or 90° for IM).					
	7. Injects vaccine using steady pressure; withdraws needle at angle of insertion.					
	8. Applies gentle pressure to injection site for several seconds with a dry cotton ball.					
	9. Properly disposes of needle and syringe in sharps container. Properly disposes of live vaccine vial.					
	10. Encourages comfort measures before, during and after the procedure.					
E. Records Procedures	1. Fully documents each immunization in patient's chart: date, lot number, manufacturer, site, VIS date, name/initials.					
	2. If applicable, demonstrates ability to use IZ registry or computer to call up patient record, assess what is due today, and update computer immunization history.					
	3. Asks for and updates patient's record of immunizations and reminds them to bring it to each visit.					

Plan of Action: **Circle desired next steps and write in the agreed deadline and date for the follow-up performance review. a.** Watch video on immunization techniques. **b.** Review office protocols. **c.** Review manuals, textbooks, wall charts or other guides. **d.** Review package inserts. **e.** Review vaccine handling guidelines or video. **f.** Observe other staff with patients. **g.** Practice injections. **h.** Read Vaccine Information Statements. **i.** Be mentored by someone who has these skills. **j.** Role play with other staff interactions with parents and patients, including age-appropriate comfort measures. **k.** Attend a skills training or other courses or training. **l.** Attend health care customer satisfaction or cultural competency training. **m.** Renew CPR certification. **Other:**_____

_____ _____ Employee Signature   Date

_____ _____ Supervisor Signature   Date

_____ Plan of Action Deadline

_____ Date of Next Performance Review

IMMUNIZATION TECHNIQUES
Safe • Effective • Caring

For 8 1/2" x 11" copies, enlarge to 155%

Immunization Site Map

Suggested sites for
toddler immunizations:

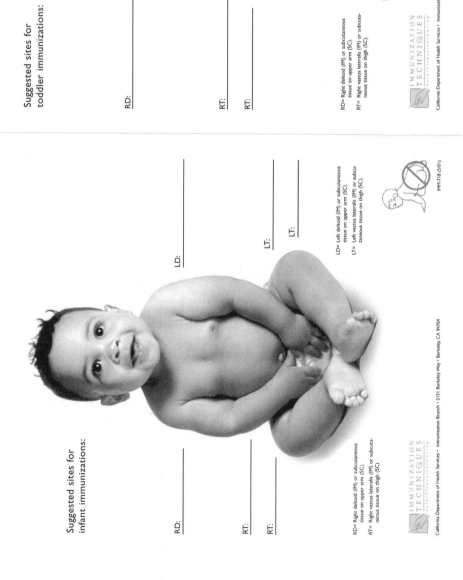

LD: _____

RD: _____

LT: _____

LT: _____

RT: _____

RT: _____

LD= Left deltoid (IM) or subcutaneous
tissue on upper arm (SC).
LT= Left vastus lateralis (IM) or subcutaneous tissue on thigh (SC).

RD= Right deltoid (IM) or subcutaneous
tissue on upper arm (SC).
RT= Right vastus lateralis (IM) or subcutaneous tissue on thigh (SC).

IMM-718 (5/01)

California Department of Health Services • Immunization Branch • 2151 Berkeley Way • Berkeley, CA 94704

IMMUNIZATION
TECHNIQUES

Immunization Site Map

Suggested sites for
infant immunizations:

LD: _____

RD: _____

LT: _____

LT: _____

RT: _____

RT: _____

LD= Left deltoid (IM) or subcutaneous
tissue on upper arm (SC).
LT= Left vastus lateralis (IM) or subcutaneous tissue on thigh (SC).

RD= Right deltoid (IM) or subcutaneous
tissue on upper arm (SC).
RT= Right vastus lateralis (IM) or subcutaneous tissue on thigh (SC).

IMM-718 (5/01)

California Department of Health Services • Immunization Branch • 2151 Berkeley Way • Berkeley, CA 94704

IMMUNIZATION
TECHNIQUES

Giving All the Doses Under 12 Months

- Needle Lengths:
  IM=1 inch   SC=5/8 inch

- Using combination
  vaccines will decrease
  the number of injections

- IM injections are given
  in the infant's thigh

- SC injections may be
  given in the arm or thigh

- Separate injection sites
  by 1-2 inches

- May consider a 5/8" needle
  for IM injections only in
  newborns less than 4 wks

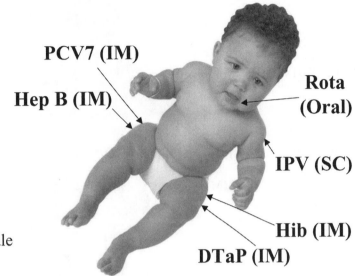

PCV7 (IM)

Hep B (IM)

Rota
(Oral)

IPV (SC)

Hib (IM)

DTaP (IM)

Alliance for Immunization in Michigan   2007 AIM Kit – Childhood Section   *December 20, 2006*

Giving All the Doses 12 Months and Older

- Needle Lengths
  IM=1 to 1.5 inches
  SC=5/8 inch

- Separate injection
  sites by 1-2 inches

- Anterolateral thigh is
  the **preferred** site for
  multiple IM injections

- Deltoid (upper arm)
  is an option for IM in
  children ≥18 mo with
  adequate muscle mass

- Using **combination vaccines**
  will decrease the number of
  injections needed to keep a
  child up-to-date

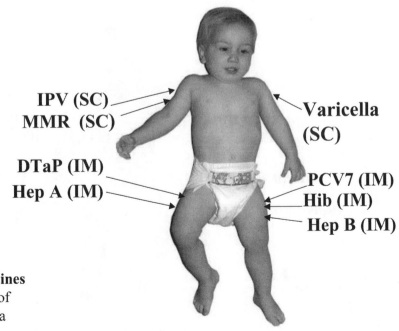

IPV (SC)
MMR (SC)

Varicella
(SC)

DTaP (IM)
Hep A (IM)

PCV7 (IM)
Hib (IM)
Hep B (IM)

Alliance for Immunization in Michigan   2007 AIM Kit – Childhood Section   *December 20, 2006*

Giving All the Doses 12 months through 5 years of age
Using Pediarix™ (DTaP/HepB/IPV) and ProQuad® (MMRV)

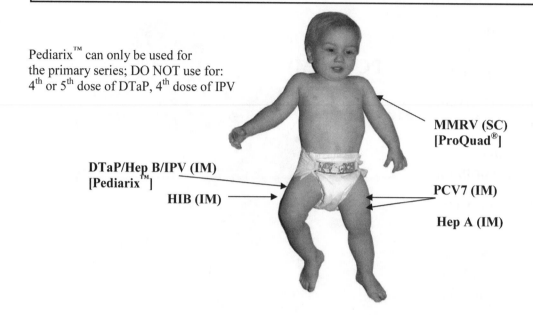

Pediarix™ can only be used for the primary series; DO NOT use for: 4th or 5th dose of DTaP, 4th dose of IPV

MMRV (SC) [ProQuad®]

DTaP/Hep B/IPV (IM) [Pediarix™]

HIB (IM)

PCV7 (IM)

Hep A (IM)

- Needle Lengths:
  IM = 1-1.5 inches
  SC = 5/8 inch
- Injection sites should be separated 1-2 inches
- The anterolateral thigh is the **preferred** site for multiple IM injections
- The deltoid (upper arm) is an option for IM in children ≥ 18 mo with adequate muscle mass

Using COMVAX™ (HepB/Hib) and ProQuad® (MMRV)

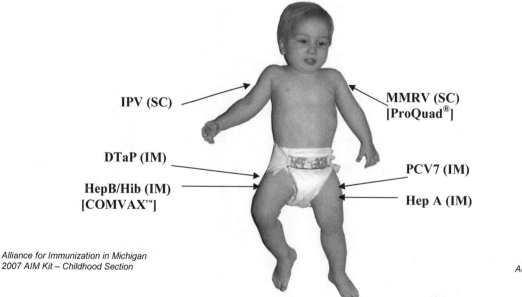

IPV (SC)

MMRV (SC) [ProQuad®]

DTaP (IM)

HepB/Hib (IM) [COMVAX™]

PCV7 (IM)

Hep A (IM)

Alliance for Immunization in Michigan
2007 AIM Kit – Childhood Section

August 23, 2006

D

Giving All the Doses Including Influenza Vaccine (TIV)

Using Pediarix™ (DTaP/HepB/IPV) and ProQuad® (MMR/Var)

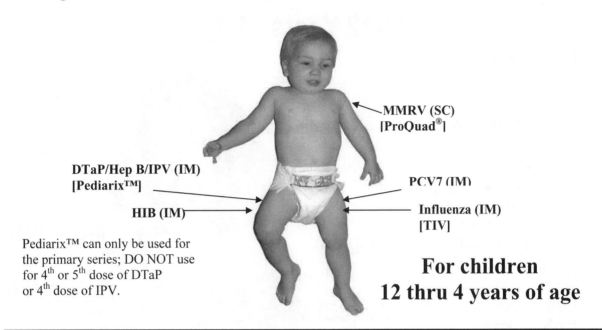

MMRV (SC)
[ProQuad®]

DTaP/Hep B/IPV (IM)
[Pediarix™]

PCV7 (IM)

HIB (IM)

Influenza (IM)
[TIV]

Pediarix™ can only be used for
the primary series; DO NOT use
for 4th or 5th dose of DTaP
or 4th dose of IPV.

**For children
12 thru 4 years of age**

◆ TIV Dosages: 6-35 mos 0.25 mL 3-8 yrs 0.5 mL	◆ 2 doses (4 weeks apart) are recommended for children 6 mo thru 8 yrs receiving any flu vaccine for the first time	◆ Children 6 mo-8 yrs who received influenza vaccine for the first time **during the previous influenza season**, and got only one dose, should receive two doses this season separated by 4 weeks

Using COMVAX™ (HepB/Hib) and ProQuad® (MMR/Var)

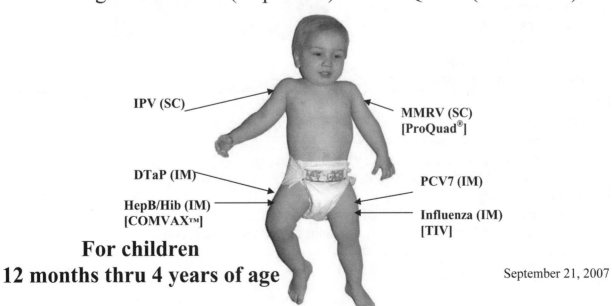

IPV (SC)

MMRV (SC)
[ProQuad®]

DTaP (IM)

PCV7 (IM)

HepB/Hib (IM)
[COMVAX™]

Influenza (IM)
[TIV]

**For children
12 months thru 4 years of age**

September 21, 2007

GIVING ALL THE DOSES
11-12 Years of Age

- Needle Lengths
  - IM= 1 to 1.5 in
  - SC= 5/8 in

- Separate injection sites by 1-2 inches

- Professional judgment is appropriate when selecting needle length for use in all children, especially small infants or larger children.

- Assess for other recommended vaccines that may be needed-
  - MMR   Polio
  - hep B   Hep A
    - influenza

- Syncope or fainting after vaccination may occur in adolescents & young adults, usually within 15 minutes of vaccination

- When giving vaccines to teens: Have the patient sit down while you are giving vaccine(s) Consider observing patients for 15-20 minutes after vaccination

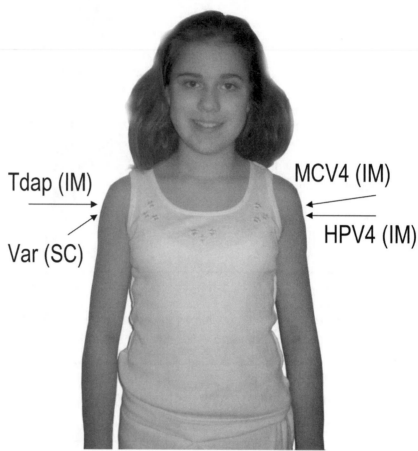

Tdap (IM)

Var (SC)

MCV4 (IM)

HPV4 (IM)

NOTE:

Var should be administered to school age children and adolescents without:
- history of 2 doses of varicella vaccine
- a healthcare provider's diagnosis of varicella disease **or** verification of history of typical varicella disease
- history of shingles

HPV4 is licensed for use in **girls only** 9-26 years of age

MMRV (ProQuad®) is licensed for children 12 months thru 12 years of age only

COMFORTING RESTRAINT

FOR IMMUNIZATIONS

• The method:

This method involves the parent in embracing the child and controlling all four limbs. It avoids "holding down" or overpowering the child, but it helps you steady and control the limb of the injection site.

• For infants and toddlers:

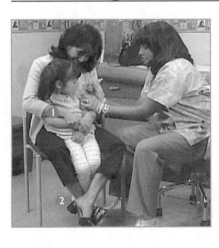

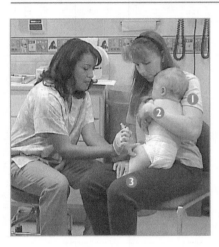

Have parent hold the child on parent's lap.

1. One of the child's arms embraces the parent's back and is held under the parent's arm.

2. The other arm is controlled by the parent's arm and hand. For infants, the parent can control both arms with one hand.

3. Both legs are anchored with the child's feet held firmly between the parent's thighs, and controlled by the parent's other arm.

• For kindergarten and older children:

Hold the child on parent's lap or have the child stand in front of the seated parent.

1. Parent's arms embrace the child during the process.

2. Both legs are firmly between parent's legs.

IMMUNIZATION
TECHNIQUES
Safe • Effective • Caring

Gray Davis, Governor—State of California
Grantland Johnson, Secretary—Health and Human Services Agency
Diana M. Bontá, R.N., Dr.P.H., Director—Department of Health Services
Immunization Branch • 2151 Berkeley Way • Berkeley, CA 94704

IMM-720 (12/01)

Injectable Vaccine Administration for Children Birth-6 years

Vaccine	Age/Reminders	Route	Site ¤	Needle*	Contraindications ⊕
Diphtheria, Tetanus, Pertussis (DTaP)	6 weeks-6 years	IM	Anterolateral Thigh **or** Deltoid±	1"-1.5" 22-25 g	Anaphylactic reaction to prior dose or component; encephalopathy without other cause within 7 days of a pertussis- containing vaccine
Haemophilus influenzae type B (Hib)	No routine doses after 59 months	IM	Anterolateral Thigh **or** Deltoid	1"-1.5" 22-25 g	Anaphylactic reaction to prior dose or component
Pneumococcal conjugate (PCV7)	No routine doses after 59 months	IM	Anterolateral Thigh **or** Deltoid	1"-1.5" 22-25 g	Anaphylactic reaction to prior dose or component
Hepatitis B (Hep B)	1st dose at birth; last dose at/after 6 months	IM	Anterolateral Thigh **or** Deltoid	1"-1.5" 22-25 g	Anaphylactic reaction to a prior dose or component (baker's yeast)
Inactivated Polio Vaccine (IPV)	For school entry: 1st dose at/ after 6 wks of age; all doses spaced at least 4 weeks apart	SC	Anterolateral Thigh **or** Lateral Upper Arm	5/8" 23-25 g	Anaphylactic reaction to a prior dose or component (neomycin, streptomycin, polymyxin B)
		IM	Anterolateral Thigh **or** Deltoid	1"-1.5 22-25 g	
Measles, Mumps, Rubella (MMR)	1st dose at/after 12 mo; 4 week interval between two doses (all ages)	SC	Anterolateral Thigh **or** Lateral Upper Arm	5/8" 23-25 g	Anaphylactic reaction to a prior dose or component (neomycin or gelatin); pregnancy
Varicella (Var)	1st dose at/after 12 mo; 3 mo interval between doses (ages 12 mo-12 yrs)	SC	Anterolateral Thigh **or** Lateral Upper Arm	5/8" 23-25 g	Anaphylactic reaction to a prior dose or component (neomycin or gelatin); pregnancy
Inactivated Influenza (TIV)	6 months and older; brand to use based on age	IM	Anterolateral Thigh **or** Deltoid	1"-1.5" 22-25 g	Anaphylactic reaction to a prior dose or component (eggs)
Hepatitis A (Hep A)	1st dose at/after 12 mo 2nd dose 6 mo later	IM	Anterolateral Thigh **or** Deltoid	1"-1.5" 22-25 g	Anaphylactic reaction to prior dose or component; hypersensitivity to alum (Havrix®: 2-phenoxyethanol)

¤ Vaccines should never be administered in the buttocks.   ⊕ See package insert for complete contraindication/component listing; may vary by brand * Professional judgment is appropriate when selecting needle length for use in all children, especially small infants or larger children.
± Use of the deltoid muscle in children 18 months and older (if adequate muscle mass is present) is an option for IM injections.   December 11, 2007

Injectable Vaccines for Selected Populations**

Vaccine	Recommendations for use and age	Route	Site ¤	Needle Length*	Contraindications⊕
Meningococcal Conjugate » (MCV4)	• For children 2-10 yrs who are at high risk for meningococcal disease • Routinely given to adolescents (1 dose) ages 11 through 18 yrs	IM	Anterolateral Thigh **or** Deltoid ±	1"-1.5" 22-25 g	Anaphylactic reaction to prior dose or component
Pneumococcal polysaccharide (PPV 23)	• For children 2 yrs and older at high risk for invasive pneumococcal disease • Given after completion of an age-appropriate PCV7 series - Minimum interval of 8 weeks between PCV7 and PPV23	IM	Anterolateral Thigh **or** Deltoid ±	1"-1.5" 22-25 g	Anaphylactic reaction to prior dose or component
		SC	Anterolateral Thigh **or** Lateral Upper Arm	5/8" 23-25g	

¤ Vaccines should never be administered in the buttocks.

* Professional judgment is appropriate when selecting needle length for use in all children, especially small infants or larger children.

⊕ See package insert for complete contraindication/component listing; components may vary by brand used

» When meningococcal vaccine is indicated and MCV4 is not available, Meningococcal polysaccharide (MPSV4) may be used for persons 2 years and older (given SC). However, if indication is for routine adolescent vaccination (ages 11-18 years), defer until MCV4 is available.

± Use of the deltoid muscle in children 18 months and older (if adequate muscle mass is present) is an option for IM injections.

** Refer to Recommended Childhood and Adolescent Immunization Schedule (available in Child/Adolescent Immunization Section of the AIM Kit) for information on the selected populations.

Alliance for Immunization in Michigan
2008 AIM Kit-Childhood Immunization Section

December 11, 2007

Michigan Department of Community Health
Jennifer M. Granholm, Governor
Janet Olszewski, Director
MDCH

Injectable Vaccine Administration for Children 7-18 Years

Vaccine	Age/Reminders	Route	Site*	Needle*	Contraindications ⊕
Tetanus, diphtheria (Td)	7 years and older	IM	Deltoid	1"-1.5" 22-25 g	Anaphylactic reaction to prior dose or component
Tetanus, diphtheria, pertussis (Tdap)	Routinely given at age 11-12 years; one dose ◉	IM	Deltoid	1"-1.5" 22-25 g	Anaphylactic reaction to prior dose or component; encephalopathy within 7 days of previous pertussis vaccine without other known cause
Hepatitis B (hep B)	1st dose at birth; last dose at/after 6 mo	IM	Deltoid	1"-1.5" 22-25 g	Anaphylactic reaction to a prior dose or component (baker's yeast)
Inactivated Polio Vaccine (IPV)	For school entry: 1st dose at/after 6 wks of age; all doses spaced at least 4 weeks apart	SC	Lateral Upper Arm	5/8" 23-25 g	Anaphylactic reaction to a prior dose or component (neomycin, streptomycin, or polymyxin B)
		IM	Deltoid	1"-1.5" 22-25 g	
Measles, Mumps, Rubella (MMR)	1st dose at/after 12 mo	SC	Lateral Upper Arm	5/8" 23-25 g	Anaphylactic reaction to a prior dose or component (neomycin, gelatin); pregnancy
Varicella (Var)	1st dose at/after 12 mo 12mo-12 yr: 3 months between dose 1 & 2	SC	Lateral Upper Arm	5/8" 23-25 g	Anaphylactic reaction to a prior dose or component (neomycin, gelatin); pregnancy
Inactivated Influenza (TIV)	Assure vaccine brand being used is age-appropriate	IM	Deltoid	1"-1.5" 22-25 g	Anaphylactic reaction to a prior dose or component (eggs)
Meningococcal Conjugate (MCV4)	Routinely given at age 11-12 yrs; catch-up all adolescents 13-18 yrs	IM	Deltoid	1"-1.5" 22-25 g	Anaphylactic reaction to a prior dose or component; history of GBS
Human Papilloma-virus (HPV4)	Females 9 through 26 years	IM	Deltoid	1"-1.5" 22-25 g	Anaphylactic reaction to prior dose or component; hypersensitivity to baker's yeast
Hepatitis A (hep A)	1st dose at/after 12 mo 2nd dose 6 mo later	IM	Deltoid	1"-1.5" 22-25 g	Anaphylactic reaction to prior dose or component; hypersensitivity to alum (Havrix®: 2-phenoxyethanol)

* Professional judgment is appropriate when selecting needle length and administration site; do not administer vaccines in buttocks
⊕ See package insert for complete contraindication listing; components may vary by brand of vaccine used
◉ Two Tdap vaccines available: Boostrix® (GSK) is licensed for persons 10-18 yrs; ADACEL™ (sanofi pasteur) licensed for persons 11-64 yrs.

December 14, 2007

Injectable Vaccines for Selected Populations**

Vaccine	Recommendation for use and age	Route	Site*	Needle Length*	Contraindications⊕
Meningococcal Polysaccharide (MPSV4)	• For children 2 years and older at high risk for meningococcal disease **and** MCV4 (conjugate) is not available • For persons with a history of Guillain-Barre syndrome (GBS)	SC	Lateral Upper Arm	5/8" 23-25g	Anaphylactic reaction to prior dose of component
Pneumococcal polysaccharide (PPV 23)	• For children 2 yrs and older at high risk for invasive pneumococcal disease	IM	Deltoid	1"-1.5" 22-25 g	Anaphylactic reaction to prior dose or component
	• Given after completion of an age-appropriate PCV7 series - Minimum interval of 8 weeks between PCV7 and PPV23	SC	Lateral Upper Arm	5/8" 23-25g	

*Professional judgment is appropriate when selecting needle length and administration site; do not administer vaccines in buttocks

⊕ See package insert for complete contraindication listing; components may vary by brand of vaccine used

** Refer to Recommended Childhood and Adolescent Immunization Schedule (available in Child/Adolescent Immunization Section of the AIM Kit on online at www.cdc.gov/vaccines) for information on the selected populations.

Alliance for Immunization in Michigan
2008 AIM Kit – Adolescent Immunization Section

Michigan Department
of Community Health
M DCH
Jennifer M. Granholm, Governor
Janet Olszewski, Director

December 14, 2007

Medical Management of Vaccine Reactions in Children and Teens

All vaccines have the potential to cause an adverse reaction. To minimize adverse reactions, patients should be carefully screened for precautions and contraindications before vaccine is administered. Even with careful screening, reactions can occur. These reactions can vary from trivial and inconvenient (e.g., soreness, itching) to severe and life threatening (e.g., anaphylaxis). If reactions occur, staff should be prepared with procedures for their management. The table below describes procedures to follow if various reactions occur.

Reaction	Symptoms	Management
Localized	Soreness, redness, itching, or swelling at the injection site	Apply a cold compress to the injection site. Consider giving an analgesic (pain reliever) or antipruritic (anti-itch) medication.
	Slight bleeding	Apply an adhesive compress over the injection site.
	Continuous bleeding	Place thick layer of gauze pads over site and maintain direct and firm pressure; raise the bleeding injection site (e.g., arm) above the level of the patient's heart.
Psychological fright and syncope (fainting)	Fright before injection is given	Have patient sit or lie down for the vaccination.
	Extreme paleness, sweating, coldness of the hands and feet, nausea, light-headedness, dizziness, weakness, or visual disturbances	Have patient lie flat or sit with head between knees for several minutes. Loosen any tight clothing and maintain an open airway. Apply cool, damp cloths to patient's face and neck.
	Fall, without loss of consciousness	Examine the patient to determine if injury is present before attempting to move the patient. Place patient flat on back with feet elevated.
	Loss of consciousness	Check the patient to determine if injury is present before attempting to move the patient. Place patient flat on back with feet elevated. Call 911 if patient does not recover immediately.
Anaphylaxis	Sudden or gradual onset of generalized itching, erythema (redness), or urticaria (hives); angioedema (swelling of the lips, face, or throat); severe bronchospasm (wheezing); shortness of breath; shock; abdominal cramping; or cardiovascular collapse	See "Emergency Medical Protocol for Management of Anaphylactic Reactions in Children and Teens" on the next page for detailed steps to follow in treating anaphylaxis.

Supplies Needed

- ☐ Aqueous epinephrine 1:1000 dilution, in ampules, vials of solution, or prefilled syringes, including epinephrine auto-injectors (e.g., EpiPen). If EpiPens are to be stocked, both EpiPen Jr. (0.15 mg) and adult EpiPens (0.30 mg) should be available.
- ☐ Diphenhydramine (Benadryl) injectable (50 mg/mL solution) and oral (12.5 mg/5 mL suspension) and 25 mg or 50 mg capsules or tablets
- ☐ Syringes: 1–3 cc, 22–25g, 1", 1½", and 2" needles for epinephrine and diphenhydramine (Benadryl)
- ☐ Pediatric & adult airways (small, medium, and large)

- ☐ Sphygmomanometer (child, adult & extra-large cuffs) and stethoscope
- ☐ Pediatric & adult size pocket masks with one-way valve
- ☐ Alcohol swabs
- ☐ Tongue depressors
- ☐ Flashlight with extra batteries (for examination of mouth and throat)
- ☐ Wrist watch
- ☐ Tourniquet
- ☐ Cell phone or access to an on-site phone

(Page 1 of 2)

www.immunize.org/catg.d/p3082a.pdf • Item #P3082a (8/06)

Immunization Action Coalition • 1573 Selby Ave. • St. Paul, MN 55104 • (651) 647-9009 • www.immunize.org • www.vaccineinformation.org

Emergency Medical Protocol for Management of Anaphylactic Reactions in Children and Teens

Signs and Symptoms of Anaphylactic Reaction

Sudden or gradual onset of generalized itching, erythema (redness), or urticaria (hives); angioedema (swelling of the lips, face, or throat); bronchospasm (wheezing); shortness of breath; shock; abdominal cramping; or cardiovascular collapse.

Treatment in Children and Teens

a. If itching and swelling are confined to the injection site where the vaccination was given, observe patient closely for the development of generalized symptoms.

b. If symptoms are generalized, activate the emergency medical system (EMS; e.g., call 911) and notify the on-call physician. This should be done by a second person, while the primary nurse assesses the airway, breathing, circulation, and level of consciousness of the patient.

c. Administer aqueous epinephrine 1:1000 dilution (i.e., 1 mg/mL) intramuscularly; the standard dose is 0.01 mg/kg body weight, up to 0.3 mg maximum single dose in children and 0.5 mg maximum in adolescents (see chart below).

d. In addition, for anaphylaxis, administer diphenhydramine either orally or by intramuscular injection; the standard dose is 1 mg/kg body weight, up to 30 mg maximum dose in children and 100 mg maximum dose in adolescents (see chart below).

e. Monitor the patient closely until EMS arrives. Perform cardiopulmonary resuscitation (CPR), if necessary, and maintain airway. Keep patient in supine position (flat on back) unless he or she is having breathing difficulty. If breathing is difficult, patient's head may be elevated, provided blood pressure is adequate to prevent loss of consciousness. If blood pressure is low, elevate legs. Monitor blood pressure and pulse every 5 minutes.

f. If EMS has not arrived and symptoms are still present, repeat dose of epinephrine every 10–20 minutes for up to 3 doses, depending on patient's response.

g. Record all vital signs, medications administered to the patient, including the time, dosage, response, and the name of the medical personnel who administered the medication, and other relevant clinical information.

h. Notify the patient's primary care physician.

Suggested Dosing of Epinephrine and Diphenhydramine				
Age Group Dose	Weight * in kg	Weight (lbs)* in lbs	Epinephrine Dose 1 mg/mL injectable (1:1000 dilution) intramuscular	Diphenhydramine (Benadryl) 12.5 mg/5 mL liquid 25 and 50 mg capsules or tabs 50 mg/mL injectable
1–6 mos	4–7 kg	9–15 lbs	0.05 mg (0.05 ml)	5 mg
7–18 mos	7–11 kg	15–24 lbs	0.1 mg (0.1 ml)	10 mg
19–36 mos	11–14 kg	24–31 lbs	0.15 mg (0.15 ml)	15 mg
37–48 mos	14–17 kg	31–37 lbs	0.15 mg (0.15 ml)	20 mg
49–59 mos	17–19 kg	37–42 lbs	0.2 mg (0.2 ml)	20 mg
5–7 yrs	19–23 kg	42–51 lbs	0.2 mg (0.2 ml)	30 mg
8–10 yrs	23–35 kg	51–77 lbs	0.3 mg (0.3 ml)	30 mg
11–12 yrs	35–45 kg	77–99 lbs	0.4 mg (0.4 ml)	40 mg
13 yrs & older	45+ kg	99+ lbs	0.5 mg (0.5 ml)	50–100 mg

*Dosing by body weight is preferred.

These standing orders for the medical management of vaccine reactions in child and teenage patients shall remain in effect for

patients of the _____ until rescinded or until _____.
      name of clinic   *date*

Medical Director's signature _____   Effective date _____

Sources: American Academy of Pediatrics. Passive Immunization. In: Pickering LK, ed. *Red Book: 2006 Report of the Committee on Infectious Diseases.* 27th ed. Elk Grove Village, IL: American Academy of Pediatrics; 2006: 64–66.

American Pharmacists Association, Grabenstein, JD, *Pharmacy-Based Immunization Delivery,* 2002.

(Page 2 of 2)

D

Medical Management of Vaccine Reactions in Adult Patients

All vaccines have the potential to cause an adverse reaction. In order to minimize adverse reactions, patients should be carefully screened for precautions and contraindications before vaccine is administered. Even with careful screening, reactions may occur. These reactions can vary from trivial and inconvenient (e.g., soreness, itching) to severe and life threatening (e.g., anaphylaxis). If reactions occur, staff should be prepared with procedures for their management. The table below describes procedures to follow if various reactions occur.

Reaction	Symptoms	Management
Localized	Soreness, redness, itching, or swelling at the injection site	Apply a cold compress to the injection site. Consider giving an analgesic (pain reliever) or antipruritic (anti-itch) medication.
	Slight bleeding	Apply an adhesive compress over the injection site.
	Continuous bleeding	Place thick layer of gauze pads over site and maintain direct and firm pressure; raise the bleeding injection site (e.g., arm) above the level of the patient's heart.
Psychological fright and syncope (fainting)	Fright before injection is given	Have patient sit or lie down for the vaccination.
	Extreme paleness, sweating, coldness of the hands and feet, nausea, light-headedness, dizziness, weakness, or visual disturbances	Have patient lie flat or sit with head between knees for several minutes. Loosen any tight clothing and maintain an open airway. Apply cool, damp cloths to patient's face and neck.
	Fall, without loss of consciousness	Examine the patient to determine if injury is present before attempting to move the patient. Place patient flat on back with feet elevated.
	Loss of consciousness	Check the patient to determine if injury is present before attempting to move the patient. Place patient flat on back with feet elevated. Call 911 if patient does not recover immediately.
Anaphylaxis	Sudden or gradual onset of generalized itching, erythema (redness), or urticaria (hives); angioedema (swelling of the lips, face, or throat); severe bronchospasm (wheezing); shortness of breath; shock; abdominal cramping; or cardiovascular collapse.	See "Emergency Medical Protocol for Management of Anaphylactic Reactions in Adults" on the next page for detailed steps to follow in treating anaphylaxis.

(continued on page 2)

Technical content reviewed by the Centers for Disease Control and Prevention, Nov. 2006.

www.immunize.org/catg.d/p3082.pdf • Item #P3082 (11/06)

Immunization Action Coalition • 1573 Selby Ave. • St. Paul, MN 55104 • (651) 647-9009 • www.immunize.org • www.vaccineinformation.org

(continued from page 1)

Emergency Medical Protocol for Management of Anaphylactic Reactions in Adults

Supplies Needed

☐ Aqueous epinephrine 1:1000 (i.e., 1 mg/mL) dilution, in ampules, vials of solution, or prefilled syringes, including epinephrine autoinjectors (e.g., EpiPen). If EpiPens are stocked, at least three adult EpiPens (0.30 mg) should be available.

☐ Diphenhydramine (Benadryl) injectable (50 mg/mL solution) and 25 mg or 50 mg capsules or tablets and syrup (12.5 mg/5 mL suspension)

☐ Syringes: 1–3 cc, 22–25g, 1", 1½", and 2" needles for epinephrine and diphenhydramine (Benadryl)

☐ Wristwatch with second hand

☐ Adult airways (small, medium, and large)

☐ Sphygmomanometer (adult and extra-large cuffs) and stethoscope

☐ Adult size pocket mask with one-way valve

☐ Alcohol swabs

☐ Tourniquet

☐ Tongue depressors

☐ Flashlight with extra batteries (for examination of the mouth and throat)

☐ Cell phone or access to an on-site phone

Signs and Symptoms of Anaphylactic Reaction

Sudden or gradual onset of generalized itching, erythema (redness), or urticaria (hives); angioedema (swelling of the lips, face, or throat); bronchospasm (wheezing); shortness of breath; shock; abdominal cramping; or cardio-vascular collapse.

Treatment in Adults

a. If itching and swelling are confined to the injection site where the vaccination was given, observe patient closely for the development of generalized symptoms.

b. If symptoms are generalized, activate the emergency medical system (EMS; e.g., call 911) and notify the on-call physician. This should be done by a second person, while the primary nurse assesses the airway, breathing, circulation, and level of consciousness of the patient.

c. Administer aqueous epinephrine 1:1000 dilution intramuscularly, 0.01 mL/kg/dose (adult dose ranges from 0.3 mL to 0.5 mL, with maximum single dose of 0.5 mL).

d. In addition, for systemic anaphylaxis, administer diphenhydramine either orally or by intramuscular injection; the standard dose is 1–2 mg/kg, up to 100 mg maximum single dose.

e. Monitor the patient closely until EMS arrives. Perform cardiopulmonary resuscitation (CPR), if necessary, and maintain airway. Keep patient in supine position (flat on back) unless he or she is having breathing difficulty. If breathing is difficult, patient's head may be elevated, provided blood pressure is adequate to prevent loss of consciousness. If blood pressure is low, elevate legs. Monitor blood pressure and pulse every 5 minutes.

f. If EMS has not arrived and symptoms are still present, repeat dose of epinephrine every 10–20 minutes for up to 3 doses, depending on patient's response.

g. Record all vital signs, medications administered to the patient, including the time, dosage, response, and the name of the medical personnel who administered the medication, and other relevant clinical information.

h. Notify the patient's primary care physician.

Sources:　1. American Academy of Pediatrics. Passive Immunization. In: Pickering LK, ed. *Red Book: 2006 Report of the Committee on Infectious Diseases.* 27th ed. Elk Grove Village, IL: American Academy of Pediatrics; 2006:64–66.
　　2. American Pharmacists Association, Grabenstein, JD, *Pharmacy-Based Immunization Delivery,* 2002.
　　3. *Got Your Shots? A Providers Guide to Immunizations in Minnesota,* Second Edition, Minnesota Department of Health, 2001:80-82.

These standing orders for the medical management of vaccine reactions in adult patients shall remain in effect for

patients of the _____ until rescinded or until _____.
　　　　　　　　　　　　name of clinic　　　　　　　　　　　　　　　　　　　　　*date*

_____　　　_____
Medical Director's signature　　　　　　　　　　Effective date

D

APPENDIX E
Vaccine Information Statements

It's federal law!
You must give your patients current Vaccine Information Statements (VISs)

To obtain a complete set of current VISs in more than 30 languages, visit IAC's website at www.immunize.org/vis

As healthcare professionals understand, the risks of serious consequences following vaccination are many hundreds or thousands of times less likely than the risks associated with the diseases that the vaccines protect against. Most adverse reactions from vaccines are mild and self-limited. Serious complications are rare, but they can have a devastating effect on the recipient, family members, and the providers involved with the care of the patient. We must continue the efforts to make vaccines as safe as possible.

Equally important is the need to furnish vaccine recipients (or the parents/legal representatives of minors) with objective information on vaccine safety and the diseases that the vaccines protect against, so that they are actively involved in making decisions affecting their health or the health of their children. When people are not informed about vaccine adverse events, even common, mild events, they can lose their trust in healthcare providers and vaccines. Vaccine Information Statements (VISs) provide a standardized way to present objective information about vaccine benefits and adverse events.

What are VISs?

VISs are developed by the staff of the Centers for Disease Control and Prevention (CDC) and undergo intense scrutiny by panels of experts for accuracy. Each VIS provides information to properly inform the adult vaccine recipient or the minor child's parent or legal representative about the risks and benefits of each vaccine. VISs are not meant to replace interactions with healthcare providers, who should answer questions and address concerns that the recipient or the parent/legal representative may have.

Use of the VIS is mandatory!

Before a healthcare provider vaccinates a child or an adult with a dose of any vaccine containing diphtheria, tetanus, pertussis, measles, mumps, rubella, polio, hepatitis A, hepatitis B, *Haemophilus influenzae* type b (Hib), influenza, pneumococcal conjugate, meningococcal, rotavirus, human papillomavirus (HPV), or varicella (chickenpox) vaccine, the provider is required by the National Childhood Vaccine Injury Act (NCVIA) to provide a copy of the VIS to either the adult recipient or to the child's parent/legal representative.

VISs are also available for pneumococcal polysaccharide vaccine, as well as various vaccines used primarily for international travelers. The use of these VISs is recommended but not currently required by federal law.

An alternative VIS—the multi-vaccine VIS—is an option to providing single-vaccine VISs when administering one or more of these routine birth-through-6-month vaccines: DTaP, hepatitis B, Hib, pneumococcal (PCV), polio (IPV), or rotavirus (RV). The multi-vaccine VIS can also be used when giving combination birth-through-6-month vaccines (i.e., Pediarix or Comvax) or when giving two or more routine birth-through-6-month vaccines together at other pediatric visits (e.g., 12–15 months or 4–6 years).

State or local health departments or individual providers may place the clinic name on the VISs, but any other changes must be approved by the director of CDC's National Center for Immunization and Respiratory Diseases.

What to do with VISs

Some of the legal requirements concerning the use of VISs are as follows:

1. Before an NCVIA-covered vaccine is administered to anyone (this includes adults!), you must give the patient or the parent/legal representative a copy of the most current VIS available for that vaccine. Make sure you give your patient time to read the VIS prior to the administration of the vaccine.

2. You must record in your patient's chart the date the VIS was given.

3. You must also record on the patient's chart the publication date of the VIS, which appears on the bottom of the VIS.

How to get VISs

All available VISs can be downloaded from the website of the Immunization Action Coalition at www.immunize.org/vis or from CDC's website at www.cdc.gov/vaccines/pubs/vis/default.htm. Ready-to-copy versions may also be available from your state or local health department.

Non-English language versions of VISs are not available from CDC; however, several state health departments have arranged for their translations. These versions do not require CDC approval. You can find VISs in more than 30 languages on the Immunization Action Coalition website at www.immunize.org/vis. To find VISs in alternative formats (e.g., audio, web-video), go to: www.immunize.org/vis/vis_audio.asp.

Most current versions of VISs

As of December 2008, the most recent versions of the VISs are as follows:

DTaP/DT/DTP	5/17/07	PCV	12/9/08
hepatitis A	3/21/06	PPSV	7/29/97
hepatitis B	7/18/07	polio	1/1/00
Hib	12/16/98	rabies	1/12/06
HPV (H. papillomavirus)	2/2/07	rotavirus	8/28/08
influenza (LAIV)	7/24/08	shingles	9/11/06
influenza (TIV)	7/24/08	Td/Tdap	11/18/08
Japan. enceph.	5/11/05	typhoid	5/19/04
meningococcal	1/28/08	varicella	3/13/08
MMR	3/13/08	yellow fever	11/9/04
Multi-vaccine VIS			9/18/08

(for 6 vaccines given to infants/children: DTaP, IPV, Hib, Hep B, PCV, RV)

"We have an obligation to provide patients and/or parents with information that includes both the benefits and the risks of vaccines. This can be done with the Vaccine Information Statements that healthcare providers are required by law to provide prior to the administration of vaccines."

Walter A. Orenstein, MD, past director, National Immunization Program, CDC

Technical content reviewed by the Centers for Disease Control and Prevention, December 2008.

www.immunize.org/catg.d/p2027.pdf • Item #P2027 (12/08)

E

E-1

Instructions for the Use of
Vaccine Information Statements

Required Use

1. Provide Vaccine Information Statement (VIS) when vaccination is given.

As required under the National Childhood Vaccine Injury Act (42 U.S.C. §300aa-26), all health care providers in the United States who administer, to any child or adult, diphtheria, tetanus, pertussis, measles, mumps, rubella, polio, hepatitis A, hepatitis B, *Haemophilus influenzae* type b (Hib), trivalent influenza, pneumococcal conjugate, meningococcal, rotavirus, human papillomavirus (HPV), or varicella (chickenpox) vaccines shall, prior to administration of each dose of the vaccine, provide a copy to keep of the relevant current edition vaccine information materials that have been produced by the Centers for Disease Control and Prevention (CDC):

- to the parent or legal representative* of any child to whom the provider intends to administer such vaccine, and
- to any adult to whom the provider intends to administer such vaccine. (In the case of an incompetent adult, relevant VISs shall be provided to the individual's legal representative.* If the incompetent adult is living in a long-term care facility, all relevant VISs may be provided at the time of admission, or at the time of consent if later than admission, rather than prior to each immunization.)

If there is not a single VIS for a combination vaccine, use the VISs for all component vaccines.

The materials shall be supplemented with visual presentations or oral explanations, as appropriate.

> *"Legal representative" is defined as a parent or other individual who is qualified under State law to consent to the immunization of a minor child or incompetent adult.

2. Record information for each VIS provided.

Health care providers shall make a notation in each patient's permanent medical record at the time vaccine information materials are provided, indicating:
(1) the edition date of the Vaccine Information Statement distributed, and
(2) the date the VIS was provided.

This recordkeeping requirement supplements the requirement of 42 U.S.C. §300aa-25 that all health care providers administering these vaccines must record in the patient's permanent medical record (or in a permanent office log):
(3) the name, address and title of the individual who administers the vaccine,
(4) the date of administration, and
(5) the vaccine manufacturer and lot number of the vaccine used.

Applicability of State Law

Health care providers should consult their legal counsel to determine additional State requirements pertaining to immunization. The Federal requirement to provide the vaccine information materials supplements any applicable State laws.

Availability of Copies

Single camera-ready copies of the vaccine information materials are available from State health departments. Copies are also available on CDC's website at www.cdc.gov/vaccines/pubs/vis.

Copies are available in English and in other languages.

Reference 42 U.S.C. §300aa-26

12/9/08

Current VIS Editions
Diphtheria, Tetanus, Pertussis (DTaP/DT): 5/17/07
Haemophilus influenzae type b: 12/16/98
Hepatitis A: 3/21/06
Hepatitis B: 7/18/07
Human Papillomavirus (HPV): 2/2/07
Inactivated Influenza: 7/24/08
Live, Intranasal Influenza: 7/24/08
Measles, Mumps, Rubella (MMR): 3/13/08
Meningococcal: 1/28/08
Pneumococcal conjugate: 12/9/08
Polio: 1/1/00
Rotavirus: 8/28/08
Tetanus, Diphtheria, (Pertussis) (Td/Tdap): 11/18/08
Varicella (chickenpox): 3/13/08
Multi-Vaccine*: 9/18/08

* This VIS is as an optional alternative when two or more routine childhood vaccines (i.e., DTaP, hepatitis B, Hib, pneumococcal, polio, or rotavirus) are administered at the same visit.

Where to Get Vaccine Information Statements

1. **The Internet.** All current VISs are available on the internet from two websites:
    - CDC (www.cdc.gov/vaccines/pubs/vis/default.htm)
    - The Immunization Action Coalition (www.immunize.org/vis/)

    VISs from these sites can be downloaded as pdf files and printed.

2. **CDC's Immunization Works CD.** This CD contains pdf files for all VIS (current as of the date the CD was issued). *Immunization Works* is usually available at CDC's immunization booth at conferences or can be ordered through CDC's online publications order form at https://www2a.cdc.gov/nchstp_od/PIWeb/niporderform.asp.

3. **State Health Departments.** CDC sends each state health department's immunization program camera-ready copies when a new VIS is published. The programs, in turn, can provide copies to providers within the state.

Audio files for most VISs can be downloaded from CDC's VIS webpage.

Text versions of VISs can also be accessed from CDC's VIS webpage. These files are compatible with screen-reader devices for use by the vision-impared.

Translations of many VISs are available in more than 30 languages from the Immunization Action Coalition's website (www.immunize.org/vis/index.htm). Languages available include:

Arabic	French	Korean	Samoan
Armenian	German	Laotian	Serbo-Croatian
Bosnian	Haitian	Marshallese	Somali
Burmese	Hindi	Polish	Spanish
Cambodian	Hmong	Porguguese	Tagalog
Chinese	Ilokano	Punjabi	Thai
Croatian	Italian	Romanian	Turkish
Farsi	Japanese	Russian	Vietnamese

E

Questions & Answers: Vaccine Information Statements

1. Should the VISs be used for adults getting vaccines as well as for children?

Yes. Under the National Childhood Vaccine Injury Act, anyone receiving a covered vaccine should be given the appropriate VIS. VISs for vaccines that are administered to both adults and children are worded so they may be used by both.

2. Are VISs "informed consent" forms?

No. People sometimes use the term "informed consent" loosely when referring to VISs. But even when vaccine information materials had tear-off sheets for parents to sign, they were not technically informed consent forms. The signature was simply to confirm that the "Duty to Warn" clause in the vaccine contract was being fulfilled.

There is no Federal requirement for informed consent. VISs are written to fulfill the information requirements of the National Childhood Vaccine Injury Act. But because they cover both benefits and risks associated with vaccinations, they provide enough information that anyone reading them should be adequately informed. Some states have informed consent laws, covering either procedural requirements (e.g., whether consent may be oral or must be written) or substantive requirements (e.g., types of information required). Check your state medical consent law to determine if there are any specific informed consent requirements relating to immunization. VISs can be used for informed consent as long as they conform to the appropriate state laws.

3. The law states that vaccine information materials be given to a child's legal representatives. Is this the same as "legal guardian?"

Not necessarily. A "legal representative" is a parent or other individual who is qualified under state law to consent to the immunization of a minor. It does not have to be the child's legal guardian (e.g., it could be a grandparent). There is not an overriding Federal definition.

4. Must the patient, parent, or legal representative physically take away a copy of each VIS, or can we simply let them read a copy and make sure they understand it?

Ideally the person getting the shot, or their representative, should actually take each VIS home. VISs contain information that may be useful later (e.g., the recommended vaccine schedule, information about what to do in the case of an adverse reaction). Patients may choose not to take the VIS, but the provider must offer them the opportunity to do so.

5. When do providers have to start using a new VIS?

The date for a new VISs required use is announced when the final draft is published in the Federal Register. Ideally, providers will begin using a new VIS immediately, particularly if the vaccine's contraindications or adverse event profile have changed significantly since the previous version.

6. How should we comply with the law for patients who cannot read the VISs (e.g., those who are illiterate or blind)?

The National Childhood Vaccine Injury Act requires providers to supplement the VISs with "visual presentations" or "oral explanations" as needed. If patients are unable to read the VISs, it is up to the provider to ensure that they have access to the information they contain. VISs can be read to these patients, or video-tapes can be used as supplements. At least one CD-ROM is being produced on which users can hear the VIS's read. Audio files and versions of VISs that are compatible with screen reader devices are available on CDC's VIS website.

7. **Why are the dates on some of the VISs so old? Are they obsolete? Why can't they be updated every year?**

VISs are updated only when they need to be. For instance, a VIS would be updated if there were a change in ACIP recommendations that affected the vaccine's adverse event profile, indications, or contraindications. If VISs were dated annually, there would be multiple editions in circulation that were identical but would have different dates. As it is, only the most recently-dated VIS for each vaccine is valid. VISs posted on CDC's VIS webpage will always be current, regardless of the edition date.

8. **Sometimes a VIS contains recommendations that is at odds with the manufacturer's package insert. Why?**

VISs are based on the ACIP's recommendations, which occasionally differ from those made by the manufac-turer. These differences may involve adverse events. For example, a package insert may mention all adverse events that were temporally associated with a vaccine during clinical trials, whereas ACIP tends to recognize only those likely to be causally linked to the vaccine.

9. **What is the reading level of VISs?**

Defining the readibility of a VIS by a traditional "grade level" measure can be difficult and misleading. Two criteria used in standard readability formulas are word length and sentence length. Neither is necessarily a reliable measure of readability. There are multi-syllable words that are widely understood and short words that are not. VISs often use bulleted lists, which a readability program might see as very long sentences (no period), even though they are actually quite easy to understand.

Applying a Fletch-Kincaid test to a VIS usually shows about a 10th grade reading level, but this should be taken with the caveats mentioned above.

In what may be a more useful measure of readability, several VISs were the subject of a series of focus groups among low literacy parents in a variety of racial and ethnic groups (including non-native English speakers) in 1998, and the participants overwhelmingly rated them easy to read and understand. Another round of focus groups is scheduled to be conducted soon, probably in 2009.

10. **Which VISs must be used?**

The appropriate VIS must be provided to the recipient of any vaccine covered by the National Childhood Vaccine Injury Act (NVCIA). VISs are available for all vaccines licensed in the United States (except BCG). Their use is strongly encouraged, whether mandated by the NCVIA or not.

11. **May providers develop their own vaccine information materials or modify the VISs?**

Providers who administer vaccines covered by the National Childhood Vaccine Injury Act are required to use the official CDC VISs. However, providers may supplement the VISs with materials of their own. Health departments or providers may add clinic name and contact information to a VIS as long as no other changes are made. Any other addition to these documents or variations from their language or format must have the prior written approval of the Director of CDC's National Center for Immunization and Respiratory Diseases.

E

12. How should we distribute VISs when the parent or legal representative of a minor is not present at the time the vaccination is given, for example during a school-based adolescent vaccination program?

CDCs legal advisors have proposed two alternatives for this situation:

- *Consent Prior to Administration of Each Dose of a Series.* With this alternative the VIS must be mailed or sent home with the student around the time of administration of each dose. Only those children for whom a signed consent is returned may be vaccinated. The program must place the signed consent in the patient's medical record.

- *Single Signature for Series.* This alternative is permissible only in those States where a single consent to an entire vaccination series is allowed under State law and in those schools where such a policy would be acceptable. The first dose of vaccine may be administered only after the parent or legal representative receives a copy of the VIS and signs and returns a statement that a) acknowledges receipt of the VIS and provides permission for their child to be vaccinated with the complete series of the vaccine (if possible, list the approximate dates of future doses); and b) acknowledges their acceptance of the following process regarding administration of additional doses:

    Prior to administration of each dose following the initial dose, a copy of the VIS will be mailed to the parent (or legal representative) who signs the original consent at the address they provide on this statement, or the VIS will be sent home with the student; and

    The vaccine information statements for the additional doses will be accompanied by a statement notifying the parent that, based on their earlier permission, the next dose will be administered to their child (state the date), unless the parent returns a portion of this statement by mail to an address provided, to arrive prior to the intended vaccination date, in which the parent withdraws permission for the child to receive the remaining doses.

The program must maintain the original consent signature and any additional dose veto statements in the patient's medical record. A record must be kept of the dates prior to additional doses that the VIS was mailed, or sent home with the adolescent.

Prior to administration of each additional dose, the provider should ask the adolescent whether he/she experienced any significant adverse events following receipt of earlier doses. If yes, the provider should consider consulting the parent or delaying the vaccination. The adolescent's response to questions about adverse reactions to previous doses should be kept in the medical record.

The following questions concern CDC's Multi-Vaccine VIS (www.cdc.gov/vaccines/pubs/vis/downloads/vis-multi.pdf).

13. Why was a Multi-Vaccine VIS developed?

It was developed with the earliest pediatric visits (i.e., birth through 6 months) in mind. Up to 6 vaccinations could be given during these visits, meaning (for the provider) that 6 individual VISs would have to be downloaded, printed and distributed and (for the patient) 6 documents would have to be read, containing much information that is duplicated. The multi-vaccine VIS is an effort to simplify and streamline this process.

14. May the existing, single-vaccine VISs still be used?

Yes. The Multi-Vaccine VIS an optional alternative to existing VISs. Providers wishing to continue using the individual VISs may do so. These will continue to be updated when recommendations change, as they have always been.

15. Must all 6 vaccines be given at the same visit for the Multi-Vaccine VIS to be used?

No. Any time two or more of the vaccines are given together it makes sense to use the Multi-Vaccine VIS. The provider should check the appropriate boxes on the first page, corresponding to vaccines given during that visit.

16. May the Multi-Vaccine VIS be used with combination vaccines, such as Pediarix or Comvax?

Yes. Just check the appropriate boxes on the first page as you would if you were administrating the individual vaccines.

17. When we record the edition date of the VISs in the patient's medical record, do we record the date on the Multi-Vaccine VIS or the dates for the individual VISs?

If you use the Multi-Vaccine VIS, record its date for each of the vaccines given that day. If there is ever a question, this will make it clear that the Multi-Vaccine VIS was used and not the individual VISs.

18. Can the Multi-Vaccine VIS be used for children older than 6 months, or for adolescents or adults getting any of these same vaccines?

It may be used for older children getting two or more of these vaccines during the same visit (e.g., a 12-month old getting Hib and PCV, or a 4-year old getting DTaP and IPV). However it should not be used for adolescents or adults. The information on this document applies to pediatric use of the vaccines. Risk factors that apply only to older persons, for example, are not discussed on this VIS. The individual VISs should be used.

19. May the Multi-Vaccine VIS be used for catch-up doses?

Yes, as long as the doses are given to children as part of the primary series or routine pediatric boosters.

20. The Multi-Vaccine VIS covers "pneumococcal" vaccine. Is it just for PCV7, or may it also be used when PPV23 is given to children?

It was designed with PCV7 specifically in mind. For PPV23, use the single VIS.

21. Will there be other Multi-Vaccine VISs, for example, for vaccines administered at 12-months or during the pre-school or adolescent-visits?

There is a multi-vaccine VIS for adolescents in development now, and plans to develop one for the 12-month vaccines as well.

CDC's Vaccine Information Statement Webpage
http://www.cdc.gov/vaccines/pubs/vis/default.htm

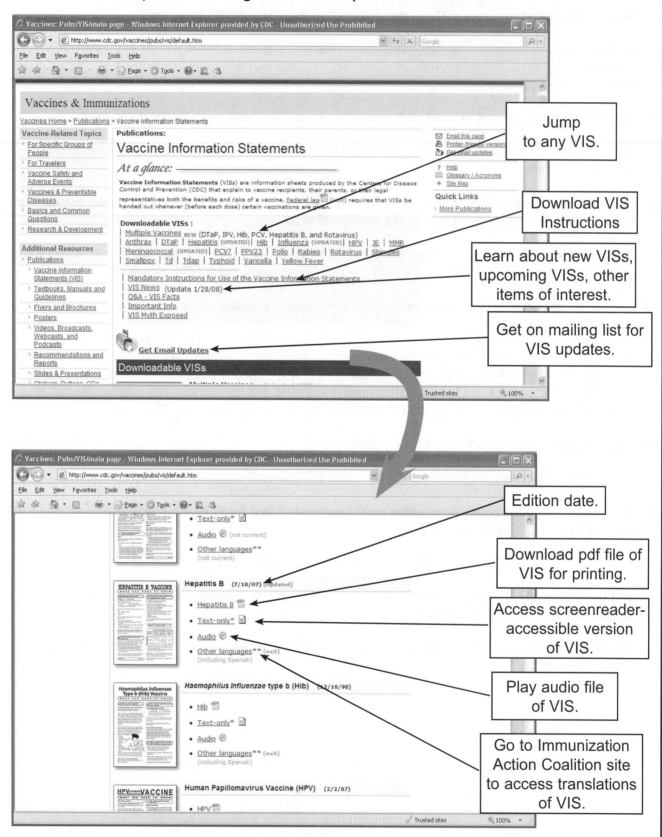

APPENDIX F
Vaccine Safety

The Vaccine Adverse Event Reporting System (VAERS)

VAERS is a national vaccine safety surveillance program co-sponsored by the Centers for Disease Control and Prevention (CDC) and the Food and Drug Administration (FDA). VAERS collects and analyzes information from reports of adverse events following immunization. Since 1990, VAERS has received over 123,000 reports, most of which describe mild side effects such as fever. Very rarely, people experience serious adverse events following immunization. By monitoring such events, VAERS can help to identify important new safety concerns.

Reporting to VAERS

Who can file a VAERS report: Anyone can submit a VAERS report. Most reports are sent in by vaccine manufacturers (42%) and health care providers (30%). The rest are submitted by state immunization programs (12%), vaccine recipients or their parent/guardians (7%), and other sources (9%).

What adverse events should be reported: VAERS encourages the reporting of any clinically significant adverse event that occurs after the administration of any vaccine licensed in the United States. Report such events even if you are unsure whether a vaccine caused them.

The National Childhood Vaccine Injury Act (NCVIA) requires health care providers to report:
- Any event listed by the vaccine manufacturer as a contraindication to subsequent doses of the vaccine.
- Any event listed in the Reportable Events Table that occurs within the specified time period after vaccination.

A copy of the Reportable Events Table can be found on the next page (F-2), or obtained by calling VAERS at 1-800-822-7967 or by downloading it from http://vaers.hhs.gov/pubs.htm.

Filing a VAERS report: Use a VAERS report form (see page F-4) to report any adverse event. You can get pre-addressed postage paid report forms by calling VAERS at 1-800-822-7967, or download a printable copy of the VAERS form from the following Internet sites:
- The VAERS Web site at http://vaers.hhs.gov/
- The Food and Drug Administration's Web site at www.fda.gov/cber/vaers/vaers.htm
- The Centers for Disease Control and Prevention Web site at www.cdc.gov/vaccines/

Instructions are included with the form. You may use a photocopy of the VAERS form to submit a report.

For more information:
- Send e-mail inquiries to info@vaers.org
- Visit the VAERS Web site at: http://vaers.hhs.gov
- Call the toll-free VAERS information line at (800) 822-7967
- Fax inquiries to the toll-free information fax line at (877) 721-0366

This information has been adapted from the VAERS website (http://vaers.hhs.gov). **F**

VAERS Table of Reportable Events Following Vaccination*

Vaccine/Toxoid	Event	Interval from Vaccination
Tetanus in any combination; DTaP, DTP, DTP-HiB, DT, Td, TT, Tdap	A. Anaphylaxis or anaphylactic shock B. Brachial neuritis C. Any acute complications or sequela (including death) of above events D. Events described in manufacturer's package insert as contraindications to additional doses of vaccine	7 days 28 days Not applicable See package insert
Pertussis in any combination; DTaP, DTP, DTP-HiB, P, Tdap	A. Anaphylaxis or anaphylactic shock B. Encephalopathy (or encephalitis) C. Any acute complications or sequela (including death) of above events D. Events described in manufacturer's package insert as contraindications to additional doses of vaccine	7 days 7 days Not applicable See package insert
Measles, mumps and rubella in any combination; MMR, MR, M, MMRV, R	A. Anaphylaxis or anaphylactic shock B. Encephalopathy (or encephalitis) C. Any acute complications or sequela (including death) of above events D. Events described in manufacturer's package insert as contraindications to additional doses of vaccine	7 days 15 days Not applicable See package insert
Rubella in any combination; MMR, MMRV, MR, R	A. Chronic arthritis B. Any acute complications or sequela (including death) of above event C. Events described in manufacturer's package insert as contraindications to additional doses of vaccine	42 days Not applicable See package insert
Measles in any combination; MMR, MMRV, MR, M	A. Thrombocytopenic purpura B. Vaccine-strain measles viral infection in an immunodeficient recipient C. Any acute complications or sequela (including death) of above events D. Events described in manufacturer's package insert as contraindications to additional doses of vaccine	7-30 days 6 months Not applicable See package insert

Oral Polio (OPV)	A. Paralytic polio
	  – in a non-immunodeficient recipient
	  – in an immunodeficient recipient
	  – in a vaccine associated community case
	B. Vaccine-strain polio viral infection
	  – in a non-immunodeficient recipient
	  – in an immunodeficient recipient
	  – in a vaccine associated community case
	C. Any sequela (including death) of above events
	D. Events described in manufacturer's package insert as contraindications to additional doses of vaccine
		
		30 days
		6 months
		Not applicable
		
		30 days
		6 months
		Not applicable
		Not applicable
		See package insert

Inactivated Polio (IPV)	A. Anaphylaxis or anaphylactic shock B. Any sequela (including death) of the above event C. Events described in manufacturer's package insert as contraindications to additional doses of vaccine	7 days Not applicable See package insert
Hepatitis B	A. Anaphylaxis or anaphylactic shock B. Any acute complications or sequela (including death) of the above event C. Events described in manufacturer's package insert as contraindications to additional doses of vaccine	7 days Not applicable See package insert
Hemophilus influenzae type b (conjugate)	A. Events described in manufacturer's package insert as contraindications to additional doses of vaccine	See package insert
Varicella	A. Events described in manufacturer's package insert as contraindications to additional doses of vaccine	See package insert
Rotavirus	A. Intussusception B. Any acute complications or sequela (including death) of the above event C. Events described in manufacturer's package insert as contraindications to additional doses of vaccine	30 days Not applicable See package insert
Pneumococcal conjugate	A. Events described in manufacturer's package insert as contraindications to additional doses of vaccine	See package insert
Hepatitis A	A. Events described in manufacturer's package insert as contraindications to additional doses of vaccine	See package insert
Influenza	A. Events described in manufacturer's package insert as contraindications to additional doses of vaccine	See package insert

* **Effective date: July 01, 2005.** The Reportable Events Table (RET) reflects what is reportable by law (42 USC 300aa-25) to the Vaccine Adverse Event Reporting System (VAERS) including conditions found in the manufacturers package insert. In addition, individuals are encouraged to report **any** clinically significant or unexpected events (even if you are not certain the vaccine caused the event) for **any** vaccine, whether or not it is listed on the RET. Manufacturers are also required by regulation (21CFR 600.80) to report to the VAERS program all adverse events made known to them for any vaccine.

Reportable Events Table Definitions

Anaphylaxis and anaphylactic shock. Anaphylaxis and anaphylactic shock mean an acute, severe, and potentially lethal systemic allergic reaction. Most cases resolve without sequelae. Signs and symptoms begin minutes to a few hours after exposure. Death, if it occurs, usually results from airway obstruction caused by laryngeal edema or bronchospasm and may be associated with cardiovascular collapse.

Brachial neuritis is defined as dysfunction limited to the upper extremity nerve plexus (i.e., its trunks, division, or cords) without involvement of other peripheral (e.g., nerve roots or a single peripheral nerve) or central (e.g., spinal cord) nervous system structures. A deep, steady, often severe aching pain in the shoulder and upper arm usually heralds onset of the condition. The pain is followed in days or weeks by weakness and atrophy in upper extremity muscle groups. Sensory loss may accompany the motor deficits, but is generally a less notable clinical feature.

Encephalopathy. For purposes of the Reportable Events Table, a vaccine recipient shall be considered to have suffered an encephalopathy only if such recipient manifests, within the applicable period, an injury meeting the description below of an acute encephalopathy, and then a chronic encephalopathy persists in such person for more than 6 months beyond the date of vaccination.

1. An ***acute encephalopathy*** is one that is sufficiently severe so as to require hospitalization (whether or not hospitalization occurred).

   a. For ***children less than 18 months of age*** who present without an associated seizure event, an acute encephalopathy is indicated by a "significantly decreased level of consciousness" (see "D" below) lasting for at least 24 hours. Those children less than 18 months of age who present following a seizure shall be viewed as having an acute encephalopathy if their significantly decreased level of consciousness persists beyond 24 hours and cannot be attributed to a postictal state (seizure) or medication.

   b. For adults and ***children 18 months of age*** or older, an acute encephalopathy is one that persists for at least 24 hours and is characterized by at least two of the following:

      i. A significant change in mental status that is not medication related: specifically a confusional state, or a delirium, or a psychosis;

      ii. A significantly decreased level of consciousness, which is independent of a seizure and cannot be attributed to the effects of medication; and

      iii. A seizure associated with loss of consciousness.

   c. Increased intracranial ***pressure*** may be a clinical feature of acute encephalopathy in any age group.

2. A "***significantly decreased level of consciousness***" is indicated by the presence of at least one of the following clinical signs for at least 24 hours or greater:

   a. Decreased or absent response to environment (responds, if at all, only to loud voice or painful stimuli);

   b. Decreased or absent eye contact (does not fix gaze upon family members or other individuals); or

   c. Inconsistent or absent responses to external stimuli (does not recognize familiar people or things).

   The following clinical features alone, or in combination, do not demonstrate an acute encephalopathy or a significant change in either mental status or level of consciousness as described above: Sleepiness, irritability (fussiness), high-pitched and unusual screaming, persistent inconsolable crying, and bulging fontanelle. Seizures in themselves are not sufficient to constitute a diagnosis of encephalopathy. In the absence of other evidence of an acute encephalopathy, seizures shall not be viewed as the first symptom or manifestation of the onset of an acute encephalopathy.

3. ***Chronic Encephalopathy*** occurs when a change in mental or neurologic status, first manifested during the applicable time period, persists for a period of at least 6 months from the date of vaccination. Individuals who return to a normal neurologic state after the acute encephalopathy shall not be presumed to have suffered residual neurologic damage from that event; any subsequent chronic encephalopathy shall not be presumed to be a sequela of the acute encephalopathy. If a preponderance of the evidence indicates that a child's chronic encephalopathy is secondary to genetic, prenatal or perinatal factors, that chronic encephalopathy shall not be considered to be a condition set forth in the Table. An encephalopathy shall not be considered to be a condition set forth in the Table if it is shown that the encephalopathy was caused by an infection, a toxin, a metabolic disturbance, a structural lesion, a genetic disorder or trauma (without regard to whether the cause of the infection, toxin, trauma, metabolic disturbance, structural lesion or genetic disorder is known).

Chronic Arthritis. For purposes of the Reportable Events Table, chronic arthritis may be found in a person with no history in the 3 years prior to vaccination of arthropathy (joint disease) on the basis of:

   a. Medical documentation, recorded within 30 days after the onset, of objective signs of acute arthritis (joint swelling) that occurred between 7 and 42 days after a rubella vaccination; and

   b. Medical documentation (recorded within 3 years after the onset of acute arthritis) of the persistence of objective signs of intermittent or continuous arthritis for more than 6 months following vaccination.

   c. Medical documentation of an antibody response to the rubella virus.

The following shall not be considered as chronic arthritis: Musculoskeletal disorders such as diffuse connective tissue diseases (including but not limited to rheumatoid arthritis, juvenile rheumatoid arthritis, systemic lupus erythematosus, systemic sclerosis, mixed connective tissue disease, polymyositis/dermatomyositis, fibromyalgia, necrotizing vasculitis and vasculopathies and Sjogren's Syndrome), degenerative joint disease, infectious agents other than rubella (whether by direct invasion or as an immune reaction), metabolic and endocrine diseases, trauma, neoplasms, neuropathic disorders, bone and cartilage disorders and arthritis associated with ankylosing spondylitis, psoriasis, inflammatory bowel disease, Reiter's syndrome, or blood disorders.

Arthralgia (joint pain) or stiffness without joint swelling shall not be viewed as chronic arthritis.

Sequela. The term "sequela" means a condition or event, which was actually caused by a condition listed in the Reportable Events Table.

WEBSITE: www.vaers.hhs.gov E-MAIL: info@vaers.org FAX: 1-877-721-0366

VACCINE ADVERSE EVENT REPORTING SYSTEM
VAERS
24 Hour Toll-Free Information 1-800-822-7967
P.O. Box 1100, Rockville, MD 20849-1100
PATIENT IDENTITY KEPT CONFIDENTIAL

For CDC/FDA Use Only

VAERS Number _____

Date Received _____

Patient Name:	Vaccine administered by (Name):	Form completed by (Name):
Last First M.I.	Responsible Physician _____	Relation ☐ Vaccine Provider ☐ Patient/Parent
Address	Facility Name/Address	to Patient ☐ Manufacturer ☐ Other
		Address *(if different from patient or provider)*
City State Zip	City State Zip	City State Zip
Telephone no. (___) _____	Telephone no. (___) _____	Telephone no. (___) _____

1. State	2. County where administered	3. Date of birth ___/___/___ mm dd yy	4. Patient age	5. Sex ☐ M ☐ F	6. Date form completed ___/___/___ mm dd yy

7. Describe adverse events(s) (symptoms, signs, time course) and treatment, if any

8. Check all appropriate:
☐ Patient died   (date ___/___/___ mm dd yy)
☐ Life threatening illness
☐ Required emergency room/doctor visit
☐ Required hospitalization (_____days)
☐ Resulted in prolongation of hospitalization
☐ Resulted in permanent disability
☐ None of the above

9. Patient recovered   ☐ YES ☐ NO ☐ UNKNOWN

10. Date of vaccination ___/___/___ mm dd yy AM PM Time ____	11 Adverse event onset ___/___/___ mm dd yy AM PM Time ____

12. Relevant diagnostic tests/laboratory data

13. Enter all vaccines given on date listed in no. 10

Vaccine (type)	Manufacturer	Lot number	Route/Site	No. Previous Doses
a.				
b.				
c.				
d.				

14. Any other vaccinations within 4 weeks prior to the date listed in no. 10

Vaccine (type)	Manufacturer	Lot number	Route/Site	No. Previous doses	Date given
a.					
b.					

15. Vaccinated at:	16. Vaccine purchased with:	17. Other medications
☐ Private doctor's office/hospital ☐ Military clinic/hospital ☐ Public health clinic/hospital ☐ Other/unknown	☐ Private funds ☐ Military funds ☐ Public funds ☐ Other/unknown	

18. Illness at time of vaccination (specify)	19. Pre-existing physician-diagnosed allergies, birth defects, medical conditions (specify)

20. Have you reported this adverse event previously?	☐ No ☐ To health department ☐ To doctor ☐ To manufacturer	*Only for children 5 and under*
		22. Birth weight _____ lb. _____ oz.	23. No. of brothers and sisters

21. Adverse event following prior vaccination (check all applicable, specify)

	Adverse Event	Onset Age	Type Vaccine	Dose no. in series
☐ In patient				
☐ In brother or sister				

Only for reports submitted by manufacturer/immunization project

24. Mfr./imm. proj. report no.	25. Date received by mfr./imm.proj.
26. 15 day report? ☐ Yes ☐ No	27. Report type ☐ Initial ☐ Follow-Up

Health care providers and manufacturers are required by law (42 USC 300aa-25) to report reactions to vaccines listed in the Table of Reportable Events Following Immunization. Reports for reactions to other vaccines are voluntary except when required as a condition of immunization grant awards.

Form VAERS-1(FDA)

"Fold in thirds, tape & mail — DO NOT STAPLE FORM"

NO POSTAGE
NECESSARY
IF MAILED
IN THE
UNITED STATES
OR APO/FPO

BUSINESS REPLY MAIL

FIRST-CLASS MAIL   PERMIT NO. 1895   ROCKVILLE, MD

POSTAGE WILL BE PAID BY ADDRESSEE

VAERS
P.O. Box 1100
Rockville MD 20849-1100

DIRECTIONS FOR COMPLETING FORM

(Additional pages may be attached if more space is needed.)

GENERAL

- Use a separate form for each patient. Complete the form to the best of your abilities. Items 3, 4, 7, 8, 10, 11, and 13 are considered essential and should be completed whenever possible. Parents/Guardians may need to consult the facility where the vaccine was administered for some of the information (such as manufacturer, lot number or laboratory data.)
- Refer to the Reportable Events Table (RET) for events mandated for reporting by law. Reporting for other serious events felt to be related but not on the RET is encouraged.
- Health care providers other than the vaccine administrator (VA) treating a patient for a suspected adverse event should notify the VA and provide the information about the adverse event to allow the VA to complete the form to meet the VA's legal responsibility.
- These data will be used to increase understanding of adverse events following vaccination and will become part of CDC Privacy Act System 09-20-0136, "Epidemiologic Studies and Surveillance of Disease Problems". Information identifying the person who received the vaccine or that person's legal representative will not be made available to the public, but may be available to the vaccinee or legal representative.
- Postage will be paid by addressee. Forms may be photocopied (must be front & back on same sheet).

SPECIFIC INSTRUCTIONS

Form Completed By: To be used by parents/guardians, vaccine manufacturers/distributors, vaccine administrators, and/or the person completing the form on behalf of the patient or the health professional who administered the vaccine.

Item 7:	Describe the suspected adverse event. Such things as temperature, local and general signs and symptoms, time course, duration of symptoms, diagnosis, treatment and recovery should be noted.
Item 9:	Check "YES" if the patient's health condition is the same as it was prior to the vaccine, "NO" if the patient has not returned to the pre-vaccination state of health, or "UNKNOWN" if the patient's condition is not known.
Item 10: and 11:	Give dates and times as specifically as you can remember. If you do not know the exact time, please indicate "AM" or "PM" when possible if this information is known. If more than one adverse event, give the onset date and time for the most serious event.
Item 12:	Include "negative" or "normal" results of any relevant tests performed as well as abnormal findings.
Item 13:	List ONLY those vaccines given on the day listed in Item 10.
Item 14:	List any other vaccines that the patient received within 4 weeks prior to the date listed in Item 10.
Item 16:	This section refers to how the person who gave the vaccine purchased it, not to the patient's insurance.
Item 17:	List any prescription or non-prescription medications the patient was taking when the vaccine(s) was given.
Item 18:	List any short term illnesses the patient had on the date the vaccine(s) was given (i.e., cold, flu, ear infection).
Item 19:	List any pre-existing physician-diagnosed allergies, birth defects, medical conditions (including developmental and/or neurologic disorders) for the patient.
Item 21:	List any suspected adverse events the patient, or the patient's brothers or sisters, may have had to previous vaccinations. If more than one brother or sister, or if the patient has reacted to more than one prior vaccine, use additional pages to explain completely. For the onset age of a patient, provide the age in months if less than two years old.
Item 26:	This space is for manufacturers' use only.

Vaccine Injury Compensation Program (VICP)

The VICP is a no-fault alternative to the traditional tort system for resolving vaccine injury claims. It was established as part of the National Childhood Vaccine Injury Act of 1986, after a rash of lawsuits against vaccine manufacturers and healthcare providers threatened to cause vaccine shortages and reduce vaccination rates.

The VICP covers all vaccines recommended by the Centers for Disease Control and Prevention for routine administration to children. It is administered jointly by the U.S. Department of Health and Human Services (HHS), the U.S. Court of Federal Claims (the Court), and the U.S. Department of Justice (DOJ). The VICP is located in the HRSA Healthcare Systems Bureau. Covered vaccines and compensible injuries are described on the "Vaccine Injury Table" (see following page - F7).

The Claims Process

An individual claiming a vaccine-related injury or death files a petition for compensation with the Court, and may be represented by an attorney. The Secretary of HHS is named as the Respondent.

An HHS physician reviews the petition to determine whether it meets the medical criteria for compensation. This recommendation is provided to the Court through a Respondent's report filed by the DOJ. The HHS position is presented by an attorney from the DOJ in hearings before a "special master," who makes the decision for compensation under the VICP. A decision may be appealed to the Court, then to the Federal Circuit Court of Appeals, and eventually to the U.S. Supreme Court.

If a case is found eligible for compensation, the amount of the award is usually negotiated between the DOJ and the petitioner's attorneys. If the attorneys can't agree, the case is scheduled for a hearing for the special master to assess the amount of compensation. Compensable claims, and even most claims found to be non-compensable, are awarded reimbursement for attorney's fees and costs. A petitioner may file a claim in civil court against the vaccine company and/or the vaccine administrator only after first filing a claim under the VICP and then rejecting the decision of the Court.

For more information, including information about restrictions that apply to filing a petition, visit the VICP website at http://www.hrsa.gov/vaccinecompensation or phone 1-800-338-2382.

For information on the Rules of the Court, including requirements for filing a petition, visit the Court's Website at http://www.uscfc.uscourts.gov/osmPage.htm or phone (202) 357-6400.

This information has been adapted from the VICP website (http://www.hrsa.gov/vaccinecompensation)

National Childhood Vaccine Injury Act: Vaccine Injury Table[a]

Vaccine	Adverse Event	Time Interval
I Tetanus toxoid-containing vaccines (e.g., DTaP, Tdap, DTP-Hib, DT, Td, TT)	A Anaphylaxis or anaphylactic shock	0-4 hours
	B Brachial neuritis	2-28 days
	C Any acute complication or sequela (including death) of above events	Not applicable
II Pertussis antigen-containing vaccines (e.g., DTaP, Tdap, DTP, P, DTP-Hib)	A Anaphylaxis or anaphylactic shock	0-4 hours
	B Encephalopathy (or encephalitis)	0-72 hours
	C Any acute complication or sequela (including death) of above events	Not applicable
III Measles, mumps and rubella virus-containing vaccines in any combination (e.g., MMR, MR, M, R)	A Anaphylaxis or anaphylactic shock	0-4 hours
	B Encephalopathy (or encephalitis)	5-15 days
	C Any acute complication or sequela (including death) of above events	Not applicable
IV Rubella virus-containing vaccines (e.g., MMR, MR, R)	A Chronic arthritis	7-42 days
	B Any acute complication or sequela (including death) of above event	Not applicable
V Measles virus-containing vaccines (e.g., MMR, MR, M)	A Thrombocytopenic purpura	7-30 days
	B Vaccine-Strain Measles Viral Infection in an immunodeficient recipient	0-6 months
	C Any acute complication or sequela (including death) of above events	Not applicable

VI Polio live virus-containing vaccines (OPV)	A Paralytic polio
	  - in a non-immunodeficient recipient
	  - in an immunodeficient recipient
	  - in a vaccine assoc. community case
		
		0-30 days
		0-6 months
		Not applicable

	B Vaccine-strain polio viral infection
	  - in a non-immunodeficient recipient
	  - in an immunodeficient recipient
	  - in a vaccine assoc. community case
		
		0-30 days
		0-6 months
		Not applicable

	C Any acute complication or sequela (including death) of above events	Not applicable
VII Polio inactivated-virus containing vaccines (e.g., IPV)	A Anaphylaxis or anaphylactic shock	0-4 hours
	B Any acute complication or sequela (including death) of above event	Not applicable
VIII Hepatitis B antigen-containing vaccines	A Anaphylaxis or anaphylactic shock	0-4 hours
	B Any acute complication or sequela (including death) of above event	Not applicable
IX *Haemophilus influenzae* type b polysaccharide conjugate vaccines	A No condition specified for compensation	Not applicable
X Varicella vaccine	A No condition specified for compensation	Not applicable
XI Rotavirus vaccine	A No condition specified for compensation	Not applicable
XII Vaccines containing live, oral, rhesus-based rotavirus	A Intussusception	0-30 days
	B Any acute complication or sequela (including death) of above event	Not applicable
XIII Pneumococcal conjugate vaccines	A No condition specified for compensation	Not applicable
XIV Any new vaccine recommended by the Centers for Disease Control and Prevention for routine administration to children, after publication by Secretary, HHS of a notice of coverage [bc]	A No condition specified for compensation	Not applicable

[a] Effective date: February 1, 2007

[b] As of **December 1, 2004**, hepatitis A vaccines have been added to the Vaccine Injury Table (Table) under this Category. As of **July 1, 2005**, *trivalent* influenza vaccines have been added to the Table under this Category. Trivalent influenza vaccines are given annually during the flu season either by needle and syringe or in a nasal spray. All influenza vaccines routinely administered in the U.S. are trivalent vaccines covered under this Category.

[c] As of **February 1, 2007**, meningococcal (conjugate and polysaccharide) and human papillomavirus (HPV) vaccines have been added to the Table under this category.

See *News* on the VICP website for more information (www.hrsa.gov/vaccinecompensation).

Qualifications and Aids to Interpretation

(1) **Anaphylaxis and anaphylactic shock** mean an acute, severe, and potentially lethal systemic allergic reaction. Most cases resolve without sequelae. Signs and symptoms begin minutes to a few hours after exposure. Death, if it occurs, usually results from airway obstruction caused by laryngeal edema or bronchospasm and may be associated with cardio-vascular collapse. Other significant clinical signs and symptoms may include the following: Cyanosis, hypotension, bradycardia, tachycardia, arrhythmia, edema of the pharynx and/or trachea and/or larynx with stridor and dyspnea. Autopsy findings may include acute emphysema which results from lower respiratory tract obstruction, edema of the hypopharynx, epiglottis, larynx, or trachea and minimal findings of eosinophilia in the liver, spleen and lungs. When death occurs within minutes of exposure and with out signs of respiratory distress, there may not be significant pathologic findings.

(2) **Encephalopathy**. For purposes of the Vaccine Injury Table, a vaccine recipient shall be considered to have suffered an encephalopathy only if such recipient manifests, within the applicable period, an injury meeting the description below of an acute encephalopathy, and then a chronic encephalopathy persists in such person for more than 6 months beyond the date of vaccination.

   (i) An acute encephalopathy is one that is sufficiently severe so as to require hospitalization (whether or not hospitalization occurred).

   (A) For children less than 18 months of age who present without an associated seizure event, an acute encephalopathy is indicated by a "significantly decreased level of consciousness" (see "D" below) lasting for at least 24 hours. Those children less than 18 months of age who present following a seizure shall be viewed as having an acute encephalopathy if their significantly decreased level of consciousness persists beyond 24 hours and cannot be attributed to a postictal state (seizure) or medication.

   (B) For adults and children 18 months of age or older, an acute encephalopathy is one that persists for at least 24 hours and characterized by at least two of the following:

   (1) A significant change in mental status that is not medication related; specifically a confusional state, or a delirium, or a psychosis;
   (2) A significantly decreased level of consciousness, which is independent of a seizure and cannot be attributed to the effects of medication; and
   (3) A seizure associated with loss of consciousness.

   (C) Increased intracranial pressure may be a clinical feature of acute encephalopathy in any age group.

   (D) A "significantly decreased level of consciousness" is indicated by the presence of at least one of the following clinical signs for at least 24 hours or greater (see paragraphs (2)(I)(A) and (2)(I)(B) of this section for applicable timeframes):

   (1) Decreased or absent response to environment (responds, if at all, only to loud voice or painful stimuli);
   (2) Decreased or absent eye contact (does not fix gaze upon family members or other individuals); or
   (3) Inconsistent or absent responses to external stimuli (does not recognize familiar people or things).

   (E) The following clinical features alone, or in combination, do not demonstrate an acute encephalopathy or a significant change in either mental status or level of consciousness as described above: Sleepiness, irritability (fussiness), high-pitched and unusual screaming, persistent inconsolable crying, and bulging fontanelle. Seizures in themselves are not sufficient to constitute a diagnosis of encephalopathy. In the absence of other evidence of an acute encephalopathy, seizures shall not be viewed as the first symptom or manifestation of the onset of an acute encephalopathy.

   (ii) Chronic encephalopathy occurs when a change in mental or neurologic status, first manifested during the applicable time period, persists for a period of at least 6 months from the date of vaccination. Individuals who return to a normal neurologic state after the acute encephalopathy shall not be presumed to have suffered residual neurologic damage from that event; any subsequent chronic encephalopathy shall not be presumed to be a sequela of the acute encephalopathy. If a preponderance of the evidence indicates that a child's chronic encephalopathy is secondary to genetic, prenatal or perinatal factors, that chronic encephalopathy shall not be considered to be a condition set forth in the Table.

(iii) An encephalopathy shall not be considered to be a condition set forth in the Table if in a proceeding on a petition, it is shown by a preponderance of the evidence that the encephalopathy was caused by an infection, a toxin, a metabolic disturbance, a structural lesion, a genetic disorder or trauma (without regard to whether the cause of the infection, toxin, trauma, metabolic disturbance, structural lesion or genetic disorder is known). If at the time a decision is made on a petition filed under section 2111(b) of the Act for a vaccine-related injury or death, it is not possible to determine the cause by a preponderance of the evidence of an encephalopathy, the encephalopathy shall be considered to be a condition set forth in the Table.

(iv) In determining whether or not an encephalopathy is a condition set forth in the Table, the Court shall consider the entire medical record.

3) **Seizure and convulsion**. For purposes of paragraphs (b)(2) of this section, the terms, "seizure" and "convulsion" include myoclonic, generalized tonic-clonic (grand mal), and simple and complex partial seizures. Absence (petit mal) seizures shall not be considered to be a condition set forth in the Table. Jerking move- ments or staring episodes alone are not necessarily an indication of seizure activity.

(4) **Sequela**. The term "sequela" means a condition or event which was actually caused by a condition listed in the Vaccine Injury Table.

(5) **Chronic Arthritis**. For purposes of the Vaccine Injury Table, chronic arthritis may be found in a person with no history in the 3 years prior to vaccination of arthropathy (joint disease) on the basis of:

(A) Medical documentation, recorded within 30 days after the onset, of objective signs of acute arthritis (joint swelling) that occurred between 7 and 42 days after a rubella vaccination;
(B) Medical documentation (recorded within 3 years after the onset of acute arthritis) of the persistence of objective signs of intermittent or continuous arthritis for more than 6 months following vaccination:
(C) Medical documentation of an antibody response to the rubella virus.

For purposes of the Vaccine Injury Table, the following shall not be considered as chronic arthritis: Musculoskeletal disorders such as diffuse connective tissue diseases (including but not limited to rheumatoid arthritis, juvenile rheumatoid arthritis, systemic lupus erythematosus, systemic sclerosis, mixed connective tissue disease, polymyositis/ dermatomyositis, fibromyalgia, necrotizing vasculitis and vasculopathies and Sjogren's Syndrome), degenerative joint disease, infectious agents other than rubella (whether by direct invasion or as an immune reaction), metabolic and endocrine diseases, trauma, neoplasms, neuropathic disorders, bone and cartilage disorders and arthritis associated with ankylosing spondylitis, psoriasis, inflammatory bowel disease, Reiter's syndrome, or blood disorders. Arthralgia (joint pain) or stiffness without joint swelling shall not be viewed as chronic arthritis for \purposes of the Vaccine Injury Table.

(6) **Brachial neuritis** is defined as dysfunction limited to the upper extremity nerve plexus (i.e., its trunks, divisions, or cords) without involvement of other peripheral (e.g., nerve roots or a single peripheral nerve) or central (e.g., spinal cord) nervous system structures. A deep, steady, often severe aching pain in the shoulder and upper arm usually heralds onset of the condition. The pain is followed in days or weeks by weakness and atrophy in upper extremity muscle groups. Sensory loss may accompany the motor deficits, but is generally a less notable clinical feature. The neuritis, or plexopathy, may be present on the same side as or the opposite side of the injection; it is sometimes bilateral, affecting both upper extremities. Weakness is required before the diagnosis can be made. Motor, sensory, and reflex findings on physical examination and the results of nerve conduction and electromyographic studies must be consistent in confirming that dysfunction is attributable to the brachial plexus. The condition should thereby be distinguishable from conditions that may give rise to dysfunction of nerve roots (i.e., radiculopathies) and peripheral nerves (i.e., including multiple mononeuropathies), as well as other peripheral and central nervous system structures (e.g., cranial neuropathies and myelopathies).

(7) **Thrombocytopenic purpura** is defined by a serum platelet count less than 50,000/mm^3. Thrombocytopenic purpura does not include cases of thrombocytopenia associated with other causes such as hypersplenism, autoimmune disorders (including alloantibodies from previous transfusions) myelodysplasias, lymphoproliferative disorders, congenital thrombocytopenia or hemolytic uremic syndrome. This does not include cases of immune (formerly called idiopathic) thrombocytopenic purpura (ITP) that are mediated, for example, by viral or fungal infections, toxins or drugs. Thrombocytopenic purpura does not include cases of thrombocytopenia associated with disseminated intravascular coagulation, as observed with bacterial and viral infections. Viral infections include, for example, those infections secondary to Epstein Barr virus, cytomegalovirus, hepatitis A and B, rhinovirus, human immunodeficiency virus (HIV), adenovirus, and dengue virus. An antecedent viral infection may be demonstrated by clinical signs and symptoms and need not be confirmed by culture or serologic testing. Bone marrow examination, if performed, must reveal a normal or an increased number of megakaryocytes in an otherwise normal marrow.

(8) **Vaccine-strain measles viral infection** is defined as a disease caused by the vaccine-strain that should be determined by vaccine specific monoclonal antibody or polymerase chain reaction tests.

(9) **Vaccine-strain polio viral infection** is defined as a disease caused by poliovirus that is isolated from the affected tissue and should be determined to be the vaccine-strain by oligonucleotide or polymerase chain reaction. Isolation of poliovirus from the stool is not sufficient to establish a tissue specific infection or disease caused by vaccine-strain poliovirus.

APPENDIX G
Data and Statistics

*Provisional

Reported Cases and Deaths from Vaccine Preventable Diseases, United States, 1950-2008*

Year	Diphtheria		Tetanus		Pertussis		Polio (paralytic)	
	Cases	Deaths	Cases	Deaths	Cases	Deaths	Cases	Deaths
1950	5,796	410	486	336	120,718	1,118	33,300	1,904
1951	3,983	302	506	394	68,687	951	28,386	1,551
1952	2,960	217	484	360	45,030	402	57,879	3,145
1953	2,355	156	506	337	37,129	270	35,592	1,450
1954	2,041	145	524	332	60,886	373	38,476	1,368
1955	1,984	150	462	265	62,786	467	28,985	1043
1956	1,568	103	468	246	31,732	266	15,140	566
1957	1,211	81	447	279	28,295	183	5,485	221
1958	918	74	445	303	32,148	177	5,787	255
1959	934	72	445	283	40,005	269	8,425	454
1960	918	69	368	231	14,809	118	3,190	230
1960	617	68	379	242	11,468	76	1,312	90
1962	444	41	322	215	17,749	83	910	60
1963	314	45	325	210	17,135	115	449	41
1964	293	42	289	179	13,005	93	122	17
1965	164	18	300	181	6,799	55	72	16
1966	209	20	235	158	7,717	49	113	9
1967	219	32	263	144	9,718	37	41	16
1968	260	30	178	66	4,810	36	53	24
1969	241	25	192	89	3,285	13	20	13
1970	435	30	148	79	4,249	12	33	7
1971	215	13	116	64	3036	18	21	18
1972	152	10	128	58	3,287	6	31	2
1973	228	10	101	40	1,759	5	8	10
1974	272	5	101	44	2,402	14	7	3
1975	307	5	102	45	1,738	8	13	9
1976	128	7	75	32	1,010	7	10	16
1977	84	5	87	24	2,177	10	19	16
1978	76	4	86	32	2,063	6	8	13

*2008 provisional data. *MMWR* 2009;57(No. 53): 1420-31.

Year	Diphtheria		Tetanus		Pertussis		Polio (paralytic)	
	Cases	Deaths	Cases	Deaths	Cases	Deaths	Cases	Deaths
1979	59	1	81	30	1,623	6	22	1
1980	3	1	95	28	1,730	11	9	2
1981	5	0	72	31	1,248	6	10	0
1982	2	1	88	22	1,895	4	12	0
1983	5	0	91	22	2,463	5	13	0
1984	1	0	74	20	2,276	7	9	0
1985	3	0	83	23	3,589	4	8	0
1986	0	0	64	22	4,195	6	10	0
1987	3	1	48	16	2,823	1	9	0
1988	2	0	53	17	3,450	4	9	0
1989	3	0	53	9	4,157	12	10	0
1990	4	1	64	11	4,570	12	6	0
1991	5	0	57	11	2,719	0	9	1
1992	4	1	45	9	4,083	5	6	0
1993	0	0	48	11	6,586	1	3	0
1994	2	0	51	9	4,617	8	8	0
1995	0	1	41	5	5,137	6	6	1
1996	2	0	36	1	7,796	4	7	0
1997	4	0	50	4	6,564	6	7	0
1998	1	1	34	7	6,279	5	2	0
1999	1	1	40	7	7,288	7	2	0
2000	1	0	35	5	7,867	12	0	0
2001	2	0	37	5	7,580	17	0	0
2002	1	0	25	5	9,771	18	0	0
2003	1	1	20	4	11,647	11	0	0
2004	0	0	34	4	25,827	16	0	0
2005	0	0	27	1	25,616	31	1**	0
2006	0	0	41	NA	15,632	NA	0	0
2007	0	0	28	NA	10,454	NA	0	0
2008*	0	0	15	NA	10,007	NA	0	0

**Vaccine-associated polio acquired outside the United States

Year	Measles		Mumps		Rubella		CRS
	Cases	Deaths	Cases	Deaths	Cases	Deaths	Cases
1950	319,124	468	NR		NR		NR
1951	530,118	683	NR		NR		NR
1952	683,077	618	NR		NR		NR
1953	449,146	462	NR		NR		NR
1954	682,720	518	NR		NR		NR
1955	555,156	345	NR		NR		NR
1956	611,936	530	NR		NR		NR
1957	486,799	389	NR		NR		NR
1958	763,094	552	NR		NR		NR
1959	406,162	385	NR		NR		NR
1960	441,703	380	NR	42	NR	12	NR
1961	423,919	434	NR	53	NR	14	NR
1962	481,530	408	NR	43	NR	8	NR
1963	385,156	364	NR	48	NR	16	NR
1964	458,083	421	NR	50	NR	53	NR
1965	261,904	276	NR	31	NR	16	NR
1966	204,136	261	NR	43	46,975	12	NR
1967	62,705	81	NR	37	46,888	16	NR
1968	22,231	24	152,209	25	49,371	24	NR
1969	25,826	41	90,918	22	57,686	29	62
1970	47,351	89	104,953	16	56,552	31	67
1971	75,290	90	124,939	22	45,086	20	44
1972	32,275	24	74,215	16	25,507	14	32
1973	26,690	23	69,612	12	27,804	16	30
1974	22,094	20	59,128	6	11,917	15	22
1975	24,374	20	59,647	8	16,652	21	32
1976	41,126	12	38,492	8	12,491	12	22
1977	57,345	15	21,436	5	20,395	17	29
1978	26,871	11	16,817	3	18,269	10	30
1979	13,597	6	14,255	2	11,795	1	57
1980	13,506	11	8,576	2	3,904	1	14
1981	3,124	2	4,941	1	2,077	5	10

Year	Measles		Mumps		Rubella		CRS
	Cases	Deaths	Cases	Deaths	Cases	Deaths	Cases
1982	1,714	2	5,270	2	2,325	4	13
1983	1,497	4	3,355	2	970	3	7
1984	2,587	1	3,021	1	752	1	2
1985	2,822	4	2,982	0	630	1	2
1986	6,282	2	7,790	0	55	1	13
1987	3,655	2	12,848	2	306	0	3
1988	3,396	3	4,866	2	225	1	2
1989	18,193	32	5,712	3	396	4	2
1990	27,786	64	5,292	1	1,125	8	32
1991	9,643	27	4,264	1	1,401	1	34
1992	2,237	4	2,572	0	160	1	11
1993	312	0	1,692	0	192	0	4
1994	963	0	1,537	0	227	0	7
1995	309	2	906	0	128	1	3
1996	508	1	751	1	238	0	2
1997	138	2	683	0	181	0	9
1998	100	0	666	1	364	0	9
1999	100	2	387	1	267	0	6
2000	86	1	338	2	176	0	8
2001	116	1	266	0	23	2	3
2002	44	0	270	1	18	0	1
2003	56	1	231	0	7	0	4
2004	37	0	258	0	10	1	0
2005	66	1	314	0	11	0	1
2006	55	NA	6,584	NA	11	NA	1
2007	43	NA	800	NA	12	NA	0
2008*	132	NA	396	NA	17	NA	0

	Hepatitis A		Hepatitis B		Haemophilus		Varicella	
Year	Cases	Deaths	Cases	Deaths	Cases	Deaths	Cases	Deaths
1966	32,859	NA	1,497	NA	NR	NR	NR	
1967	38,909	NA	2,458	NA	NR	NR	NR	
1968	45,893	NA	4,829	NA	NR	NR	NR	
1969	48,416	NA	5,909	NA	NR	NR	NR	
1970	56,797	NA	8,310	NA	NR	NR	NR	
1971	59,606	NA	9,556	NA	NR	NR	NR	
1972	54,074	NA	9,402	NA	NR	NR	164,114	122
1973	50,749	NA	8,451	NA	NR	NR	182,927	138
1974	40,358	NA	10,631	NA	NR	NR	141,495	106
1975	35,855	NA	13,121	NA	NR	NR	154,248	83
1976	33,288	NA	14,973	NA	NR	NR	183,990	106
1977	31,153	NA	16,831	NA	NR	NR	188,396	89
1978	29,500	NA	15,016	NA	NR	NR	154,089	91
1979	30,407	129	15,452	260	NR	NR	199,081	103
1980	29,087	112	19,015	294	NR	NR	190,894	78
1981	25,802	93	21,152	394	NR	NR	200,766	84
1982	23,403	83	22,177	375	NR	NR	167,423	61
1983	21,532	82	24,318	438	NR	NR	177,462	57
1984	22,040	77	26,115	465	NR	NR	221,983	53
1985	23,210	80	26,611	490	NR	NR	178,162	68
1986	23,430	65	26,107	557	NR	NR	183,243	47
1987	25,280	77	25,916	595	NR	NR	213,196	89
1988	28,507	70	23,177	621	NR	NR	192,857	83
1989	35,821	88	23,419	711	NR	NR	185,441	89
1990	31,441	76	21,102	816	NR	NR	173,099	120
1991	24,378	71	18,003	912	2,764	17	147,076	81
1992	23,112	82	16,126	903	1,412	16	158,364	100
1993	24,238	95	13,361	1041	1,419	7	134,722	100
1994	26,796	97	12,517	1120	1,174	5	151,219	124
1995	31,582	142	10,805	1027	1,180	12	120,624	115
1996	31,032	121	10,637	1082	1,170	7	83,511	81

Year	Hepatitis A		Hepatitis B		Haemophilus		Varicella	
	Cases	Deaths	Cases	Deaths	Cases	Deaths	Cases	Deaths
1997	30,021	127	10,416	1,030	1,162	7	98,727	99
1998	23,229	114	10,258	1,052	1,194	11	82,455	81
1999	17,047	134	7,694	832	1,309	6	46,016	48
2000	13,397	106	8,036	886	1,398	6	27,382	44
2001	10,609	83	7,843	769	1,597	11	22,536	26
2002	8,795	76	7,996	762	1,743	7	22,841	32
2003	7,653	54	7,526	685	2,013	5	20,948	16
2004	5,970	58	6,741	643	2,085	11	26,659	19
2005	4,488	43	5,119	642	2,304	4	32,242	13
2006	3,579	NA	4,713	NA	2,436	NA	48,445	NA
2007	2,979	NA	4,519	NA	2,541	NA	40,146	NA
2008*	2,340	NA	3,513	NA	2,547	NA	26,924	NA

Notes
NA - Not Available
NR - Not nationally reportable
CRS: Congenital Rubella Syndrome

Prior to 1966, hepatitis A and B were not separated from other types of hepatitis. Prior to 1978, deaths from hepatitis A and B were not separated from deaths from other types of hepatitis.

Haemophilus (Hi) reporting includes all serotypes and all ages. In 2008, 27 cases of invasive Hi type B disease were reported among children <5 years of age.

Varicella was removed from the nationally notifiable disease list in 1991. In 2008, varicella cases were reported from 33 states, the District of Columbia, Guam, and Puerto Rico.

Sources:
Final totals for 2007: *MMWR* 2008;57(33):903-13.
Final totals for 2006: *MMWR* 2007;56(33):851-64.
Final totals for 2005: *MMWR* 2006;55(32):883-93.
Final totals for 2004: Summary of Notifiable Diseases, United States, 2004. *MMWR* 2006;53(53):18-19.
Reportable disease (1950-2003): Earlier editions of Summary of Notifiable Diseases, published annually in *MMWR*.

Deaths: National Center for Health Statistics Mortality Report for respective years.

March 2009

Impact of Vaccines in the 20th & 21st Centuries

Disease	20th Century Annual Morbidity	2007 Total	% Decrease
Smallpox	48,164	0	100
Diphtheria	175,885	0	100
Pertussis	147,271	10,454	93
Tetanus	1,314	28	98
Polio (paralytic)	16,316	0	100
Measles	503,282	43	>99.9
Mumps	152,209	800	99.5
Rubella	47,745	12	>99.9
Congenital rubella	823	0	100
Haemophilus influenzae (<5 years)	20,000 (est)	202 (serotype B or unknown serotype)	99

Sources:
1. CDC. Impact of vaccines universally recommended for children – United States, 1900-1998. *MMWR* 1999;48(12): 243-8

2. CDC. Notice to Readers: Final 2007 Reports of Notifiable Diseases. *MMWR* 2008;57(33):903-13

3/20/09

Vaccine Coverage Levels – United States, 1962-2007

Year	DTP3+	DTP4+	Polio3+	MMR*	Hib3+	Var	PCV3+	HepB3+	Combined 4-3-1	Combined 4-3-1-3
1962	67.3									
1963	71.4									
1964	74.6									
1965	72.7									
1966	74.0									
1967	77.9			60.0						
1968	76.8			61.5						
1969	77.4			61.4						
1970	76.4			58.4						
1971	77.8			62.2						
1972	74.1			62.8						
1973	71.7		59.5	61.0						
1974	72.4		60.0	63.4						
1975	73.2		63.6	65.5						
1976	72.7		61.3	66.3						
1977	69.6		62.6	65.0						
1978	66.6		59.5	63.6						
1979	64.4		59.7	66.5						
1980	66.0		58.9	66.6						
1981	68.1		59.2	66.8						
1982	67.1		57.0	67.6						
1983	65.4		56.9	66.3						
1984	65.0		53.2	65.8						
1985	63.6		53.6	61.2						
1986†										
1987†										
1988†										
1989†										

Year	DTP3+	DTP4+	Polio3+	MMR*	Hib3+	Var	PCV3+	HepB3+	Combined 4-3-1	Combined 4-3-1-3
1990†										
1991	68.8		53.2	82.0						
1992	83.0	59.0	72.4	82.5	28.2			8.0	68.7	55.3
1993	88.2	72.1	78.9	84.1	55.0			16.3	67.1	
1994	93.0	77.7	83.0	89.0	86.0			37.0	75.0	
1995	94.7	78.5	87.9	87.6	91.7			68.0	76.2	74.2
1996	95.0	81.1	91.1	90.7	91.7	16.0		81.8	78.4	76.5
1997	95.5	81.5	90.8	90.5	92.7	25.9		83.7	77.9	76.2
1998	95.6	83.9	90.8	92.0	93.4	43.2		87.0	80.6	79.2
1999	95.9	83.3	89.6	91.5	93.5	57.5		88.1	79.9	78.4
2000	94.1	81.7	89.5	90.5	93.4	67.8		90.3	77.6	76.2
2001	94.3	82.1	89.4	91.4	93.0	76.3		88.9	78.6	77.2
2002	94.9	81.6	90.2	91.6	93.1	80.6	40.8	89.9	78.5	77.5
2003	96.0	84.8	91.6	93.0	93.9	84.8	68.1	92.4	82.2	81.3
2004	95.9	85.5	91.6	93.0	93.5	87.5	73.2	92.4	83.5	82.5
2005	96.1	85.7	91.7	91.5	93.9	87.9	82.8	92.9	83.1	82.4
2006	95.8	85.2	92.9	92.4	93.4	89.3	87.0	93.4	83.2	82.3
2007	95.5	84.5	92.6	92.3	92.6	90.0	90.0	92.7	82.8	81.1

*Previously reported as measles-containing vaccine (MCV).
†No national coverage data were collected from 1986 through 1990.

Var: varicella vaccine

Combined 4-3-1: Four or more doses of DTP/DTaP/DT, three or more doses of poliovirus vaccine, and one or more doses of any measles-containing vaccine.

Combined 4-3-1-3: Four or more doses of DTP/DTaP/DT, three or more doses of poliovirus vaccine, one or more doses of any measles-containing vaccine, and three or more doses of *Haemophilus influenzae* type b vaccine.

Data prior to 1993 were collected by the National Health Interview Survey and represent 2-year-old children. Data from 1993 are from the National Immunization Survey and represent 19-35 month-old children. Different methods were used for the two surveys.

Most recent publication: CDC. National, State, and Local Area Vaccination Coverage Among Children Aged 19-35 Months – United States, 2007. *MMWR* 2008;57(35);961-66.

APPENDIX H
Immunization Resources

Centers for Disease Control and Prevention
and
National Center for Immunization & Respiratory Diseases (NCIRD)

Contact Information & Resources

Telephone
Immunization Call Center
800-232-4636 (800-CDC-INFO)
Contact CDC-INFO 24 hours a day, 7 days a week, in English or Spanish, with questions concerning immunizations or vaccine-preventable diseases, to find the location of immunization clinics near you, or to order single copies of immunization materials from NCIRD.

E-Mail
nipinfo@cdc.gov
Healthcare providers can send their immunization or vaccine-preventable disease related questions to this e-mail address. You will get an answer from a CDC immunization expert, usually within 24 hours.

Internet
NCIRD: http://www.cdc.gov/vaccines
Vaccine Safety: http://www.cdc.gov/od/science/iso or http://www.cdc.gov/vaccines/vac-gen/safety/default.htm
Hepatitis: http://www.cdc.gov/hepatitis
Influenza: http://www.cdc.gov/flu
Travelers' Health: http://wwwn.cdc.gov/travel

Calendar of upcoming events, online access to publications such as ACIP statements and Vaccine Information Statements, online publications ordering, vaccine safety information, latest pediatric and adult immunization schedules, downloadable Clinic Assessment Software Application (CASA), Frequently Asked Questions, PowerPoint slide presentations, links to other immunization sites, and much more.

NCIRD Training & Education Resources. Download NCIRD's curriculum brochure: http://www.cdc.gov/vaccines/ed/curric-brochure.htm

Publications may be ordered through NCIRD's online order form: http://www.cdc.gov/vaccines/pubs/default.htm

IAC's Online Directory of Immunization Resources

Visit our website to find the Immunization Action Coalition's online directory of immunization resources. Continually updated, it keeps you in the know about immunization and viral hepatitis issues and resources. Use it to gain access to hundreds of reliable sources of information with the click of a mouse. Here's what you'll find:

- **Books and Periodicals:** Standard resources for providers, as well as helpful and informative books for patients and parents.

- **CDC Materials**: Ordering information for CDC-produced materials; links to frequently requested items, live satellite broadcasts, and websites; and a listing of telephone and email information services.

- **Continuing Educational Opportunities for Health Professionals:** Listings and links for providers needing CMEs, CNEs, CEUs, or just to stay current.

- **Email News Services:** Information about how to sign up to receive periodic email updates from several immunization-related organizations.

- **Government Agencies:** Links to most federal agencies (e.g., CDC, FDA) and state health departments.

- **Hotlines:** Information about toll-free hotlines for providers and patients.

- **IAC Materials:** Links to IAC's ready-to-print educational pieces for providers, patients, and parents—and much more.

Visit us:
www.immunize.org/resources

- **International Organizations:** Links to organizations (e.g., WHO, PAHO, GAVI) providing information on international immunization and hepatitis issues.

- **Other Immunization Partners:** Links to other organizations and professional societies that provide immunization information.

- **Videos and More:** Helpful videos, DVDs, and other electronic formats for providers, patients, and parents to learn more about immunization and viral hepatitis.

To get free weekly updates on new immunization resources, subscribe to IAC's news service, IAC Express, at www.immunize.org/subscribe

www.immunize.org/news.d/6012resr.pdf • Item #U6012 (1/07)

Immunization Action Coalition • 1573 Selby Ave. • St. Paul, MN 55104 • (651) 647-9009 • www.immunize.org • www.vaccineinformation.org

H

H-2

Sample IAC Print Materials

These, and many other useful materials for both providers and patients, can be downloaded free of charge from the IAC's website at http://www.immunize.org/catg.d/free.htm

Vaccine Administration Record
for Children and Teens
http://www.immunize.org/catg.d/p2022b.pdf

Standing Orders for Administering
Influenza Vaccine to Adults
http://www.immunize.org/catg.d/p3074.pdf

Screening Questionnaire
for Child and Teen Immunization
http://www.immunize.org/catg.d/p4060.pdf

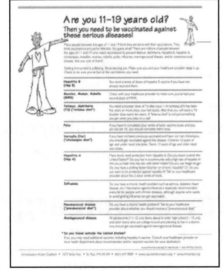

Are You 11-19 Years Old?
http://www.immunize.org/catg.d/11teens8.pdf

Temperature Log for Vaccines (Fahrenheit)
http://www.immunize.org/catg.d/p3039pdf

"Handy" resources

Practical information
about immunization
and vaccine-
preventable diseases

Subscribe to
IAC's FREE publications

It's so easy to subscribe to IAC's 3 print periodicals—
Needle Tips, Vaccinate Adults, and *Vaccinate Women*—
and email news service *IAC Express.*
Just go to www.immunize.org/subscribe, follow the directions,
and you're done!

Visit www.immunize.org

Hundreds of free, ready-to-copy immunization and viral
hepatitis print materials for your patients and staff and many other
free resources, including VISs in more than 30 languages

Visit www.vaccineinformation.org

Disease and vaccine information for the public
and healthcare professionals (photos & videos, too!)

www.immunize.org/news.d/u6005.pdf • Item #U6005 (8/08)

Immunization Action Coalition • 1573 Selby Ave. • St. Paul, MN 55104 • (651) 647-9009 • www.immunize.org • www.vaccineinformation.org

DVD: Immunization Techniques "Safe, Effective, Caring"

[VHS version]

Add to Cart
for credit cards only

View Cart

Order Form
for all payment types

The video "Immunization Techniques: Safe, Effective, Caring" is now available on DVD. Every clinic in the United States that delivers vaccination services should have a copy of this 35-minute video available for clinic staff. This video teaches best practices about how to administer intramuscular (IM) and subcutaneous (SC) vaccines to infants, children, and adults. It is designed for use as a "hands-on" instructional program for new staff as well as a refresher course for experienced health professionals.

The DVD provides discussion of all the following:
- Anatomic sites
- Choice of needle size
- Vaccines and routes of administration
- Demonstrations of infants, toddlers, kindergartners, and adults being vaccinated
- How to "draw up" doses of vaccine

Features
- 35-minute DVD on immunization techniques
- English and dubbed-Spanish versions

The DVD disk includes English- and Spanish-language versions of the following print materials
- Presenter's notes
- "Comforting Restraint," a poster that clearly shows parents how to hold a child during vaccination
- "Be there for your child," a poster that presents ideas parents can use before, during, and after vaccination to make the experience easier for their child.

The DVD also includes the following print materials in English only:
- Skills checklist to help you document that your staff is well trained.
- "Immunization Record and History," a chart that allows health professionals to document vaccine administration information for each of the recommended childhood vaccines
- A resource list that directs parents to sources of reliable immunization information

New price effective October 1, 2007: $10.50 each

For quotes on larger quantities, call 651-647-9009 or email admininfo@immunize.org

Developed by the California Department of Health Services Immunization Branch in collaboration with a team of national experts

http://www.immunize.org/shop/toolkit_iztechdvd.asp

Vaccine Storage and Handling Toolkit

Everything you want to know about vaccine storage and handling in one place!

- Forms
- Posters
- Checklists
- Interactive Game
- Videos
- Storage & Handling Guidelines
- Contact Information

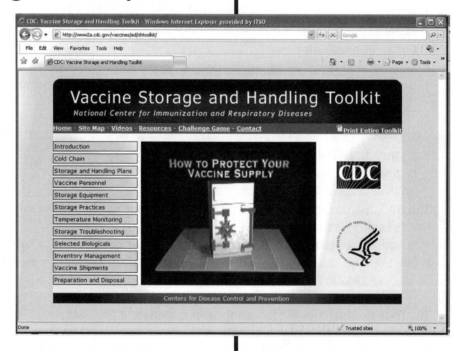

Online at www.2a.cdc.gov/vaccines/ed/shtoolkit